The John Harvard Library

Cotton Mather

Magnalia Christi Americana

Cotton Mather

Magnalia Christi Americana

Books I and II

Edited by Kenneth B. Murdock
With the assistance of Elizabeth W. Miller

The Belknap Press of
Harvard University Press
Cambridge, Massachusetts, and
London, England
1977

*F
7
.M4
1977*

Library of Congress Cataloging in Publication Data

Mather, Cotton, 1663–1728.
    Magnalia Christi Americana, books I and II.

    (The John Harvard Library)
    Includes bibliographical references and index.
        1. New England—History—Colonial period, ca. 1600–
1775. 2. New England—Church history. 3. New England
—Biography. I. Murdock, Kenneth Ballard, 1895–1975.
II. Miller, Elizabeth W. III. Title. IV. Series.
F7.M4 1976   974'.02   73-76383
ISBN 0–674–54155–3

FOREWORD

In 1926 the late Professor Stanley T. Williams of Yale asked me to prepare *Selections from Cotton Mather* as one of the volumes in The American Authors Series, which he was then editing for Harcourt, Brace, and Company. In doing this I became interested in the *Magnalia* and decided to prepare an edition of it, more accurate and fully annotated than the two printed in the nineteenth century. Williams and other scholars joined in the project, but it soon became clear that to do the edition we had in mind would take years, and the cost of printing would be great.

Meanwhile, unknown to us, the Reverend William Wallace Fenn had made a hobby of what he called his "knitting"—the tracing down of the sources of Mather's quotations and Biblical allusions, and the correction of misprints in the text. He entered his findings on a thousand or more cards, each containing one or more of his notes. Shortly after he died in 1952, his widow, knowing my interest in the *Magnalia*, gave these cards to be used in writing my proposed edition, thereby providing me with much material nowhere else available.

Meanwhile also the late George W. Robinson had, unknown to me, virtually finished an edition of the *Magnalia* of his own, introducing some new material, altering some passages in order to make them more readable, elaborating on others he thought deserving of special attention. In spite of the good qualities of his book, he could find no publisher for it. After his death, however, the Harvard University Press, which by then had agreed to publish my edition in its John Harvard Library, procured Robinson's pages and notes and turned them over for my use.

I became especially indebted to the work of Thomas J. Holmes, who, with support from Mr. and Mrs. William G. Mather, brought out in 1940 his *Cotton Mather, A Bibliography of His Work*. This work, in three volumes, supplies rich material for the student of the *Magnalia*, and its author helped me constantly in the preparation of my edition by giving time and thought to many problems which, without his aid, would have baffled me.

The John Harvard Library edition of the *Magnalia* was made possible by the work of many scholars who in various ways supplied material—

George Lyman Kittredge and Chester Noyes Greenough, for example, and many others, such as Mason Hammond, William Jepson, the late Perry Miller, Alan Heimert, Leonard Miller, and William L. Lane.

From 1961 until 1964 I served as director of the Harvard University Center of Italian Renaissance Studies in Florence, Italy, and thus was able to do little if anything on the edition of the *Magnalia*. For this period Dr. George McCandlish in Cambridge worked in my place, but he then undertook teaching at the George Washington University, which gave him little time for anything else.

Fortunately Elizabeth Miller was persuaded by the Harvard University Press to join with me in finishing this volume. I owe to her more than to any of the others who have contributed to the making of the Harvard *Magnalia*.

K.B.M.

THE TEXT

This edition of the *Magnalia* follows as faithfully as possible the 1702 edition, except that the modern "s" replaces the long "s" wherever used in the original text. The desirability of reproducing that text instead of "modernizing" it seems to the editors unquestionable.

A use of italics excessive to the modern eye was a characteristic of all seventeenth-century books. However, preservation of Mather's italics is essential for understanding his prose. He employs them for emphasis, for proper names, for foreign words and phrases. He uses them often in lieu of quotation marks and no less often to allude without direct quotation to proverbs or other popular sayings, or to commonplaces familiar to scholars. To read the *Magnalia* in a text which ignores the italics or preserves them only sporadically and at random (as the nineteenth-century editions of the work did) is to run the risk of attributing to Mather sentences he did not write or epigrammatic sayings which were not his, and to miss entirely many of the Biblical allusions, almost always in italics, which he used to illuminate a theme, to drive home a point, or to reveal his basic thought and purpose in writing.

His use of capital letters is often erratic, but frequently they serve to make plain the structure of a passage by accenting key words or by marking out the essential elements in a pun or some other rhetorical device. In similar manner, his capitalization calls attention to Biblical phrases or words which are fraught with typological overtones especially relevant to his purposes.

Scores of spellings which are obviously printers' errors or slips of the author's pen have been corrected. The punctuation of the original has also been altered when necessary to make a sentence intelligible to modern readers; however, the seventeenth-century practice of punctuating numerals, especially in dates, by periods rather than commas has been retained in order to avoid a tedious multiplication of emendations. All alterations are noted in the records of emendations, which give both the emended and the original readings so that readers may easily reconstruct the text as it was first printed. Dates in Mather's text are given as printed in 1702. He used the Old Style calendar, in which March was the first month of the year. Whenever necessary, endnotes clarify the chronology.

Mather in the *Magnalia* reprints wholly or in part certain of his writings published earlier. In so doing he, or perhaps the printers, made slight typographical changes and other minor alterations. These are ignored in the present edition. Occasionally, however, Mather makes additions or deletions. These are pointed out in endnotes when they seem to the editors to indicate shifts in his thinking or to shed light on his methods and motives in composing the *Magnalia*.

K.B.M.

TECHNICAL APPARATUS

The lines of the text are numbered in flights of 99, regardless of section divisions, with every fifth line carrying a line number, and each line 99 carrying its number.

Emendations are identified by line numbers, and are recorded immediately below the text on the pages to which they pertain. Those made by Cotton Mather himself bear his initials.

Footnotes are numbered either major division by major division, or section by section, identified and keyed by superior figures in the text, and printed at the bottom of the page on which the reference occurs. They have been limited to information immediately useful for making the text comprehensible to the reader. Identification of persons and definitions of words are provided only when such knowledge is not available in standard dictionaries. Biblical references are given for passages in the book which cannot be fully understood without some knowledge of their source and context in Holy Writ, and of their metaphorical or typological significance. Otherwise they are relegated to endnotes with, when necessary, other examples and comments. An asterisk at the end of a footnote indicates that there is further related information in an endnote keyed to the same page and line. Mather's occasional minor alterations in Biblical texts or phrases which do not change their import are not annotated.

Endnotes are grouped by major divisions, such as Attestation or Book, and are printed at the end of the volume. They are identified by the page and line numbers to which they apply. It should be noted that endnotes are not necessarily tied to footnotes, and the reader should consult them independently.

The endnotes serve a variety of functions. They identify Mather's sources, if luck has been with the editors, both primary and secondary. They furnish explanatory detail, historical background, elucidation of theological and ecclesiastical matters. In many cases, they explicate and amplify guarded or ambiguous references by Mather to events he wished, for one reason or another, to elide or to present in a particular light. They also, on occasion, confess the editors' failure to track down an allusion or to identify a source. Cross-references to later Books of the *Magnalia* are to the 1702 edition. The editors have felt throughout that only by a considerable amplitude of annotation could they fulfill two major purposes of this edition: to contribute to the significance of the *Magnalia* as the history of the great works of Christ in America and to present a study of that extraordinary young man, Cotton Mather, who wrote it.

                                                                    E.W.M.

Contents

The map on the following page was photographed from the 1702 edition of the *Magnalia* by courtesy of the Houghton Library, Harvard College Library.

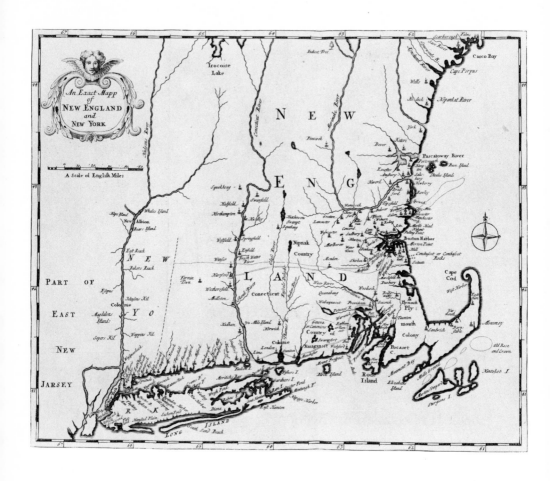

An Exact Mapp of NEW ENGLAND and NEW YORK

A Scale of English Miles

Cotton Mather

Magnalia Christi Americana

COTTON MATHER

Cotton Mather was born in Boston on February 12, 1662/63. Both his grandfathers, John Cotton, in whose honor he was named, and Richard Mather, had been leaders of the first generation of Congregational ministers in New England. His father, Increase, was in 1664 to be ordained as minister of the Second (or "Old North") Church of Boston and soon thereafter to become the most powerful divine in the colony, influential in both ecclesiastical and political affairs.

As a boy Cotton Mather studied at the Boston Latin School, first under Benjamin Tompson, "a Man of great Learning and Wit . . . well acquainted with *Roman* and *Greek* Writers" and some talent as a poet, and then under "the famous *Ezekiel Cheever*," renowned for his piety, learning, and skill as a teacher. Mather displayed "laudable Proficiency." When wintry weather prevented him from taking the long walk to school, he read at home in his father's library and "much employed" himself "*in Church History*."

By the time he was twelve he could speak Latin, "had composed many *Latin* Exercises, both in prose and verse," and "conversed with *Cato, Corderius, Terence, Tully, Ovid*, and *Virgil*." In Greek he "had gone through a great part of the New Testament" and had "read considerably in *Isocrates* and Homer." He had also begun to study Hebrew. Admitted to Harvard, he kept up the pace, perfecting his Hebrew, "composing Systems of *Logic* and *Physic*," going over "the Use of the *Globes*," proceeding "in *Arithmetic* as far as was ordinary," and, "in a Word, describing the Circle of all the Academical Studies." In 1678, when he was only sixteen, he took his A.B. degree, the youngest student who had ever received it at Harvard. On August 9, 1681, he received his M.A.

According to his son, Samuel, who published in 1729 a eulogistic biography of him, "There was one Thing, which, from his Cradle seem'd to have a dark and sad Aspect upon his Usefulness . . . an *uncommon Impediment in his Speech*." Whether he had this affliction from birth may be questioned, but there is good evidence that by the time he was in his twelfth year he suffered from it. In October 1674, his father and mother prayed together because of his "Impediment," begging "God's mercy in this particular" in the hope that He would "in some comfortable measure remove this evill." There is no reason to doubt Samuel's statement that because of his "Stammering" Cotton, while in college, "for some Time" almost "laid aside the Tho'ts of being a *Minister*," and "with great Application studied Physic" in order to prepare himself for "the Calling of a Physician."

Elijah Corlet, a wise old schoolmaster in Cambridge, heard of his plight, sought him out, and gave him advice which helped him to conquer his handicap. Thanks to this he was able on August 22, 1680, successfully to preach his first sermon. Appropriately he chose as his theme "Our blessed SAVIOUR as the glorious *Physician of Souls*," and took for his first text part of Luke 4.18: "He hath sent me to heal the brokenhearted."

Other sermons followed and were well received, and on February 23, 1681, just after he was eighteen, he accepted the invitation of the Second Church to serve as his father's assistant there. Less than a year later the church "chose him for their *Pastor*, and desired his *Ordination* as such over them," to serve as co-minister with his father, their "Teacher." "He for some Time *declined*," though he continued to assist in all the parochial duties of the church.

He was not ordained until three years later and then wrote in his diary, "Thou, O Lord, art stronger than I, and hast prevailed!" According to his son, one reason for his initial refusal to accept the pastorship was his "*modest* Opinion, and low Apprehension of himself and his Talents," which led him to "*fear and quake exceedingly*, about entring into sacred Orders." But there seem to have been other causes for the long delaying of his ordination. Increase Mather himself, when the Church "did unanimously elect" his son as their pastor, was "very backward in consenting," because of his "Relation to him," but since "the church could not agree in calling any other . . . gave way to their Importunity." And, although the vote to appoint Cotton had been unanimous, some doubt of its wisdom developed. On April 5, 1685, the day when the date of his ordination was to be fixed by the members of the church, the "*Congregation*" was "*thinner* than ordinary" and his "Heart began to sink." He had heard three days before that "the extreme Criticalness of the Time, with regard unto" the "publick Affayrs" of the colony had "raised such a Diversitie . . . in the Brethren of our Church, about the Conveniencie of" his "*Ordination at this Time*, that there was like to bee some Division." In a "secret FAST" he gave himself to God and was assured that "Hee would bee with" him. In a prayer he promised that he would never cherish resentment "of any *Wrong* or *Sleight*, which any of the Church might heretofore have ill treated" him with. "The Design of Satan, to embarass the Concerns" of Mather's settlement as pastor was duly defeated "by a most uniting Work of God upon the Spirits of the people" and on May 13, 1685, he was ordained. He remained pastor of the Second Church until his death on February 13, 1727/28.

The Church was his central concern. He devoted himself to its pastorate with fanatic zeal and terrifying energy, and tried to relate to it all his activities and interests. His conception of the duty of a minister was all-embracing. Not content with visiting the sick, helping the impoverished, chastising backsliders, and preaching spiritual values and the nature of piety, he felt he must regulate the conduct of his flock in every aspect of life. He strove to discover and teach new means of serving God and new ways of proving the boundless extent of the divine power. Since, as Mather saw it, the entire universe and the whole history of mankind revealed this power, there was virtually no limit to the range of education he must provide. This meant constant writing of sermons, daily reading and memorizing of the Bible and its commentators, studying history and science, and feverish searching for effective methods of instruction. And, of course, he tried day by day to assess his shortcomings and spent hours in fasting and praying for divine forgiveness.

On May 6, 1684, he married Abigail Phillips, the daughter of Colonel John Phillips of Charlestown. She lived until November, 1702, a "lovely Consort," devoted to her husband as he was to her. Nine children were born to them but only four outlived their mother. Yet, in spite of bereavements, frequent ill health, and other "afflictions," Cotton never neglected his ministry, and his belief in the rightness of God's decrees, however inscrutable, never flagged.

One source of his zealous faith and restless effort to "Do Good" was certainly his family background. Both his grandfathers had been pioneer "saints" in Massachusetts; his father was carrying on their tradition. Must he not seek to follow the same path and devote himself to keeping New England a land in which righteous living and "true religion" could flourish? What toil or sacrifice could be too great a price to pay with such a goal in view? His family pride led, unfortunately, to faults as well as virtues. Some elements of his complicated character probably resulted from the nervous strain he was subjected to as a child, and some of his least attractive traits can be understood when one remembers what his upbringing must have been. The first-born son of Increase Mather, "the greatest of the native Puritans" in New England, and the obvious heir apparent to his dominion, young Cotton must at all costs be brought up to achieve supremacy in piety, learning, and authority. Naturally he was given "undue stimulus and a forced culture" and "his religious nature, at the outset, was forced above his strength, and beyond what his health could bear." He "was encouraged to leap into sainthood." At school, his "boyish intellect" was "stimulated by a more than boyish ambition," and the praise of his teachers encouraged an overweening vanity. As his son put it, he "bid fair to be *great*" even "while he was yet young" because "he *believed* he should be so; he *expected* it." When still in his teens he declared, "I beleeve that I am a chosen Vessel, and that the Lord will pour mercy unto me, till I have arrived unto a Fulness of eternal Glory . . . It will bee so!" On another occasion he confided to his diary, "Lord, I know Thou wilt . . . improve mee in eminent Services for thy Name. Lord, I know Thou will signalize mee, as thou hast my Father, my Grandfathers, and my Uncles before mee. Hallelujah." Once, before he was ordained, he was, he thought, visited by an angel who brought a message from "the Lord Jesus" assuring him that he was to achieve great things. Faced by a winged guest clad in "white and shining" garments, he was disturbed by the thought that the message might have been sent by Satan rather than by Christ, but he seems to have easily convinced himself that he had indeed been blessed by a visitation from heaven. Some years later he wrote: "There is one good *Angel* . . . peculiarly My *Angel*."

The vanity he revealed in his youth persisted throughout his life; so did his worldly ambition. He grew jealous of those who threatened to surpass him and savage in his denunciation of those who did not accept his word as law. His tone in speech or writing was often annoyingly dictatorial. He recognized his faults and, "prostrate in the Dust on his study floor," bewailed his "vileness" and declared himself "the most loathsome Creature in the world." He confessed his sins and promised God that he would conquer them, but too often forgot his vows. In his diaries, his accounts of his abject confessions are often followed by assertions of confidence that pardon would surely be granted, and, in moods of elation, he expressed with what seems perilously like arrogance his belief that as one chosen by God he could communicate with Him more directly than less favored mortals. Highly sensitive, irritable, and constantly exhausting himself nervously and physically in his passionate pursuit of godliness and renown, he often gave way to fits of rage, and as long as he lived he alternated between quasi-hysterical "ecstasies and raptures" and "ascetic mortifications and vigils."

Had he lived a quarter-century earlier his struggle for sainthood might have been less arduous. He was born in trying times. His grandfathers had preached to "Watchful . . . Fruitful and Prayerful Christians, and Humble *Walkers with* GOD," who were able to demonstrate that they had undergone a genuine religious experience of "conversion" and to give tangible proof of their "regeneration." But by the time Increase Mather was ordained as minister of the Second Church, there were signs of "decay." The population of Boston had increased, and many children of the first Congregational settlers of the town lacked the religious fervor which had brought their parents to New England. Some of them, although professing piety, were less concerned with salvation in the next world than with material prosperity in this. In the next two decades the situation became worse. Increase Mather in 1674 (the year in which Cotton entered Harvard) preached a sermon bewailing the decline of the "power of godliness" in New England. He reminded his hearers that "The Interest of *New-England* was Religion, which did distinguish us from other *English Plantations*; they were built upon a Worldly design, but we upon a Religious design; . . . now, we begin to espouse a Worldly Interest, and so to chuse a new God, therefore no wonder that War is like to be in the gates. I cannot but admire the Providence of God, that he should threaten . . . us with a generation of men that are notorious for that sin of Worldliness, as if the Lord would make us see what our great sin is, in the Instruments of our trouble." The "Instruments" Mather had in mind were probably not simply backsliding Bostonians, but Charles II, whose accession to the throne in 1661 ended the non-conformist domination in England; the French colonists perilously close to the boundaries of New England; and the Indians, who grew increasingly restless as the colonists, induced by motives economic and worldly rather than religious, occupied more and more of their territory.

Increase continued: "*Without doubt the Lord Jesus hath a peculiar respect unto this place, and for this people. This is Immanuels Land.* Christ by a wonderful Providence hath dispossessed Satan, who reigned . . . in these Ends of the Earth for Ages . . . and here the Lord hath caused . . . *New Jerusalem* to come down from Heaven; He dwels in this place: therefore, . . . he will scourge us for our backslidings. So doth he say, *Rev.* 3.19 *As many as I love, I rebuke and chasten.*"

The prophecy was fulfilled. In 1675 the Indians went to war against the colonists and by August of the next year had destroyed a dozen New England towns and partially burned many others. Several thousand colonists had been killed. Here surely was a drastic rebuke and chastening of the errant people of "Immanuels Land." Other events confirmed God's determination to scourge New England. In 1676, Increase's house and the meeting house of the Second Church were burned, together with some dozens of other buildings, and three years later another fire destroyed most of the business center of Boston. "*Pestilential* sicknesses did sometimes become *epidemical*"; there were "multiplied *Shipwrecks*," and "Enemies prey'd on our Vessels and our Sailors."

In May 1679, the Massachusetts General Court, following the request of Increase Mather and eighteen other ministers, called a synod of representatives of the churches to determine "What are the Evils that have provoked the Lord to bring his Judgments on New-England?" and "What is to be done, that so those Evils may be Reformed?" The report of its first session was drawn up by Increase Mather himself and

published as *The Necessity of Reformation*. This had some effect.
"Churches were stirred up to renewed activity" and some "young
people" were persuaded to "undertake the Christian life"; but the
synod proved to be "a palliative rather than a cure" for the ills of New
England, and God's wrath was not appeased.

The ministers of the Lord were not alone in deploring the course of
events in the colony. For some time Charles II had been concerned
about New England's virtual independence of royal control. His advisers reported that New England acted with little "reguard to Old
England" and that its people were "al most upon the very brink of
renouncing any dependance of the Crowne." In 1678 Edward Randolph
had been appointed collector of the king's revenue in Massachusetts.
An Anglican and royalist, he detested the Massachusetts nonconformists, and he sent to London a variety of charges against them. He went
farther and vigorously urged the English government to revoke the
charter of Massachusetts and replace its locally elected officers with
agents appointed by the king. Late in 1683 Charles II sent to Boston a
"declaration" that unless there was "full *Submission,* and *entire Resignation* . . . to his Pleasure, a *Quo Warranto*" would be prosecuted against
their Charter. Increase Mather opposed yielding. In January 1684, at
the request of the Deputies of Boston he spoke at a meeting of the town's
Freemen, assuring them that to submit to "*his Majesties Pleasure*" would
be a grave sin. "If," he said, "we make a *full Submission* . . . we fall into
the *Hands of Men* Immediately. But if we do it not, we still keep ourselves
in the *Hands* of GOD; we trust ourselves with his Providence . . . Who
knows what GOD may do for us?" The deputies promptly refused to
approve the Council's vote to send a conciliatory answer to Charles.

The Mathers—Cotton at this time still not ordained but eagerly
supporting his father's position—represented a large group, called by
Randolph the "faction," made up principally of the clergy and their
devout disciples. But they were opposed by others, probably even more
numerous, whom Randolph praised as "moderates." Some of these
were pious folk who had no serious quarrel with congregationalism
but were still loyal Englishmen and not ready to disobey the king;
others with little or no religious interest saw no reason for defiance and
regarded as unwise anything which might anger Charles II to the point
of inflicting dire penalties or even resorting to force of arms. Still others,
inclined to anglicanism, were hostile to the Congregationalists and felt
that no royal tyranny could be worse than, or even as bad as, the
tyranny they were subjected to by the nonconformist clergy in Boston.

The colony was divided against itself and the royal government took
matters into its own hands. The Court of Chancery declared the
Massachusetts charter void. To the "faction" this was a crushing blow.

What would become of the nonconformist churches? How would the king punish those who had most stoutly refused to yield to his will?

For a time the government in Massachusetts continued as it had under the charter. It was not until April 1685 that the news of King Charles's death and the accession to the throne of James II reached New England. Cotton Mather devoted the day on which the new monarch was proclaimed in Boston to "Humiliations, and Supplications, before the Lord," begging for deliverance from "the Confusions with which the Protestant Religion and Interest, were threatned by the Accesion of that Prince . . . especially in our own unhappy Colony." Charles II had on his deathbed declared himself a Roman Catholic, but James II had been known as a papist ever since 1672. That Massachusetts, deprived of its charter, was in his power alarmed hosts of New Englanders, including even those "moderates" who were Anglicans but hostile to Rome.

The events in Massachusetts which most concerned the Mathers during the fifteen years after the annulment of the charter are recorded in the life of Sir William Phips in Book II of the *Magnalia*. The prestige of the Mathers was enhanced during the regime of Sir Edmund Andros, who was in 1686 appointed by James II Royal Governor of New England. They combated him by all means in their power, and won the support not only of their pious followers but of many others who resented the new taxes and fees he imposed, and foresaw increasing danger to their pocket-books if his regime continued.

James II issued in April 1687 a Declaration of Indulgence, suspending penalties for religious offenses and removing religious tests or oaths as qualifications for office. Eager to replace the protestant Church of England by a new established church subservient to Rome, he hoped that by winning the support of the nonconformists and increasing their political influence as well as that of the Catholics, he could defeat the Anglican establishment and clear the way for the realization of his dream. Many of the nonconformist groups failed at first to recognize his aim and assured him of their gratitude for his declaration. In Boston, Increase Mather "moved that our churches (and not the ministers only) might Thank the King . . . which was readily complyed with by 10 churches." It was suggested that the record of their action should be taken to London by "some one . . . who might there obtain an Interest in such NonConformists as have the Kings ear; and in special take care for the well settlement of the Colledge."

Increase Mather, after graduating from Harvard, had gone abroad in 1657, taken his M.A. degree at Trinity College, Dublin, and preached to congregations in Ireland, England, and Guernsey. By the time he returned to Boston in 1661 he had achieved a considerable recognition among his fellow ministers abroad, some of whom were in 1687 still leaders. Since 1685 he had been president of Harvard College. Who was better fitted to convey New England's gratitude to the king, present to him the colonists' complaints against Andros, and urge him to restore the old charter of Massachusetts?

On April 4, 1688, he sailed for England, as a representative of the Boston churches. In his nearly four years of dealing first with James II and then with William III and Mary II, he proved himself a good diplomat, "an ecclesiastical statesman, a Yankee Mazarin" who "without sacrificing his dignity, or compromising principles . . . cultivated all sorts of people, from peers and court ladies, to the humblest dissenters, who might be of some assistance to his cause."

Meanwhile Cotton Mather, left as the sole minister of the Second Church, was busier than ever. Increase in London worried lest he work too hard and wrote to John Richards, a member of the congregation, "I am afraid you permit him to undertake more works than his weake nature is able to go through with. For your own sake as well as mine, do not let him kill Himselfe. He will do it, if you do not hinder him." But in spite of his father's admonition and any "hindrance" Richards provided, Cotton continued to work strenuously, preaching and writing, involving himself in politics, taking an active part in the revolt against Andros on April 18, 1689, and wrote himself the "Declaration" which was publicly read on that day. Whether it was then known in Massachusetts that William III and Mary II had already been proclaimed sovereigns of England is not clear. In any case it took courage to join in the insurrection. Even if William and Mary had been crowned, what assurance was there that they would regard New Englanders who had rebelled against a Royal Governor as anything but opponents of the monarchy, whoever the king and queen might be?

Fortunately Increase Mather in London was able to dispel any doubts the new rulers may have had about the loyalty of the Massachusetts rebels. Although he failed to persuade William to restore the original charter, he induced him to grant a new one which gave the colony some at least of the "righs and privileges" it had earlier enjoyed. And, as a mark of good will, the king permitted Mather to nominate the first Royal Governor and the members of his Council to take office in 1692 under the new charter. He chose as Governor Sir William Phips, who had been "converted" by a sermon he had preached in 1674, baptized by Cotton Mather, and admitted to membership in the Second Church.

On May 14, 1692, Increase Mather and Phips arrived in Boston. Cotton Mather had written in his diary a fortnight before: "Wee have not our former *Charter*, but wee have . . . one which much better suits our Circumstances. And instead, of my being made a Sacrifice to wicked *Rulers*, all the *Councellours* of the Province, are of my own Father's Nomination; and my *Father-in-Law*, with several *related* unto mee, and several *Brethren* of my own church, are among them. The *Governour* of the Province is not my Enemy, but . . . one of my own Flock, and one of my dearest Friends."

Sir William had at once to deal with a mad witch hunt which had begun in Salem Village, some twenty miles from Boston. Dozens of supposed witches were in jail in the nearby town of Salem, awaiting trial, and a hysterical search for others was spreading farther each day. The governor appointed a special court to meet in Salem to try the accused. By the time it finished its work, nineteen suspects had been found guilty of witchcraft and hanged, and another, who refused to plead guilty or not guilty, had been pressed to death in accordance with an old English law.

Horrible as the affair was, it was a comparatively minor episode in the dire record of witchcraft delusions in many countries for centuries before the Salem Village outbreak and, outside New England, even thereafter. It is important to remember that, as Perry Miller pointed out, "The intellectual history of New England up to 1720 can be written as though" the persecution in Massachusetts had never taken place. "It had no effect on the ecclesiastical or political situation, it does not figure in the institutional or idealogical development" of New England.

The *Magnalia* gives a summary account of the witchcraft episode as Cotton Mather saw it four years after it ended. Any reader who wishes to study the details of the whole sad story will find in Mather's pages, together with the notes and bibliographical references in this edition, all that he needs for understanding the course of events.

So far as the Mathers are concerned, the essential facts are that Cotton wrote in June 1692 *The Return of Several Ministers*, a document which he and others of the clergy submitted to the governor and council in response to their request. It warned the "witch court" against relying on "spectral evidence" as the sole basis for convicting the accused. The *Magnalia* explains adequately the nature of this "evidence," commonly accepted in witch trials in England and elsewhere. The ministers also pointed out other ways in which the court should correct its procedure. Had the advice given in the *Return* been followed, many of the accused would have been saved, but the magistrates paid little or no attention to it.

Throughout the period of the trials and even before, Cotton argued that those who said they had been tormented by the devil or his agents should be examined not in open court but privately. If possible they should be brought by fasting and prayer to repulse Satan and frustrate his diabolic campaign. In 1688 Cotton had taken into his own house a child who appeared to be afflicted by the devil, and together with others of the clergy had succeeded in curing her delusion. After the trials began he offered to harbor six others and to try to save them by the same method, but the court refused him permission.

The five essential sections of the *Return* of June 15 are given in the *Magnalia*. The full text was not printed until early November of 1692, when it was included in the postscript to Increase Mather's *Cases of Conscience Concerning Evil Spirits*. This book was written at the request of a group of ministers who met at Cambridge on August 1. Six "witches" had already been hanged, and Mather and his colleagues were alarmed by the court's failure to heed the *Return*. Shortly after October 3, Mather's finished manuscript was sent to the governor, with the endorsement of the ministers of eleven towns and three of the Congregational churches in Boston. By then fourteen more persons had been hanged in Salem, a half-dozen more had been condemned, and fifty others were in jail awaiting trial.

The *Cases* repeated the warnings of the *Return* but argued its points more vigorously and supported them by references to a variety of authorities. And, in two memorable sentences, it made absolutely clear Increase Mather's position and, presumably, that of his son: "It were better that ten suspected Witches should escape, than that one innocent Person should be Condemned," and "I had rather judge a Witch to be an honest woman, than judge an honest woman as a Witch."

By October 12, Phips had read the manuscript and had been deeply impressed. On the 26th his council voted to call a meeting to seek light on the "right way as to the witchcrafts." The Salem court interpreted this as, in effect, a dismissal. Three days later Phips confirmed this and suspended the trials until January, when the Supreme Court was to convene with instructions not to condemn any "witch" on the basis of "spectral evidence." It tried fifty-two of the accused and acquitted all but three. These the governor reprieved and later pardoned. Sir William declared that "the stop put to the first method of proceedings . . . dissipated the blak cloud that threatened this Province with destruccion." There was never again a trial for witchcraft in New England. Thus, "Increase Mather . . . brought the murders to an end by his *Cases of Conscience*."

At least a fortnight before the *Cases* was printed, Cotton Mather had brought out his strangely confused and hastily written book, *The Wonders of the Invisible World*, "Published by the Special Command of His EXCELLENCY, the Governour of the Province of the Massachusetts-Bay." Earlier, probably in mid-September, Phips had asked him to write an account of some of the Salem trials. As Royal Governor he had received from England sharp queries about the court's proceedings. In Massachusetts manuscript copies of Increase Mather's *Cases* had been widely circulated, and there were signs of growing opposition to the judges Phips had appointed. He hoped that a record of a few of the trials, carefully selected and adroitly commented on, might help him to reply to his English interrogators and check the New England critics' hostility to the court. Some of the judges, notably William Stoughton, the chief justice, and Samuel Sewall, were men of influence and supporters of Sir William's regime, and he was eager to protect them from attack. But who would write the sort of book he wanted? Not Increase Mather, since he was writing a severe critique of the court's methods. But what about Cotton? He was less powerful, certainly, but was pastor of an important church and renowned as a writer.

On September 22nd, the day of the last execution in Salem, he was called to meet with Stoughton and two other judges, Samuel Sewall and John Hathorne, and the clerk of the court, Stephen Sewall. He was promised records of the trials, and both Samuel Sewall and Stoughton, who was not only chief justice but also lieutenant governor, pledged him their support if he would write the book Phips wanted.

He was caught in a painful dilemma. He agreed with his father's criticisms of the witchcraft trials. Could he now with a clear conscience write anything in defense of the judges which would satisfy them and the governor, unless he hid his real feelings and dealt only in half-truths? On the other hand, could he take the consequences of a refusal to follow the magistrates' wish? His father, by virtue of his age, experience, and achievement, could afford to rebuke them, but Cotton, not yet thirty, still had his way to make. He was passionately eager for fame and power, and for success he must preserve the good will of such local potentates as Stoughton and Sewall.

Ambition conquered scruples. He agreed to write the book and, clearly terrified and unhappy, set about the task. He dashed off a prefatory section, "The Author's Defence," left a blank sheet for a statement approving his labors which he hoped Stoughton would supply, and wrote a curious little foreword, which began: "I live by *Neighbours* that force me to produce these undeserved Lines." At this point he paused and sent all he had written to the chief justice. He was rewarded by a fulsome letter of praise and gratitude, signed "Your assured Friend, William Stoughton." Thus stimulated, he plunged on, adding to his manuscript some pages which had little or no relevance to his ostensible purpose. Then, at last, Stephen Sewall delivered some of the court's records of five of the Salem trials. Mather settled down to write his version of them, trying to demonstrate that in these cases at least the court had not acted improperly. Samuel Sewall and Stoughton read his account in proof and wrote an endorsement of it as a true report of the "matters of Fact and Evidence" and a correct "Prospect" of the "Methods of Conviction." This Mather promptly dispatched to the printer. Still unable to control his pen, he added to the book a sermon on "The Devil Discovered," and some extracts from an account of witchcrafts in Sweden. The whole desperate hodge-podge was hurried through the press and put on sale probably about October 15.

Here and there in the book are passages which reveal what Mather actually thought about the magistrates' mistakes—their reckless reliance on "spectral evidence," their unwise method of conducting the first investigation of each of the accused, and their failure to treat the "afflicted" as he had recommended. But for the most part these passages are so swamped by other material and so cautiously phrased that the reader must agree with Perry Miller's verdict that the *Wonders* was a "false book, produced by a man whose heart was not in it," which failed "to convey except by its utter confusion, what Cotton Mather really believed" about the judges' acts in Salem.

The book must have been a source of embarrassment to his father. Devoted to his son, Increase could not openly censure what he had done. He loyally added to his *Cases* a "Postscript" asserting that he had read and approved of Cotton's work "before it was printed." The basic difference between it and Increase's *Cases* was not one of disagreement on ideas and principles but a contrast between an honest book, presenting its author's beliefs directly and forcefully, and a time-serving publication, shaped to win the approval of men who, even though misguided, could be useful to its writer.

Once the last of the accused in Salem was freed, even those who "reviled" the *Wonders* when it first appeared did not trouble to press their attack. Cotton Mather, his father, and the judges of the court lost neither standing nor influence. In the election of members of the Council in 1693 all the nine magistrates who had condemned the supposed witches were chosen, together with two-thirds of those whom Increase had asked King William to appoint as councillors.

The election of 1693, although it was in no way affected by the witchcraft trials, boded ill for the Mathers. Most of the councillors that Increase had persuaded the king to appoint when the new charter was granted had previously been members of the council. Of those who had not, only a few were elected. Plainly the voters preferred those whom they had in the past chosen themselves to those they had not but who had been nominated by Mather in England. Two councillors whom Mather did not include in the list he gave the king, but who were elected in 1693, were Elisha Cooke and Thomas Oakes. Both had served with him and Sir Henry Ashurst, as agents of Massachusetts in the effort to induce William III to restore the old charter. When it became clear that the king would not restore it, Cooke refused to sign an acceptance of the new one, which was approved by Mather and Ashurst. Oakes, although he may have signed, did so reluctantly.

Cooke may well have been envious of the respect shown Mather by eminent political figures and clergymen in England and have felt that he had been relatively ignored and his advice given little weight. Certainly he was interested in his own political advancement, perhaps more interested than he was in congregationalism or even the old charter. He set out to organize in Boston a coalition against Mather. There were, he knew, a number of believers in the original "New England Way" who resented the new charter because it took away some of the means by which the Congregational churches had kept their political power. Also there were many who, loyal to the Church of England (an Anglican church had been established in Boston in 1686), resented the dominance of the Congregational ministers and the appointment of Phips, one of their disciples, as governor. Others, not concerned with religious affairs, hated the idea of having the chief officer of Massachusetts appointed by the king instead of, as in the past, by the representatives of the people. Harping on such loosely defined but emotionally inflammatory slogans as "the original rights and privileges of the colony," or "liberty, the great heritage of Englishmen," Cooke put together an oddly assorted "faction" which, under his skillful leadership, rapidly gained ground.

When in 1693 he was elected to the Council, Phips overruled the vote. The new charter gave the royal governor the right to veto the election to the council of anyone of whom he disapproved. Sir William's use of this power supplied Cooke with priceless political ammunition. His action could easily be decried as a tyrannical defiance of the will of the people. And, although it is not certain that Phips acted on Mather's advice, it was easy to spread the idea that he had. By so doing Cooke could appeal to those who professed devotion to the "rights of Englishmen" and also to devout Congregationalists by warning them that one of their leaders was exercising a political authority in government which the saintly founders of the reformed church in Massachusetts would not have claimed. Cooke was elected to the council again in 1694 and this time there was no veto.

Phips was under fire. A good sailor and soldier, a successful discoverer of "Treasures . . . Long in the Bottom of the *Ocean* laid," he had too little political skill and too hot a temper to lead a New England split by warring factions. Charges against him were sent to England, and he was summoned there to defend himself. He left Boston on November 17, 1694, was well received in London, but died in February before any investigation of the complaints against him had been made. The government in New England was taken over by none other than William Stoughton.

Sir William's death initiated the political decline of the Mathers. Stoughton was on the whole well inclined toward them but by no means as devoted an ally as Phips had been. They were identified with Sir William; his foes were theirs and were all too ready to blame them for his faults. To keep their dominant position they must engage in a struggle against heavy odds. Surrender was, of course, unthinkable.

Cotton Mather wrote book after book and preached sermon after sermon, urging "reformation," renewal of the covenants of the churches, and a return to the righteousness of their founders. He also began work on the *Magnalia*, which was in large part designed as a jeremiad against the sinful backslidings of New England. But the Mathers' enemies proved to be stronger than they. In the six years following Phip's death they lost two major battles. One concerned the control of Harvard College, the other the preservation of the pristine "purity" of the Congregational churches.

Increase Mather had twice refused the presidency of Harvard, and accepted it in 1685 only when it was agreed that he might live in Boston in order to carry on his ministry at the Second Church. He promised, however, to manage the annual commencements, and to make frequent visits to the college to inspect its affairs.

Harvard had been governed under a Massachusetts charter by a Corporation made up of a President, a Treasurer, and five Fellows. This body had full authority, subject only to the advice and approval of the "Overseers"—the Governor, Deputy Governor, and "Assistants" of the colony, together with the Congregational ministers of Boston and the six adjoining towns. When the charter of the colony was invalidated, the college's charter was also, but the Corporation continued to rule as before, pending a new charter or a restoration of the old one. In England Increase Mather had tried unsuccessfully to persuade William to grant one or the other, and was advised that the best way to proceed would be for the General Court of Massachusetts Bay to incorporate Harvard and submit this Act of the Court to the king for his approval, which, Mather was told, there was reason to hope he would grant.

Accordingly, almost as soon as Phips arrived in Boston in 1692, Increase drew up a new charter, which was approved by the Court, signed by the governor, and sent to London. Clearly designed to put Harvard entirely under the control of the Congregational clergy and their disciples, it made no provision for "Overseers" but left the entire government of the college to a self-perpetuating Corporation. Increase Mather was, of course, named as President, with John Richards, a member of his own church, as Treasurer. The eight Fellows were Cotton

Mather, of the same church, the ministers of the other two congregations in Boston, those of three adjoining towns, and William Brattle and John Leverett, who had for many years while Mather was president taken care of the everyday operation of Harvard. It was indeed "a very close and clerical Corporation" which the Mathers could easily dominate. But it was too "close and clerical" to please King William, and he refused to approve it.

There followed a period in which various plans for a collegiate charter were drawn up but failed. Increase Mather yearned to be sent to England to plead with the king but, in spite of the support of many of the clergy, could not persuade the General Court to let him go. Cooke was active and succeeded in getting an official decree that the president of Harvard must live at the college, hoping that Mather would not obey and thus could be removed from office. He did twice try living in Cambridge, but hated it, and on July 3, 1701, returned to Boston, after having three days before asked the general court to find a new president. On August 1 the Court invited Samuel Willard, who had for a year been vice president, to accept the presidency, but he, like Mather, was unwilling to live in Cambridge. This presented no difficulty to Increase's opponents. Willard was given all the powers of the president but was officially designated as vice president. This transparent device can have deceived no one and was for Mather an addition of insult to injury.

Cotton Mather, of course, was furious, and at "Mr. Wilkins's shop" created a scene. He talked so loudly that he could be heard in the street, declaring that his father had been "used . . . worse than a Neger." A little later, again at Mr. Wilkins's, and refusing to go "unto the inner room," he accused the governor's council of "*Lying, Hypocrisy*" and "Tricks."

By 1701 the Mathers had been defeated in another campaign, one waged against those who seemed to them dangerous innovators within the Congregational fold, and, in Cotton's words, sought "utterly" to "subvert our churches." This seemed the more outrageous because two of the subversive ringleaders were William Brattle and John Leverett, Increase's right-hand men at Harvard. They and their followers were theologically sound; their "subversion" was their advocacy of some changes in ritual and polity which today seem both innocent and "liberal." The most important of the innovations they sought was the authorization of ministers to admit to communion and full church membership anyone of "visible sanctity" without a relation of a religious experience proving "conversion" or "regeneration." The rebels also held that the choice of a minister should be made by vote of all male adult members of the congregation who contributed to the maintenance of their church, whether or not they were communicants.

Early in 1698, Leverett, William and Thomas Brattle, and a group of merchants and other prosperous and influential men in Boston, decided to establish a new church. They chose as its first minister Benjamin Colman, a Harvard graduate of 1692. Colman, who was then in England, accepted, and after obtaining Presbyterian ordination there, arrived in Boston in November, 1699. By then Thomas Brattle had given a plot of land known as "Brattle Close," and others had supplied funds for building on it a simple wooden meeting house.

On November 17th, a "Manifesto" was published, stating the principles on which the "Brattle Street Church" (often called the "Manifesto Church") was founded. The document provoked heated criticisms from various ministers. Cotton Mather declared that a Satanic "Shake unto the Churches of New England" had begun and called Colman's followers "ignorant, arrogant, obstinate, and full of Malice." A superficial truce was somehow patched up, however, and on the last day of January, 1700, both Mathers joined other Congregational ministers in Boston in a service at the new meeting house. Increase preached and Cotton "pray'd excellently and pathetically for Mr. Colman and his Flock." To this comment Samuel Sewall added: "Twas a close dark day."

For the Mathers it was indeed. Increase promptly published his *Order of the Gospel Professed and Practised by the Churches of Christ in New England*, a hard-hitting denunciation of the ideas and practice of the new church, but it was quickly and effectively answered. For a time a hot debate raged, but the controversy gradually ceased to be a matter of general concern. The new church went its way and the older churches theirs.

Increase Mather had fought and lost and was "left at sixty-two just what he had been at twenty-five, and what he remained all the rest of his life—nothing but the Minister of the Second Church in Boston." But, embittered as he was, he could find consolation in the knowledge that by virtue of his age and experience he still commanded respect, and that his service in his ministry had won him the enduring affection of his congregation and many other good citizens of Boston. Cotton Mather, who had vociferously supported his father in the battle at Harvard and the effort to check the "subversion" of the "Manifesto Church," had no such consolation.

There is no doubt that he hoped some day to be president of the college as his father had been and longed to achieve an influence comparable to Increase's in politics and church leadership. The goal had not been reached, and the events of 1700 and 1701 made it unlikely that it ever would be. He had, to be sure, many admirers in his congregation, and some renown as a preacher and as a prolific writer; he had in nineteen years produced some twenty more books or pamphlets than Increase had in thirty-eight. But much that he had published was hastily written and

repetitive, and his eager rushing into print whenever a controversy arose
and the intemperate tone of some of his pages had won him more foes
than friends. Early in 1700 he wrote: "It is represented unto mee, as if
my *Opportunities to glorify* . . . *Christ*, were like to bee much abridged and
abated, if not almost wholly extinguished: that . . . Prejudices were like
to prevail against mee, in the *apostatizing Generation*," and "that whereas
I had enjoy'd singular Advantages to do good, by the Way of the *Press*
People were now prejudiced against mee for printing so many Books,
and it will be necessary for mee to desist from the Printing of any more."

Later in 1700 there arrived from London a book which assailed both
Mathers but aimed its sharpest shafts against Cotton. Robert Calef's
More Wonders of the Invisible World was a heated criticism of what its
author considered to have been the part played by the ministers, especially the two leaders of the Second Church, during the witch trials eight
years before. Calef seems to have been a cloth merchant of Boston. He
was no scholar but a man of common sense. Although anticlerical, he
was a faithful reader of the Bible and as early as 1693 had interested
himself in the witchcraft persecutions. He began to gather what information he could, collected fuller records of the Salem trials than Cotton
Mather had when he concocted his *Wonders of the Invisible World*, and
wrote to him and to other ministers asking them for comments on his
ideas about the witchcraft affair. For the most part they seem to have
treated his requests with scant courtesy, refusing to answer, or, in the
case of Cotton Mather, threatening him with a libel suit.

Calef's book is clumsily constructed and hard to read, but is nonetheless a courageous attempt to defend an important thesis. Like most men
of his time in Old and New England, he believed that there were witches
—"Scriptures else were vain which assign their punishment to be by
death." He shared the common view that "there are possessions" by
Satan and that "the bodies of the possest have hence been . . . afflicted."
But he insisted, as Perry Miller has put it, that the Bible gives no "explicit
rules for detecting the witch," so "learned theories concerning the nature
of the sin or its evidences are 'humane inventions'—mere 'traditions'
of men foisted onto Scripture, exactly on a par with the superstitions of
Rome." He inveighed especially against the "assumption to which all
theorizers subscribed, the notion that a witch enters explicit 'covenant'
with the Devil" and declared it to be utterly without textual foundation.

Calef's book was finished in 1697 but not printed until 1700, and then
in London. It was too late to accomplish anything by raking over the
dead coals of the Salem trials. Samuel Sewall had already publicly
acknowledged that, as a member of the first Salem witch court, he had
followed methods and accepted evidence which he feared had cost some
innocent people their lives, although, of course, he did not question that

there were witches or that the law required that they be tried and, if found guilty, put to death. By 1700 most New Englanders shared his opinion and were eager to forget the whole dismal affair of 1692. No one seems to have paid much attention to Calef's book, except those directly attacked in it—notably the Mathers—and those who welcomed anything that might weaken the influence of the Congregational clergy.

The book has been ably studied and summarized by several careful scholars. The only reason for mentioning it here is the fact that nearly two decades after the trials ended, when belief in witchcraft was no longer general, it became the principal source of the persistent myth which portrays Cotton Mather as the chief originator of the witchcraft hysteria, a villain who egged on the judges in their bloody work and gloated over the executions—a myth unhappily still cherished by some writers of fiction and drama and a few hasty historians.

This is understandable. As he went on with his work, Calef, justly angered by Cotton Mather's cavalier treatment of his queries, devoted many pages to virulent denunciations of him, often more abusive than respectful of truth. He enlarged the scope of his attack on the clergy to cover their political position and influence in matters that had little or no relation to the Salem affair. Thus he included derogatory passages on Increase Mather's agency in England, his acceptance of the new charter, and Phips's regime as governor. Calef declared, "It has been an observation of long continuance, that matters of State seldom prosper, when managed by the clergy." Here, obviously, was grist for Elisha Cooke's political mill, and it has been suggested but never proved that he or one of his henchmen aided Calef in writing the *More Wonders* and arranged for its publication in 1700, when the Mathers were fighting against odds and resentment of clerical domination in "matters of state" was rife.

The story that Increase Mather had the book publicly burned at Harvard may be true, although it has thus far been traced back no farther than 1809. Both Mathers did, however, collaborate in the production of an answer, refuting much that Calef had written, and successfully disposing of most of his charges, in a style often as vituperative as his own.

It was published in Boston in 1701 as *Some Few Remarks Upon a Scandalous Book, against the Government and Ministry of New-England.* It was "Composed . . . by several Persons belonging to the Flock of some of the Injured Pastors," in other words, by members of the Mathers' congregation. Increase contributed an "Instrument" defending his agency in England; Cotton furnished a letter answering Calef's strictures against him, and a short postscript disavowing authorship of the *Some Few Remarks* except for the letter itself.

Calef's work deserves to be read for his sensible theory about the unsound basis traditionally relied on in New England and abroad for the discovery and trial of witches. But any dispassionate reader interested in the actual relation of the clergy to the witchcraft delusion of 1692 should also make his way through the pages of *Some Few Remarks* as an antidote to the *More Wonders'* reckless ignoring or distorting of the facts. Although Cotton declared that, even after the *Remarks* appeared, Calef, the "vile fool," was employed by "the Enemies of the Churches . . . to go on, with more of his filthy Scribbles," nothing seems to have come of it. Little is known about the "fool's" career after 1700, except that he "held several town offices in Boston and Roxbury" and "died on April 13, 1719."

For the reader of the *Magnalia* the details of Cotton Mather's career from 1701 until his death in 1728 are not important. The Cotton Mather who finished the *Magnalia* before he was forty was a very different man from the Cotton Mather who in the last twenty-eight years of his life achieved more that now seems praiseworthy than he ever had before. His major characteristics, good and bad, were unchanged. His ambition, vanity, and nervous instability persisted, but so did his passionate devotion to his church. Although he never became as powerful as his father had been, many of the pious still recognized him as a leader. He worked hard trying to form societies dedicated to such good purposes as the maintenance of peace, the building up of churches in poor communities, the relief of needy ministers, the distribution of religious tracts, the conversion of Indians, and the education of slaves, imitating as far as possible the many reform societies which were active in England. He was especially interested in the training of children and seems to have been liked by them, and continued to be generous in giving time and money to aid the poor and afflicted.

Busy as he was, he somehow found time for study and writing. He had always been an eager scholar and all too fond of seeing his work in print. He became even more so after 1700, probably because he hoped that the circulation of his writings might not only stimulate piety but also win abroad the appreciation and renown which he felt ungrateful and backsliding New England had denied him. In the years before 1701 he published ninety-four books as well as a number of "Attestations," prefaces, postscripts, and other minor contributions to works by others. By 1728 he had added to the list more than three hundred other items. Among these were several of his most readable and best known books—his *Bonifacius* (1710), later to be called "Essays to Do Good" and praised by Benjamin Franklin; *The Christian Philosopher* (1720), a compendium of scientific data, chiefly drawn from other writers but well selected and admirably presented; and the *Manuductio ad Ministerium, Directions For a Candidate of the Ministry* (1726), which reveals both its author's wide reading and his literary taste. He also completed the manuscripts of his *Biblia Americana*, described in his General Introduction to the *Magnalia* but never printed, and his *Angel of Bethesda,* a collection of medical lore, also still unprinted except for a few sections.

In his writing after 1700 Mather often concerned himself with science, and especially medicine, harking back to interests he had developed when at Harvard he had studied to be a physician. Some years before 1721 he heard of inoculation as a means of preventing smallpox, and when in that year an epidemic of the disease broke out in Boston, he persuaded Dr. Zabdiel Boylston to experiment with the hitherto virtually unknown method. Opposed by the other doctors in the town and by most of its people, Mather wrote in defense of Boylston, helped him in every other way he could, and showed his own faith in what he was convinced was a beneficent medical innovation by having his own son Samuel inoculated.

He corresponded with many scientists, divines, and other scholars abroad. Among them were John Woodward, then famous as a geologist and botanist, who wrote occasionally on medicine; William Whiston, a mathematician and a man of wide learning, who helped to call attention to some important points in ecclesiastical history; John Desaguliers, a scientist, esteemed by Newton and inventor of the planetarium who won the Copley gold medal of the Royal Society; Peter King, who wrote in 1691 a book on early church history which interested John Locke and was later elevated to the peerage and made Lord Chancellor of England; and even Sir Richard Blackmore, physician to King William and Queen Mary, who had an unfortunate passion for writing epics which are remembered today only for their dullness. Mather exchanged letters also with August Herman Francke, a German protestant, a pietist, and a scholar learned in Hebrew, Greek, and Biblical exegesis, and even with Danish missionaries in India.

He managed all this in spite of financial worries, continuing abuse from some of the "godless," and, worst of all, family tragedies. His second wife, whom he married in 1703, died in 1713. She bore him six children but only one outlived him. His third wife became insane. His eldest son, Increase, was a scapegrace whose vagaries gave him much pain, but he loved him, struggled hard to reform him, and was profoundly grieved by his death at sea in 1724.

He had also to contend with his realization that times were changing, and for the worse. His hope of preserving in Massachusetts the religious zeal of his grandfathers was clearly doomed to failure. Bravely, although often deeply distressed, he tried to adapt himself to new ideas and to find ways by which they might be used in God's service. He continued to confide to his diary bitter reflections on those who had abandoned the old standards of New England congregationalism but in his writing and teaching became more and more tolerant. He was determined to preserve the basic elements of holiness, even though the methods he had once advocated were no longer possible to follow.

His son Samuel wrote that his "Domestic Honours" were "but *small*"; his countrymen did not honor him "so much as he honored them." Abroad he fared better. In 1710 he was given by the University of Glasgow the honorary degree of Doctor of Divinity, and in 1713 he was elected a Fellow of the Royal Society in England—the first minister in New England ever to receive this distinction.

Two hundred years after his death some of his achievements came to be better understood and more cordially extolled than they ever were by his contemporaries in New England. He was in 1954 called by two historians of science "the first significant figure in American medicine," who "deserves, moreover, a place in the history of western medicine as a whole." A biologist noted in 1935 that Mather wrote the earliest account of plant hybridization then known. Recent historians of philosophy and ideas have pointed out that *The Christian Philosopher* is "the finest example of the way in which Newtonian science came to America and was disseminated" there "as a welcome support to the Christian religion." The older Calvinistic view was that man was "vile" and that "nature was rather awful than beautiful, a manifestation of God's dread power rather than of His love for mankind." *The Christian Philosopher*, however, emphasized the beauty and orderliness of the divine planning of the universe, so that "to study nature" was "to realize God's goodness" and to "appreciate" Him "by the exercise of observation and reason." The book "expresses as no earlier American book had done the beginning of the more liberal philosophy of the eighteenth century." As for the *Manuductio*, it also "appears to mark . . . the beginnings of a new era" and reveals "a heightened consciousness of stylistic issues that could not have been exhibited by a seventeenth century divine." It "illustrates for us, more cogently, perhaps, than any other American writing of the period, what contradictory winds of doctrine were blowing" in the late seventeenth century and the early eighteenth. "The element of Humanism originally combined with the theology" was "beginning to crowd it out." Mather had for years inclined toward the idea "that the function of religion is well doing, that he who contributes to the welfare of mankind glorifies God," and that "the first concern of the minister is to find out opportunities to do good." From the vantage point of the present it is refreshing to find Mather emphasizing in one of his last books this idea rather than the older grim "Puritan"view of man's relation to God.

On his deathbed he was asked by his son "what Sentence or Word . . . he would have me think on constantly," and replied, "Remember only that one word *Fructuosus*." It was his fruitfulness as a scholar and writer that the "united Pastors of the Town" chose to praise most when they joined with the Second Church in eulogizing "their deceased colleague." Among them was Benjamin Colman of the Brattle Street Church, who, nearly three decades before, had been denounced by the Mathers and had given them as good as they sent. In 1728, "commanded" by love for Christ and for Mather himself, he chose to "draw a veil" over Cotton's failings and said: "It was *Conversation* and Acquaintance with him, in his familiar and occasional Discourses and private Communications, that discovered the vast compass of his Knowledge and the Projections of his Piety . . . Here he excell'd; here he shone; being exceeding communicative, and bringing out of his *Treasury* things new & old, without measure . . . His Wit, and Fancy, his Invention, his Quickness of thought, and ready Apprehension . . . were all consecrated to God . . . and out of his Abundance . . . overflow'd . . . richness and brightness, pleasure and profit."

Others praised his hospitality. Over the door of his study, "a large, yett a warm chamber" lined with books, he had written "Be Short," but when his friends sought him out there "he would always entertain" them "with Ease & Pleasure, even in his Studying Hours." He would on such occasions "advance Himself in learning, by the most artful Repetition of the more agreable Passages He had lately been reading," adding his "Remarks or Improvements upon them," thus digesting them, and making them more "perfectly . . . his own." Thomas Prince, later to be called "the Father of American Bibliography," marvelled at how much Mather had read and studied, and "What a vast Amassment of *Learning* He had grasp'd."

He said in his *Manuductio* that a scholar need not, and should not, be "an Odd, Starv'd, Lank sort of a thing, who . . . lived only on *Hebrew Roots* all his Days." He himself was not. Genuinely in love with learning, he had learned to read seven languages and, "with a little Study," to write them, and was happiest when, surrounded by his books, he could "feast" himself "with the Sweets of all the *Sciences* which the more polite Part of Mankind ordinarily present unto." "I am entertained," he wrote, "with all kinds of *Histories* ancient and modern," and "the Curiosities which, by all sorts of learning, are brought unto the curious. These *Intellectual* Pleasures are far beyond any *Sensual* ones."

Both Mathers were ardent book collectors, but Cotton's library became even greater than his father's. By 1700 he estimated that he owned "several Thousands of Books," and he added more each year of his life. Probably by the time of his death, the total had risen to four thousand, and John Dunton's statement that "Mr. Mather's library" was "the Glory of *New-England*, if not of all *America*," is borne out by such records as we have of its contents. They make it clear that his interests were many and varied and that he often chose books as much for their literary quality as for their scholarly importance.

As a reader he was primarily a smatterer, constantly skimming through whole volumes in search of passages containing ideas which he thought he could develop in his own way or which might serve him as appropriate quotations for use in his own writing. He did not "trouble himself" with any books "but those that were likely to bring him something *New*, and so increase his Knowledge. In two or three minutes turning thro' a Volumn, he cou'd easily tell whether it wou'd make Additions to the Store of his Ideas. If it cou'd not, He quickly laid it by." If it could, he read only "those Parts . . . that represented something *Novel*, which he Pencil'd as he went along, and at the End reduc'd the Substance" to entries in his notebooks, or "Quotidiana" as he called them, "to be review'd at Leisure." Thus he read with "wonderful Celerity," and as he grew older "there were but few Books published that would take him *much* to read." Although, judged by present day standards, he had grave defects as a scholar, which the *Magnalia* all too plainly reveals, he showed in it and his other writings a first-hand knowledge of many authorities familiar only to the most erudite of his time and probably known to very few of his compatriots in New England.

Enough has been said about Cotton Mather's faults of character and his inability to conquer them. But Barrett Wendell, who understood him better than any other of his biographers, was right in saying: "There is still good ground for believing it was a good man they buried on Copp's Hill one February day in the year 1728." A strangely complex creature of flesh and blood, he could neither understand nor control the conflicting strains in his nature. He longed for triumphs he was not equipped to achieve and passionately sought for a holiness he was temperamentally unfitted to attain. Tortured by his failures and unduly proud of his successes, he was at times convinced that he was deservedly doomed to damnation, and at others confident that he was a special favorite of the Lord. But, whatever his mood and however obsessed he was by his dreams of sainthood or eternal punishment, he never flinched in his efforts to serve God. He strove doggedly in his writing, preaching, and daily struggles to convert the unregenerate, whatever the cost in weariness and strain, to keep alive what he conceived to be the essential elements of faith and piety. It was this determined striving in the face of odds which made him, in spite of his shortcomings, "a good man."

BIBLIOGRAPHICAL NOTES

Four full-length biographies of Cotton Mather have been printed thus far, and a fifth, by Professor David Levin, is soon to be published. Of the four, the best are *The Life of . . . Cotton Mather* (Boston, 1729) by his son Samuel, a book excessively eulogistic and tiresome in style but with material found nowhere else, and Barrett Wendell's *Cotton Mather, The Puritan Priest* (New York, 1891; reprinted Cambridge, Mass., 1926; and with an introduction by Alan Heimert, New York, 1963), which in spite of some minor errors is still the best balanced life of his subject. Ralph and Louise Boas, *Cotton Mather, Keeper of the Puritan Conscience* (New York, 1928) has some interesting suggestions on Mather's psychology, but is in most of its pages trite or superficial. A. P. Marvin's *Life and Times of Cotton Mather* (Boston, 1892) is now completely outmoded.

Essential for understanding Mather's life are his "Reserved and Revised Memorials," diaries he kept year by year, often revising or deleting passages in order to portray himself in the most favorable light. Nevertheless, the diaries are excellent guides for understanding his life, character, and motives. Worthington C. Ford in 1911–12 published in two volumes all the diaries then known as *The Diary of Cotton Mather* (7 MHS *Collections*, vols. 7 and 8). The diary for 1712, discovered in 1912, was edited with notes by William R. Manierre II and published in 1964 by the University Press of Virginia.

Indispensable for the study of Mather's life are Thomas J. Holmes, *Cotton Mather: A Bibliography of His Works* (3 vols., Harvard University Press, Cambridge, Mass., 1940) and Holmes's *Increase Mather, A Bibliography* (2 vols., Cambridge, 1931). Both supply not only careful bibliographical details but extremely valuable biographical material. Useful also for understanding Cotton Mather are passages in the "Autobiography" of his father, Increase, printed with an introduction and some notes by M. G. Hall (*Proceedings of the American Antiquarian Society*, vol. 71, part 2, pp. 271–360). For Cotton Mather's ancestors and relatives, see "The Pedigree of the Family of Mather" in the 1852/53 edition of the *Magnalia*, 1:lii–xliii. The effect of Mather's ancestry on his boyhood has been ably discussed in Chandler Robbins, *History of the Second Church . . . in Boston* (Boston, 1852).

Increase Mather's sermon in 1674 was published in Boston in the same year as *The Day of Trouble Is Near*. The reasons for the synod of 1679 and its results are given in chapter 13 of Williston Walker, *Creeds and Platforms of Congregationalism* (New York, 1893; reprinted with an introduction by Douglas Horton, Boston, 1960). The "pestilential sicknesses . . . epidemical," "multiplied Shipwrecks," and "enemies" preying on "Vessels and Sailors" are listed in *Magnalia*, Book V, part 4, section 1. An example of the New Englanders' disregard for the English government is in *The Diary of John Evelyn* (ed. E. S. DeBeer, 6 vols., Oxford, 1955), 3:579–580 and note. Increase Mather's opposition to accepting Charles II's "Declaration" of 1683 is in Cotton Mather's *Parentator, Memoirs of . . . Increase Mather* (Boston, 1724), p. 91, taken from Increase's "Autobiography" (Hall, p. 308), as was his wish that thanks be sent to James II for his Declaration of Indulgence (Hall, p. 320). The praise for Mather's skill as a diplomat comes from Samuel E. Morison, *Harvard College in the Seventeenth Century* (2 vols., Cambridge, Mass., 1936), 1:488. His letter to John Richards and another of the same tenor are in the Massachusetts Historical Society and quoted with its permission. They were called to the attention of the editors by Mr. Richard Simmons of the School of History in the University of Birmingham.

Perry Miller's remark on the relative unimportance of the witchcraft tragedy is from *The New England Mind from Colony to Province* (Cambridge, Mass., 1953), p. 191. There is abundant material on the affair in Holmes, *Increase Mather*, and *Cotton Mather, passim. The Return of Several Ministers*, complete with its eight sections, is in Chadwick Hansen, *Witchcraft at Salem* (New York, 1969), pp. 123–125. For Increase Mather's "It were better," etc., and his "I had rather judge," etc., see Murdock, *Increase Mather* (Cambridge, Mass., 1925), p. 300. Phips's declaration that the end of the first method of judging the supposed witches "dissipated the blak cloud" over the "Province," is in Holmes, *Increase*, 1:128, following Phips's letter to London on February 21, 1693, printed in *Calendar of State Papers*, Colonial Series, America and West Indies, No. 112. For the various editions of Cotton Mather's *The Wonders of the Invisible World*, see Holmes, *Cotton Mather*, 3:1234–1246.

Morison's *Harvard College* (1:490) supplies the comment on the governing board of the college. Cotton Mather's outburst of rage at Mr. Wilkins's shop is described in *The Diary of Samuel Sewall* (5 MHS *Collections*, vols. 5, 6, 7), 2:43–44; Mather recorded in his *Diary* (1:326) his dislike of the "innovators." The following comments on the nature of their "subversion" are taken from Miller's *Colony to Province*, p. 242. The whole story of the founding of the Brattle Street Church and its "Manifesto" is succinctly told in Walker, *Creeds*, pp. 472–480.

George L. Burr, *Narratives of the Witchcraft Cases* (New York, 1914, reprinted 1946) has in pages 296–393 Calef's *More Wonders*, with some omissions but useful notes. There are valuable comments in Miller's *Colony to Province*, pp. 245–252. Cf. also W. F. Poole, "Witchcraft in Boston," in Justin Winsor, ed., *Memorial History of Boston* (4 vols., Boston, 1880–1881), 2:167–169. Dr. John Eliot (1754–1813) published the *New England Biographical Dictionary* in 1809. For Calef after 1700, see DAB.

The editions prior to 1940 of *Bonifacius* or "Essays to do Good," *The Christian Philosopher*, and the *Manuductio ad Ministerium* are listed in Holmes, *Cotton*, 1:89–95, 324–338, 129–138; 2:617–636. For Benjamin Franklin's praise of the *Bonifacius*, see Holmes, 1:92–93. David Levin, ed., *Bonifacius, An Essay Upon the Good* (Cambridge, Mass., 1966), in his "Introduction" examines Mather's purpose in writing the *Bonifacius*. An excellent essay, "Notes on the Christian Philosopher," by Theodore Hornberger, is in Holmes, 1:133–137; Perry Miller's "A Note on the Manuductio ad Ministerium" is in Holmes, 2:630–635. A facsimile of this book with a biographical note by Holmes and K. B. Murdock was published for the Columbia University Press, New York, 1938. A small part of *The Angel of Bethesda* was published with that title in 1722 (Holmes, 1:40–44), but the full text remains in manuscript at the American Philosophical Society. The "Proposals" for its publication and some selections from the text are in Otto T. Beall, Jr., and Richard H. Shryock, *Cotton Mather: First Significant Figure in American Medicine* (Baltimore, 1924), pp. 127–234.

The increased esteem accorded some of Cotton Mather's writings in the present century is exemplified by Conway Zirkle's crediting him with being the first to give an account of plant hybridization. (See his "Some Forgotten Records of Hybridization," in the American Genetic Association *Journal of Heredity*, vol. 23, no. 11.) For praise given to Mather's *Christian Philosopher*, see Murdock, *Selections from Cotton Mather* (New York, 1926, reprinted New York, 1960), p. li, with references to I. Woodbridge Riley, *American Thought from Puritanism to Pragmatism* (New York, 1923) and *American Philosophy: The Early Schools* (New York, 1907).

The eulogies of Cotton Mather after his death, extolling his hospitality and good talk with visitors as well as his delight in learning, are described in Murdock, *Selections*, chapter II, pp. xxv–xxx, and notes.

THE *MAGNALIA*

The first mention of the *Magnalia* in Cotton Mather's Diary was written some time in July 1693. "I foresaw," he said, that "the Church-History of this countrey" might do a great "service . . . for the Church of God, not only here, but abroad in Europe." He consulted other ministers, who encouraged him, and began his work on the book late in 1693 or very early in 1694. By 1695 he had completed five biographies intended for inclusion in it, and four of his admirers in Boston subsidized their publication in a small volume called *Johannes in Eremo*. To it was appended an advertisement for his "Church-History of New England, with a Schaeme of the Whole Work," which outlined in all essentials his plan for the contents and structure of the book. His purpose in writing was also defined in the "Schaeme": to "preserve the true principles . . . good practices, and famous occurrences, temptations and salvations, of the churches in my country, from corruption and oblivion; and assist the interests of religion in the churches abroad, with the experiences of a renowned plantation, settled in a new world, purely for the sake of the most reformed religion." His work, Mather wrote, was to include "biographies" of persons who were "stars of the first magnitude in our heavens." Part of his intention, he added, was to check the "fearful degeneracy . . . rushing, in upon" New England churches, arising from the "dangers of our loosing" important elements "in our first faith" and of "giving up the essentials of that church order, which was the very END of these colonies." New Englanders, he declared, were falling away from "the greatness and . . . goodness" of the first settlers. He feared that New England, "planted with a . . . noble vine," henceforth gave "a prospect of affording only the degenerate plants of a *Strange Vine*." In other words, the "Church-History" was planned to be not only a glorification of New England's past achievements and of its saintly founders, but also a jeremiad against the backsliders of a later generation.

On January 7, 1698, there arrived from England William Turner's *Compleat History of the Most Remarkable Providences . . . Which Have Hapned in This Present Age*, a folio volume published in London some months before by John Dunton. Mather was surprised and delighted to discover that the book contained an advertisement by Dunton which announced " *The Church-History of New England* is now almost finished, including the lives of the most eminent divines of that countrey . . . down to . . . 1696. 'Tis written by Mr. Cotton Mather . . . from whom I shall receive the manuscript copy as soon as compleated; and being a large work, 'twill be printed in folio by way of subscription."

Mather was well aware that the book could not be published in New England. No printer there had either the equipment or the necessary capital. Dunton's advertisement seemed to assure that it could be brought out soon in London. He promptly made "supplications" for "direction from Heaven" about the "time and way" of sending the manuscript abroad and the "methods of its publication."

In 1698 his "Church-History" was indeed "almost finished." By late March of 1697 John Higginson had read the manuscript, or most of it, and had finished his Attestation to it. Mather had completed the first draft of his General Introduction and most of the rest of the book itself. But there remained the problem of how to send it safely. There was need for a reliable agent to take care of the bulky manuscript on the long voyage to England and, once there, to deal with the printers. It was not until June 4, 1700, that Mather wrote in his Diary "I this Day putt up my *Church-History*, and pen down Directions about the publishing it. It is a work of near 300 sheets; and has lain by me, diverse years, for want of a fitt opportunity to send it. A Gentleman, just now sailing for *England* undertakes the care of it; and by his Hand I send it for *London*."

The "gentleman" seems to have been Edward Bromfield, a Boston merchant, and a good friend of Mather, who had contributed to the cost of printing the *Johannes in Eremo*. He sailed for England on June 14, 1700. Just what he did with Mather's manuscript when he arrived in London is not clear. Unless John Dunton, by no means a trustworthy character, had by 1700 already decided not to publish it and had informed Mather of his change of heart, it seems certain that Bromfield must have taken Mather's cherished pages first to him. If he did, his errand was fruitless. In Dunton's *Life and Errors*, first published in 1705, he wrote of Mather's "Conversation" and "Writings" as "living evidences that he had read much," but added: "There are many that will not allow him the prudence to make a seasonable use of it. His Library is very large and numerous; but, had his Books been fewer when he wrote his 'History', it would have pleased us better." This suggests that Dunton did see the manuscript, but felt that it was too heavily burdened with learned allusions and erudite references to succeed.

There is definite evidence that, whatever Dunton's part in the affair, Mather's precious pages and his "Instructions" for their publishing were very soon after they arrived in London committed to the care of the Reverend John Quick, minister to a Presbyterian congregation in Bartholomew Close, Smithfield. Increase Mather had years before preached there for Quick, who was of course known to Cotton Mather by hearsay. With the manuscript of the "Church-History" in hand,

Quick promptly had printed and circulated a sheet of "Proposals For Printing *Magnalia Christi Americana* . . . By the Reverend and Learned *COTTON MATHER*, M. of A. and Pastor of the North Church in *BOSTON, N. E.*" The document listed the "Titles and Contents" of the work, and praised it for "the rich and curious Variety of its Materials" and the "Fidelity and Impartiality observed by its author." Quick declared the *Magnalia* had "been long desired by many Learned and Godly Men" and offered it to "Publick" subscribers at twenty shillings for each copy "of 240 sheets more or less," ten to be paid in advance and ten when the finished book was delivered. Anyone who presented six subscriptions was to be given a seventh copy without charge.* Quick obviously hoped that there would be enough advance subscriptions to encourage someone to undertake the publication of the book. Indeed, he optimistically believed that some booksellers known to him would buy Mather's manuscript for one hundred guineas or their equivalent in bound volumes and would agree to print the work on paper of good quality and adorn it with "the best chart of New England," "the best topographicall delineation of Boston," and a mezzotint portrait of its author.

Mather, worrying about the fate of his manuscript, seems to have heard nothing from Quick for nearly two years after it was given to Bromfield, but he did have word from someone in England that to print his "*Church-History* . . . would cost about 600 lb.," that "the Booksellers" were "cold about it," and that "the Proposals for Subscriptions" were "of an uncertain and tedious Event." However, on June 13, 1701, he received from Bromfield a letter sent from London on March 28 which reported, "There is one Mr. *Robert Hackshaw*, a very serious and Godly man who proposed to print the *Ecclesiastical History* . . . AT HIS OWN CHARGE . . . not with any Expectation of Gain to himself, but for the Glory of God."

Excited by this news, Mather at once despatched to Hackshaw an order which he was instructed to present to Quick, demanding that the manuscript be given to him. Quick, however, stoutly refused to give up the precious pages unless Hackshaw would assure him that the printing would proceed "speedily" and that he would "have the correcting of the sheets, as they" were "wrought off from the press." He pointed out that Mather had written him that he wanted the book published expeditiously and the proofs corrected by him, but Hackshaw refused to agree.

However "serious and godly" he may have been, he was a shrewd business man, and his concern with the *Magnalia* stemmed as much from commercial motives as from a desire to advance piety. He was a merchant and had in his warehouse a large supply of inferior paper which he had

---

* I am deeply indebted to Mrs. W. B. Almon who sent me her copy of the "Proposals," so far as I know the only one extant, and allowed me to print some excerpts from it.

not been able to sell. Knowing that Thomas Parkhurst, a well-known London publisher, had already issued several books by Cotton Mather, he decided to try to persuade him to print the "Church-History" and for this purpose to buy from him at a low price the stock of paper he was eager to dispose of. Hard pressed by Quick, Hackshaw revealed his plan. He declared that he would have nothing to do with the printing. "I have," he said, "treated with Mr. Parkhurst, who will buy the paper of me, & print it, provided I will take off an hundred books wch I intend to send to N. E[ngland] & the Caribee Islands, there to be disposed of . . . I have left all to Parkhurst, who will take a fortnight's time to peruse it, & then He will tell me, whether He will print it or no." Quick continued to insist that he must have the right to correct the proofs, and summoned the "Booksellers" whom he had been sure would produce the book. They did not appear, and at last he reluctantly delivered to Hackshaw Mather's manuscript and "the additional prints" Mather had sent "to be inserted in their proper place."

Parkhurst, after seeing Mather's pages, fell in with Hackshaw's plan and issued with him new "Proposals" for subscriptions to the *Magnalia*. Dunton, who had been taught his trade by Parkhurst and was devoted to him, printed in December 1701 in his periodical, "The Post-Angel," a notice of these "Proposals" which, he announced, had been "lately published." He included some phrases from Quick's earlier advertisement and expatiated on Cotton Mather's virtues and the "Glory" of his library, in a tone quite unlike that of his comments on Mather's book in his *Life and Errors* already quoted. Dunton also announced that the printing of the *Magnalia* would be finished "about *Lady-Day*, next" —that is, March 25, 1702. It seems in fact to have been completed at least a week earlier.

Mather meanwhile had for some time heard little or nothing about the fate of his "Church-History." At last there came a letter from Quick, dated March 19, 1702, giving his version of the whole story and bewailing the failure of his "fair designes, hopes, & endeavours" for the book. These, he wrote, were "now vanished into Smoak." He declared himself "most of all grieved for the Paper & character, which compareing with the specimens herewith sent you will certainly affect & afflict you, for they doe me very much." The letter cannot have reached Boston much before mid-April. Mather was then in no position to compare the paper sent him with that used by Parkhurst or to judge the type used for the *Magnalia*. It was not until October 30 that he at last saw his book in print. On that day "a gentleman" who had bought a copy in "*New Castle* in *England*" arrived in Boston with it.

Mather at once devoted himself to "solemn THANKSGIVING unto God for His Watchful and gracious Providence over that Work and the

Harvest of so many Prayers, and Cares, and Tears, and Resignations, as
I had employ'd upon it." Bromfield, who had come back to New England,
called on him late in the afternoon and joined with him in his "prayers
to God."

As soon as he had a chance to leaf through the *Magnalia*, Mather's
rejoicing was sharply checked. Printed without proof-reading, the book
was riddled with errors. What could its unhappy author do to prove that
he was not responsible for them? Copies of the *Magnalia* had been sold
in England for some months, and it was too late to correct the mistakes
in them. It was certain that other copies would very soon arrive in
Boston. All Mather could do was to make sure that none of these were
sold without some correction of their misprints. There was not time
enough for him to read through the whole work, page by page, but he
did hastily run through the crowded pages and made up a list of corrections, had it printed, and distributed it to the Boston booksellers for
insertion in whatever copies they might sell. Making no effort to correct
all the many faults in punctuation, he did in his sheets of "Errata" give
the proper readings for some one hundred and fifty instances of the typesetters' carelessness, but in his hurried examination of the folio pages
failed to detect nearly as many more.

The book had a mixed reception. In October 1703 Mather had letters
from England with "surprising informations" about its "acceptance . . .
from one end of England unto the other" and the "influence" it was
"like to have upon the evangelical interests." He was told that in 1702
and 1703 "an abridgement of the *Magnalia* was proposed" at an "assembly of ministers" in England, but the Reverend Vincent Alsop, then a
powerful figure among nonconformists, declared that the proposal was
"very improper . . . 'Tis impossible to abridge it! You injure it if you go
to do it. There is nothing Superfluous in it: Instead of . . . Epitomizing
go do as I have done; read all of it no less than twice over: No man that
has a relish for Piety or Variety can ever be weary of Reading it."

In 1708, John Oldmixon, an English pamphleteer and journalist rather
than a historian, sounded a quite different note. In his *The British Empire
in America*, in which he relied on the *Magnalia* for much of his material,
he ungratefully complained of Mather's "*Puns, Anagrams, Acrosticks,
Miracles, Prodigies, Witches, Speeches, Epistles,* and other Incumbrances."
Later in his book Oldmixon wrote: "*The History of New-England* . . . by
Cotton Mather, a *Man* of *Fame* in his Country, as appears by the barbarous
Rhimes before it in Praise of the Author, is a sufficient proof, that a Man
may have read hundreds of Latine Authors . . . have spent his Youth in
a College, and . . . bred up in Letters, yet have neither Judgment to
know how to make a Discourse perspicuous, nor Eloquence to express
his Sentiments so that they may please and perswade, the easiest way to

Conviction . . . Of all the Books that ever came from the Press with the venerable Title of a History, 'tis impossible to shew one . . . so confus'd in the Form, trivial in the Matter, and so faulty in the Expression." Mather was, of course, furious, and called Oldmixon's book "the most foolish and faithless Performance" in the writing of history "that ever Mankind was abused withal."

The *Boston Courant*, a newspaper whose editors enjoyed outraging the pious, published in 1710 some verses by John Banister, which shed light on what Mather's enemies then thought of him:

> The mad enthusiast, thirsting after fame,
> By endless volum'ns thought to raise a name.
> With undigested trash he throngs the Press;
> Thus striving to be greater, he's the less,
>
> . . . .
>
> . . . Parkhurst says, *Satis fecisti*,
> My belly's full of your Magnalia Christi.
> Your crude Divinity, and History
> Will not with a censorious age agree."

Increase Mather showed this "libel" to Judge Samuel Sewall, who summoned Banister to court. In spite of a letter from Cotton Mather himself, arguing against it, the culprit was fined.

Another English historian, Daniel Neal, later famous for his *History of the Puritans*, made use of Mather's *Magnalia*, and in his *History of New England*, printed in London in 1720, spoke well of it and its author. He wrote that Mather "with great Diligence and *Industry* . . . collected a Variety of useful Materials, for the Ecclesiastical and Civil History" which he "publish'd . . . to the world in *Folio* . . . The Dr., is certainly a Gentleman of great Probity and Vertue . . . as capable of knowing the Truth of the Facts he relates as any Man living . . . His great Integrity and Diligence deserve the Publick Thanks of his Country." But Neal qualified his praise with a note of criticism which cannot have pleased Mather: "Had the Dr.," he wrote, "put his *Materials* a little closer together, and disposed them in another Method, his Work would have been more acceptable to this Part of the World."

"The Dr." magnanimously wrote Neal that his *History* was the "Reverse of what was done by the malicious and Satanic pen of one Oldnixon (some such name)"—a characteristic Matherian pun on "Oldmixon" and "Old Nick's son"—"whose History of N.E. has far more Lies than pages in it." Mather did allow himself to say that Neal's work had "certain passages . . . which might call for a little further Elucidation," but nonetheless helped to get for him a Harvard degree of M.A.

Probably the most savage of the critics of Mather and his books was

Dr. William Douglass, who had in 1721 bitterly opposed his effort to introduce in Boston inoculation for smallpox. The feud between the two men continued for years. Douglass reportedly declared that to point out all the errors of the *Magnalia* would be to copy the whole book. Mather's attacks on Douglass were no less hyperbolic.

The criticisms levelled against the "Church-History" during Mather's lifetime have been often repeated and elaborated in later years. The strange fate of his book in the centuries since 1728 would have seemed to Mather a "remarkable providence," a divine chastisement for his sins. Although no one has ever read his "Church-History" as he wrote it, or ever will unless the original manuscript some day comes to light, its critics have not hesitated to blame its author for mistakes not his own. The sheet of "Errata" he prepared was not included in most of the copies of the 1702 edition, nor was it used by the editors of those of 1820 and 1853–1855, although the introduction to the latter of these announced that its text had been corrected according to Mather's "Errata."

The *Magnalia*, perhaps partly because of its bulk, has become more famous than any of his other books and is often regarded as his most important work. He did not consider it so. It was a product of his youth, finished when he was still in his thirties, and even while he was preparing it he gave more of his "*Thought* and *Hope*" to toiling on "another and greater" book, his "Biblia Americana," an immense tome which throughout his life he seems to have considered his major achievement. But the "Biblia" was, to his grief, never printed; the *Magnalia* was and has been more widely commented on than any of his other writings, some of which certainly are no less worthy of attention, stylistically more expert, and more revealing of his thought and intellectual calibre. Unfortunately the faults—and virtues—of his "Church-History" have again and again been used as bases for sweeping judgments of his character and place in literature, without serious evaluation of the more mature and more carefully composed works of the last two decades of his life.

After his death his "Church-History" seems to have been read, or at least dipped into, by historians who found in it data not available elsewhere, and, presumably, by such pious nonconformists as still revered the founders of the New England churches. But by 1800 much of its source material had been printed elsewhere; many nonconformists no longer followed the "faith and order" of the Congregationalists of seventeenth-century New England, and were no longer much concerned with their "Acts and Monuments." Biblical criticism had made impossible the acceptance of many of the interpretations of Holy Writ which seemed unimpeachable to Mather and his predecessors. The time-honored belief that throughout the history of the universe and mankind every phenomenon or event, however strange or incredible, directly reflected God's omnipotent exercise of his inscrutable "Providence," became weakened as scientists demonstrated that many of the quasi-miraculous "wonders" in which Mather delighted could be explained by natural causes. More and more, those which could not be so explicated were regarded merely as evidence of the credulity of a bygone and unenlightened age.

In 1818, William Tudor, the first editor of the *North American Review*, published a long essay on the *Magnalia* which admirably sums up the then prevailing attitude toward the book. He wrote: "In this effeminate period . . . a fair perusal of Mather's *Magnalia* is an achievement not to be slighted . . . 800 folio pages in close double columns, even of the most desirable matter, might well cause hesitation. What then must be the effect of a chaotick mass of history, biography, obsolete creeds, witch-craft, and Indian wars, interspersed with bad puns, and numerous quotations in Latin, Greek and Hebrew which rise up like so many decayed, hideous stumps to arrest the eye and deform the surface?" Tudor went on to say that it might hereafter be said that he "was the last (and possibly the first) individual who, bona fide, perused the whole" *Magnalia*. His conclusion was: "Those who are interested in the early history of our country . . . if they wish to obtain a general view of the state's society and manners . . . will probably nowhere find so many materials for this . . . as in the work of this credulous, pedantick, and garrulous writer." But he added "that for accuracy in historical occurences," readers would "do well to rely upon other authorities." In 1853 James Savage even more vigorously castigated Mather for his inaccuracies, declaring that he "published more errors of carelessness than any writer of the history of New England."

Many of the errors in the *Magnalia* were, as has been pointed out, chargeable to its printers and not its author. Mather's handwriting was on the whole legible but had, of course, individual pecularities. Many of these baffled the typesetters, who, it should be noted, managed to make misprints even when they worked from printed copy. There are, however, scores of mistakes which were plainly Mather's own. Some of these were certainly "careless." His conviction that the "Biblia" was destined to be his most important work distracted him from the *Magnalia* and led him to hurry it to completion in order that he might give more time to the larger work he had already begun. While haste accounts for some of his inaccuracies, others reveal not carelessness but a deliberate concealment of evidence which might put the New England churches and its founders in a bad light. Still others glossed over or distorted the arguments of those who challenged the old "New England way."

Tudor's opinion that the *Magnalia* was "chaotic" was shared by many others. So in part it was, but it was not wholly formless. Mather's original plan as given in the "Schaeme" appended to the *Johannes in Eremo* was sound enough. Each of the seven "Books" of the *Magnalia* was to be devoted to a major theme or related themes, all traditionally regarded as proper for an "Ecclesiastical History." But Mather, never weary of seeing his work in print, unfortunately yielded to temptation and included in his *Magnalia*, completely or in part, many of his previously printed sermons and other writings. Some of these fitted in well enough but many were superfluous or irrelevant in the context of his "Church-History." As late as 1698 he tacked on to Book II the *Pietas in Patriam*, his life of Sir William Phips, which had already been printed in a London edition. Its length was disproportionate with the space given to other governors of Massachusetts who had been more important "Shields of the Churches" than Sir William. But Phips was a devoted disciple of Increase and Cotton Mather and a member of their church. Cotton's Diary makes it plain that he conceived of the *Pietas* as "a piece of pamphleteering" in defence of his father's acceptance of the new Royal Charter of 1691 and his recommendation of Phips for the governorship. Many of its pages were therefore out of place in a "Church-History." So were some of the other "prints" he sent to England in 1700 with instructions to add them in their proper places to the manuscript of the *Magnalia*. The structure of the work would have been more coherent had he kept them at home.

He was especially outraged by Oldmixon's assertion, later concurred in by others, that the *Magnalia* was "trivial in the matter of it." He retorted with a heavily sarcastic passage in which he listed the exalted themes heard in the book. "The *Marvellous Work* of GOD in Producing and Maintaining and Afflicting and Relieving of Colonies *in a Matchless Manner* Formed upon the Noble Intentions of *Pure* and *Undefiled* Religion: The Wise Measures *Taken* by the *Best of Men* to establish that Religion ... seen in the Lives of such Men; and as choice Materials as a Church-History can be composed of; these are *Trivial Matters*!" Still fuming, Mather went on to ridicule Oldmixon's own idea of "important matter" as "ludicrous" and listed as examples his record of how two Indians went fishing and hunting and met only two moose; how geese flying south in October presaged cold weather; how " (O Marvellous) it snow'd in November"; how a boy once had his feet frostbitten; and how four men in one week killed twenty-six partridges.

Oldmixon's book was not as "ludicrous" as Mather painted it, nor was the material of the *Magnalia* as "trivial" as Oldmixon declared. The quarrel was between two authors, one of them concentrating on matters appropriate, as he believed, to "Ecclesiastical History," the other a general historian, properly concerned with the social, political, economic, and military affairs of the colony. Other critics of the *Magnalia* persisted in calling it a "history of New England," but Mather seems never to have referred to it as such until years after it was published. Although the subsidiary title pages which he, or more probably his printers, prefixed to each of its seven Books did have "The New English History," the first page of the volume with its full title made perfectly clear the historical genre to which the book belonged and the fact that it was not designed as a "general history" of the sort Oldmixon attempted.

By 1702 the principles generally accepted by church historians in the seventeenth century were so no longer, and the prestige of their histories had waned. Mather, however, deliberately clung to the old standards and in his choice of material and method followed the practice of scores of historiographers for centuries before his day. Early in Section 4 of his General Introduction he wrote that "of all History . . . the *Palm* is to be given unto *Church History*." This he quoted almost verbatim from a treatise on history and historians by Degory Wheare, the first occupant of the chair of modern history at Oxford, who had died more than fifty years before the *Magnalia* was finished. In the same section of the Introduction Mather made plain the pious purposes—no longer so much admired as they once had been—which he hoped his book would serve. Higginson's Attestation to it, written in 1697, when he was more than eighty years old, also buttressed these purposes in his list of seven ways in which he believed Mather's work might serve "Great and Good Ends."

To Oldmixon, reading the book for data on the political and economic history of the colonies, all this was useless and tiresome. He likened the *Magnalia* to a schoolboy's exercise of twenty years earlier and regarded church history of the sort Mather revered as out of date. So in large measure it was. Although Wheare's book was used as a text at Cambridge University as late as the beginning of the eighteenth century, it was by then probably valued for its catalogue of historians of all kinds and its comments on them rather than for its emphasis on the special nobility of church history.

Granting that Cotton Mather's "Ecclesiastical History of New-England," in its choice of material and method of presentation, followed principles in large part obsolete in 1702, it seems only fair in judging the book to keep in mind what those principles were. In order to do so the significance of Mather's general title, *Magnalia Christi Americana*, must be understood. He seems not to have decided on it until his manuscript was ready to send to London, where, apparently following his instructions, Quick placed it at the head of the title page and also used it in his "Proposals." Part of the Greek text of Acts 2.11 had been translated in the Vulgate, "magnalia dei," which, in the 1599 English version and that of the King James Bible, became "wonderful works of God." The word had been used in the seventeenth century in the titles of at least a half-dozen books recording "wonders" of one sort or another. Mather's "Magnalia Christi Americana" was probably suggested by John Vicar's *Magnalia Dei Anglicana*, published in London in 1646, and would then and earlier have needed no explanation.

"The idea of providence" was, as Herschel Baker has written, "the broadest and most persistently employed principle of causality in Renaissance historiography." This idea was based on the conviction that everything that happened in the created universe, "from the fall of a sparrow through the vicissitudes of private men and the calamities of rulers to the wheeling of the stars," exemplified God's all-powerful control of men and the universe and His divine purpose, which, however inscrutible it seemed, "was bound to be benign." History, Wheare maintained, was "nothing but Moral Philosophy, cloaked in Examples." Not only the "wonders" recorded in the Bible, but every event in history exemplified God's omnipotence and the nature of His will. To neglect this was to blind oneself to the "Moral Philosophy" which was essential for sound historiography.

Historians in the early seventeenth century accepted this theory, and followed this tenet even when they wrote of contemporary occurrences. George Carleton, Bishop of Chichester, compiled a collection of lively narratives of England's history during the reigns of Queen Elizabeth and James I and called it *A Thankfull Remembrance of Gods Mercie*. Among the examples cited of this "mercie" were the defeat of the Spanish Armada and the discovery of the Gunpowder Plot—examples used for the same purpose by Sir Thomas Browne in his *Religio Medici*.

Mather, in writing his "Ecclesiastical History," knew well that the recording of providential wonders had been for centuries an essential part of most such histories. The ecclesiastical history written by Eusebius, sometimes called "the father of church history," had been "from first page to last the working of Providence," and scores of other writers had followed suit.

In the seventeenth century the interest in God's "illustrious providence" was so great that dozens of "providence Books" were published, most of them written by others than historians. These were essentially catalogues of striking "wonders" in the world God had made and the no less amazing rewards and punishments He bestowed upon its inhabitants. Increase Mather's *Essay For The Recording of . . . Providences*, printed in Boston in 1684, was basically such a book, and Cotton Mather, before he began to write the *Magnalia*, seems to have toyed with the idea of making it primarily a record of "the more illustrious Discoveries of the Divine *Providence* in the Government of the World." One of those that they read and studied was Samuel Clarke's *A Mirrour or Looking-Glasse both for Saints and Sinners*, which was so popular that it had three editions in two years. The book, commonly known as "Clarke's Examples," was typical of its genre. It was divided into one hundred and thirty-six chapters, each made up of quotations or bits of information which exemplified in one way or another the awe-inspiring dispensations of God. The topics range from "Apparitions" through "Hereticks and Schismaticks plagued by God," to "Warre, and the evills of it" and the "Vanity of all earthly things."

The audience for such volumes in the seventeenth century was not limited to the man in the street who relished them because of their sensational tales of marvels. "Providence Books" were taken seriously and often quoted by sober scholars. Their compilers usually gave their source for each entry—ancient writers still esteemed, and scores of later scientists, travelers, and pundits of all sorts. Some such books were published after 1700, but by then the market for them had declined. Oldmixon, therefore, naturally considered Mather's recording of "magnalia" as an example of absurd "credulity."

Dozens of later writers have also called Mather "credulous," and with reason. For him, unfortunately perhaps, "wonders" had a special appeal. The drama of the contest between God and his angels and the devil's iniquitous agents fascinated him. He saw himself as a participant in the struggle, beset by evil temptations but, strengthened by his "own Angel," determined to resist and to fight on the side of the Lord. God's "magnalia" were intensely real to him, sometimes more real than the events of his own little world. In moments of depression the contemplation of wonders could reassure him of God's ability to forgive; in moments of elation they supported his conviction that he had won God's special favor.

Many of the "magnalia" he recorded did not, however, represent "credulity." Some were vouched for by respected authorities; not all of the strange phenomena he described had in 1700 been explained by scientists or by historians. In some cases, at least, he warned his readers that the truth of a "wonder" was not capable of proof. Before making a final judgment on the extent of his "credulity" it is well to note the way in which he introduces some of his strange tales. His passage in Section 6 of the General Introduction describing the remarkable behavior of a Spanish lake was, for instance, preceded by the phrase "they say"— precisely the words used by a recent editor of Eusebius in his translation of the Greek phrase which that ancient historian used when he included in his history a "wonder" for the truth of which he could not vouch.

Mather's passion for crowding his pages with accounts of "magnalia" had undoubtedly helped to win for him the title of "pedant." Professor Gay has recently written that "No American writer has been given the title more often than Cotton Mather" or "deserved the epithet more than he." Most commentators on the *Magnalia* have agreed. In 1878

Moses Coit Tyler called Mather's pedantry "gigantic, stark, untempered, rejoicing in itself, unconscious of shame, filling all space in his books like an atmosphere." His mind was so possessed by the books he had read, that his most common thought had to force its way into utterance through "dense hedges and jungles of quotation."

Mather was prepared for such assaults. In his General Introduction he prophesied that some "Learned Men . . . terrified by the Reproaches of *Pedantry*, which little Smatterers at Reading and Learning" had "by their *Quoting Humours* brought upon themselves," would decry "the best way of Writing" which he used. That way involved "embellishing" his work with "multiplied References to other and former Concerns, closely couch'd, for the Observation of the Attentive, in almost every Paragraph." He steadfastly held to his belief that "a little salt of antiquity" made "style more pleasing" and that his quotations and learned allusions were "as choice Flowers as most . . . in Ancient or Modern Writings." Many of the "Flowers" included in his history were, however, irrelevant to their context; others served no purpose except to parade his learning.

When, for example, he calls New England a country where "Recompenses never were in fashion," he contrasts this niggardliness with the munificence with which Ptolemy rewarded Strabo for his labors. This by itself is appropriate enough and drives home Mather's point, but it is followed by a listing of three other instances of generosity of no use except as illustrations of the extent of his knowledge—in this case a knowledge derived from a single anthology.

Similar examples of "pedantry" can easily be found by any reader. One of them at least represents not merely "pedantry" but something close to scholarly chicanery. In the long section on history in Mather's Introduction to the *Magnalia*, virtually all of his quotations come from Degory Wheare's book or from Johann Alsted's *Encyclopaedia*. He does not name either Wheare or Alsted, calling one "a Learned *Professor of History*" and the other simply "a worthy writer." The title of Wheare's book is not given and Alsted's is masked as his "*Historica*"—the title of one section of the *Encyclopaedia* and a clue unlikely to be very helpful to any reader.

Mather's pedantry has, however, sometimes been exaggerated. It does not deserve such sweeping denunciation as Tyler's. Nor is it possible to agree with Tudor, who soundly condemned Mather's many quotations in Latin, Greek and Hebrew.

By 1700, to be sure, the crusade for the vernacular was in full swing. Edmund Bohun, in his translation of Degory Wheare's *De Ratione* . . . *Legendi Historias*, rejoiced at the number of classical authors who had been put into English, and ridiculed the "Morose gentlemen" who, familiar with Greek and Latin, regarded the translations of them into

English as enemies "to learning and learned men" whose efforts would destroy "esteem for the learned tongues," and thus "deprive the world of all learning." But in spite of Bohun and other advocates of the vernacular, Latin, Greek, and Hebrew kept their prestige for many years after the *Magnalia* was printed. The three languages were those of the Bible and revered as such, especially among theologians and religious historians. Nor can Mather's crowded citations of Biblical texts have seemed "pedantic" to such scholars in 1700 or in the decades thereafter. Holy Writ was the word of God and therefore most worthy of study. English versions were of course useful, but serious scholars were not content to rely wholly upon them.

Definitions of the words *pedant* and *pedantry* change according to the intellectual climate in each period. Much that seems "pedantic" now, or seemed so in the eighteenth century, was not so regarded in the seventeenth. Even today a careful scholar, who regards his meticulous reporting of all the evidence for his conclusions as the real meat of his work, may find himself accused of poisonous "pedantry" by those who read as they run or those who regard the author's subject as unimportant.

To a considerable degree each individual makes his judgment of what is or is not pedantry on the basis of his own interests and ideas. Many pages in the *Magnalia* seem to me indubitably pedantic, but one can pronounce such a verdict upon the whole book, I believe, only if he ignores or fails to understand much that it contains. Some of Mather's "dense hedges and jungles of quotation" which at first sight appear blantant pedantry can, I think, be shown to contribute essentially to the exposition of his theme.

In his *Manuductio ad Ministerium*, published twenty-four years after the *Magnalia*, Mather wrote: "There has been a deal of a do about a STYLE ... there is a *Way of Writing* wherein the Author endeavours that the Reader may have *something to the* Purpose in every Paragraph . . . The *Paragraph* is embellished with *Profitable References*, even to something beyond what is *directly* spoken." The writer's "composures are . . . a *Cloth of Gold* . . . stuck with as many Jewels, as the Gown of a Russian Embassador. This Way of Writing has been decried . . . and is at this Day more than ever so . . . A Lazy, Ignorant, Conceited Sett of authors, would perswade the whole Tribe" to lay it aside. "But, however *Fashion* and *Humour* may prevail, they must not think that the Club at their *Coffee-House* is, *All* the *World* . . . there will always be those who will . . . think that the real Excellency of a book will never ly in *saying of little* . . . If a more Massy *Way of Writing* be never so much digusted at This Day a *Better Gust* will come on." "In the mean time," Mather continued, "Nothing appears to me more Impertinent and ridiculous than the

Modern Way . . . of *Criticising* . . . The Blades that set up for *Criticks* . . .
appear to me . . . as *Contemptible*, as they are a *Supercilious* Generation
. . . No Two of them have the same *Style* . . . nor can you easily find any
one thing wherein they agree for their *Style*, except perhaps a perpetual
Care to give us Jejune and Empty Pages, without such *Touches of Erudition*
. . . as may make the discourses less *Tedious*, and more *Enriching*, to the
Mind of him that peruses them. There is much Talk of a Florid Style,
obtaining among the Pens, that are most in Vogue; but how often would
it puzzle one, even with the best Glasses, to find the flowres! . . . Every man
will have his own style, which will distinguish him as much as his gate."

This is the position Mather held when he wrote the Introduction to
the *Magnalia*. He knew as well as Oldmixon did that the style of the *Magnalia* was outmoded in 1702. So it seemed to those who took the
"Augustan" writers of the reign of Queen Anne as models. Later, in the
romantic period, other standards of style came into fashion. These perhaps account for Tyler's vehement attack when in 1878 he discussed
Mather's prose. Usually a gentle and unbiased critic, he was passionate
in his hatred of the "fantastic" or "baroque" style. That style, he felt,
expelled "the beautiful from thought, from sentiment, from language."
For him the "baroque" writers were victims of "that perverse and
detestable literary mood that held sway in different countries of Christendom during the sixteenth and seventeenth centuries. Its birthplace was
Italy; New England was its grave; Cotton Mather was its last great
apostle."

By the end of the nineteenth century, however, fashion had shifted
once more, and Barrett Wendell saw Mather's writing in a different light.
He repeated the charges that the *Magnalia* was "flung together, not
composed at all," and was "full of superstitions now incredible" and
"hasty errors." But, admitting all this, Wendell declared that the style
of the *Magnalia* seemed to him "remarkably good," although it was
"prolix, often overloaded with pedantic quotations," and "now and then
fantastic in its conceits." Wendell, widely read in sixteenth- and seventeenth-century English literature, saw these faults as those of "Mather's
time" and declared that "in the whole book" he "had not found a line
that" was "not perfectly lucid, nor many paragraphs that, considering
the frequent dullness" of its subject, he "could honestly call tiresome."
"The *Magnalia*," he declared, "has merits which dispose me to rate it
among the great works of English literature in the seventeenth century."

Early in our own century interest in the "baroque" or "fantastic"
style began to be even more favorably regarded. Many of the sixteenth-
and seventeenth-century writers whom Tyler had denounced as disciples
of "degenerate euphemism" began once more to be carefully read,
studied, and praised by scholars and critics. Some of these found the

Magnalia more intelligible and less easily condemned than most of their predecessors had. Austin Warren, like Wendell thoroughly familiar with the literature of the Elizabethan age and that of Charles I, has discussed the *Magnalia* in a brilliant essay, "Grandfather Mather and his Wonder Book," and, without minimizing its faults, has called attention to some of its literary virtues. He reminded its readers that Cotton Mather could and did "write in other styles," but in his "History" followed his "taste for complexity, allusiveness, and, in general, for opulence." The *Magnalia*, Warren writes, is a book "which like Browne's *Vulgar Errors* . . . or Fuller's *Worthies* can always be 'read in' with delight. It comes near to being a masterpiece—whether of fact or mythology scarcely matters. In many ways it is, as its author designed it, a conscious masterpiece written in the Baroque style, one of the last and latest works anywhere written in such a style—belatedly Baroque, as its author's view of the world is also dominantly (despite his innoculatory innovations and philanthropies) belatedly Baroque."

"Baroque," a name originally given to a school of painting, is now often applied to a "fantastic" literary style, full of ornamental devices, elaborate verbal flights, rich in metaphor, and crowded with wordplays. It is fortunately not necessary here to describe in detail the "baroque" elements in the *Magnalia*, since Professor Manierre has analyzed them in his valuable study on its verbal patterns. Among these patterns was the frequent use of many kinds of alliteration, some chosen for their stylistic effect, others to display Mather's verbal ingenuity, and still others to elucidate and emphasize passages Mather considered especially important. Another of his favorite artifices was the repetition of key words or phrases. Such repetition was, as Manierre points out, "a standard characteristic" of the New England sermon. In order to keep their listeners' attention on the Biblical text "Mather's fellow preachers were not averse to using the same words over and over again . . . in order to gain clarity, precision, and less often, emphasis." In some cases, Mather employed repetition to supply overtones to his text. Thus the reiteration of "Desarts" and "Trial of Faith" near the end of Section 7 of Chapter 2 of Book I unmistakably linked the first settlers at Plymouth with Abraham and his followers. In the same way reiteration of "World" in Book I, chapter 1, section 3, taken in its context, implied that the settlement of New England was part of a great victory of the "Church of Christ."

Mather was in love with words, proud of his vocabulary, and often intemperate in his use of it. "He was seldom satisfied with one word if he could use two, or with two if he could use three." This "may partly result from the customary Puritan desire for exactness . . . even at the expense of brevity," and may also have been influenced by Elizabethan translators who often used two words to translate one in order to make its meaning clear. Mather did not hesitate to use even more to serve the same purpose. Moreover, he longed "to present everything in its strongest colors," and "delighted in piling adjective on adjective and adverb on adverb." A good example is in his description of Theophilus Eaton in Book II of the *Magnalia*: "He was Affable, Courteous, and generally *Pleasant* but *Grave* perpetually; and . . . Cautelous and Circumspect in his Discourses and Modest in his Expressions."

Mather, like many other writers of his time and earlier, doted on paradoxes. Among the examples cited by Manierre are: "He was chosen a *Magistrate* of *New-England* before *New-England* it self came into *New-England* (*Magnalia*, Book II, "Pater Patriae: Or, The Life of Samuel Bradstreet"); and "He . . . bore this *Affliction* unto his *Dying Day;* having been taught by the Affliction to *Die Daily*, as long as he *Lived*" (Book II, "Publicola Christianus. The Life of Edward Hopkins," section 5). Such paradoxes as these were essentially puns, and the *Magnalia* is noted for its abundant punning, a form of wit which no doubt pleased its author and his contemporaries more than it has later readers. The "punning habit," Manierre writes, "perfectly exemplifies Mather's custom of putting to use every rhetorical device available to him . . . Whatever had proved useful to other writers" he "appropriated to his own purposes; verbal techniques, that others used seldom, unobtrusively, and with restraint, Mather used without restraint, extravagantly, and in exaggerated form."

This is illustrated not only in his punning but also in his studding the *Magnalia* with anagrams. Few of these were of his own making, and in his life of John Wilson, published in 1695 in his *Johannes in Eremo* and reprinted in Book III of the *Magnalia*, he paraphrased a line in William Camden's *Remains*, disparaging "Annagrammatizing" as "a certain little Sport of Wit." Nonetheless, always in search of "wonders," he was fascinated by Camden's elaboration of the notion that the letters of a word or name might be so manipulated as to reveal cabalistically God's mysterious will.

Manierre shrewdly points out that "to be fully appreciated Mather's prose should be read aloud." This seems to me an important observation. For those who have so read the *Magnalia*, Wendell among them, Mather's style becomes more "lucid" and more praiseworthy than to those who have never listened to the sound of his prose. This suggests, I think, that Mather was by temperament in no way fitted to be a historian. His talent was for preaching and for expression in the spoken word, and not for sober recording and evaluation of historical data on the printed page. He began the *Magnalia* when he was only thirty-four, but he had already won some fame for his prowess in the pulpit. Expert in oral exhortation and polemic discourse and a master of the jeremiad, he found the sermon the readiest and perhaps the most effective medium for instructing and inspiring those who were eager to understand and follow the precepts of the Bible, and for warning the ignorant and godless of the need to mend their ways. More than half of the books which he had published before the *Magnalia* and reprinted there, wholly or in part, were sermons; scores of the other passages he borrowed from his earlier works were so in effect.

His experience in preaching "Constant *Sermons*, usually more than once, and perhaps three or four times in a Week," had taught him the value of many of the stylistic devices he used in his "history." Wordplay of all sorts, he discovered, pleased his listeners, and held their attention; the repetition of words and phrases helped them to follow his thought. Even the godless could be roused from their lethargy by puns, anagrams, and paradoxes; any specially sonorous sentence, delivered with the oratorical skill of which he was a master, could, when deftly introduced in a difficult passage, rouse even the weariest in his audience.

It is easy to imagine that when he settled himself in his study and began to write anything, sermon or not, he heard echoing in his ears the sound of his own voice in the pulpit. Sometimes this led his pen to prose which is as successful when read on the printed page as it was when spoken in the meeting-house; at other times it betrayed him into a style which in print seems florid, tiresomely repetitive, and even at times trivial in content.

Especially useful for the preacher were "Examples" of God's providence and His "wonders"—rewarding His faithful servants, punishing the wicked, and manipulating the entire universe. Recording such "Examples" was traditionally, as has been already pointed out, a staple part of ecclesiastical histories. Scores of ministers in Mather's time and before found such a device virtually essential. Mather himself wrote in his "Quotidiana": "Examples, as by a secret charm, draw out the heart unto imitations. When we press holiness, people think, our doctrine is calculated for *Angels* and *Spirits* that have divested themselves of the concernments of flesh and blood and so go away with prejudice. But when they read the lives of persons that had like passions, temptations, necessities with themselves, with what holy diligence they carried on their hopes of a blessed eternity, it has a marvellously convictive influence upon them."

Mather here was thinking primarily of biography as a means of winning readers to holiness. He knew that "Examples" of God's unlimited power manifested in "wonders," however incredible and dubiously supported by fact, could, whether printed or preached, serve the same purpose and remind saints and sinners alike of the omnipotence of the Almighty.

In the "Epistle to the Reader" of his *Mirrour or Looking Glass*, Samuel Clarke, for years a successful preacher, wrote: "I have collected the eminentest, and most remarkable Examples . . . and reduced them under several heads distinguished into several Chapters . . . and . . . have now this third time published them to the world . . . I have also sometimes set down more pleasant stories, which may have their use, and prevent tediousness to the reader." It may well be that Cotton Mather's "tall stories" do not always represent "credulity" but rather his realization that in writing as in preaching "tediousness" was dangerous.

Many of Mather's stylistic vagaries in the *Magnalia*, its untidy structure, his choice of material, and its "pedantry," can, I think, be understood, if not excused, if one realizes that he was concerned to reach more than one audience. A devoted pastor, he wanted to give his flock at the Second Church the instruction he felt they needed. Some of his congregation, nonmembers and by no means devout, would, he hoped, be beguiled by strange "Examples." Others, although pious readers of the Bible, were unable to interpret some of its knottier texts. He was sure that these good men would welcome the scores of Biblical quotations, accompanied by reminders of their context and meaning, and would rejoice in adding from his pages to their store of information. He was at the same time eager to establish his prestige among his clerical brethren in New England, men for the most part learned and well read, whom he hoped to impress by demonstrating in the *Magnalia* an erudition even greater than theirs.

By 1697, moreover, the handwriting on the wall must have warned him that his father's and his own supremacy in Congregational circles was soon to end, and that his writing was no longer appreciated as it once had been. Accordingly he longed to win abroad the renown his countrymen were more and more loath to grant him. He was determined, therefore, to prove himself equal in scholarship to the English writers most revered for their learning. Ambitious for the respect of the renowned foreign scholars he worshipped and envied, he felt they would surely acknowledge the breadth of his reading and the profundity of his scholarship as demonstrated by pages crowded with allusions, quotations, and scraps of learned exegesis. With this in mind he used in his "history" a variety of what may be figuratively called "languages."

The first of these was based on the culture of the English Renaissance. Mather had been brought up in his father's library, which abounded in classics and the works of sixteenth- and early-seventeenth-century writers. In college he found the curriculum based largely on books of the same vintage, and when, still young, he began to collect his own library, which was in time to become even greater than his father's, he chose for the most part similar volumes. The classics were of special importance.

The *Magnalia* opens with an echoing of Virgil, and here and there throughout the book there are instances of Mather's belief that the story of the exile of the founding fathers and their building of a "city on a hill" was an epic comparable to the *Aeneid*. The analogy is by no means systematically maintained, but nonetheless shows, as do many of his other classical allusions, Mather's respect for the "language" of the Renaissance.

The technique of the jeremiad called for another "language," based primarily on the Bible but furnished by theologians with a pattern and mode of its own. With its constantly reiterated theme of God's sure punishment of stubborn sinners, the jeremiad sermon was considered especially suitable for arousing a luke-warm audience, or a congregation made up in part of unbelievers. It was Mather's hope that the language of the jeremiad would prove as effective in print as from the pulpit.

A third "language" was typology, based on the idea that the Old Testament foreshadowed the New. For centuries theologians had revered the Bible as a supreme authority; after the Reformation nonconformists insisted that it was the only source of truth. Recognizing that the two testaments often disagreed, they maintained that any person, object, or event in the Old Testament might prefigure someone or something in the New. Though theologians differed as to the precise nature of such "types" and "antitypes," the basic significance of both was generally agreed upon.

Mather wrote in his General Introduction to the *Magnalia* that "good *Men*" would be grateful "to have all the *Typical* Men and things in our *Book of Mysteries*," the Bible, "accommodated with their *Antitypes*." He had himself a special interest in typology. In Dublin his uncle Samuel had at some time before 1671 delivered a long series of sermons on it which Samuel's brother, Nathanael, put together in a book, *The Figures or Types of the Old Testament. By Which Christ and the Heavenly Things of the Gospel were preached and Shadowed to the People of God of Old*. Nathanael published this in 1683. Mather received the book soon after it came from the press and read it avidly. There he found many typological interpretations of Biblical words, phrases, and allusions with which he loaded the pages of the *Magnalia*. Some of his first readers, like many since, no doubt failed to grasp their import, but the better informed of his contemporaries understood them at once and admired the ingenuity with which he fitted them into his text.

Mather's basic "language" in the *Magnalia* was, of course, that of the Bible. So far as any man ever has, he knew it by heart. It has been said that when Milton wrote *The Reason of Church-Government* he knew so well the "verbal mannerisms, thought patterns, and language of the King James version" that it is "difficult to say where the Bible leaves off and . . . [Milton] begins." The same is true of Mather in the *Magnalia*. He did not, however, limit himself to a single version of the Scriptures, but studied several, together with the interpretations of their commentators. Often he quoted his sources exactly, but almost as often he altered them slightly, without changing their meaning, in order to adapt them to his context. Now and then he relied on single words or phrases to remind his readers of passages in Holy Writ which seemed to him relevant to his subject.

For him the Bible was the one guide to truth, and its style was the one most worthy of emulation. He believed, as had John Donne, that the Scriptures were the most "eloquent Books" the world had ever known. Its "Figures and Tropes" surpassed those of the Greek and Latin "Poets and Orators"; the Holy Ghost's "manner of expressing himselfe" was as "powerful" as it was "eloquent." Sure of this, Mather turned constantly to the Bible for instruction and inspiration, and in preaching or writing "spoke Bible."

His ardent bibliolatry accounts for some of the duller and more tangled pages of the *Magnalia*. Again and again, however, his mastery of the language and methods of Scripture served him in good stead.

In attempting to please a variety of readers by managing four "languages," Mather undertook a task beyond his power. Certain of his defects might have been avoided had he been content to limit its scope. As it is, the book is renowned as much for its failures as for its successes. A few critics, to be sure, have been sufficiently impressed by its good qualities—especially the effectiveness of a number of the biographies—to forgive or forget its more turgid pages. To some it has presented a terrifying revelation of New England's "Puritanism" and its culture, while others have cherished it as a faithful depiction of a golden age.

It seems to me that to assess fairly its sprawling pages one must, as I have already suggested, regard it as not in essence a history at all but rather as an extended tract, a series of sermons, a nostalgic meditation. It was not, I think, in any way typical of the literary or historiographical standards of its day, nor is it a portrait of the "Puritan character." It stands as a completely idiosyncratic document, one which none of Mather's contemporaries could, or would, have written.

It was the creation of a young man, vain, blind to his own shortcomings, inordinately proud of his ancestors, and obsessed by the notion that he had been elected by God to record His wonders and to win others to His service. In pursuing this purpose Mather concerned himself more with glorifying a past which never was than with understanding the realities of the cramped world in which he lived. Shocked by the indifference of his compatriots to the splendor of that past, in chapter after chapter he intoned jeremiads against the evils of his day and lost himself in dreams of a future which was never to be.

But by some indefinable magic—or as Mather would have said, by "God's Providence"—the *Magnalia* preserves its vitality. It is still read, or pretended to be, and argued about; it is still quoted, and there are those who see in it a minor masterpiece. Perhaps it survives despite its glaring faults because of some dozens of pages which, even when devoted to themes and theses antipathetic to modern readers, rival in style and in their reflection of Puritan thought any others written in the American colonies by a member of Mather's generation. More than anything else, however, the *Magnalia's* life depends on the vividness of its author's presentation of his dream, or what might be called its autobiographical evocation of an extraordinarily complex Puritan mentality—a mentality and a dream which, *mutatis mutandis*, often bears resemblances to thinking and dreams common in our own lifetime.

BIBLIOGRAPHICAL NOTES

The story of the publication of Mather's *Church-History* is told in George Noyes Greenough's "A Letter relating to the Publication of Cotton Mather's *Magnalia*," in the Colonial Society of Massachusetts, *Transactions* (1924–1926), 26:296–307.

For the news of the "acceptance" of the *Magnalia*, see Mather, *Diary*, 1:498, and for Vincent Alsop's praise see Samuel Mather, *Life of . . . Cotton Mather*, p. 85; and Cotton Mather, *Memoirs . . . of The Life . . . of . . . Increase Mather* (Boston, 1724), Introduction, pp. vii–viii.

The full text of Banister's doggerel is in Sewall's *Letter Book*, 1:407, and Increase Mather's charge against him, together with Cotton's attempt to reduce his punishment, is in Sewall, *Papers*, 2:290–291. For Douglass see T. J. Holmes, *Cotton Mather*, *passim*, and Mather's *Diary*, 2:624–625 and notes. For the "Biblia Americana," see *Diary*, 1:230, and *Magnalia*, General Introduction, section 5.

For James Savage's attack on Mather's careless errors see the 1853 edition of his *History of New England from 1630 to 1649;* for Cotton Mather's use of his *Pietas in Patriam* as a "piece of pamphleteering," see Holmes, *Cotton Mather*, 2:807.

Mather's sarcastic reply to Oldmixon's assertion that the *Magnalia* dealt with trivialities was published in his *Parentator* (1724), pp. x–xii; two years later he continued his attack, in his *Manuductio ad Ministerium*, by calling Oldmixon "the most foolish and faithless Performance in this Kind, that ever Mankind was abused withal." Greenough's "Letter Relating to the Publication of Cotton Mather's *Magnalia*," mentioned above, discussed at some length, on pp. 308–310, the meaning and use of the word "Magnalia."

For Herschel Baker on the "idea of providence," see his *The Race of Time* (University of Toronto Press, 1967), pp. 64–65. Mather plainly knew Degory Wheare's *Method and Order of Reading Histories*, printed in 1685 and again in 1694, and probably also his *Relectiones Hyemales*, the fourth and fifth editions of which appeared in 1662 and 1684. See also Eusebius, *The History of the Church from Christ to Constantine*, translated by G. A. Williamson (New York, 1966), p. 22.

For Mather's pedantry see Peter Gay, *A Loss of Mastery* (University of California Press, 1966), p. 60; and Moses Coit Tyler, *History of American Literature, 1607–1765* (New York, 1878), or more conveniently, Cornell University Press, 1949, pp. 335–336.

The reference to New England as not given to "recompenses" is from the General

Introduction of the *Magnalia*, as are Mather's " Learned *Professor*" and his "worthy writer."

Professor Austin Warren's essay was published in *The Sewanee Review* for January-March, 1964, pp. 96–115; the quoted passages are on pp. 98, 110, and 111. For the "baroque characteristics" in the *Magnalia*, see Professor William R. Manierre II's "Verbal Patterns in Cotton Mather's Magnalia" (*Quarterly Journal of Speech*, December, 1961); "Cotton Mather and the Biographical Parallel" (*American Quarterly*, Summer, 1961); and "Some Characteristic Mather Redactions" (*New England Quarterly*, December, 1958).

THE IDEA OF THE WILDERNESS OF THE NEW WORLD IN COTTON MATHER'S *MAGNALIA CHRISTI AMERICANA*

George H. Williams

Commencing his recital of the mighty works of Christ in the New World, Cotton Mather declared that "*Geography* must now find work for a *Christiano-graphy*" of the entire Western hemisphere, that "*Ballancing half* of the Globe" which had long lain concealed from the rest of the world. Mather was convinced that the North American wilderness had been providentially "*Spied out*" as the "*Resting-place*" or "*Hiding-place*" for "*Reformed CHURCHES*," where the "*Evangelical,* and *Ecclesiastical,* and very remarkable Transactions*" to be recounted in his history should be enacted. He was even attracted by the opinion of some learned men that the reference in Philippians 2.10 to the bowing of every knee of "things *under* the earth" at the name of Jesus might be an allusion to all American inhabitants (aborigines or colonists) "who are *Antipodes* to those of the other *Hemisphere*." Mather, however, had to get around the fact that it had been an Italian Catholic navigator, sailing with royal support from Catholic Spain, who discovered the New World, and that consequently in many parts of the hemisphere "idolatry" in Christian guise had gained a foothold. He found it very helpful, therefore, to interpret the New World wilderness biblically as at once a place of refuge and a realm of demonic temptations and assaults, both a place of disciplinary tutelage and a potential paradise.

In explaining further the projection of the religious conflict of the Old World into the arena of the New, Mather found it also useful to attach equal importance to "the *Concealing* of *America*" until "the fulness of Time was come for the Discovery." He noted the swift succession of three memorable developments in human affairs at about the turn of the fifteenth century, namely, "the *Resurrection of Literature*," "the opening of *America*," "the *Reformation of Religion*." He speculated that even though the devil had probably seduced the aboriginal inhabitants into America in order to populate it with those who presumably would ever thereafter be "out of the sound of the *Silver Trumpets* of the *Gospel*," the devil had reckoned ill; for God in His providence was so to arrange human affairs that the Europeans prepared by Him to fill the waste places would enter the devilish American desert only after literature had been reborn, the art of printing had been acquired, and the religion to be transplanted had been restored to the perfection of its apostolic "*Golden Age*."

The providential preparation on one side of the ocean for the trans-plantation of the true reformed faith did not include any alleviation of the perils of passage over the ocean or of the hardships of settlement in a "Rough and Bleak *Winter*," but it did include a recent decimation of the aboriginal population by a fearful plague which left the enfeebled survivors disposed to meet with "humble Regards" the elect planters come to occupy their land. Apart from this small consolation, the "American" or the "Indian" desert or wilderness was for the "New-English Israel," "*this little* Israel," admittedly as bleak and hazardous as it was for the incompletely reformed "Church of England-men" in Virginia, or for the popish French to the North and Spaniards to the South.

For Puritans the wilderness of the New World was "dark," "desolate," "horrible," "horrid," "howling," "mighty," "squalid," "terrible," "vast," "waste," and "wretched." Though some of these adjectives had a Biblical resonance they were for Mather, on one level, simply descriptive of the harsh realities of the untamed physical environment—its peril and discomfort—in which the Puritans had come to settle. But the "wilderness" had for Mather other and nonliteral meanings. In his employment of the term in a metaphorical or typological sense, Mather drew not only directly from scriptures but also indirectly from a complex monastic and mystical tradition about the function of the outer and inner desert in Christian life and experience. Basic to his conception of the Puritan "*Errand into the Wilderness*" were the biblically saturated, non-literal senses of the word that provided him with a literary-typological, a providential, and an eschatological framework for his densely elaborated picture of a pilgrim people, a little Israel, in the vast New Canaan of the Western hemisphere. Mather never developed the "*Christiano-graphy*" he called for except in literary conceits and scriptural allusions; nevertheless, his understanding of the wilderness in moral, spiritual, and eschatological senses is everywhere apparent.

Like other New England divines, Mather found in the wilderness experience of the Israelites and of the earliest Christians as recorded in the New Testament a wide range of signification and practical application. He could refer in general to Biblical deserts or to particular deserts in which memorable episodes had taken place, as well as to subsequent scriptural reflections on these episodes at various stages in the growth of Israel and the early Church, from Abraham's setting forth from Ur of the Chaldees to John the Baptist's preparing the way of the Lord in the wilderness of Judaea (Bk. III, p. 6, par. VII).*

The most notable Biblical desert was, of course, the wilderness of the Sinai peninsula traversed for forty years by the Israelites after their

---

* References to Books I and II are to this edition; references to subsequent books are to the 1702 edition.

escape from Egyptian bondage and before their entry into the Promised Land of Canaan. However, the seventeenth-century Puritans of New England were both theologically and as Englishmen constrained from exploiting this episode in its entirety as a Biblical analogy or type of their escape from bondage to the High-Church Laudian establishment in England. It is true that Mather likens the Indians to the Canaanites and other tribes without the Law and readily compares the colonists in their peregrinations to the "*Erratick Church of Israel*" (Bk. III, p. 11) in the wilderness of Sinai; but the fact that the Puritan New Englanders in the seventeenth century professed unquestioning loyalty to their king (or protector) in England inhibited their full use of the imagery of Exodus. They could not openly identify their sovereign as a latter-day Pharaoh, nor old England as an Egypt. England was, rather, the home of the still insufficiently reformed, yet always beloved, church and kingdom of God's very special people, of whom the Puritans in the overseas diaspora were but the more advanced, reformed, and disciplined contingent. Accordingly, the New England Puritans did not directly liken their crossing of the Atlantic to the passage through the Red Sea (as was later attractive in the perspective of the impending and then the accomplished American Revolution). Notably, they did not liken the American wilderness to the wilderness of Sinai as the scene of some new disclosure of the Law, a dispensational renewal of the covenant (Exod. 19.1–6; Acts 7.38). This was because the Puritans thought of their errand in the wilderness as the perfecting of the Reformation rather than as the quest for a new mandate in doctrine, cultus, and the moral code. Mather, to be sure, made *selective* use of the epic, forty-year experience of Israel in the desert in flight from Egypt and in the gradual approach to Canaan. For example, he fondly referred to the Puritan refugees, in muted allusion to the surreptitious petitions of the Israelites to their Egyptian sovereign, as being "let go," that they "might hold a feast unto God in the wilderness" (Exod. 5.1) in order "to serve" (7.17) and "to worship the Lord in the wilderness" (8.28) according to the pure principles of the reformed religion. And with the Pilgrims' pastor John Robinson, Mather could agree that the Lord had "more Truth yet to break forth out of his holy Word" and that the Bay Puritans, too, might therefore come "to embrace *further light*" concerning the manner of repristination or reformation within the stipulations of the church covenants of gathered saints (*Magnalia*, Bk. I, chap. 3, sect. 8). With the prefatory attestator of the *Magnalia*, John Higginson of Salem, Mather wholly agreed that "farther practical reformation" or the complete recovery of pristine Christian usage and doctrine would attend the voluntary exile in the wilderness, for the very simplification of cultus in a rude environment would necessarily lead to "a *perfect reformation*" (*Magnalia*, Attestation, p. 70). But none of these strenuous reformers of the Reformation, be it John Robinson or John Cotton in the first generation or their interpreters John Higginson or Cotton Mather, could ever have thought of reformation, however radical, as a new revelation or a new covenantal dispensation. That their descendants in and around Boston would one day plausibly interpret their new truth breaking forth and their further light dawning as a latter-day sanction for the espousal of fresh draughts of revelation from the Holy Spirit would have been anathema. For them reformation meant restitution and return. It did not mean a new Sinai and a new covenant, teaching new duties. Accordingly, Mather carefully avoided any metaphorical or typological exploitation of the central action of the wilderness pilgrimage in Exodus, the handing down of the Decalogue from Sinai. He never suggested a new dispensation in the wilderness of the New World—only a new opportunity. He could never think of New Englanders as anything more than an advance party in time and space of godly Protestant Englishmen, beloved and favored by the Almighty above all the tribes in the new covenant in Christ.

Since restoration and renewal was his theme, Mather, without failing to exploit aspects of the wilderness of Exodus, was even more interested in the mystically nuptial wilderness of Canticles (3.16, 8.5), the wilderness in which the heavenly bridegroom encounters the pure ecclesiastical bride (the Puritan church). Still more, Mather's is the protective wilderness of the righteous remnant, the refuge of Revelation 12.6, to which the woman with child, symbolic of the Church, flees from the dragon in the last days. Besides this notably apocalyptic passage and other references in the New Testament to the wilderness as a resting place or hiding place, Mather found others in the Old Testament as well.

In his strong eschatological emphasis, Mather gave attention even to Joseph Mede's strange conjecture in *Clavis Apocalyptica* (1627) that the American hemisphere might "escape the *Conflagration* of the *Earth*" expected at the descent of Christ from heaven at the Second Advent; but he insisted that the regenerated pilgrims to the New World (as distinguished from the devilish aborigines), instead of not participating in the blessedness of the renovated world during the "*Thousand Years* of *Holy Rest*," might in the American hemisphere so live and discipline themselves as to "anticipate the State of the *New-Jerusalem*." The fact that Mather was thinking more often of a wilderness of God's quasi-constitutional covenant with the whole of his people at the beginning of Israel's history imparted to his American annals something of the tonality and coloration of the apocalyptic. His preference for the mystical or the eschatological rather than the covenantal wilderness thus goes far to explain the intensity of his narrative, which, though dense with archival and biographical detail, is no mere chronicle but a theodicy of the New

English Israel renewed, regenerated, and ever ready to face "wilderness temptations," moving confidently toward a cosmic vindication of the faith.

By the term "wilderness temptations," Mather had in mind the trials of faith known alike to the Israelites in the Sinai desert, to Jesus tempted in the wilderness by Satan, and to the "little flock" of Jesus' eschatological sermon (Luke 12.32) and of his eschatological warning to flee (Matt. 24.16). More specifically, these wilderness trials were modeled on the temptations to idolatry that beset the wandering Israelites during forty years (Ps. 95.8; Heb. 3.8), enticing them into a temporary abandonment of their shepherds and an overturning of the divinely sanctioned law, and luring them to return to their condition of servitude before the flight. For the Puritans these temptations of the wilderness were "persecutions," "hardships," "Streights," "Wants," and what Mather once called the "*Littlenesses* of a *Wilderness*" (Bk. III, p. 105), with special reference to the privations suffered by learned men remote from the seats of culture.

The New England Puritans in Mather's interpretation were "the People of the *Design*" (Bk. III, p. 75), of a more "Glorious Reformation" (Bk. III, p. 11), the "*Peculiar People*" of the Great God of Heaven, of the Lord of Hosts, of the Lord Jesus Christ, constituting in four colonies or "squadrons" an "army" in the American wilderness, a "*Theocracy*." The distinctive feature of the regenerated *gens pro Christo* of the New England Congregationalist colonies was that they considered themselves to be sojourners (aliens) or pilgrims (exiles) (I Pet. 2.11) on earth, owning a citizenship in heaven (Phil. 3.20), acknowledging spiritual allegiance to Christ as lord of the whole society and as personal lord of each duly gathered, regenerated congregational fellowship of believers. Within the theocracy the Puritans considered themselves independent in polity, covenant, and creed of any shepherds or pastors from outside the local visible church or congregation, that is, of any external bishop (overseer) or of any synod of presbyters (elders). Thus, they believed, they could truly worship God perfectly and walk uprightly in their daily lives. Indeed, to change the imagery from "Lord" to "Shepherd," they had, as a company of pasturing flocks under various pastors, followed Christ as the chief "Pastor" and only "Overseer" into the wilderness. Many elected, regenerate pastors, answerable alone to the "*great* and *good Shepherd*" invisible above, fed their congregations as flocks grazing in the wilderness (Bk. III, p. 11).

At one point, Mather characterizes the wilderness into which the Puritans had followed Christ as "*a Land not sown*" (Bk. IV, p. 169). To this familiar Biblical locution for the desert may be related the references in the *Magnalia* to the wilderness as potentially a garden of the Lord. In the language of this metaphor the religious colonies were plantings or plantations of the Lord; and in one place Mather quotes the lieutenant governor of New England as having once declared: "*God sifted three Nations, that he might bring choice Grain into this Wilderness*" (Bk. III, p. 5). The "*General Considerations for the Plantation of New-England*" that were drawn up in 1629 in England to enunciate the purposes of the plantation declared: "The *whole Earth* is the *Lord's Garden,* and he hath given it to the Sons of *Adam,* to be Tilled and Improved by them." We should remember, however, that the allusions in the *Magnalia* and in all the Puritan literature to a garden in the wilderness are much more than references to fruitful clearings in the forests of New England. Their horticultural language reflected not so much the actualities of colonial agriculture as the whole Biblical cycle of experience with the shifting boundaries between wilderness and cultivated land and the intricate complex of moral and spiritual meanings which was the Puritans' inheritance from the prophetic literature of the Old Testament.

The Israelites, like all the peoples of the Fertile Crescent insofar as they depended upon rain for their gardens, grainfields, orchards, and pastures, dreaded the desert and feared the wilderness and their encroachment in times of unseasonable drought upon the sown lands. But unlike all the surrounding peoples, they had had a formative experience of collective redemption, tutelage, and covenantal organization in the desert itself. Their prophets repeatedly reminded the Israelites settled in agricultural Canaan that God had most loved them when they were wandering in the wilderness, when He came to them as lover to the beloved (Hos. 2.14ff.; Jer. 2.2), and they often sought to recall the Israelites to the purity and justice of their nomadic desert past. Again and again minorities within Israel (like the Rechabites, later the Essenes, and finally the followers of John the Baptist) tried to renew the covenant of righteousness in the simplicities and austerities of the wilderness. Thus, in Biblical literature the wilderness or desert had both a negative and a positive connotation, and in either case it was understood not only literally but also spiritually as a state or condition willed by God for His chosen for their punishment, their purgation, their protection, or their illumination.

When the Scriptures presented the wilderness as an evil but as nevertheless willed by God, the term was in effect a metaphor of God's wrath. When the Scriptures used "wilderness" in a positive sense, it was essentially a metaphor of God's grace. As a metaphor of God's wrath, Jerusalem—even as it was receiving the seasonal rains—could be called a blasted wilderness. The Hebrews understood that not only could their sown land be turned literally into a desert by a want of seasonal rain, withheld by God in punishment, but also Israel could become spiritually

a wasteland through disobedience. And likewise they knew from agricultural and spiritual experience that the wilderness could by God's
grace be turned into a garden, and blossom as the rose (Isa. 35.1).

Back of these gardens and deserts was the Biblical account of the
Great Garden, of man's fall from Paradise into the wilderness of this
world because of his primeval disobedience. And just as in early
Christian, monastic, and sectarian history, highly disciplined Christians
regarded their sanctified community—their church of the martyrs, their
conventual congregation, or their saintly sect—as a provisional restoration of Paradise, an oasis in the desert of the world, so Mather and his
contemporaries thought of their church and commonwealth in the wilderness as a "garden of spices." They were equally certain of the means by
which the American wilderness would be turned into a paradise, "the
Garden of *New-England*" (Bk. IV, p. 181): by total obedience to Christ,
the Second and Last Adam.

The garden-wilderness metaphor was susceptible of a variety of applications. When it referred to the realm of education in New England, it
became the "nursery" or "seminary in the wilderness." Mather called
Harvard University, for example, a seminary in the wilderness, devoting
the whole of Book IV to it and to its alumni. He came close to suggesting
that this seedbed in the wilderness was a foreshadowing of that garden
which is the paradise of spiritual delights. In Mather's day the word
"seminary" as a seedbed of ministers or priests had entered the international vocabulary of religion as a Catholic contribution following the
Council of Trent. Mather was probably only vaguely aware of the word's
Catholic connotation, but he twice calls Harvard a "Happy *Seminary*"
and the context would seem to indicate that Mather thought of his
beloved college as "happy" in contrast to many an unhappy seminary of
dark and obscurantist doctrine. He looked back in veneration to Emmanuel College in old Cambridge as a "Seminary of Puritans," and the
same metaphor served him to describe the Puritan college in the wilderness as a "learned seminary," a "nursery" and a "seedbed" in the New
World (Bk. IV, p. 134).

On the title page of Book IV, devoted to the university in new
Cambridge and to "the LIVES of some Eminent Persons, who were
Plants of Renown growing in that NURSERY," Mather linked the seminary metaphor in a special way with the scriptural wilderness-paradise
motif. In his life of Thomas Shepard of the first church gathered in what
is now Cambridge, he referred to the "many *Monsters*" (antinomianism,
familism, and so on) which arose to threaten the flocks of Christ pasturing
in the wilderness. Making the most of the pastor's surname, he credited
the "vigilance" of Shepard with the deliverance of all the flocks, not only
of his own, from these dangers, with the consequence that when the

foundation of Harvard was to be laid, "*Cambridge* rather than any other place, was pitch'd upon to be the Seat of that happy Seminary" (Bk. III, p. 87). Here the pastoral and horticultural metaphors are brought together. Elsewhere they are conflated in a sustained attempt to provide for Harvard College the highest possible Biblical sanction against all detractors of clerical education. Mather also placed Harvard in what might be called an evangelical monastic tradition, quoting from the former Premonstratensian abbot Thomas Stange (d. 1559), who had converted his abbey of Ilfeld in the Harz Mountains into a "*Protestant Colledge*," "a school of the knowledge of God, a teaching place for logical minds" (Bk. IV, p. 125). Mather at another point reprinted the memoirs of a Harvard student who, in allusion to a famous letter of the monkish scholar Jerome ("Make your cell, your paradise"), called his small but precious library his "*Paradice*" (Bk. IV, p. 217). He also referred floridly to the prospering Long Island parish of another Harvard alumnus as becoming, through the hard labors of teaching and ruling, "(what *Paradise* was called), *An Island of the Innocent*" (Bk. III, p. 95).

Indeed, for Cotton Mather, Harvard College was in the direct line of the schools of the prophets. The seminary in Cambridge took its place as the most recent in the half legendary history of the transfer of licit knowledge (*translatio studii*) from Paradise through "the universities of Palestine" (Mather often called his new Cambridge *Kirjath Sepher*— Bk. IV, p. 126—the City of Books) to the University of Paris (where the four faculties were likened to the four rivers of Paradise), to old Cambridge, and to John Calvin's Academy in Geneva.

Without directly naming Harvard a provisional paradise like medieval Paris, Mather was content to call it a seminary in the full metaphorical sense by describing it as "a river, without the streams whereof, these regions would have been mere unwatered places for the devil." The university was thus not only a seedbed but also a river of grace that irrigated the desert of the New World. Its matured seedlings, taking root in distant parishes, were envisaged as turning each into a forecourt of the heavenly paradise. Mather likened Harvard, with its ministerial and magisterial alumni, both to the temple in Jerusalem and to a river flowing from beneath Zion into the desert. Just as the stream flowing beneath the temple in Jerusalem, understood eschatologically, irrigated the moral desert, so did the college revitalize and nourish the land. The allusions here are numerous. He quotes an unamed Greek historian concerning "the *Temples* built by *Constantine*" at Jerusalem (Bk. IV, p. 126). This is probably a reference to the *Vita Constantini* of Eusebius of Caesarea, who calls the basilica erected by the order of the emperor "on the very spot which witnessed the Saviour's sufferings," "a new Jerusalem" or Zion. At this point, Eusebius, the historian of the Church of the ancient world, merely suggests that "this was that second and new Jerusalem spoken of in the predictions of the prophets." Cotton Mather, the historian of the "reformed" churches of the New World, in his devotion to the new Zion in Cambridge is more fervent and more direct. Here Mather's vision of Harvard as a river flowing from beneath Zion into a dry place is at once an allusion to the river of the gladdened city of the Psalmist (46.4), to the fountain of the heavenly Jerusalem (Rev. 21.6), and to the waters that issue from "out the sanctuary" of the new Zion of the prophet Ezekiel (47.12) and make glad the wilderness round about Zion envisioned by the prophet Isaiah (35.1ff.). Of his father, Increase Mather, rector or president of the university, Cotton Mather declares that "he does to this Day continue his Endeavours to keep alive that *River*, the Streams whereof have *made glad* this *City of God*" (Bk. IV, p. 131).

At this point the Matherian speculation about the university of budding divines and magistrates as a seminary or seedbed in the wilderness joins with the much more ancient scriptural, monastic, scholastic reflection on the ascetic cell or the academic study or the *studium generale* as a portion of Paradise precariously restored. In the seminary understood as a garden in the protective wilderness of the New World, under the tutelage of Christ and through the operations of the Holy Spirit, the covenantal community of learning could now, according to Mather, licitly pursue, in utter obedience to *Veritas*, that very knowledge which had once been, because of inordinate desire and disobedience, the occasion of man's fall from Paradise. The idea of Puritan Harvard as "a happy seminary"—through whose precincts flowed the rivers of Eden before the fall, irrigating New England by streams of divine grace—and also "a school of the prophets" in continuous succession with the great schools of Christendom—back to Cambridge and medieval Paris, back to Athens, back further to the imagined schools of the prophets, cannot be over-emphasized if we would understand the power and purposefulness which the idea of the *translatio studii*, the transfer of learning in orderly succession from Paradise to the wilderness of the New World, gave to the builders of the first center of learning in New England.

The frequency and variety of Mather's wilderness language prompted the author of the biographical memoir in the 1852 edition of the *Magnalia* to remark that Mather's expressions about wilderness and remoteness, though common in the seventeenth century—and he proceeded to cite a dozen instances in other writers—seemed "peculiarly odd" in mid-nineteenth-century America, and he thereupon suggested that in another century and a half "they may be viewed as something more than odd." The memorialist was quite right. To speak of what has become in the meantime the technologically most advanced society in the world as "this far remote and vast wilderness" quietly registers the tremendous historical accomplishment that separates us from the provincial author of the *Magnalia*. Yet the non-literal meanings of "wilderness" in Mather have still an incantatory power and haunting relevance.

REFERENCES

Frederick Bussby, "An Ecclesiastical Seminarie and College," *Journal of Ecclesiastical History*, IV (1953), 154–161.

Peter N. Carroll, *Puritanism and the Wilderness: The Intellectual Significance of the New England Frontier, 1629–1700* (New York, 1969).

Kenneth B. Murdock, "Clio in the Wilderness: History and Biography in Puritan New England," *Church History*, XXIV (1955), 221–238.

James A. O'Donohoe, *Tridentine Seminary Legislation: Its Sources and Its Formation*, Bibliotheca Ephemeridum Theologicarum Lovaniensium, IX (1957), 157.

George H. Williams, "Seminary in the Wilderness," *Harvard Library Bulletin*, XII (1959), 369–400; XIV (1960), 27–58.

——*Wilderness and Paradise in Christian Thought* (New York, 1962).

——"The Puritans' Conception of Their First University in New England, 1636," *Archiv für Reformationsgeschichte*, LVII (1966), Nos. 1 and 2.

——"Christian Attitudes Toward Nature," *Christian Scholar's Review*, II (Fall 1972), 3–35, 112–126.

Magnalia Christi Americana :

OR, THE

Ecclesiastical History

OF

NEVV-ENGLAND,

FROM

Its First Planting in the Year 1620. unto the Year
of our LORD, 1698.

In Seven BOOKS.

I. Antiquities : In Seven Chapters. With an Appendix.
II. Containing the Lives of the Governours, and Names of the Magistrates of *New-England*: In Thirteen Chapters. With an Appendix.
III. The Lives of Sixty Famous Divines, by whose Ministry the Churches of *New-England* have been Planted and Continued.
IV. An Account of the University of *Cambridge* in *New-England*; in Two Parts. The First contains the Laws, the Benefactors, and Vicissitudes of *Harvard College*; with Remarks upon it. The Second Part contains the Lives of some Eminent Persons Educated in it.
V. Acts and Monuments of the Faith and Order in the Churches of *New-England*, passed in their Synods; with Historical Remarks upon those Venerable Assemblies; and a great Variety of Church-Cases occurring, and resolved by the Synods of those Churches : In Four Parts.
VI. A Faithful Record of many Illustrious, Wonderful Providences, both of Mercies and Judgments, on divers Persons in *New-England*: In Eight Chapters.
VII. *The Wars of the Lord.* Being an History of the Manifold Afflictions and Disturbances of the Churches in *New-England*, from their Various Adversaries, and the Wonderful Methods and Mercies of God in their Deliverance : In Six Chapters : To which is subjoined, An Appendix of Remarkable Occurrences which *New-England* had in the Wars with the *Indian* Salvages, from the Year 1688, to the Year 1698.

By the Reverend and Learned *COTTON MATHER*, M. A.
And Pastor of the North Church in *Boston*, *New-England*.

LONDON:

Printed for *Thomas Parkhurst*, at the *Bible* and *Three
Crowns* in *Cheapside*. MDCCII.

This title page, the title page of the original volume, was photographed from the 1702 edition of the *Magnalia* by courtesy of the Houghton Library, Harvard University.

In the original edition, the title page of the first Book, "Antiquities," followed on the next recto, as it does here, preceding the Attestation.

ANTIQUITIES.

The First Book

OF THE

New-English History.

REPORTING,

The DESIGN where-*on*,	The several COLONIES
The MANNER where-*in*,	of NEW-ENGLAND
And the PEOPLE where-*by*,	were Planted.

WITH

A NARRATIVE of many Memorable Passages,

Relating to the

Settlement of these Plantations;

AND

An Ecclesiastical MAP of the Country.

By the Endeavour of

COTTON MATHER.

Tantæ Molis erat, pro CHRISTO condere Gentem.

LONDON,

Printed for *Thomas Parkhurst*, at the *Bible* and *Three
Crowns* in *Cheapside* near *Mercers Chappel*, 1702.

This title page was photographed from the 1702 edition of the *Magnalia* by courtesy of the Houghton Library, Harvard University.

Line 17, "So much labor did it cost to establish a people for Christ," is an adaptation of the *Aeneid* I.36.

AN
ATTESTATION[1]
TO THIS
Church-History
OF
NEW-ENGLAND.

5

IT hath been deservedly esteemed, one of the great and wonderful
Works of God in this *Last Age*,[2] that the Lord stirred up the Spirits of
so many Thousands of his Servants, to leave the *Pleasant Land of England*,
10 the Land of their *Nativity*, and to transport themselves, and Families,
over the *Ocean Sea*, into a *Desert Land*,[3] in *America*, at the Distance of a
Thousand Leagues from their own Country; and this, meerly on the Account of *Pure and Undefiled Religion*, not knowing how they should have
their *Daily Bread*, but trusting in God for *That*, in the way of *seeking first the*
15 *Kingdom of God, and the Righteousness thereof*: And that the Lord was pleased
to grant such a gracious *Presence* of his with them, and such a *Blessing*
upon their Undertakings, that within a few Years a *Wilderness* was
subdued before them, and so many *Colonies* Planted, *Towns* Erected,
and *Churches* Settled, wherein the true and living God in Christ Jesus, is
20 worshipped, and served, in a place where time out of mind, had been

---

[1] John Higginson (1616–1708), the author of the Attestation, came to Massachusetts from
England in 1629 with his father, Francis, who was ordained minister of the First Church in
Salem in that year. Francis died in 1630. In 1660 John Higginson became pastor of the same
church and served it until his death. In 1697, when the Attestation was written, he was one of
the oldest and most respected ministers in New England. A close friend of the Mathers, he was
called by Cotton a "true *Simeon*" (Luke 2.25–35), and "my Reverend Father." Higginson
also wrote prefaces for Mather's *Winter-Meditations* (Boston, 1693) and his *Everlasting Gospel*
(Boston, 1700). See Thomas J. Holmes, *Cotton Mather: A Bibliography* (3 vols., Cambridge,
Mass, Harvard University Press, 1940), 3:1221; 1:340.*

[2] "Wonderful Works of God": i.e., "magnalia dei." See introductory essay "The Magnalia,"
and Acts 2.11. "*Last Age*," the most recent age, the one just passed, carried here also the sense
of the "last" before the end of time.*

[3] See Deut. 32.10. Higginson here, as elsewhere in the Attestation, uses a Biblical phrase
to liken the pilgrimage of the first settlers of New England to that of the Children of Israel.
See introductory essay "The Idea of the Wilderness."

nothing before, but *Heathenism, Idolatry,* and *Devil-worship*; and that the Lord has added so many of the Blessings of *Heaven* and *Earth* for the Comfortable Subsistence of his People in these *Ends of the Earth*.[4] Surely of this *Work,* and of this *Time,* it shall be said, *What hath God wrought?*

25 And, *This is the Lord's doing, it is marvellous in our Eyes!* Even so (*O Lord*) *didst thou lead thy People, to make thy self a glorious Name!*[5] Now, *One Generation passeth away, and another cometh.* The *First Generation* of our Fathers, that began this Plantation of *New-England,* most of them in their *middle Age,* and many of them in their *declining Years,* who, *after they had served the*

30 *Will of God,* in laying the *Foundation* (as we hope) of *many Generations,*[6] and given an *Example* of true *Reformed Religion* in the *Faith* and *Order* of the Gospel,[7] according to their best Light from the *Words* of God, they are now *gathered unto their Fathers.* There hath been *another Generation* succeeding the *First,* either of such as come over with their Parents very

35 Young, or were born in the Country, and these have had the managing of the *Publick Affairs* for many Years, but are apparently *passing away,* as their *Fathers* before them. There is also a *Third Generation,* who are grown up, and begin to stand thick upon the Stage of *Action,*[8] at this Day, and these were all born in the Country, and may call *New-England*

40 their *Native Land.* Now, in respect of what the Lord hath done for these Generations, succeeding one another, we have abundant cause of Thanksgiving to the Lord our God, who hath so Increased and Blessed this People, that from a *Day of small things,* he has brought us to be, what we now are. We may set up an *EBENEZER,* and say, *Hitherto the Lord*

45 *hath helped us.*[9] Yet in respect of our *Present State,* we have need earnestly to *Pray,* as we are directed, *Let thy Work farther appear unto thy Servants, and let thy Beauty be upon us, and thy Glory upon our Children; Establish thou the Works of these our hands; yea, the Works of our hands, Establish thou them.*[10]

---

25 *doing/doings*

[4] For "*Presence,*" "*Blessing,*" see Exod. 32.29, 33.14; for "*Wilderness* subdued," Num. 32.22, 29; Josh. 18.1; I Chron. 22.18; for "Blessings of *Heaven* and *Earth,*" Gen. 49.25; for "*Ends of the Earth,*" Pss. 48.10, 98.3; Acts 13.47.

[5] For "*What hath God wrought?*" see Num. 23.23; for "*marvellous in our eyes,*" Ps. 118.23; for "*make thyself a glorious Name!*" Isa. 63.14.

[6] For "*served the will of God,*" see Acts 13.36; for "*Foundation of many Generations,*" Isa. 58.12.*

[7] Cotton Mather in the *Magnalia* presents the founders of the New England churches and their creed and polity ("*Faith* and *Order*") as good "examples," which should be followed by their descendants. Cf. James 5.10; I Pet. 2.21; and introductory essay "The Magnalia." "Reformed religion" is often used for Protestantism in general, but Cotton Mather commonly applies the phrase "true reformed religion" to Genevan Calvinism.*

[8] "Action" is used here literally, as in I Sam. 2.3: "The Lord is a God of knowledge, and by him actions are weighed," and metaphorically, as action on a stage. See General Introduction p. 90, ll. 26–32.

[9] Eben-ezer was the name of the commemorative stone which Samuel set up after the victory of Mizpeh, "saying, Hitherto hath the LORD helped us" (I Sam. 7.12).*

[10] Ps. 90.16–17.*

For, if we look on the *Dark side*,[11] the *Humane side* of this Work, there is
50 much of *Humane Weakness* and *Imperfection*, hath appeared in all that hath
been done by *Man*, as was acknowledged by our *Fathers* before us. Neither
was *New-England* ever without some *Fatherly Chastisements* from God;
shewing that He is not Fond of the *Formalities* of any People upon Earth,
but expects the *Realities* of *Practical Godliness*, according to our Profession
55 and Engagement unto him. Much more may we, the *Children* of such
Fathers, lament our *Gradual Degeneracy* from that *Life* and *Power of Godliness* that was in them, and the many *Provoking Evils* that are amongst us;
which have moved our God severely to witness against us,[12] more than in
our *first Times*, by his *lesser Judgments* going before, and his *Greater
60 Judgments* following after; He shot off his *Warning-pieces first*, but his
Murthering-pieces[13] have come after them, in so much as in these Calamitous Times, the Changes of Wars of *Europe* have had such a malignant
Influence upon US in *America*, that we are at this Day *Greatly diminished
and brought low, through Oppression, Affliction, and Sorrow.*[14]

65 And yet if we look on the *Light side*, the *Divine side* of this Work, we may
yet see, that the *Glory of God* which was with our *Fathers*, is not wholly
departed from us their *Children*; there are as yet many *Signs* of his *Gracious
Presence* with us, both in the way of his *Providences*, and in the use of his
Ordinances, as also in and with the *Hearts* and *Souls*[15] of a considerable
70 number of his People in *New-England*, that we may yet say as they did,
*Thy Name is Upon us, and thou art in the midst of us, therefore, Lord, Leave us
not!* As *Solomon* prayed, so may we, *The Lord our God be with us, as he was
with our Fathers; Let him not leave nor forsake us; but incline our Hearts to keep
his Commandments.* And then, *That he would maintain his own, and his Peoples
75 Cause, at all times, as the matter may require.*[16]

For the Lord our God hath in his infinite Wisdom, Grace and Holiness,
contrived and established His *Covenant*, so as he will be the God of his
People, and of their *Seed* with them, and after them, *in their Generations*;

---

[11] "*Dark side*," and "*Light side*" at the beginning of the next paragraph, refer metaphorically
to the light and dark sides of the pillar of cloud and fire, which guided the Children of Israel
on their wilderness pilgrimage and was light to them but dark to their pursuers (Exod. 14.19–
20). "*Humane*" (human) is contrasted with "*Divine*" in the first line of the next paragraph.*

[12] For "*Chastisements*," see Deut. 8.5, 11.2; for "Profession," "Engagement," the declaration
of belief in God's law and promise to obey it, see I Tim. 6.12; Heb. 10.23; for "*Provoking Evils*,"
i.e., evil ways which provoke God to "witness against us," see I Kings 14.15; Ps. 78.17, 40;
Ezek. 20.43.*

[13] "Warning-pieces": guns sounded as alarms. "Murthering-pieces": small cannons or
mortars (sometimes called "murderers").*

[14] The Massachusetts colonists feared the hostile French in Canada and depended on military
support from England against them. They were therefore deeply concerned with the "changes"
(vicissitudes, "ups and downs") of Anglo-French relations and England's political strategy in
Europe.*

[15] For "*Glory of God* . . . with our *Fathers*," see Exod. 16.7, 10, 24.16–17; for "*Ordinances*,"
Exod. 18–20; for "*Hearts* and *Souls*," Josh. 23.14.

[16] The italicized passages in these lines are based on Jer. 14.9 and I Kings 8.57–59.

and in the Ministerial Dispensation of the *Covenant of Grace*, in, with, and
80 to his *visible Church*, He hath promised *Covenant-Mercies* on the Condition
of *Covenant-Duties*.[17] *If my People, who are called by my Name, shall humble
themselves, and pray, and seek my Face, and turn from their wicked ways, then
will I hear their Prayers, forgive their Sins, and heal their Land; and mine Eyes,
and mine Heart, shall be upon them perpetually for Good!* [18] That so the *Faith-*
85 *fulness* of God may appear in all Generations for ever, that if there be any
Breach between the *Lord* and his *People*, it shall appear plainly to lye on
his *Peoples* part. And therefore he has taken care, that his own *Dealings*
with his People in the Course of his *Providence*, and their *Dealings* with him
in the Ways of *Obedience* or *Disobedience*, should be *Recorded*, and so
90 transmitted for the Use and Benefit of After-times, from Generation to
Generation; as, (*Exodus* 17. 14.) *The Lord said unto* Moses, *write this for a
Memorial in a Book*; and, (*Deut.* 31. 19.) *Write ye this Song for you, that it
may be a Witness for me against the Children of* Israel; and (*Psal.* 102. 18.) *This
and that shall be written for the Generation to come, and the People that shall be*
95 *created shall praise the Lord.* Upon this Ground it was said (in *Psal.* 44. 1.)
*We have heard with our Ears, O God, and our Fathers have told Us, what Work
thou didst in their Days in times of Old, how thou castest out the Heathen, and
plantedst them*; (so likewise in *Psal.* 78. v. 3 to the 8th.) Upon the same ac-
99 count it may be said, (*Psal.* 45. last.)[19] *I will make thy Name to be remembered
to all Generations:* And this is one Reason why the *Lord* commanded so
great a part of the *Holy Scriptures* to be written in an *Historical way*, that
the wonderful Works of God towards his Church and People, and their
Actings towards him again, might be *known unto all Generations:* And
5 after the *Scripture-time*, so far as the *Lord* in his *Holy Wisdom* hath seen
meet, He hath stirred up some or other to write the *Acts and Monuments*[20]
of the Church of God in all Ages; especially since the *Reformation of*

---

[17] For "established His *Covenant . . . in their Generations*," see Gen. 17.7, 9. It was on the basis
of Genesis 17 that Puritans constructed their covenant theology. In the Covenant of Grace,
God contracted to redeem and glorify those who engaged themselves, through faith, to submit
to His ordinances. The Church Covenant was a compact between God and a company of
Christians within the Covenant of Grace who pledged themselves to worship together and to
"walke together by the assistance [mercies] of his Spirit, in all such wayes [duties] of holy
worship." Since, in this life, there could be no absolute assurance of the determinations of
God's secret will, it was acknowledged that the "visible church" must be understood to consist
only of "visible saints," those who by their ability to make public profession of an experience
of saving grace were deemed "justified" and therefore eligible for church membership and the
enjoyment of the sacraments.*
[18] II Chron. 7.14–16.
[19] "45. last": Ps. 45.17.
[20] "Scripture-time": the period historically recorded in the Bible; "Monuments": documents, records, or, in general, anything that by its survival commemorates a person, period,
action, or event. "Acts and Monuments," here and on the title page of the *Magnalia*, refers to
the famous *Acts and Monuments* written by the Protestant reformer John Foxe (1516–1587),
which in the seventeenth century was widely read and much valued in England and the
colonies.*

Religion from Antichristian Darkness,[21] was *vigorously* and in a great measure *successfully* endeavoured in the foregoing Century, by such
10 Learned and Pious Persons, as the Lord inclined and inabled thereunto.

And therefore surely, it hath been a Duty incumbent upon the People of God, in this our *New-England*, that there should be extant, a true *History* of the Wonderful Works of God in the late Plantation of this part of *America*; which was indeed planted, not on the account of any *Worldly*
15 *Interest*, but on a Design of Enjoying and Advancing the true *Reformed Religion*, in a *Practical way*: And also of the *Good Hand of God* upon it from the beginning unto this Day, in granting such a measure of *Good Success*, so far as we have attained: Such a Work as this hath been much *Desired*,[22] and long *Expected*, both at home and abroad, and too long Delayed by
20 *Us*, and sometimes it hath seemed a hopeless thing ever to be attained, till God raised up the Spirit of this Learned and Pious Person, one of the Sons of the *Colledge*, and one of the Ministers of the *Third Generation*, to undertake this Work. His Learning and Godliness, and *Ministerial Abilities*, were so Conspicuous, that at the Age of *Seventeen Years*, he was
25 called to be a publick Preacher[23] in *Boston*, the *Metropolis* of the whole English *America*; and within a while after that, he was ordained *Pastor*[24] of the same Church, whereof his own *Father* was the *Teacher*, and this at the unanimous Desire of the People, and with the Approbation of the *Magistrates*, *Ministers* and *Churches*, in the Vicinity of *Boston*. And after
30 he had, for divers Years, approved himself in an exemplary way, and obliged his *Native Country*, by publishing many useful *Treatises*,[25] suitable to the *Present State* of Religion amongst us, he set himself to write the *Church-History of New-England*, not at all omitting his Ministerial Employments; and in the midst of many Difficulties, Tears and Temptations,
35 having made a diligent Search, Collecting of proper *Materials*, and Selecting the choicest *Memorials*,[26] he hath, in the Issue, within a few Months, contrived, composed, and methodized the same into this

[21] Most "reformed" Protestants regarded the period from A.D. 606 until the Reformation as one of "Antichristian Darkness." In 606 Bishop Bonifacius III of Rome established himself as pope, with supreme authority over the whole church, thus initiating the "Popish *Supremacy*" abhorred by the reformers.*

[22] When Higginson wrote, no general history of New England and its people had been published since Edward Johnson's, best known by its subtitle, "The Wonder-Working Providence of Sion's Saviour in New England" (London, 1653). One had been "expected," since the Reverend William Hubbard was known to have finished his in 1682. This, however, had not yet been printed. Higginson's listing below of the reasons that the *Magnalia* was useful indicates why a history was "desired."*

[23] One accepted as a preacher but not appointed to office in any church.*

[24] The larger churches in New England had two ministers, one a "Teacher" and the other a "Pastor."*

[25] Holmes, *Cotton Mather*, lists sixty-one works by Mather printed before 1697—books of his own, and prefaces, letters, and "Attestations" contributed by him to volumes written by others—all of which, from the point of view of pious Congregationalists, were "useful."

[26] Any writings or objects which served to preserve the memory of persons or events.*

Form and Frame which we here see: So that it deserves the name of,
THE CHURCH-HISTORY OF NEW-ENGLAND.

40   But as I behold this Exemplary Son of *New-England,* while thus
Young and Tender, at such a rate Building the *Temple of God,* and in a
few Months dispatching such a piece of *Temple-work*[27] as this is; a Work
so notably adjusted and adorned, it brings to mind the Epigram upon
young *Borellus:*

45   *Cum Juveni tantam dedit Experientia Lucem,*
                Tale ut promat opus, quam Dabit illa Seni?[28]

As for *my self,* having been, by the Mercy of God, now above *Sixty
eight Years* in *New-England,* and served the Lord and his People in my
weak Measure, *Sixty Years* in the Ministry of the Gospel, I may now
50 say in my Old Age, *I have seen all that the Lord hath done for his People in*
New-England, and have known the Beginning and Progress of these
Churches unto this Day; and having read over much of this *History,*
I cannot but in the Love and Fear of God, bear witness to the *Truth
of it*; viz. That this present *Church-History of* New England, Compiled
55 by Mr. *Cotton Mather,* for the Substance, End and Scope of it, is, as far
as I have been acquainted therewithall, *according to Truth.*

The manifold *Advantage,* and *Usefulness* of this present *History,* will
appear, if we consider the Great and Good *Ends* unto which it may be
serviceable; As,
60 *First,* That a plain Scriptural Duty of *Recording the Works of God unto
After-times,* may not any longer be omitted, but performed in the best
manner we can.

Secondly, That by the Manifestation of the *Truth of things,* as they have
been and are amongst us, the *Misrepresentations* of *New-England* may be
65 removed and prevented; for, *Rectum est sui & obliqui Index.*[29]

Thirdly, That the True *Original* and *Design* of this Plantation may not
be lost, nor buried in *Oblivion,* but known and remembred for ever,
[*Psal.* 111. 4. *He hath made his wonderful Works to be remembred. Psal.* 105. 5.
Remember ye the marvellous Works which he hath done.]
70 *Fourthly,* That God may have the *Glory* of the Great and Good *Works*

[27] David was told by God that the "house of the Lord" he had hoped to construct would be built by his son, Solomon, who would rule over Israel. Solomon built the temple while he was still "young and tender" (I Chron. 22.5–10, 29.1). Higginson here likens the young Cotton Mather to Solomon and the *Magnalia* to a temple.*

[28] "When experience has given the youth light so great that he may produce such a work, what light will she give to the mature man?" Borellus was Pierre Borel (1620–1689), a French physician and scholar who wrote on medicine and natural history.*

[29] "Uprightness is an index not only of itself but also of what is crooked or untrue." Here the meaning is that Mather's truth makes plain the falseness of the misrepresentations of New England by some other writers.*

which he hath done for his People in these Ends of the Earth, [As in *Isaiah* 63. 7. *I will mention the loving Kindness of the Lord, and the Praises of the Lord, according to all the Great Goodness and Mercy he has bestowed on us.*]

 Fifthly, That the *Names* of such Eminent Persons as the Lord made use
75 of, as *Instruments* in his hand, for the beginning and carrying on of this Work, may be embalmed, and preserved, for the Knowledge and Imitation of Posterity; for *the Memory of the Just is Blessed.*

 Sixthly, That the present Generation may remember the *Way* wherein the Lord hath led his People in this *Wilderness,* for so many Years past
80 unto this Day; [according to that in *Deut.* 8. 2. *Thou shalt remember all the way wherein the Lord hath led thee in the Wilderness this Forty Years, to humble thee, and to prove thee, and to know what was in thy Heart, whether thou wouldest keep his Commandments or no.*] All considering Persons cannot but observe, that our *Wilderness*-condition hath been full of *humbling, trying,*
85 *distressing Providences.* We have had our *Massahs* and *Meribahs*;[30] and few of our Churches but have had some remarkable *hours of Temptation* passing over them, and God's End in all has been to *prove us,* whether, according to *our Profession,* and *his Expectation,* we would *keep his Commandments, or not.*

90 *Seventhly,* That the *Generations to come* in *New-England,* may *know the God of their Fathers, and* may *serve him with a perfect Heart and willing Mind*; as especially the *first Generation* did before them; and that they may set *their hope in God, and not forget his Works, but keep his Commandments.* (Psal. 78. 7.)

 Eighthly, And whereas it may be truly said, (as *Jer.* 2.3, 21.) *That when*
95 *this People began to follow the Lord into this Wilderness, they were, Holiness to the Lord, and he planted them as a noble Vine*; Yet if in process of time, when they are *greatly increased and multiplied,* they should so far Degenerate, as to forget the *Religious Design* of their Fathers, and forsake the Holy Ways
99 of God, (as it was said of them in *Hosea* 4. 7. *As they were increased, so they sinned against the Lord*) and so that many Evils and Troubles will befall them; *Then* this Book may be for a *Witness against them*; and yet thro' the Mercy of God, may be also a means to *Reclaim* them, and cause them to *Return* again unto the Lord, and his Holy Ways, that He may *Return*
5 again in Mercy unto them; even unto the *many Thousands* of New-England.

 Ninthly, That the Little Daughter of *New-England* in *America,* may bow

---

94 Jer. 2.3, 21./Jer. 23.21

[30] In the wilderness the thirsty Children of Israel murmured against Moses, "tempting" God by their rebellion. He listened to Moses' plea and brought water out of the rock in Horeb. Moses "called the name of the place Massah and Maribah, because of the chiding" (Maribah: "quarrel," "strife") of the people and their tempting (Massah: "Testing," "trial") of the Lord (Exod. 17.1–7). "Prove": to make trial of, or test—the usual meaning of the word in the 1611 English Bible.*

down her self to her Mother *England*, in *Europe*, presenting this *Memorial* unto her; assuring her, that tho' by some of her *Angry Brethren*, she was forced to make a *Local Secession*, yet not a *Separation*, but hath always re-
10 tained a Dutiful Respect to the *Church of God in* England; and giving some account to her, how graciously the Lord has dealt with her self in a *Remote Wilderness*, and what she has been doing all this while; giving her thanks for all the *Supplies* she has received from her; and because she is yet in her *Minority*, she craves her farther *Blessing* and *Favour* as the Case
15 may require; being glad, if what is now presented to her, may be of any use, to help forward the *Union* and *Agreement* of her *Brethren*, which would be some Satisfaction to her for her undesired Local Distance from her Dear *England*; and Finally, promising all that Reverence and Obedience which is due to her Good *Mother*, by virtue of the *Fifth* Commandment.[31] And
20 *Lastly*, That this present *History* may stand as a *Monument*, in relation to future times, of a fuller and better *Reformation* of the Church of God, than it hath yet appeared in the World. For by this *Essay* it may be seen, that a *farther Practical Reformation* than that which began at the first coming out of the Darkness of *Popery*, was aimed at, and endeavoured by a great
25 Number of *Voluntary Exiles*, that came into a *Wilderness* for that very end, that hence they might be free from humane *Additions* and *Inventions* in the Worship of God, and might practice the *positive part* of Divine *Institutions*, according to the Word of God. How far we have attained this Design, may be judged by this *Book*. But we beseech our Brethren, of our own and
30 of other *Nations*, to believe that we are far from thinking that we have attained a *perfect Reformation*. Oh, *No!* Our Fathers did in their time acknowledge, there were many *Defects* and *Imperfections* in our Way, and yet we believe they did as much as could be expected from Learned and Godly Men in their Circumstances; and we, their *Successors*, are far short
35 of them in many respects, meeting with many *Difficulties* which they *did not*; and *mourning* under many *Rebukes* from our God which they *had not*, and with trembling Hearts observing the *Gradual Declinings* that are amongst us from the Holy Ways of God; we are forced to cry out, and say, *Lord, what will become of these Churches in time? And what wilt thou do for*
40 *thy great Name?* And yet in the Multitude of our Thoughts and Fears, the *Consolations of God refresh our Souls*, that all those that *in Simplicity and*

---

[31] Most New England Congregationalists insisted, as Higginson does in the preceding paragraph, that they respected "the *Church of God in* England" and had not separated from it, but had been forced to make a geographical "secession" from it by "*Angry Brethren*"—notably Charles I, Archbishop Laud, and those Anglicans who opposed full "reformation," and in polity and ritual followed too closely the Church of Rome. The colonists hoped to establish reformed churches which would serve as examples for their mother country. They were encouraged by the accession to the throne of William and Mary, since both were staunch Protestants, untainted by Rome. They hoped also that under the new regime some agreement might be found which would enable Anglicans, Presbyterians, and Congregationalists to live and worship in harmony.*

Godly Sincerity do serve the Lord, and his People in their Generation (tho they should miss it in some things) they shall deliver their own Souls, they are accepted of the Lord, and *their Reward is with him;*[32] and in the ap-
45 proaching Days of a better *Reformation*, the *sincere*, tho' *weak* Endeavours of the Servants of God, that went before them, will be also accepted of the Saints in those times of greater Light and Holiness, that are to come; and when the Lord shall make *Jerusalem* (or, the true Church of God, and the true Christian Religion) *a Praise in the Earth, and the Joy of many*
50 *Generations*,[33] then the *Mistakes* of *these times* will be rectified; and that which is of *God* in any of his Churches, now in any Part of the World, will be owned and improved unto an higher Degree of *Practical Godliness*, that shall continue for many Generations succeeding one another, which hitherto hath been so rare a thing to be found in the World.

55 I shall now draw to a *Conclusion*, with an *Observation* which hath visited my Thoughts: That the Lord hath blessed the Family of the *MATHERS*, amongst us, with a singular Blessing, in that no less than *Ten* of them, have been accepted of him, to serve the Lord and his People in the Ministry of the Gospel of Jesus Christ; of whom, as the
60 Apostle said in another case, tho' *some are fallen asleep*, yet the *greatest part remain unto this Day;*[34] I do not know the like in our *New-England*, and perhaps it will be found rare to parallel the same in other Countries. Truly I have thought, it hath been a Reward of *Grace*, with respect unto the *Faithfulness* they have expressed, in asserting, clearing, maintaining,
65 and putting on [35] for the Practice of that great Principle, of the *Propagation of Religion* in these Churches, viz. *The Covenant-State and Church-membership of the Children born in these Churches*,[36] together with the *Scripture Duties* appertaining thereunto, and that by vertue of God's *Covenant of Grace*, established by God with his People, and their Seed with them, and after
70 them in their Generations. And this has been done especially by Mr. *Richard Mather* the Father, and by Mr. *Increase Mather* his Son, and by Mr. *Cotton Mather* his Son, the Author of this present Work.

I shall give the Reader the Satisfaction to enumerate this happy *Decemvirate*.

[32] Gen. 15.1; Isa. 40.10, 62.11.*
[33] Isa. 62.7, 60.15.
[34] I Cor. 15.6.
[35] Pushing on, hastening onward.
[36] A reference to the Mathers' support of the "Half-Way Covenant," agreed to by a synod in Boston in 1662. Originally membership in the churches had been restricted to those who could give a "personal relation" of a religious experience proving that they had been converted by the work of God's spirit in their hearts and were thus truly "regenerate." Their children were allowed baptism and church membership but denied communion unless they could meet the same test their parents had. The 1662 Covenant provided that, if they lived godly lives, their offspring in turn might have the same relation to the church that they had.*

75   1. *Richard Mather,* Teacher of the Church in *Dorchester.*[37]

2. *Samuel Mather*: He was the first Fellow of *Harvard-Colledge* in *Cambridge* in *New-England,* and the first Preacher at *North-Boston,* where his *Brother* and his *Nephew* are now his Successors. He was afterwards one of the Chaplains in *Magdalen-Colledge* in *Oxford*; after that, a *Senior Fellow* of

80   *Trinity-Colledge* in *Dublin,* and Pastor of a Church in that City, where he died.

3. *Nathanael Mather*; which succeeded his Brother *Samuel* as Pastor of that *Church* in *Dublin,* and is now Pastor of a *Church* in *London.*

4. *Eleazar Mather*: He was Pastor of the Church at *Northampton* in

85   *New-England,* and much esteemed in those parts of the Country: He died when he was but Thirty two years old.

5. *Increase Mather*; who is known in both *Englands.*[38] These four were the Sons of *Richard Mather.*

6. *Cotton Mather,* the Author of this History.

90   7. *Nathanael Mather.* He died at the *Nineteenth* Year of his Age; was a *Master of Arts*; began to preach in private. His Piety and Learning was beyond his Years. The History of his *Life and Death* was written by his *Brother,* and there have been *Three Editions* of it printed at *London.* He dyed here at *Salem,* and over his Grave there is written, *THE ASHES OF*

95   *AN HARD STUDENT, A GOOD SCHOLAR, AND A GREAT CHRISTIAN.*

8. *Samuel Mather*; he is now a publick Preacher. These three last mentioned, are the Sons of *Increase Mather.*

99   9. *Samuel Mather,* the Son of *Timothy,*[39] and Grandson of *Richard*

---

93   He/Ht

[37] Richard Mather (1596–1669), a minister in Lancashire, was in 1634 forbidden to continue preaching because of his nonconformity and came in the next year to Massachusetts with his wife and children. Two of his sons, Samuel (1626–1671), and Nathanael (1631–1697), graduated from Harvard College and entered the ministry, but soon went back to England. Richard, however, served as minister of the church in Dorchester from 1636 until his death. He was especially renowned as an expositor of doctrine and an organizer of the polity of the New England churches. Two sons were born to him in Massachusetts. One, Eleazar (1637–1669), became minister of the church at Northampton; the other, Increase (1639–1723), followed the example of his older brothers and after leaving Harvard went abroad. He preached in Ireland, England, and Guernsey, but after Charles II came to the throne in 1661, realizing that as a nonconformist he could not hope to make a career in England, he returned to Boston, where he was in 1664 ordained Teacher of the Second Church.*

[38] Increase Mather married in 1662 Maria Cotton, the daughter of John Cotton (1585–1652), probably the most powerful of the Massachusetts Congregational clergy of the first generation. Increase and Maria had three sons. The first was Cotton; the second, Nathanael (1669–1688), who studied for the ministry but died before he was old enough to have a pastorate; and the third, Samuel (1674–1733), M.A. Harvard 1693, who left Boston for England some time before 1698 and, after experience as a "publick Preacher," became minister of the Congregational church in Witney, Oxfordshire.*

[39] Timothy Mather (1628–1664), Richard's son, did not go to college and seems to have been a farmer and businessman, whose behavior somewhat distressed his ministerial relatives. His brother Nathanael wrote: "I desyre to mourn over poor Tim's case . . . that his heart should

Mather; He is the Pastor of a Church in *Windsor*; a Pious and a Prudent Man; who has been an happy Instrument of uniting the Church and Town, amongst whom there had been great Divisions.

5   10. *Warham Mather*, the Son of *Eleazar Mather*, and by his Mother Grandson to the Reverend Mr. *Warham*, late Pastor of the Church in *Windsor:* He is now also a publick Preacher. Behold, an happy Family, the *Glad sight* whereof, may well inspire even an Old Age past Eighty, with *Poetry* enough to add this,

Epigramma in *MATHEROS.*

10   *O Nimium Dilecte Deo, Venerande MATHERE,*
      Gaudens tot Natos Christi numerare Ministros!
      Det Deus ut tales insurgant usque Matheri,
      Et Nati Natorum, & qui Nascentur ab illis.
      Has inter stellas fulgens, Cottone Mathere,
15   *Patrum tu sequeris vestigia semper adorans,*
      Phosphorus ast aliis!——[40]

    Now the Lord our God, the Faithful God, that *keepeth Covenant and Mercy to a thousand Generations,* with his People; let him incline the Heart of this People of *New-England,* to keep Covenant and Duty towards their
20 God, to walk in his Ways, and keep his Commandments, that he may bring upon them the Blessing of *Abraham,* the Mercy and Truth unto *Jacob,* the sure Mercies of *David,* the Grace and Peace that cometh from God the Father, and the Lord Jesus Christ; and that the *Grace* of our Lord Jesus Christ may be in and with these Churches, from one Genera-
25 tion to another, until the Second Coming[41] of our Lord and Saviour Jesus Christ! *Unto him be Glory and Dominion, for Ever and Ever.   Amen.*
                                                            John Higginson.

Salem, the 25th of the
First Month 1697.[42]

---

13   *Nati Natorum/Nati, Natorum*   15   *adorans/ad orans*

---

work in so quite contrary a way argues a very evill and unhumbled frame" (4 MHS *Coll.* 8:18). Warham Mather (1666–1745), the son of Eleazar of Northampton, seems never to have been ordained, although he was a "publick Preacher" in various towns. His mother was the daughter of John Warham (1595–1670), M.A. Oxford, who was for a time preacher at Exeter, Devonshire, but in 1630 came to New England. There he was junior minister at the First Church in Dorchester before going to Windsor.*

   40 "Epigram on the Mathers: O venerable Mather family, beloved of God; rejoicing to number so many ministers of Christ as sons! God grant that such Mathers may continue to arise, and sons of sons, and children born to them. Cotton Mather, shining among these stars, do thou ever in adoration follow the footsteps of the fathers, thyself a morning star."*

   41 See Acts 1.11; cf. John 21.23; Heb. 9.27.*

   42 "25th of the First Month 1697," i.e., March 25, 1697.

A Prefatory Poem,[1]

On that Excellent Book, Entituled,

Magnalia Christi Americana

Written by the Reverend

5   Mr. *COTTON MATHER*, Pastor of a Church at *Boston, New-England.*

To the Candid Reader.

S *Truck with huge Love*, of what to be possest,
   I much despond, good Reader, in the *quest*;
Yet help me, if at length it may be said,[2]
10   Who first the *Chambers of the South* display'd?
Inform me, Whence the *Tawny People* came?
Who was their Father, *Japhet, Shem,* or *Cham?*[3]
And how they straddled to th' *Antipodes,*
To look *another World* beyond the Seas?
15   And when, and why, and where they last broke ground,
What Risks they ran, where they first Anchoring found?[4]
Tell me their Patriarchs, Prophets, Priests and Kings,
Religion, Manners, Monumental things:
What *Charters* had they? What Immunities?[5]
20   What Altars, Temples, Cities, Colonies,
Did they erect? Who were their publick Spirits?[6]

---

[1] Nicholas Noyes (1647–1717), the author of this poem and the two anagram verses which follow, was co-minister with John Higginson at the church in Salem. He had some reputation as a poet, owned the largest library in Salem, and is said to have been a man "of good learning."*

[2] These clumsy lines seem to mean: "Smitten with great love for what there is to learn, I am despondent when I search for it and therefore ask the reader to help me." "Possest" is here used in the obsolete sense of "furnished with knowledge, instructed in."

[3] For "*Chambers of the South,*" see Job 9.9. "*Tawny People*": the American Indians. "*Japhet . . . Cham*": the sons of Noah.*

[4] "Straddled to th' *Antipodes*": strode across the world. "Look": seek for. "Broke ground": weighed anchor. "Anchoring": anchorage.

[5] "Charters" and "Immunities" were words of special significance for Massachusetts settlers. Their original charter had been revoked and in 1691 replaced by one which some of them thought deprived them of important privileges (immunities) they had formerly enjoyed. See introductory essay, "Cotton Mather," and *Magnalia*, Bk. II, Appendix, "Pietas in Patriam," sec. 14.

[6] Public-spirited men.*

Where may we find the *Records* of their Merits?
What Instances, what glorious Displays
Of Heav'ns high Hand, commenced in their dayes?
25 These things in *Black Oblivion* covered o'er,
(As they'd ne'er been) lye, with a thousand more.
A vexing Thought, that makes me scarce forbear
To stamp, and wring my Hands, and pluck my Hair,
To think, what Blessed *Ignorance*[7] hath done,
30 What fine Threads *Learnings* Enemies have spun,
How well Books, Schools, and Colledge may be spar'd,
So *Men* with *Beasts*[8] may fitly be compar'd!
Yea, how *Tradition*[9] leaves us in the lurch,
And who, nor stay at home, nor go to Church:
35 The *Light-within-Enthusiasts*, who let fly
Against our *Pen and Ink Divinity*;[10]
Who boldly do pretend (but who'll believe it?)
If *Genesis* were lost, they could retrieve it;
Yea, all the *Sacred Writ*; Pray let them try
40 On the *New World*, their *Gift of Prophecy*.[11]
For all them, the *New Worlds Antiquities*,
Smother'd in everlasting Silence lies;
And its *First Sachims*[12] mention'd are no more,
Than they that *Agamemnon* liv'd before.[13]
45 The poor *Americans* are under blame,
Like them of old, that from *Tel-melah* came,
Conjectur'd once to be of *Israel's* Seed,
But no *Record* appear'd to prove the Deed:

26 ne'er/ne er

[7] An ironic reference to the proverbial saying that, among Catholics, ignorance is the mother of devotion.*

[8] "Man . . . hath no understanding; but is compared unto the beasts that perish": Ps. 49.20, in the version used in the Psalter of the English *Book of Common Prayer*.*

[9] Noyes here plays on the two meanings of "*Tradition*": one, the now obsolete "surrender" or "betrayal," and the other, usual today, "a statement, belief, or practice transmitted from generation to generation." The good "tradition" of New England, Noyes felt, had been "betrayed" by the ignorant.*

[10] "*Enthusiasts*": those who claimed to have divine revelation, held extravagant and visionary theological opinions, or were given to excessive religious emotionalism. The specific reference is to the Quakers, who professed to live by an "inner light" given by God, but the passage alludes also to the Antinomians and others who, from the point of view of the orthodox, were heretics. Throughout the *Magnalia*, "enthusiasts" has this connotation. "*Pen and Ink Divinity*": the theology of the New England churches, based on learned study and interpretation of the Bible, and scoffed at by some of the "enthusiasts."*

[11] Cf. I Cor. 13.2: "Though I have the gift of prophecy . . . and have not charity, I am nothing."

[12] Chiefs of American Indian tribes.

[13] Cf. Horace, *Odes* IV.ix.25.

And like *Habajah's* Sons, that were put by ⎫

50   The *Priesthood*, Holy things to come not nigh,   ⎬

For having lost their *Genealogy*.[14]   ⎭

Who can past things to memory command,

Till one with *Aaron's Breast-plate*[15] up shall stand?

Mischiefs Remediless such Sloth ensue;

55   God and their Parents lose their Honour due,

And Childrens Children suffer on that Score,

Like Bastards cast forlorn at any Door;

And they and others put to seek their Father,

For want of such a *Scribe* as *COTTON MATHER*;

60   Whose Piety, whose Pains, and peerless Pen,

Revives *New-England*'s nigh-lost Origin.

    Heads of our *Tribes*, whose *Corps*[16] are under ground,

Their Names and Fames in *Chronicles*[17] renown'd,

Begemm'd on *Golden Ouches*[18] he hath set,

65   Past Envy's Teeth, and Times corroding Fret:

Of *Death* and *Malice*, he has brush'd off the Dust,

And made a *Resurrection of the Just:*[19]

And clear'd the Lands Religion of the Gloss,

And *Copper-Cuts* of *Alexander Ross*.[20]

70   He hath related *Academic* things,

And paid their *First-Fruits*[21] to the King of Kings;

And done his *Alma Mater* that just Favour,

To shew *Sal Gentium* hath not lost its Savour.

He writes like an *Historian*, and *Divine*,

75   Of *Churches, Synods, Faith,* and *Discipline.*

Illustrious Providences are display'd,

Mercies and Judgments are in colours laid;

---

69   *Copper-Cuts/Coppe-Cuts*

[14] Ezra 2.59–62; Neh. 7.61–64.

[15] Aaron's breastplate was set with stones with the "names of the children of Israel" (Exod. 28.15–29). New England needed a similar reminder of "past things."

[16] "*Heads* of our *Tribes*": a Biblical phrase, e.g., Num. 30.1. "*Corps*": corpses.*

[17] "*Chronicles*" here refers both to the Biblical books, I and II Chronicles, and to the historical and biographical accounts of early days of New England.

[18] Exod. 28.11.

[19] Luke 14.14.

[20] Alexander Ross (1591–1654), a chaplain to Charles I, in his Πανσεβεια: *Or, A View of All Religions in the World*, first published in London in 1653, declared that the tenets of the "*Independents of* New-England" savored "of nothing but of pride, carnall security, blasphemy, and slighting of Gods written word" (4th ed., London, 1664, pp. 390–391). To the second and later editions of the book there was appended *Apocalypsis: Or, The Revelation of . . . Heresie*, which contained seventeen "Copper-cuts" of notorious heretics.*

[21] Book IV of the *Magnalia*, an account of Harvard College and some of its graduates, deals with "academic things." Its title, *Sal Gentium*, is translated in the King James Bible, Matt. 5.13, "salt of the earth." For "*First-Fruits*," see God's command, Exod. 22.29: "Thou shalt not delay to offer the first of thy ripe fruits . . . the firstborn of thy sons shalt thou give unto me."*

Salvations wonderful by Sea and Land,
Themselves are *Saved* by his Pious Hand.[22]
80   The *Churches Wars*, and various *Enemies*,
Wild *Salvages*, and wilder *Sectaries*,
Are notify'd for them that after rise.[23]
    This *well-instructed Scribe* brings *New* and *Old*,[24]
And from his *Mines* digs richer things than Gold;
85   Yet freely gives, as *Fountains*[25] do their Streams,
Nor more than they, Himself, by giving, drains.
He's all *Design*, and by his *Craftier Wiles*[26]
Locks fast his Reader, and the Time beguiles:
Whilst *Wit* and *Learning* move themselves aright,
90   Thro' ev'ry line, and *Colour* in our sight,
So interweaving *Profit* with *Delight*;
And curiously inlaying both together,
That he must needs find Both, who looks for either.
    His *Preaching, Writing*, and his Pastoral Care,
95   Are very much, to fall to one Man's share.
This added to the rest, is admirable,
And proves the Author *Indefatigable*.
Play is his Toyl, and *Work* his Recreation,
99   And his *Inventions* next to Inspiration.[27]
His *Pen*[28] was taken from some *Bird of Light*,
Addicted to a swift and lofty Flight.
Dearly it loves *Art, Air*, and *Eloquence*,
And hates *Confinement*, save to *Truth* and *Sense*.

[22] Noyes alludes to Bk. V of the *Magnalia*, "The Faith and the Discipline"; and to Bk. VI, "Illustrious . . . Discoveries . . . of the Divine Providence" and "Remarkable Mercies and Judgments." "Colours laid": rhetorical modes or figures, set down (laid) in writing. Here Mather enjoys a play on words: he "*Saved*" (preserved) "*Salvations*" by recording them.

[23] The "*Churches' Wars*" and "*Enemies*" are "*notify'd*" (taken notice of) in Bk. VII of the *Magnalia*. By Anglicans, nonconformists were called "sectaries" (members of a schismatical or heretical sect); by the New England Congregationalists, the word was applied to those who challenged their orthodoxy.

[24] Matt. 13.52: "Therefore every scribe which is instructed unto the kingdom of heaven is like unto a man . . . which bringeth forth out of his treasure things new and old."

[25] Samuel Mather, *The Figures or Types of the Old Testament* (London, 1705), p. 143: "There is nothing more frequent in Scripture, then to express the Spirit [of Christ] by Water." See, for example, Isa. 44.3, Rev. 21.6, and introductory essay, "The Idea of the Wilderness."*

[26] "*Design*" probably refers to Mather's plan for the organization of the book and also to his purpose in writing it. "*Craftier Wiles*": skillful or ingenious devices, without the suggestion of deceit or evil scheming now suggested by the words.

[27] "*Inventions*": in rhetoric sometimes discoveries or selections of topics to be treated; also works or writings produced by exercise of the mind or imagination, literary compositions. "Inspiration" in theological writing is often used for an influence of the Spirit of God or of some divinity or supernatural being, especially the divine influence under which the Bible was said to have been written. The line therefore likens the *Magnalia* to Holy Writ, as being an inspired book.

[28] "Pen" is used here both as "feather" and as a pen made from one, thus relating to the "Bird of Light" and its virtues in the following three lines. In this context "Air" may carry a suggestion of "melody or harmony."

5   Allow what's known; they who write Histories,
     Write many things they see with others Eyes;
     'Tis fair, where nought is feign'd, nor undigested,
     Nor ought,[29] but what is credibly attested.
     The Risk is his; and seeing others do,
10   Why may not I speak mine Opinion too?
       The *Stuff* is true, the *Trimming* neat and spruce,
     The Workman's good, the Work of publick use;
     Most piously design'd, a publick Store,[30]
     And well deserves the publick Thanks, and more.
15   *Nicholas Noyes*, Teacher of the Church at *Salem*.

Reverendo Domino,
D. COTTONO *MADERO,*[1]

Libri Utilissimi, cui Titulus, *Magnalia Christi Americana,*
Authori Doctissimo, ac Dilectissimo,
5   Duo Ogdoastica, & bis duo Anagrammata, dat Idem, *N. Noyes.*[2]

Cottonus Maderus.[3]

Anagr. $\begin{cases} \textit{Est duo Sanctorum.} \\ \textit{Natus es Doctorum.} \end{cases}$

Nomina Sanctorum, *quos Scribis, clara* duorum
10   *Nomine Cerno Tuo; Virtutes Lector easdem*
     Candidus inveniet Tecum, Charitate refertas.
     Doctrina Eximius Doctos, Pietate piosque

---

[29] In the seventeenth century a common spelling for "aught."
[30] A public storage place, a warehouse.

---

[1] "Mather" was sometimes spelled "Madder" and probably occasionally so pronounced.*
[2] "To the Reverend Master Cotton Mather, the most learned and esteemed author of the very useful book called *Magnalia Christi Americana*, Nicholas Noyes presents two eight-line verses and two anagrams." For anagrams and their popularity in Mather's time, see introductory essay "The Magnalia." The Latin texts are translated by L. F. Robinson.

[3]   Cotton Mather
Anagram $\begin{cases} \text{It consists of Two Saints.} \\ \text{Thou art a Descendant of the Learned.} \end{cases}$
Lo! in thy name TWO SAINTS' names I behold—
Saints whose good deeds are in this book enroll'd—
Whose virtues candid readers can but find
Not only in thy book, but in thy mind.
Learned and pious, with a master's eye,
Thou canst depicture learned piety.
   CHILD OF THE LEARNED! noble is thy race,
But nobler art thou as a child of grace;
Third of thy line! thy heritage receive,
And these prophetic Anagrams believe.

The two saints were Cotton Mather's two grandfathers, John Cotton and Richard Mather. They were "doctors," i.e., "learned men," and could be thought of as successors of the prophets and apostles.*

Tu bene describis; describere nescit ut alter.
Doctorum es Natus, *Domino Spirante Renatus;*
15 *De bene quæsitis gaudeto Tertius Hæres;*
Nomen præsagit, nec non Anagrammata, vates.

Cottonus Maderus.[4]

Anagr. $\begin{cases} \textit{Unctas demortuos.} \\ \textit{Senatus Doctorum.} \end{cases}$

20 Unctas demort'os, *decoratur Laude* Senatus
Doctorum, *Merita, fit præsens præterita ætas,*
Huic exempla patent, & postera Progenitores
Non ignorabit, patriisque superbiet Actis;
More, Fide, cultu, quoque patrissare studebit;
25 *Gratum opus est Domino, Patriæ nec inutile nostræ;*
Orbi fructificat. Fer Fertilitatis Honorem,
Scribendo Vitas alienas, propria scripta est.

Celeberrimi

COTTONI MATHERI,

Celebratio;

Qui Heroum Vitas, in sui-ipsius & illorum Memoriam
5 sempiternam, revocavit.[1]

Quod Patrios Manes revocasti a Sedibus altis,
Sylvestres Musæ grates, Mathere, *rependunt.*
Hæc nova Progenies, veterum sub Imagine, cælo

13   *describis;/describis,*   *ut/at*

4
Cotton Mather
Anagram $\begin{cases} \text{Thou embalmest the Dead.} \\ \text{A Senate of Learned Men.} \end{cases}$
THOU HAST EMBALMED THE DEAD! Thy truthful praise
'Round LEARNING'S SENATE wreathes immortal bays.
Thy magic pen the Past the Present makes,
And we seem honoured for our fathers' sakes.
Nor shall our pride end here: each future age
Shall claim the honours, sparkling on thy page,
Shall still revere the founders of the State,
Their worship, faith, and virtues imitate.
Thy God shall bless the labour of thy mind,
Thy country's boon, a treasure to mankind.
Though here thou writest others' lives, yet thine
Shall glow resplendent in each living line.

[1] "An honor for the widely honored Cotton Mather, who has recalled the lives of heroes, as an eternal memorial to them and to himself." The author of the poem which follows, Benjamin Tompson (1642–1714), was Mather's first teacher at school. The inscription on his tombstone celebrated him as a "learned Schoolmaster & Physician" and the "Renowned Poet" of New England.*

Arte Tua Terram visitans, aemissa, salutat.
10 *Grata Deo Pietas; Grates persolvimus omnes:*
Semper Honos, Nomenque Tuum, Mathere, *manebunt.*[2]

Is the Bles'd *MATHER Necromancer*[3] turn'd,
To raise his Countries Father's Ashes Urn'd?
Elisha's Dust, Life to the Dead imparts;
15 This Prophet, by his more *Familiar Arts,*
Unseals our *Hero's* Tombs, and gives them Air;
They Rise, they Walk, they Talk, Look wond'rous Fair;
Each of them in an Orb of *Light* doth shine,
In Liveries of *Glory* most Divine.
20   When ancient Names I in thy Pages met,
Like Gems on *Aaron's* costly Breast-plate set;
Methinks Heaven's open, while Great *Saints* descend,
To wreathe the Brows, by which their *Acts* were penn'd.

B. Thompson.

To the Reverend

Mr. *COTTON MATHER,*

ON HIS

History of New-England.

5   IN this Hard Age, when Men such Slackness show,
      To pay *Loves* Debts, and what to *Truth* we owe,
You to step forth, and such Example shew,
In paying what's to God and Country due,
Deserves *our* Thanks: *Mine* I do freely give:

[2] Translated by R. G. Gummere in his *The American Colonial Mind and the Classical Tradition* (Cambridge, Mass., Harvard University Press, 1963), p. 145:

Since thou hast called from their dwellings on high these spirits departed,
Mather, the forest-born Muses with gratitude hereby reward thee.
Here a new offspring, in guise of the ancients, descending from Heaven,
Brought back to earth by the skill of thy pen, stand here in thy honor.
With hearts that are grateful to God, we thank thee in bountiful measure.
The glory and name of a Mather shall bide with us now and forever.

[3] Tompson here indulges in a touch of humor. Cotton Mather would have been outraged by any serious suggestion that he practised necromancy. Necromancers were "abominations unto the Lord" (Deut. 18.11–12). "Elisha's Dust" refers to II Kings 13.21—a dead man put among the bones in Elisha's sepulchre "revived, and stood up on his feet." "Familiar" is used by Tompson for a play on words. In summoning the dead, necromancers were aided by "familiars"—demons or evil spirits. Mather, Tompson says, uses more "Familiar" (i.e., more usual and comprehensible) arts in reviving the memory of New England's heroes.*

10   'Tis fit that with the *Raised Ones*[1] you Live.
         Great your Attempt. No doubt some Sacred Spy,
      That Leiger[2] in your Sacred Cell did ly,
      Nurs'd your first Thoughts, with gentle Beams of Light,
      And taught your Hand Things past to bring to sight:
15   Thus led by secret sweetest Influence,
      You make Returns to God's good Providence:
      Recording how that mighty Hand was nigh,
      To Trace out Paths not known to mortal Eye,
      To those brave Men, that to this Land came o'er,
20   And plac'd them safe on the *Atlantick Shore*:
      And how the same Hand did them after save,
      And say, *Return*, oft on the Brink o'th' Grave;
      And gave them room to spread, and bless'd their Root,
      Whence, hung with Fruit, now many Branches shoot.
25   Such were these *Heroes*, and their *Labours* such,
      In their Just Praise, Sir, who can say too much?
      Let the Remotest parts of Earth behold,
      New-England's Crowns[3] excelling *Spanish Gold*.
      Here be Rare Lessons set for us to Read,
30   That Off-springs are of such a Goodly Breed.
      The *Dead Ones* here, so much *Alive* are made,
      We think them speaking from Bles'd *Eden*'s Shade;
      Hark! How they check the Madness of this Age,
      The Growth of Pride, fierce Lust, and worldly Rage.
35   They tell, we shall to *Clam-banks* come again,[4]
      If Heaven still doth Scourge us all in vain.
         But, Sir, upon your Merits heap'd will be,
      The *Blessings* of all those that here shall see
      Vertue Embalm'd; *This Hand joins* to put on
40   The *Lawrel* on your Brow, so justly won.
                  Timothy Woodbridge, Minister of *Hartford*.[5]

39 *joins/seems* C.M.

[1] Raised to Heaven. Cf. Luke 14.14: "Thou shalt be recompensed at the resurrection of the just."

[2] "Leiger" (or "leaguer" or "ledger"), now obsolete, often signified an agent, an ambassador, frequently an ambassador of the Gospel. "To lie leiger" meant to reside in the capacity of a commissioner or ambassador.

[3] New England's heroes were figuratively its chief or "crowning" ornaments. There is a play on words: "Crowns" were also coins, like the "Spanish gold" brought back by the Elizabethan voyagers. For "Dead Ones . . . speaking," cf. Abel, who "being dead yet speaketh," Heb. 10.11.

[4] "To Clam-banks come again" presumably means to be reduced to subsisting solely on clams.

[5] Timothy Woodbridge (1656–1732) was born in England, graduated from Harvard in 1673, and became minister of the First Congregational Church in Hartford, Connecticut, and a founder, trustee, and Fellow of Yale College.*

Ad Politum Literaturæ, atque Sacrarum Literarum Antistitem,

Angliæque Americanæ Antiquarium Callentissimum,

Reverendum Dominum,

D. COTTONUM MATHERUM,

5   Apud Bostonenses V. D. M.[1]

Epigramma.

Cottonus Matherus.

Anagr.

Tu tantum Cohors es.

10   Epigramma.

Ipse, vales Tantum, Tu, *mi memorande MATHERE,*
Fortis pro Christo Miles, es *ipse* cohors.[2]

A Pindaric.

Art thou *Heavens Trumpet?*[3] sure by the *Archangel* blown;
15   Tombs Crack, Dead Start, Saints Rise, are seen and known,
And *Shine* in Constellation;[4]
From ancient Flames here's a New *Phœnix*[5] flown,
To shew the World, when Christ Returns, he'll not Return alone.

                              J. Danforth, V. D. M. *Dorcestr.*[6]

1   Literarum/Literaturum   C.M.

[1] Translated by L. F. Robinson: "To That Oracle of Polite Learning and Sacred Literature, and Accomplished Historian of New-England, The Reverend Mr. Cotton Mather, Minister at Boston." "V.D.M.": "Verbi Dei Minister," minister of God's word.

[2] "An Epigram. / Cotton Mather, / Anagram. / Thou art alone a host. / Epigram.

        Thou, noble Mather, though thou wouldst not boast,
        In Christian warfare ART ALONE A Host."

[3] I Thess. 4.16: "For the Lord himself shall descend from heaven . . . with the voice of the archangel, and with the trump of God: and the dead in Christ shall rise first." In typology "Trumpet" is often associated with "Ministers of the Gospel" who "*lift up their Voices like a Trumpet*" (Isa. 58.1). "The faithful discharge and execution of their Office is expressed by *blowing of the Trumpet,* Hos. 8.1; Ezek. 33.3, 4, 5" (S. Mather, *Figures,* p. 437).*

[4] The "Saints" "*Shine* in Constellation" because, in typology, the ministers were often called the "candle-sticks" of the churches. In the heavens, the "seven Stars that shine" in their "tops . . . *are the Angels of the seven Churches*" (Rev. 1.20). For an enumeration of the "types" represented by candlesticks, see S. Mather, *Figures,* p. 391, and endnote to General Introduction p. 93, l. 55.

[5] "New *Phoenix*": presumably Cotton Mather, risen from the ashes of his sainted ancestors.

[6] John Danforth (1660–1730), A.B. A.M., Harvard, and Fellow 1697–1707, was minister of the church in Dorchester from 1682 until his death. He was an industrious writer of verse.*

To the Learned and Reverend

Mr. *COTTON MATHER,*

On his Excellent *Magnalia.*

SIR,

M Y Muse will now by Chymistry[1] draw forth
The Spirit of your Names Immortal worth.

Cottonius Matherus.

Anagr.

Tuos Tecum ornasti.[2]

While thus the Dead in thy rare Pages Rise,
Thine,[3] *with thy self, thou dost Immortalize.*
To view the Odds, thy Learned *Lives* invite,
'Twixt *Eleutherian* and *Edomite.*[4]
But all succeding Ages shall despair,
A Fitting Monument for *thee* to Rear.
Thy own Rich Pen (Peace, silly *Momus,*[5] Peace!)
Hath given them a Lasting *Writ of Ease.*[6]

Grindal Rawson, Pastor of *Mendon.*[7]

11   *thou/thon*

[1] For the "chemistry" of anagrams see introductory essay, "The Magnalia."
[2] "Two with thyself you adorn."
[3] Mather's ancestors who had died.
[4] "To view the Odds . . . 'Twixt": to see the difference between. "Lives": the biographies in the *Magnalia.* Mather called the "Friends of the Reformation" "Eleutherians," and their foes the "Idumaeans" or Edomites—enemies of Israel from whose stock the house of Herod sprang.*
[5] Momus, in Greek mythology, was the personification of censoriousness, ridicule, and mockery.
[6] In law, a certificate of discharge or release; hence release from all burdens and cares.
[7] Grindal (Grindall) Rawson (1659–1715), Cotton Mather's classmate at Harvard, was minister at Mendon, Massachusetts, from 1684 to 1715, and was "a faithful labourer among the Indians."*

In Jesu Christi

MAGNALIA AMERICANA,

Digesta in Septem Libros,

Per Magnum, Doctissimumque Virum,

D. Cottonum Matherum,

J. Christi Servum, Ecclesiæque Americano Bostoniensis
Ministrum Pium & Disertissimum.[1]

5

SUnt *Miracla Dei*, sunt & *Magnalia Christi*,
  Qua patet *Orbis*. Erant ultra *Garamantas*,[2] & *Indos*
Maxuma, quæ paucis licuit cognoscere. Sed, quæ
Cernis in *America*, procul unus-quisque videbit.
  Vivis, ubi fertur nullum vixisse. Videsque
Mille homines, res multas, Incunabula mira.
Strabo sile, qui *Magna* refers. *Vesputius* autem
Primis scire *Novum* potuit conatibus *Orbem*.
Et dum *Magna* docet te *Grotius*,[3] Unde repletos
Esse per *Americam*, volucresque, hominesque, Deosque.
Dumque libet, tibi scire licet *Nova* viscera rerum.
  Nullus erat, nisi brutus homo: Sine lege, Deoque.
Numa[4] dat Antiquis, *Solon*que & Jura *Lycurgus*.
Hic nihil, & nullæ (modo sic sibi vivere) Leges.
Jam decreta vide, & Regum diplomata, curque,
Ne sibi vivat homo, nostrorum vivere Regi est.
Dic tot habendo Deos, legisque videndo peritos,
Centenosque viros, celebres virtute, Statumque
Quem *Novus Orbis* habet; *Quantum mutatus ab illo est!*[5]

10

15

20

25

17 Esse/Ecce   18 Dumque/Deumque C.M.
26 *est!/es!*

[1] Translated by L. F. Robinson: "A Poem, Concerning The Mighty Works of Jesus Christ in America, Arranged in Seven Books, By that Great and Most Learned Man, Mr. Cotton Mather, A Servant of Jesus Christ, and of a Church at Boston in America the Pious and Most Eloquent Minister."

[2] A powerful ancient tribe in Africa.*

[3] Amerigo Vespucci (Americus Vespucius, *c*.1451–1512), Italian navigator, who claimed to have reached the American continent before Columbus and whose name was given to it. See *Magnalia*, Bk. I, chap. 1, sec. 3. Hugo Grotius (1583–1645), famous as a jurist and statesman and sometimes called the founder of international law, wrote a dissertation on the origin of the peoples on the American continent.*

[4] Numa Pompilius, in legend the second king of Rome (715–673 B.C.), was supposed to have founded many of its institutions.

[5] Virgil, *Aeneid* II.274.

Res bona. Nec sat erit, & Rege & Lege beatum,
Posse vehi super Astra. *Deum* tibi noscere, fas est.
Nil Lex, nil *Solon*, nil & sine *Numine Numa.*[6]

30   Sit *Deus*, ignotosque *Deos* fuge. Multa Poetæ
De *Jove* finxerunt, *Neptuno* & *Marte*, Diisque
Innumerabilibus. *Magnique Manitto* pependit
Non conversa Deo Gens *Americana, Manitto*,[7]
Quem velut *Artificem* colit, & ceu *Numen* adorat.

35   E tenebris Lux est. In abysso cernere Cœlum est,
Ignotumque Deum,[8] notum INDIS, *Biblia Sancta
Indica, Templa, Preces, Psalmos*, multosque *Ministros.*
Ut *Christum* discant, *Indorum* Idiomate *Numen*
Utitur, & sese patefecit ubique locorum.

40   Plura canam. Veterem *Schola* sit dispersa per *Orbem*,
Et tot *Athenæis* scatet *Anglus, Belga, Polonus,*
Germanus, Gallusque. Sat est *Academia nostra.*[9]
Extra *Orbem Novus Orbis* habet, quod habetur in *Orbe.*
Dat *Cantabrigiæ Domus Harvardina* Cathedram

45   Cuilibet, & cur non daret *Indis*, Proselytisque?
Trans Mare non opus est ad *Pallada* currere. *Pallas*
Hic habitat, confertque *Gradus*;[10] modo *Pallada* discas,
Desistasque gradum. Quantum *Sapientia* confert!
Forte novas, pluresque artes *Novus Orbis* haberet.

50   Quotquot in *America* licet *Admiranda* supersint,
Singula non narro. Nec opus tibi singula narrem.
Multa fidem superant, multorum Exempla docebunt;
Plura quot *Orbis* habet *Novus Admiranda*, quot artes;
Et quot in *America* degunt ubicunque *Coloni.*

55   Deque *Veneficiis* quid erit tibi noscere? Lusus
Sperne Diabolicos. Sunt hic *Magnalia Christi.*
Ne timeas Umbram. Corpus sine corpore spectrum est.
Pax rara in terris. Ætas quasi ferrea.[11] *Bellum*

---

[6] A play on "Numa," the king, and "Numen," god—"a king without a god."

[7] "Manitto" (manitou, manetto, etc.), applied by the North American Indians to a supernatural power or powers, or specifically to a deity. Here the author clearly regards it as the name of a god.

[8] "*Ignotum Deum*": the Christian God previously unknown to the Indians. "*Biblica Sancta Indica*": the translation of the Bible into the language of the Indians by John Eliot (1604–1690), first published in Cambridge, Massachusetts, in 1663. Cotton Mather's life of Eliot, *The Triumphs of the Reformed Religion in America* (Boston, 1691), was reprinted in the *Magnalia*, Bk. III, pt. 3, pp. 170–210.*

[9] Harvard College, founded in 1636.

[10] Pallas Athena, in Greek mythology the goddess of knowledge and the arts and sciences, who personified the spirit of truth and divine wisdom. "Gradus," in English "step," was often used to refer to the *Gradus ad Parnassum*, a famous dictionary of prosody much studied as a textbook.*

[11] The "iron age," in classical mythology, was the last and worst of the four ages of the world.

      Sceptra gerens, gladiosque ferox ubicunque Noverca est.

60   Destruit omnia, destruit oppida, destruit artes.

      Mars nulli cedit. Nihil exitialius armis.

      Testis adest. *Europa* docet lacrymabile *Bellum*,

      Hispani, Belgæ, Germani, & quotquot in *Orbe*

      Sunt Veteri, Rigidisq; plagis vexantur & armis.

65   Quas *Sectas* vetus *Orbis* habet, quæ dogmata Carnis?

      Primum *Roma* locum tenet, *Enthusiasta* secundum,

      Arminius tandem, *Menno* & *Spinosa* sequuntur.[12]

      Quisque incredibiles poterit dignoscere *Sectas?*

      Non tot cernuntur fidei discrimina, nec tot

70   Hæreticos *novus Orbis* habet, quod & Enthea res est.

      Tu dilecte *Deo*, cujus *Bostonia* gaudet

      Nostra Ministerio, seu cui tot scribere Libros,

      Non opus, aut labor est, & qui *Magnalia Christi*

      Americana refers, scriptura plurima. Nonne

75   Dignus es, agnoscare inter *Magnalia Christi?*

      Vive *Liber*, totique *Orbi Miracula* monstres,

      Quæ sunt extra *Orbem. Cottone*, in sæcula vive;

      Et dum Mundus erit, vivat tua Fama per *Orbem.*

80   Henricus Selijns,[13]

               Ecclesiæ Neo-Eboracenfis Minister Belgicus.

Dabam, Neo-Eboraci
   Americana, 16 Oct.
   1697.

[12] Jacobus Arminius (Jacob Hermansen or Hermanns, 1560–1609), a celebrated Dutch theologian and leader of the "Arminian movement," challenged the Calvinist doctrine of predestination and insisted that Jesus died for all men and not only for the "elect." The terms "Arminian" and "Arminianism" were often loosely used, and in old England and New were sometimes applied to Anglican followers of Archbishop Laud, even when they were not actual supporters of Arminius' doctrine. Menno Simons (1492–1559), a Frisian reformer, founded the Mennonite sect, which had many members in the seventeenth and eighteenth centuries in Europe and in some of the colonies in North America. By New England standards they were definitely "heretical," as was Spinoza, the famous Dutch philosopher (1632–1677).*

[13] Henricus Selijns (Selyns, 1636–1701) was minister of the Dutch Reformed Church at New York from 1682 until his death.* His poem in the *Magnalia* is freely translated by L. F. Robinson:

      The wondrous works of God and Christ abound,
      Wherever nature reigns or man is found.
      Some, known to few, have been revealed before,
      Beyond the Indies and the Afric shore.
      But what God *here* hath wrought, in this our age,
      All shall behold, emblazoned on thy page.
        Strange is thy dwelling-place. Thy home is where
      'Twas thought no creature breathed the vital air.
      Yet there a mighty future is begun.
      And men and things a race of empire run.
      Strabo! thy many marvels tell no more,
      No proud discovery known in ancient lore

Can match that wondrous waif Vesputio found,
A WORLD—NEW WORLD—at ocean's farthest bound.
   Let Grotius fancy whence, in ancient time,
Came the first people of this Western clime,
Whence their religion and ancestral line:
MATHER! a deeper, loftier theme is thine.
   The savage race, who once were masters here,
Nor law nor God inspired with wholesome fear:
They no Lycurgus, Numa, Solon knew,
To frame their code, and fix its sanctions too.
Self-will alone was law: but now we see
Our royal charters sent across the sea,
To teach our wills their loyal bond to own
To England's statutes and our sovereign's throne.
Look at our courts, our rulers, small and great,
Our civil order and compacted State;
See these where once the lawless savage ranged,
And then, like old Aeneas, say, "How changed!"
   'Tis well. But not enough are laws and kings
To raise our souls to Heaven and heavenly things.
We must know GOD, and in his ways be taught;
Without such knowledge, men and states are nought.
   The LORD is GOD! The ancient poets feign
Their Pantheon of pagan gods in vain.
In vain the unconverted Indians raise
Their forest altars in Manitou's praise;
For light shines out of darkness: the Unknown
And dreadful God the *Indian* calls his own.
The Indian has his Christian psalms and prayer,
His Christian temple, and his pastor there;
God speaks the Indian's language, rude and wild,
To teach His mercy to the forest-child.
   And more! though Science older climes befits,
And Europe swarms with academic wits,
Yet see scholastic shades these wilds adorn.
Such as the Old World may not wisely scorn.
That world we left; but Science has made known,
Out of the world, a *new* world of our own:
A hemisphere, imperial let to rise—
In arts proficient, and in Learning wise.
We have a Cambridge; where to rich and poor
Young HARVARD opes a hospitable door;
Its liberal texts no ban of ignorance fix
On Indians or converted heretics.
For Wisdom's halls we need not cross the seas;
Here Wisdom dwells and here confers degrees
Since Wisdom ever honours toil and pains,
And high *degrees* true merit always gains,
Perchance Philosophy and Science here
Will find new secrets and a broader sphere.
I will not, need not, tell our marvels o'er;
Many exceed belief, and many more
Might teach mankind how noble is the pace
In human progress of our exile-race.
   I need not speak of witchcrafts: go! despise
The devil's arts—his agents and his lies.
Here is the standard of the Cross unfurled,
And JESUS' "MIGHTY WORKS" astound the world.
Scorn of the goblin horde to be afraid—

Shapes without substance, shadows of a shade.
How rare is peace! War thunders its alarms;
The Age is Iron—with the ring of arms!
War sacks great cities; mars, with sounds of strife,
All social arts and every joy of life.
Europe is drench'd in blood: War's iron heel
And fiery scourge her writhing millions feel.
The blood of Frenchmen, Dutch and German slain,
Imbrues the soil of Italy and Spain;
While banded kings the sword of slaughter wield,
And humbler thrones afford a battle-field.
Then in the Old World see how sects uphold
A war of dogmas in the Christian fold:
Lo! Rome stands first; Fanaticism next,
And then Arminius with polemic text;
Then anabaptist Menno, leading on
Spinoza, with his law-automaton.
Who shall of sects the true meridian learn?
Their longitude and latitude discern?
We of the Western World cannot succeed
In conjuring up such difference of creed,
Or to Uncovenanted grace assign
So many heretics in things divine.
Beloved of God! whose ministry hath bless'd
Our Boston and the Churches of the West;
Who, without seeming toil, hast nobly wrought
Within thy breast exhaustless mines of thought,
And here recordest, as by God's commands,
" *The Mighty Works of Christ in Western Lands.*"
Say, dost thou not THYSELF deserve a place
Among those "Mighty Works" of Sovereign Grace?
Immortal MATHER! 'tis thy page alone
To Old World minds makes New World wonders known;
And while the solid Earth shall firm remain,
New World and Old World shall thy praise retain.

HENRY SELIJNS,
Pastor of a Dutch Reformed Church at New York

Dated at New York, October 16, 1697.

A General
INTRODUCTION.

'Ερῶ δὲ τοῦτο, τῆς τῶν ἐντευξομένων ὠφελείας ἔνεκα.

Dicam hoc propter utilitatem eorum qui Lecturi sunt hoc opus. Theodoret.[1]

5 §. 1. **I** WRITE the *Wonders* of the CHRISTIAN RELIGION, flying from the Depravations[2] of *Europe*, to the *American Strand:*[3] And, assisted by the Holy Author of that *Religion*, I do, with all Conscience of *Truth*, required therein by Him, who is the *Truth* it self, Report the *Wonderful Displays* of His Infinite Power, Wisdom, Goodness, and Faith-
10 fulness, wherewith His Divine Providence hath *Irradiated* an *Indian Wilderness.*

I Relate the *Considerable Matters*, that produced and attended the First Settlement of COLONIES, which have been Renowned for the Degree of REFORMATION, Professed and Attained by *Evangelical Churches*,
15 erected in those *Ends of the Earth:* And a *Field* being thus prepared, I proceed unto a Relation of the *Considerable Matters* which have been acted thereupon.

I first introduce the *Actors*, that have, in a more exemplary manner served those *Colonies*; and give *Remarkable Occurrences*, in the exemplary
20 LIVES of many *Magistrates*, and of more *Ministers*, who so *Lived*, as to leave unto Posterity, *Examples* worthy of *Everlasting Remembrance.*

I add hereunto, the *Notables* of the only *Protestant University*, that ever *shone* in that Hemisphere of the *New World*; with particular Instances of *Criolians*,[4] in our *Biography*, provoking[5] the *whole World*, with vertuous
25 Objects of Emulation.

3 ἐντευξομένων/ἐντευξαμένων   4 Theodoret/Theodorit

[1] "This I say for the benefit of those who may happen to read the book." Theodoret (A.D. *c.*393–457), Greek theologian, exegete, church historian, and for a time bishop of Cyrrhus.*
[2] "Deprave" was in Mather's day sometimes used for "deprive." Here Mather may have intended a pun on "deprivations" in its sense of depriving an ecclesiastic of a benefice or preferment. A number of early New Englanders had suffered such "deprivations" in England.
[3] Cf. George Herbert, "The Church Militant," ll. 235–236, in *Works*, ed. F. E. Hutchinson (Oxford, Clarendon Press, 1941), p. 196:

> Religion stands on tiptoe in our land,
> Readie to passe to the *American* strand.*

[4] "*Criolians*" (Creolians): people of European (sometimes African) descent born or natural-ized in America.*
[5] For "Provoking," see Rom. 11.14. Paul strives to "provoke" the Gentiles to emulation in order to "save some of them."

I introduce then, the *Actions* of a more Eminent Importance, that have signalized those *Colonies*; Whether the *Establishments*, directed by their *Synods*; with a Rich Variety of *Synodical* and *Ecclesiastical* Determinations;[6] or, the *Disturbances*, with which they have been from all sorts of *Tempta-*

30 *tions* and *Enemies* Tempestuated; and the *Methods* by which they have still weathered out each *Horrible Tempest*.

And into the midst of these *Actions*, I interpose an entire *Book*, wherein there is, with all possible Veracity, a *Collection* made, of *Memorable Occurrences*, and amazing *Judgments* and *Mercies*, befalling many *particular*

35 *Persons* among the People of *New-England*.

Let my Readers expect all that I have promised them, in this *Bill of Fare*; and it may be they will find themselves entertained[7] with yet many other Passages, above and beyond their Expectation, deserving likewise a room in *History*: In all which, there will be nothing, but the *Author's*

40 too mean way of preparing so great Entertainments, to Reproach the Invitation.

§. 2. The Reader will doubtless desire to know, what it was that

—tot Volvere casus
Insignes Pietate Viros, tot adire Labores,
45   *Impulerit.*[1]

And our *History* shall, on many fit Occasions which will be therein offered, endeavour, with all *Historical* Fidelity and Simplicity, and with as little Offence as may be, to satisfie him. The Sum of the Matter is, That from the very Beginning of the REFORMATION in the *English Nation*, there

50 hath always been a Generation of *Godly Men*, desirous to pursue the *Reformation of Religion, according to the Word of God, and the Example of the best Reformed Churches*;[2] and answering the Character of *Good Men*, given by *Josephus*,[3] in his Paraphrase on the words of *Samuel* to *Saul*, μηδὲν ἄλλο πραγθήσεσθαι καλῶς ὑφ' ἑαυτῶν νομίζοντες ἢ ὅτι ἂν ποιήσωσι τοῦ θεοῦ

55 κεκελευκότος. *They think they do nothing Right in the Service of God, but what they do according to the Command of God.* And there hath been another Generation of Men, who have still employed the *Power* which they have

---

37   *Fare*/Fair   C.M.

[6] Judicial or authoritative decisions or settlements of churches and synods.

[7] "Entertain" in the sense of occupying one's attention. Cf. Dryden's comment: "It [history] has always been the most delightful entertainment of my life."*

---

[1] "Did drive men of such wondrous goodness to traverse so many perils, to face so many trials." An adaptation of Virgil, *Aeneid* I.9–11.

[2] Mather quotes here the Solemn League and Covenant agreed on by the Scots and the English Parliament in 1643.*

[3] Flavius Josephus (first century A.D.) wrote a history of the Jews from the creation of the world to the outbreak of the war with Rome in 67.*

generally still had in their Hands, not only to stop the Progress of the
Desired *Reformation*, but also, with Innumerable Vexations, to Persecute
60 those that most Heartily wished well unto it. There were many of the
Reformers, who joyned with the Reverend *JOHN FOX*, in the *Complaints*
which he then entred in his *Martyrology*, about the *Baits of Popery* yet left
in the Church, and in his *Wishes: God take them away, or else us from them,
for God knows, they be the Cause of much Blindness and Strife amongst Men!* They
65 Zealously decried the *Policy* of complying always with the *Ignorance* and
Vanity of the *People*; and cried out earnestly for *Purer Administrations* in the
House of God, and more *Conformity* to the *Law of Christ*, and *Primitive
Christianity*: While others would not hear of going any further than the
First Essay of Reformation. 'Tis very certain, that the *First Reformers* never
70 intended, that what *They* did, should be the *Absolute Boundary* of *Reformation*, so that it should be a Sin to proceed any further; as, by their own
going beyond *Wickliff*,[4] and *Changing* and *Growing* in their own *Models*[5]
also, and the Confessions of *Cranmer*,[6] with the *Scripta Anglicana* of *Bucer*,
and a thousand other things, was abundantly demonstrated. But after a
75 Fruitless Expectation, wherein the truest Friends of the *Reformation* long
waited, for to have that which *Heylin*[7] himself owns to have been the
Design of the *First Reformers*, followed as it should have been, a Party very
unjustly arrogating to themselves, the Venerable Name of, *The Church of*
England, by Numberless Oppressions, grievously *Smote those their Fellow-*
80 *Servants*.[8] Then 'twas that, as our Great *OWEN*[9] hath expressed it,
*Multitudes of Pious, Peaceable Protestants, were driven, by their Severities, to
leave their Native Country, and seek a Refuge for their Lives and Liberties, with
Freedom, for the Worship of God, in a Wilderness, in the Ends of the Earth.*

§. 3. It is the History of these PROTESTANTS, that is here attempted:
85 PROTESTANTS that highly honoured and affected *The Church of*
ENGLAND, and humbly Petition to be a *Part* of it: But by the Mistake
of a few powerful *Brethren*, driven to seek a place for the Exercise of the
Protestant Religion, according to the Light of their Consciences, in the
Desarts of *America*. And in this Attempt I have proposed, not only to

63 Church,/Church;   *Wishes:*/*Wishes*,   else/ease
65 decried/decreed   C.M.   72 *Wickliff*/*Wicklift*

[4] John Wycliffe (d. 1384), English anti-papal reformer and translator of the Bible into English.*
[5] Creedal or institutional patterns or designs.
[6] Thomas Cranmer (1489–1556), first Protestant archbishop of Canterbury, was burned at the stake for heresy in the reign of Queen Mary I. "Confessions" is used here in the sense of "statements of faith." Martin Bucer (Butzer, 1491–1551), German Protestant, was professor of theology at Cambridge University from 1549 to 1551.*
[7] Peter Heylin (1600–1662), Anglican historian and ardent opponent of the Puritans.*
[8] Matt. 24.49–51. "Smote their fellow servants" suggests that the Anglican opposers of reformation ate and drank "with the drunken" and were to be punished with "the hypocrites."*
[9] John Owen (1616–1683), eminent English Congregational nonconformist.*

90 preserve and secure the Interest of *Religion*, in the Churches of that little
Country *NEW-ENGLAND*, so far as the Lord Jesus Christ may please to
Bless it for that End, but also to offer unto the Churches of the *Reformation*,
abroad in the World, some small *Memorials*, that may be serviceable unto
the Designs of *Reformation*, whereto, I believe, they are quickly to be
95 awakened. I am far from any such Boast, concerning these Churches,
That they have Need of Nothing, I wish their *Works* were more *perfect before
God*. Indeed, that which *Austin*[1] called *The Perfection of Christians*, is like
to be, until the Term for the *Antichristian Apostasie*[2] be expired, *The
99 Perfection of Churches* too; *Ut Agnoscant se nunquam esse perfectas*.[3] Nevertheless, I perswade my self, that *so far as they have attained*, they have given
Great Examples of the *Methods* and *Measures*, wherein an *Evangelical Reformation* is to be prosecuted, and of the *Qualifications* requisite in the Instruments that are to prosecute it, and of the *Difficulties* which may be most
5 likely to obstruct it, and the most likely *Directions* and *Remedies* for those
Obstructions. It may be, 'tis not possible for me to do a greater Service
unto the Churches on the *Best Island* of the Universe, than to give a distinct Relation of those *Great Examples* which have been occurring among
Churches of *Exiles*, that were driven out of that *Island*, into an horrible
10 *Wilderness*, meerly for their being Well-willers unto the *Reformation*. When
that Blessed Martyr *Constantine*[4] was carried, with other Martyrs, in a
Dung-Cart, unto the place of Execution, he pleasantly said, *Well, yet we
are a precious Odour to God in Christ*. Tho' the *Reformed Churches* in the
American Regions, have, by very Injurious Representations of their
15 Brethren (all which they desire to Forget and Forgive!) been many
times thrown into a *Dung-Cart*; yet, as they have been a *precious Odour to
God in Christ*, so, I hope, they will be a *precious Odour* unto *His People*; and
not only *Precious*, but *Useful* also, when the *History* of them shall come to be
considered. A *Reformation of the Church* is coming on, and I cannot but
20 thereupon say, with the dying *Cyrus* to his Children in *Xenophon*, Ἐκ τῶν
προγεγενημένων μανθάνετε, αὐτὴ γὰρ ἀρίστη διδασκαλία. *Learn from the
things that have been done already, for this is the best way of Learning*. The
Reader hath here an Account of *The Things that have been done already*.
Bernard[5] upon that Clause in the *Canticles*, [*O thou fairest among Women*]
25 has this ingenious Gloss, *Pulchram, non omnimodo quidem, sed pulchram inter
mulieres cam dicit, videlicet cum Distinctione, quatenus et ex hoc amplius reprimatur*,

---

21 προγεγενημένων/προγεγεννημένων   26 *dicit/docet*   *quatenus et ex/quatenus ex*
25 *omnimodo/omnimode*

[1] St. Augustine (A.D. 354–430).   [2] Cf. Attestation, p. 67, l. 8.
[3] "That they know themselves to be by no means perfect."*
[4] A Norman martyr (d. 1542).*
[5] St. Bernard of Clairvaux (1090–1153), commenting on Song of Solomon 1.8: "He says
that she is fair, not in a universal sense, but fair among women, plainly with a distinction, to
which extent his praise is qualified and she may know what she lacks."*

& sciat quid desit sibi. Thus I do not say, That the Churches of *New-England* are the most *Regular*[6] that can be; yet I do say, and am sure, That they are very like unto those that were in the *First Ages* of Christianity.
30 And if I assert, That in the *Reformation* of the Church, the State of it in those *First Ages*, is to be not a little considered, the Great *Peter Ramus*,[7] among others, has emboldened me. For when the Cardinal of *Lorrain*,[8] the *Mæcenas* of that Great Man, was offended at him, for turning *Protestant*, he replied, *Inter Opes illas, quibus me ditasti, has etiam in æternum*
35 *recordabor, quod Beneficio, Poessiacæ Responsionis tuæ didici, de Quindecim a Christo sæculis, primum vere esse aureum, Reliqua, quo longius abscederent esse nequiora, atque deteriora: Tum igitur cum fieret optio, Aureum sæculum delegi.*[9] In short, The *First Age* was the *Golden Age*: To return unto *That*, will make a Man a *Protestant*, and I may add, a *Puritan*. 'Tis possible, That our Lord
40 Jesus Christ carried some Thousands of *Reformers* into the Retirements of an *American Desart*, on purpose, that, with an opportunity granted unto many of his Faithful Servants, to enjoy the precious *Liberty* of their *Ministry*, tho' in the midst of many *Temptations* all their days, He might there, *To* them first, and then *By* them, give a *Specimen* of many Good Things,
45 which He would have His Churches elsewhere aspire and arise unto: And *This* being done, He knows whether there be not *All done*, that *New-England* was planted for; and whether the Plantation may not, soon after this, *Come to Nothing*. Upon that Expression in the Sacred Scripture, *Cast the unprofitable Servant into Outer Darkness*,[10] it hath been imagined by some,
50 That the *Regiones Exteræ* of America, are the *Tenebræ Exteriores*,[11] which the *Unprofitable* are there condemned unto. No doubt, the Authors of those Ecclesiastical Impositions and Severities, which drove the English Christians into the *Dark Regions* of *America*, esteemed those *Christians* to be a very *unprofitable* sort of Creatures. But behold, ye *European* Churches,
55 There are *Golden Candlesticks*[12] [more than *twice Seven times Seven!*] in the midst of this *Outer Darkness*: Unto the *upright* Children of *Abraham*, here hath arisen *Light in Darkness*. And let us humbly speak it, it shall be *Profitable* for you to consider the *Light*, which from the midst of this *Outer*

46 knows whether/knows not whether   C.M.

6 "Regular" in the sense of observing a single set rule. New England churches differed among themselves on minor points of organization and practice.

7 Petrus Ramus (Pierre de la Ramée, 1515–1572), French anti-Aristotelian logician, anti-scholastic philosopher, and educational reformer.

8 Charles de Guise (1524–1574), Archbishop and Duke of Rheims and Cardinal of Lorraine, was a patron of Ramus, who on occasion addressed him as his "Maecenas."

9 "Among all the treasures with which you enriched me I shall always remember what I learned, thanks to your reply at Poissy, that 'of the fifteen centuries since Christ, the first is golden; the rest, the more distant they are from Christ's time, the more wicked and corrupt they are.' Hence when a choice was to be made I chose the golden age."*

10 Matt. 25.30; see also 8.12.

11 *Regiones Exterae*: outer regions; *Tenebrae Exteriores*: outer darkness.

12 Metaphorical for churches. Rev. 1.12, 20, 2.5.*

Darkness, is now to be Darted over unto the other side of the *Atlantick*
60 *Ocean*. But we must therewithal ask your Prayers, that these *Golden*
Candlesticks may not *quickly* be *Removed out of their place!*

§. 4. But whether *New England* may *Live* any where else or no, it must
Live in our *History!*

HISTORY, in general, hath had so many and mighty Commenda-
65 tions from the Pens of those Numberless Authors, who, from *Herodotus* to
Howel,[1] have been the professed Writers of it, that a tenth part of them
Transcribed, would be a Furniture for a *Polyanthea in Folio*.[2] We, that
have neither liberty, nor occasion, to quote those Commendations of
History, will content our selves with the Opinion of one who was not
70 much of a *profess'd Historian*, expressed in that passage, whereto all
Mankind subscribe, *Historia est Testis temporum, Nuntia vetustatis, Lux*
veritatis, vita memoriæ, magistra vitæ.[3] But of all *History* it must be confessed,
that the *Palm* is to be given unto *Church History*; wherein the *Dignity*, the
Suavity,[4] and the *Utility* of the *Subject* is transcendent. I observe, that for
75 the Description of the *whole World* in the Book of *Genesis*, that *First-born*
of all Historians, the great *Moses*, employes but *one* or *two* Chapters, whereas he employes, it may be *seven times* as many Chapters, in describing that
one little *Pavilion, The Tabernacle*. And when I am thinking, what may
be the Reason of this *Difference*, methinks it intimates unto us, That the
80 *Church* wherein the Service of God is performed, is much more Precious
than the *World*, which was indeed created for the Sake and Use of the
Church. 'Tis very certain, that the greatest Entertainments must needs
occur in the History of the *People*, whom the *Son* of God hath *Redeemed*
and *Purified* unto himself, as a *Peculiar People*,[5] and whom the *Spirit* of
85 God, by *Supernatural Operations* upon their Minds, does cause to live like
Strangers in *this World*, conforming themselves unto the *Truths* and *Rules*
of his Holy Word, in Expectation of a *Kingdom*, whereto they shall be in
another and a better *World* advanced. Such a *People* our Lord Jesus
Christ hath procured and preserved in all Ages *visible*;[6] and the Dispensa-
90 tions of his *wonderous Providence* towards this People (for, *O Lord, thou do'st*
lift them up, and cast them down!)[7] their Calamities, their Deliverances, the

77   employes/implies   C.M.

[1] William Howell (1638?–1683), author of a general *History of the World* (London, 1680–
1685). Cotton Mather commends him in the *Manuductio*, p. 59.

[2] A large anthology; a collection of commonplaces arranged alphabetically. Such collections
were used by many orators and writers.*

[3] "History is the witness of periods of time, the messenger of antiquity, the light of truth,
the life of memory, and the instructress of life."*

[4] Sweetness, agreeableness.*

[5] A people set apart from others by special qualities, as, for example, the Jews as God's
chosen people.

[6] That is, "visible" as a group of believers, a church.

[7] Ps. 102.10.

Dispositions which they have still discovered,[8] and the considerable *Persons* and *Actions* found among them, cannot but afford Matters of *Admiration* and *Admonition*, above what any other Story can pretend un-
95 to: 'Tis nothing but *Atheism* in the Hearts of Men, that can perswade them otherwise. Let any Person of good Sense peruse the History of *Herodotus*, which, like a River taking Rise, where the *Sacred Records* of the *Old Testament* leave off, runs along smoothly and sweetly, with Relations
99 that sometimes perhaps want an *Apology*, down until the *Grecians* drive the *Persians* before them. Let him then peruse *Thucydides*, who from *Acting* betook himself to *Writing*,[9] and carries the ancient State of the *Grecians*, down to the twenty first Year of the *Peloponnesian Wars* in a manner, which *Casaubon*[10] judges to be *Mirandum potius quam imitandum*. Let him
5 next Revolve[11] *Xenophon*, that *Bee* of *Athens*, who continues a Narrative of the *Greek Affairs*, from the *Peloponnesian Wars*, to the Battle of *Mantinea*, and gives us a *Cyrus* into the bargain, at such a rate, that *Lipsius* reckons the Character of a *Suavis, Fidus & Circumspectus Scriptor*,[12] to belong unto him. Let him from hence proceed unto *Diodorus Siculus*,[13] who, besides a
10 rich Treasure of *Egyptian, Assyrian, Lybian* and *Grecian*, and other *Antiquities*, in a Phrase, which according to *Photius*'s Judgment, is ἱστορία μαλιστὰ πρεπούσῃ, *of all most becoming an Historian*, carries on the Thread begun by his Predecessors, until the End of the Hundred and nineteenth *Olympiad*; and where he is defective, let it be supplied from *Arianus*,[14] from *Justin*,
15 and from *Curtius*, who in the relish of *Colerus* is, *Quovis melle dulcior*.[15] Let him hereupon consult *Polybius*,[16] and acquaint himself with the Birth

8 *Suavis/Suavi*

[8] "Still" in the sense of "ever more and more." Thus God's chosen people have ever more and more revealed ("discovered") the divine order and arrangement of events.

[9] Thucydides (fifth century B.C.) was active in political life before he wrote his famous history.

[10] Isaac Casaubon (1559–1614), Hellenist and Calvinist theologian: "To be admired rather than imitated."*

[11] Study or read.

[12] Xenophon was given the epithet *apis attica* because of the honeyed sweetness of his words. In the battle of Mantinea (362 B.C.), the Boeotians defeated the Spartans, but Epaminondas, the Theban general who had successfully challenged Sparta's hegemony, lost his life. Xenophon's *Cyropaedia* gives an idealized account of the boyhood and training of Cyrus the Great. Justus Lipsius (1547–1606), who praises Xenophon as "An agreeable, faithful and careful writer," was a Flemish philologist and critic.*

[13] Diodorus Siculus, first-century B.C. Greek historian. Photius (c.820–c.895), who commended Diodorus' "Phrase"—i.e., diction or style—was Patriarch of Constantinople; he made a collection of extracts and abridgments from classical authors, many of whom were historians. The ancient Greeks measured time by "Olympiads," four-year periods, counting from 776 B.C. Hence the end of the 119th Olympiad was 301 B.C.*

[14] Flavius Arrianus was a Greek historian and philosopher of the second century A.D.; Marcus Junianus Justinus (fl. second half of the second century) and Curtius Rufus (fl. A.D. c.50) were Roman historians; Christoph Coler, or Colerus (fl. 1592–1604), was professor of history at Altdorf.*

[15] "Sweeter than honey."

[16] Books 1–5 are all that have been preserved of Polybius' Roman history, which covered the period from the 129th Olympiad (264–261 B.C.) to 146 B.C.

and Growth of the *Roman Empire*, as far as 'tis described, in *Five* of the *Forty* Books composed by an Author, who with a Learned *Professor of History* is, *Prudens Scriptor, si quis alius.*[17] Let him now run over the Table
20 of the *Roman* Affairs, compendiously given by *Lucius Florus*,[18] and then let him consider the Transactions of above three hundred Years reported by *Dionysius Halicarnassæus*,[19] who, if the Censure of *Bodin*[20] may be taken, *Græcos omnes & Latinos superasse videatur.*[21] Let him from hence pass to *Livy*,[22] of whom the famous Critick says, *Hoc solum ingenium (de Historicis*
25 *Loquor) populus Romanus par Imperio suo habuit*, and supply those of his *Decads* that are lost, from the best Fragments of Antiquity, in others (and especially *Dion* and *Salust*)[23] that lead us on still further in our way. Let him then proceed unto the Writers of the *Cesarean*[24] times, and first revolve *Suetonius*, then *Tacitus*, then *Herodian*,[25] then a whole Army more
30 of *Historians*, which now crowd into our *Library*; and unto all the rest, let him not fail of adding the Incomparable *Plutarch*, whose Books they say, *Theodore Gaza*[26] preferred above any in the World, next unto the Inspired Oracles of the *Bible:* But if the Number be still too little to satisfie an *Historical Appetite*, let him add *Polyhistor*[27] unto the number, and all
35 the *Chronicles* of the following Ages. After all, he must sensibly acknowledge, that the two short Books of *Ecclesiastical History*, written by the Evangelist *Luke*, hath given us more *glorious Entertainments*, than all these voluminous Historians if they were put all together.[28] The *Atchievements* of one *Paul* particularly, which that Evangelist hath *Emblazon'd*, have more
40 *True Glory* in them, than all the Acts of those Execrable *Plunderers* and *Murderers*, and irresistible *Banditti* of the World, which have been dignified with the Name of *Conquerors*. *Tacitus* counted *Ingentia bella, Expugnationes*

[17] "A discreet [wise] writer, if any be." The "learned Professor" is Degory Wheare (1573–1647), first professor of modern history at Oxford.*
[18] Lucius Annaeus Florus (fl. second century A.D.) wrote an abridged history of Rome to the time of Augustus.*
[19] Dionysius of Halicarnassus (first century B.C.) wrote a history of Rome.
[20] Jean Bodin (1530–1596), French political philosopher. "Censure" is used in the sense of critical opinion, with no pejorative connotation.
[21] "Seems to have surpassed all the Greek and Roman [historians]."*
[22] Titus Livius (Livy, 59 B.C.–A.D. 17). His history of Rome was divided into decades (Decads) after his death. Mather quotes "the famous critic" Casaubon: "As for historians, the Romans had this one genius worthy of their empire."*
[23] Dio Cassius (Dion, A.D. *c.*155–*c.*235) wrote a history of Rome, of which twenty-five books survive; Gaius Sallustius Crispus (Sallust, *c.* 86–*c.*35 B.C.) also wrote a history of Rome, of which only fragments exist.
[24] That is, imperial.
[25] Herodian (A.D. *c.*170–*c.*240), author of a Roman history covering the years 180–238.
[26] Greek scholar (1398–1475), professor of Greek at Ferrara, translated Aristotle and Theophrastus into Latin.*
[27] Alexander Cornelius (Polyhistor, i.e., "very learned," fl. first century B.C.), compiler of geographical and historical accounts of many countries.*
[28] Both the third Gospel and the Book of the Acts are traditionally ascribed to Luke.

urbium, fusos captosque Reges,[29] the Ravages of *War*, and the glorious
Violences, whereof great Warriors make a wretched Ostentation, to be the
45 *Noblest Matter* for an *Historian*. But there is a *Nobler*, I humbly conceive,
in the planting and forming of *Evangelical Churches*, and the *Temptations*,
the *Corruptions*, the *Afflictions*, which assault them, and their *Salvations*
from those Assaults, and the Exemplary *Lives* of those that Heaven employs to be Patterns of *Holiness* and *Usefulness* upon Earth: And unto such
50 it is, that I now invite my Readers; Things, in comparison whereof, the
Subjects of many other Histories, are of as little weight, as the Questions
about Z, the last Letter of our Alphabet, and whether H is to be pronounced with an Aspiration, where about whole Volumes have been
written, and of no more Account, than the Composures of *Didymus*.[30]
55 But for the *manner* of my treating this *Matter*, I must now give some account unto him.

§. 5. *Reader!* I have done the part of an *Impartial Historian*, albeit not
without all occasion perhaps, for the Rule which a worthy Writer, in his
Historica, gives to every Reader, *Historici Legantur cum Moderatione &*
60 *venia, & cogitetur fieri non posse ut in omnibus circumstantiis sint Lyncei*.[1] *Polybius*
complains of those *Historians*, who always made either the *Carthagenians*
brave, and the *Romans* base, or *e contra*, in all their Actions, as their
Affection for their own *Party* led them. I have endeavoured, with all
good Conscience, to decline this writing meerly for a *Party*, or doing like the
65 Dealer in History, whom *Lucian*[2] derides, for always calling the Captain
of his own Party an *Achilles*, but of the adverse Party a *Thersites*:[3] Nor
have I added unto the just Provocations for the Complaint made by the
Baron *Maurier*,[4] That the *greatest part of Histories* are but so many
Panegyricks composed by *Interested Hands*, which *elevate Iniquity to the Heavens*,
70 like *Paterculus*, and like *Machiavel*, who propose *Tiberius Cesar*, and *Cesar
Borgia*, as Examples fit for *Imitation*, whereas *True History* would have
Exhibited them as Horrid *Monsters*, as very *Devils*.[5] 'Tis true, I am not of

54 Composures/Composure   63 endeavoured/eadeavoured
60 *Lyncei/Lymei* C.M.

[29] "Huge wars, cities taken by storm, kings captive or routed."*
[30] An Alexandrian grammarian of the end of the first century B.C., said to have written four
thousand books, in which "Composures," according to Seneca, he investigated problems
"the answers to which if found were forthwith to be forgotten."*

---

[1] "Let historians be read with moderation and indulgence, and let it be considered that it
is impossible for them always to be like Lynceus," who, in Greek mythology, was famous for
sharp sight.*
[2] Greek satirist of the second century A.D.*
[3] In Homer, an insolent and ugly Greek slain by Achilles.
[4] Louis Aubery, sieur du Maurier (d. 1687), author of a history of the Netherlands.*
[5] Caius Velleius Paterculus (*c.*19 B.C.–A.D. *c.*30), whose epitome of Roman history was
marred by excessive praise of Tiberius and the infamous Nero; Machiavelli admired Cesare
Borgia, Duke of Valentinois (*c.*1476–*c.*1507), Italian cardinal and military leader notorious
for cruelty and fraud.

the Opinion, that one cannot merit the Name of an *Impartial Historian,* except he write bare *Matters of Fact,* without all *Reflection;* for I can tell

75 where to find this given as the Definition of *History, Historia est rerum gestarum, cum laude aut vituperatione, Narratio:*[6] And if I am not altogether a *Tacitus,* when *Vertues* or *Vices* occur to be Matters of *Reflection,* as well as of *Relation,*[7] I will, for my Vindication, appeal to *Tacitus* himself, whom *Lipsius* calls one of the *Prudentest* (tho' *Tertullian,* long before, counts

80 him the *Lyingest*) of them who have Inriched the World with *History:* He says, *Præcipuum munus Annalium reor, ne virtutes sileantur, utque pravis Dictis, Factisque ex posteritate & Infamia metus sit.*[8] I have not *Commended* any Person, but when I have really judg'd, not only *That* he *Deserved* it, but also that it would be a Benefit unto Posterity to know, Wherein he

85 deserved it: And my Judgment of *Desert,* hath not been *Biassed,* by Persons being of my own particular Judgment in matters of *Disputation,* among the Churches of God. I have been as willing to wear the Name of *Simplicius Verinus,*[9] throughout my whole undertaking, as he that, before me, hath assumed it: Nor am I like Pope *Zachary,*[10] impatient so much

90 as to hear of any *Antipodes.* The Spirit of a *Schlusselbergius,*[11] who falls foul with Fury and Reproach on all who differ from him; The Spirit of an *Heylin,* who seems to count no Obloquy too hard for a *Reformer;* and the Spirit of those (*Folio-writers* there are, some of them, in the English Nation!) whom a Noble Historian[12] Stigmatizes, as, *Those Hot-*

95 *headed, Passionate Bigots, from whom, 'tis enough, if you be of a Religion contrary unto theirs, to be defamed, condemned and pursued with a thousand Calumnies.* I thank Heaven I Hate it with all my Heart. But how can the *Lives* of the *Commendable* be written without *Commending* them? Or, is that Law of

99 *History* given in one of the eminentest pieces of *Antiquity* we now have in our hands, wholly antiquated, *Maxime proprium est Historiæ, Laudem rerum egregie gestarum persequi?*[13] Nor have I, on the other side, forbore to mention many *Censurable* things, even in the Best of my Friends, when the things, in my opinion, were *not Good;* or so bore away for *Placentia,* in the

5 course of our Story, as to pass by *Verona;*[14] but been mindful of the Direc-

---

[6] "History is the story of events, with praise or blame."*
[7] Matters for considered judgment and comment.*
[8] "I regard it as the first duty of history not to let virtues be uncelebrated and to hold up as a terror the censure of posterity for bad words and deeds."*
[9] "Honest Truthful," pseudonym used occasionally by Salmasius (Claude de Saumaise, 1588–1653), classical professor at Leyden.
[10] Saint Zacharias, pope from 741 to 752, condemned Bishop Vergilius of Salzburg for writing a tract on the Antipodes.*
[11] Conrad Schlüsselburg (1543–1619), Lutheran theologian and controversialist.
[12] The "Noble Historian" has not yet been identified by the editors.*
[13] "It is in the highest degree the property of history to record praise of good deeds."*
[14] Punning on the place names *Placentia* (in post-classical Latin "suavity," "courteousness") and *Verona* (which suggests *verum,* "true"), Mather is in effect saying, "I thought it better to be truthful than pleasing."*

tion which *Polybius* gives to the Historian, *It becomes him that writes an History, sometimes to extol Enemies in his Praises, when their praise-worthy Actions bespeak it, and at the same time to reprove the best Friends, when their Deeds appear worthy of a reproof; in-as much as History is good for nothing, if*
10   *Truth (which is the very Eye of the Animal) be not in it.* Indeed I have thought it my duty upon all accounts, (and if it have proceeded unto the degree of a *Fault*, there is, it may be, something in my *Temper* and *Nature*, that has betray'd me therein) to be more sparing and easie, in thus mentioning of *Censurable* things, than in my *other Liberty*: [15] A writer of *Church-History*,
15   should, I know, be like the *builder of the Temple*, one of the *Tribe* of *Naphthali*;[16] and for this I will also plead my *Polybius* in my Excuse; *It is not the Work of an Historian, to commemorate the Vices and Villanies of Men, so much as their just, their fair, their honest Actions: And the Readers of History get more good by the Objects of their Emulation, than of their Indignation.* Nor
20   do I deny, that tho' I cannot approve the Conduct of *Josephus*, (whom *Jerom* not unjustly nor ineptly calls, *The Greek Livy*) when he left out of his *Antiquities*, the Story of the *Golden Calf*, and I don't wonder to find *Chamier*, and *Rivet*,[17] and others, taxing him for his *Partiality* towards his Country-men; yet I have left unmentioned some *Censurable Occurrences* in
25   the *Story* of our *Colonies*, as things no less *Unuseful* than *Improper* to be raised out of the Grave, wherein *Oblivion* hath now buried them; lest I should have incurred the *Pasquil*[18] bestowed upon Pope *Urban*, who employing a *Committee* to Rip up the *Old Errors* of his Predecessors, one clap'd a pair of Spurs upon the heels of the Statue of St. *Peter*; and a
30   Label from the Statue of St. *Paul* opposite thereunto, upon the Bridge, ask'd him, *Whither he was bound?* St. *Peter* answered, *I apprehend some Danger in staying here; I fear they'll call me in Question for denying my Master.* And St. *Paul* replied, *Nay, then I had best be gone too, for they'll question me also, for Persecuting the Christians before my Conversion.* Briefly, My Pen shall
35   Reproach none, that can give a Good Word unto any Good Man that is not of their *own Faction*, and shall *Fall out* with none, but those that can *Agree* with no body else, except those of their own *Schism*. If I draw any sort of Men with *Charcoal*, it shall be, because I remember a notable passage of the *Best Queen* that ever was in the World, our late Queen

---

[15] Mather claims the liberty both to "censure" and to "commend," and prefers the latter.

[16] Naphtali, the son of Jacob, was known for his "goodly words," and Hiram, of the tribe of Naphtali, was "filled with wisdom and understanding," and helped build Solomon's temple.*

[17] Daniel Chamier (1565–1621), French Calvinist theologian; André Rivet (1572–1651), French Calvinist Biblical scholar and polemicist.

[18] A lampoon, a satirical squib, affixed to some public place, often a statue; so called after an imaginary Roman, Pasquin, to whom anonymous lampoons were ascribed. When the "Pasquil" was illustrated by a comic drawing, a "Label," or balloon-shaped outline, contained words supposedly spoken by the person represented.*

40　*Mary.*[19] Monsieur *Jurieu,*[20] that he might Justifie the Reformation in
　Scotland, made a very black Representation of their old Queen *Mary*;[21]
　for which, a certain *Sycophant* would have incensed our Queen *Mary*
　against that Reverend Person, saying, *Is it not a Shame that this Man,*
　without any Consideration for your R*oyal Person, should dare to throw such*
45　*Infamous Calumnies upon a Queen, from whom your* R*oyal Highness is descended?*
　But that Excellent Princess replied, *No, not at all*; *Is it not enough that by*
　fulsome Praises great Persons be lull'd asleep all their Lives; *But must Flattery*
　accompany them to their very Graves? How should they fear the Judgment of
　Posterity, if Historians be not allowed to speak the Truth after their Death? But
50　whether I do my self *Commend,* or whether I give my Reader an oppor-
　tunity to *Censure,* I am careful above all things to do it with *Truth*; and
　as I have considered the words of *Plato, Deum indigne & graviter ferre, eum*
　quis ei similem hoc est, virtute præstantem, vituperet, aut laudet contrarium :[22] So
　I have had the *Ninth Commandment*[23] of a greater *Law-Giver* than *Plato,* to
55　preserve my care of *Truth* from first to last. If any Mistake have been any
　where committed, it will be found meerly *Circumstantial,*[24] and wholly
　Involuntary; and let it be remembred, that tho' no *Historian* ever merited
　better than the Incomparable *Thuanus,*[25] yet learned Men have said of *his*
　Work, what they never shall truly say of *ours,* that it contains *multa*
60　*falsissima & indigna.*[26] I find *Erasmus* himself mistaking *One* Man for *Two,*
　when writing of the Ancients. And even our own English Writers too are
　often mistaken, and in Matters of a very late Importance, as *Baker,* and
　Heylin, and *Fuller,*[27] (professed Historians) tell us, that *Richard Sutton,*[28] a
　single Man, founded the *Charter-House*; whereas his Name was *Thomas,*
65　and he was a married Man. I think I can Recite such Mistakes, it may be
　Sans Number occurring in the most credible Writers; yet I hope I shall
　commit none such. But altho' I thus challenge, as my due, the Character
　of an *Impartial,* I doubt I may not challenge *That* of an *Elegant Historian.*
　I cannot say, whether the *Style,* wherein this *Church-History* is written, will
70　please the Modern *Criticks :* But if I seem to have used ἁπλουστάτῃ

40 *Jurieu*/*Juvien* C.M.

[19] Mary II and her husband William III were declared joint monarchs in 1688 to succeed
her deposed father James II.

[20] Pierre Jurieu (1637–1713), French Protestant theologian and polemicist.*

[21] Mary Stuart, Queen of Scots (1542–1587). Her son, James I of England, was the great-
grandfather of Mary II, as also of William III.

[22] "It is to act unworthily and offensively toward God, to abuse anyone who is like him
excelling in virtue, or to praise the opposite of such a one."*

[23] "Thou shalt not bear false witness against thy neighbor": Exod. 20.16; Deut. 5.20.

[24] That is, non-essential, incidental or unimportant.

[25] Jacques Auguste de Thou (1553–1617), French magistrate, historian, and poet.

[26] "Much that is most false and unworthy."*

[27] Sir Richard Baker (1568–1645), historian and writer on religious subjects. Thomas
Fuller (1608–1661), English divine and historian.

[28] Thomas Sutton (1532–1611) in 1611 bought the Charterhouse in London and established
there a hospital and a school for boys.*

συντάξει γραφῆς, a Simple, Submiss, Humble *Style*,[29] 'tis the same that
Eusebius[30] affirms to have been used by *Hegesippus*,[31] who, as far as we
understand, was the first Author (after *Luke*) that ever composed an entire Body of *Ecclesiastical History*, which he divided into *Five Books*, and
75 Entitled, ὑπομνήματα τῶν ἐκκλησιαστικῶν πράξεων.[32] Whereas *others*, it
may be, will reckon the *Style* Embellished with too much of *Ornament*,
by the multiplied References to other and former Concerns, closely
coach'd, for the Observation of the *Attentive*, in almost every Paragraph;
but I must confess, that I am of his mind who said, *Sicuti sal modice cibis*
80 *aspersus Condit, & gratiam saporis addit, ita si paulum Antiquitatis admiscueris,*
Oratio fit venustior.[33] And I have seldom seen that Way of Writing faulted,
but by those, who, for a certain odd Reason, sometimes find fault, *That*
the Grapes are not ripe. These *Embellishments* (of which yet I only—*Veniam*
pro laude peto[34]) are not the puerile Spoils of *Polyanthea*'s; but I should have
85 asserted them to be as choice *Flowers* as most that occur in Ancient or
Modern Writings, almost unavoidably putting themselves into the
Authors Hand, while about his Work, if those words of *Ambrose*[35] had
not a little frighted me, as well as they did *Baronius*,[36] *Unumquemque*
Fallunt sua scripta.[37] I observe that Learned Men have been so terrified by
90 the Reproaches of *Pedantry*, which little Smatterers at Reading and Learning have, by their *Quoting Humours* brought upon themselves, that, for to
avoid all Approaches towards that which those Feeble Creatures have
gone to[38] imitate, the best way of Writing has been most injuriously
deserted. But what shall we say? The Best way of Writing, under Heaven,
95 shall be the Worst, when *Erasmus* his Monosyllable Tyrant will have it
so![39] And if I should have resign'd my self wholly to the Judgment of
others, What way of Writing to have taken, the Story of the two Statues
made by *Policletus*[40] tells me, what may have been the Issue: He contrived

---

29 "The simplest style of writing." "Submiss": submissive, that is, a simple, restrained,
humble style.
30 Eusebius (*c.*260–*c.*340), Bishop of Caesarea, called "the father of church history" because
of his monumental history of the Christian Church.
31 Hegesippus (fl. 150–180), Christian writer, fragments of whose works are preserved in
Eusebius' history.
32 "Memoirs of Ecclesiastical Affairs."
33 "Just as salt discreetly spread on food seasons it, and increases its flavor, so to mix in a
little of antiquity makes style more pleasing."*
34 "Indulgence, rather than praise, I ask."*
35 Ambrose (*c.*340–*c.*397), one of the fathers of the Latin Church, was Bishop of Milan.
36 Cesar Baronius (Caesare Baronio, 1538–1607), cardinal, librarian of the Vatican, and
Catholic apologist, wrote *Annales Ecclesiastici*, based extensively on then unpublished Vatican
materials.
37 "Everyone is deceived by his own writings."*
38 That is, have attempted to.
39 A reference to Erasmus' adage, "A master (δεσπότης) needs only monosyllables: yes
or no; the servant needs longer words to entreat and cajole."*
40 Polycletus (Polyclitus) the Elder, Greek architect and sculptor (fifth century B.C.).*

99 one of them according to the Rules that best pleased himself, and the other according to the Fancy of every one that look'd upon his Work: The former was afterwards Applauded by all, and the latter Derided by those very Persons who had given their Directions for it. As for such *Unaccuracies* as the *Critical* may discover, *Opere in longo,*[41] I appeal to the

5 *Courteous,* for a favourable Construction of them; and certainly they will be favourably Judged of, when there is considered the *Variety* of my *other Employments,* which have kept me in continual Hurries, I had almost said, like those of the *Ninth Sphere,*[42] for the few Months in which this Work has been *Digesting.*[43] It was a thing well thought, by the wise Designers of

10 *Chelsey-Colledge,* wherein able *Historians* were one sort of Persons to be maintained;[44] That the Romanists do in one Point condemn the Protestants; for among the Romanists, they don't burden their *Professors* with any *Parochial Incumbrances*; but among the *Protestants,* the very same *Individual* Man must *Preach, Catechize,* Administer the *Sacraments,* Visit the

15 Afflicted, and manage all the parts of *Church-Discipline*; and if any *Books* for the Service of Religion, be written, Persons thus *extreamly incumbred* must be the Writers. Now, of all the Churches under Heaven, there are none that expect so much *Variety* of Service from their Pastors, as those of *New-England*; and of all the Churches in *New-England,* there are none that

20 require more, than those in *Boston,* the Metropolis of the English *America*; whereof *one* is, by the Lord Jesus Christ, committed unto the Care of the unworthy Hand, by which this *History* is compiled. Reader, Give me leave humbly to mention, with him in *Tully, Antequam de Re, Pauca de Me*![45] Constant *Sermons,* usually more than once, and perhaps three or four

25 times, in a Week, and all the other Duties of a *Pastoral Watchfulness,* a very *large Flock* has all this while demanded of me; wherein, if I had been furnished with as many *Heads* as a *Typheus,* as many *Eyes* as an *Argos,* and as many *Hands* as a *Briareus,*[46] I might have had Work enough to have employ'd them all; nor hath my *Station* left me free from Obligations to

30 spend very much time in the *Evangelical Service* of *others* also. It would have been a great *Sin* in me, to have *Omitted,* or *Abated,* my Just Cares, to *fulfil my Ministry in these things,* and in a manner *Give my self wholly to them.* All the time I have had for my *Church-History,* hath been perhaps only,

---

[41] "In a long work."

[42] In Ptolemaic astronomy the ninth (crystalline) sphere accounted for the precession of the equinoxes.

[43] That is, thinking over and arranging methodically in the mind, receiving and considering, or, in an older sense, ripening or maturing in the mind.

[44] King James's College, founded in the borough of Chelsea in 1610, "was intended for a spiritual garrison, where learned divines should study and write in maintenance of all controversies against the Papists." The foundation provided for two resident historians.*

[45] Marcus Tullius Cicero: "Before coming to the subject, a little about myself."*

[46] In Greek mythology Typhoeus is a hundred-headed monster; Argus, the all-seeing, hundred-eyed son of Zeus; and Briareus, the hundred-armed son of Heaven and Earth.

or chiefly, that, which I might have taken else for less profitable Recrea-
35 tions; and it hath all been done by *Snatches*. My Reader will not find me
the Person intended in his *Litany,* when he says, *Libera me ab homine unius
Negotii :*[47] Nor have I spent *Thirty Years* in shaping this my *History,* as
Diodorus Siculus did for his, [and yet both *Bodinus* and *Sigonius*[48] complain
of the Σφαλματα[49] attending it.] But I wish I could have enjoy'd entirely
40 for this Work, one quarter of the little more than *Two Years* which have
roll'd away since I began it; whereas I have been forced sometimes wholly
to throw by the Work whole Months together, and then resume it, but
by a stolen hour or two in a day, not without some hazard of incurring
the *Title* which *Coryat*[50] put upon his History of his Travels, *Crudities
45 hastily gobbled up in five Months. Protogenes* being seven Years in drawing a
Picture, *Apelles* upon the sight of it, said, *The Grace of the Work was much
allay'd by the length of the Time.*[51] Whatever else there may have been to
take off the *Grace of the Work,* now in the Readers hands, (whereof the
Pictures of Great and Good Men make a considerable part) I am sure
50 there hath not been the *length of the Time* to do it. Our English Martyrolo-
ger, counted it a sufficient *Apology,* for what Meanness might be found in
the first Edition of his *Acts and Monuments,* that it was *hastily rashed up*[52]
in about fourteen Months: And I may Apologize for this Collection of our
Acts and Monuments, that I should have been glad, in the little more than
55 *Two Years* which have ran out, since I enter'd upon it, if I could have
had one half of *About fourteen Months* to have entirely devoted thereunto.
But besides the *Time,* which the *Daily Services* of *my own* first, and then
many *other* Churches, have necessarily call'd for, I have lost abundance of
precious *Time,* thro' the feeble and broken State of my *Health,* which hath
60 unfitted me for *Hard Study;* I can do nothing to purpose at *Lucubrations.*[53]
And yet, in this *Time* also of the two or three Years last past, I have not
been excused from the further Diversion of *Publishing* (tho' not so many
as they say *Mercurius Trismegistus*[54] did,) yet more than a *Score* of other
Books, upon a copious Variety of other Subjects, besides the composing

36 *Litany/Littany*   63 did,) yet/did, yet)
37 *Negotii/Negotis*

[47] "Deliver me from a man of but one interest."*
[48] Carlo Sigonio (*c.*1520–*c.*1584), Italian writer and philologist.*
[49] Faults.
[50] Thomas Coryat (Coryate or Coriat, 1577?–1617), English courtier famous for his travels.*
[51] Protogenes and Apelles were Greek painters of the fourth century B.C.*
[52] Put together hastily.*
[53] Nocturnal studies.
[54] Hermes Trismegistus (Hermes the thrice-great), identified with the Egyptian Thoth, was called the "scribe of the Gods." According to tradition, he was the author of everything discovered by the human mind, contained in forty-two sacred "Hermetic" books. Over the years certain papyri or works on temple walls were claimed as part of them. In the third and following centuries, the name became a convenient pseudonym for various occult or alchemic writing.

65 of several more, that are not yet published. Nor is this neither all the
Task that I have in this while had lying upon me; for (tho' I am very
sensible of what *Jerom* said, *Non bene fit, quod occupato Animo fit*;[55] and of
Quintilian's Remark, *Non simul in multa intendere Animus totum potest*;[56])
when I applied my mind unto this way of serving the Lord JESUS
70 CHRIST in my Generation,[57] I set upon another and a greater, which
has had, I suppose, more of my *Thought* and *Hope* than this, and wherein
there hath passed me, for the most part, *Nulla dies sine linea*.[58] I considered,
That all sort of *Learning* might be made gloriously Subservient unto the
Illustration of the *Sacred Scripture*; and that no *professed Commentaries* had
75 hitherto given a thousandth part of so much *Illustration* unto it, as might
be given. I considered, that Multitudes of *particular Texts*, had, especially
of later Years, been more notably *Illustrated* in the *Scattered Books* of
Learned Men, than in any of the *Ordinary Commentators*. And I consider'd,
That the *Treasures* of *Illustration* for the Bible, dispersed in many hundred
80 Volumes, might be fetch'd all together by a Labour that would resolve
to *Conquer all things*; and that all the *Improvements* which the *Later-ages*
have made in the *Sciences*, might be also, with an inexpressible Pleasure,
call'd in, to assist the *Illustration* of the *Holy Oracles*, at a Rate that hath
not been attempted in the vulgar *Annotations*; and that a common degree
85 of *Sense*, would help a Person, who should converse much with these
things, to attempt sometimes also an *Illustration* of his own, which might
expect some Attention. Certainly, it will not be ungrateful unto good
Men, to have innumerable *Antiquities*,[59] *Jewish, Chaldee, Arabian, Grecian*
and *Roman*, brought home unto us, with a *Sweet Light* Reflected from
90 them on the *Word*, which is our *Light:*[60] Or, To have all the *Typical*
Men and things in our *Book of Mysteries*, accommodated with their
Antitypes:[61] Or, To have many Hundreds of References to our dearest
Lord Messiah, discovered in the Writings which *Testifie of Him*, oftner than
the most of Mankind have hitherto imagined: Or, To have the *Histories*
95 of all Ages, coming in with punctual and surprising *Fulfillments* of the
Divine *Prophecies*, as far as they have been hitherto fulfilled; and not meer
Conjectures, but even Mathematical and Incontestable *Demonstrations*,

83 assist/Christ C.M.

[55] "What is done with an occupied mind, is not well done."*
[56] "One cannot put his whole mind on many things at the same time." Marcus Fabius
Quintilianus (A.D. *c*.35–*c*.95) was a celebrated Roman rhetorician.*
[57] As David did in his; cf. Acts 13.36.
[58] "No day without a line."*
[59] Remains or monuments of antiquity, ancient relics, particularly records of earlier times,
as, for example, the *Antiquitates Judaicae* of Josephus.
[60] Ps. 119.105, 130; Prov. 6.23.
[61] "*Book of Mysteries*": the Bible. "Mysteries" here means religious truths known only
from divine revelation. "*Antitypes*": things which have been shadowed forth or represented
by a "type" or symbol. See prefatory essay, "The Magnalia."

given of *Expositions* offered upon the *Prophecies*, that yet remain to be
99 accomplished: Or, To have in *One Heap*, Thousands of those *Remarkable
Discoveries of the deep things of the Spirit of God*, whereof *one* or *two*, or a few,
sometimes, have been, with good Success accounted Materials enough to
advance a Person into *Authorism*; or to have the delicious *Curiosities* of
Grotius, and *Bochart*, and *Mede*, and *Lightfoot*, and *Selden*, and *Spencer*,[62]
5 (carefully selected and corrected) and many more Giants in Knowledge,
all set upon one Table. Travellers tell us, That at *Florence* there is a rich
Table, worth a thousand Crowns, made of Precious Stones neatly inlaid;
a Table that was fifteen Years in making, with no less than thirty Men
daily at work upon it; even such a Table could not afford so rich Enter-
10 tainments, as one that should have the Soul-feasting Thoughts of those
Learned Men together set upon it. Only 'tis pitty, that instead of one
poor feeble *American*, overwhelm'd with a thousand other Cares, and
capable of touching this Work no otherwise than in a Digression, there
be not more than Thirty Men daily employ'd about it. For, when the
15 excellent Mr. *Pool*[63] had finished his Laborious and Immortal Task, it
was noted by some considerable Persons, *That wanting Assistance to Collect
for him many miscellaneous Criticisms, occasionally scattered in other Authors,
he left many better Things behind him than he found.* At more than all this, our
Essay is levell'd, if it be not anticipated with that Epitaph, *Magnis
20 tamen excidit ausis.*[64] Designing accordingly, to give the Church of God such
displays of his blessed Word, as may be more Entertaining for the Rarity
and Novelty of them, than any that have hitherto been seen together in
any *Exposition*; and yet such as may be acceptable unto the most Judicious,
for the Demonstrative Truth of them, and unto the most Orthodox, for
25 the regard had unto the *Analogy of Faith* in all, I have now, in a few
Months, got ready an huge number of *Golden Keys* to open the *Pandects*[65]
of Heaven, and some thousands of charming and curious and singular
Notes, by the *New Help* whereof, the *Word of* CHRIST *may run and be
glorified.* If the *God of my Life*, will please to spare my Life [my yet Sinful,
30 and Slothful, and thereby Forfeited Life!] as many years longer as the
Barren Fig-tree had in the Parable,[66] I may make unto the Church of God,

---

19   *Magnis/agnis*

[62] Samuel Bochart (1599–1667), French Biblical scholar, orientalist, and Huguenot pastor;
Joseph Mede (1586–1638), Biblical scholar, philologist, and historian; John Lightfoot (1602–
1675), Hebraist and Biblical critic, master of Catharine Hall, Cambridge; John Selden
(1584–1654), jurist, historian and orientalist; John Spencer (1630–1693), master of Corpus
Christi College, Cambridge, theologian and Hebraist, laid foundations of science of com-
parative religion with his *De Legibus Hebræorum* (Cambridge, Eng., 1685).*
[63] Matthew Poole (1624–1679), Puritan divine, graduate of Emmanuel College, Cambridge,
and author of a synopsis of Biblical commentaries.*
[64] "And though he greatly failed, more greatly dared."*
[65] A body of laws.*
[66] Luke 13.6–9: three years plus one more.

an humble Tender of our BIBLIA AMERICANA,[67] a Volumn enrich'd with better things than all the Plate of the *Indies*; YET NOT I,
BUT THE GRACE OF CHRIST WITH ME.[68] My Reader sees, why
35 I commit the Fault of a περιαυτία,[69] which appears in the mention of
these Minute-passages;[70] 'tis to excuse whatever other Fault of Inac-
curacy, or Inadvertency, may be discovered in an History, which hath
been a sort of Rapsody[71] made up (like the Paper whereon 'tis written!)
with many little Rags, torn from an Employment, multifarious enough
40 to overwhelm one of my small Capacities.

> *Magna dabit, qui magna potest; mihi parva potenti*
> *Parvaque poscenti, parva dedisse sat est.*[72]

§. 6. But shall I prognosticate thy Fate, now that,

> *Parve (sed invideo) sine me, Liber, ibis in Urbem.*[1]

45 *Luther*, who was himself owner of such an Heart, advised every Historian
to get the *Heart of a Lion*; and the more I consider of the Provocation,
which this our *Church-History* must needs give to that Roaring Lion, who
has, through all Ages hitherto, been tearing the Church to pieces, the
more occasion I see to wish my self a *Cœur de Lion*.[2] But had not my Heart
50 been Trebly Oak'd and Brass'd[3] for such Encounters as this our History
may meet withal, I would have worn the Silk-worms Motto, *Operitur
dum Operatur*,[4] and have chosen to have written *Anonymously*; or, as
Claudius Salmasius calls himself *Walo Messalinus*, as *Ludovicus Molinæus* calls
himself *Ludiomæus Colvinus*, as *Carolus Scribanius* calls himself *Clarius
55 Bonarscius*, (and no less Men than *Peter du Moulin*, and Dr. *Henry More*,
stile themselves, the one *Hippolytus Fronto*, the other *Franciscus Paleo-*

---

54 *Clarius/Clarus*

[67] Mather's large Biblical commentary, never published, but extant in manuscript. See
prefatory essay, "The Magnalia."*

[68] I Cor. 15.10; cf. Gal. 2.20.

[69] "Talking about oneself."

[70] Small particulars, minutiae; work of fugitive minutes.

[71] Here in the obsolete sense of a literary work consisting of disconnected or miscellaneous
pieces.

[72] "He who is able will give great things; for me, who am able to do little and ask for little,
it is enough to have given little."*

---

[1] "O little book, though I am envious, you will go without me to the city."*

[2] Richard I, Coeur de Lion (1157–1199), favorite hero of troubadours, romancers, and
medieval chroniclers of the Crusades, became by metaphorical extension the symbol of
extraordinary accomplishments.

[3] Made strong by oak and brass, as a ship (or possibly a shield) might be.

[4] "It is hidden while it works."*

politanus.)⁵ Thus I would have tried, whether I could not have Ana-
grammatized⁶ my Name into some Concealment; or I would have
referr'd it to be found in the second Chapter of the second Syntagm of
60 *Selden de Diis Syris.*⁷ Whereas now I freely confess, 'tis COTTON
MATHER that has written all these things;

*Me, me, ad sum qui scripsi; in me convertite Ferrum.*⁸

I hope 'tis a right Work that I have done; but we are not yet arrived
unto the *Day, wherein God will bring every Work into Judgment* (the Day of the
65 *Kingdom* that was promised unto *David*) and a Son of *David*⁹ hath as
Truly as Wisely told us, that until the arrival of that Happy Day, this
is one of the *Vanities* attending Humane Affairs; *For a right VVork a Man
shall be envied of his Neighbour.* It will not be so much a Surprise unto me,
if I should live to see our *Church-History* vexed with *Anie-mad-versions*¹⁰ of
70 Calumnious Writers, as it would have been unto *Virgil*, to read his
Bucolicks reproached by the *Antibucolica* of a *Nameless Scribbler*, and his
Æneids travestied by the *Æneidomastix* of *Carbilius*: Or *Herennius* taking
pains to make a Collection of the *Faults*, and *Faustinus* of the *Thefts*, in
his incomparable Composures:¹¹ Yea, *Pliny*,¹² and *Seneca* themselves, and
75 our *Jerom*, reproaching him, as a Man of no Judgment, nor Skill in
Sciences; while *Pædianus* affirms of him, that he was himself, *Usque adeo
invidiæ Expers, ut si quid erudite dictum inspiceret alterius, non minus gauderet
ac si suum-esset.*¹³ How should a Book, no better laboured than this of
ours, escape *Zoilian* Outrages,¹⁴ when in all Ages, the most exquisite

62 *in/tu* C.M.

⁵ Molinæus: Lewis du Moulin (1606–1680), nonconformist controversialist, Camden
Professor of Ancient History at Oxford; Carolus Scribanius (1561–1629), Belgian Jesuit
scholar; Pierre du Moulin (Hippolytus Fronto Caracotta, 1568–1658), French Protestant
divine and professor of philosophy at Leyden; Henry More (1614–1687), theologian and
philosopher.
⁶ Mather's name was "anagrammatized" in the Prefatory Poems by Nicholas Noyes, John
Danforth, and Grindal Rawson.*
⁷ Selden won fame as an orientalist with his *De Diis Syris.* "Syntagma": section of a systematically arranged treatise.
⁸ "It is I who have written; turn the sword against me."*
⁹ Solomon.*
¹⁰ A Matherian play on "animadversions" (criticisms or comments, usually implying
censure) and "any mad versions," with "version" in the sense of an account embodying a
particular point of view.
¹¹ Philo Herennius, of Byblus, a grammarian of the first century A.D. Little is known of
Carbilius (Carvilius) Pictor and Perilius Faustinus except that they were critics of Virgil.*
¹² Pliny the Younger: Gaius Plinius Caecilius Secundus (A.D. *c.*62–*c.*113), Roman author,
nephew of the elder Pliny, who wrote the famous "Natural History."*
¹³ Quintus Ascanius Pedianus (first century A.D.), Roman historian and grammarian, wrote,
in defense of Virgil: "He was so incapable of envy that if he saw anything learnedly said by
someone else he was as delighted as if it had been his own."*
¹⁴ Zoilus (fourth century B.C.), a Greek rhetorician, criticized Homer so severely that he
was called "the scourge of Homer."

80 Works have been as much vilified, as *Plato*'s by *Scaliger*, and *Aristotle*'s by
    Lactantius?[15] In the time of our K. *Edward* VI. there was an Order to
    bring in all the Teeth of St. *Apollonia*,[16] which the People of his one
    Kingdom carried about them for the Cure of the *Tooth ach*; and they
    were so many, that they almost fill'd a Tun. Truly *Envy* hath as many
85 *Teeth* as Madam *Apollonia* would have had, if all those pretended
    Reliques had been really hers. And must all these *Teeth* be fastned on
    thee, *O my Book?* It may be so! And yet the *Book*, when ground between
    these *Teeth*, will prove like *Ignatius* in the *Teeth* of the furious Tygers,
    The whiter Manchet for the Churches of God.[17] The greatest and fiercest
90 Rage of *Envy*, is that which I expect from those IDUMÆANS,[18] whose
    Religion is all Ceremony, and whose Charity is more for them who deny
    the most Essential things in the Articles and Homilies of the Church of
    England, than for the most Conscientious Men in the World, who manifest
    their being so, by their Dissent in some little Ceremony: Or those Persons
95 whose Hearts are notably expressed in those words used by one of them
    ['tis *Howel*[19] in his *Familiar Letters*, Vol. 1. Sect. 6. Lett. 32.] *I rather pitty,*
    than hate, Turk or Infidel, for they are of the same Metal, and bear the same
    Stamp, as I do, tho' the Inscriptions differ; If I hate any, 'tis those Schismaticks
99 *that puzzle the sweet Peace of our Church; so that I could be content to see an*
    Anabaptist go to Hell on a Brownists Back.[20] The Writer whom I last quoted,
    hath given us a Story of a young Man in *High-Holbourn*,[21] who being after
    his death Dissected, there was a Serpent with divers tails, found in the
    left Ventricle of his Heart. I make no question, that our Church History
5   will find some Reader disposed like that Writer, with an Heart as full
    of Serpent and Venom as ever it can hold: Nor indeed will they be able to
    hold, but the Tongues and pens of those angry Folks, will scourge me as
    with Scorpions, and cause me to feel (if I will feel) as many Lashes as
    Cornelius Agrippa[22] expected from their Brethren, for the Book in which

----

[15] Julius Caesar Scaliger (Guilio Cesare Scaliger or Della Scale, 1484–1558), Italian philologist and physician; Lucius Caelius Lactantius Firmianus (*c.*260–*c.*330), Christian writer
so famous for his style that he was called the "Christian Cicero."*

[16] Apollonia (*c.*250), a Christian martyr in Alexandria, whose teeth were knocked out before
she was burned.*

[17] Ignatius (d. *c.*107), Bishop and martyr of Antioch. Manchet was a small loaf of the
finest wheaten bread.*

[18] See Prefatory Poems p. 83, l. 13 and endnote thereto.

[19] James Howell (1594?–1666), English traveler, writer, and for a time historiographer-royal.*

[20] Anabaptists did not believe in infant baptism; Brownists accepted the "separatist"
doctrines of Robert Browne (1550?–1633?) and advocated complete separation from the
Church of England.

[21] One of the most ancient streets in London. In the seventeenth century, the area immediately to the south of High Holborn became a center of poverty and crime (see Walter Thorn-
bury, *Old and New London*, 6 vols., London, 1897, 2:526 ff.), and was hence a likely place of
residence for a young man possessed by Satan. For the Serpent as Satan, see Gen. 3.1–14;
Rev. 12.9, 20.2.

[22] Heinrich Cornelius Agrippa von Nettesheim (1486–1535), German physician and
philosopher.*

10 he exposed their Vanities. A Scholar of the great JUELS,[23] made once about, fourscore Verses, for which the Censor of *Corpus Christi* Colledge in the beginning of Queen *Maries* Reign, publickly and cruelly scourged him, with one Lash for every Verse. Now in those Verses, the young Man's Prayers to the Lord JESUS CHRIST, have this for part of the

15 answer given to them.

Respondit Dominus, spectans de sedibus altis,
Ne dubites recte credere, parve puer.
Olim sum passus mortem, nunc occupo dextram
Patris, nunc summi sunt mea regna poli.
20 *Sed tu, crede mihi, vires Scriptura resumet,*
Tolleturque suo tempore missa nequam.

In English.

The Lord beholding from his Throne, reply'd,
Doubt not, *O Youth*, firmly in me confide:
25 I dy'd long since, now sit at the Right Hand
Of my bless'd Father, and the World command.
Believe me, *Scripture* shall regain her sway,
And wicked *Mass* in due time fade away.

Reader, I also expect nothing but *Scourges* from that Generation, to
30 whom the *Mass-book* is dearer than the *Bible*. But I have now likewise confessed another Expectation, that shall be my Consolation under all. They tell us, That on the highest of the *Capsian* Mountains in *Spain*, there is a Lake, whereinto if you throw a Stone, there presently ascends a Smoke, which forms a dense Cloud, from whence issues a Tempest of
35 Rain, Hail, and horrid Thunder-claps, for a good quarter of an hour. Our Church-History will be like a Stone cast into that Lake, for the furious Tempest which it will raise among some, whose Ecclesiastical Dignities have set them, as on the top of Spanish Mountains. The Catholick Spirit of Communion wherewith 'tis written, and the Liberty
40 which I have taken, to tax the Schismatical Impositions and Persecutions of a Party, who have always been as real Enemies to the English Nation, as to the Christian and Protestant Interest, will certainly bring upon the whole Composure, the quick Censures of that Party, at the first cast of

16   *Respondit/Respondet*

[23] John Jewel (1522–1571), Fellow of Corpus Christi College, Oxford, and Bishop of Salisbury.*

their look upon it. In the Duke of *Alva*'s Council of twelve Judges, there
45 was one *Hessels* a *Flemming*, who slept always at the Trial of Criminals, and
when they wak'd him to deliver his Opinion, he rub'd his Eyes, and cry'd,
between sleeping and waking, *Ad patibulum! ad Patibulum!* To the Gallows
with 'em![24] [And, by the way, this Blade was himself, at the last, condemned unto the Gallows, without an Hearing!] As quick Censures must
50 this our Labour expect from those who will not bestow waking thoughts
upon the Representations of Christianity here made unto the World;
but have a Sentence of Death always to pass, or at least, Wish, upon
those Generous Principles, without which, 'tis impossible to maintain
the Reformation: And I confess, I am very well content, that this our
55 Labour takes the Fate of those Principles: Nor do I dissent from the
words of the Excellent *VVhitaker* upon *Luther, Fœlix ille, quem Dominus eo
Honore dignatus est, ut Homines nequissimos suos haberet inimicos.*[25] But if the
old Epigrammatist, when he saw Guilty Folks raving Mad at his Lines,
could say—

60   *Hoc volo; nunc nobis carmina nostra placent:*[26]

Certainly an Historian should not be displeased at it, if the Enemies of
Truth discover their Madness at the true and free Communications of
his History; and therefore the more Stones they throw at this Book, there
will not only be the more Proofs, that it is a Tree which hath good Fruits[27]
65 growing upon it, but I will build my self a Monument with them,
whereon shall be inscribed, that Clause in the Epitaph of the Martyr
Stephen:

          Excepit Lapides, cui petra Christus erat.[28]

Albeit perhaps the *Epitaph,* which the old *Monks* bestow'd upon
70 *Wickliff,*[29] will be rather endeavour'd for me, (*If I am thought worth one!*)
by the Men, who will, with all possible *Monkery,* strive to stave off the
approaching *Reformation.*

68 *erat./erat:*

[24] Fernando Alvarez de Toledo (1507–1582), third Duke of Alva, Governor General of the
Netherlands, 1567, was famous for his "Council of Blood," which condemned to death thousands of opponents of the Spanish rulers in the Netherlands.*
[25] William Whitaker (1548–1595), professor of divinity and master of St. John's College,
Cambridge. "Happy he whom God has dignified with the honor of having the worst of men
as his enemies."*
[26] "That is what I want; now my verses please me."*
[27] Matt. 3.10, 7.17–19, 12.33.*
[28] Saint Stephen, the first Christian martyr, was stoned to death. "He whose rock was
Christ received the stone."*
[29] In the epitaph Wycliffe is called, among other things, the "devil's instrument" and
the "Church's Enemy." "Monkery": conduct or practices characteristic of monks, especially
conduct marked by the faults or abuses with which Protestants charged monasticism.*

But since an Undertaking of this Nature, must thus encounter so much Envy, from those who are under the Power of the *Spirit that works in the* 75 *Children of Unperswadeableness*,[30] methinks I might perswade my self, that it will find another sort of Entertainment from those Good Men who have a better Spirit in them: For, as the Apostle *James* hath noted, (so with Monsieur *Claude*[31] I read it) *The Spirit that is in us, lusteth against Envy*; and yet even in *us* also, there will be the *Flesh*, among whose Works, 80 one is *Envy*, which will be *Lusting* against the *Spirit*. All Good Men will not be satisfied with every thing that is here set before them. In my own Country, besides a considerable number of loose and vain Inhabitants risen up, to whom the Congregational Church-Discipline, which cannot Live well, where the Power of Godliness dyes, is become distastful for the 85 Purity of it; there is also a number of eminently Godly Persons, who are for a Larger[32] way, and unto these my Church-History will give distast, by the things which it may happen to utter, in favour of that Church-Discipline on some few occasions; and the Discoveries which I may happen to make of my Apprehensions, that *Scripture*, and *Reason*, and 90 *Antiquity* is for it; and that it is not far from a glorious Resurrection. But that, as the Famous Mr. *Baxter*,[33] after Thirty or Forty Years hard Study, about the true Instituted Church-Discipline, at last, not only own'd, but also invincibly prov'd, That it is *The Congregational*; so, The further that the *Unprejudiced Studies* of Learned Men proceed in this Matter, the more 95 generally the *Congregational Church-Discipline* will be pronounced for. On the other side, There are some among us, who very strictly profess the *Congregational Church-Discipline*, but at the same time they have an unhappy Narrowness of Soul, by which they confine their value and Kindness too much unto their own Party; and unto those my *Church History* 99 will be offensive, because my Regard unto our own declared Principles, does not hinder me from giving the Right hand of Fellowship[34] unto the valuable Servants of the Lord Jesus Christ, who find not our Church-Discipline as yet agreeable unto their present Understandings and 5 Illuminations. If it be thus in my own Country, it cannot be otherwise in

95 for./for

[30] See Eph. 2.2; Col. 3.6.*
[31] Jean Claude (1619–1687), French Huguenot divine, whose translation of James 4.5 Mather follows here.
[32] "Larger": here in the obsolete or archaic sense of "freer," "less restrained."*
[33] Richard Baxter (1615–1691), eminent English Puritan divine.*
[34] Gal. 2.9. In the Congregational churches of New England, the ceremonial giving of the right hand of fellowship constituted an affirmation of the autonomy of individual churches, and of their independence of both synods and bishops. Thus when a church of visible saints "called" a minister, his ordination was sealed by the right hand of fellowship, and when new churches were organized their congregations, together with representatives of neighboring churches, exchanged the right hand of fellowship in recognition of the new church as a "true" church established in accordance with Gospel ordinances.

That whereto I send this account of my own. Briefly, as it hath been said, That if all *Episcopal* Men were like Archbishop *Usher*, and all *Presbyterians* like *Stephen Marshal*, and all *Independents* like *Jeremiah Burroughs*, the Wounds of the Church would soon be healed;[35] my Essay to carry that

10 Spirit through this whole Church-History, will bespeak Wounds for it, from those that are of another Spirit. And there will also be in every Country those Good Men, who yet have not had the Grace of Christ so far prevailing in them, as utterly to divest them of that piece of Ill Nature which the Comedian resents, *In homine Imperito, quo nil quicquam*

15 *Injustius, quia nisi quod ipse facit, nil recte factum putat.*[36]

However, All these things, and an hundred more such things which I think of, are very small Discouragements for such a Service as I have here endeavoured. I foresee a Recompence,[37] which will abundantly swallow up all Discouragements! It may be *Strato* the Philosopher counted himself

20 well recompensed for his Labours, when *Ptolomy* bestow'd fourscore Talents on him. It may be *Archimelus* the Poet counted himself well recompensed, when *Hiero* sent him a thousand Bushels of Wheat for one little Epigram: And *Saleius* the Poet might count himself well recompensed, when *Vespasian* sent him twelve thousand and five hundred *Philippicks*;

25 and *Oppian* the Poet might count himself well recompensed, when *Caracalla* sent him a piece of Gold for every Line that he had inscribed unto him.[38] As I live in a Country where such Recompences never were in fashion; it hath no Preferments for me, and I shall count that I am well Rewarded in it, if I can escape without being heavily Reproached,

30 Censured and Condemned, for what I have done: So I thank the Lord, I should exceedingly Scorn all such mean Considerations, I seek not out for Benefactors, to whom these Labours may be Dedicated: There is ONE to whom all is due! From Him I shall have a Recompence: And what Recompence? The Recompence, whereof I do, with inexpressible

35 Joy, assure my self, is this, *That these my poor Labours will certainly serve the Churches and Interests of the Lord Jesus Christ.* And I think I may say,

---

[35] James Ussher (1581–1656), Archbishop of Armagh in Ireland, and a scholar learned in patristic literature, tried to reconcile the strict Anglicans and the nonconformists; Marshall (1594–1655), a Presbyterian divine, was an influential advocate of liturgical and episcopal reform; and Burroughs (Burroughes, 1599–1646), a Congregational divine, presented the case of the "independents" to Parliament in 1644.*

[36] "There is nothing more unjust than a man without knowledge of the world; he thinks nothing right except what he has done himself." The "Comedian" was Terence; see *Adelphoe* I.ii.88–89.

[37] Cf. Luke 14.14.

[38] Strato, Greek peripatetic philosopher (fl. 288 B.C.); Ptolemy I (Soter, d. 283 B.C.), king of Egypt and founder of the great library in Alexandria; Archimelus (fl. 220 B.C.), Greek poet and epigrammatist; Hieron II, King of Syracuse (*c.*270–*c.*216 B.C.); Saleius Bassus (first century A.D.), poet and grammarian of Cilicia; Vespasian (A.D. 9–79), Roman Emperor 68–79; Oppian, third-century Greek didactic poet; Caracalla, Roman Emperor 212–217. Philippics were gold coins of King Philip of Macedon.*

That I ask to live no longer, than I count a Service unto the Lord Jesus Christ, and his Churches, to be it self a glorious Recompence for the doing of it. When *David* was contriving to build the House of God, there
40 was that order given from Heaven concerning him, *Go tell* David, *my Servant.* The adding of *that* more than *Royal Title* unto the Name of *David,* was a sufficient Recompence for all his Contrivance about the House of God.[39] In our whole *Church-History,* we have been at work for the House of the Lord Jesus Christ, [Even that *Man* who is the *Lord*
45 *God,* and whose *Form* seems on that occasion represented unto His *David.*] And herein 'tis Recompence enough, that I have been a *Servant* unto that heavenly Lord. The greatest *Honour,* and the sweetest *Pleasure,* out of *Heaven,* is to Serve our Illustrious Lord JESUS CHRIST, who hath *loved us, and given himself for us*; and unto whom it is infinitely reason-
50 able that we should *give our selves,* and all that we *have* and *Are:* And it may be the *Angels* in *Heaven* too, aspire not after an higher Felicity.

Unto thee,[40] *therefore, O thou Son of God, and King of Heaven, and Lord of all things, whom all the Glorious Angels of Light, unspeakably love to Glorifie; I humbly offer up a poor History of Churches, which own thee alone for their*
55 *Head, and Prince, and Law-giver; Churches which thou hast purchas'd with thy own Blood, and with wonderful Dispensations of thy Providence hitherto protected and preserved; and of a People which thou didst Form for thy self, to shew forth thy Praises. I bless thy great Name, for thy inclining of me to, and carrying of me through, the Work of this History: I pray thee to sprinkle the Book of this History*
60 *with thy Blood,*[41] *and make it acceptable and profitable unto thy Churches, and serve thy Truths and Ways among thy People, by that which thou hast here prepared; for 'tis* THOU *that hast prepar'd it for them.* Amen.

Quid sum? Nil. Quis sum? Nulles. Sed Gratia CHRISTI, Quod sum, quod Vivo, quodque Laboro, facit.[42]

---

46 *David.*]/*David*]

[39] For the "House of God," see II Sam. 7.1–5, 18–29; cf. Heb. 3.6.

[40] The italicized paragraph which begins here and dedicates the *Magnalia* to God is largely made up of Biblical words, phrases, and allusions, just as is the prayer with which Higginson ended his Attestation. Mather's dedication is an example of his use of the words of Holy Writ as a special "language," particularly in passages which he considers of importance, or, as in this case, climactic. See prefatory essay, "The Magnalia."

[41] Even as Moses sprinkled the Book of the Covenant with blood: Exod. 24.6–8.*

[42] "What am I? Nothing. Who am I? Nobody. But the grace of Christ has brought it about that I am, that I live, and that I work."*

The First BOOK.

ANTIQUITIES:

OR,

A FIELD prepar'd for Considerable Things to be Acted
thereupon.

The INTRODUCTION.

אי״ה[1]

I T *was as long ago, as about the middle of the former Century, that under the*
Influences of that admirable Hero *and* Martyr, *of the* Protestant Religion,
Gasper Coligni, *the great Admiral of* France, *a Noble and Learned Knight*
called Villegagnon,[2] *began to attempt the Settlement of some Colonies in*
AMERICA, (*as it was declared*) for the Propagation of that Religion. *He*
Sailed with several Ships of no small Burthen, till be arriv'd at Brasile;[3] *where*
he thought there were now shown him Quiet Seats, *for the retreat of a People*
harrass'd already with deadly Persecutions, and threatned with yet more Calamities.
Thence *he wrote Home Letters unto that glorious* Patron *of the* Reform'd
Churches,[4] *to inform him, That he had now a fair Prospect of seeing those*
Churches *erected, multiply'd and shelter'd in the Southern Regions of the* New
World; *and requested him, That* Geneva *might supply them with* Pastors *for*
the planting of such Churches in these New Plantations. *The Blessed* Calvin,
with his Collegues, thereupon sent of their Number Two *Worthy Persons, namely*
Richerius *and* Quadrigarius, *to assist this Undertaking; and unto these were*
joined several more, especially Lerius, *and, who became a Leader to the rest,*

---

28 *as/not* C.M.   31 Villegagnon/Villagagnon

---

1 "If the Lord wills." *

2 Gaspard de Coligny (Gaspard II, 1519–1572), a Huguenot convert, and a leader of the
Protestant party in France. He was one of the first victims of the St. Bartholomew's Day
massacre. Nicholas Durand, seigneur de Villegagnon (*c.*1510–1571), was a professional soldier
and adventurer. Coligny sent Villegagnon to Brazil with six hundred colonists in 1555. The
"declared" purpose, to propagate the Protestant religion, while genuine with Coligny, proved
false with Villegagnon.

3 The site of the French settlement in Brazil was a small island in the bay of Rio de Janeiro.

4 John Calvin, from 1541 the effective head of the Geneva theocracy.

Corquillerius, an eminent Man, for the Cause of Christianity, then residing at
45 *Geneva.*[5] *Embark'd in three Ships, well fitted, they came to the* American
Country, whither they had been invited; and they soon set up an Evangelical
Church Order, in those Corners of the Earth where God in our Lord Jesus
Christ had never before been called upon. But it was not long before some unhappy
Controversies *arose among them, which drove their Principal Ministers into*
50 *Europe again, besides those* Three *that were Murthered by their* Apostate
Governour, whose Martyrdom Lerius *procured* Crispin *to Commemorate in*
his History,[6] *but I now omit in this of ours,* Ne me Crispini scrinia lecti
compilasse putes:[7] *And as for the People that staid behind, no other can be*
Learn'd, but that they are entirely lost, *either in* Paganism *or* Disaster:[8] *In this,*
55 *more unhappy sure, than that* Hundred Thousand *of their Brethren who were*
soon after Butcher'd at Home, in that horrible Massacre, *which then had not,*
but since hath, *known a Parallel.*[9] *So has there been utterly* lost *in a little time,*
A Country intended for a Receptacle of Protestant Churches on the
American Strand. *It is the most Incomparable* De Thou, *the Honourable President*
60 *of the Parliament at* Paris, *an Historian whom* Casaubon *Pronounces,* A Singular Gift of Heaven, to the last Age, for an Example of Piety and Probity,
that is our Author,[10] *(besides others) for* this History.

 'Tis now time for me to tell my Reader, that in our Age *there has been another*
Essay, made not by French, *but by* English PROTESTANTS, *to fill a certain*
65 *Country in* America *with* Reform'd Churches; *nothing in* Doctrine, *little in*
Discipline, *different from that of* Geneva. *Mankind will pardon me, a Native*
of that Country, if smitten with a just Fear of incroaching and ill-boding Degeneracies,[11] *I shall use my Modest Endeavours to prevent the* Loss *of a Country,*
so signaliz'd for the Profession *of the purest Religion, and for the* Protection *of*
70 *God upon it, in that Holy Profession. I shall count my Country* lost, *in the* Loss
of the Primitive Principles, *and the Primitive* Practices,[12] *upon which it was at*

52 lecti/lecti,
53 compilasse/compitasse

67   *ill-boding/ill-bodied*   C.M.

[5] Pierre Richer (Richier, *c.*1505–1580), Guillaume Chartier (*c.*1525–1581), and Jean de
Lery (Lerius, 1534–1613), whose *Histoire d'un voyage fait en la terre du Brésil* (La Rochelle,
1578) had many printings, were Huguenot pastors, although Lery was not ordained until
after his return to Geneva; Philippe de Corquilleray, sieur du Pont, was an old man living
in retirement when appointed leader of the expedition.

[6] The apostate governor was Villegagnon.*

[7] "That you may not suspect me of having rifled the portfolios of the excellent Crispin."*

[8] In 1560 the French island fort was captured by a Portuguese expedition, and a later
Portuguese attack, in 1567, destroyed the French settlements, which by then had spread to the
mainland.

[9] The "horrible massacre" was that of the Huguenots in France the night of August 23–24
(St. Bartholomew's), 1572; the "parallel" was the massacre of the Protestants in Ireland in
1641.*

[10] That is, the author used as source.*

[11] Mather hoped that his book would help to arrest the "Degeneracies" into which the
community had fallen. See introductory essay "The Magnalia."

[12] Cf. Attestation p. 66, l. 1 – p. 67, l. 8, and endnotes to p. 66, l. 6 and p. 67, l. 8.

first Established: But certainly one good way to save that Loss, *wou'd be to do something that the Memory of the* great Things[13] done for us by our God *may not be* lost, *and that the Story of the Circumstances attending the* Foundation

75 *and* Formation *of this Country, and of its* Preservation *hitherto, may be impartially handed unto Posterity. THIS is the Undertaking whereto I now Address my self; and now,* Grant me thy Gracious Assistances, O my God; that in this my Undertaking I may be kept from every false way: But that sincerely aiming at thy Glory in my Undertaking, I may find my

80 Labours made Acceptable and Profitable unto thy Churches, and Serviceable unto the Interests of thy Gospel; so let my God think upon me for Good; and spare me according to the greatness of thy Mercy in the Blessed Jesus, *Amen.*

CHAP. I.

85 Venisti tandem?[1] *Or Discoveries of* AMERICA, *tending to, and ending in, Discoveries of* NEW-ENGLAND.

§. 1. IT is the Opinion of some, though 'tis *but* an *Opinion,* and *but* of *some* Learned Men, That when the Sacred Oracles of Heaven assure us, *The Things under the Earth* are some of those, whose *Knees are to bow*

90 *in the Name of Jesus,*[2] by those *Things* are meant the Inhabitants of *America,* who are *Antipodes* to those of the other *Hemisphere.* I would not Quote any Words of *Lactantius,*[3] tho' there are *some* to Countenance this Interpretation, because of their being so *Ungeographical:* Nor would I go to strengthen the Interpretation by reciting the Words of the *Indians* to the first

95 *White Invaders* of their Territories, *We hear you are come from under the World to take our World from us.*[4] But granting the *uncertainty* of such an Exposition, I shall yet give the Church of God a certain Account of those *Things,* which in *America* have been Believing and Adoring the glorious *Name* of

99 Jesus; and of that Country in *America,* where those *Things* have been

---

[13] For the "great things," "Magnalia," see Ps. 126.3, and introductory essay "The Magnalia."

---

[1] "Hast thou come at last!"*
[2] Phil. 2.10.
[3] Lactantius rejected the existence of any antipodes on the grounds that nothing was "so blockish as to beleeue there are men whose feet are higher then their heads, or that those thinges there hang, which with vs lye on the ground."*
[4] Cf. William Strachey, *History of Travel into Virginia Brittania,* as quoted by L. B. Wright, *The Elizabethans' America* (Cambridge, Mass., Harvard University Press, 1965), p. 207: of Powhatan, "as more fearing than harmed at any time with the danger and mischief which he saith we intend unto him by taking away his land from him and conspiring to surprise him."

attended with Circumstances most remarkable. I can contentedly allow
that *America* (which as the Learned *Nicolas Fuller*[5] Observes, might more
justly be called *Columbina*) was altogether unknown to the *Penmen* of the
Holy Scriptures, and in the *Ages* when the Scriptures were Penned. I
5 can allow, that those Parts of the Earth, which do not include *America*,
are in the inspired Writings of *Luke*, and of *Paul*, stiled; *All the World*.[6]
I can allow, that the Opinion of *Torniellus*, and of *Pagius*, about the
Apostles Preaching the Gospel in *America*, has been sufficiently refuted
by *Basnagius*.[7] But I am out of the reach of Pope *Zachary*'s Excommunica-
10 tion.[8] I can assert the Existence of the *American Antipodes*: And I can
Report unto the *European* Churches great Occurrences among these
Americans. Yet I will Report every one of them with such a Christian and
exact Veracity, that no Man shall have cause to use about any one of
them, the Words which the great *Austin* (as *great* as he was) used about
15 the Existence of *Antipodes*: it is a Fable, and, *nulla ratione credendum*.[9]

§. 2. If the *Wicked One in whom the whole World lyeth*,[1] were *he*, who like
a *Dragon*, keeping a Guard upon the spacious and mighty *Orchards* of
America, could have such a *Fascination* upon the Thoughts of Mankind,
that neither this *Ballancing half* of the Globe should be considered in
20 *Europe* till a little more than two Hundred Years ago, nor the *Clue* that
might lead unto it, namely, the *Loadstone*, should be known, till a
Neapolitan[2] stumbled upon it, about an Hundred Years before; yet the
over-ruling *Providence* of the *great God* is to be acknowledged, as well in
the *Concealing* of America for so long a time, as in the *Discovering* of it,
25 when the fulness of Time was come for the Discovery: For we may count
America to have been concealed, while Mankind in the other *Hemisphere*
had lost all Acquaintance with it, if we may conclude it had any from
the Words of *Diodorus Siculus*, That *Phœnecians* were by great Storms
driven off the Coast of *Africa*, far *Westward*, ἐπὶ πολλὰς ἡμέρας, *for many*
30 *Days together*, and at last fell in with an Island of prodigious Magnitude;
or from the Words of *Plato*, that beyond the Pillars of *Hercules* there was
an Island in the *Atlantick* Ocean, ἅμα λιβύης κὰι Ασίας μείζων, *larger than*
Africa and Asia *put together*: Nor should it pass without Remark, that

15 *Antipodes*:/*Antipodes*;

[5] Nicholas Fuller (1557?–1626), English Hebraist and philologist.*
[6] Luke 2.1; Acts 11.28; Rom. 3.19.
[7] Agostino Tornielli (1543–1622) and Antoine Pagi (1624–1699) were Catholic scholars
and historians; Samuel Basnage de Flottemanville (1638–1721), an exiled Huguenot pastor
and ecclesiastical historian.*
[8] For "Pope *Zachary's* Excommunication," see footnote to General Introduction p. 98, l. 89.
[9] "Utterly incredible."*

[1] Cf. I John 5.19.*
[2] Flavio Gioia (fl. end of the thirteenth century), an Italian pilot of Amalfi.*

Three most memorable things which have born a very great Aspect upon
35 *Humane Affairs,* did near the same time, namely at the Conclusion of the
Fifteenth, and the beginning of the *Sixteenth Century,* arise unto the World:
The First was the *Resurrection of Literature*; the Second was the opening of
America; the Third was the *Reformation* of *Religion.* But, as probably, the
Devil seducing the first Inhabitants of *America* into it, therein aimed at the
40 having of them and their Posterity out of the sound of the *Silver Trumpets*
of the *Gospel,* then to be heard through the *Roman Empire*; if the *Devil*
had any Expectation, that by the Peopling of *America,* he should utterly
deprive any *Europeans* of the Two Benefits, *Literature* and *Religion,* which
dawned upon the miserable World, one just *before,* t'other just *after,* the
45 first famed *Navigation* hither, 'tis to be hop'd he will be disappointed of
that Expectation. The *Church* of God must no longer be wrapp'd up in
Strabo's Cloak:[3] *Geography* must now find work for a *Christiano-graphy* in
Regions far enough beyond the Bounds wherein the *Church* of God had
thro' all former Ages been circumscribed. Renown'd *Churches* of Christ
50 must be gathered where the Ancients once Derided them that look'd for
any *Inhabitants.* The Mystery[4] of our Lord's Garments, made *Four Parts,*
by the Soldiers that cast *Lots* for them,[5] is to be accomplished in the good
Sence put upon it by *Austin,* who if he had known *America* could not have
given a better *Quadripartita vestis Domini Jesu, quadripartitam figuravit ejus.*
55 *Ecclesiam, toto scilicet, qui quatuor partibus constat, terrarum orbe diffusam.*[6]

§. 3. Whatever Truth may be in that Assertion of one who writes;
If we may credit any Records besides the Scriptures, I know it might be said and
proved well, that this New World was known, and partly Inhabited by Britains,[1]
or by Saxons *from* England, *Three or Four Hundred Years before the* Spaniards
60 *coming thither*; which Assertion is Demonstrated from the Discourses
between the *Mexicans* and the *Spaniards* at their first Arrival; and the
Popish *Reliques,* as well as *British* Terms and Words, which the *Spaniards*
then found among the *Mexicans,* as well as from undoubted Passages, not
only in other Authors, but even in the *British* Annals also. Nevertheless,
65 Mankind generally agree to give unto *Christopher Columbus,* a *Genoese,* the
Honour of being the First *European* that opened a way into these Parts

---

55   *terrarum/terraram*   C.M.   64   also./also:

[3] Strabo (*c.*63 B.C. – A.D. 24), the Greek geographer, compared the shape of the habitable
world to that of a cloak.*
[4] An incident in the life of Christ regarded as having a mystical significance; by extension,
a religious truth known only by divine revelation.
[5] John 19.23.
[6] "The parting of the garments of our Lord Jesus into four pieces was a type of a like division
of His Church which is distributed through the four quarters of the globe."*

---

[1] Ancient Britons as distinguished from Anglo-Saxons; Welshmen. Similarly "British,"
below, means Welsh.*

of the World. It was in the Year 1492. that this famous Man, acted[2] by
a most vehement and wonderful *Impulse,* was carried into the *Northern
Regions* of this vast Hemisphere, which might more justly therefore have
70 receiv'd its *Name* from *Him,* than from *Americus Vesputius* a *Florentine,*
who in the Year 1497. made a further Detection of the more *Southern
Regions* in this Continent. So a *World,* which has been one great Article
among the *Res deperditæ* of *Pancirollus,*[3] is now *found out,* and the Affairs
of the *whole World* have been affected by the finding of it. So the *Church*
75 of our Lord Jesus Christ, well compared unto a *Ship* is now *victoriously*
sailing round the *Globe* after Sir *Francis Drake*'s renowned Ship, called
The Victory,[4] which could boast,

Prima ego velivolis ambivi cursibus orbem.[5]

And yet the Story about *Columbus* himself must be corrected from the
80 Information of *De la Vega,*[6] That one *Sanchez,* a Native of *Huelva* in *Spain,*
did before him find out these Regions. He tells us, That *Sanchez* using to
Trade in a small Vessel to the *Canaries,* was driven by a furious and tedious
Tempest over unto these Western Countries; and at his return he gave to
Colon, or *Columbus,* an account of what he had seen, but soon after died of
85 a Disease he had got on his dangerous Voyage. However, I shall expect
my Reader e're long to grant, that some things done since by Almighty
God for the *English* in these Regions, have exceeded all that has been
hitherto done for any other Nation: If this *New World* were not found out
first by the *English*; yet in those regards that are of all the *greatest,* it seems
90 to be found out more *for* them than any other.

§. 4. But indeed the two *Cabots,* Father and Son,[1] under the Commission of our King *Henry* VII. entering upon their generous[2] Undertakings in the Year 1497. made further Discoveries of *America,* than
either *Columbus* or *Vesputius*; in regard of which notable Enterprizes, the
95 younger of them had very great Honours by the Crown put upon him,
till at length he died in a good Old Age, in which Old Age King *Edward*
VI. had allowed him an Honourable Pension. Yea, since the *Cabots,*

80 *Huelva/Helva*

[2] Actuated.
[3] Guido Panciroli (1523–1599), Italian jurisconsult, wrote a book on "things lost," the
arts and inventions of the ancients.*
[4] The *Victory* was Magellan's ship; Drake's was the *Golden Hind.**
[5] "I first went about the world in my sail-driven coursings."*
[6] Garcilaso de la Vega (*c.*1535–1616), called "Inca," his father being a conquistador, his
mother a noble Inca lady, wrote on both Inca history and the Spanish conquest.*

[1] John (1450–1498) and Sebastian (1474–1557), Italian navigators and explorers.*
[2] Gallant, high-spirited.

employ'd by the King of *England*, made a Discovery of this *Continent* in
99 the Year 1497. and it was the Year 1498. before *Columbus* discovered any
part of the *Continent*; and *Vesputius* came a considerable time after both
of them; I know not why the *Spaniard* should go *unrivall'd* in the claim of
this *New World*, which from the *first finding* of it is pretended unto. These
Discoveries of the *Cabots* were the Foundation of all the *Adventures*, with
5 which the *English Nation* have since followed the *Sun*, and *scrued*[3] themselves
into an Acquaintance on the hither side of the *Atlantick* Ocean. And now
I shall *drown* my Reader with my self in a tedious Digression, if I enumerate all the Attempts made by a *Willoughby*, a *Frobisher*, a *Gilbert*, and besides many others, an Incomparable *Rawleigh*, to settle *English* Colonies
10 in the Desarts of the Western *India*.[4] It will be enough if I entertain him
with the History of that *English* Settlement, which may, upon a Thousand
accounts, pretend unto more of *True English* than all the rest, and which
alone therefore has been called *New-England*.

§. 5. After a discouraging Series of Disasters attending the Endeavours
15 of the *English* to swarm into *Florida*,[1] and the rest of the Continent unto
the Northward of it, called *Virginia*, because the first *White* Born in those
Regions was a *Daughter*, there Born to one *Ananias Dare*, in the Year
1585.[2] the Courage of one Captain *Bartholomew Gosnold*, and one Captain
Bartholomew Gilbert,[3] and several other Gentlemen, served them to make
20 yet more Essays upon the like Designs. This Captain *Gosnold* in a small
Bark, on *May* 11.[4] 1602. made Land on this Coast in the Latitude of
Forty-Three; where, tho' he liked the *Welcome* he had from the Salvages
that came aboard him, yet he disliked the *Weather*, so that he thought it
necessary to stand more Southward into the Sea. Next Morning he found
25 himself Embayed within a mighty Head of Land; which Promontory,
in remembrance of the *Cod-Fish* in great quantity by him taken there,

---

5   *scrued*/*served* C.M.   18   the/The
8   Frobisher/Frobrisher   18   one Captain *Bartholomew*/one *Bartholo-*
17 there/then   *mew* C.M.

---

[3] Screwed, here in the sense of constrained themselves with a great effort.

[4] Sir Hugh Willoughby died (1554) on a voyage in search of the Northwest Passage; Sir
Martin Frobisher (1535?–1594) led explorations in Greenland and accompanied Drake to
the West Indies in 1586; Sir Humphrey Gilbert (1539?–1583) was stepbrother to Sir Walter
Raleigh, with whom he undertook a voyage of exploration of the eastern seaboard of America
in 1578. Sir Walter Raleigh planted the first English colony at Roanoke, Virginia, in 1585.
"Western *India*": according to Purchas (*Purchas his Pilgrimage*, London, 1614, p. 451), "The
name of India, is now applied . . . even to whole America, through the errour of Columbus . . .
who . . . thought that they had met with Ophir, and the Indian Regions of the East."*

---

[1] By Florida here must be understood the southern parts of Virginia, particularly the
Roanoke colony.*

[2] Virginia Dare was born August 18, 1587, not 1585.*

[3] Bartholomew Gilbert (d. 1603) and Bartholomew Gosnold (d. 1607) made a trading
and reconnoitering voyage to the New England coast in 1602.*

[4] The correct date was May 14.*

he called *Cape-Cod*, a Name which I suppose it will never lose, till Shoals
of *Cod-Fish* be seen swimming upon the top of its highest Hills. On this
Cape, and on the Islands to the Southward of it,[5] he found such a com-
30 fortable Entertainment from the *Summer-Fruits*[6] of the Earth, as well as
from the *Wild Creatures* then ranging the Woods, and from the *wilder
People* now surprized into Courtesie, that he carried back to *England* a
Report of the Country, better than what the *Spies* once gave of the *Land
flowing with Milk and Honey*.[7] Not only did the Merchants of *Bristol* now
35 raise a considerable Stock to Prosecute these Discoveries, but many other
Persons of several Ranks Embarked in such Undertakings; and many
Sallies into *America* were made; the exacter Narrative whereof I had
rather my Reader should *purchase* at the expence of consulting *Purchas*'s
Pilgrims,[8] than endure any *stop* in our hastening Voyage unto the
40 𝔥𝔦𝔰𝔱𝔬𝔯𝔶 𝔬𝔣 𝔞 𝔑𝔢𝔴-𝔈𝔫𝔤𝔩𝔦𝔰𝔥 𝔍𝔰𝔯𝔞𝔢𝔩.

§. 6. Perhaps my Reader would gladly be informed how *America*
came to be *first Peopled*; and if *Hornius*'s Discourses, *De origine Gentium
Americanarum*, do not satisfie him, I hope shortly the most Ingenious
Dr. *Woodward*, in his *Natural History of the Earth*, will do it.[1] In the mean
45 time, to stay thy Stomach, Reader, accept the Account which a very
sensible *Russian*, who had been an Officer of Prime Note in *Siberia*, gave
unto Father *Avril*.[2] Said he, 'There is beyond the *Obi* a great River called
'*Kawoina*, at the Mouth whereof, discharging it self into the *Frozen Sea*,
'there stands a spacious Island very well Peopled, and no less considerable
50 'for Hunting an Animal, whose Teeth are in great esteem. The Inhabi-
'tants go frequently upon the side of the *Frozen Sea* to Hunt this Monster;
'and because it requires great Labour with Assiduity, they carry their
'Families usually along with them. Now it many times happens, that
'being surprized with a Thaw, they are carried away, I know not whither,
55 'upon huge peices of Ice that break off one from another. For my part,
'I am perswaded that several of those Hunters have been carried upon
'these floating pieces of Ice to the most Northern Parts of *America*, which
'is not far from that Part of *Asia* that jutts out into the Sea of *Tartary*. And

5 Martha's Vineyard, Nantucket, Newport.
6 For Biblical "*Summer-Fruits*," see, e.g., II Sam. 16.1, 2.*
7 Num. 13.26, 27.*
8 Samuel Purchas, *Purchas his Prilgrimes* (London, 1625).*

1 Georg Horn (1620–1670), German historian and professor; his *De Originibus Americanis*
was published at The Hague, 1652. John Woodward (1664–1728), English geologist and
physician; his *Natural History* was published in London, 1695. Mather sent to him prior to the
writing of the *Magnalia* various contributions to be offered to the Royal Society for publication,
and Woodward seems to have been instrumental in securing his election to the Society.
"Shortly" is used here in the sense of briefly, concisely.*
2 Philippe Avril, French Jesuit missionary, traveled through Tartary in the course of an
attempted expedition to China. He detoured into Russia in the effort to obtain a passport for
his further journey.*

'that which confirms me in this Opinion, is this, That the *Americans* who
60 'Inhabit that Country, which advances farthest towards that Sea, have
'the same *Physiognomy* as those Islanders. Thus the *Vayvode*[3] of *Smolensko.*
But all the concern of this our History, is to tell how *English People* first
came into *America*; and what *English People* first came into that Part of
America, where this History is composed. Wherefore, instead of reciting
65 the many *Adventures* of the *English,* to visit these Parts of the World, I
shall but repeat the Words of one Captain *Weymouth,*[4] an *Historian,* as
well as an *Undertaker* of those *Adventures*; who Reports, *That one main End
of all these Undertakings, was to plant the Gospel in these dark Regions of* America. How well the most of the *English* Plantations have answered this
70 *main End,* it *mainly* becomes them to consider: However, I am now to tell
Mankind, that as for *One* of these *English* Plantations, this was not only a
main End, but the *sole End* upon which it was erected. If they that are
solicitous about the Interests of the *Gospel,* would know *what* and *where*
that Plantation is; be it noted, That all the vast Country from *Florida*
75 to *Nova-Francia,*[5] was at first called *Virginia*; but this *Virginia* was distinguished into *North Virginia* and *South Virginia,* till that Famous
Traveller Captain *John Smith,* in the Year 1614. presenting unto the Court
of *England* a Draught[6] of *North Virginia,* got it called by the Name of
NEW-ENGLAND; which Name has been ever since allowed unto my
80 Country, as unto the most *Resembling Daughter,* to the chief Lady of the
European World.[7] Thus the Discoveries of the Country proceeded so far,
that K. *James* I. did by his *Letters Patents* under the Great Seal of *England,*
in the 18th Year of his Reign, give and grant unto a certain Honourable
Council Established at *Plymouth,* in the County of *Devon,* for the Planting,
85 Ruling, and Ordering, and Governing of *New-England* in *America,* and
to their Sucessors and Assigns, all that Part of *America,* lying and being
in Breadth, from *Forty Degrees* of Northerly Latitude, from the Equinoctial
Line, to the *Forty-Eighth Degree* of the said Northerly Latitude Inclusively;
and the *Length* of, and within all the Breadth aforesaid, throughout all
90 the *firm Lands* from Sea to Sea. This at last is the Spot of *Earth,* which the
God of Heaven *Spied out* for the Seat of such *Evangelical,* and *Ecclesiastical,*
and very remarkable Transactions, as require to be made an 𝕳𝖎𝖘𝖙𝖔𝖗𝖞;
here 'twas that our Blessed 𝕵𝖊𝖘𝖚𝖘 intended a *Resting-place,* must I say?
Or only an *Hiding-place* for those *Reformed CHURCHES,* which have given

61   *Smolensko/Smotensko*

[3] An elected sovereign, or governor of a province.
[4] George Weymouth (Waymouth, fl. 1601–1612), in 1605 made a voyage of reconnaissance
to the coast of New England for a group projecting colonization.*
[5] "New France," the French settlements in Canada.
[6] Map.*
[7] Old England.*

95 him a little Accomplishment of his Eternal Father's Promise unto him; to be; we hope, yet further accomplished, *of having the utmost Parts of the Earth for his Possession?*[8]

§. 7. The Learned *Joseph Mede*[1] conjectures that the *American Hemi-*
99 *sphere* will escape the *Conflagration* of the *Earth*, which we expect at the descent of our Lord JESUS CHRIST from *Heaven:* And that the People here will not have a share in the Blessedness which the *Renovated World* shall enjoy, during the *Thousand Years* of *Holy Rest* promised unto the Church of God:[2] And that the Inhabitants of these Regions, who were
5 Originally *Scytheans*, and therein a notable fulfilment of the Prophecy, about the *Enlargement of* Japhet, will be the *Gog* and *Magog* whom the *Devil* will seduce to Invade the *New-Jerusalem*, with an Envious Hope to gain the *Angelical Circumstances* of the People there.[3] All this is but Conjecture; and it may be 'twill appear unto some as little probable, as that
10 of the later *Pierre Poiret*[4] in his *L'Oeconomie Divine*, that by *Gog* and *Magog* are meant the *Devils* and the *Damned*, which he thinks will be let loose at the end of the *Thousand Years*, to make a furious, but a fruitless Attempt on the glorified Saints of the *New-Jerusalem*. However, I am going to give unto the *Christian Reader* an *History* of *some feeble Attempts* made in the
15 *American Hemisphere* to anticipate the State of the *New-Jerusalem*, as far as the unavoidable *Vanity* of *Humane Affairs*, and *Influence* of *Satan* upon them would allow of it; and of *many worthy Persons*, whose Posterity, if they make a *Squadron* in the *Fleets* of *Gog* and *Magog*, will be *Apostates* deserving a Room, and a Doom with the *Legions* of the *Grand Apostate*,
20 that will deceive the Nations to that *Mysterious Enterprize*.

CHAP. II.

Primordia:[1] *Or, The Voyage to* NEW-ENGLAND, *which produced the First Settlement of* NEW-PLYMOUTH; *with an Account of many Remarkable and Memorable Providences relating to that Voyage.*

25 §. 1. A Number of devout and serious *Christians* in the *English Nation*, finding the *Reformation* of the *Church* in that Nation, according to the WORD OF GOD, and the Design of many among the *First*

---

[8] Ps. 2.8.

---

[1] See endnote to General Introduction p. 93, ll. 46–48.
[2] Cf. endnote to Attestation p. 73, l. 25.
[3] See Gen. 9.27; Rev. 20.7–10.
[4] Pierre Poiret (1646–1719), Huguenot minister and mystic.*

---

[1] "The first beginnings."

Reformers, to labour under a sort of *hopeless Retardation,* they did, *Anno* 1602.
in the *North* of *England,* enter into a COVENANT, wherein expressing
30 themselves desirous, not only to attend the *Worship* of our Lord Jesus
Christ, with a freedom from humane *Inventions* and *Additions,* but also to
enjoy *all* the Evangelical Institutions of that Worship, they did like those
Macedonians, that are *therefore* by the Apostle *Paul* commended, *give
themselves up, first unto God, and then to one another.*[2] These Pious People
35 finding that their Brethren and Neighbours in the Church of *England,*
as then *established by Law,* took offence at these their Endeavours after a
Scriptural Reformation; and being loth to live in the continual *Vexations,*
which they felt arising from their *Non-Conformity* to things which their
Consciences accounted *Superstitious* and *Unwarrantable,*[3] they peaceably
40 and willingly embraced a *Banishment* into the *Netherlands;* where they
settled at the City of *Leyden,* about Seven or Eight Years after their First
Combination. And now in that City this People sojourned, an Holy
CHURCH of the Blessed JESUS, for several Years under the Pastoral
Care of Mr. *John Robinson,* who had for his *Help* in the *Government* of the
45 Church, a most Wise, Grave, good Man, Mr. *William Brewster,* the ruling
Elder.[4] Indeed Mr. *John Robinson* had been in his *younger* time, (as very
good Fruit hath sometimes been, before Age hath *Ripened* it) *Sowred*
with the Principles of the most Rigid *Separation,* in the maintaining
whereof he composed and published some little Treatises, and in the
50 Management of the Controversie made no Scruple to call the incomparable Dr. *Ames*[5] himself, Dr. *Amiss,* for opposing such a Degree of
Separation. But this worthy Man suffered himself at length to be so far
convinced by his Learned *Antagonist,* that with a most Ingenious *Retracta-
tion,* he afterwards writ a little Book[6] to prove the *Lawfulness* of one thing,
55 which his mistaken *Zeal* had formerly impugned. Several Years, even till
1625. and about the *Fiftieth* Year of his own Age, continued he a Blessing
unto the whole Church of God, and at last, when he dy'd, he left behind
him in his immortal Writings, a *Name* very much embalm'd among the
People that are best able to judge of *Merit;* and even among such, as

55 impugned. Several/impugned several
C.M.

[2] II Cor. 8.5.
[3] The Puritans denounced as "Superstitious" what they considered the residues of popery
in Church of England ecclesiastical forms, and as "Unwarrantable" anything in either dogma
or polity which they found not directly enjoined by Scripture.
[4] John Robinson (1576?–1625); until his death, the Plymouth colony hoped he would
rejoin them. William Brewster (1567–1644) continued as elder of the church at Plymouth in
New England.*
[5] William Ames (1576–1633), English Puritan divine, was for some years resident in Leyden
before becoming professor of theology at Franeker. It was from his *Medulla Sacrae Theologicae*
that Puritan thinking largely derived; hence he was "incomparable" to Mather.*
[6] *A Treatise on the Lawfullness of Hearing Ministers in the Church of England* (Amsterdam, 1634).*

60 about the Matters of *Church-Discipline*, were not of his Perswasion. Of
such an eminent Character was he, while he *lived*, that when *Arminianism*[7]
so much prevailed, as it then did in the *low Countries*, those famous
Divines, *Polyander*, and *Festus Hommius*,[8] employed this our Learned
Robinson to dispute publickly in the University of *Leyden* against *Episcopius*,[9]
65 and the other Champions of that Grand *Choak-weed*[10] *of true Christianity:*
And when he *Died*, not only the *University*, and Ministers of the City,
accompanied him to his *Grave*, with all their accustomed *Solemnities*, but
some of the Chief among them with sorrowful Resentments[11] and
Expressions affirmed, *That all the Churches of our Lord Jesus Christ had*
70 *sustained a great Loss by the Death of this worthy Man.*

§. 2. The *English Church* had not been very long at *Leyden* before they
found themselves encountred with many Inconveniencies. They felt that
they were neither for *Health*, nor *Purse*, nor *Language* well accommodated;
but the concern which they most of all had, was for their *Posterity*. They
75 saw, that whatever *Banks* the *Dutch* had against the Inroads of the *Sea*,
they had not sufficient Ones against a *Flood* of manifold *Profaneness*. They
could not with *Ten Years Endeavour* bring their Neighbours, particularly
to any suitable Observation of the LORD's DAY; without which they
knew, that all *practical Religion* must wither Miserably. They beheld some
80 of their *Children*, by the Temptations of the Place, which were especially
given in the licentious Ways of many *Young People*, drawn into dangerous
Extravagancies. Moreover, they were very loth to lose their Interest in
the *English Nation*; but were desirous rather to enlarge their *King's
Dominions*. They found themselves also under a very strong disposition of
85 *Zeal*, to attempt the Establishment of 𝕮𝖔𝖓𝖌𝖗𝖊𝖌𝖆𝖙𝖎𝖔𝖓𝖆𝖑 𝕮𝖍𝖚𝖗𝖈𝖍𝖊𝖘 in the
remote Parts of the World; where they hoped they should be reached by
the Royal Influence of their *Prince*, in whose *Allegiance* they chose to live
and die; at the same time likewise hoping that the *Ecclesiasticks*, who had
thus driven them out of the Kingdom into a *New World*, for nothing in the
90 World but their *Non-Conformity* to certain *Rites*, by the Imposers confessed
Indifferent,[1] would be *ashamed* ever to persecute them with any further
Molestations, at the distance of a Thousand Leagues. These *Reasons* were
deeply considered by the *Church*; and after many *Deliberations*, accompanied with the most solemn *Humiliations* and *Supplications* before the
95 God of Heaven, they took up a *Resolution*, under the conduct of Heaven,

---

[7] Jacobus Arminius (1560–1609), unlike the Calvinists, held that Christ died for all men,
not just the elect, and that divine sovereignty is not compatible with free will in man.*
[8] Johannes Polyander a Kerckhoven (1568–1646), professor of theology at Leyden. Festus
Hommius (1576–1642), pastor of the Walloon church at Leyden.*
[9] Simon Episcopius (Bisschop, 1583–1643), Dutch theologian and professor at Leyden.*
[10] The chokeweed, a species of broomrape, a parasitic herb which chokes other plants.*
[11] Feelings or emotions of any kind.

---

[1] That is, not essential in points of faith or ecclesiastical polity.

to REMOVE into *AMERICA*; the opened Regions whereof had now filled all *Europe* with Reports. It was resolved, that *part* of the Church should go before their Brethren, to *prepare* a place for the Rest; and where-as the *Minor part* of younger and stronger Men were to go first, the *Pastor* was to stay with the *Major*, till *they* should see cause to follow. Nor was there any occasion for this Resolve, in any weariness which the *States* of *Holland* had of their Company, as was basely *whispered* by their Adversaries; therein like those who of old assign'd the same cause for the Departure of the *Israelites* out of *Egypt:* For the Magistrates of *Leyden* in their Court, reproving the *Walloons*, gave this Testimony for our *English*; *These English have lived now Ten Years among us, and yet we never had any Accusation against any one of them*; *whereas your Quarrels are continual*.

§. 3. These good People were now *satisfy'd*, they had as plain a command of Heaven to attempt a Removal, as ever their Father *Abraham* had for his leaving the *Caldean* Territories; and it was nothing but such a *Satisfaction* that could have carried them thro' such, otherwise insuperable Difficulties, as they met withal. But in this Removal the *Terminus ad Quem* was not yet resolved upon. The Country of *Guiana* flattered them with the Promises of a *perpetual Spring*, and a Thousand other comfortable Entertainments. But the probable disagreement of so *Torrid* a Climate unto *English Bodies*; and the more dangerous Vicinity of the *Spaniards* to that Climate; were Considerations which made them fear that Country would be *too Hot* for them. They rather propounded some Country bordering upon *Virginia*; and unto this purpose, they sent over Agents[1] into *England*, who so far treated not only with the *Virginia Company*,[2] but with several great Persons about the Court;[3] unto whom they made Evident *their Agreement with the French reformed Churches in all things whatsoever, except in a few small accidental Points*; that at last, after many tedious *Delays*, and after the loss of many *Friends* and *Hopes* in those delays, they obtained a *Patent* for a quiet Settlement in those Territories; and the Archbishop of *Canterbury* himself[4] gave them some Expectations that they should never be disturbed in that Exercise of Religion, at which they aimed in their Settlement; yea, when Sir *Robert Nanton*, then Principal Secretary of State unto King *James*,[5] moved his Majesty to give way, *that such a People might enjoy their Liberty of Conscience under his gracious Protection in America, where they would endeavour the Advancement of his Majesty's Dominions, and the Enlargement of the Interests of the Gospel*;

---

[1] The agents were Robert Cushman and John Carver.

[2] The Virginia Company was in 1606 chartered by the king, with rights of trade and settlement between 34 and 41 degrees north latitude.

[3] One of the principal persons "about the Court" with whom the agents met was Sir Edwin Sandys (1561–1629).

[4] George Abbot (1562–1633), archbishop, 1611–1633.*

[5] Sir Robert Naunton (1563–1635), secretary of state, 1618–1623.*

the King said, *it was a good and honest Motion*. All this notwithstanding,
35 they never made use of that *Patent*:[6] But being inform'd of *NEW-
ENGLAND*, *thither* they diverted their Design, thereto induced by sundry
Reasons; but particularly by *this*, that the Coast being extreamly well
circumstanced for *Fishing*, they might therein have some immediate
Assistance against the hardships of their First Encounters. Their Agents
40 then again sent over to *England*, concluded *Articles* between *them* and such
Adventurers,[7] as would be concerned with them in their present Under-
takings. *Articles*, that were indeed sufficiently *hard* for those poor Men,
that were now to transplant themselves into an horrid *Wilderness*. The
Diversion of their Enterprize from the *First* State and Way of it, caus'd an
45 unhappy Division among those that should have Encourag'd it; and
many of *them* hereupon fell off. But the *Removers* having already sold their
Estates, to put the Money into a *Common Stock*, for the welfare of the
Whole; and their *Stock* as well as their *Time*, spending so fast as to threaten
them with an *Army* of Straits, if they delayed any longer; they nimbly
50 dispatcht the best *Agreements* they could, and came away furnished with
a Resolution for a large Tract of Land in the *South-West* Parts of *New-
England*.

§. 4. All things now being in some Readiness, and a couple of Ships,
one called, *The Speedwell*, t'other, *The May-flower*, being hired for their
55 Transportation, they solemnly set apart a Day for *Fasting* and *Prayer*;
wherein their Pastor preached unto them upon *Ezra* 8. 21. *I proclaimed a
Fast there, at the River* Ahava, *that we might afflict our selves before our God, to
seek of him a right way for us, and for our little ones, and for all our substance.*

After the fervent Supplications of this Day, accompanied by their
60 affectionate Friends, they took their leave of the pleasant City, where
they had been *Pilgrims* and *Strangers* now for Eleven Years. *Delft-Haven*
was the Town, where they went on Board one of their Ships,[1] and there
they had such a mournful parting from their Brethren, as even *drowned*
the *Dutch* Spectators themselves, then standing on the *Shore*, in Tears.
65 Their excellent *Pastor*, on his Knees, by the *Sea-side*, poured out their
mutual Petitions unto God; and having wept in one another's Arms, as
long as the *Wind* and the *Tide* would permit them, they bad *Adieu*. So
sailing to *Southampton* in *England*, they there found the other of their
Ships come from *London*, with the rest of their Friends that were to be the

---

41 *Adventurers/Adventures* C.M.

---

6 Because of their "Resolution" to seek a place of settlement farther north, a Patent, or
franchise to settle, from the Virginia Company was not valid.*
7 London merchants and others who furnished, or "adventured," the money for the enterprise.

---

1 The *Speedwell*.

70 *Companions of the Voyage.* Let my Reader place the *Chronology* of this
Business on *July* 2.[2] 1620. And know, that the faithful *Pastor* of this
People immediately sent after them a *Pastoral Letter*; a Letter filled with
Holy Counsels unto them, to settle their *Peace* with God in their own
Consciences, by an exact *Repentance* of all Sin whatsoever, that so they
75 might more easily bear all the Difficulties that were now before them; and
then to maintain a good *Peace.* with one another, and beware of giving or
taking *Offences*; and avoid all Discoveries of a *Touchy Humour*; but use
much *Brotherly Forbearance*, [where, by the way, he had this remarkable
Observation, *In my own experience few or none have been found that sooner give*
80 *Offence, than those that easily take it; neither have they ever proved sound and*
profitable Members of Societies, who have nourished this Touchy Humour;] as
also to take heed of a *private Spirit*,[3] and all *retiredness of Mind in each Man,*
for his own proper Advantage; and likewise to be careful, that the *House of*
God, which *they* were, might not be shaken with unnecessary *Novelties* or
85 *Oppositions:* Which LETTER afterwards produced most happy Fruits
among them.

§. 5. On *August* 5th, 1620. they set Sail from *Southampton*; but if it
shall, as I believe it *will*, afflict my Reader to be told what Heart-breaking
Disasters befel them, in the very beginning of their Undertaking, let him
90 glorifie God, who carried *them* so well through *their* greater Affliction.

They were by bad *Weather* twice beaten back, before the came to the
Land's End: But it was judged, that the *Badness* of the *Weather* did not
retard them so much as the *deceit* of a *Master*,[1] who, grown *Sick* of the
Voyage, made such Pretences about the Leakiness of his Vessel, that they
95 were forced at last wholly to dismiss that lesser Ship from the Service.
Being now all stowed into *one Ship*,[2] on the *Sixth* of *September* they put to
Sea; but they met with such terrible Storms, that the principal Persons
on Board had serious Deliberations upon returning Home again;
99 however, after long beating upon the *Atlantick* Ocean, they fell in with
the Land at *Cape-Cod*, about the *Ninth* of *November* following, where going
on Shore they fell upon their Knees, with many and hearty Praises unto
God, who had been *their Assurance*, when they were *afar off upon the Sea,*
and was to be further *so*, now that they were come to the *Ends of the*
5 *Earth.*

But why at this *Cape*? *Here* was not the Port which they intended; *this*
was not the Land for which they had provided. There was indeed a most

---

78 where, by the way,/whereby the way   93 who, grown/who grown

---

[2] The correct date was July 22.*
[3] Cf. endnote to Prefatory Poems p. 74, l. 21.

---

[1] Of the *Speedwell*, by name "Mr. Reinolds."*
[2] The *Mayflower.*

wonderful *Providence* of God, over a Pious and a Praying People, in this *Disappointment!* The most *crooked Way* that ever was gone, even that of
10 *Israel's* Peregrination *thro' the Wilderness*, may be called *a right Way*, such was the *way* of this little *Israel*, now going *into* a *Wilderness*.[3]

§. 6. Their design was to have sat down somewhere about *Hudson's* River; but some of their Neighbours in *Holland* having a Mind themselves to settle a Plantation there, secretly and sinfully contracted with the
15 Master of the Ship, employed for the Transportation of these our English *Exiles*, by a more *Northerly* Course, to put a Trick upon them. 'Twas in the pursuance of this *Plot*, that not only the *Goods*, but also the *Lives* of all on Board were now hazarded, by the Ships falling among the Shoals of *Cape-Cod:* Where they were so entangled among dangerous *Breakers*, thus
20 late in the Year, that the *Company* got at last into the *Cape-Harbour, Broke off* their Intentions of going any further. And yet behold the watchful Providence of God over them that seek him! This *False-dealing* proved a *Safe-dealing* for the good People against whom it was used. Had they been carried according to their desire unto *Hudson's River*, the *Indians* in those
25 Parts were at this time so Many, and so Mighty, and so Sturdy, that in probability all this little feeble Number of Christians had been Massacred by these bloody *Salvages*, as not long after some others were: Whereas the good Hand of God now brought them to a Country wonderfully prepared for their Entertainment, by a sweeping *Mortality* that had lately
30 been among the Natives. *We have heard with our Ears, O God, our Fathers have told us, what work thou didst in their Days, in the times of Old; how thou dravest out the Heathen with thy Hand, and plantedst them; how thou did'st afflict the People, and cast them out!*[1] The *Indians* in these Parts had newly, even about a Year or Two before, been visited with such a prodigious Pesti-
35 lence; as carried away not a *Tenth*, but *Nine Parts* of *Ten*, (yea, 'tis said, *Nineteen* of *Twenty*) among them: So that the *Woods* were almost cleared of those pernicious Creatures, to make Room for a *better Growth*. It is Remarkable, that a *Frenchman* who not long before these Transactions, had by a Shipwreck been made a Captive among the *Indians* of this
40 Country, did, as the Survivers reported, just before he dy'd in their Hands, tell those *Tawny Pagans, that God being angry with them for their Wickedness, would not only destroy them all, but also People the place with another Nation, which would not live after their Brutish Manners.* Those Infidels then Blasphemously reply'd, *God could not kill them;* which Blasphemous mistake
45 was confuted by an horrible and unusual *Plague*, whereby they were

---

[3] For "*Israel's* Peregrination," see Exod. 13.17–18. "*Right*" is used here in the obsolete sense of straight, not bent, as opposed to "*crooked*" above. For crooked and right ways, see Ps. 125.5, Prov. 2.15, and Gen. 24.48; I Sam. 12.23; II Pet. 2.15.

---

[1] Ps. 44.1–2.

consumed in such vast Multitudes, that our *first Planters* found the Land almost covered with their unburied Carcases; and they that were left *alive*, were smitten into awful and humble Regards of the *English*, by the Terrors which the Remembrance of the *Frenchman's* Prophesie had Im-
50 printed on them.

§. 7. Inexpressible the Hardships to which this *chosen Generation* was now exposed! Our Saviour once directed his Disciples to deprecate *a flight in the Winter*; but these Disciples of our Lord were now arrived at a very *Cold* Country, in the beginning of a Rough and Bleak *Winter*; the
55 *Sun* was withdrawn into *Sagittarius*,[1] whence he shot the penetrating *Arrows* of *Cold*; feathered with nothing but *Snow*, and pointed with *Hail*; and the *Days* left them to behold the *Frost*-bitten and *Weather*-beaten face of the *Earth*, were grown shorter than the *Nights*, wherein they had yet more trouble to get shelter from the increasing Injuries of the *Frost* and
60 *Weather*. It was a relief to those Primitive Believers, who were cast on Shore at *Malta*, *That the Barbarous People show'd them no little Kindness, because of the present Rain, and because of the Cold*. But these Believers in *our* Primitive Times, were more afraid of the *Barbarous People* among whom they were now cast, than they were of the *Rain, or Cold*: These *Barbarians*
65 were at the first so far from accommodating them with *Bundles of Sticks* to *Warm* them, that they let Fly other sorts of *Sticks* (that is to say, *Arrows*) to *Wound* them: And the very *Looks* and *Shouts* of those *Grim Salvages*, had not much less of Terrour in them, than if they had been so many *Devils*. It is not long since I compared this remove of our Fathers,
70 to that of *Abraham*, whereas I must now add, that if our Father *Abraham*, called out of *Ur*, had been directed unto the *Desarts* of *Arabia*, instead of the *Land flowing with Milk and Honey*, the *Trial of his Faith* had been greater than it was; but such was the *Trial of the Faith* in these holy Men, who followed the Call of God into *Desarts* full of dismal Circumstances. All
75 this they chearfully underwent, in hope, that they should settle the *Worship* and *Order* of the Gospel, and the *Kingdom* of our Lord Jesus Christ in these Regions, and that thus enlarging the *Dominion*, they should thereby so Merit the *Protection* of the Crown of *England*, as to be never abandoned unto any further *Persecutions*, from any Party of their *Fellow*
80 *Subjects*, for their Consciencious Regards unto the *Reformation*. Their Proposal was, *Exiguam sedem Sacris, Litusque rogamus, Innocuum, & cunctis undamq; auramq; Patentem*.[2]

81 *Litusque/Littusque*

[1] The ninth sign of the zodiac, corresponding to late November and early December; also a zodiacal constellation, which the Greeks described as a centaur drawing his bow to shoot an arrow.
[2] "And now crave a scant home for our religion, a harmless landing place, and air and water free to all."*

§. 8. Finding at their Arrival, that what other Powers they had, were
made useless by the *undesigned Place* of their Arrival; they did, as the
85 *Light of Nature* it self directed them, immediately in the Harbour, sign an
Instrument,[1] as a Foundation of their future and needful *Government*;
wherein Declaring themselves the Loyal Subjects of the Crown of
England, they did combine into a *Body Politick*, and solemnly engage
Submission and Obedience to the *Laws, Ordinances, Acts, Constitutions* and
90 *Officers*, that from time to time should be thought most convenient for the
general Good of the *Colony*. This was done on *Nov.* 11th, 1620. and they
chose one Mr. *John Carver*,[2] a Pious and Prudent Man; their Governour.

Hereupon they sent Ashore to look a convenient Seat for their intended Habitation: And while the Carpenter was fitting of their Shallop,
95 *Sixteen Men* tender'd themselves, to go, by Land, on the Discovery.
Accordingly on *Nov.* 16th, 1620. they made a dangerous Adventure;
following five *Indians*, whom they spied Flying before them, into the
Woods for many Miles; from whence, after two or three Days Ramble,
99 they returned with some *Ears* of *Indian Corn*, which were an *Eshcol*[3] for
their Company; but with a poor and small Encouragement, as unto any
Scituation.[4] When the Shallop was fitted, about thirty more went in it
upon a further Discovery; who prospered little more, than only to find a
little *Indian Corn*, and bring to the Company some Occasions of doubtful
5 Debate, whether they should *here* fix their Stakes. Yet these Expeditions
on Discovery had this one Remarkable Smile of Heaven upon them;
that being made before the *Snow* covered the Ground, they met with some
Indian Corn; for which, 'twas their purpose honestly to pay the Natives
on demand; and this Corn served them for *Seed* in the Spring following,
10 which else they had not been seasonably furnished withal. So that it
proved, in Effect, their Deliverance from the *Terrible Famine*.

§. 9. The Month of *November* being spent in many *Supplications* to
Almighty God, and *Consultations* one with another, about the Direction
of their Course; at last, on *Dec.* 6. 1620. they manned the Shallop with
15 about eighteen or twenty Hands, and went out upon a *third Discovery*. So
bitterly Cold was the Season, that the Spray of the Sea lighting on their
Cloaths, glazed them with an immediate Congelation; yet they kept
Cruising about the Bay of *Cape-Cod*, and that Night they got safe down the
Bottom of the Bay. There they Landed, and there they tarried that Night;

---

[1] "Powers": the Virginia Company Patent. For Puritans, the "Light of Nature" consisted
of the common principles of reason in man which persisted after the Fall, and by which,
even without the light of grace, he could discern the difference between good and bad. The
"Instrument" was the Mayflower Compact.*

[2] John Carver (*c.*1576–1621), deacon of the church as well as governor of the colony.

[3] That is, a cluster of grapes. In the Old Testament (Num. 13.23), the name of the fertile
valley from which Moses' spies brought back a cluster of grapes as a sign of its riches.*

[4] An old spelling for "Situation," preserved in the name of the town of "Scituate" on the
coast above Plymouth.

20 and unsuccessfully Ranging about all the next Day, at Night they made
a little *Barricado* of Boughs and Logs, wherein the most weary slept. The
next Morning after Prayers, they suddenly were surrounded with a
Crue[1] of *Indians*, who let Fly a Show'r of *Arrows* among them; whereat
our distressed handful of *English* happily recovering their Arms, which
25 they had laid by from the Moisture of the Weather, they vigorously
discharged their *Muskets* upon the Salvages, who astonished at the strange
Effects of such *Dead-doing Things*, as *Powder* and *Shot*, fled apace into the
Woods; but not one of ours was wounded by the *Indian* Arrows that flew
like *Hail* about their Ears, and pierced through sundry of their *Coats:*
30 For which they returned their solemn Thanks unto God their Saviour;
and they call'd the place by the Name of, *The First Encounter*. From hence
they coasted along, till an horrible *Storm* arose, which tore their *Vessel*
at such a rate, and threw them into the midst of such dangerous *Breakers*,
it was reckoned little short of *Miracle* that they escaped alive. In the End
35 they got under the Lee of a small *Island*, where going Ashore, they kindled
Fires for their succour against the Wet and Cold; it was the Morning
before they found it was an *Island*, whereupon they rendred their Praises
to him, that *hitherto had helped them*;[2] and the Day following, which was,
The Lord's Day, the difficulties now upon them, did not hinder them from
40 spending it in the devout and pious Exercises of a *Sacred Rest*. On the
next Day they sounded the *Harbour*, and found it fit for Shipping; they
visited the *Main Land* also, and found it accommodated with pleasant
Fields and Brooks; whereof they carried an encouraging Report unto
their Friends on Board. So they resolved that they would *here* pitch their
45 Tents; and Sailing up to the *Town* of *Plymouth* [as with an hopeful *Prolep-
sis*, my Reader shall now call it; for otherwise, by the *Indians* 'twas called,
Patuxet;] on the Twenty-fifth Day of *December* they began to erect the
First House that ever was in that memorable Town; an House for the
general Entertainment of their Persons and Estates: And yet it was not
50 long before an unhappy Accident burnt unto the Ground their House,
wherein some of their principal Persons then lay Sick; who were forced
nimbly to Fly out of the fired House, or else they had been blown up with
the *Powder* then Lodged there. After this, they soon went upon the Building of more little *Cottages*; and upon the settling of good *Laws*, for the
55 better Governing of such as were to Inhabit those *Cottages*. They then
resolved, that until they could be further strengthned in their Settlement,
by the Authority of *England*, they would be governed by *Rulers* chosen
from among themselves, who were to proceed according to the Laws of
England, as near as they could, in the Administration of their Govern-

[1] That is, "crew."
[2] I Sam. 7.12.*

60 ment; and such other *By-Laws*, as by Common Consent should be judged
necessary for the Circumstances of the Plantation.

§. 10. If the Reader would know, how these good People fared the
rest of the Melancholy *Winter*; let him know, That besides the Exercises
of Religion, with other Work enough, there was the *care of the Sick* to take
65 up no little part of their Time. 'Twas a most heavy Trial of their Patience,
whereto they were called the first Winter of this their *Pilgrimage*, and
enough to convince them, and remind them, that they were but *Pilgrims*.¹
The *Hardships* which they encountred, were attended with, and productive
of *deadly Sicknesses*; which in two or three Months carried off more than
70 *Half* their Company. They were but meanly provided against these
unhappy *Sicknesses*; but there died sometimes *Two*, sometimes *Three* in a
Day; till scarce *Fifty* of them were left alive; and of those *Fifty*, sometimes
there were scarce *Five* well at a time to look after the Sick. Yet their
profound Submission to the Will of God, their Christian Readiness to
75 help one another, accompanied with a joyful Assurance of another and
better World, carried them chearfully thro' the Sorrows of this *Mortality*:
Nor was there heard among them a continual *Murmur* against those who
had by *unreasonable Impositions* driven them into all these Distresses. And
there was this *Remarkable Providence* further in the Circumstances of this
80 *Mortality*, that if a *Disease* had not more easily fetcht so many of this
Number away to Heaven, a *Famine* would probably have destroy'd them
all, before their expected Supplies from *England* were Arrived. But what
a wonder was it that all the Bloody Salvages far and near did not cut
off this *little Remnant*!² If he that once muzzled the *Lions* ready to devour
85 the Man of Desires,³ had not *Admirably*, I had almost said, *Miraculously*
restrained them, *These* had been all devoured! But this People of God
were come into a *Wilderness* to *Worship Him*;⁴ and so *He* kept their
Enemies from such Attempts, as would otherwise have soon *annihilated*
this Poor Handful of Men, thus far already diminished. They saw no
90 *Indians* all the Winter long, but such as at the first Sight always ran away;
yea, they quickly found, that God had so turned the Hearts of these
Barbarians, as more to *Fear*, than to *Hate* his People thus cast among them.
This blessed People was as *a little Flock of Kids*, while there were many
Nations of *Indians* left still as Kennels of *Wolves* in every Corner of the
95 Country. And yet the *little Flock* suffered no damage by those Rabid
Wolves! We may and should say, *This is the Lord's Doing, 'tis marvellous
in our Eyes*.⁵

95 Rabid/Rapid

¹ Heb. 11.13.
² Isa. 1.9.*
³ Dan. 6.22. "Man of Desires": a man "greatly loved."*
⁴ Exod. 3.18.*
⁵ Ps. 118.23; quoted by Matt. 21.42.

But among the many Causes to be assigned for it, one was *This*. It was
99 afterwards by *Them* confessed, that upon the Arrival of the *English* in
these Parts, the *Indians* employ'd their *Sorcerers*, whom they call *Powaws*,
like *Balaam*, to *Curse* them, and let loose their *Demons* upon them, to
Shipwreck them, to Distract them, to Poison them, or any way to Ruin
them. All the noted *Powaws* in the Country spent three Days together in
5 Diabolical *Conjurations*, to obtain the Assistances of the *Devils* against the
Settlement of these our *English*; but the *Devils* at length acknowledged
unto them, that they could not hinder those People from their becoming
the *Owners* and *Masters* of the Country; whereupon the *Indians* resolved
upon a good Correspondence with our *New-Comers*; and God convinced
10 them, that there was no *Enchantment* or *Divination* against such a People.

§. 11. The doleful *Winter* broke up sooner than was usual. But our
crippled Planters were not more comforted with the early advance of the
Spring, than they were surpriz'd with the appearance of two *Indians*,
who in broken *English* bade them, *Welcome Englishmen!* It seems that one
15 of these *Indians* had been in the Eastern Parts of *New-England*, acquainted
with some of the *English* Vessels that had been formerly *Fishing* there; but
the other of the *Indians*, and he from whom they had most of Service,
was a Person provided by the very singular Providence of God for that
Service. A most wicked Ship-master being on this Coast a few Years
20 before,[1] had wickedly Spirited away more than Twenty *Indians*; whom
having enticed them aboard, he presently stowed them under Hatches,
and carried them away to the *Streights*,[2] where he sold as many of them as
he could for *Slaves*. This avaritious and pernicious *Felony* laid the Foundation of grievous Annoyances to all the *English* Endeavours of Settlements,
25 especially in the Northern Parts of the Land for several Years ensuing.
The *Indians* would never *forget* or *forgive* this Injury; but when the *English*
afterwards came upon this Coast, in their *Fishing-Voyages*, they were
still assaulted in an Hostile manner, to the Killing and Wounding of many
poor Men by the angry *Natives*, in revenge of the wrong that had been
30 done them; and some intended *Plantations* here were hereby utterly
nipt in the *Bud*. But our good God so order'd it, that one of the stoln
Indians, called *Squanto*,[3] had escaped out of *Spain* into *England*; where he
lived with one Mr. *Slany*, from whom he had found a way to return into
his own Country, being brought back by one Mr. *Dermer*,[4] about half a

---

[1] Thomas Hunt (d. *c*.1620), shipmaster; commander of one of the two vessels on John Smith's
voyage to New England in 1614.*
[2] The Straits of Gibraltar.
[3] Squanto (Tisquantum, d. 1622), a Patuxet Indian.
[4] "Mr. *Slany*" was treasurer of the Newfoundland Company; Thomas Dermer, a gentleman
employed by the Council for New England, explored the New England coast in 1615–1618,
and returned in 1619, on which voyage he visited Patuxet, June 1620, bringing Squanto
with him.*

35 Year before our honest *Plymotheans* were cast upon this Continent. This *Indian* (with the other) having received much Kindness from the *English*, who he saw generally condemned the Man that first betrayed him, now made unto the *English* a return of that Kindness: And being by his Acquaintance with the *English Language*, fitted for a Conversation with
40 them, he very kindly informed them what was the present Condition of the other *Indians*; instructed them in the way of ordering their *Corn*; and acquainted them with many other things, which it was necessary for them to understand. But *Squanto* did for them a yet greater benefit than all *this*: For he brought *Massasoit*, the chief *Sachim*, or Prince of the
45 *Indians* within many Miles, with some Scores of his Attenders, to make our People a kind Visit; the Issue of which Visit was, that *Massasoit* not only entred into a firm Agreement of *Peace* with the *English*, but also they declared and submitted themselves to be Subjects of the King of *England*; into which *Peace* and *Subjection* many other *Sachims* quickly after
50 came, in the most voluntary manner that could be expressed. It seems this unlucky *Squanto* having told his Countrymen how easie it was for so great a Monarch as K. *James* to destroy them all, if they should hurt any of his People, he went on to terrifie them with a ridiculous *Rhodomantado*,[5] which they Believed, that this People kept the *Plague* in a
55 Cellar (where they kept their *Powder*) and could at their pleasure let it loose to make such Havock among them, as the Distemper had already made among them a few Years before. Thus was the *Tongue of a Dog* made useful to a feeble and sickly *Lazarus!*[6] Moreover, our *English Guns*, especially the *great* ones, made a formidable *Report* among these Ignorant
60 *Indians*; and the hopes of enjoying some Defence by the *English*, against the Potent Nation of *Narraganset-Indians*, now at War with *these*, made them yet more to Court our Friendship. This very strange Disposition of things, was extreamly advantageous to our distressed *Planters*: And who sees not herein the special *Providence* of the God *who disposeth all?*

65 ## CHAP. III

Conamur Tenues Grandia:[1] *Or, A Brief Account of the Difficulties, the Deliverances, and other Occurrences, thro' which the Plantation of* New-Plymouth *arrived unto the Consistency of a Colony.*

51 Countrymen/Conntrymen

[5] A boastful, arrogant speech.
[6] Luke 16.20–21.

---

[1] "Weak we attempt great things."*

§. 1. SEtting aside the just and great Grief of our *new Planters* for the
immature Death of their Excellent Governour,[2] succeeded by
the Worthy Mr. *Bradford*, early in the *Spring* after their first Arrival, they
spent their *Summer* somewhat comfortably, Trading with the *Indians* to
the Northward of their Plantation; in which Trade they were not a little
assisted by *Squanto*, who within a Year or two Dy'd among the *English*;
but before his Death, desired them to Pray for him, *That he might go to
the* Englishman's God *in Heaven*. And besides the assistance of *Squanto*,
they had also the help of another *Indian*, called *Hobbamok*, who continued
faithful unto the *English* Interests as long as he liv'd; tho' he sometimes
went in Danger of his Life among his Countrymen for that Fidelity. So
they jogg'd on till the Day *Twelvemonth* after their first Arrival; when
there now arrived unto them a good Number more of their old Friends
from *Holland*, for the *strengthening* of their new Plantation: But inasmuch
as they brought not a sufficient stock of Provisions with them, they rather
weakened it, than *strengthened* it.

If *Peter Martyr*[3] could magnifie the *Spaniards*, of whom he reports,
They led a miserable Life for three days together with parched Grain of Maize
only, and that not unto satiety; what shall I say of our *Englishmen*, who would
have thought a little *parched Indian Corn* a mighty *Feast?* But they wanted
it, not only three Days together; no, for two or three Months together,
they had no kind of *Corn* among them: Such was the scarcity, accompanied with the disproportion of the *Inhabitants* to the *Provisions*. However,
Peter Martyr's Conclusion may be ours, *With their Miseries this People
opened a way to those new Lands, and afterwards other Men came to Inhabit
them with ease, in respect of the Calamities which these Men have suffered*. They
were indeed very often upon the very point of *Starving*; but in their
Extremity the God of Heaven always furnished them with some *sudden
Reliefs*; either by causing some Vessels of *Strangers* occasionally to look
in upon them, or by putting them into a way to catch *Fish* in some convenient Quantities, or by some other surprizing Accidents; for which
they render'd unto Heaven the Solemn *Thanks* of their Souls. They kept
in such good *Working case*,[4] that besides their Progress in *Building*, and
Planting, and *Fishing*, they formed a sort of a *Fort*, wherein they kept a
Nightly *Watch* for their security against any Treachery of the *Indians*;
being thereto *awakened* by an horrible Massacre, which the *Indians* lately
made upon several Hundreds of the *English* in *Virginia*.[5]

§. 2. In one of the first Summers after their sitting down at *Plymouth*,

[2] John Carver.*
[3] Peter Martyr (Pietro Martire d'Anghiera, 1455–1526), wrote a history of Spanish explorations in America from 1492 to 1526.*
[4] Condition for work.
[5] In the late spring of 1622, Bradford received a letter "from a stranger," giving details
of the massacre, on March 22, of nearly four hundred Virginia settlers.*

a terrible *Drought* threatned the Ruin of all their Summers *Husbandry*. From about the middle of *May* to the middle of *July*, an extream hot *Sun*
10 beat upon their Fields, without any *Rain*, so that all their *Corn* began to Wither and Languish, and some of it was irrecoverably parched up. In this Distress they set apart a Day for *Fasting* and *Prayer*, to deprecate the Calamity that might bring them to *Fasting* thro' *Famine*; in the Morning of which Day there was no sign of any *Rain*; but before the
15 Evening the Sky was overcast with Clouds, which went not away without such easie, gentle, and yet plentiful *Showers*, as reviv'd a great part of their decay'd *Corn*, for a comfortable Harvest. The *Indians* themselves took notice of this Answer given from Heaven to the Supplications of this Devout People; and one of them said, *Now I see that the* Englishman's
20 God *is a good God; for he hath heard you, and sent you Rain, and that without such Tempest and Thunder as we use to have with our Rain; which after our* Powawing *for it, breaks down the Corn; whereas your Corn stands whole and good still; surely, your God is a good God.* The *Harvest* which God thus gave to this pious People, caused them to set apart another Day for Solemn
25 *Thanksgiving* to the glorious *Hearer of Prayers!*

§. 3. There was another most wonderful *Preservation*, vouchsafed by God unto this little Knot of Christians. One Mr. *Weston*,[1] a Merchant of good Note, interested at first in the *Plymouth* Design, afterwards deserted it; and in the Year 1622, sent over two Ships with about Sixty Men, to
30 begin a Plantation in the *Massachuset-Bay*. These Beginners being well refreshed at *Plymouth*, travelled more Northward unto a place known since by the Name of *Weymouth*; where these *Westonians*, who were *Church of England-men*, did not approve themselves like the *Plymotheans*, a pious, honest, industrious People; but followed such bad Courses, as had
35 like to have brought a Ruin upon their Neighbours, as well as themselves. Having by their *Idleness* brought themselves to *Penury*, they stole Corn from the *Indians*, and many other ways provoked them; although the Governour of *Plymouth* Writ them his very sharp disapprobation of their Proceedings. To satisfie the exasperated Salvages, divers of the *Thieves*
40 were *Stockt* and *Whipt*, and one of them at last put to *Death* by this miserable Company; which did no other Service than to afford an occasion for a *Fable* to the Roguish *Hudibras*,[2] for all Accommodation was now *too late*. The *Indians* far and near entred into a *Conspiracy* to cut off these abusive *English*; and least the Inhabitants of *Plymouth* should
45 revenge that Excision of their Countrymen, they resolv'd upon the Murther of *them* also. In pursuance of this *Plot*, Captain *Standish*,[3] the

---

[1] Thomas Weston (*c.*1574–*c.*1644), merchant-adventurer and colonist.*
[2] The chief character in the famous satirical poem *Hudibras*, by Samuel Butler, which often aimed its shafts at the Puritans.*
[3] Myles Standish (*c.*1584–1656).*

Commander of the *Militia* of *Plymouth*, Lodging on a Night, with Two or Three Men in an *Indian* House, the *Indians* proposed that they might begin the Execution of their Malice by the Assassination of the Captain, 50 as soon as ever he should be fallen asleep. However, the *watchful* Providence of God so ordered it, that the Captain could not *Sleep* all that Night; and so they durst not meddle with him. Thus was the beginning of the *Plot* put by: But the whole Plot came another way to be discovered and prevented. *Massasoit*, the Southern *Sachim*, falling Sick, the Gover-55 nour of *Plymouth* desired a couple of Gentlemen, whereof one was that good Man, Mr. *Winslow*,[4] to visit this poor *Sachim*: Whom, after their long Journey, they found lying at the point of Death with a Crue of Hellish *Powaws*, using their ineffectual *Spells* and *Howls* about him to Recover him. Upon the taking of some *English Physick*, he presently revived; and 60 thus regaining his lost Health, the Fees he Paid his *English* Doctor were, *A Confession of the Plot among several Nations of the* Indians, *to destroy the* English. He said, that they had in vain sollicited *him* to enter into that bloody Combination; but his Advice was, that the Governour of *Plymouth* should immediately take off the *principal Actors* in this Business, where-65 upon the rest being terrify'd, would soon desist. There was a Concurrence of many things to confirm the Truth of this Information; wherefore Captain *Standish* took Eight resolute Men with him to the *Westonian* Plantation; where pretending to Trade with the *Indians*, divers of the Conspirators began to Treat him in a manner very Insolent. The Captain, 70 and his little *Army* of *Eight Men*, (Reader, allow them for their *Courage* to be called so) with a prodigious Resolution, presently killed some of the Chief among these *Indians*, while the rest, after a short Combate, ran before him as fast as their Legs could carry them; nevertheless, in the midst of the Skirmishes, an *Indian* Youth ran to the *English*, desiring to 75 be with them; and declaring that the *Indians* waited but for their finishing Two *Canoo*'s, to have surprized the Ship in the Harbour, and have Massacred all the People; which had been finished, if the Captain had not arrived among them just in the *nick of Time* when he did: And an *Indian* Spy detained at *Plymouth*, when he saw the Captain return from 80 this Expedition, with the *Head* of a famous *Indian* in his *Hand*, then with a faln and frighted Countenance, acknowledged the whole Mischief intended by the *Indians* against the *English*. Releasing this Fellow, they sent him to the *Sachim* of the *Massachusets*, with Advice of what he must look for, in Case he committed any Hostility upon the Subjects of the King 85 of *England*; whereof there was this Effect, that not only that *Sachim* hereby terrified, most humbly begg'd for *Peace*, and pleaded his Ignorance of his Mens Intentions; but the rest of the *Indians*, under the same Terror,

[4] Edward Winslow (1595–1655), Assistant, 1624–1646; Governor of Plymouth Colony, 1633, 1636, 1644.

withdrew themselves to Live in the unhealthful *Swamps*, which prov'd Mortal to many of them. One of the *Westonians* was endeavouring to
90 carry unto *Plymouth* a Report of the Straits and Fears which were come upon them, and this Man losing his *Way*, saved his Life; taking a wrong Track, he escaped the Hands of the Two *Indians*, who went on hunting after him; however e're he reached *Plymouth*, care had been already taken for these wretched *Westonians* by the earlier and fuller Communications
95 of *Massasoit*. So was the Peace of *Plymouth* preserved, and so the *Westonian* Plantation broke up, went off, and came to nothing: Altho' 'twas much wished by the Holy *Robinson*, that some of the poor Heathen had been *converted* before any of them had been *Slaughtered*.

99   §. 4. A certain *Gentleman*[1] [if nothing in the following Story contradict *that Name*] was employed in obtaining from the Grand Council of *Plymouth* in *England*, a Patent in the Name of these Planters for a convenient quantity of the Country, where the Providence of God had now disposed them. This Man speaking *one* Word for *them*, spake *two* for *himself:* And surrep-
5 titiously procured the Patent in his own Name, reserving for himself and his Heirs an huge Tract of the Land; and intending the *Plymotheans* to hold the rest as *Tenants* under him. Hereupon he took on Board many *Passengers* with their Goods; but having Sailed no further than the *Downs*, the Ship sprang a Leak; and besides this Disaster, which alone
10 was enough to have stopt the Voyage, one Strand of their Cable was accidentally cut; by which means it broke in a stress of Wind; and they were in extream danger of being wrack'd upon the *Sands*. Having with much Cost recruited their *Loss*, and encreased the Number of their *Passengers*, they put out again to Sea; but after they had got half Way, one
15 of the saddest and longest Storms that had been known since the Days of the Apostle *Paul*,[2] drove them home to *England* again, with a Vessel well nigh torn to pieces, tho' the Lives of the People, which were above an Hundred, mercifully preserved. This Man, by all his tumbling backward and forward, was by this time grown so *Sick* of his *Patent*, that he
20 *vomited* it up; he assigned it over to the Company, but they afterwards obtained *another*, under the Umbrage[3] whereof they could now more effectually carry on the Affairs of their New *Colony*. The Passengers went over afterwards in another Vessel; and quickly after that another Vessel of Passengers also arrived in the Country: Namely, in the Year 1623.

---

1   in/and   C.M.   9   Disaster/Dissaster

[1] John Peirce, of whom little is known except that he was a citizen of London; the patent was dated June 1, 1621.*
[2] Acts 27.14 to end of chapter.
[3] "Umbrage," in the obsolete sense of shelter or protection. The "they" who obtained, in 1629, another patent from the Council for New England were adventurers formerly associated with Peirce in plans for New England settlement.*

25 Among these Passengers were divers Worthy and Useful Men, who were come to *seek the Welfare of this little* Israel; tho' at their coming they were as diversly affected, as the Rebuilders of the Temple at *Jerusalem:* Some were *grieved* when they saw *how bad* the Circumstances of their Friends were, and others were *glad* that they were *no worse.*[4]

30 §. 5. The Immature Death of Mr. *Robinson* in *Holland,* with many ensuing Disasters, hindred a great part of the *English* Congregation at *Leyden,* from coming over to the *Remnant here separated from their Brethren.* Hence it was, that altho' this *Remnant* of that Church were blessed with an *Elder*[1] so *apt to Teach,* that he attended all the other Works of a *Minister;*
35 yet they had not a *Pastor* to dispence the *Sacraments* among them, till the Year 1629, when one Mr. *Ralph Smith*[2] undertook the Pastoral Charge of this Holy *Flock.* But long before that, namely, in the Year 1624. the *Adventurers* in *England,* with whom this Company held a *Correspondence,*[3] did send over unto them a *Minister,*[4] who did them no manner of good; but
40 by his Treacherous and Mischievous Tricks at last utterly destroyed that *Correspondence.* The first *Neat-Cattel,*[5] namely, Three *Heifers* and a *Bull,* that ever were brought into this Land, now coming with him, did the Land certainly better Service than was ever done by *him,* who sufficiently forgot that Scriptural Emblem of a Minister, *The Ox Treading out the Corn.*[6] This
45 Minister at his first arrival did caress them with such extream Showes of Affection and Humility, that they were very much taken with him; nevertheless, within a little while, he used most malignant Endeavours to make *Factions* among them, and confound all their *Civil* and *Sacred* Order. At last there fell into the Hands of the Governour his *Letters*
50 home to *England,* filled with wicked and lying Accusations against the People; of which things being shamefully Convicted, the Authority Sentenced him to be expell'd the *Plantation,* only they allowed him to stay *Six Months,* with secret Reservations and Expectations to release him from that Sentence, if he approved himself sound in the *Repentance*
55 which he now expressed. *Repentance,* I say; for he did now publickly in the *Church* confess with Tears, that the *Censure of the Church was less than he deserved;* he acknowledged, *That he had slanderously abus'd the good People, and that God might justly lay Innocent Blood to his Charge; for he knew not what*

45 Showes/Showers C.M.

---

[4] Neh. 2.10, 13, 17–20.

[1] William Brewster.*
[2] Ralph Smith (d. 1661), of strong separatist leanings, was minister at Plymouth from 1629 to 1636.*
[3] Commercial intercourse, business relations.
[4] John Lyford came to Plymouth in 1624 and died in Virginia about 1627.*
[5] Animals of the ox kind.
[6] Deut. 25.4, quoted I Cor. 9.9 and I Tim .5.18.

hurt might have come thro' his Writings; for the Interception whereof he now blessed
60 *God; and that it had been his manner to pick up all the Evil that was ever spoken*
against the People; but he shut his Ears and Eyes against all the Good; and that
if God should make him a Vagabond in the Earth, he were just in doing so; and
that those Three things, Pride, Vain-glory, *and* Self-love, *had been the Causes*
of his Miscarriages. These things he uttered so Pathetically, that they again
65 permitted him to Preach among them; and some were so perswaded of
his *Repentance*, that they profess'd they would fall down on their Knees,
that the Censure pass'd on him should be remitted. But, *Oh* the *deceitful*
Heart of Man! After *Two Months* time, he so notoriously renewed the
Miscarriages which he had thus bewailed, that his own Wife, through
70 her Affliction of Mind at his *Hypocrisie*, could not forbear declaring her
Fears, that God would bring some heavy Judgment upon their Family,
not only for *these*, but some former Wickednesses by him committed,
especially as to fearful Breaches of the *Seventh Commandment*, which he had
with an *Oath* denied, tho' they were afterwards evinced. Wherefore upon
75 the whole, being banished from hence, because his Residence[7] here was
utterly Inconsistent with the *Life* of this *Infant-Plantation*; he went into
Virginia, where he shortly after ended his own *Life*. Quickly after these
Difficulties, the Company of *Adventurers* for the support of this Plantation,
became rather *Adversaries* to it; or at least, a, *Be you warmed and filled;*[8]
80 a few good Words were all the help they afforded it; *they* broke to pieces,
but the *God of Heaven* still supported it.

§. 6. After these many Difficulties were thus a little surmounted, the
Inhabitants of this *Colony* Prosecuted their Affairs at so vigorous and successful a rate, that they not only fell into a comfortable way, both of *Plant-*
85 *ing* and of *Trading*; but also in a few Years there was a notable number of
Towns to be seen settled among them, and very considerable *Churches*
walking, so far as they had *attained*, in the *Faith* and *Order* of the Gospel.
Their *Churches*, flourished so considerably, that in the Year 1642. there
were above a dozen Ministers, and some of those Ministers were *Stars*
90 *of the first Magnitude*, shining in their several *Orbs* among them. And as
they *proceeded* in the Evangelical Service and Worship of our Lord Jesus
Christ, so they *prospered* in their Secular Concernments. When they first
began to divide their *Lands*, they wisely contrived the Division so, that
they might keep close together for their mutual Defence; and then their
95 Condition was very like that of the *Romans* in the time of *Romulus*, when
every Man contented himself with *Two Acres* of Land; and as *Pliny* tells
us, *It was thought a great Reward for one to receive a Pint of Corn from the People*
of Rome, *which Corn they also pounded in Mortars.* But since then their

---

[7] That is, "being banished from hence, because, on the whole, his residence," etc.

[8] James 2.16: "Go in peace, be ye warmed and filled; and yet ye give them not the things needful to the body; what doth it profit?"

99 Condition is marvellously altered and amended: *Great Farms* are now seen among the Effects of this good Peoples Planting; and in their *Fishing*, from the catching of *Cod*, and other Fish of less Dimensions, they are since passed on to the catching of *Whales*, whose *Oil* is become a *Staple-Commodity* of the Country: *Whales*, I say, which living and moving

5 *Islands*, do now find a way to this Coast, where, notwithstanding the desperate hazards run by the *Whale-Catchers* in their thin *Whale-Boats*, often torn to pieces by the stroaks of those enraged Monsters; yet it has been rarely known that any of them have miscarried. And within a few Days of my Writing this Paragraph, a *Cow* and a *Calf* were caught at *Yarmouth*

10 in this Colony; the *Cow* was Fifty Five Foot long, the *Bone* was Nine or Ten Foot wide; a *Cart* upon Wheels might have gone in at the Mouth of it; the *Calf* was twenty Foot long, for unto such vast *Calves*, the *Sea-Monsters draw forth their Breasts*. But so does the good God here give his People to *suck the abundance of the Seas!*

15   §. 7. If my Reader would have the *Religion* of these Planters more exactly described unto him; and I have told him that many Hundreds of Holy Souls, having been *ripened* for Heaven under the Ordinances of God in this Colony; and having left an Example of wonderful Prayerfulness, Watchfulness, Thankfulness, Usefulness, exact Conscienciousness, Piety,

20 Charity, Weanedness from the things of this World, and Affection to the things that are above, are now at rest with the Blessed Jesus, whose *Names*, tho' not Recorded in *this Book*, are yet entred in the *Book of Life*; and I hope there are still many Hundreds of their Children, even of the Third and Fourth Generation, resolving to *follow them as they followed*

25 *Christ*. I must refer him to an account given thereof by the Right Worshipful *Edward Winslow*, Esq; who was for some time the *Governour* of the Colony. He gives us to understand, that they are entirely of the same Faith with the Reformed Churches in *Europe*, only in their *Church-Government* they are Endeavourous after *a Reformation more thorough* than

30 what is in many of them; yet without any uncharitable *Separation* from them. He gives Instances of their admitting to Communion among them the Communicants of the *French*, the *Dutch*, the *Scotch* Churches, meerly by Virtue of their being so; and says, *We ever placed a large difference between those that grounded their Practice on the Word of God, tho' differing from*

35 *us in the Exposition and Understanding of it, and those that hated such Reformers and Reformation, and went on in Antichristian Opposition to it, and Persecution of it*: After which, he adds, '*Tis true, we profess and desire to practice* a Separation *from the World, and the Works of the World*; *and as the Churches of Christ are all* Saints by Calling, *so we desire to see the Grace of God shining*

40 *forth (at least* seemingly, *leaving secret things to God) in all we admit into* Church-Fellowship *with us, and to keep off such as openly wallow in the Mire of their Sins, that neither the Holy things of God, nor the Communion of Saints, may be leavened or polluted thereby. And if any joining to us formerly, either when*

we lived at Leyden *in* Holland, *or since we came to* New-England, *have with*
45 *the Manifestation of their Faith, and Profession of Holiness, held forth therewith*
Separation from the Church of England; *I have divers times, both in the one place,*
and in the other, heard either Mr. Robinson *our Pastor, or Mr.* Brewster *our*
Elder, stop them forthwith, shewing them that we required no such thing at their
Hands; but only to hold forth Faith in Christ Jesus, Holiness in the Fear of God,
50 *and Submission to every Ordinance and Appointment of God.* Thus he. It is true
there have been some *Varieties* among this People, but still I suppose the
Body of them do with Integrity espouse and maintain the Principles upon
which they were first Established: However, I must *without Fear* of offending express my *Fear,* that the *Leaven* of that rigid Thing, they call *Brown-*
55 *ism,*[1] has prevailed sometimes a little of the furthest in the *Administrations*
of this Pious People. Yea, there was an *Hour of Temptation,* wherein the
fondness of the People for the *Prophecyings*[2] *of the Brethren,* as they called
those Exercises; that is to say, the *Preachments* of those whom they call'd
Gifted Brethren, produced those Discouragements unto their *Ministers,*
60 that almost all the *Ministers* left the Colony; apprehending themselves
driven away by the Insupportable Neglect and Contempt, with which
the People on this occasion treated them. And this *dark Hour* of *Eclipse,*
upon the *Light* of the Gospel, in the Churches of the Colony, continued
until their Humiliation and Reformation before the *Great Shepherd of the*
65 *Sheep,* who hath since then blessed them with a *Succession* of as Worthy
Ministers as most in the Land. Moreover, there has been among them one
Church, that have *Questioned* and *Omitted* the Use of *Infant-Baptism;*
nevertheless, there being many good Men among those that have been of
this Perswasion, I do not know that they have been *Persecuted* with any
70 harder Means, than those of kind *Conferences* to reclaim them. There
have been also some unhappy *Sectaries,* namely, *Quakers* and *Seekers,*
and other such *Energumens,*[3] [pardon me, *Reader,* that I have thought
them so] which have given uggly Disturbances to these *Good-Spirited*
Men in their *Temple-Work;* but they have not prevailed unto the Sub-
75 version of the *First Interest.*

Some little *Controversies* likewise have now and then arisen among them
in the Administration of their *Discipline;* but *Synods* then regularly called,
have usually and presently put into *Joint* all that was apprehended *out.*
Their chief *Hazard* and *Symptom of Degeneracy,* is in the Verification of that
80 Old Observation, *Religio peperit Divitias, & Filia devoravit Matrem:*
Religion brought forth *Prosperity,* and the *Daughter* destroy'd the *Mother.*
Though one would expect, that as they grew in their *Estates,* they would

82 Though one/The one C.M.

[1] For Brownism, see footnote 20 to General Introduction p. 108, l. 1.*
[2] Lay preaching.*
[3] Demoniacs, enthusiasts, fanatical devotees.*

grow in the Payment of their *Quit-rents* unto the God who *gives them Power to get Wealth,* by more liberally supporting his *Ministers* and *Ordinances*
85 among them; the most likely way to save them from the most miserable *Apostacy*; the neglect whereof in some former Years, began for a while to be punished with a sore *Famine of the Word*; nevertheless, there is danger lest the *Enchantments* of this World make them to forget *their Errand into the Wilderness*: And some woful Villages in the Skirts of the
90 Colony, beginning to live without the *Means of Grace* among them, are still more Ominous Intimations of the danger. May the God of *New-England* preserve them from so great a Death!

§. 8. Going now to take my leave of this little *Colony,* that I may Converse for a while with her *Younger Sisters,* which yet have outstript her in
95 growth exceedingly, and so will now draw all the Streams of *her* Affairs into *their Channels,* I shall repeat the Counsel which their Faithful *Robinson* gave the first Planters of the Colony, at their parting from him in *Holland.* Said he, [to this purpose.]
99 'Brethren, We are now quickly to part from one another; and whether 'I may ever live to see your Faces on Earth any more, the God of Heaven 'only knows. But whether the Lord have appointed *that* or no, I charge 'you before *God,* and before his Blessed *Angels,* that you *follow me* no 'further than you have seen me *follow the Lord Jesus Christ.*
5 'If God reveal any thing to you by any *other* Instrument of *his,* be as 'ready to receive it, as ever you were to receive any Truth by *my* Ministry; 'for I am verily perswaded, I am very confident the Lord hath *more* 'Truth yet to break forth out of his Holy Word. For my part, I cannot 'sufficiently bewail the Condition of the *Reformed Churches,* who are come
10 'to a *Period*[1] in Religion; and will go at present no further than the 'Instruments of their first *Reformation.* The *Lutherans* can't be drawn to go 'beyond what *Luther* saw: Whatever part of his Will our good God has 'imparted and revealed unto *Calvin,* they will rather Die than Embrace 'it. And the *Calvinists,* you see, stick fast where they were left by that great
15 'Man of God, who yet *saw not all things.*
'This is a Misery much to be *lamented*; for tho' they were *Burning and Shining Lights* in their Times, yet they penetrated not into the *whole Counsel of God*; but were they now living, they would be as willing to 'embrace *further Light,* as that which they *first* received. I beseech you to
20 'remember it; it is an Article of your *Church-Covenant,* That you will *be ready to receive whatever Truth shall be made known unto you from the Written Word of God.* Remember *that,* and every other Article of your most Sacred 'Covenant. But I must herewithal exhort you to take heed what you

22 Remember/Remmber

[1] A full stop.

'receive as *Truth*; examine it, consider it, compare it with the other
25 '*Scriptures of Truth*, before you do receive it. For it is not possible the
'*Christian World* should come so lately out of such thick *Antichristian*
'*Darkness*, and that *Perfection of Knowledge* should break forth at once. I
'must also advise you to abandon, avoid and shake off the Name of
'*Brownist:* It is a meer *Nick-Name*, and a *Brand* for the making of Religion,
30 'and the Professors of Religion, odious unto the *Christian World*. Unto this
'End, I should be extreamly glad, if some *Godly Minister* would go with
'you, or come to you, before you can have my Company. For there
'will be no difference between the *Unconformable Ministers* of *England* and
'you, when they come to the practice of Evangelical Ordinances out of
35 'the Kingdom. And I would wish you by all Means to close with the
'*Godly People* of *England*; study *Union* with them in all things, wherein
'you can have it without Sin, rather than in the least measure to affect a
'*Division* or *Separation* from them. Neither would I have you loth to take
'another *Pastor* besides *my self*; in as much as a Flock that hath Two
40 '*Shepherds* is not thereby endangered, but secured.

So adding some other things of great Consequence, he concluded most
affectionately, commending his departing *Flock* unto the Grace of God,
which now I also do the Offspring of that Holy *Flock*.

CHAP. IV.

45 Paulo Majora![1] *Or, The* Essays *and* Causes *which produced the Second, but
largest Colony of* NEW-ENGLAND; *and the manner wherein the First
Church of this* New-Colony *was gathered.*

§. 1. WORDS full of *Emphasis*, are those which my Reader may find
Written by a Learned and Pious Minister of the Church of
50 *England*;[2] and I hope I may without offence tender to the Reader the
Words of *such* an Author.

'Some among us (*writes he*) are angry with *Calvin* for calling Humane
'*Rites, Tolerabiles Ineptias*;[3] they will not at the great Day be *such* unto

---

32 my/any   34 they/you

[1] "A somewhat loftier strain."*

[2] Probably John Williams (1582–1650), Dean of Westminster from 1620, Bishop of Lincoln
from 1621, and ultimately Archbishop of York. Admired by James I, he was selected for
the lord-keepership after the fall of Bacon, a post he filled with great worldly wisdom for three
years until dismissed by Charles I. In both his episcopal character and his public life, he
showed a hatred of extremes and strove to effect compromise both between king and parliament
and Laud and the nonconformists.*

[3] "Bearable trifles."*

'the rigorous Imposers, who made them *the Terms of Communion.* How will
55 'you at that Day lift up your Faces before your Master and your Judge,
'when he shall demand of you, *what is become of those his Lambs which you*
'*drove into the Wilderness by needless Impositions?*

The Story of the Flocks thus *driven into the Wilderness* has begun to be
related: And we would relate it without all Intemperate Expressions of
60 our anger against our *Drivers,* before whom the People must *needs go,* as
they did: It becomes not an *Historian,* and it less becomes a *Christian,* to
be *Passionate.* Nevertheless, *Poetry* may *dare* to do something at the
Description of that which *drove* those *Drivers;* and with a few Lines fetch'd
from the most famous *Epic Poem* of Dr. *Blackmore,*[4] we will describe the
65 Fury.

> ——*A* Fury *crawl'd from out her Cell,*
> *The Bloodiest Minister of* Death *and* Hell.
> *A monstrous Shape, a foul and hideous Sight,*
> *Which did all* Hell *with her dire Looks affright.*
> 70 *Huge full-gorg'd* Snakes *on her lean Shoulders hung,*
> *And* Death's *dark Courts with their loud hissing rung.*
> *Her* Teeth *and* Claws *were* Iron, *and her* Breath
> *Like Subterranean* Damps, *gave present* Death.
> *Flames worse than* Hell's, *shot from her Bloody* Eyes,
> 75 *And* Fire! *and* Sword! *Eternally she cries.*
> *No certain Shape, no Feature regular,*
> *No Limbs distinct in th' odious* Fiend *appear.*
> *Her Squalid, Bloated Belly did arise,*
> *Swoll'n with black* Gore *to a prodigious Size:*
> 80 *Distended vastly by a might Flood*
> *Of slaughter'd* Saints, *and constant* Martyr's *Blood.*
> *A* Monster *so deform'd, so fierce as this,*
> *It self a* Hell, *ne're saw the dark* Abyss!
> Horror *till now, the uggliest Shape esteem'd,*
> 85 *So much out-done, an* harmless Figure *seem'd.*
> Envy, *and* Hate, *and* Malice *blush'd to see*
> *Themselves* Eclips'd *by such Deformity.*
> *Her Feav'rish Heat drinks down a Sea of* Blood;
> *Not of the* Impious, *but the* Just *and* Good:
> 90 *'Gainst whom she burns with unextinguish'd* Rage,
> *Nor can th' Exhausted* World *her Wrath asswage.*

It was PERSECUTION; a *Fury* which we consider not as possessing
the Church of England, but as inspiring a *Party* which have unjustly

84 Horror/Horrow C.M.

[4] For Sir Richard Blackmore, see introductory essay "The Magnalia."*

Challenged the Name of *the Church of* England, and which, whenever *the*
95 *Church of* England shall any more encourage her *Fall*, will become like
that of the *House* which our Saviour saw Built upon the *Sand*.

§. 2. There were more than a few attempts of the *English*, to People
and Improve the Parts of *New-England*, which were to the Northward of
99 *New-Plymouth*; but the Designs of those Attempts being aim'd no higher
than the Advancement of some *Worldly Interests*, a constant Series of
Disasters had confounded them, until there was a Plantation[1] erected
upon the nobler Designs of *Christianity*; and that Plantation, tho' it has
had more Adversaries than perhaps any one upon Earth; yet, *having*
5 *obtained help from God, it continues to this Day.* There have been very fine
Settlements in the *North-East* Regions; but what is become of them? I
have heard that one of our Ministers[2] once Preaching to a Congregation
there, urged them to approve themselves a *Religious People* from this
Consideration, *That otherwise they would contradict the main end of Planting*
10 *this Wilderness*; whereupon a well-known Person, then in the Assembly,
cry'd out, *Sir, You are mistaken, you think you are Preaching to the People at*
the Bay; *our main End was to catch Fish.* Truly 'twere to have been wished,
that something more excellent had been the *main End* of the *Settlements*
in that brave Country, which we have, even long since the arrival of that
15 more Pious Colony at the *Bay*, now seen dreadfully *unsettled*, no less than
twice at least, by the Sword of the Heathen,[3] after they had been replen-
ished with many *Hundreds* of People, who had thriven to many *Thousands*
of Pounds; and had all the force of the *Bay* too, to assist them in the maintaining of their Settlements. But the same or the like inauspicious things
20 attended many other Endeavours, to make Plantations upon such a
Main End in several other Parts of our Country, before the Arrival of
those by whom the *Massachuset* Colony was at last formed upon more
glorious *Aims:* All proving like the Habitations of the *foolish, cursed before*
they had taken root. Of all which *Catastrophes*, I suppose none was more sud-
25 den than that of Monsieur *Finch*, whom in a Ship from *France*, trucking
with the *Massachuset-Natives*; those Bloody Salvages, coming on Board
without any other *Arms*, but *Knives* concealed under *Flaps*, immediately
Butchered with all his Men, and set the Ship on Fire. Yea, so many
Fatalities attended the *Adventurers* in their Essays, that they began to
30 suspect that the *Indian* Sorcerers had laid the place under some *Fascina-*
tion; and that the *English* could not prosper upon such *Enchanted Ground*,
so that they were almost afraid of *Adventuring* any more.

§. 3. Several Persons in the West of *England*, having by Fishing-
Voyages to Cape *Ann*, the Northern Promontory of the *Massachuset-Bay*,

2   had/has   24   *Catastrophes/Catastrophe's*

[1] That is, the Massachusetts Bay Colony.
[2] "One of our Ministers" has not been identified.*
[3] By the Pequot War, 1637, and King Philip's War, 1675–1676.

35 obtained some Acquaintance with those Parts; the News of the good
Progress made in the New Plantation of *Plymouth,* inspired the renowned
Mr. *White,*[1] Minister of *Dorchester,* to prosecute the Settlement of such
another Plantation here for the Propagation of *Religion.* This good Man
engaged several Gentlemen about the Year 1624. in this Noble Design;[2]

40 and they employ'd a most Religious, Prudent, Worthy Gentleman, one
Mr. *Roger Conant,*[3] in the Government of the Place, and of their Affairs
upon the Place; but thro' many Discouragements, the Design for a while
almost fell unto the Ground. The great Man greatly grieved hereat,
wrote over to this Mr. *Roger Conant,* that if he and three Honest Men more

45 would yet stay upon the Spot, he would procure a *Patent* for them, and
send them over *Friends, Goods, Provisions,* and what was necessary to
assist their Undertakings. Mr. *Conant,* then looking out a Scituation more
Commodious for a *Town,* gave his Three disheartned Companions to
understand, that he did believe God would make this Land a Receptacle

50 for his People, and that if *they* should leave him, yet *he* would not stir;
for he was confident he should not long want Company; which Confidence of his caused them to abandon the thoughts of leaving him. Well,
it was not long before the Council of *Plymouth* in *England,* had by a
Deed[4] bearing Date, *March* 19. 1627. sold unto some Knights and

55 Gentlemen about *Dorchester,* viz. Sir *Henry Roswel,* Sir *John Young,*
Thomas Southcott, John Humphrey, John Endicot, and *Simon Whetcomb,* and
their Heirs and Assigns, and their Associates for ever, that Part of *New-
England* which lyes between a great River call'd *Merimack,* and a certain
other River there call'd *Charles River,* in the bottom of the *Massachuset-*

60 *Bay.* But shortly after this, Mr. *White* brought the aforesaid Honourable
Persons into an Acquaintance with several other Persons of Quality
about *London;* as, namely, Sir *Richard Saltonstall, Isaac Johnson, Samuel
Adderly, John Ven, Matthew Cradock, George Harwood, Increase Nowel, Richard
Perry, Richard Bellingham, Nathanael Wright, Samuel Vassal, Theophilus*

65 *Eaton, Thomas Goff, Thomas Adams, John Brown, Samuel Brown, Thomas
Hutchings, William Vassal, William Pinchon,* and *George Foxcraft.* These
Persons being associated unto the former, and having bought of them
all their Interest in *New-England* aforesaid, now consulted about settling
a *Plantation* in that Country, whither such as were then called *Non-*

54 *March* 19. 1627. sold/*March* 19. 1627.
Sold

[1] John White (1575–1648), minister in Dorchester, England, one of the chief founders of
the Massachusetts Bay Colony and active in the securing of its charter.*
[2] The Dorchester Company of Adventurers, formed in 1623 by a group of West Country
merchants and others.*
[3] Roger Conant (*c.*1592–1679) was in charge of the settlement during its last year.*
[4] The deed was granted to this group as the New England Company for a Plantation in
Massachusetts Bay.*

70 *Conformists*, might with the Grace and Leave of the King make a peaceable *Secession*, and enjoy the Liberty and the Exercise of their own Perswasions, about the Worship of the Lord Jesus Christ. Whereupon Petitioning the King to confirm what they had thus purchased with a New *Patent*, he granted them one, bearing Date from the Year 1628. which gave them a

75 Right unto the Soil, holding their Titles of Lands, as of the Mannor of *East Greenwich* in *Kent*,[5] and in common *Soccage*. By this *Charter* they were empowered yearly to *Elect* their own Governour, Deputy-Governour and Magistrates; as also to make such *Laws* as they should think suitable for the Plantation: But as an acknowledgment of their dependance upon

80 *England*, they might not make any Laws Repugnant unto those of the Kingdom; and the Fifth part of all the *Oar*[6] of *Gold* or *Silver* found in the Territory, belong'd unto the Crown. So, soon after Mr. *Cradock*[7] being by the Company chosen Governour, they sent over Mr. *Endicott*[8] in the Year 1628. to carry on the Plantation, which the *Dorchester*-Agents[9] had

85 lookt out for them, which was at a Place called *Nahumkeick*. Of which place I have somewhere met with an odd Observation, that the Name of it was rather *Hebrew* than *Indian*; for נחום *Nahum*, signifies Comfort, and חיק *Keik*, signifies an *Haven*; and our *English* not only found it an *Haven of Comfort*, but happened also to put an *Hebrew Name* upon it; for they

90 call'd it *Salem*, for the *Peace* which they had and hoped in it; and *so it is called unto this Day*.

§. 4. An Entrance being thus made upon the Design of Planting a Country of *English* and *Reformed* Churches; they that were concerned for the Plantation, made their Application to Two Non-Conformist

95 Ministers, that they would go over to serve the *Cause of God and of Religion* in the beginning of those *Churches*. The one of these was Mr. *Higginson*,[1] a Minister in *Leicestershire*, silenced for his Non-Conformity; the other was Mr. *Skelton*,[2] a Minister of *Lincolnshire*, suffering also for his Non-

99 Conformity: Both of which were Men eminent for Learning and Virtue, and who thus driven out of their Native Country, sought their Graves on the *American-Strand*, whereon the Epitaph might be inscribed that was

---

78 *Laws* as/*Laws*   94 Non-Conformist/Non-Conformists

[5] That is, according to the same form of land tenure by which the manor of East Greenwich was held.*

[6] Ore; a standard stipulation.

[7] Matthew Cradock (or Craddock, d. 1641), was a London merchant and large shareholder of East India Company stock. He served as governor of the Massachusetts Bay Company until the transfer of the Charter to America.

[8] John Endecott (*c.*1589–1665); see *Magnalia*, Bk. II, chap. 5, sec. 4.

[9] The "*Dorchester*-Agents" were, of course, Conant and his group, who had removed to "*Nahumkeick*" after the collapse of the Cape Ann settlement.*

---

[1] Francis Higginson (1586–1630), well known as a nonconformist minister in England, who, although he lived only one year in New England, left a strong impress on its theological history.*

[2] Samuel Skelton (1584–1634).*

on *Scipio*'s, *Ingrata Patria, ne Mortui quidem habebis Ossa*.[3] These Ministers came over to *Salem*, in the Summer of the Year 1629. and with these
5 there came over a considerable number of Excellent Christians, who no sooner arrived, but they set themselves about the Church-Work, which was their *Errand* hither.

'Tis true, there were two other *Clergy-Men*,[4] who came over about the same time; nevertheless, there has been very little Account given of their
10 Circumstances; except what a certain little *Narrative-Writer*[5] has offered us, by saying, *There were Two that began to hew Stones in the Mountains, for the Building of the Temple here; but when they saw all sorts of Stones would not fit in the Building, the one betook himself to the Seas again, and the other to Till the Land*; for which cause, burying all further mention of them among the
15 *Rubbish*, in the *Foundation* of the Colony, we will proceed with our Story; which is now to tell us, That the Passage of these our *Pilgrims* was attended with many Smiles of Heaven upon them. They were blessed with a Company of honest *Seamen*; with whom the Ministers and Passengers constantly served God, Morning and Evening; *Reading, Expound-*
20 *ing* and *Applying* the Word of God, *singing* of His Praise, and *seeking* of His Face; to which Exercises they added on the *Lord's Day* two Sermons, and a *Catechising:* And sometimes they set apart an whole Day for *Fasting* and *Prayer*, to obtain from Heaven a good success in their Voyage, especially when the Weather was much against them, whereto they had
25 very Remarkable Answers; but the *Seamen* said, *That they believed these were the First* Sea-*Fasts that ever were kept in the World*. At length, *Per varios Casus, per Tot Discrimina Rerum*,[6] they Landed at *the Haven of Rest* provided for them.

§. 5. The persecuted Servants of God, under the *English* Hierarchy,
30 had been in *a Sea of Ice mingled with Fire*; tho' the *Fire* scalded them, yet such Cakes of *Ice* were over their Heads, that there was no getting out: But the *Ice* was now broken, by the *American* Offers of a Retreat for the pure Worshippers of the Lord into a *Wilderness*.

The Report of the 𝕮𝕳𝖆𝖗𝖙𝖊𝖗 granted unto the Governour and Company
35 of the *Massachuset-Bay*, and the Entertainment and Encouragement, which Planters began to find in that *Bay*, came with a, —*Patrias, age, desere Sedes*,[1] and caused many very deserving Persons to transplant them-

21 Face/Peace C.M.

[3] "Ungrateful fatherland! Thou wilt not even hold my lifeless bones."*
[4] Francis Bright, an Oxford man, who came with Higginson and Skelton in 1629, and William Blackstone (1595–1675), who had come to New England in 1623.*
[5] Captain Edward Johnson (1598–1672), one of the founders of Woburn, a militia captain and a leading citizen.*
[6] "Through divers mishaps, through so many perilous chances."*

[1] "Come, leave your native land."*

selves and their Families into *New-England*. *Gentlemen* of Ancient and
Worshipful Families, and *Ministers* of the Gospel, then of great Fame at
40 Home, and *Merchants, Husbandmen, Artificers*, to the Number of some
Thousands, did for Twelve Years together carry on this Trans-plantation.
It was indeed a *Banishment*, rather than a *Removal*, which was undergone
by this glorious Generation, and you may be sure sufficiently *Afflictive* to
Men of Estate, Breeding and Conversation.[2] As the *Hazard* which they
45 ran in this Undertaking was of such *Extraordinariness*, that nothing less
than a strange and strong Impression from *Heaven* could have thereunto
moved the Hearts of such as were in it; so the *Expence* with which they
carried on the Undertaking was truly *Extraordinary*. By Computation, the
Passage of the *Persons* that peopled *New-England*, cost at least Ninety
50 Five Thousand Pound: The Transportation of their first small Stock of
Cattel great and small, cost no less than Twelve Thousand Pound, besides
the Price of the *Cattel* themselves: The *Provisions* laid in for Subsistence,
till *Tillage* might produce more, cost Forty Five Thousand Pounds; the
Materials for their first Cottages cost Eighteen Thousand Pounds; their
55 Arms, Ammunition and Great Artillery, cost Twenty Two Thousand
Pounds; besides which Hundred and Ninety Two Thousand Pounds, the
Adventurers laid out in *England*, what was not Inconsiderable. About an
Hundred and Ninety Eight Ships were employed in passing the *Perils of the
Seas*, in the Accomplishment of this Renowned Settlement; whereof, by
60 the way, but *one* miscarried in those *Perils*.

Briefly, The God of Heaven served as it were, a *Summons* upon the
Spirits of His People in the English Nation; stirring up the Spirits of
Thousands which never saw the *Faces* of each other, with a most Unanimous Inclination to leave all the Pleasant Accommodations of their
65 Native Country, and go over a Terrible *Ocean*, into a more Terrible
Desart, for the *pure Enjoyment of all his Ordinances*. It is now Reasonable
that before we pass any further, the *Reasons* of this Undertaking should
be more exactly made known unto *Posterity*, especially unto the *Posterity*
of those that were the *Undertakers*, lest they come at length to Forget and
70 Neglect *the true Interest of* New-England. Wherefore I shall now Transcribe
some of *them* from a Manuscript, wherein they were then tendred unto
Consideration.

General Considerations for the Plantation of New-England.

'*First*, It will be a Service unto the *Church* of great Consequence, to
75 'carry the *Gospel* into *those* Parts of the World, and Raise a *Bulwark*
'against the Kingdom of *Antichrist*, which the *Jesuites* labour to Rear
'up in *all* Parts of the World.

[2] In the obsolete sense of consorting with others, living together.

'*Secondly*, All other Churches of *Europe* have been brought under
'*Desolations*; and it may be feared that the like Judgments are coming
80 'upon *Us*; and who knows but God hath provided this place to be a
'*Refuge* for many, whom he means to save out of the *General Destruction*.

'*Thirdly*, The Land grows weary of her *Inhabitants*, insomuch that *Man*,
'which is the most precious of all Creatures, is here more vile and base
'than the Earth he treads upon: *Children, Neighbours* and *Friends*, especially
85 'the *Poor*, are counted the greatest *Burdens*, which if things were right,
'would be the chiefest Earthly *Blessings*.

'*Fourthly*, We are grown to that Intemperance in all *Excess of Riot*, as
'no mean *Estate* almost will suffice a Man to keep Sail with his *Equals*,
'and he that fails in it, must live in Scorn and Contempt: Hence it comes
90 'to pass, that all *Arts* and *Trades* are carried in that Deceitful Manner,
'and Unrighteous Course, as it is almost Impossible for a good upright
'Man to maintain his constant Charge, and live comfortably in them.

'*Fifthly*, The *Schools* of Learning and Religion are so corrupted, as
'(besides the unsupportable Charge of Education) most Children, even
95 'the Best, Wittiest, and of the Fairest Hopes, are perverted, corrupted,
'and utterly overthrown, by the multitude of evil Examples and Licen-
'tious Behaviours in those *Seminaries*.

'*Sixthly*, The *whole Earth* is the *Lord's Garden*, and he hath given it to
99 'the Sons of *Adam*, to be Tilled and Improved by them: Why then should
'we stand Starving here for Places of Habitation, and in the mean time
'suffer whole Countries, as profitable for the use of Man, to lye waste
'without any Improvement?

'*Seventhly*, What can be a better or nobler Work, and more worthy
5 'of a *Christian*, than to erect and support a *reformed particular Church*[3] in its
'Infancy, and unite our Forces with such a Company of Faithful People,
'as by a timely Assistance may grow Stronger and Prosper; but for want
'of it, may be put to great Hazards, if not be wholly Ruined.

'*Eighthly*, If any such as are known to be Godly, and live in Wealth
10 'and Prosperity here, shall forsake all this to join with this *Reformed*
'*Church*, and with it run the Hazard of an hard and mean Condition, it
'will be an Example of great Use, both for the removing of *Scandal*, and
'to give more *Life* unto the *Faith* of God's People in their Prayers for the
'*Plantation*, and also to encourage others to join the more willingly in it.
15 §. 6. Mr. *Higginson*, and Mr. *Skelton*, and other good People that
arrived at *Salem*, in the Year 1629. resolved, like their Father *Abraham*,
to begin their Plantation with *calling on the Name of the Lord*. The great
Mr. *Hildersham*[1] had advised our first Planters to agree fully upon their

---

[3] That is, a single or individual church organized according to congregational polity.

[1] Arthur Hildersham (1563–1632), a prominent Puritan and conspicuous enemy of Separation.*

Form of *Church Government*, before their coming into *New-England*; but
20 they had indeed agreed little further than in this general Principle, *That
the Reformation of the Church was to be endeavoured according to the written
Word of God.* Accordingly ours, now arrived at *Salem*, consulted with their
Brethren at *Plymouth*, what Steps to take for the more exact Acquainting
of themselves *with*, and Conforming themselves *to*, that *written Word:*
25 And the *Plymotheans*, to their great Satisfaction, laid before them what
Warrant, they judged, that they had in the *Laws* of our Lord Jesus Christ,
for every Particular in their *Church Order.*

Whereupon having the Concurrence and Countenance of their
Deputy Governour, the Worshipful *John Endicot*, Esq; and the approving
30 Presence of Messengers from the Church of *Plymouth*, they set apart the
Sixth Day of *August*, after their Arrival, for *Fasting* and *Prayer*, for the
settling of a *Church-State* among them, and for their making a *Confession
of their Faith*, and entering into an Holy *Covenant*, whereby that *Church-
State*² was formed.

35 Mr. *Higginson* then became the Teacher, and Mr. *Skelton* the Pastor,
of the Church thus constituted at *Salem*; and they lived very *peaceably* in
Salem together, till the Death of Mr. *Higginson*, which was about a
Twelvemonth after, and then of Mr. *Skelton*, who did not long survive
him. Now the *Covenant* whereto these *Christians* engaged themselves,
40 which was about Seven Years after solemnly *renewed*³ among them, I
shall here lay before all the *Churches* of God, as it was then expressed and
inforced.

*We Covenant with our Lord, and one with another; and we do Bind our selves
in the presence of God, to walk together in all his Ways, according as he is pleased
45 to reveal himself unto us in his blessed Word of Truth; and do explicitely, in the
Name and Fear of God, profess and protest to walk as followeth, thro' the Power
and Grace of our Lord Jesus Christ.*

*We Avouch the Lord to be our God, and our selves to be his People, in the truth
and simplicity of our Spirits.*

50 *We Give our selves to the Lord Jesus Christ, and the Word of his Grace for the
Teaching, Ruling and Sanctifying of us in Matters of Worship and Conversation,
resolving to cleave unto him alone for Life and Glory, and to reject all contrary
Ways, Canons, and Constitutions of Men in his Worship.*

*We Promise to walk with our Brethren, with all Watchfulness and Tenderness,
55 avoiding Jelousies and Suspicions, Back-Bitings, Censurings, Provokings, secret
Risings of Spirit against them; but in all Offences to follow the Rule of our Lord
Jesus, and to bear and forbear, give and forgive, as he hath taught us.*

*In Publick or Private, we will willingly Do nothing to the Offence of the Church;
but will be willing to take Advice for our selves and ours, as occasion shall be
60 presented.*

---

² Church-estate; church body-politic.
³ Probably on the occasion of the ordination of Hugh Peter as pastor in 1636.*

We will not in the Congregation be forward either to show our own Gifts and Parts in Speaking or Scrupling, or there discover the Weakness or Failings of our Brethren; but attend an orderly Call thereunto, knowing how much the Lord may be dishonoured, and his Gospel, and the Profession of it, slighted by our Distempers 65 *and Weaknesses in Publick.*

We Bind our selves to study the Advancement of the Gospel in all Truth and Peace; both in Regard of those that are within or without; no way slighting our Sister Churches, but using their Counsel, as need shall be; not laying a Stumbling-block before any, no, not the Indians, whose good we desire to promote; and so to 70 *converse, as we may avoid the very appearance of Evil.*

We do hereby promise to carry our selves in all lawful Obedience to those that are over us, in Church or Commonwealth, knowing how well-pleasing it will be to the Lord, that they should have Encouragement in their Places, by our not grieving their Spirits thro' our Irregularities.

75 *We Resolve to approve our selves to the Lord in our particular Callings; shunning Idleness, as the Bane of any State; nor will we deal hardly or oppressingly with any, wherein we are the Lord's Stewards.*

Promising also unto our best Ability to Teach our Children and Servants the Knowledge of God, and of His Will, that they may serve Him also; and all this 80 *not by any strength of our own, but by the Lord Christ; whose Blood we desire may sprinkle this our Covenant made in His Name.*

By this *Instrument* was the *Covenant of Grace* Explained, Received, and Recognized, by the *First Church* in this Colony, and *applied* unto the Evangelical Designs of a *Church-Estate* before the Lord: This *Instrument* 85 they afterwards often read over, and renewed the *Consent* of their Souls unto every Article in it; especially when their Days of *Humiliation* invited them to lay hold on particular Opportunities for doing so.

So you have seen the *Nativity* of the *First Church* in the *Massachuset-*Colony.

90 §. 7. As for the Circumstances of *Admission* into this Church, they left it very much unto the Discretion and Faithfulness of their Elders, together with the Condition of the Persons to be admitted. Some were admitted by expressing their Consent unto their *Confession* and *Covenant*; some were admitted after their first Answering to *Questions* about *Religion*, 95 propounded unto them; some were admitted, when they had presented in *Writing* such things, as might give *Satisfaction* unto the People of God concerning them; and some that were admitted, *Orally* adressed the People of God in such Terms, as they thought proper to ask their 99 *Communion* with; which *Diversity* was perhaps more *Beautiful*, than would have been a more *Punctilious Uniformity:* But none were admitted without regard unto a Blameless and Holy *Conversation*. They did all agree with their Brethren of *Plymouth* in this Point, *That the Children of the Faithful were Church-Members, with their Parents; and that their Baptism was a Seal of*

5 *their being so*; only before their admission to Fellowship in a *Particular Church*, it was judged Necessary, that being free from Scandal, they should be examined by the *Elders* of the Church, upon whose Approbation of their *Fitness*, they should Publickly and Personally own the *Covenant*; so they were to be received unto the Table of the Lord: And accordingly

10 the Eldest Son of Mr. *Higginson*,[1] being about Fifteen Years of Age, and laudably Answering all the Characters expected in a *Communicant*, was then so Received.

§. 8. It is to be Remembred, that some of the Passengers, who came over with those of our first *Salemites*, observing that the Ministers did

15 not use the *Book of Common-Prayer* in their Administrations; that they Administred the *Baptism* and the *Supper* of the Lord, without any unscriptural *Ceremonies*; that they resolved upon using *Discipline* in the Congregation against Scandalous Offenders, according to the Word of God; and that some *Scandalous* Persons had been denied *Admission* into

20 the Communion of the Church; they began (*Frankford*-Fashion)[1] to raise a deal of Trouble hereupon. *Herodiana Malitia, nascentem persequi Religionem!*[2] Of these there were especially *Two* Brothers;[3] the one a Lawyer, the other a Merchant, *both* Men of Parts, Estate and Figure in the Place. These gather'd a Company together, *separate* from the publick Assembly;

25 and *there* the *Common-Prayer-Worship* was after a sort upheld among such as would resort unto them. The Governour perceiving a Disturbance to arise among the People on this Occasion, sent for the *Brothers*; who accused the Ministers, as *departing from the Orders of the Church of England*; adding, *That they were Separatists, and would be shortly Anabaptists*; but for

30 themselves, *They would hold unto the Orders of the Church of England*. The Answer of the Ministers to these Accusations, was, *That they were neither* Separatists *nor* Anabaptists; *that they did not separate from the Church of* England, *nor from the Ordinances of God there, but only from the Corruptions and Disorders of that Church: That they came away from the* Common-Prayer *and*

35 Ceremonies, *and had suffered much for their Non-conformity in their Native Land; and therefore being in a place where they might have their Liberty, they neither could nor would use them; inasmuch as they judged the Imposition of these things to be a sinful Violation of the Worship of God.* The Governour, the Council, the People, generally approved of the Answer thus given by the

40 Ministers; but these Persons returned into *England* with very furious *Threatnings* against the Church thus Established; however the *threatned*

[1] John Higginson (1616–1708).*

[1] Mather is here referring to a dispute over the use of the Prayer Book among English nonconformist exiles in Frankfurt during the reign of Mary I.*
[2] "Herod-like malice, bent on crushing the infant church."*
[3] Samuel and John Browne.*

Folks have *lived so long*, that the *Church* has *out-lived* the grand *Climacterical*[4] Year of Humane Age; it now Flourishing more than *Sixty-three* Years after its first Gathering under the Pastoral Care of a most Reverend and 45 Ancient Person, even Mr. *John Higginson*, the *Son* of that excellent Man who laid the Foundations of that Society.

CHAP. V.

Peregrini Deo Curæ:[1] *Or*, *The Progress of the* New-Colony; *with* some *Account of the* Persons, *the* Methods, *and the* Troubles, *by which it came to* 50 Something.

§. 1. THE *Governour* and *Company* of the *Massachuset-Bay* then in *London*, did in the Year 1629. after exact and mature Debates, Conclude, that it was most Convenient for the *Government*, with the Charter of the Plantation, to be transferred into the Plantation it self; and an 55 *Order of Court* being drawn up for that End, there was then Chosen a New *Governour*, and a New *Deputy-Governour*, that were willing to remove themselves with their Families thither on the first Occasion. The Governour was *John Winthrop*, Esq;[2] a Gentleman of that Wisdom and Virtue, and those manifold Accomplishments, that After-Generations must reckon 60 him no less a *Glory*, than he was a *Patriot* of the Country. The Deputy-Governour was *Thomas Dudley*, Esq;[3] a Gentleman, whose *Natural* and *Acquired* Abilities, joined with his excellent *Moral* Qualities, Entitled him to all the great Respects with which his Country on all Opportunities treated him. Several most Worthy *Assistants*[4] were at the same time 65 chosen to be in this *Transportation*; moreover, several other *Gentlemen* of prime Note, and several famous *Ministers* of the Gospel, now likewise embarked themselves with these Honourable *Adventurers:* Who Equipped a *Fleet*, consisting of Ten or Eleven Ships, whereof the Admiral[5] was, *The Arabella* (so called in Honour of the Right Honourable the Lady 70 *Arabella Johnson*,[6] at this time on Board) a Ship of Three Hundred and

---

[4] All years denoted by multiples of seven (climacterics) were considered liable to change in health or fortune, but the Grand Climacteric (9 × 7) was deemed especially critical.

---

[1] "Strangers are under the care of God."*

[2] For John Winthrop (1588–1649), see *Magnalia*, Bk. II, chap. 4.

[3] For Thomas Dudley (1576–1653), see *Magnalia*, Bk. II, chap. 5, sec. 1.

[4] An Assistant was an elected member of the governor's council in the early Massachusetts Bay and Plymouth colonies.

[5] That is, the flagship of the fleet.*

[6] Lady Arbella Johnson, sister to the fourth Earl of Lincoln, was the wife of Isaac Johnson, one of the Assistants and reputed to be the richest of the immigrants.*

Fifty Tuns; and in some of the said Ships there were Two Hundred Passengers; all of which Arrived before the middle of *July*, in the Year 1630. safe in the Harbours of *New-England*.[7] There was a time when the *British Sea*[8] was by *Clement*,[9] and the other Ancients, called, 'Ωκεανὸς
75 ἀπέραντος, *The unpassable Ocean*. What then was to be thought of the vast *Atlantick Sea* on the Westward of *Britain?* But this *Ocean* must now be *passed!* An Heart of Stone must have dissolved into *Tears* at the Affectionate *Farewel*, which the Governour and other Eminent Persons took of their Friends, at a *Feast* which the Governour made for them, a little
80 before their going off; however they were acted[10] by Principles that could carry them thro' *Tears* and *Oceans*; yea, thro' *Oceans of Tears:* Principles that enabled them to leave, *Dulcia Limina, atq; amabilem Larem, quem & parentum memoria, atq; ipsius* (to use *Stupius* words) *Infantiæ Rudimenta Confirmant*.[11] Some very late *Geographers* do assure us, that the
85 Breadth of the *Atlantick Sea* is commonly over-reckoned by *Six*, by *Eight*, by *Ten* Degrees. But let that Sea be as narrow as they please, I can assure the Reader the passing of it was no little *Trial* unto those worthy People that were now to pass it.

§. 2. But the most notable Circumstance in their *Farewel*, was their
90 Composing and Publishing of what they called, *The humble request of His Majesties Loyal Subjects, the Governour and Company lately gone for* New-England, *to the rest of their Brethren in and of the Church of* England; *for the obtaining of their Prayers, and the removal of Suspicions and Misconstructions of their Intentions*. In this Address of theirs, notwithstanding the trouble
95 they had undergone for desiring to see the Church of *England Reformed* of several things, which they thought its *Deformities*, yet they now called the Church of *England* their *Dear Mother*; acknowledging that such *Hope* and *Part* as they had obtained in the *Common Salvation* they had *sucked from*
99 *her Breasts*; therewithal entreating their many *Reverend Fathers and Brethren* to recommend them unto the Mercies of God, in their constant Prayers, as a *Church* now springing out of their own Bowels. *You are not Ignorant* (said they) *that the Spirit of God stirred up the Apostle* Paul, *to make a continual mention of the Church at* Philippi, *which was a Colony from* Rome;
5 *let the same Spirit, we beseech you, put you in Mind, that are the Lord's Remembrancers, to pray for us without ceasing, who are the weak* Colony *from your*

74 *Clement/Clements*   83 *Infantiæ/Infamiæ* C.M.

7 The *Arbella* entered port on June 12. The last vessel, the *Ambrose*, arrived by July 6.*
8 The English Channel.*
9 Clement of Alexandria (d. *c.*215), one of the church fathers.*
10 That is, actuated.
11 "Pleasant abodes and lovely home, confirmed by the memory of parents and the early lessons there imbibed in the very principles which now make them objects of persecution." Stupius (Jean Baptiste Stouppe, *c.*1620–1700), a soldier of fortune, author, secret agent, and for a time minister of the French church in London.*

selves. And after such Prayers, they Concluded, *What Goodness you shall extend unto us, in this or any other Christian Kindness, we your Brethren in Christ shall Labour to Repay, in what Duty we are or shall be able to perform; promising*
10 *so far as God shall enable us, to give him no rest on your Behalfs; wishing our Heads and Hearts may be Fountains of Tears for your everlasting Welfare, when we shall be in our Poor Cottages in the Wilderness, overshadowed with the Spirit of Supplication, thro' the manifold Necessities and Tribulations, which may not altogether unexpectedly, nor we hope unprofitably, befal us.*
15 §. 3. *Reader,* If ever the *Charity* of a Right Christian, and Enlarged Soul, were exemplarily seen in its proper *Expansions,*[1] 'twas in the Address which thou hast now been Reading: But if it now puzzel the Reader to Reconcile these Passages with the *Principles* declared, the *Practices* followed, and the *Persecutions* undergone, by these *American Reformers,* let
20 him know, that there was more than one *Distinction,* whereof these excellent Persons were not Ignorant. First, They were able to Distinguish between the *Church of England,* as it *contained* the whole *Body of the Faithful,* scattered throughout the Kingdoms, tho' of different Perswasions about some *Rites* and *Modes* in Religion; many Thousands of whom our *Nov-*
25 *Angles* knew could comply with many things, to which *our Consciences* otherwise enlightned and perswaded could not yeild such a Compliance: And the *Church of England,* as it was *confined* unto a certain Constitution by *Canons,* which pronounced *Ipso Facto,* Excommunicate all those who should affirm that the *Worship* contained in the Book of *Common-Prayer,*
30 and *Administrations of Sacraments,* is unlawful, or that any of the *Thirty Nine Articles* are Erroneous, or that any of the *Ceremonies* commanded by the Authority of the Church might not be Approved, Used and Subscribed; and which will have to be *Accursed* all those, who maintain that there are in the Realm any other Meetings, Assemblies or Congregations
35 of the King's Born Subjects, than such as by the Laws of the Land are allowed, which may rightly Challenge to themselves the Name of *True* and *Lawful Churches:* And by which, all those that refuse to *Kneel* at the Reception of the Sacrament, and to be present at Publick *Prayers,* according to the *Orders* of the Church, about which there are prescribed
40 many Formalities of *Responses,* with Bowing at the *Name* of 𝕵𝖊𝖘𝖚𝖘, are to be denied the *Communion*; and all who dare not submit their Children to be *Baptized* by the Undertaking of *God-Fathers,* and receive the *Cross* as a dedicating Badge of *Christianity,* must not have *Baptism* for their Children:

24 *Nov-/Nor-* C.M.

[1] In the Puritan vocabulary, "*Charity*" means Christian love; a "Right Christian" is a true, an orthodox (according to nonconformist doctrine) Christian; an "Enlarged Soul" is a soul with increased capacity for the religious affections; "proper Expansions" signify full spiritual development.*

Besides an *Et Cætera* of how many more *Impositions!*[2] Again, they were
45 able to distinguish between the *Church of England*, as it kept the true
Doctrine of the *Protestant Religion*, with a Disposition to pursue the *Reformation* begun in the former Century, among whom we may Reckon such
Men, as the famous *Assembly of Divines* at *Westminster*,[3] who all but *Eight*
or *Nine*, and the *Scots*, had before then lived in *Conformity*; and *the Church*
50 *of England*, as limiting that Name unto a certain *Faction*, who together
with a *Discipline* very much *Unscriptural*, vigorously prosecuted the
Tripartite Plot of *Arminianism* and Conciliation with *Rome*, in the *Church*,
and unbounded *Prerogative* in the *State*;[4] who set themselves to Cripple
as fast as they could the more Learned, Godly, Painful[5] *Ministers* of the
55 Land, and Silence and Ruin such as could not Read a *Book for Sports on
the Lord's Days*;[6] or did but use a *Prayer* of their own Conceiving,[7] before or
after Sermon; or did but Preach in an *Afternoon*, as well as in a Morning,
or on a *Lecture*, or on a *Market*,[8] or in aniwise discountenance *Old* Superstitions, or *New* Extravagancies; and who at last threw the Nation into
60 the lamentable Confusions of a *Civil War*. By the Light of this *Distinction*,
we may easily perceive what *Church of England* it was, that our *New-
England* Exiles called, *Their Mother*; though their *Mother* had been so
harsh to them, as to turn them out of Doors, yet they highly honoured
Her; believing that it was not so much their *Mother*, but some of their
65 angry *Brethren*; abusing the Name of their *Mother*, who so harshly treated
them; and all the harm they wished her, was to see her put off those *Ill
Trimmings*, which at her first coming out of the Popish *Babylon*, she had
not so fully laid aside. If any of those *envious Brethren* do now call these
Dissenters, as not very long since a great Prelate in a Sermon did, *The
70 Bastards of the Church of England*, I will not make the Return which was
made upon it by a Person of Quality then present; but instead thereof
humbly Demand, who are the *Truer Sons* to the Church of *England*; they
that hold all the *Fundamentals of Christianity* embraced by that Church,
only Questioning and Forbearing a few *Disciplinary*[9] *Points*, which are

[2] The canons of 1640 required the clergy to forswear any attempt to alter the ecclesiastical hierarchy—"archbishops, bishops, deans . . . et cetera." Puritans objected that "et cetera" required them to swear to they knew not what.*
[3] The assembly was summoned by the Long Parliament in 1643 to confer on questions relative to the liturgy, discipline, and government of the Church of England. It included representatives of both houses of Parliament, English divines, and, after the promulgation of the Solemn League and Covenant, Scottish commissioners.*
[4] That is, Erastians, who supported the ascendancy of the state in ecclesiastical matters.
[5] Painstaking, diligent.
[6] The Book of Sports, first issued by James I in 1617, authorized and fostered such Sunday sports as archery and dancing in an attempt to counteract the strict Puritan observance of the Sabbath. Reissued by Archbishop Laud in 1633, it was ordered to be read in all churches.*
[7] "Set" prayers, that is, those read from the Prayer Book, were particularly repugnant to the Puritans.*
[8] That is, a weekday lecture, or a lecture on a market day.*
[9] That is, pertaining to church polity or discipline.

75 confessed *Indifferent*[10] by the greatest Zealots for them; or they that have
made *Britain* more unhabitable than the *Torrid Zone* for the poor *Non-
Conformists*, by their *hot* pressing of those *Indifferencies*, as if they had been
the only *Necessaries*, in the mean time utterly subverting the *Faith* in the
important Points of *Predestination, Free-will, Justification, Perseverance*,[11] and
80 some other things, which that Church requires all her Children to give
their *Assent* and *Consent* unto? If the *Former*; *then*, say I, the First Planters
of *New England* were *Truer Sons* to the Church of *England*, than that part
of the *Church*, which, then by their misemploying their heavy *Church-keys*,
banished them into this Plantation. And indeed, the more Genuine
85 among the most Conformable *Sons of the Church*, did then accordingly
wish all Prosperity to their *New-English* Brethren; in the Number of
whom I would particularly Reckon that faithful Man, Mr. *Edward
Symons*, Minister of *Rayne* in *Essex*; who in a Discourse printed *Anno*
1637,[12] does thus Express himself, *Many now promise to themselves nothing
90 but successive Happiness at* New-England; *which for a time, thro' God's Mercy,
they may enjoy; and I pray God, they may a long time, but in this World there is
no Happiness perpetual.* Nor would I on this Occasion leave unquoted some
notable Words of the Learned, Witty,[13] and Famous Dr. *Fuller*, in his
Comment on *Ruth*, Page 16.[14] *Concerning our Brethren which of late left this
95 Kingdom, to advance a Plantation in* New-England, *I think the Counsel best,
that King* Joash *prescribed unto* Amaziah, Tarry at Home: *Yet as for those
that are already gone, far be it from us to conceive them to be such, to whom we
may not say,* God speed: *But let us Pity them, and Pray for them. I conclude of
99 the two* Englands, *what our Saviour saith of the two Wines*, No Man having
tasted of the Old, presently desireth the New; for he saith, The Old is
better.

§. 4. Being happily arrived at *New-England*, our new Planters found
the difficulties of a rough and hard *Wilderness* presently assaulting them:
5 Of which the worst was the *Sickliness* which many of them had contracted

76 *Zone* for/*Zone*? For C.M.   88 *Rayne*/*Rayn*

    [10] Things not essential in point of doctrine or polity.
    [11] "*Predestination*": the divine decree by which certain persons are infallibly guided to eternal
salvation.
    "*Free-will*": according to Puritan theory, in the physical or natural world, the will of man
is free, and therefore he is sufficiently free, despite predestination, to be responsible for his
deeds.
    "*Justification*": a legal metaphor, connoting not so much to make righteous as to pronounce
righteous, whereby God, in His mercy, treats man as though he were righteous.
    "*Perseverance*": used technically to mean steady continuance, after conversion, in the
faith and life proper to the attainment of eternal life.
    [12] The sermon, entitled "A Wise Man's Carriage in Evill Times," was preached at a public
lecture at Stortford August 3, 1637, on the text Amos 5.13.*
    [13] That is, wise.
    [14] Thomas Fuller's *Comment* was published in 1654. Mather makes some omissions from
Fuller's text.

by their other difficulties. Of those who soon dy'd after their first Arrival, not the least considerable was the Lady *Arabella*, who left an Earthly *Paradice* in the Family of an *Earldom*, to Encounter the Sorrows of a *Wilderness*, for the Entertainments of a *pure Worship* in the *House of God*;
10 and then immediately left that *Wilderness* for the Heavenly *Paradise*, whereto the Compassionate *Jesus*, of whom she was a *Follower*, called her. We have Read concerning a Noble Woman of *Bohemia*, who forsook her Friends, her Plate, her House and All; and because the Gates of the City were Guarded, crept through the Common-Sewer, that she might enjoy
15 the *Institutions* of our Lord at another Place where they might be had. The Spirit which acted[1] that Noble Woman, we may suppose carried this Blessed Lady thus to and thro' the Hardships of an *American* Desart. But as for her Virtuous Husband, *Isaac Johnson*, Esq;

———*He try'd*
20 *To Live without her, lik'd it not, and Dy'd.*

His *Mourning* for the Death of his Honourable Consort was too bitter to be extended a *Year*; about a Month after *her* Death, *his* ensued, unto the extream loss of the whole Plantation. But at the *End* of this *perfect and upright Man*, there was not only *Peace*, but *Joy*; and his *Joy* particularly
25 expressed it self, *That God had kept his Eyes open so long as to see* One Church *of the Lord Jesus Christ gathered in these Ends of the Earth, before his own going away to Heaven.* The *Mortality* thus threatning of this New Plantation, so *enlivened* the Devotions of this good People, that they set themselves by *Fasting* and *Prayer* to obtain from God the removal of it; and their Brethren
30 at *Plymouth* also attended the like Duties on their Behalf: The Issue whereof was, that in a little time they not only had *Health* restored, but they likewise enjoyed the special Direction and Assistance of God in the further Prosecution of their Undertakings.

§. 5. But there were Two terrible Distresses more, besides that of
35 *Sickness*, whereto this People were exposed in the beginning of their Settlement: Tho' a most seasonable and almost unexpected *Mercy from Heaven* still rescued them out of those Distresses. One thing that sometimes extreamly exercised[1] them, was a *Scarcity of Provisions*; in which 'twas wonderful to see their *Dependance* upon God, and God's *Mindfulness* of
40 them. When the parching Droughts of the *Summer* divers times threatned them with an utter and a total Consumption[2] to the Fruits of the Earth, it was their manner, with *Heart-melting*, and I may say, *Heaven-melting* Devotions, to *Fast* and *Pray* before God; and on the very Days, when they

---

[1] Actuated.

[1] In the sense of harassed.
[2] In the sense of decay, wasting away, destruction.

poured out the Water of their *Tears* before him, he would *shower down the*
45 *Water* of his *Rain* upon their Fields; *while they were yet speaking, he would
hear them;* insomuch that the Salvages themselves would on that Occasion
admire *the Englishman's God!* But the *Englishmen* themselves would
Celebrate their Days of *Thanksgiving* to him. When their *Stock* was likewise wasted so far, which divers times it was, that they were come *to the*
50 *last Meal in the Barrel,* just then, unlook'd for, arrived several Ships from
other Parts of the World loaden with Supplies, among which, One was
by the *Lord Deputy of Ireland*[3] sent hither, altho' he did not know the
Necessities of the Country, to which he sent her; and if he had *known* them,
would have been thought as unlikely as any Man living to have helpt
55 them: In these Extremities, 'twas marvellous to see how *Helpful* these
good People were to one another, following the Example of their most
liberal Governour *Winthrop,* who made an *equal Distribution* of what he
had in his own Stores among the Poor, *taking no thought for to Morrow!* And
how *Content* they were; when an Honest Man,[4] as I have heard, inviting
60 his Friends to a Dish of *Clams,* at the Table gave Thanks to Heaven, who
*had given them to suck the abundance of the Seas, and of the Treasures hid in the
Sands!*

Another thing that gave them no little Exercise, was *the Fear of the
Indians,* by whom they were sometimes *Alarm'd.* But this Fear was won-
65 derfully prevented, not only by *Intestine Wars* happening then to fall out
among those *Barbarians,* but chiefly by the *Small-Pox,* which prov'd a
great Plague unto them, and particularly to one of the *Princes*[5] in the
Massachuset-Bay, who yet seemed hopefully to be *Christianiz'd* before he
Dy'd. This Distemper getting in, I know not how, among them, swept
70 them away with a most prodigious Desolation, insomuch that altho' the
English gave them all the assistances of *Humanity* in their Calamities, yet
there was, it may be, not *One* in *Ten* among them left alive, of those
few that liv'd, many also *fled* from the Infection, leaving the Country a
meer *Golgotha* of unburied Carcases; and as for the *rest,* the *English* treated
75 them with all the Civility imaginable; among the Instances of which
Civility, let this be reckoned for *One,* that notwithstanding the *Patent*
which they had for the Country, they fairly *purchased* of the Natives the
several *Tracts* of Land which they afterwards *possessed.*

§. 6. The People in the Fleet that arriv'd at *New-England,* in the Year
80 1630, left the Fleet almost, as the *Family* of *Noah* did the *Ark,* having a
whole World before them to be peopled. *Salem* was already supplied with

---

72   alive; of/alive of   C.M.   73   liv'd,/liv'd.   C.M.

---

[3] Sir Thomas Wentworth; the vessel was the *St. Patrick.**
[4] The "Honest Man" has not been identified.*
[5] Sagamore John.*

a competent Number of Inhabitants; and therefore the Governour, with most of the Gentlemen that Accompanied him in his Voyage, took their first Opportunity to prosecute further Settlements about the bottom of the
85 *Massachuset-Bay:* But where-ever they sat down, they were so mindful of their *Errand into the Wilderness,* that still one of their *First Works* was to gather a *Church* into the *Covenant* and *Order* of the Gospel. First, There was a Church thus gathered at *Charles-Town,* on the North side of *Charles's* River; where keeping a Solemn *Fast* on *August* 27. 1630, to Implore the
90 Conduct[1] and Blessing of Heaven on their Ecclesiastical Proceedings, they chose Mr. *Wilson,*[2] a most Holy and Zealous Man, formerly a Minister of *Sudbury,* in the County of *Suffolk,* to be their Teacher; and altho' he now submitted unto an *Ordination,* with an *Imposition of such Hands* as were by the Church invited so to pronounce the Benediction of
95 Heaven upon him; yet it was done with a *Protestation* by all, that it should be only as a sign of his *Election* to the Charge of his *New Flock,* without any Intention that he should thereby Renounce the Ministry he had received in *England.* After the gathering of the Church at *Charles-Town,* there
99 quickly followed another at the Town of *Dorchester.*

And after *Dorchester* there followed another at the Town of *Boston,* which Issued out of *Charles-Town;* one Mr. *James*[3] took the Care of the Church at *Charles-Town,* and Mr. *Wilson* went over to *Boston,* where they that formerly belonged unto *Charles-Town,* with Universal Approbation be-
5 came a *distinct Church* of themselves. To *Boston* soon succeeded a Church at *Roxbury;* to *Roxbury,* one at *Lyn;* to *Lyn,* one at *Watertown;* so that in one or two Years time there were to be seen *Seven Churches*[4] in this Neighbourhood, all of them attending to what the *Spirit* in the *Scripture said unto them;* all of them *Golden Candelsticks,* illustrated with a very sensible[5]
10 *Presence* of our Lord Jesus Christ among them.

§. 7. It was for a matter of *Twelve Years*[1] together, that Persons of all Ranks, well affected unto *Church-Reformation,* kept sometimes *Dropping* and sometimes *Flocking*[2] into *New-England,* tho' some that were coming into *New-England* were not suffered so to do. The Persecutors of those
15 *Puritans,* as they were called, who were now *Retiring* into that *Cold Country*

10 among/amoug

[1] In the sense of direction, guidance.
[2] John Wilson (*c.*1591–1667) came out with Winthrop, and became, first, teacher and then pastor of the First Church. See *Magnalia,* Bk. III, pt. 1, chap. 3.
[3] Thomas James (1595–1682), A.B. Emmanuel College, Cambridge, was ordained in England and again in Charlestown, where he served as minister from 1632 to 1636.
[4] Mather's order of the foundation of the seven churches seems inaccurate. Dorchester was founded before Boston, and Watertown at least as soon.*
[5] In the sense of discernible, evident.

[1] That is, from 1628 to 1640.*
[2] That is, either coming a few at a time, or in great numbers.

from the *Heat* of their Persecution, did all that was possible to hinder as many as was possible from enjoying of that *Retirement*. There were many *Countermands* given to the Passage of People that were now steering of this *Western Course*; and there was a sort of *Uproar* made among no small
20 part of the Nation, that this People should not be *let go*. Among those bound for *New-England*, that were so stopt, there were especially Three Famous Persons, whom I suppose their Adversaries would not have so studiously detained at Home, if they had *foreseen* Events; those were *Oliver Cromwel*, and Mr. *Hampden*, and Sir *Arthur Haselrig*: [3] Nevertheless,
25 this is not the only Instance *of Persecuting Church-men's* not having the *Spirit of Prophecy*. But many others were diverted from an intended Voyage hither by the pure *Providence* of God, which had *provided* other Improvements for them; and of this take one Instance instead of many. Before the woful Wars which broke forth in the *Three Kingdoms*, there were
30 divers Gentlemen in *Scotland*,[4] who being uneasie under the *Ecclesiastical Burdens* of the Times, wrote unto *New-England* their Enquiries, Whether they might be there suffered freely to Exercise their *Presbyterian Church-Government?* And it was freely answered, *That they might*. Hereupon they sent over an Agent, who pitched upon a Tract of Land near the Mouth
35 of *Merimack River*, whither they intended then to Transplant themselves: But altho' they had so far proceeded in their Voyage, as to be *Half-Seas* thorough;[5] the manifold Crosses they met withal, made them give over their Intentions; and the Providence of God so ordered it, that some of those very Gentlemen were afterwards the *Revivers* of that well-known
40 *Solemn League and Covenant*,[6] which had so great an Influence upon the following Circumstances of the Nations. However, the number of those who did actually arrive at *New-England* before the Year 1640. have been computed about *Four Thousand*; since which time far more have gone out of the Country than have come to it; and yet the God of Heaven so
45 smiled upon the *Plantation*, while under an *easie* and *equal* Government, the Designs of Christianity in well-formed *Churches* have been carried on, that no History can *parallel* it. That saying of *Eutropius* about *Rome*, which hath been sometimes applied unto the Church, is capable of some Application to this little part of the Church: *Nec Minor ab Exordio, nec major*
50 *Incrementis ulla*.[7] Never was any Plantation brought unto such a Con-

24 *Hampden/Hambden*   25 *Church-men's/Church-mens*

[3] John Hampden (1594–1643) and Sir Arthur Haselrig (Hesilrige, d. 1661), were Puritan statesmen and parliamentary leaders.*
[4] The leaders were two ministers, Robert Blair and John Livingston.*
[5] Halfway across, or "through," the ocean.
[6] The Solemn League and Covenant (1643) pledged noblemen and commons of the kingdoms of England, Scotland, and Ireland to maintenance of the Church of Scotland, reformation of the Church of England, and uniformity of the churches of the British Isles.*
[7] Eutropius (d. *c*.610), Roman historian. "Never was anything more mean in inception or more mighty in progress."*

siderableness, in a space of time so Inconsiderable! An *Howling Wilderness* in a few Years became a *Pleasant Land*, accommodated with the *Necessaries*, yea, and the *Conveniencies* of *Humane Life*; the *Gospel* has carried with it a *fulness of all other Blessings*; and (albeit, that Mankind generally, as far as
55 we have any Means of enquiry, have increased, in one and the same given Proportion, and so no more than *doubled* themselves in about Three-Hundred and Sixty Years, in all the past Ages of the World, since the fixing of the present Period of Humane Life) the Four-Thousand *First Planters*, in less than Fifty Years, notwithstanding all *Transportations* and
60 *Mortalities*, increased into, they say, more than an *Hundred Thousand*.

CHAP. VI.

—Qui Trans Mare Currunt.—[1] *Or, The* Addition *of several other Colonies to the former; with some other Considerables*[2] *in the* Condition *of these later Colonies.*

65 §. I. IT was not long before the *Massachuset* Colony was become like an *Hive*, overstock'd with *Bees*; and many of the new Inhabitants entertained thoughts of *swarming* into Plantations extended further into the Country. The Colony might fetch its own Description from the Dispensations of the Great God, unto his Ancient *Israel*, and say, *O*
70 *God of Hosts, Thou hast brought a Vine out of* England; *Thou hast cast out the Heathen and planted it; Thou preparedst room before it, and didst cause it to take deep root, and it filled the Land; the Hills were covered with the shadow of it, and the Boughs thereof were like the goodly Cedars; she sent out her Boughs unto the Sea.*[3] But still there was one stroak wanting for the compleat Accommo-
75 dation[4] of the Description; to wit, *she sent forth her Branches unto the River*; and this therefore is to be next attended. The Fame of *Connecticut* River, a Long, Fresh, Rich *River* (as indeed the Name *Connecticut* is Indian for *a long River*) had made a little *Nilus* of it, in the Expectations of the good People about the *Massachuset-Bay*: Whereupon many of the Planters
80 belonging especially to the Towns of *Cambridge, Dorchester, Watertown* and *Roxbury*, took up Resolutions to Travel an Hundred Miles *Westward* from those Towns, for a further Settlement upon this Famous *River*. When the Learned *Fernandius* had been in the *Indies*, he did in his Preface

62   Trans Mare/Transmare   74–75   Accommodation/Accommodations

1 "Those who cross the sea."*
2 In the sense of things worthy to be considered or noted; notable.
3 Ps. 80.7–11; "England" replaces "Egypt."
4 Agreement, conformity.

to his Commentaries afterwards published, give this Account of it; *Deo*
85 *sic volente, prodii in remotissimos usq; Indos, tam non avidus lucis & gloriæ, ut
eam vere dixerim, ultro elegerim mei ipsius adhuc viventis verissimam Sepulturam.*[5]
Reader, come with me now to behold some Worthy, and Learned, and
Genteel Persons going to be *Buried Alive* on the Banks of *Connecticut*,
having been first *Slain*[6] by the Ecclesiastical Impositions and Persecu-
90 tions of *Europe*.

§. 2. It was in the Year 1635. that this Design was first formed; and
the Disposition of the Celebrated Mr. *Thomas Hooker*,[1] with his People
now in *Cambridge*, to engage in the Design, was that which gave most
Life unto it. They then sent their Agents to view the Country, who re-
95 turned with so Advantageous a Report, that the next Year there was a
great *Remove* of good People thither: On this Remove, they that went
from *Cambridge* became a Church upon a Spot of Ground now called
Hartford; they that went from *Dorchester* became a Church at *Windsor*;
99 they that went from *Watertown* sat down at *Wethersfield*; and they that
left *Roxbury* were *In-Churched* higher up the River at *Springfield*, a place
which was afterwards found within the Line of the *Massachuset*-Charter.
Indeed the *first* Winter after their going thither proved an *hard* one; and
the grievous Disappointments which befel them, thro' the unseasonable
5 Freezing of the *River*, whereby their Vessel of *Provisions* was detained at
the Mouth of the River, Threescore Miles below them, caused them to
Encounter with very Disastrous Difficulties. Divers of them were hereby
obliged in the Depth of Winter to Travel back into the *Bay*; and some
of them were frozen to Death in the Journey.

10 However, such was their Courage, that they Prosecuted their *Plantation-
Work* with speedy and blessed Successes; and when Bloody *Salvages* in
their Neighbourhood, known by the Name of *Pequots*, had like to have
nipt the Plantation in the Bud by a cruel War, within a Year or two after
their Settlement, the marvellous Providence of God immediately ex-
15 tinguished that *War*, by prospering the *New-English* Arms, unto the utter
subduing of the Quarrelsome Nation, and affrightning of all the other
Natives.

§. 3. It was with the Countenance and Assistance of their Brethren in
the *Massachuset-Bay*, that the First Planters of *Connecticut* made their

---

[5] "By God's permission, I penetrated into the remotest parts of India, actuated less by
curiosity or ambition than by a desire to say, with truth, that I had voluntarily sought out a
spot where I was in reality buried alive." Antonio Fernandez (1558?–1628), a Portuguese
Jesuit priest, taught in the universities of Coimbra and Evora in his native land, and served
for a time in the Portuguese outpost of Goa in India.*
[6] Here in the obsolete sense of "smitten" or "stricken."

---

[1] Thomas Hooker (1586?–1647), Fellow of Emmanuel College and lecturer at Chelmsford,
England, came out to New England with John Cotton on the *Griffin* in 1633. He was first
pastor of the church in Cambridge. See *Magnalia*, Bk. III, pt. 1, Appendix.*

20 Essays thus to Discover and Cultivate the remoter Parts of this mighty
Wilderness; and accordingly several Gentlemen went furnished with
some kind of *Commission* from the Government of the *Massachuset-Bay*, for
to maintain some kind of Government among the Inhabitants, till there
could be a more orderly Settlement. But the Inhabitants quickly per-
25 ceiving themselves to be without the *Line* of the *Massachuset-Charter*,
entred into a Combination among themselves, whereby with mutual
Consent they became a *Body-Politick*, and framed a Body of necessary
Laws and *Orders*,[1] to the Execution whereof they chose all necessary
Officers, very much, tho' not altogether after the form of the Colony from
30 whence they Issued. So they jogg'd on for many Years; and whereas
before the Year 1644. that Worthy Gentleman, *George Fenwick*, Esq;[2] did
on the behalf of several Persons of Quality begin a Plantation about the
Mouth of the River, which was called *Say-Brook*, in Remembrance of
those Right Honourable Persons, the Lord *Say*, and the Lord *Brook*, who
35 laid a Claim to the Land thereabouts, by Virtue of a Patent granted by
the Earl of *Warwick*;[3] the Inhabitants of *Connecticut* that Year purchased
of Mr. *Fenwick* this Tract of Land. But the Confusions then Embarassing
the Affairs of the *English* Nation, hindered our *Connecticotians* from seeking
of any further Settlement, until the Restoration of K. *Charles* II. when
40 they made their Application to the King for a *Charter*, by the Agency of
their Honourable Governour, *John Winthrop*, Esq;[4] the most accomplished Son of that Excellent Person, who had been so Considerable in
the Foundations of the *Massachuset*-Colony. This Renowned *Virtuoso*[5] had
justly been the Darling of *New-England*, if they had only considered his
45 Eminent Qualities, as he was a *Christian*, a *Gentleman*, and a *Philosopher*,
well worthy to be, as he was, a Member of the *Royal-Society*; but it must
needs further endear his Memory to his Country, that God made him
the Instrument of obtaining for them, as he did from the King of *England*,
as amply priviledged a *Charter*[6] as was ever enjoy'd perhaps by any
50 People under the Cope[7] of Heaven. Under the Protection and Encouragement of this *Charter* they flourished many Years; and many Towns being

---

[1] The *Fundamental Orders*, formed by voluntary compact in 1639.*

[2] George Fenwick (1603–1657), active in the colonization of Connecticut, came to America
in 1639 and settled at the mouth of the Connecticut River. He returned to England in 1645.*

[3] William Fiennes (1582–1662), first Viscount Saye and Sele, was a prominent Puritan;
he acquired land in both Connecticut and New Hampshire. Lord Brooke (Robert Greville,
1608–1643) was a Puritan member of the House of Lords. Robert Rich (1587–1658), second
Earl of Warwick, was a member of the Council for New England and an active champion of
the parliamentary cause.*

[4] John Winthrop, Jr. (1606–1676), was governor of Connecticut continuously from 1659
to 1676. See *Magnalia*, Bk. II, chap. 11.

[5] One who has a general interest in arts and sciences, or who pursues special investigations
in one of them.

[6] The Connecticut Charter was granted April 23, 1662.*

[7] In the obsolete figurative sense of canopy, vault, or expanse.

successively erected among them, their *Churches* had *Rest, and walked in the Fear of God, and in the Comfort of the Holy Spirit.*[8]

§. 4. The *Church-Order* observed in the Churches of *Connecticut*, has been
55 the same that is observed by their *Sisters* in the *Massachuset-Bay*; and in this *Order* they lived exceeding peaceably all the Eleven Years that Mr. *Hooker* lived among them. Nevertheless there arose at length some unhappy Contests in one Town[1] of the *Colony*, which grew into an Alienation that could not be cured without such a Parting, and yet, indeed, hardly
60 so kind a Parting, as that whereto once *Abraham* and *Lot* were driven. However, these Little, Idle, Angry *Controversies*, proved Occasions of *Enlargements* to the Church of God; for such of the Inhabitants as chose a *Cottage in a Wilderness*, before the most beautiful and furnished Edifice, overheated with the *Fire* of Contention, removed peaceably higher up
65 the River, where a whole County of Holy *Churches*[2] has been added unto the number of our Congregations.

§. 5. But there was one thing that made this Colony to become very considerable; which thing remains now to be considered. The well-known Mr. *Davenport*, and Mr. *Eaton*,[1] and several Eminent Persons that
70 came over to the *Massachuset-Bay*, among some of the First Planters, were strongly urged, that they would have settled in this *Bay*; but hearing of another *Bay* to the South-West of *Connecticut*, which might be more capable to entertain those that were to follow them, they desired that their Friends at *Connecticut* would purchase of the Native Proprietors for
75 *them*, all the Land that lay between themselves and *Hudson's* River, which was in part effected. Accordingly removing thither in the Year 1637.[2] they seated themselves in a pleasant *Bay*, where they spread themselves along the *Sea-Coasts*; and one might have been suddenly, as it were surprized with the sight of such notable Towns, as first *New-Haven*;
80 then *Guilford*; then *Milford*; then *Stamford*; and then *Brainford*, where our Lord Jesus Christ is Worshipped in *Churches* of an Evangelical Constitution; and from thence, if the Enquirer made a Salley over to *Long Island*, he might there also have seen the Churches of our Lord beginning to

---

80   *Brainford,/Brainford*   82   made/make

---

[8] Acts 9.31.

---

[1] Wethersfield.*'
[2] "County of Holy *Churches*": at Springfield, Hadley, and Hatfield.*

---

[1] John Davenport (1597–1670) early evidenced his interest in the Massachusetts Bay Company by contributing £50. Interdicted from preaching in both England and Holland, in 1637 he and his close friend Theophilus Eaton (1590–1658), a London merchant, emigrated to New England. Davenport became the first pastor, Eaton the first governor of the independent New Haven colony. See *Magnalia*, Bk. III, pt. 1, chap. 4; Bk. II, chap. 9.*

[2] They sailed from Boston March 30, 1638, and on April 18 kept their first Sabbath in New Haven.

take root in the Eastern Parts of that Island. All this while this *Fourth*
85 *Colony* wanted the legal *Basis* of a *Charter* to build upon; but they did by
mutual Agreement form them selves into a *Body-Politick*, as like as they
judg'd fit unto the other Colonies in their Neighbourhood; and as for
their *Church-Order*, it was generally, *Secundum Usum Massachusettensem*.[3]

§. 6. Behold, a Fourth Colony of *New-English* Christians, in a manner
90 *stoln* into the World, and a Colony, indeed, *constellated* with many Stars
of the *First Magnitude*. The Colony was under the Conduct of as Holy,
and as Prudent, and as Genteel Persons as most that ever visited these
Nooks of *America*; and yet *these* too were Try'd with very humbling
Circumstances.

95 Being *Londoners*, or Merchants, and Men of Traffick and Business, their
Design was in a manner wholly to apply themselves unto *Trade*; but the
Design failing, they found their great Estates to sink so fast, that they
must quickly *do something*. Whereupon in the Year 1646. gathering to-
99 gether almost all the Strength which was left 'em, they Built one Ship
more, which they fraighted for *England* with the best part of their Tradable[1] Estates; and sundry of their Eminent Persons Embarked themselves
in her for the Voyage. But, alas, the Ship was never after heard of! She
foundred in the Sea; and in her were lost, not only the *Hopes* of their
5 future Trade, but also the *Lives* of several Excellent Persons, as well as
divers *Manuscripts* of some great Men in the Country, sent over for the
Service of the Church, which were now buried in the Ocean. The *fuller
Story* of that *grievous Matter*, let the Reader with a just Astonishment accept from the Pen of the Reverend Person, who is now the Pastor of
10 *New-Haven*. I wrote unto him for it, and was thus Answered.

Reverend and Dear Sir,
'IN Compliance with your Desires, I now give you the Relation of that
'   *Apparition* of a *Ship in the Air*, which I have received from the most
'Credible, Judicious and Curious Surviving Observers of it.
15 'In the Year 1647.[2] besides much other Lading, a far more Rich
'Treasure of Passengers, (Five or Six of which were Persons of chief Note
'and Worth in *New-Haven*) put themselves on Board a *New Ship*, built at
'*Rhode-Island*, of about 150 Tuns; but so walty,[3] that the Master, (*Lam-*
'*berton*) often said she would prove their Grave. In the Month of *January*,
20 'cutting their way thro' much Ice, on which they were accompanied
'with the Reverend Mr. *Davenport*, besides many other Friends, with

---

[3] "According to the Massachusetts usage."

[1] That may be dealt with in the way of trade, marketable.*
[2] The date was actually 1645/46.
[3] Crank or unsteady; this passage cited by the NED to illustrate use.*

'many Fears, as well as Prayers and Tears, they set Sail. Mr. *Davenport*
'in Prayer with an observable *Emphasis* used these Words, *Lord, if it be*
'*thy pleasure to bury these our Friends in the bottom of the Sea, they are thine*;
25 '*save them!* The Spring following no Tidings of these Friends arrived
'with the Ships from *England: New-Haven's* Heart began to fail her: This
'put the Godly People on much *Prayer*, both Publick and Private, *That*
'*the Lord would (if it was his Pleasure) let them hear what he had done with their*
'*dear Friends, and prepare them with a suitable Submission to his Holy Will*. In
30 '*June* next ensuing, a great *Thunder-storm* arose out of the *North-West*:
'after which, (the *Hemisphere*[4] being serene) about an Hour before Sun-
'set a SHIP of like Dimensions with the aforesaid, with her Canvas and
'Colours abroad[5] (tho' the Wind Northernly) appeared in the Air
'coming up from our Harbour's Mouth, which lyes Southward from the
35 'Town, seemingly with her *Sails* filled under a fresh Gale, holding her
'Course North, and continuing under Observation, Sailing against the
'Wind for the space of half an Hour. *Many* were drawn to behold this
'great Work of God; yea, the very *Children* cry'd out, *There's a Brave*
'*Ship!* At length, crouding up as far as there is usually *Water* sufficient for
40 'such a Vessel, and so near some of the Spectators, as that they imagined
'a Man might hurl a Stone on Board her, her *Maintop* seem'd to be
'blown off, but left hanging in the Shrouds; then her *Missen-top*; then
'all her *Masting* seemed blown away by the Board: Quickly after the
'*Hull* brought unto a Careen,[6] she overset, and so vanished into a smoaky
45 'Cloud, which in some time dissipated, leaving, as everywhere else, a
'clear Air. The admiring[7] Spectators could distinguish the several Col-
'ours of each Part, the Principal Riging, and such Proportions, as
'caused not only the generality of Persons to say, *This was the Mould of*
'*their Ship, and thus was her Tragick End:* But Mr. *Davenport* also in publick
50 'declared to this Effect, *That God had condescended, for the quieting of their*
'*afflicted Spirits, this Extraordinary Account of his Soveraign Disposal of those*
'*for whom so many Fervent Prayers were made continually.* Thus I am, Sir,

Your Humble Servant,

James Pierpont.[8]

55   Reader, There being yet living so many Credible Gentlemen, that
were Eye-Witnesses of this *Wonderful* Thing, I venture to Publish it for
a thing as *undoubted*, as 'tis *wonderful*.

But let us now proceed with our Story. Our *Colony* of *New Haven*
apprehended themselves Disadvantageously seated for the Affairs of

---

[4] In early usage, half of the celestial sphere; the sky above us.
[5] That is, with sails spread and flag displayed.
[6] That is, heeled over on her side.
[7] Wondering.
[8] James Pierpont (1660–1714) was pastor of the First Congregational Church of New Haven from 1685 to 1714.*

60 *Husbandry*; and therefore upon these Disasters they made many Attempts
of *removing* into some other Parts of the World. One while they were
invited unto *Delaware-Bay*, another while they were invited unto *Jamaica*;
they had offers made them from *Ireland* also, after the Wars there were
over; and they entred into some Treaties about the City of *Galway*,
65 which they were to have had as a small *Province* to themselves. But the
God of Heaven still strangely disappointed all these Attempts; and whereas they were concerned how their *Posterity* should be able to live, if they
must make *Husbandry* their main shift for their Living; that *Posterity* of
theirs by the good Providence of God, instead of coming to Beggary and
70 Misery, have thriven wonderfully: The Colony is improved with many
Wealthy *Husbandmen*, and is become no small part of the best *Granary*
for all *New-England*. And the same good Providence has all along so
preserved them from annoyance by the *Indians*, that altho' at their first
setting down there were few Towns but what wisely perswaded a Body of
75 *Indians* to dwell near them; whereby such Kindnesses passed between
them, that they always dwelt peaceably together; nevertheless there are
few of those Towns, but what have seen their Body of *Indians* utterly
Extirpated by nothing but *Mortality* wasting them.

§. 7. But what is now become of *New-Haven* Colony? I must Answer,
80 *It is not:* And yet it has been growing ever since it first *was*. But when
Connecticut Colony Petitioned the Restored King for a 𝕮𝔥𝔞𝔯𝔱𝔢𝔯,[1] they
procured *New-Haven* Colony to be annexed unto them in the same *Charter*;
and this, not without having first the private Concurrence of some
Leading Men in the Colony; tho' the Minds of *others* were so uneasie about
85 the Coalition, that it cost some time after the Arrival of the *Charter* for
the Colony, like *Jephtah*'s Daughter, to bewail her Condition before it
could be quietly complied withal. Nevertheless they have lived ever since,
One Colony, very happily together, and the *God of Love and Peace* has
remarkably dwelt among them: However, these Children of God have
90 not been without their *Chastisements*, especially in the Malignant *Fevers*
and *Agues*, which have often proved very Mortal in most or all of their
Plantations.

§. 8. While the *South-West* Parts of *New-England* were thus filled with
New Colonies, the *North-East* Parts of the Country were not forgotten.
95 There were ample Regions beyond the Line of the *Massachuset-Patent*,
where new Settlements were attempted, not only by such as designed a
Fishing-Trade at Sea, or a *Bever*-Trade on Shore; nor only by some that
were uneasie under the *Massachuset*-Government in a *Day of Temptation*,[1]

64 *Galway/Galloway*

[1] The Connecticut Charter was granted by Charles II in 1662.*

[1] A reference to the Antinomian controversy of 1636–1637 concerning the nature and
primacy of grace in the drama of salvation, and the relation of sanctification to the justification
of a true believer.*

99 which came upon the First Planters; but also by some very serious
Christians, who propounded the Enlargement and Enjoyment of our
Lord's Evangelical Interests in those Territories. The Effects of these
Excursions were, That several well-constituted Churches were gathered
in the Province of *East-Hampshire*,[2] besides one or two in the Province of
5 *Main*, whereto were added a large number of other Congregations,
wherein weekly *Prayers* and *Sermons* were made, altho' the Inhabitants
belonging to those Congregations, proceeded not so far as to all the
Ordinances of a more compleat *Church-State* among them. That which
contributed more than a little to the growth of *Christianity* in those Parts
10 of *New-England*, was the Application, which the People being tired with
many Quarrelsome Circumstances about their Government, made unto
the *General Court* of the *Massachuset-Bay*, to be taken under their Protection; which Petition of theirs being answered by that *General Court*,
surely after a more Charitable and Accountable manner, than such
15 Authors as *Ogilby* in his *America* have represented it, [*Vos magis Historicis,
Lectores, Credite veris!*][3] there followed many Successful Endeavours to
spread the good Effects and Orders of the *Gospel* along that Coast.

But thus was the Settlement of *New-England* brought about; these were
the *Beginnings*, these the *Foundations* of those *Colonies*, which have not
20 only enlarged the *English Empire* in some Regards more than any other
Outgoings of our Nation, but also afforded a Singular Prospect of
Churches erected in an *American* Corner of the World, on purpose to
express and pursue the Protestant *Reformation*.

CHAP. VII.

25 Hecatompolis:[1] *Or, A Field which the Lord hath Blessed.*
A *MAP* of the Country.

IT is proper that I should now give the Reader an *Ecclesiastical Map* of
the Country, thus Undertaken. Know then, that although for now
more than Twenty Years, the *Blasting Strokes*[2] of Heaven upon the Secu-

---

2 Effects/Effect   5 *Main/Mam*

[2] New Hampshire; the settlements along the Piscataqua as distinguished from those in Hampshire County in western Massachusetts.
[3] "Readers, rather trust truthful historians than such."*

---

[1] Having a hundred cities.
[2] The secular *"Blasting Strokes"* included King Philip's War, the annulment of the Massachusetts Charter in 1684, the impositions of Sir Edmund Andros as royal governor from 1686 until the colonists deposed him in April 1689, and the disastrous expedition against Quebec and Montreal in 1690.*

30 lar Affairs of this Country have been such, as rather to *Abate* than *Enlarge* the growth of it; yet there are to be seen in it at this present Year 1696,[3] these *Colonies, Counties,* and *Congregations.*

¶ *The Numbers and Places of the Christian Congregations, now Worshipping our Lord Jesus Christ, in the several Colonies of* New-England, *and the Names of* 35 *the Ministers at this time employed in the Service of those Congregations.*[4]

Notandum, Where the Name of any Minister hath *H.C.* added unto it in our Catalogue, it is to be understood that *Harvard-Colledge* was the *Mother,* in whose Arms that Minister was Educated.

I. **I**N Plymouth *Colony there are Three Counties; and the several Congregations*
40 *therein are thus Accommodated.*

Plymouth County Ministers.

Bridgewater, Mr. *James Keith.*
Duxbury, Mr. *Ichabod Wiswall,* H. C.
Marshfield, Mr. *Edward Thompson,* H. C.
45 *Middlebury,*[5] Mr. [*Thomas Palmer.*]
Plymouth, Mr. *John Cotton,* H. C.[6]
Scituate, which hath two Churches, Mr. *Jeremiah Cushing,* H. C. Mr. *Deodate Lawson.*

Barnstable County Ministers.

50 *Barnstable,* Mr. *Jonathan Russel,* H. C.
Eastham, Mr. *Samuel Treat,* H. C.
Falmouth, Harwich, Manamoyet,[7] Mr. *Nathanael Stone,* H. C.

43   *Wiswall/Wiswul*

[3] Just when Mather wrote his list of ministers is difficult to determine, but it is probable that it was finished by early 1697.

[4] Mather's list of ministers has many omissions and errors. Some of the errors were clearly those of the printers; others resulted from his attempt to spell names given him by word of mouth or from his use of documents the orthography of which was phonetic. For misspellings that are easily intelligible no notes are given; those that are not are corrected in the text and listed as emendations. When Mather gives only the surname of a minister the Christian name is, whenever possible, inserted in brackets in the text. When he lists no minister for a town or area but one is known to have existed, the name is also given in brackets. When there is no clear evidence that there was a minister, endnotes supply available data. Footnotes are given also when two or more men listed have the same name and when earlier pages in the *Magnalia* give data on a minister. Identifications of others are not given, but endnotes give the principal sources of information on them.*

[5] Now Middleborough, Massachusetts.

[6] John Cotton of Plymouth was Cotton Mather's uncle.*

[7] Now Chatham, Massachusetts.

Rochester,[8] Mr. [*Samuel*] *Arnold*, [Jr.]
Sandwich, Mr. *Rowland Cotton*, H. C.
55 *Yarmouth*, Mr. *John Cotton*, H. C.[9]

Bristol County Ministers.

Bristol, Mr. *John Sparhawk*, H. C.
Dartmouth, Perishing without Vision.[10]
Freetown,[11]
60 *Little-Compton*, Mr. *Eliphelet Adams*, H. C.
Swansy,[12] [Mr. *Samuel Luther*, Mr. *Thomas Barnes.*]
Tanton, Mr. *Samuel Danforth*, H. C.

Hereto an Ecclesiastical Reckoning may annex the Islands of

Martha's Vineyard, Mr. *Ralph Thacher*, Mr. [*Jonathan*] *Dunham*, besides
65   *Indian* Churches and Pastors.
Nantucket, Indian Pastors.
Newport in *Rode Island*, Mr. *Nathanael Clap*, H. C.

II. I*N* Massachuset *Colony are Four Counties, and the several Congregations
     in them are so supplied.*

70   The County of *Suffolk* Ministers.

Boston, Of the *Old* Church, Mr. *James Allen*, Mr. *Benj. Wadsworth*, H. C.
Of the *North* Church, Mr. *Increase Mather*, President of the Colledge, and
    his Son *Cotton Mather*, H. C.
Of the *South* Church, Mr. *Samuel Willard*, H. C.
75 Besides these, there is in the Town a small Congregation that Worship
    God with the Ceremonies of the Church of *England*; served generally
    by a Change of Persons, occasionally visiting these Parts of the World.[13]
And another small Congregation of *Antipedo-Baptists*, wherein Mr.
    [*John*] *Emblen* is the settled Minister.
80 And a *French* Congregation of Protestant *Refugees*, under the Pastoral
    Cares of Monsieur [*Pierre*] *Daille*.
Braintree, Mr. *Moses Fisk*, H. C.

64 *Dunham/Denham*   79   *Emblen/Emblin*
74 *Willard/Wilward* C.M.

8 Now Marion, Massachusetts.
9 John Cotton of Yarmouth (1661–1706) was Cotton Mather's cousin.
10 Without a minister and thus deprived of the light of the Gospel.*
11 Now part of Fall River and Fairhaven, Massachusetts.*
12 Swansea, when Mather wrote, had two Baptist churches, but no Congregational one.
13 In 1686 a group of Anglicans in Boston joined in an Episcopal service, and formed an
Episcopal Church Society, led by the Reverend John Ratcliffe. He ministered to the Society
until 1689, when he was succeeded by Samuel Myles.*

Dedham, Mr. *Joseph Belcher*, H. C.
Dorchester, Mr. *John Danforth*, H. C.[14]
85 *Hingham*, Mr. *John Norton*, H. C.
Hull, Mr. *Zechariah Whitman*, H. C.
Medfield, Mr. *Joseph Baxter*, H. C.
Mendon, Mr. *Grindal Rawson*, H. C.
Milton, Mr. *Peter Thacher*, H. C.
90 *Roxbury*, Mr. *Nehemiah Walter*, H. C.
Weymouth, Mr. *Samuel Torrey*, H. C.
Woodstock, Mr. *Josiah Dwight*, H. C.
Wrentham, Mr. *Samuel Man*, H. C.

The County of *Middlesex* Ministers.

95 *Billerica*, Mr. *Samuel Whiteing*, H. C.
Cambridge, Mr. *William Brattle*, H. C.[15]
Charles-Town, Mr. *Charles Morton*.
Chelmsford, Mr. *Thomas Clark*, H. C.
99 *Concord*, Mr. *Joseph Eastabrook*, H. C.
Dunstable, Mr. *Thomas Weld*, H. C.
Groton, Mr. *Gershom Hobart*, H. C.
Lancaster, Mr. *John Whiteing*, H. C.
Malborough, Mr. *William Brinsmead*, H. C.
5 *Malden*, Mr. *Michael Wigglesworth*, H. C.
Medford, Mr. *Simon Bradstreet*, H. C.
Newtown,[16] Mr. *Nehemiah Hobart*, H. C.
Oxford,[17]
Reading, Mr. *Jonathan Pierpont*, H. C.
10 *Sherborn*, Mr. *Daniel Gookin*, H. C.
Stow,[18] Mr.
Sudbury, Mr. *James Sherman*.
Watertown East, Mr. *Henry Gibbs*, H. C.
West,[19] Mr. *Samuel Angier*. H. C.
15 *Woburn*, Mr. *Jabez Fox*, H. C.
Worcester,[20]

[14] See note on John Danforth in the Prefatory Poems to the *Magnalia*, p. 82, l. 19n.
[15] See introductory essay "Cotton Mather," p. 15.
[16] Known as Cambridge Village when Hobart began to preach there in June 1672, subsequently became Newton.
[17] Oxford, Massachusetts, had a French Protestant church for a few years, with Daniel Bondet as its minister, but he left Oxford before Mather wrote. There was no Congregational church in Oxford until 1721.
[18] Stow had no church until 1700.
[19] Later incorporated as Waltham.
[20] Worcester was settled in 1688, but was attacked by Indians and no permanent settlement was made until 1713.

The County of *Essex* Ministers.

Amesbury, [Mr. *Thomas Wells*.]
Andover, Mr. *Francis Dane*, and Mr. *Thomas Barnard*, H. C.
20 *Beverly*, Mr. *John Hale*, H. C.
Boxford,[21]
Bradford, Mr. *Zechariah Symmes*, H. C.
Glocester, Mr. *John Emerson*, H. C.
Haveril, Mr. *Benjamin Rolfe*, H. C.
25 *Ipswich*, Mr. *William Hubbard*, H. C. and Mr. *John Rogers*, H. C.
And Village,[22] Mr. *John Wise*, H. C.
Lyn, Mr. *Jeremiah Shepard*, H. C.
Manchester, Mr. *John Emerson*, H. C.
Marblehead, Mr. *Samuel Cheever*, H. C.
30 *Newbury*, East, Mr. [*Christopher*] *Toppan*, H. C.
West, Mr. *Samuel Belcher*, H. C.
Rowly, Mr. *Edward Payson*, H. C.
Salem, Mr. *John Higginson*, and Mr. *Nicholas Noyse*, H. C.[23]
And Village,[24] Mr. *Samuel Paris*, H. C.
35 *Salsbury*, Mr. *Caleb Cushing*, H. C.
Topsfield, Mr. *Joseph Capen*, H. C.
Wenham, Mr. *Joseph Gerish*, H. C.

The County of *Hampshire*[25] Ministers.

Deerfield, Mr. *John Williams*, H. C.
40 *Endfield*,[26] Mr.
Hatfield, Mr. *William Williams*, H. C.
Hadley, Mr. [*Isaac Chauncy*, H. C.]
Northampton, Mr. *Solomon Stoddard*, H. C.
Springfield, Mr. *Daniel Brewer*, H. C.
45 *Southfield*, Mr. *Benjamin Ruggles*, H. C.
Westfield, Mr. *Edward Taylor*, H. C.

To which, if we add the Congregations in *Piscataqua*.[27]

Dover, Mr. *John Pike*, H. C.
Exeter, Mr. *John Clark*, H. C.

19 *Dane/Dean*   30 *Toppan/Tappin*

[21] Boxford had no minister until 1702.
[22] Ipswich Village, now Essex, Massachusetts.
[23] John Higginson wrote the Attestation to the *Magnalia* and Noyes contributed the first of the Prefatory Poems to it.*
[24] Salem Village, now Danvers.
[25] The County of Hampshire became in part Connecticut.
[26] Enfield, Connecticut, had no minister from 1689 until 1697.*
[27] Piscataqua was the name of the river and bay which divided New Hampshire from Maine.

50 *Hampton*, Mr. *John Cotton*,[28] H. C.
Newcastle, Mr. *Samuel Moodey*, H. C.
Portsmouth, Mr. *Joshua Moodey*, H. C.

And in the Province of *Main*.

Isle of *Sholes*,[29]
55 *Kittery*, [Mr. *John Newmarch*, H. C.]
Wells, *York*, Mr. [*John*] *Hancock*, H. C.

III.   I*N* Connecticut-*Colony there are Four Counties, and the several Congregations therein are illuminated by these Preachers of the Gospel.*

Hartford County Ministers.

60 *Farmington*, Mr. *Samuel Hooker*, H. C.
Glastenbury, Mr. *Timothy Stevens*, H. C.
Hadham, Mr. *Jeremiah Hobart*, H. C.
Hartford, Old Church, Mr. *Timothy Woodbridge*, H. C.
New Church, Mr. *Thomas Buckingham*, H. C.
65 *Middletown*, Mr. *Noadiah Russel*, H. C.
Simsbury, Mr. *Dudly Woodbridge*, H. C.
Waterbury, Mr. *Jeremiah Peck*, H. C.
Wethersfield, Mr. *Steven Mix*, H. C.
Windsor, Mr. *Samuel Mather*, H. C.
70 And *Farms*, Mr. *Timothy Edwards*, H. C.
Windham, Mr. *Samuel Whiting*.

New-London-County Ministers.

Killingworth, Mr. *Abraham Pierson*, H. C.
Lebanon,[30]
75 *Lyme*, Mr. *Moses Noyse*, H. C.
New-London, Mr. *Gurdon Saltonstal*, H. C.
Norwich, Mr. *James Fitch*.
Pescamsik,[31] Mr. *Joseph Mors*, H. C.
Preston, Mr. *Salmon Treat*, H. C.
80 *Saybrook*, Mr. *Thomas Buckingham*.
Stonington, Mr. *James Noyse*, H. C.

70	*Farms/Farme*	76	*Gurdon/Gordon*
75	*Lyme/Linne* C.M.	79	*Salmon Treat/Samuel Tread*

[28] John Cotton (1658–1710) was Mather's cousin and was with him at Harvard.*
[29] The Isles of Shoals, off the New Hampshire coast, had no regular minister from 1692 until about 1698 but probably had occasional preachers from time to time.
[30] Lebanon, Connecticut, had no church before 1699.
[31] Pescamsik was an Indian name, possibly misprinted from Mather's script.*

New-Haven-County Ministers.

Brainford, Mr. *Samuel Russel*, H. C.
Derby, Mr. *John James*, H. C.
85 *Guilford*, Mr. *Thomas Ruggles*, H. C.
Milford, Mr. *Samuel Andrews*, H. C.
New-Haven, Mr. *James Pierpoint*, H. C.
Wallingford, Mr. *Samuel Street*, H. C.

Fairfield-County Ministers.

90 *Danbury*, Mr. *Seth Shove*, H. C.
Fairfield, Mr. *Joseph Web*, H. C.
Fairfield Village, Mr. *Charles Chauncey*, H. C.
Greenwich, Mr. *Joseph Morgan*.
Norwalk, Mr. *Steven Buckingham*, H. C.
95 *Rye*, Mr. [*Nathanael*] *Bowers*, H. C.
Stamford, Mr. *John Davenport*, H. C.
Stratford, Mr. *Israel Chauncey*, H. C.
Woodbury, Mr. *Zachariah Walker*, H. C.

99   REMARKS *upon the Catalogue of Plantations.*

§. 1. THERE are few Towns to be now seen in our List, but what were existing in this Land before the dreadful *Indian War*, which befel us Twenty Years ago; and there are few Towns broken up within the then *Massachuset-Line* by that War, but what have revived out of 5 their *Ashes.* Nevertheless the many Calamities, which have ever since been wasting of the Country, have so nipt the *growth* of it, that its later Progress hath held no Proportion with what was *from the Beginning*; but yet with such variety, that while the *Trained Companies*[1] of some Towns are no bigger than they were Thirty or Forty Years ago, others are as 10 big again.

§. 2. The Calamities that have carried off the Inhabitants of our several Towns have not been all of *one sort*; nor have all our Towns had an equal share in *any sort.* Pestilential *Sicknesses* have made fearful Havock in divers Places, where the *Sound* perhaps have not been enough to tend 15 the *Sick*; while others have not had one touch from that *Angel of Death.* And the *Sword* hath cut off *Scores* in sundry Places, when others, it may be, have not lost a Man by that *Avenger.*

§. 3. 'Tis no *unusual*, though no *universal* Experiment[2] among us,

[1] Companies of citizen soldiery; trainbands.
[2] Experience.

that while an excellent, laborious, illuminating *Ministry* has been con-
20 tinued in a Town, the place has thriven to admiration; but ever since
that Man's time, they have gone down the Wind in all their Interests. The
Gospel has evidently been the *making* of our Towns, and the Blessings
of the *Upper* have been accompanied with the Blessings of the *Nether-*
springs. Memorable also is the Remark of *Slingsby Bethel,* Esq; in his
25 most Judicious Book of *The Interest of Europe. Were not the cold Climate of*
New-England *supplied by good Laws and Discipline, the Barrenness of that*
Country would never have brought People to it, nor have advanced it in Consideration
and Formidableness above the other English *Plantations, exceeding it much in*
Fertility, and other Inviting Qualities.
30 §. 4. Well may 𝔑𝔢𝔴-𝔈𝔫𝔤𝔩𝔞𝔫𝔡 lay claim to the *Name* it wears, and to a
Room in the tenderest Affections of its Mother, the *Happy Island!* For as
there are few of our Towns but what have their *Names-sakes* in England,
so the Reason why most of our Towns are called what they are, is because
the Chief of the First Inhabitants would thus bear up[3] the *Names* of the
35 particular Places there from whence they came.
§. 5. I have heard an Aged *Saint,*[4] near his Death chearfully thus
Express himself; 'Well, I am going to Heaven, and I will there tell the
'Faithful, who are gone long since from *New-England,* thither, that
'though they who gathered our Churches are all Dead and gone, yet
40 'the Churches are still Alive, with as numerous Flocks of Christians as
'ever were among them. Concerning the most of the *Churches* in our
Catalogue, the Report thus carried unto *Heaven,* I must now also send
through the *Earth;* but if with, *As Numerous,* we could in every Respect
say, *As Gracious,* what Joy unto all the Saints, both in *Heaven* and on
45 *Earth,* might be from thence occasioned!

23 *Upper*/U*pper*

[3] That is, "preserve."
[4] John Eliot (1604–1690), ordained Teacher of the Church of Roxbury, 1632. Soon thereafter he embarked on the long evangelical ministry which earned him the name of Apostle
to the Indians.*

The BOSTONIAN EBENEZER.[1]

SOME

Hiftorical Remarks

On the State of

B O S T O N,

The *Chief Town* of *New-England,* and of the *Englifh*
A M E R I C A.

With Some

Agreeable[2] Methods

FOR

Preferving and Promoting the *Good State* of THAT, as
well as any *other Town* in the like Circumftances.

Humbly Offered by a Native *of* BOSTON.

Ezek. 48. 35. *The Name of the City from that Day fhall be,* T H E
L O R D I S T H E R E.

*Vrbs Metropolis, ut fit maximæ Auttoritatis, conftituatur præcipuum pietatis Exemplum
& Sacrarium.* Aphor. Polit. 3

The Hiftory of *B O S T O N,* Related and Improved.[4]

At Bofton *Lecture,* 7. d. 2. m.[5] 1698.

---

[1] This heading was photographed from the 1702 edition of the *Magnalia,* by courtesy of the Houghton Library, Harvard University. Line numbers and footnote references have been added. The paper is a reprint of the first of two lectures published at Boston in 1698 under this title.*

[2] Suitable.

[3] "A metropolitan city, in order to exercise the greatest authority, should become a special exemplar and depository of piety."*

[4] That is, made use of for spiritual edification.

[5] The seventh day of the second month [Old Style].

65 REmarkable and Memorable was the Time, when an *Army* of Terrible
Destroyers was coming against one of the *Chief Towns* in the Land of
Israel. God rescued the *Town* from the Irresistible Fury and Approach
of those *Destroyers*, by an immediate Hand of Heaven upon them. Upon
that Miraculous Rescue of the *Town*, and of the whole Country, whose
70 Fate was much enwrapped in it, there follow'd that Action of the Prophet
SAMUEL, which is this Day to be, with some Imitation, Repeated in
the midst of thee, O *BOSTON*, *Thou Helped of the Lord.*

I SAM. VII. 12.

Then SAMUEL *took a Stone, and set it up,—and called the Name of it,*
75 𝖈𝖇𝖊𝖓𝖊𝖟𝖊𝖗, *saying, Hitherto the Lord hath Helped us.*

THE thankful Servants of God have used sometimes to Erect Monuments of *Stone*, as durable Tokens of their *Thankfulness* to God for
Mercies received in the places thus distinguished. *Jacob* did so; *Joshua*
did so; and *Samuel* did so; but they so did it, as to keep clear of the Trans-
80 gression forbidden in *Lev.* 26. 1. *Ye shall not set up any Image of Stone in*
your Land, for to Bow down unto it.
   The *Stone* Erected by *Samuel*, with the Name of *Ebenezer*, which is as
much as to say, *A Stone of Help*; I know not whether any thing might be
Writ upon it, but I am sure there is one thing to be now *Read* upon it,
85 by our selves, in the Text where we find it: Namely, thus much,
   That a People whom the God of Heaven hath remarkably helped in their
Distresses, ought greatly and gratefully to acknowledge what 𝖍𝖊𝖑𝖕 *of Heaven they*
have received.
   Now 'tis not my Design to lay the Scene of my Discourse as far off as
90 *Bethcar*, the place where *Samuel* set up his *Ebenezer*. I am immediately to
transfer it into the Heart of *Boston*, a place where the *Remarkable Help*
received from Heaven by the People, does loudly call for an *Ebenezer*. And
I do not ask you to change the Name of the Town into that of 𝖍𝖊𝖑𝖕-𝕾𝖙𝖔𝖓𝖊 [1]
as there is a Town in *England* of that Name, which may seem the *English*
95 of 𝖈𝖇𝖊𝖓𝖊𝖟𝖊𝖗, but my *Sermon* shall be this Day, your *Ebenezer*, if you will
with a Favourable and a Profitable Attention Entertain it. May the Lord
Jesus Christ accept me, and assist me now to *Glorifie him* in the *Town*
where I drew my first sinful Breath; a *Town* whereto I am under great
99 Obligations for the precious Opportunities to *glorifie him*, which I have
quietly and publickly enjoy'd therein for near Eighteen Years together.

80 *any/an*

   [1] Helpston: Helpeston, in Northamptonshire.

O my Lord God, remember me, I pray thee, and strengthen me this once, to speak from thee unto thy People!

And now, Sirs, That I may set up an *EBENEZER* among you, there
5 are these things to be Inculcated.

I. Let us *Thankfully*, and *Agreeably*, and *Particularly* acknowledge *what* 𝕳𝖊𝖑𝖕 we have received from the God of Heaven, in the Years that have rouled over us. While the Blessed Apostle *Paul*, was, as it should seem, yet short of being *Threescore* Years Old, how affectionately did he set up
10 an *Ebenezer*, with an acknowledgment in *Acts* 26. 22. *Having obtained help of God, I continue to this Day!* Our Town is now *Threescore and Eight* Years Old; and certainly 'tis time for us, with all possible Affection, to set up our *Ebenezer*, saying, *Having obtained help from God, the Town is continued until almost the Age of Man is passed over it!* The Town hath indeed *Three*
15 *Elder Sisters*[1] in this Colony, but it hath wonderfully *outgrown* them all; and her Mother, Old *Boston*, in *England* also; yea, within a few Years after the first Settlement it *grew* to be, 𝕿𝖍𝖊 𝕸𝖊𝖙𝖗𝖔𝖕𝖔𝖑𝖎𝖘 𝖔𝖋 𝖙𝖍𝖊 𝖜𝖍𝖔𝖑𝖊 𝕰𝖓𝖌𝖑𝖎𝖘𝖍 𝕬𝖒𝖊𝖗𝖎𝖈𝖆. Little was *this* expected by them that first settled the Town, when for a while 𝕭𝖔𝖘𝖙𝖔𝖓 was proverbially called, 𝕷𝖔𝖘𝖙 𝕿𝖔𝖜𝖓, for the mean and
20 sad Circumstances of it.[2] But, O *Boston*, it is because thou hast *obtained help from God*, even from the Lord Jesus Christ, who for the sake of his *Gospel*, Preached and once prized here, undertook thy Patronage. When the World and the Church of God had seen *Twenty-Six* Generations, a *Psalm* was Composed, wherein that Note occurs with *Twenty-Six* Repe-
25 titions; *His Mercy endureth for ever.* Truly there has not one Year passed over this Town, *Ab Urbe Condita*,[3] upon the Story whereof we might not make that Note, our *Ebenezer*; *His Mercy endureth for ever.* It has been a Town of great Experiences. There have been several Years wherein the *Terrible* 𝕱𝖆𝖒𝖎𝖓𝖊 hath terribly stared the Town in the Face: We have been
30 brought sometimes unto the *last Meal* in the Barrel; we have cry'd out with the Disciples, *We have not Loaves enough to feed a Tenth Part of us!* But the fear'd *Famine* has always been kept off; always we have had Season-able and Sufficient Supplies after a surprizing manner sent in unto us: Let the *Three last Years* in this thing most eminently Proclaim the Good-
35 ness of our Heavenly *Shepherd* and *Feeder*. This has been the *help* of our God; *Because his Mercy endureth for ever!* The *Angels of* 𝕯𝖊𝖆𝖙𝖍 have often

6 and/aud

---

[1] Salem, Charlestown, and Dorchester.
[2] In 1630 the settlers in Charlestown, fearing that the supply of fresh water there would prove insufficient, moved across the Charles River to "Trimountain," as the Boston peninsula was then called, where there was a spring which could meet their needs. Winthrop renamed the peninsula Boston. The area, however, had little hay or timber, and was connected with the more fruitful mainland only by one narrow road. For a time, therefore, Boston was exceeded in population and prosperity by neighboring towns, notably Dorchester.*
[3] "From the founding of the city."*

Shot the *Arrows of* 𝕯𝖊𝖆𝖙𝖍 into the midst of the Town; the *Small-Pox* has especially 𝖋𝖔𝖚𝖗 𝕿𝖎𝖒𝖊𝖘 been a *great Plague* upon us: How often have there been Bills desiring Prayers for more than an Hundred Sick on one Day in
40 one of our Assemblies? In *one Twelve-month*, about one *Thousand* of our Neighbours have one way or other been carried unto their long Home: And yet we are after all, many more than *Seven Thousand* Souls of us at this Hour living on the Spot. Why is not, a, *Lord, have Mercy upon us*, written on the Doors of our abandon'd Habitations? This hath been the
45 *help* of our *God*, because *his Mercy endureth for ever.* Never was any Town under the Cope of Heaven more liable to be laid in 𝕬𝖘𝖍𝖊𝖘, either through the *Carelesness*, or through the *Wickedness* of them that *Sleep* in it. That such a *Combustible heap* of Contiguous Houses yet stands, it may be called, A *Standing Miracle*; it is not because *the Watchman keeps the City:* Perhaps
50 there may be too much cause of *Reflection* in that thing, and of *Inspection too*; no, *It is from thy watchful Protection, O thou keeper of* Boston, *who neither Slumbers nor Sleeps.* 𝕿𝖊𝖓 𝕿𝖎𝖒𝖊𝖘 has the *Fire* made notable *Ruins* among us, and our *good Servant* been almost our *Master:* But the *Ruins* have mostly and quickly been Rebuilt. I suppose, that many more than a *Thousand Houses*
55 are to be seen on this little piece of Ground, all fill'd with the undeserved Favours of God. Whence this Preservation? This hath been the *help* of our *God*, because *his Mercy endureth for ever!* But if ever this Town saw a *Year of Salvations*, transcendently such was the 𝕷𝖆𝖘𝖙 𝖄𝖊𝖆𝖗 unto us. A Formidable *French Squadron* hath not Shot one Bomb into the midst of
60 thee,[4] O thou *Munition of Rocks*; our Streets have not run with Blood and Gore, and horrible devouring Flames have not raged upon our Substance: Those are *Ignorant*, and *Unthinking*, and *Unthankful* Men, who do not own that we have narrowly escaped as dreadful things, as *Carthagena*, or *Newfoundland*,[5] have suffered. I am sure our more considerate Friends
65 Beyond-Sea were very *Suspicious*, and well nigh *Despairing*, that Victorious *Enemies* had swallowed up the Town. But *thy Soul is escaped, O* Boston, *as a Bird out of the Snare of the Fowlers.* Or if you will be Insensible of *this*, ye *vain Men*, yet be sensible, That an *English Squadron* hath not brought among us the tremendous *Pestilence*, under which a Neighbouring
70 *Plantation* hath undergone prodigious Desolations.[6] *Boston*, 'tis a marvellous

---

[4] In 1697 the Bostonians had expected an attack from a "formidable Squadron of about fifteen French Men of War," but the threat came to nothing.*

[5] Cartagena, the principal port of New Granada (Colombia), was seized and pillaged of an enormous prize of precious metals by the Baron de Pointis in May 1697. The brutal attack on Newfoundland occurred during the winter of 1696–1697.*

[6] Mather refers to an English fleet which arrived in Boston Harbor in July 1693, after a "disastrous Expedition" against the French in Martinique. During the voyage to Massachusetts two-thirds of the sailors and soldiers aboard died of some pestilence. Mather glosses over the fact that the disease cost the lives of many in Boston by saying that the city did not suffer from as "tremendous a *Plague*" or as "prodigious Desolations" as did a "Neighbouring *Plantation*." His object was to demonstrate God's special mercies to Boston rather than to emphasize the afflictions undergone.*

thing a *Plague* has not laid thee Desolate! Our Deliverance from our *Friends* has been as full of astonishing *Mercy*, as our Deliverance from our *Foes*.[7] We read of a certain City in *Isa.* 19. 18. called, *The City of Destruction*. Why so? some say, Because delivered from *Destruction*. If that be so,

75 then hast thou been a *City of Destruction:* Or I will rather say, *A City of Salvation:* And this by the *help* of God; because *his Mercy endureth for ever.* Shall I go on? I will. We have not had the *Bread of Adversity* and the *Water of Affliction*, like many other places. But yet all this while *Our Eyes have seen our Teachers.* Here are several *Golden Candlesticks* in the Town.

80 *Shining and Burning Lights* have illuminated them. There are gone to shine in an *higher Orb* Seven Divines that were once the *Stars* of this Town, in the Pastoral Charge of it; besides many others, that for some Years gave us transient Influences. *Churches* flourishing with much Love, and Peace, and many *Comforts of the Holy Spirit*, have hitherto been our greatest

85 *Glory.* I wish that some sad *Eclipse* do not come e're long upon this *Glory!* The Dispensations of the *Gospel* were never enjoy'd by any Town with more *Liberty* and *Purity* for so long a while together. Our *Opportunities* to draw near unto the Lord Jesus Christ in his *Ordinances*, cannot be parallell'd. *Boston*, thou hast been *lifted up to Heaven*; there is not a Town

90 upon *Earth*, which, on some Accounts, has more to answer for. Such, O such has been our *help* from our God, because *his Mercy endureth for ever.*

II. Let us acknowledge 𝔚𝔥𝔬𝔰𝔢 *Help* it is that we have received, and not *Give the Glory of our God unto another.* Poorly *Helped* had we been, I may tell you, if we had none but *Humane Help* all this while to depend upon. The

95 Favours of our Superiors we deny not; we forget not the Instruments of our *Help*. Nevertheless, this little *outcast Zion*, shall, with my Consent, Engrave the Name of no MAN upon her *Ebenezer!* It was well confess'd in *Psal.* 108. 12. *Vain is the help of Man!* It was well counsell'd in *Psal.*

99 146. 3. *Put not your trust in Princes, nor in the Son of man, in whom there is no Help.*

Wherefore, *First*, Let 𝔊𝔬𝔡 in our Lord 𝔍𝔢𝔰𝔲𝔰 𝔠𝔥𝔯𝔦𝔰𝔱, have the *Glory* of *bestowing* on us all the *help* that we have had. When the Spirit of God came upon a Servant of his, he cried out unto *David*, in 1 *Chron.* 12. 18. *Thy*

5 *God helpeth thee.* This is the voice of God from Heaven to *Boston* this Day, *Thy God hath helped thee: Thou hast by thy Sin destroyed thy self, but in thy God hath been.thy help.* A Great Man[1] once building an Edifice, caused an Inscription of this Importance to be written on the Gates of it, *Such a place Planted me, such a place Watered me,* and *Cæsar gave the Increase.* One

10 that pass'd by with a witty Sarcasm, wrote under it, *Hic Deus nihil fecit;*

10 Sarcasm/Sacarsm

7 *"Friends,"* the English; *"Foes,"* the French.

----

1 Hadrian VI, pope from 1522 to 1523.*

i. e. *God, it seems, did nothing for this Man.* But the Inscription upon our *Ebenezer*, owning what *help* this Town hath had, shall say, *Our God hath done all that is done!* Say then, *O helped 𝕭oston*, say as in *Psal.* 121. 2. *My help is from the Lord which made Heaven and Earth.* Say as in *Psal.* 94. 17.
15 *Unless the Lord had been my help, my Soul had quickly dwelt in silence.* And boldly say, '*Tis only because the Lord has been my helper, that Earth and Hell have never done all that they would unto me.*

Let our Lord JESUS CHRIST be praised as our Blessed *Helper:* That *Stone* which the *Foolish Builders* have *refused*, Oh! Set up that *Stone*; even
20 that *high Rock*, set him on high in our Praises, and say, That *That is our Ebenezer*. 'Tis our Lord JESUS CHRIST, who in his Infinite Compassions for the Town hath said, as in *Isa.* 63. 5. *I looked, and there was none to help*; *therefore my own Arm hath brought Salvation* unto it. It is foretold concerning the Idolatrous Roman Catholicks, That together with the Lord
25 Jesus Christ, they shall *Worship* other *Mauzzim*; that is to say, other *Protectors*. Accordingly, all their Towns ordinarily have singled out their *Protectors* among the *Saints* of Heaven; such a *Saint* is Entituled unto the *Patronage* of such a Town among them, and such a *Saint* for another: Old 𝕭oston, by Name, was but Saint 𝕭otolph'𝖘 𝕿own. Whereas Thou, O
30 *Boston*, shalt have but one *Protector* in Heaven, and that is our Lord JESUS CHRIST. Oh! Rejoice in him alone, and say, *The Lord is my Fortress and my Deliverer!* There was a Song once made for a *Town*, which in its Distresses had been *helped* wondrously; and the First Clause in that Song, [you have it in *Isa.* 26. 1.] may be so rendred, *We have a strong*
35 *Town*; *Salvation* [or JESUS the Lord, whose Name hath *Salvation in it*] *will appoint Walls and Bulwarks.* Truly what *helps* we have had we will Sing, '*Tis our JESUS that hath appointed them.* The Old Pagan Towns were sometimes mightily Solicitous to conceal the Name of the particular God that they counted their *Protector, Ne ab hostibus Evocatus, alio commigraret.*[2]
40 But I shall be far from doing my Town any damage, by Publishing the Name of its *Protector*; no, let all Mankind know, that the Name of our *Protector* is JESUS CHRIST: For, *Among the Gods there is none like unto thee, O LORD: Nor is any help like unto thine: And there is no Rock like to our God.*

Yea, when we ascribe the Name of *Helper* unto our Lord JESUS
45 CHRIST, let us also acknowledge that the Name is not sufficiently Expressive, Emphatical and Significant. *Lactantius* of old blamed the Heathen for giving the highest of their Gods no higher a Title than that of *Jupiter*, or *Juvans Pater, i. e. An helping Father*; and he says, *Non intelligit Divina Beneficia, qui se a Deo tantummodo Juvari putat:* The *Kindnesses* of

36 *helps*/*help*

[2] "Lest invoked by the enemy, he should take up residence elsewhere."*

50 God are not understood by that Man, who makes no more than an *Helper* of him. Such indeed is the penury of our Language, that we cannot Coin a more *Expressive Name.* Nevertheless, when we say, The Lord JESUS CHRIST hath been our *Helper*, let us intend more than we express; *Lord, thou hast been All unto us.*

55   *Secondly*, Let the 𝕾𝖆𝖈𝖗𝖎𝖋𝖎𝖈𝖊 of our Lord Jesus Christ most Explicitely have the *Glory* of *Purchasing* for us all our *Help*. What was it that procured an *Ebenezer* for the People of God? We read in 1 *Sam.* 7. 9. Samuel *took a Sucking Lamb, and offered it a Burnt-Offering wholly unto the Lord*; *and* Samuel *cried unto the Lord for* Israel, *and the Lord heard him.* Shall I tell 60 you? Our Lord Jesus Christ is that *Lamb of God*; and he has been a *Lamb slain as a Sacrifice*; and he is a *Sacrifice* pleadable not only for *Persons*, but also for *Peoples* that belong unto him. To teach us this Evangelical and Comfortable *Mystery*, there was *a sacrifice for the whole Congregation* prescribed in the *Mosaic* Pædagogy. 'Tis notorious that the *Sins* of this 65 Town have been many Sins, and mighty Sins; the *Cry* thereof hath *gone up to Heaven.* If the Almighty God should from Heaven Rain down upon the Town an *horrible Tempest* of Thunderbolts, as he did upon the Cities *which he overthrew in his Anger, and repented not,* it would be no more than our unrepented Sins deserve. How comes it then to pass that we have 70 had so much *help* from Heaven after all? Truly the *Sacrifice* of our Lord Jesus Christ has been pleaded for *Boston*, and *therefore* say, *Therefore* it is that the Town is not made a *Sacrifice* to the Vengeance of God. God sent *help* to the Town that was the very *Heart* and *Life* of the Land that he had a pity for: But why so? He said in *Isa.* 37. 35. *I will defend this Town, to* 75 *save it for my Servant* David's *sake.* Has this Town been *Defended?* It has been for the sake of the *Beloved* JESUS; therefore has the Daughter of *Boston* shaken *her Head* at you, O ye Calamities that have been Impending over *her Head.* O *helped* and happy Town! Thou hast had those Believers in the midst of thee, that have pleaded this with the great God; *Ah! Lord,* 80 *Thou hast been more Honoured by the Sufferings of our Lord Jesus Christ, than thou couldst be Honoured by overwhelming this Town with all the Plagues of thy Just Indignation. If lhou wilt Spare, and Feed, and Keep, and Help this poor Town, the Sufferings of our Lord Jesus Christ shall be own'd as the Price of all our help.* 'Tis *this* that hath procured us all our *Help:* 'Tis *this* that must 85 have all our *Praise.*

    Thirdly, Let the Lord be in a special manner *Glorified* for the Ministry of his good 𝖆𝖓𝖌𝖊𝖑𝖘, in that *help* that has been Ministred unto us. A *Jacob* lying on a *Stone*, saw the *Angels* of God *helping* him. We are setting up an *Ebenezer*; but when we lay our Heads and our Thoughts upon the *Stone*, 90 let us then see, *The Angels of God have helped us.* When *Macedonia* was to have

57   1 *Sam.*/2 *Sam.*   83   *Price/Prize*

some *help* from God, an *Angel*, whom the Apostle in *Acts* 16. 9. saw
Habited like a *Man of* Macedonia, was a Mean[3] of its being brought
unto them. There is abundant Cause to think, That every Town in which
the Lord Jesus Christ is Worshipped, hath an *Angel* to watch over it.
95 The Primitive Christians were perswaded from the Scriptures of Truth
to make no doubt of this, *Quod per Civitates distributæ sunt Angelorum
præfecturæ*.[4] When the Capital Town of *Judea* was rescued from an Invasion, we read in 2 Kings 19. 35. *The Angel of the Lord WENT OUT,*
99 *and smote the Camp of the* Assyrians. It should seem there was an *Angel*
which did Reside in, and Preside over the Town, who *went out* for that
amazing Exploit. And is it not likely, that *the Angel of the Lord WENT
OUT for to smite the Fleet of the* Assyrians[5] with a Sickness, which the last
Summer hindred their Invading of this Town? *The Angel of* BOSTON
5 was concerned for it! Why have not the *Destroyers* broke in upon us, to
Prey upon us with sore *Destruction?* 'Tis because we have had *a Wall
of Fire* about us; that is to say, a Guard of *Angels*, those *Flames of Fire* have
been as a *Wall* unto us. It was an *Angel* that *help'd* a *Daniel* when the
Lions would else have swallowed him up. It was an *Angel* that *help'd* a *Lot*
10 out of the Fires that were coming to consume his Habitation. It was an
Angel that *help'd* an *Elias* to *Meat* when he wanted it. They were *Angels*
that *help'd* the whole People of God in the Wilderness to their *Daily
Bread:* Their *Manna* was *Angel's Food:* And is it nothing that such *Angels*
have done for this Town, think you? Oh! Think not so. Indeed if we
15 should go to thank the *Angels* for doing these things, they would zealously
say, *See thou do it not!* But if we thank their Lord and ours for his employing them to do these things, it will exceedingly gratifie them. Wherefore,
Bless ye the Lord, ye his Angels; *and Bless the Lord*, O my Town, for those *his
Angels*.

20   III. Let the *help* which we have *hitherto* had from our God, encourage
us to *hope* in him for 𝔐𝔬𝔯𝔢 𝔥𝔢𝔩𝔭 hereafter, *as the Matter may require.* The
help that God had given to his People of Old was Commemorated, as
with *Monumental Pillars*, conveying down the Remembrance of it unto
their Children. And what for? We are told in *Psal.* 78. 7. *That they might*
25 *set their hope in God, and not forget the Works of God.* I am not willing to say
how much this Town may be threatned, even with an *Utter Extirpation.*
But this I will say, The *Motto* upon all our *Ebenezers*, is, 𝔥𝔬𝔭𝔢 𝔦𝔫 𝔊𝔬𝔡 !
𝔥𝔬𝔭𝔢 𝔦𝔫 𝔊𝔬𝔡 ! The *Use* of the *former help* that we have had from God,
should be an *hope* for *future help* from him, that is *a present help in the time*
30 *of Trouble.* As in the Three First Verses of the *Eighty-fifth* Psalm Six times

---

[3] In the obsolete sense of an intermediary agent, an intercessor, a mediator between God
and man.
[4] "That governments of angels are distributed throughout the cities."*
[5] That is, the French fleet.*

over there occurs, *Thou hast, Thou hast:* All to usher in this; *Therefore thou WILT still do so.* O let our *Faith* proceed in that way of Arguing in 2 *Cor.* 1. 10. *The Lord hath delivered, and he doth deliver, and in him we trust that he will still deliver.* We are today Writing, *Hitherto the Lord hath helped*

35 *us*; let us Write under it, *And we hope the Lord has more help for us in the time of need!* It may be some are purposing suddenly and hastily to *leave* the Town through their Fears of the Straits that may come upon it. But I would not have you be too sudden and hasty in your Purposes, as too many have been unto their *After-Sorrow.* There was a time when People

40 were so Discouraged about a *Subsistence* in the Principal Town of the *Jews,* that they talk'd of plucking up Stakes and flying away; but the Minister of God came to them, [and so do I to you this Day!] Saying, in *Isa.* 30. 7. *I cried concerning this, their strength is to sit still! Boston* was no sooner come to some *Consistence*[1] Threescore Years ago, but the People

45 found themselves plunged into a sad *Non-plus* what way to take for a *Subsistence.* God then immediately put them into a way, and *hitherto the Lord has helped us!* The Town is at this Day full of *Widows* and *Orphans,* and a multitude of them are very *helpless* Creatures. I am astonish'd how they live! In that Church whereof I am the Servant, I have counted the

50 *Widows* make about a *Sixth Part* of our Communicants, and no doubt in the whole Town the proportion differs not very much. Now stand still, my Friends, and behold the *help* of God! Were any of these ever *starved* yet? No, these *Widows* are every one in some sort provided for. And let me tell you, ye Handmaids of the Lord, you shall be *still* provided for!

55 The Lord, whose *Family* you belong unto, will conveniently and wonderfully provide for you; if you say, and Oh! Say of him, *The Lord is my Helper, I will not fear!*

What shall I say? When *Moses* was ready to faint in his *Prayers* for his People, we read in *Exod.* 17. 12. *They took a Stone, and put it under him.*

60 Christians, there are some of you who abound in *Prayers,* that the *help* of God may be granted unto the Town; the Town is much upheld by those *Prayers* of yours. Now that you may not faint in your *Prayers,* I bring you a *Stone:* The *Stone,* 'tis our *Ebenezer;* or, The Relation of the *help* that *hitherto* the Lord hath given us.

65 IV. Let all that bear 𝔓𝔲𝔟𝔩𝔦𝔠𝔨 𝔒𝔣𝔣𝔦𝔠𝔢 in the Town contribute all the *help* they can, that may continue the *help* of God unto us. *Austin* in his *Confessions* gives thanks to God, that when he was an *helpless Infant,* he had a *Nurse* to *help* him, and one that was both able and willing to *help* him. Infant-*Boston,* thou hast those whom the *Bible* calls *Nursing-Fathers.* Oh

---

31   occurs/occurrs   34   today/to Day

[1] Settled condition; state of rest.

70 be not *froward*, as thou art in thy Treating of thy *Nurses*; but give thanks
to God for them. I forget my self; 'tis with the *Fathers* themselves that
I am concerned.

When it was demanded of *Demosthenes*, what it was that so long preserved *Athens* in a flourishing State, he made this Answer, *The Orators*
75 *are Men of Learning and Wisdom, the Magistrates do Justice, the Citizens love*
Quiet, and the Laws are kept among them all. May *Boston* flourish in such happy
Order!

And first, You may assure your selves that the 𝔐𝔦𝔫𝔦𝔰𝔱𝔢𝔯𝔰 of the Lord
Jesus Christ among you will be *Joyful* to approve themselves, as the Book
80 of God has called them, *The Helpers of your Joy.* O our dear *Flocks*, we
owe you our *All*; all our *Love*, all our *Strength*, all our *Time*; we *watch for*
you as those that must give an account: And I am very much mistaken if we
are not willing to *Die* for you too, if called unto it. If our Lord Jesus
Christ should say to us, *My Servant, if you'll Die to Night, you shall have this*
85 *Reward; The People that you Preach to shall be all Converted unto me!* I think
we should with Triumphing Souls reply, *Ah! Lord, Then I'll Die with all*
my Heart. Sirs, we should go away *Rejoycing with Joy unspeakable and full of*
Glory. I am satisfied, that the most Furious and Foul-mouth'd Reviler
that God may give any of us to be *Buffeted* withal, if he will but come to
90 sober Thoughts, he will say, That there is not any *One Man* in the Town,
but the *Ministers* wish that Man as well as they do their own Souls, and
would gladly serve that Man by Day or by Night, in any thing that it
were possible to do for him. Wherefore, O our beloved People, I beseech
you leave off, leave off to throw *Stones* at your *Ebenezers*. Instead of *that*
95 *pray for us*, and *strive together with us in your Prayers to God for us.* Then with
the *help* of Christ we'll promise you, we will set our selves to observe what
Special Truths may be most needful to be Inculcated upon you, and we
will Inculcate them. We will set our selves to observe the *Temptations*
99 that beset you, the *Afflictions* that assault you, and the *Duties* that are
incumbent on you; and we will accommodate our selves unto them. We
will set our selves to observe what Souls among you do call for our more
particular Addresses, and we will Address them faithfully, and even *Travel*[1]
in *Birth* for them. Nor will we give over *Praying*, and *Fasting*, and *Crying*
5 to our great LORD for you until we Die. Whatever other *Helpers* the
Town enjoys, they shall have that Convenience in *Ezra* 5. 2. *With them*
were the Prophets of God, helping them. Well then, let the rest of our Worthy
Helpers lend an *helping* Hand for the promoting of those things wherein
the Weal of the Town is wrapped up! When the *Jews* thought that a
10 *Defiling* thing was breaking in among them, in *Acts* 21. 28. *They cried*
out, Men of Israel, *help.* Truly there is Cause to make that Cry, *Men of*

[1] Travail, labor.

Boston, *help!* For Ignorance, and Prophaneness, and Bad Living, and the worst things in the World, are breaking in upon us.

And now will the JUSTICES of the Town set themselves to consider,
15 *How they may help to suppress all growing Vices among us?*

Will the CONSTABLES of the Town set themselves to consider, *How they may help to prevent all Evil Orders among us?*

There are some who have the Eye of the *Town* so much upon them, that the very Name of TOWNS-MEN is that by which they are distinguished.
20 Sirs, Will *you* also consider *how to help the Affairs of the Town, so as that all things may go well among us?*

Moreover, may not SCHOOL-MASTERS do much to instil Principles of *Religion* and *Civility*, as well as other Points of good Education into the Children of the *Town?* Only let the *Town* well Encourage its well
25 deserving *School-Masters.*

There are some other *Officers;* but concerning *all*, there are these Two things to be desired. First, It is to be desired, That such *Officers* as are *Chosen* among us, may be chosen in the *Fear of God.* May none but *Pious* and *Prudent* Men, and such as *Love* the Town, be chosen to serve it. And,
30 Secondly, It is to be desired, That *Officers* of several sorts would often come together for *Consultation.* Each of the sorts by themselves, may they often come together to consult, *What shall we do to serve the Town in those Interests which are committed unto our Charge?* Oh! What a Deplorable thing will it be for Persons to be entrusted with *Talents,* [your Opportunities
35 to serve the *Town* are so many *Talents!*] and they never seriously consider, *What good shall I do with my Talents in the place where God hath Station'd me?*

And will the REPRESENTATIVES of the Town be considered among the rest, as entrusted with some singular Advantages for our *help!*
40 *The Lord give you Understanding in all things.*

V. God *help* the Town to manifest all that 𝔓iety which a Town so *helped* of him is obliged unto! When the People of God had been carried by his *help* through their Difficulties, they set up *Stones* to keep in mind how he had *helped* them: And something was Written on the *Stones:*
45 But what was Written! See *Josh.* 8. 32. *Joshua wrote upon the Stones a Copy of the Law.* Truly upon those *Ebenezers* which we set up, we should Write the *Law* of our God, and Recognize the Obligations which the *help* of our God has laid upon us to keep it.

We are a very Unpardonable Town, if after all the *help* which our God
50 has given us, we do not ingenuously enquire, *What shall we render to the Lord for all his Benefits?* Render! Oh! Let us our selves thus answer the Enquiry; *Lord, we will render all Possible and Filial Obedience unto thee, because hitherto thou hast helped us: Only do thou also help us to render that Obedience!*

13 the World/World

Mark what I say; if there be so much as one *Prayerless House* in such a *Town*
55 as this, 'tis Inexcusable! How Inexcusable then will be all *Flagitious*
Outrages? There was a Town, ['twas the Town of *Sodom!*] that had been
wonderfully saved out of the Hands of their Enemies. But after the *help*
that God sent unto them, the Town went on to Sin against God in very
prodigious Instances. At last a provoked God sent a *Fire* upon the Town
60 that made it an Eternal Desolation. Ah, *Boston*, beware, beware, lest the
Sins of *Sodom* get footing in thee! And what were the Sins of *Sodom?* We
find in Ezek. 16. 49. *Behold, this was the Iniquity of* Sodom; *Pride, Fulness of*
Bread, and Abundance of Idleness was in her; neither did she strengthen the Hand
of the Poor and the Needy; there was much Oppression there. If you know
65 of any *Scandalous Disorders* in the Town, do all you can to suppress them,
and redress them: And let not those that send their Sons hither from other
Parts of the World, for to be improved in *Virtue*, have cause to complain,
That after they came to Boston *they lost what little Virtue was before Budding*
in them: That in Boston *they grew more Debauched and more Malignant than*
70 *ever they were before!* It was noted concerning the Famous Town of *Port-*
Royal in *Jamaica*, which you know was t'other Day swallow'd up in a
Stupendous *Earthquake*,[1] that just before the *Earthquake* the People were
violently and scandalously set upon going to *Fortune-Tellers* upon all
Occasions: much notice was taken of this *Impiety* generally prevailing
75 among the People: But none of those wretched *Fortune-Tellers* could foresee, or forestal the direful *Catastrophe*. I have heard that there are *Fortune-*
Tellers in this Town sometimes consulted by some of the sinful Inhabitants. I wish the Town could be made too Hot for these *Dangerous*
Transgressors. I am sure the preservation of the Town from horrendous
80 *Earthquakes*, is one thing that bespeaks our *Ebenezers*; 'tis from the Merciful
help of our God unto us. But beware, I beseech you, of those *provoking*
Evils that may expose us to a Plague, exceeding all that are in the Catalogue of the *Twenty-eighth of Deuteronomy*. Let me go on to say, What, shall
there be any *Bawdy-Houses* in such a Town as this! It may be the Neigh-
85 bours, that could Smoke 'em,[2] and Rout 'em, if they would, are loth to
Stir, for fear of being reputed *Ill Neighbours*. But I say unto you, that you
are *Ill Neighbours* because you do it not: All the Neighbours are like to
have their Children and Servants Poisoned, and their Dwellings laid in
Ashes, because you do it not. And Oh! That the 𝔇rinking-ℌouses in the
90 Town might once come under a laudable *Regulation*. The Town has an
Enormous Number of them; will the *Haunters* of those *Houses* hear the Counsels of Heaven? For *You* that are the *Town-Dwellers*, to be oft, or long in
your *Visits* of the *Ordinary*,[3] 'twill certainly expose you to Mischiefs more

---

[1] June 7, 1692.*
[2] Expose and drive out.
[3] An inn or tavern.

than ordinary. I have seen certain *Taverns*, where the Pictures of horrible
95 *Devourers*[4] were hang'd out for the *Signs*; and, thought I, 'twere well if
such *Signs* were not sometimes too too *Significant:* Alas, Men have their
Estates *devoured*, their Names *devoured*, their Hours *devoured*, and their very
Souls *devoured*, when they are so besotted, that they are not in their
99 Element, except they be Tipling at such Houses. When once a Man is
bewitched with the *Ordinary*, what usually becomes of him? He is a *gone
Man*; and when he comes to Die, he'll cry out as many have done,
Ale-Houses are Hell-Houses! Ale-Houses are Hell-Houses! But let the *Owners*
of those *Houses* also now hear our Counsels. *Oh! Hearken to me, that God
5 may hearken to you another Day!* It is an *Honest*, and a *Lawful*, tho' it be not
a very *Desireable* Employment, that you have undertaken: You may
Glorifie the Lord Jesus Christ in your Employment if you will, and benefit
the Town considerably. There was a very godly Man that was an *Inn-
keeper*, and a great Minister of God could say to that Man, in 3 *John* 2.
10 *Thy Soul prospereth.* O let it not be said of you, since you are fallen into
this Employment, *Thy Soul withereth!* It is thus with too many: Especially,
when they that get a *License* perhaps to Sell Drink out of Doors, do stretch
their *License* to Sell within Doors. Those *Private Houses*,[5] when once a
Professor of the Gospel comes to *Steal* a Living out of them, it commonly
15 precipitates them into abundance of wretchedness and confusion. But
I pray God assist you that keep *Ordinaries*, to keep the *Commandments* of
God in them. There was an *Inn* at *Bethlehem* where the Lord JESUS
CHRIST was to be met withal. Can *Boston* boast of many such? Alas,
too ordinarily it may be said, *There is no Room for him in the Inn!* My
20 Friends, let me beg it of you, banish *the unfruitful works of Darkness* from
your *Houses*, and then the *Sun of Righteousness* will shine upon them. Don't
countenance *Drunkenness, Revelling*, and *Mis-spending* of precious Time in
your Houses. Let none have the *Snares of Death* laid for them in your
Houses. You'll say, *I shall Starve then!* I say, *better Starve than Sin:* But you
25 *shalt not.* It is the Word of the Most High, *Trust in the Lord, and do Good,
and verily thou shalt be Fed.* And is not *Peace of Conscience* with a *Little*,
better than those *Riches*, that will shortly melt away, and then run like
Scalding Metal down the very Bowels of thy Soul?

What shall I say more? There is one Article of *Piety* more to be Rec-
30 ommended unto us all; and it is an Article which all *Piety* does exceed-
ingly turn upon, that is, 𝕿𝖍𝖊 𝕾𝖆𝖓𝖈𝖙𝖎𝖋𝖎𝖈𝖆𝖙𝖎𝖔𝖓 𝖔𝖋 𝖙𝖍𝖊 𝕷𝖔𝖗𝖉'𝖘 𝕯𝖆𝖞: Some very
Judicious Persons have observed, that as *they sanctified the Lord's Day,
Remisly or Carefully, just so their Affairs usually prospered all the ensuing Week.*
Sirs, you cannot more consult the Prosperity of the Town, in all its

97   their Hours/they Hours   C.M.

4 In Mather's day, both a Red Lion and a Red Lyon, as well as a Green Dragon, appeared
on tavern signs.*
5 That is, unlicensed drinking houses.*

35 Affairs, than by Endeavouring that the *Lord's Day* may be exemplarily *Sanctified*. When People about *Jerusalem* took too much Liberty on the *Sabbath*, the Ruler of the Town *Contended* with them, and said, *Ye bring wrath upon* Israel, *by prophaning the Sabbath*. I fear, I fear there are many among us, to whom it may be said, *Ye bring wrath upon* Boston, *by pro-*
40 *phaning the Sabbath*. And what *Wrath?* Ah, Lord, *prevent it!* But there is an awful Sentence in *Jer*. 17. 27. *If ye will not hearken unto me, to sanctifie the Sabbath Day, then will I kindle a Fire on the Town, and it shall Devour, and shall not be Quenched*.

Finally, Let the *Piety* of the Town manifest it self in a due Regard unto
45 the **Institutions** of him whose *help* has *hitherto* been a *Shield* unto us. Let the *Ark* be in the Town, and God will *Bless* the Town! I believe it may be found, that in the *Mortal Scourges* of Heaven, which this Town has felt, there has been a *discernable Distinction* of those that have come up to attend all the *Ordinances* of the Lord Jesus Christ, in the Communion of his
50 *Churches*. Though these have had, as 'tis fit they should, a Share in the *Common Deaths*, yet the *Destroying Angel* has not had so great a proportion of these in his Commission, as he has had of others. Whether *this* be so, or no, to uphold, and support, and attend the *Ordinances* of the Lord Jesus Christ in *Reforming Churches*, this will Entitle the Town to the *help*
55 of Heaven; for, *Upon the Glory there shall be a defence!* There were the Victorious Forces of *Alexander*, that in going backward and forward, pass'd by *Jerusalem* without Hurting it. Why so? Said the Lord in *Zech*. 9. 8. *I will encamp about my House, because of the Army*. If our God have an *House* here, he'll Encamp about it. *Nazianzen*,[6] a famous Minister of the Gospel,
60 taking his farewel of *Constantinople*, an old Man that had sat under his Ministry, cried out, *Oh! My Father, Don't you dare to go away, you'll carry the whole Trinity with you!* How much more may it be cried out, *If we lose or slight the Ordinances of the Lord Jesus Christ, we forego the help of all the Trinity with them!*

65 VI. Extraordinary **Equity** and **Charity**, as well as *Piety*, well becomes a Town that hath been by the *help* of God so Extraordinarily signalized. A Town marvellously *helped* by God, has this foretold concerning it, in *Isa*. 1. 26. *Afterward thou shalt be called, the City of Righteousness, the faithful City*. May the *Ebenezers* of this Town render it *a Town of Equity*, and a *Town*
70 *of Charity!* Oh! There should be none but *fair Dealings* in a Town wherewith Heaven has dealt so favourably. Let us *Deal fairly* in *Bargains*; *Deal fairly* in *Taxes*; *Deal fairly* in paying Respects to such as have been *Benefactors* unto the Town. 'Tis but *Equity*, that they who have been *old Standers*[1] in the Town, and both with *Person* and *Estate* served the Town
75 unto the utmost for many Years together, should on all proper Occasions be considered. For *Charity*, I may indeed speak it without Flattery, this

6 St. Gregory of Nazianzen (329–389), one of the four great fathers of the Eastern church.*

1 That is, residents of long standing.

Town has not many Equals on the Face of the Earth. Our Lord Jesus Christ from Heaven wrote unto the good People of a Town in the lesser *Asia*, [*Rev.* 2. 19.] *I know thy Works and Charity.* From that Blessed Lord
80 I may venture to bring that Message unto the good People of this Town; *the glorious Lord of Heaven knows thy works, O* Boston, *and all thy Charity.* This is a *poor* Town, and yet it may be said of the *Bostonians*, as it was of the *Macedonians, their deep Poverty hath abounded unto the Riches of their Liberality.* O ye bountiful People of God, all your *daily Bounties* to the
85 Needy, all your *Subscriptions* to send the *Bread of Life* abroad unto places that are perishing in Wickedness, all your *Collections* in your Assemblies as often as they are called for; *all these Alms are come up for a Memorial before God!* The Lord Jesus Christ in Heaven hath beheld your *helpfulness*, and *readiness to every good Work*; and he hath requited it with his *helpful*
90 *Ebenezers.* It was said, in *Isa.* 32. 8. *The Liberal deviseth Liberal things, and by Liberal things he shall stand.* There are some in this Town that are always *devising Liberal things*, and our Lord Jesus Christ lets the Town *stand* for the sake of those! Instead of *exhorting* you to *Augment* your *Charity*, I will rather utter an *Exhortation*, or at least a *Supplication*, that you may not
95 *abuse* your *Charity* by misapplying of it. I remember I have Read, that an Inhabitant of the City *Pisa*[2] being asked why their Town so went, as it then did, unto decay? He fetched a deep sigh, and said, *Our young Men are too Prodigal, our old Men are too Affectionate, and we have no Punishment*
99 *for those that spend their Years in Idleness.* Ah! the last stroak of that complaint I must here sigh it over again. *Idleness*, alas! *Idleness* increases in the Town exceedingly: *Idleness*, of which there never came any *Goodness*; *Idleness*, which is a *reproach to any People. We* work hard all Summer, and the *Drones* count themselves wrong'd if they have it not in the Winter
5 divided among them. The *Poor* that can't *Work*, are Objects for your *Liberality.* But the *Poor* that can *Work* and won't, the best *Liberality* to them is to *make* them. I beseech you, Sirs, find out a Method quickly, that the *Idle Persons* in the Town may earn their *Bread*; it were the best piece of *Charity* that could be shown unto them, and *Equity* unto us all. Our
10 *Beggars* do shamefully grow upon us, and such *Beggars* too as our Lord Jesus Christ himself hath expresly forbidden us to Countenance. I have Read a Printed Sermon which was Preached before *Both Houses of Parliament*, the *Lord Mayor and Aldermen* of *London*, and the *Assembly of Divines*;[3] the greatest Audience then in the World: And in that Sermon the Preacher
15 had this passage; *I have lived in a Country where in Seven Years I never saw a Beggar, nor heard an Oath, nor looked upon a Drunkard.* Shall I tell you where that *Utopia* was? 'Twas *NEW-ENGLAND!* But they that go from hence must now tell another Story.

[2] The man of Pisa remains unidentified.
[3] By Hugh Peter on April 2, 1645.*

VII. May the 𝕮𝖍𝖆𝖓𝖌𝖊𝖘, and especially the 𝕵𝖚𝖉𝖌𝖒𝖊𝖓𝖙𝖘 that have come
20 upon the Town, direct us what *help* to petition from the *God of our Salvations.* The *Israelites* had formerly seen *Dismal Things,* where they now set
up their *Ebenezer:* The *Philistines* had no less than Twice beaten them
there, and there taken from them the *Ark* of God. Now we are setting up
our *Ebenezer,* let us a little call to mind some *Dismal Things* that we have
25 seen; the *Ebenezer* will go up the better for it.

We read in 1 *Sam.* 6. 18. concerning *the Great Stone of Abel.* Some say,
That *Adam* erected that *Stone,* as a *Grave-stone* for his *Abel,* and wrote that
Epitaph upon it, *Here was poured out the Blood of the Righteous ABEL.* I
know nothing of *This*; the Names, I know, differ in the Original; but as
30 we may erect many a *Stone* for an *Ebenezer,* so we may erect many a *Great
Stone of ABEL,* that is to say, we may write MOURNING and SOR-
ROW, upon the Condition of the Town in various Examples. Now from
the *Stones* of *Abel,* we will a little gather what we should wish to write
upon the *Stones* of our *Ebenezer.*

35 What *Changes* have we seen in point of 𝕽𝖊𝖑𝖎𝖌𝖎𝖔𝖓? It was noted by *Luther,
He could never see good Order in the Church last more than Fifteen Years together
in the Purity of it.* Blessed be God, *Religion* hath here flourished in the
Purity of it for more than *Fifteen Years together.* But certainly the *Power
of Godliness* is now grievously decay'd among us. As the Prophet of old
40 Exclaimed in *Joel* 1. 2. *Hear this, ye old Men, and give Ear, ye Inhabitants;
has this been in your Days?* Thus may I say, *Hear this, ye old Men, that are the
Inhabitants of the Town:* Can't you Remember that *in your Days,* a Prayerful, a Watchful, a Fruitful Christian, and a well Governed Family, was
a more common Sight, than it is now in *our Days?* Can't you Remember
45 that *in your Days* those abominable Things did not *show their Heads,* that
are now *Bare-faced* among us? Here then is a Petition to be made unto
our God; *Lord, help us to Remember whence we are fallen, and to Repent, and
to do the first Works.*

Again, What *Changes* have we seen in Point of 𝕸𝖔𝖗𝖙𝖆𝖑𝖎𝖙𝖞? By *Mortality*
50 almost all the *Old Race* of our *First Planters* here are carried off; the *Old
Stock* is in a manner expired. We see the fulfilment of that Word in
Eccl. 1. 4. *One Generation passeth away, and another Generation cometh.* It
would be no unprofitable thing for you to pass over the several Streets,
and call to mind, *Who lived here so many Years ago?* Why? In *that place*
55 lived such an one; and in *that place* lived such an one. But, *Where are
they Now?* Oh! They are *Gone*; they are *Gone* into that Eternal World,
whither *we* must quickly follow them. Here is another Petition to be made
unto our God; *Lord, help us to Number our Days, and Apply our Hearts unto
Wisdom, that when the places that now know us, do know us no more, we may be
60 gone into the City of God.*

Furthermore, What *Changes* have we seen in point of 𝕻𝖔𝖘𝖘𝖊𝖘𝖘𝖎𝖔𝖓𝖘? If some that are now *Rich*, were once *Low* in the World, 'tis possible, more that were once *Rich*, are now brought very *Low*. Ah! *Boston*, Thou hast seen the *Vanity* of all *Worldly Possessions*. One fatal Morning,[1] which laid

65 Fourscore of thy *Dwelling-houses*, and Seventy of thy *Ware-houses*, in a Ruinous Heap, not Nineteen Years ago, gave thee to Read it in Fiery Characters. And an huge *Fleet* of thy Vessels,[2] which they would make if they were all together, that have miscarried in the late War, has given thee to Read more of it. Here is one Petition more to be made unto our

70 God: *Lord, help us to ensure a better and a lasting Substance in Heaven, and the good part that cannot be taken away.*

   In fine, How dreadfully have the *Young People* of *Boston* perished under the *Judgments* of God! A renowned Writer among the *Pagans* could make this Remark; There was a Town so Irreligious and Atheistical, that they

75 did not pay their *First-fruits* unto God: (which the *Light of Nature* taught the Pagans to do!) and, says he, they were by a sudden Desolation so strangely destroy'd, that there were no Remainders either of the *Persons*, or of the *Houses*, to be seen any more. Ah, *my Young Folks*, there are few *First-fruits* paid unto the Lord Jesus Christ among you. From hence it

80 comes to pass, that the consuming Wrath of God is every Day upon you. *New-England* has been like a *Tott'ring House*, the very *Foundations* of it have been shaking: But the House thus over-setting by the *Whirlwinds* of the Wrath of God, hath been like *Job's* House; *It falls upon the Young Men, and they are Dead!* The Disasters on our *Young Folks* have been so multiplied,

85 that there are few Parents among us, but what will go with *Wounded Hearts* down unto their Graves: Their daily Moans are, *Ah, my Son cut off in his Youth! My Son, my Son!* Behold then the *help* that we are to ask of our God; and why do we, with no more Days of *Prayer* with *Fasting*, ask it? *Lord, help the young People of* Boston *to Remember thee in the Days of their*

90 *Youth, and sanctifie unto the Survivers the terrible things that have come upon so many of that Generation.*

   And now as *Joshua* having reasoned with his People, a little before he Died, in *Josh.* 24. 26, 27. *Took a Great STONE, and set it up, and said unto all the People, Behold, this Stone shall be a witness unto you, lest ye deny your*

95 *God.* Thus we have been this Day setting up a STONE, even an *Ebenezer* among you; and I conclude, earnestly testifying unto you, *Behold this Stone shall be a witness unto you, that the Lord* JESUS CHRIST *has been a good Lord unto you; and if you seek him, he will be still found of you; but if you*

99 *forsake him, he will cast you off for ever.*

                     The End of the First Book.

    [1] August 8, 1679.
    [2] The fleet returning from the unsuccessful expedition against Quebec in 1690.*

Ecclesiarum Clypei.

The Second BOOK

OF THE

New Englifh Hiftory :

CONTAINING THE

LIVES

OF THE

GOVERNOURS, and the *Names* of the MA-
GISTRATES, that have been SHIELDS
unto the CHURCHES of *NEW-ENGLAND*,
(until the Year 1686.)

Perpetuated by the Eſſay of COTTON MATHER.

Priſcaq; ne Veteris vaneſcat Gloria Sæ&i,
Vivida defenſant, quæ Monumenta damur.

Qui Aliis præſunt, tanto privatis Hominibus Meliores eſſe Oportet,
Quanto Honoribus & Liquitate antecellunt. Panorinitan.

Nondum hæc, quæ nunc tenet Sæculum, Negligentia
Dei Venerat. Liv. l. 3.

Optimus quiſq; Nobiliſſimus. Plato.

LONDON:

Printed for *Thomas Parkhurſt*, at the *Bible* and *Three*
Crowns in *Cheapſide.* 1702.

This title page of The Second Book is photographed from the 1702 edition of the *Magnalia*,
courtesy of the Houghton Library, Harvard University. The five Latin items are translated
below. The printers' errors in lines 13–14 and 16 were noted by Mather himself.

13 *Sæcti* should read *Saecli*   16 *Liguitate* should read *Dignitate*
14 *damur* should read *damus*   Panorinitan *should read* Panormitan

¹ Heading: "Shields unto the Church."*

² "The ancient glory of that elder age does not vanish while living monuments remain to defend it."*

³ "As for those who are in authority over others, it behooves them to be as much more virtuous than private citizens as they surpass them in honors and dignity." The "Panormitan" was Antonius Beccadelli (1394–1471), a native of Palermo, which in Latin was called "Panormus" and its people "Panormitani."*

⁴ "Not yet had that neglect of veneration of the Deity, which now marks the age, begun to appear."*

⁵ "Whoever is noblest is best."*

INTRODUCTION.

' *TWERE to be wish'd that there might never be any* English Translation *of*
25 *that* Wicked Position *in* Machiavel, Non requiri in Principe veram
pietatem, sed sufficere illius quandam umbram, & simulationem Ex-
ternam.[1] *It may be there never was any Region under Heaven happier than poor*
New-England *hath been in* Magistrates, *whose* True Piety *was worthy to be
made the* Example *of* After-Ages.

30   Happy hast thou been, O Land! *in* Magistrates, *whose Disposition to
serve the Lord Jesus Christ, unto whom they still considered themselves accountable,
answered the good Rule of* Agapetus, Quo quis in Republica Majorem
Dignitatis gradum adeptus est, eo Deum Colat Submissius:[2] Magistrates,
whose Disposition to serve the People that chose them to Rule over them, argued
35 *them sensible of that great Stroak in* Cicero, Nulla Re propius Homines ad
Deum Accedunt, quam salute Hominibus danda:[3] Magistrates, *acted
in their Administrations by the Spirit of a* Joshua.[4] *When the* Wise Man[5]
observes unto us, That Oppression makes a Wise Man Mad, *it may be
worth considering, whether the* Oppressor *is not intended rather than the Op-*
40 pressed *in the Observation.* '*Tis very certain that a* Disposition to Oppress
other Men, does often make those that are otherwise very Wise Men, *to forget the
Rules of* Reason, *and commit most* Unreasonable *Exorbitancies.* Rehoboam[6]
in some things acted wisely; *but this Admonition of his Inspired Father could not
restrain him from* acting madly, *when the Spirit of* Oppression *was upon him.*
45 *The Rulers of* New-England *have been* Wise Men, *whom that* Spirit of
Oppression *betray'd not into this* Madness.

    The Father of Themistocles *disswading him from Government, show'd him
the* Old Oars *which the Marriners had now thrown away upon the* Sea-shores
with Neglect and Contempt; and said, That People would certainly treat their
50 Old Rulers with the same Contempt. *But, Reader, let us now take up our
Old Oars with all possible Respect, and see whether we can't still make use of
them to serve our little Vessel. But this the rather, because we may with an easie
turn change the Name into that of* Pilots.

38 Oppression/Oppressions

[1] "For a prince, true piety is not required; a shadow and pretence of it is enough."*
[2] "The higher the rank one has obtained in the state, the more humbly let him worship God." Agapetus was deacon of the church in Constantinople and mentor to Justinian.*
[3] "In nothing do men more nearly approach divinity than in doing good to their fellow men."*
[4] Joshua was actuated by a desire to make the Israelites serve God: Num. 32.12.*
[5] The "Wise Man" was Solomon: Eccles. 7.7.
[6] Rehoboam, the son of Solomon: I Kings 14.13.*

The Word GOVERNMENT, *properly signifies the* Guidance of a Ship:
55 Tully[7] *uses it for that purpose*; *and in* Plutarch, *the Art of* Steering a Ship, *is*,
Τέχνη κυβερνητική. New-England *is a little* Ship, *which hath Weathered many
a Terrible* Storm; *and it is but reasonable that they who have sat at the* Helm *of
the* Ship, *should be remembred in the* History *of its Deliverances.*

Prudentius *calls* Judges, The Great Lights of the Sphere; Symmachus[8]
60 *calls* Judges, The better part of Mankind. *Reader, Thou art now to be entertained with the* Lives *of* Judges *which have deserved that Character. And the*
Lives *of those who have been called,* Speaking Laws, *will excuse our History
from coming under the Observation made about the Works of* Homer, *That the
Word,* LAW, *is never so much as once occurring in them. They are not written*
65 *like the* Cyrus *of* Xenophon, *like the* Alexander *of* Curtius, *like* Virgil's
Æneas, *and like* Pliny's Trajan: *But the Reader hath in every one of them a Real
and a Faithful History. And I please my self with hopes, that there will yet be
found among the Sons of* New-England, *those Young Gentlemen by whom the
Copies given in this History will be written after; and that saying of Old* Chaucer
70 *be remembred*, To do the Genteel Deeds, that makes the Gentleman.

63   *Works/Work*   C.M.

---

[7] That is, Cicero.*

[8] Aurelius Clemens Prudentius (348–*c.*410), the chief Christian poet of the early church,
practiced at the bar and had a successful career in civil administration. Quintus Aurelius
Symmachus (345–410), pagan orator, statesman, and letter-writer.*

The Second BOOK

OF THE

New English History.

75

CHAP. I.

Galeacius Secundus.[1] *The LIFE of* WILLIAM BRADFORD, *Esq;*
Governour of PLYMOUTH *COLONY.*

Omnium Somnos, illius vigilantia defendit, omnium otium illius Labor, omnium Delicias
illius Industria, omnium vacationem illius occupatio.[2]

80 §. 1. IT has been a Matter of some Observation, that although *York-*
shire be one of the largest Shires in *England,* yet, for all the *Fires*
of Martyrdom which were kindled in the Days of Queen *Mary,* it afforded
no more *Fuel* than one poor *Leaf*; namely, *John Leaf,* an Apprentice, who
suffered for the *Doctrine* of the *Reformation* at the same Time and Stake with
85 the Famous *John Bradford.*[3] But when the Reign of Queen *Elizabeth*
would not admit the *Reformation* of *Worship* to proceed unto those Degrees, which were proposed and pursued by no small number of the
Faithful in those Days, *Yorkshire* was not the least of the Shires in *England*
that afforded Suffering *Witnesses* thereunto. The *Churches* there *gathered*
90 were quickly molested with such a raging *Persecution,* that if the Spirit of
Separation in them did carry them unto a further *Extream* than it should
have done, one blameable Cause thereof will be found in the *Extremity*
of that *Persecution.* Their *Troubles* made that *Cold*[4] Country too *Hot* for
them, so that they were under a necessity to *seek* a Retreat in the *Low*
95 *Countries*; and yet the watchful Malice and Fury of their Adversaries
rendred it almost impossible for them to *find* what they sought. For them

78 *Delicias/Delitias*

  1 "The Second Galeacius." The first Galeazzo Carracioli, exiled from Italy when he was
converted to Protestantism.*
  2 "His watchfulness secures the sleep of all, his labor the ease of all, his diligence the pleasures
of all, his employment the freedom of all."*
  3 John Bradford (1510?–1555), while Fellow of Pembroke Hall, Cambridge, was the teacher
of John Whitgift. A popular preacher, he was made chaplain to Edward VI in 1553. Martyred
in Smithfield July 1, 1555.*
  4 That is, "cold" to reformation; cf. Matt. 24.12.

to leave their *Native Soil*, their *Lands* and their *Friends*, and go into a *Strange Place*, where they must hear *Forreign Language*, and live *meanly*
99 and *hardly*, and in other Imployments than that of *Husbandry*, wherein they had been Educated, *these* must needs have been such *Discouragements* as could have been Conquered by none, save those who *sought first the Kingdom of God, and the Righteousness thereof.* But that which would have made these Discouragements the more Unconquerable unto an ordinary
5 Faith, was the terrible Zeal of their Enemies to Guard all *Ports*, and Search all *Ships*, that none of them should be carried off. I will not relate the *sad things* of this kind, then *seen* and *felt* by this People of God; but only exemplifie those *Trials* with one short Story. Divers of this People having Hired a *Dutchman* then lying at *Hull*, to carry them over to *Holland*, he
10 promised faithfully to take them in between *Grimsby* and *Hull*; but *they* coming to the Place a Day or Two too soon, the appearance of such a Multitude alarmed the *Officers* of the Town adjoining, who came with a great Body of *Soldiers* to seize upon them. Now it happened that one Boat full of *Men* had been carried Aboard, while the *Women* were yet in a *Bark*
15 that lay Aground in a Creek at Low-Water. The *Dutchman* perceiving the *Storm* that was thus beginning *Ashore*, swore by the *Sacrament* that he would stay no longer for any of them; and so taking the Advantage of a Fair Wind then Blowing, he put out to *Sea* for *Zealand.* The Women thus left near *Grimsby Common*, bereaved of their Husbands, who had been
20 hurried from them, and forsaken of their Neighbours, of whom none durst in this Fright stay with them, were a very rueful Spectacle; some crying for *Fear*, some shaking for *Cold*, all dragg'd by Troops of *Armed* and *Angry* Men from one Justice to another, till not knowing what to do with them, they e'en dismiss'd them to shift as well as they could for
25 themselves. But by their singular *Afflictions*, and by their Christian *Behaviours*, the *Cause* for which they exposed themselves did gain considerably. In the mean time, the Men at Sea found Reason to be glad that their Families were not with them, for they were surprized with an *horrible Tempest*, which held them for Fourteen Days together, in Seven whereof
30 they saw not *Sun, Moon* or *Star*, but were driven upon the Coast of *Norway.* The *Mariners* often despaired of Life, and once with doleful shrieks gave over all, as thinking the Vessel was Foundred: But the Vessel rose again, and when the *Mariners* with sunk Hearts often cried out, *We Sink! We Sink!* The Passengers without such Distraction of Mind, even while
35 the Water was running into their Mouths and Ears, would chearfully Shout, *Yet, Lord, thou canst save! Yet Lord, thou canst save!* And the Lord accordingly brought them at last safe unto their *Desired Haven:* And not long after helped their Distressed Relations thither after them, where

indeed they found upon almost all Accounts *a new World,* but a World
40 in which they found that they must live like *Strangers* and *Pilgrims.*

§. 2. Among those Devout People was our *William Bradford,* who was
Born *Anno* 1588. in an obscure Village call'd *Austerfield,*[1] where the People
were as unacquainted with the *Bible,* as the *Jews* do seem to have been
with *part* of it in the Days of *Josiah;* a most Ignorant and Licentious
45 *People,* and *like unto their Priest.* Here, and in some other Places, he had a
Comfortable *Inheritance* left him of his Honest Parents, who died while
he was yet a Child, and cast him on the Education, first of his *Grand
Parents,* and then of his *Uncles,* who devoted him, like his Ancestors, unto
the Affairs of *Husbandry.* Soon and long Sickness kept him, as he would
50 afterwards thankfully say, from the *Vanities of Youth,* and made him the
fitter for what he was afterwards to undergo. When he was about a
Dozen Years Old, the Reading of the *Scriptures* began to cause great
Impressions upon him; and those Impressions were much assisted and
improved, when he came to enjoy Mr. *Richard Clifton*'s[2] Illuminating
55 Ministry, not far from his Abode; he was then also further befriended,
by being brought into the Company and Fellowship of such as were then
called *Professors;* though the Young Man that brought him into it, did
after become a Prophane and Wicked *Apostate.* Nor could the *Wrath* of
his *Uncles,* nor the *Scoff* of his *Neighbours* now turn'd upon him, as one of
60 the *Puritans,* divert him from his Pious Inclinations.

§. 3. At last beholding how fearfully the Evangelical and Apostolical
Church-Form, whereinto the Churches of the *Primitive Times* were cast
by the good Spirit of God, had been *Deformed* by the *Apostacy* of the
Succeeding Times; and what little Progress the *Reformation* had yet made in
65 many Parts of *Christendom* towards its Recovery, he set himself by Reading, by Discourse, by Prayer, to learn whether it was not his Duty to
withdraw from the Communion of the *Parish-Assemblies,* and *engage* with
some *Society* of the Faithful, that should keep close unto the *Written
Word* of God, as the *Rule* of their *Worship.* And after many Distresses of
70 Mind concerning it, he took up a very Deliberate and Understanding[1]
Resolution of doing so; which *Resolution* he chearfully Prosecuted, although
the provoked *Rage* of his Friends tried all the ways imaginable to reclaim
him from it, unto all whom his Answer was, *Were I like to endanger my
Life, or consume my Estate by any ungodly Courses, your Counsels to me were very*

42 *Austerfield/Ansterfield*

[1] In the West Riding of Yorkshire.
[2] Richard Clifton (1553–1616), rector of the church at Babworth and later (1606) pastor
of the congregation gathered at Scrooby, which he accompanied to Amsterdam, where he
joined the exiled English church.

[1] Discerning.

75 *seasonable: But you know that I have been Diligent and Provident in my Calling,*
and not only desirous to augment what I have, but also to enjoy it in your Company;
to part from which will be as great a Cross as can befal me. Nevertheless, to keep
a good Conscience, and walk in such a Way as God has prescribed in his Word,
is a thing which I must prefer before you all, and above Life it self. Wherefore,
80 *since 'tis for a good Cause that I am like to suffer the Disasters which you lay before*
me, you have no Cause to be either angry with me, or sorry for me; yea, I am not only
willing to part with every thing that is dear to me in this World for this Cause, but
I am also thankful that God has given me an Heart so to do, and will accept me so to
suffer for him. Some lamented him, *some* derided him, *all* disswaded him:
85 Nevertheless the more they did it, the more fixed he was in his Purpose
to seek the Ordinances of the Gospel, where they should be dispensed
with most of the *Commanded Purity*; and the *sudden Deaths* of the chief
Relations which thus lay at him, quickly after convinced him what a
Folly it had been to have quitted his *Profession*, in Expectation of any
90 Satisfaction from them. So to *Holland* he attempted a removal.

§. 4. Having with a great Company of Christians Hired a Ship to
Transport them for *Holland*, the Master perfidiously betrayed them into
the Hands of those *Persecutors*, who Rifled and Ransack'd their Goods,
and clapp'd their Persons into Prison at *Boston*, where they lay for a
95 Month together. But Mr. *Bradford* being a Young Man of about *Eighteen*,
was dismissed sooner than the rest, so that within a while he had Opportunity with some others to get over to *Zealand*, through *Perils* both by
Land and *Sea* not inconsiderable; where he was not long Ashore e're a
99 *Viper* seized on his Hand, that is, an Officer, who carried him unto the
Magistrates, unto whom an envious Passenger had accused him as having
fled out of *England*. When the Magistrates understood the True Cause of
his coming thither, they were well satisfied with him; and so he repaired
joyfully unto his Brethren at *Amsterdam*, where the Difficulties to which
5 he afterwards stooped in Learning and Serving of a *Frenchman* at the
Working of *Silks*, were abundantly Compensated by the *Delight* wherewith he sat under the *Shadow* of our Lord in his purely dispensed Ordinances. At the end of Two Years, he did, being of Age to do it, convert
his Estate in *England* into Money; but Setting up for himself, he found
10 some of his Designs by the *Providence* of God frowned upon, which he
judged a *Correction* bestowed by God upon him for certain Decays of
Internal Piety, whereinto he had fallen; the *Consumption* of his *Estate* he
thought came to prevent a *Consumption* in his *Virtue*. But after he had
resided in *Holland* about half a Score Years, he was one of those who bore
15 a part in that Hazardous and Generous[1] Enterprize of removing into
New-England, with part of the *English* Church at *Leyden*, where at their

---

[1] Gallant.

first Landing, his dearest Consort accidentally falling Overboard, was drowned in the *Harbour*; and the rest of his Days were spent in the Services, and the Temptations, of that *American Wilderness.*

20 §. 5. Here was Mr. *Bradford* in the Year 1621. unanimously chosen the *Governour* of the Plantation: The Difficulties whereof were such, that if he had not been a Person of more than Ordinary Piety, Wisdom and Courage, he must have sunk under them. He had with a Laudable Industry been laying up a Treasure of *Experiences,* and he had now occa-
25 sion to use it: Indeed nothing but an *Experienced* Man could have been suitable to the Necessities of the People. The Potent Nations of the *Indians,* into whose Country they were come, would have cut them off, if the Blessing of God upon *his* Conduct had not quell'd them; and if his Prudence, Justice and Moderation had not over-ruled them, they had
30 been ruined by their own *Distempers.* One *Specimen* of his Demeanour is to this Day particularly spoken of. A Company of Young Fellows that were newly arrived, were very unwilling to comply with the Governour's Order for *Working* abroad on the Publick Account; and therefore on *Christmass-Day,* when he had called upon them, they excused themselves,
35 with a pretence that it was against their *Conscience* to *Work* such a Day. The Governour gave them no Answer, only that he would spare them till they were better informed; but by and by he found them all at *Play* in the Street, sporting themselves with various Diversions; whereupon Commanding the Instruments of their Games to be taken from them, he
40 effectually gave them to understand, *That it was against his Conscience that they should play whilst others were at Work; and that if they had any Devotion to the Day, they should show it at Home in the Exercises of Religion, and not in the Streets with Pastime and Frolicks;* and this gentle Reproof put a final stop to all such Disorders for the future.
45 §. 6. For Two Years together after the beginning of the Colony, whereof he was now Governour, the poor People had a great Experiment of *Man's not living by Bread alone;* for when they were left all together without one Morsel of *Bread* for many Months one after another, still the good Providence of God relieved them, and supplied them, and this for
50 the most part out of the *Sea.* In this low Condition of Affairs, there was no little Exercise for the *Prudence* and *Patience* of the Governour, who chearfully bore his part in all: And that *Industry* might not flag, he quickly set himself to settle *Propriety* among the New Planters; foreseeing that while the whole Country labour'd upon a *Common Stock,* the *Husbandry*
55 and *Business* of the Plantation could not *flourish,* as *Plato* and others long since dream'd that it would, if a *Community* were established. Certainly, if the Spirit which dwelt in the *Old Puritans,* had not inspired these *New-*

20 1621. unanimously/1621. Unanimously

Planters, they had sunk under the Burden of these Difficulties; but our *Bradford* had a *double Portion* of that Spirit.

60 §. 7. The Plantation was quickly thrown into a *Storm* that almost overwhelmed it, by the unhappy Actions of a Minister[1] sent over from *England* by the *Adventurers* concerned for the Plantation; but by the Blessing of Heaven on the Conduct of the Governour, they Weathered out that *Storm*. Only the *Adventurers* hereupon breaking to pieces, threw up

65 all their Concernments with the *Infant Colony*; whereof they gave this as one Reason, *That the Planters dissembled with His Majesty, and their Friends in their Petition, wherein they declared for a Church-Discipline, agreeing with the* French *and others of the Reforming Churches in* Europe. Whereas 'twas now urged, that they had admitted into their Communion a Person, who at

70 his Admission utterly *renounced* the Churches of *England*, (which Person by the way, was *that* very Man who had made the Complaints against them) and therefore though they denied the *Name* of *Brownists*, yet they were the *Thing*. In Answer hereunto, the very Words written by the Governour were these; *Whereas you Tax us with dissembling about the* French

75 Discipline, *you do us wrong, for we both hold and practice the* Discipline *of the* French *and other* Reformed *Churches (as they have published the same in the* Harmony of Confessions) *according to our Means, in Effect and Substance. But whereas you would tie us up to the* French Discipline *in every Circumstance, you derogate from the* Liberty *we have in Christ Jesus. The Apostle* Paul *would*

80 *have none to* follow him *in any thing, but wherein he* follows Christ; *much less ought any Christian or Church in the World to do it. The* French *may err, we may err, and other Churches may err, and doubtless do in many* Circumstances. *That Honour therefore belongs only to the* Infallible Word of God, *and* pure Testament of Christ, *to be propounded and followed as the* only *Rule and*

85 *Pattern for Direction herein to all Churches and Christians. And it is too great Arrogancy for any Men or Church to think, that he or they have so sounded the Word of God unto the bottom, as precisely to set down the Churches Discipline without Error in Substance or Circumstance, that no other without blame may digress or differ in any thing from the same. And it is not difficult to shew that the* Reformed

90 Churches *differ in many* Circumstances *among themselves.* By which Words it appears how far he was free from that *Rigid Spirit* of *Separation*, which broke to pieces the *Separatists* themselves in the *Low Countries*, unto the great Scandal of the *Reforming Churches*. He was indeed a Person of a *well-temper'd Spirit*, or else it had been scarce possible for him to have kept

95 the Affairs of *Plymouth* in so good a *Temper* for *Thirty Seven* Years together; in every one of which he was chosen their Governour, except the *Three Years*, wherein Mr. *Winslow*, and the *Two Years*, wherein Mr. *Prince*, at the choice of the People, took a *turn* with him.

---

[1] John Lyford.*

99 §. 8. The *Leader* of a People in a *Wilderness* had need be a *Moses*; and if a *Moses* had not led the People of *Plymouth-Colony*, when this Worthy Person was their Governour, the People had never with so much Unanimity and Importunity still called *him* to lead them. Among many Instances thereof, let this one piece of *Self-denial be told for a Memorial of*
5 *him, wheresoever this History shall be considered.* The Patent of the Colony was taken in *his* Name, running in these Terms, *To* William Bradford, *his Heirs, Associates and Assigns:* But when the number of the *Freemen* was much Increased, and many New *Townships* Erected, the *General Court* there desired of Mr. *Bradford,* that he would make a Surrender of
10 the same into *their Hands,* which *he* willingly and presently assented unto, and confirmed it according to their Desire by his *Hand* and *Seal,* reserving no more for himself than was his *Proportion,* with others, by *Agreement.* But as he found the Providence of Heaven many ways *Recompencing* his many Acts of *Self-denial,* so he gave this Testimony to the Faithfulness of
15 the Divine Promises; *That he had forsaken Friends, Houses and Lands for the sake of the Gospel, and the Lord gave them him again. Here* he prospered in his *Estate*; and besides a Worthy *Son* which he had by a former Wife, he had also Two Sons and a Daughter by another, whom he Married in this Land.
20 §. 9. He was a Person for *Study* as well as *Action*; and hence, notwithstanding the Difficulties through which he passed in his Youth, he attained unto a notable Skill in *Languages*; the *Dutch* Tongue was become almost as Vernacular to him as the *English*; the *French* Tongue he could also manage; the *Latin* and the *Greek* he had Mastered; but the *Hebrew* he
25 most of all studied, *Because,* he said, *he would see with his own Eyes the Ancient Oracles of God in their Native Beauty.* He was also well skill'd in *History,* in *Antiquity,* and in *Philosophy*; and for *Theology* he became so versed in it, that he was an *Irrefragable Disputant* against the *Errors,* especially those of *Anabaptism,* which with Trouble he saw rising in his
30 Colony; wherefore he wrote some Significant things for the Confutation of those Errors. But the *Crown* of all was his Holy, Prayerful, Watchful and Fruitful *Walk with God,* wherein he was very Exemplary.
§. 10. At length he fell into an Indisposition of Body, which rendred him unhealthy for a whole *Winter*; and as the *Spring* advanced, his Health
35 yet more declined; yet he felt himself not what he counted *Sick,* till one *Day*; in the *Night* after which, the God of Heaven so fill'd his Mind with *Ineffable Consolations,* that he seemed little short of *Paul,* rapt up unto the *Unutterable* Entertainments of *Paradise.* The next Morning he told his Friends, *That the good Spirit of God had given him a Pledge of his Happiness*
40 *in another World, and the First-fruits of his Eternal Glory:* And on the Day following he died, *May* 9. 1657. in the 69th Year of his Age, lamented by
41 Age, lamented/Age. Lamented

all the Colonies of *New-England*, as a Common Blessing and Father to them all.

O mihi si Similis Contingat Clausula Vitæ! [1]

45 *Plato*'s brief Description of a *Governour*, is all that I will now leave as his Character, in an

EPITAPH.

Νομεὺς Τροφὸς ἀγέλης ἀνθρωπίνης [2]

MEN are but FLOCKS: BRADFORD beheld their Need,
50 *And long did them at once both* Rule *and* Feed.

CHAP. II.

SUCCESSORS.

Inter Omnia quæ Rempublicam, ejusq; fælicitatem conservant, quid utilius, quid præstantius, quam Viros ad Magistratus gerendos Eligere, summa prudentia & Virtute
55 *preditos, quiq; ad Honores obtinendos, non Ambitione, non Largitionibus, sed Virtute & Modestia sibi parent adytum!* [1]

§. 1. THE Merits of Mr. *Edward Winslow*, the Son of *Edward Winslow,* Esq; of *Draughtwich*, in the Country of *Worcester*,[2] obliged the Votes of the *Plymouthean* Colony (whereto he arrived in the Year 1624.
60 after his Prudent and Faithful Dispatch of an Agency in *England*, on the behalf of that Infant Colony) to chuse him for many Years a Magistrate, and for Two or Three their *Governour*. Travelling into the *Low-Countries*, he fell into Acquaintance with the *English Church* at *Leyden*, and joining himself to them, he Shipped himself with that part of them which
65 first came over into *America*; from which time he was continually engaged in such extraordinary Actions, as the assistance of that People to encounter their more than ordinary Difficulties, called for. But their *Publick* Affairs then requiring an *Agency* of as wise a Man as the Country

---

[1] "O if only the end of my life could be the same."*
[2] "Shepherd and feeder of the flocks of men."*

---

[1] "Among all the things that preserve the commonwealth and its happiness, what is more useful, what more excellent, than to choose for public office men endowed with prudence and virtue, and who win honors, not by currying favor, not by distributing largesse, but who serve in the temple with virtue and modesty."*
[2] Droitwich. "Country" is here used in the sense of "county."*

could find at *Whitehall* for them, he was again prevail'd withal in the
70 Year 1635. to appear for them at the *Council-board*; and his appearance
there proved as *Effectual*, as it was very *Seasonable*, not only for the Colony
of *Plymouth*, but for the *Massachusets* also, on very important Accounts.
It was by the Blessing of God upon his wary and proper Applications,
that the Attempts of many Adversaries to overthrow the whole Settle-
75 ment of *New-England*, were themselves wholly overthrown; and as a small
Acknowledgment for his great Service therein, they did, upon his return
again, chuse him their *Governour*. But in the Year 1646. the place of
Governour being reassumed by Mr. *Bradford*, the *Massachuset*-Colony
Addressed themselves unto Mr. *Winslow* to take another Voyage for
80 *England*, that he might there procure their Deliverance from the Designs
of many Troublesome Adversaries that were Petitioning unto the *Parliament* against them; and this *Hercules* having been from his very early Days
accustomed unto the crushing of that sort of *Serpents*, generously undertook another *Agency*, wherein how many good Services he did for *New-
85 England*, and with what Fidelity, Discretion, Vigour and Success he
pursued the Interests of that Happy People, it would make a large History
to relate, an *History* that may not now be expected until the *Resurrection
of the Just*. After this he returned no more unto *New-England*; but being
in great Favour with the greatest Persons then in the Nation, he fell into
90 those Imployments wherein the whole Nation fared the better for him.
At length he was imployed as one of the *Grand Commissioners* in the Expedition against *Hispaniola*, where a *Disease* (rendred yet more *uneasie*
by his Dissatisfaction at the strange miscarriage of that Expedition)
arresting him, he died between *Domingo* and *Jamaica*, on *May* 8. 1655. in
95 the Sixty-first Year of his Life, and had his Body Honourably committed
unto the *Sea*.

§. 2. Sometimes during the *Life*, but always after the *Death* of Governour *Bradford*, even until his own, Mr. *Thomas Prince*[1] was chosen
99 𝔊𝔬𝔟𝔢𝔯𝔫𝔬𝔲𝔯 of *Plymouth*. He was a Gentleman whose *Natural Parts* exceeded his *Acquired*; but the want and worth of *Acquired Parts* was a thing
so sensible unto him, that *Plymouth* perhaps never had a greater *Mæcenas*
of *Learning* in it: It was he that in spite of much Contradiction, procured
Revenues for the Support of *Grammar-Schools*[2] in that Colony. About the
5 time of Governour *Bradford*'s Death, *Religion* it self had like to have *died*
in that Colony, through a *Libertine* and *Brownistick* Spirit then prevailing

---

83   crushing/crusting   2   *Mæcenas*/*Mecænas*

---

[1] More commonly, Thomas Prence (cf. Charles M. Andrews, *Colonial Period* [4 vols., New Haven, Yale University Press, 1934–1938], 1:286, 290, 296).

[2] Apparently in 1673, the year of his death, Prence gave funds to be used for grammar schools to teach both "humane learning, and good litterature."*

among the People, and a strange Disposition to Discountenance the *Gospel-Ministry*, by setting up the *Gifts of Private Brethren* in Opposition thereunto. The good People being in extream Distress from the Prospect
10 which this matter gave to them, saw no way so likely and ready to save the Churches from Ruin, as by the *Election* of Mr. *Prince* to the place of *Governour*; and this Point being by the Gracious and Marvellous Providence of the Lord Jesus Christ gained at the next *Election*; the *Adverse Party* from that very time sunk into Confusion. He had Sojourned for a
15 while at *Eastham*, where a Church was by his means gathered; but after this time he returned unto his former Scituation at *Plymouth*, where he resided until he died, which was *March* 29. 1673. when he was about *Seventy-Three* Years of Age: Among the many Excellent Qualities which adorned him as *Governour* of the Colony, there was much notice taken of
20 that *Integrity*, wherewith indeed he was most *exemplarily* qualified: Whence it was that as he ever would refuse any thing that look'd like a *Bribe*; so if any Person having a Case to be heard at Court, had sent a Present unto his Family in his absence, he would presently send back the value thereof in Money unto the Person. But had he been only a private
25 *Christian*, there would yet have been seen upon him those Ornaments of *Prayerfulness*, and *Peaceableness*, and profound Resignation to the Conduct of the *Word* of God, and a strict *Walk* with God, which might justly have been made an *Example* to a whole Colony.

§. 3. Reader, If thou would'st have seen the true Picture of *Wisdom*,
30 *Courage* and *Generosity*, the Successor of Mr. *Thomas Prince* in the Government of *Plymouth* would have represented it. It was the truly Honourable *Josiah Winslow*, Esq; the first Governour that was Born in *New-England*, and one well worthy to be an Example to all that should come after him: A True *English Gentleman*, and (that I may say all at once) the *True Son*
35 of that Gentleman whom we parted withal no more than Two Paragraphs ago. His Education and his Disposition was that of a *Gentleman*; and his many Services to his Country in the *Field*, as well as on the *Bench*, ought never to be Buried in *Oblivion*. All that *Homer* desired in a *Ruler*, was in the Life of this Gentleman expressed unto the Life; to be, *Fortis in*
40 *Hostes*, and, *Bonus in Cives*.[1] Though he hath left an *Off-spring*,[2] yet I must ask for *One Daughter* to be remembered above the rest. As of Old, *Epaminondas* being upbraided with want of Issue, boasted that he left behind him one Daughter, namely, the Battel of *Leuctra*, which would render him Immortal; so our General *Winslow* hath left behind him his
45 Battel at the Fort of the *Narragansets*, to Immortalize him: *There* did he

39 *Fortis/Fortes* C.M.

[1] "Brave against the enemy, good to his subjects."*
[2] A son, Isaac.

with his own *Sword* make and shape a *Pen* to Write his History. But so large a *Field* of Merit is now before me, that I dare not give my self the liberty to Range in it lest I lose my self. He died on *Dec.* 18. 1680.

Jam Cinis est, & de tam magno restat Achille,
50   *Nescio quid; parvam quod non bene compleat Urnam.*[3]

§. 4. And what *Successor*[1] had *he?* Methinks of the Two last Words in the wonderful Prediction of the *Succession,* Oracled unto King *Henry* VII. *LEO, NULLUS,*[2] the First would have well suited the Valiant *Winslow* of *Plymouth*; and the last were to have been wish'd for him that followed.

55   CHAP. III.

Patres Conscripti[1]: *Or, ASSISTENTS.*

THE GOVERNOURS of *New-England* have still had *Righteousness the Girdle of their Loins, and Faithfulness the Girdle of their Reins,* that is to say, *Righteous* and *Faithful* Men about them, in the *Assistance* of such
60 *Magistrates* as were called by the *Votes* of the *Freemen* unto the Administration of the Government, (according to their *Charters*) and made the *Judges of the Land.* These Persons have been such *Members* of the *Churches,* and such *Patrons* to the *Churches,* and generally been such Examples of Courage, Wisdom, Justice, Goodness and Religion, that it is fit our
65 *Church-History* should remember them. The Blessed *Apollonius,* who in a set Oration Generously and Eloquently Pleaded the Cause of *Christianity* before the *Roman Senate,* was not only a Learned Person, but also (if *Jerom* say right) a *Senator* of Rome. The *Senators* of *New-England* also have pleaded the Cause of *Christianity,* not so much by *Orations,* as by *Practising*
70 of it, and by *Suffering* for it. Nevertheless, as the *Sicyonians* would have no other Epitaphs written on the Tombs of their *Kings,* but only their *Names,* that they might have no Honour, but what the Remembrance

---

49 *magno/magus* C.M.

---

[3] "Now he is but dust; and of Achilles, once so great, there remains a pitiful handful, hardly enough to fill an urn."*

---

[1] Thomas Hinckley (1618–1706), the last governor of the Plymouth Colony, served from 1680 to 1692 except for the years of the Andros regime.
[2] "A lion, then no one."*

---

[1] "Enrolled fathers," that is, senators.*

of their Actions and Merits in the Minds of the People should procure for them; so I shall content my self with only reciting the *Names* of these
75 Worthy Persons, and the *Times* when I find them first chosen unto their Magistracy.

MAGISTRATES in the Colony of New-Plymouth.

THE good People, soon after their first coming over, chose Mr. *William Bradford* for their Governour, and added Five *Assistents*, whose
80 Names, I suppose, will be found in the Catalogue of them, whom I find sitting on the *Seat of Judgment* among them, in the Year 1633.

Edward Winslow, Gov.
William Bradford.
Miles Standish.
85 *John Howland.*

John Alden.
John Done.[2]
Stephen Hopkins.
William Gilson.

Afterwards at several times were added,

Thomas Prince.	1634.[3]	*Thomas Southworth.*	1652.
William Collier.	1634.	*James Cudworth.*	1656.
Timothy Hatherly.	1636.	*Josiah Winslow.*	1657.
90 *John Brown.*	1636.	*William Bradford.* F.	1658.
John Jenny.	1637.	*Thomas Hinkley.*	1658.
John Atwood.	1638.	*James Brown.*	1665.
Edmund Freeman.	1640.	*John Freeman.*	1666.
William Thomas.	1642.	*Nathanael Bacon.*	1667.
95 *Thomas Willet.*	1651.		

Thus far we find in a Book Entituled, *New-England's Memorial,* which was Published by Mr. *Nathanael Morton,* the Secretary of *Plymouth* Colony, in the Year 1669.[4] Since then there have been added at several
99 times,[5]

Constant Southworth.	1670.	*John Thatcher.*	[1682.]
Daniel Smith.	1674.	*John Walley.*	[1684.]
Barnabas Lothrop.	1681.	[*John Cushing.*]	[1689.]

---

[2] Or Doane; Mather corrects Morton's *Memoriall* (p. 89), which has Dove.

[3] In 1634 Prince, or Prence, was elected governor; in 1635 an Assistant.

[4] Mather's tabulation, which gives the first year in which a man was elected to the Assistants, is culled from Morton's annual election lists.

[5] Dates and name in brackets supplied from the *Plymouth Colony Records,* 6:9, 58, 97, 150, 205. Daniel Smith's first election to the Assistants was in 1679, not 1674.

CHAP. IV.

5　Nehemias Americanus.[1] *The LIFE of* JOHN WINTHROP, *Esq*; *Governour of the* MASSACHUSET *COLONY.*

Quicunq; Venti erunt, Ars nostra certe non aberit.[2] Cicer.

§. 1. LET *Greece* boast of her patient *Lycurgus*, the *Lawgiver*, by whom *Diligence, Temperance, Fortitude* and *Wit* were made the *Fashions*
10　of a therefore Long-lasting and Renowned Commonwealth: Let *Rome* tell of her Devout *Numa*, the *Lawgiver*, by whom the most Famous Commonwealth saw *Peace* Triumphing over extinguished *War*, and cruel *Plunders*, and *Murders* giving place to the more mollifying Exercises of his *Religion*. Our *New-England* shall tell and boast of her 𝔚𝔦𝔫𝔱𝔥𝔯𝔬𝔭, a *Lawgiver*,
15　as patient as *Lycurgus*, but not admitting any of *his* Criminal Disorders; as Devout as *Numa*, but not liable to any of *his* Heathenish Madnesses; a *Governour* in whom the Excellencies of *Christianity* made a most improving Addition unto the *Virtues*, wherein even without *those* he would have made a *Parallel* for the Great Men of *Greece*, or of *Rome*, which the Pen of
20　a *Plutarch* has Eternized.

§. 2. A stock of *Heroes* by right should afford nothing but what is *Heroical*; and nothing but an extream Degeneracy would make any thing less to be expected from a Stock of *Winthrops*. Mr. *Adam Winthrop*, the Son of a Worthy Gentleman wearing the same Name, was himself a
25　Worthy, a Discreet, and a Learned Gentleman, particularly Eminent for *Skill* in the *Law*, nor without Remark for *Love* to the *Gospel*, under the Reign of King *Henry* VIII. And Brother to a Memorable *Favourer* of the *Reformed Religion* in the Days of Queen *Mary*, into whose Hands the Famous Martyr *Philpot*[1] committed his *Papers*, which afterwards made no
30　Inconsiderable part of our *Martyr-Books*. This Mr. *Adam Winthrop* had a Son of the same Name also, and of the same Endowments and Imployments with his Father; and this Third *Adam Winthrop* was the Father of that Renowned *John Winthrop*, who was the Father of *New-England*, and the Founder *of a Colony*, which upon many Accounts, like *him* that Founded
35　it, may challenge the *First Place* among the *English* Glories of *America*. Our 𝔍𝔬𝔥𝔫 𝔚𝔦𝔫𝔱𝔥𝔯𝔬𝔭 thus Born at the Mansion-House of his Ancestors, at *Groton* in *Suffolk*, on *June* 12. 1587.[2] enjoyed afterwards an agreeable Education. But though he would rather have Devoted himself unto the

---

[1] "The American Nehemiah."*
[2] "But whatever winds may blow, such skill as I have will not be wanting."*

[1] John Philpot (1516–1555), Archdeacon of Winchester, was burned at the stake in Smithfield December 18, 1555.*
[2] The correct date is January 12, 1587/88.

Study of Mr. *John Calvin*, than of Sir *Edward Cook*;[3] nevertheless, the
40 Accomplishments of a *Lawyer*, were those wherewith Heaven made his
chief Opportunities to be Serviceable.

§. 3. Being made, at the unusually early Age of *Eighteen*, a *Justice of
Peace*, his Virtues began to fall under a more general Observation; and
he not only so *Bound himself to the Behaviour* of a *Christian*, as to become
45 Exemplary for a Conformity to the *Laws* of *Christianity* in his own Conversation, but also discovered a more than ordinary Measure of those
Qualities, which adorn an *Officer of Humane Society*. His *Justice* was Impartial, and used the *Ballance* to weigh not the *Cash*, but the *Case* of those
who were before him: *Prosopolatria*, he reckoned as bad as *Idololatria*:[1]
50 His *Wisdom* did exquisitely Temper things according to the *Art of Governing*, which is a Business of more Contrivance than the *Seven Arts* of the
Schools:[2] *Oyer* still went before *Terminer*[3] in all his Administrations: His
Courage made him *Dare to do right*, and fitted him to stand among the
Lions, that have sometimes been the *Supporters* of the Throne: All which
55 Virtues he rendred the more Illustrious, by *Emblazoning* them with the
Constant *Liberality* and *Hospitality* of a *Gentleman*. This made him the
Terror of the Wicked, and the *Delight* of the Sober, the *Envy* of the many,
but the *Hope* of those who had any *Hopeful Design* in Hand for the Com-
mon Good of the Nation, and the Interests of Religion.

60 §. 4. Accordingly when the *Noble Design* of carrying a Colony of
Chosen People into an *American* Wilderness, was by *some* Eminent Persons
undertaken, *This* Eminent Person was, by the Consent of all, *Chosen* for
the *Moses*, who must be the Leader of so great an Undertaking: And indeed nothing but a *Mosaic Spirit* could have carried him through the
65 *Temptations*, to which either his *Farewel* to his *own Land*, or his *Travel*[1] in
a *Strange Land*, must needs expose a Gentleman of his *Education*. Wherefore having Sold a fair Estate of Six or Seven Hundred a Year, he Transported himself with the Effects of it into *New-England* in the Year 1630.
where he spent it upon the Service of a famous Plantation founded and
70 formed for the Seat of the most *Reformed Christianity*: And continued
there, conflicting with *Temptations* of all sorts, as many Years as the *Nodes*[2]
of the *Moon* take to dispatch a Revolution. Those Persons were never

---

[3] Sir Edward Coke (1552–1634), Lord Chief Justice, author of the *Institutes of the Laws of
England.**

---

[1] That is, "Man-worship is as bad as Idol-worship." *Prosopolatria*, derived from πρόσωπον,
person, and λατρεία, worship or veneration.*
[2] The seven arts of the medieval schools: the trivium (grammar, rhetoric, dialectic) and the
quadrivium (arithmetic, geometry, astronomy, music).
[3] "Oyer," to hear; "Terminer," to determine.*

---

[1] In the double sense of "travel" and "travail."
[2] The time required for a revolution of the nodes of the moon is 18.6 years. Winthrop died
March 26, 1649.

concerned in a *New-Plantation*, who know not that the unavoidable
Difficulties of such a thing, will call for all the *Prudence* and *Patience* of a
75 Mortal Man to Encounter therewithal; and they must be very insensible
of the Influence, which the *Just Wrath* of Heaven has permitted the *Devils*
to have upon *this World*, if they do not think that the Difficulties of a
New-Plantation, devoted unto the *Evangelical Worship* of our Lord Jesus
Christ, must be yet more than Ordinary. How *Prudently*, how *Patiently*,
80 and with how much Resignation to our Lord Jesus Christ, our brave
Winthrop waded through these *Difficulties*, let Posterity Consider with
Admiration. And know, that as the *Picture* of this their *Governour*, was,
after his *Death*, hung up with Honour in the *State-House* of his Country,
so the *Wisdom, Courage*, and Holy *Zeal* of his *Life*, were an Example well-
85 worthy to be Copied by all that shall succeed in *Government*.

§. 5. Were he now to be consider'd only as a *Christian*, we might therein
propose him as greatly Imitable. He was a very *Religious* Man; and as he
strictly kept his *Heart*, so he kept his *House*, under the Laws of *Piety*; *there*
he was every Day constant in Holy Duties, both Morning and Evening,
90 and on the *Lord's Days*, and *Lectures*; though he *wrote* not after the Preacher,[1] yet such was his *Attention*, and such his *Retention* in *Hearing*, that he
repeated unto his *Family* the *Sermons* which he had heard in the Congregation. But it is chiefly as a *Governour* that he is now to be consider'd.
Being the *Governour* over the considerablest Part of *New-England*, he
95 maintain'd the Figure and Honour of his Place with the Spirit of a true
Gentleman; but yet with such obliging *Condescention* to the Circumstances
of the Colony, that when a certain troublesome and malicious Calumni-
ator, well known in those Times, printed his Libellous *Nick-Names* upon
99 the chief Persons here, the worst *Nick-Name* he could find for the Governour, was *John Temper-well*;[2] and when the Calumnies of that ill Man
caused the Arch-Bishop to Summon one Mr. *Cleaves* before the King, in
hopes to get some Accusation from him against the Country, Mr.
Cleaves[3] gave such an Account of the Governour's laudable Carriage in
5 all Respects, and the serious Devotion wherewith Prayers were both
publickly and privately made for His Majesty, that the King expressed
himself most highly *Pleased* therewithal, only *Sorry*, that so Worthy a
Person should be no better Accommodated than with the Hardships of
America. He was, indeed, a *Governour*, who had most exactly studied that

---

99 *Nick-Name/Nich-Name*

[1] That is, did not take down the preacher's words in writing.
[2] Thomas Morton refers to Winthrop as Joshua, not John, Temperwell in his *New English Canaan*, p. 162.
[3] George Cleaves (Cleeve, Cleeves) was deputy president for Alexander Rigby, M.P., of the province of Ligonia in Maine, and had also received a letter of agency from Sir Ferdinando Gorges.*

10 Book, which pretending to Teach *Politicks*, did only contain *Three Leaves*,
and but *One Word* in each of those Leaves, which Word was, 𝔐𝔬𝔡𝔢𝔯𝔞𝔱𝔦𝔬𝔫.
Hence, though he were a Zealous Enemy to all *Vice*, yet his *Practice* was
according to his *Judgment* thus expressed; *In the Infancy of Plantations,
Justice should be administred with more Lenity than in a settled State; because*
15 *People are more apt then to Transgress; partly out of Ignorance of new Laws and
Orders, partly out of Oppression of Business, and other Straits.* [𝔏𝔢𝔫𝔱𝔬 𝔈𝔯𝔞𝔡𝔲,]
*was the old Rule; and if the Strings of a new Instrument be wound up unto their
heighth, they will quickly crack.* But when some Leading and Learned Men
took Offence at his Conduct in this Matter, and upon a *Conference* gave
20 it in as their Opinion, *That a stricter Discipline was to be used in the beginning
of a Plantation, than after its being with more Age established and confirmed,* the
Governour being readier to see *his own* Errors than *other Mens*, professed
his Purpose to endeavour their Satisfaction with less of *Lenity* in his
Administrations. At that *Conference* there were drawn up several other
25 *Articles* to be observed between the Governour and the rest of the Magistrates, which were of this Import: *That* the *Magistrates*, as far as might be,
should aforehand ripen their *Consultations*, to produce that *Unanimity*
in their *Publick Votes*, which might make them liker to the *Voice of God*;
that if Differences fell out among them in their Publick Meetings, they
30 should speak only to the *Case*, without any Reflection, with all due
Modesty, and but by way of *Question*; or Desire the deferring of the *Cause*
to further time; and after *Sentence* to intimate privately no *Dislike*; *that*
they should be more *Familiar*, Friendly and Open unto each other, and
more frequent in their *Visitations*, and not any way expose each other's
35 *Infirmities*, but seek the *Honour* of each other, and all the Court; *that* One
Magistrate shall not *cross* the Proceedings of another, without first
advising with him; and *that* they should in all their Appearances abroad,
be so circumstanced as to prevent all Contempt of Authority; and *that*
they should Support and Strengthen all *Under Officers*. All of which *Articles*
40 were observed by no Man more than by the *Governour* himself.

§. 6. But whilst he thus did as our *New-English Nehemiah*, the part of a
Ruler in Managing the Publick Affairs of our *American Jerusalem*, when
there were *Tobiahs* and *Sanballats* enough to vex him, and give him the
Experiment of *Luther*'s Observation, *Omnis qui regit, est tanquam signum, in*
45 *quod omnia Jacula, Satan & Mundus dirigunt;*[1] he made himself still an
exacter *Parallel* unto that Governour of *Israel*, by doing the part of a
Neighbour among the distressed People of the *New-Plantation*. To teach
them the *Frugality* necessary for those times, he abridged himself of a

---

32 intimate/imitate C.M.   43 *Tobiahs/Tobijahs*

[1] "Every one who rules is like a mark against which Satan and the World aim all their
darts."*

Thousand comfortable things, which he had allow'd himself elsewhere:
50 His *Habit* was not that *soft Raiment*, which would have been disagreeable
to a *Wilderness*; his *Table* was not covered with the *Superfluities* that would
have invited unto *Sensualities: Water* was commonly his *own Drink*,
though he gave Wine to *others*. But at the same time his *Liberality* unto
the Needy was even beyond measure Generous; and therein he was
55 continually causing *The Blessing of him that was ready to Perish to come upon
him, and the Heart of the Widow and the Orphan to sing for Joy:* But none more
than those of Deceas'd *Ministers*, whom he always treated with a very
singular Compassion; among the Instances whereof we still enjoy with
us the Worthy and now Aged Son of that Reverend *Higginson*, whose
60 Death left his Family in a wide World soon after his arrival here, publickly
acknowledging the Charitable *Winthrop* for his *Foster-Father*.[2] It was of
tentimes no small Trial unto his *Faith*, to think, *How a Table for the People
should be furnished when they first came into the Wilderness!* And for very many
of the People, his *own good Works* were needful, and accordingly employed
65 for the answering of his *Faith*. Indeed, for a while the Governour was the
Joseph, unto whom the whole Body of the People repaired when their
Corn failed them: And he continued Relieving of them with his *open-
handed Bounties*, as long as he had any Stock to do it with; and a lively
Faith to *see* the return of the *Bread after many Days*, and not *Starve* in the
70 Days that were to pass till that *return* should be *seen*, carried him chearfully
through those Expences. Once it was observable, that on *Feb*. 5. 1630.
when he was distributing the last Handful of *the Meal in the Barrel* unto
a Poor Man distressed by the Wolf *at the Door*, at that Instant they spied
a Ship arrived at the Harbour's Mouth Laden with *Provisions* for them
75 all. Yea, the Governour sometimes made his own *Private Purse* to be the
Publick; not by *sucking* into it, but by *squeezing* out of it; for when the
Publick Treasure had nothing in it, he did himself defray the Charges of
the *Publick*. And having learned that Lesson of our Lord, *That it is better to
Give, than to Receive*, he did, at the General Court when he was a Third
80 time chosen Governour, make a Speech unto this purpose, *That he had
received Gratuities from divers Towns, which he accepted with much Comfort and
Content; and he had likewise received Civilities from particular Persons, which he
could not refuse without Incivility in himself: Nevertheless, he took them with a
trembling Heart, in regard of God's Word, and the Conscience of his own Infirmities;*
85 *and therefore he desired them that they would not hereafter take it Ill if he refused
such Presents for the time to come.* 'Twas his Custom also to send some of his

80 make/made C.M.

[2] John Higginson, author of the Attestation. For his father, Francis Higginson, see Bk. III, pt. 2, chap. 1. John was only fourteen years old at the time of his father's death, and he was educated through the care of Winthrop and others.

Family upon Errands, unto the Houses of the Poor about their *Meal-time*, on purpose to *spy* whether they *wanted*; and if it were found that they *wanted*, he would make *that* the Opportunity of sending Supplies unto
90 them. And there was one Passage of his *Charity* that was perhaps a little *unusual:* In an hard and long Winter, when *Wood* was very scarce at *Boston*, a Man gave him a private *Information*, that a needy Person in the Neighbourhood stole *Wood* sometimes from *his* Pile; whereupon the Governour in a seeming Anger did reply, *Does he so? I'll take a Course with*
95 *him; go, call that Man to me, I'll warrant you I'll cure him of Stealing!* When the Man came, the Governour considering that if he had *Stoln*, it was more out of *Necessity* than *Disposition*, said unto him, *Friend, It is a severe Winter, and I doubt you are but meanly provided for Wood*; wherefore I would have you
99 *supply your self at my Wood-Pile till this cold Season be over.* And he then Merrily asked his Friends, *Whether he had not effectually cured this Man of Stealing his Wood?*

§. 7. One would have imagined that so *good* a Man could have had no *Enemies*; if we had not had a daily and woful Experience to Convince
5 us, that *Goodness* it self will *make* Enemies. It is a wonderful Speech of *Plato*, (in one of his Books, *De Republica*) *For the trial of true Vertue, 'tis necessary that a good Man* μηδὲν γὰρ ἀδικῶν δόξαν ἐχέτω τὴν μεγίστην ἀδικίας. *Tho' he do no unjust thing, should suffer the Infamy of the greatest Injustice.* The Governour had by his unspotted *Integrity*, procured himself
10 a great Reputation among the *People*; and then the Crime of *Popularity* was laid unto his Charge by such, who were willing to deliver him from the Danger of having *all Men speak well of him*. Yea, there were Persons eminent both for Figure and for Number, unto whom it was almost *Essential* to *dislike* every thing that came from *him*; and yet *he* always
15 maintained an Amicable Correspondence with them; as believing that they acted according to their Judgment and Conscience, or that their Eyes were held by some *Temptation* in the worst of all their Oppositions. Indeed, his *right Works* were so many, that they exposed him unto the *Envy* of his Neighbours; and of such *Power* was that *Envy*, that sometimes
20 he could not *stand before it*; but it was by *not standing* that he most effectually *withstood* it all. Great Attempts were sometimes made among the *Freemen*, to get him left out from his Place in the *Government* upon little Pretences, lest by the too *frequent Choice* of One Man, the *Government* should cease to be by *Choice*; and with a particular aim at *him*, Sermons
25 were Preached at the Anniversary Court of *Election*, to disswade the *Freemen* from chusing *One Man* Twice together. This was the Reward of his *extraordinary Serviceableness!* But when these Attempts *did* succeed, as they sometimes *did*, his Profound *Humility* appeared in that *Equality of Mind*, wherewith he applied himself cheerfully to serve the Country in

10 Reputation/Repntation

30 whatever Station their *Votes* had allotted for him. And one Year when the
Votes came to be Numbered, there were found Six less for Mr. *Winthrop*,
than for another Gentleman who then stood in Competition: But several
other Persons regularly Tendring their *Votes* before the *Election* was
published, were, upon a very frivolous Objection, refused by some of the
35 Magistrates, that were afraid lest the *Election* should at last fall upon Mr.
Winthrop: Which though it was well perceived, yet such was the *Self-
denial* of this *Patriot*, that he would not permit any Notice to be taken of
the Injury. But these *Trials* were nothing in Comparison of those harsher
and harder *Treats*,[1] which he sometimes had from the *Frowardness* of not
40 a few in the Days of their *Paroxisms*; and from the *Faction* of some against
him, not much unlike that of the *Piazzi*[2] in *Florence* against the Family
of the *Medices:* All of which he at last Conquered by Conforming to the
Famous *Judges* Motto, *Prudens qui Patiens*.[3] The Oracles of God have said,
Envy is rottenness to the Bones; and *Gulielmus Parisiensis*[4] applies it unto
45 Rulers, who are as it were the *Bones* of the Societies which they belong
unto: *Envy*, says he, *is often found among them, and it is rottenness unto them.*
Our *Winthrop* Encountred this *Envy* from others, but Conquered it, by
being free from it himself.

§. 8. Were it not for the sake of introducing the Exemplary Skill of
50 this Wise Man, *at giving soft Answers*, one would not chuse to Relate those
Instances of *Wrath*, which he had sometimes to Encounter with; but he
was for his *Gentleness*, his *Forbearance*, and his *Longanimity*,[1] a Pattern so
worthy to be Written *after*, that something must here be Written *of* it.
He seemed indeed never to speak any other Language than that of
55 *Theodosius*,[2] *If any Man speak evil of the Governour, if it be thro' Lightness, 'tis
to be contemned; if it be thro' Madness, 'tis to be pitied; if it be thro' Injury, 'tis to
be remitted.* Behold, Reader, the *Meekness of Wisdom* notably exemplified!
There was a time when he received a very sharp Letter from a Gentleman, who was a Member of the Court,[3] but he delivered back the Letter
60 unto the Messengers[4] that brought it with such a Christian Speech as
this, *I am not willing to keep such a matter of Provocation by me!* Afterwards the
same Gentleman was compelled by the scarcity of Provisions to send

56 *it be thro'/it thro'* C.M.

[1] In the obsolete sense of "treatments."
[2] The Pazzi were a powerful Florentine family who in 1478 conspired to kill Giuliano and
Lorenzo de Medici while at mass. Giuliano was killed, but Lorenzo was only wounded.*
[3] "He is prudent who is patient."*
[4] Gulielmus Alvernus, or Guillaume d'Auvergne (d. 1249), celebrated French theologian
and philosopher, became known as Guillaume de Paris after he was created Bishop of Paris
in 1228.*

[1] Patience, forbearance.
[2] Fourth-century Roman emperor of the East.*
[3] Thomas Dudley (see chap. 5).*
[4] John Haynes (see chap. 5, sec. 2) and Thomas Hooker (see Bk. III, pt. 1, Appendix).*

unto him that he would Sell him some of his Cattel;[5] whereupon the
Governour prayed him to accept what he had sent for as a *Token* of his
65 Good Will; but the Gentleman returned him this Answer, *Sir, your
overcoming of your self hath overcome me*; and afterwards gave Demonstration
of it. The *French* have a saying, That *Un Honeste Homme, est un Homme mesle!*
A *good* Man is a *mixt* Man; and there hardly ever was a more sensible
Mixture of those Two things, *Resolution* and *Condescention*, than in this good
70 Man. There was a time when the Court of *Election*, being for fear of
Tumult, held at *Cambridge, May* 17. 1637. the Sectarian part of the Country, who had the Year before gotten a *Governour*[6] more unto their Mind,
had a Project now to have confounded the *Election*, by demanding that
the *Court* would consider a *Petition* then tendered before their Proceeding
75 thereunto. Mr. *Winthrop* saw that this was only a Trick to throw all into
Confusion, by putting off the *Choice* of the *Governour* and *Assistents* until
the *Day* should be over; and therefore he did, with a strenuous *Resolution*,
procure a disappointment unto that mischievous and ruinous Contrivance. Nevertheless, Mr. *Winthrop* himself being by the Voice of the Free-
80 men in this Exigence chosen the *Governour*, and all of the other Party
left out, that ill-affected Party discovered the *Dirt* and *Mire*, which
remained with them, after the *Storm* was over; particularly the *Serjeants*,
whose Office 'twas to attend the *Governour*, laid down their *Halberts*;
but such was the *Condescention* of this Governour; as to take no present
85 Notice of this Anger and Contempt, but only Order some of his own
Servants to take the *Halberts:* And when the Country manifested their
deep Resentments of the Affront thus offered him, *he* prayed them to
overlook it. But it was not long before a Compensation was made for these
things by the *doubled Respects* which were from all Parts paid unto him.
90 Again, there was a time when the Suppression of an *Antinomian* and *Familistical* Faction, which extreamly threatned the Ruin of the Country,
was generally thought much owing unto this Renowned Man; and
therefore when the Friends of that Faction could not wreak their Displeasure on him with any *Politick* Vexations, they set themselves to do it
95 by *Ecclesiastical* ones. Accordingly when a Sentence of *Banishment* was
passed on the Ringleaders of those Disturbances, who

—Maria & Terras, Cœlumq; profundum,
Quippe ferant, Rapidi, secum, verrantque; per Auras;[7]

71   1637. the/1637. The   98   *verrantque/vertantque*
95   *Ecclesiastical/Ecclesistical*

[5] The "Cattel" were "a fat hog or two."*

[6] Henry Vane, son of Sir Henry Vane, comptroller of the king's household, arrived in Boston
in October 1635. On November 1 he was admitted a member of the First Church of Boston.
(See below chap. V, sec. 3.)*

[7] "Would surely bear off with them in wild flight seas and lands and the vault of heaven,
sweeping them through space."*

99 many at the Church of *Boston*, who were then that way too much inclined,
most earnestly solicited the Elders of that Church, whereof the Governour
was a *Member*, to call him forth as an *Offender* for passing of that Sentence.
The *Elders* were unwilling to do any such thing; but the Governour
understanding the *Ferment* among the *People*, took that occasion to make a
5 Speech in the Congregation to this Effect. '*Brethren*, Understanding that
'some of you have desired that I should Answer for an *Offence* lately
'taken among you; had I been callled upon so to do, I would, *First*,
'Have advised with the Ministers of the Country, whether the *Church*
'had Power to call in Question the *Civil Court*; and I would, *Secondly*,
10 'Have advised with the rest of the *Court*, whether I might discover their
'Counsels unto the *Church*. But though I know that the Reverend *Elders*
'of this Church, and some others, do very well apprehend that the
'*Church* cannot enquire into the Proceedings of the *Court*; yet for the
'Satisfaction of the weaker who do not apprehend it, I will declare my
15 'Mind concerning it. If the *Church* have any such Power, they have it
'from the Lord Jesus Christ; but the Lord Jesus Christ hath disclaimed
'it, not only by *Practice*, but also by *Precept*, which we have in his Gospel,
'*Mat.* 20. 25, 26.[8] It is true indeed, that *Magistrates*, as they are *Church-*
'*Members*, are accountable unto the *Church* for their Failings; but that is
20 'when they are out of their Calling. When *Uzziah* would go offer Incense
'in the *Temple*, the Officers of the *Church* called him to an account, and
'withstood him; but when *Asa* put the Prophet in Prison, the Officers
'of the *Church* did not call *him* to an account for *that*. If the *Magistrate*
'shall in a *private way* wrong any Man, the *Church* may call him to an
25 'Account for it; but if he be in Pursuance of a Course of *Justice*, though
'the thing that he does be *unjust*, yet he is not accountable for it before
'the *Church*. As for my self I did nothing in the Causes of any of the
'*Brethren*, but by the Advice of the *Elders* of the *Church*. Moreover, in the
'*Oath* which I have taken there is this Clause, *In all Causes wherein you are*
30 '*to give your Vote, you shall do as in your Judgment and Conscience you shall see*
'*to be Just, and for the publick Good*. And I am satisfied, it is most for the
'Glory of God, and the *publick Good*, that there has been such a *Sentence*
'passed; yea, those *Brethren* are so divided from the *rest* of the Country
'in their Opinions and Practices, that it cannot stand with the *publick*
35 '*Peace* for them to continue with us; *Abraham* saw that *Hagar* and *Ishmael*
'must be sent away. By such a Speech he marvellously convinced, satisfied
and mollified the *uneasie Brethren* of the Church; *Sic cunctus Pelagi cecidit*
Fragor—.[9] And after a little patient waiting, the *differences* all so wore
away, that the Church, meerly as a Token of Respect unto the Governour,

---

[8] "Ye know that the princes of the Gentiles exercise dominion over them, and they that
are great exercise authority upon them. But it shall not be so among you: but whosoever will
be great among you, let him be your minister."
[9] "Even so all the roar of ocean sank."*

40 when he had newly met with some *Losses* in his Estate, sent him a Present
of several *Hundreds* of Pounds. Once more there was a time, when some
active Spirits among the *Deputies* of the Colony, by their endeavours not
only to make themselves a *Court of Judicature*, but also to take away the
Negative by which the *Magistrates* might check their *Votes*, had like by
45 over-driving to have run the whole Government into something too
Democratical. And if there were a Town in *Spain* undermined by *Coneys*,
another Town in *Thrace* destroyed by *Moles*, a Third in *Greece* ranversed
by *Frogs*, a Fourth in *Germany* subverted by *Rats*; I must on this Occasion
add, that there was a Country in *America* like to be confounded by a
50 *Swine*. A certain *stray Sow* being found, was claimed by Two several
Persons with a Claim so equally maintained on both sides, that after
Six or Seven Years *Hunting* the Business, from one Court unto another, it
was brought at last into the *General Court*, where the final Determination
was, *that it was impossible to proceed unto any Judgment in the Case*. However
55 in the debate of this Matter, the *Negative* of the *Upper-House* upon the
Lower in that Court was brought upon the Stage; and agitated with
so hot a Zeal, that a *little more and all had been in the Fire*. In these Agita-
tions the Governour was informed that an offence had been taken by
some eminent Persons, at certain Passages in a Discourse by him written
60 thereabout; whereupon with his usual *Condescendency*, when he next
came into the General Court, he made a Speech of this Import. 'I
'understand, that some have *taken* Offence at something that I have lately
'written; which *Offence* I desire to remove now, and begin this Year in a
'reconciled State with you all. As for the *Matter* of my Writing, I had
65 'the Concurrence of my *Brethren*; it is a Point of *Judgment* which is not at
'my own disposing. I have examined it over and over again, by such
'*Light* as God has given me, from the Rules of *Religion, Reason* and *Custom*;
'and I see no cause to Retract any thing of it: Wherefore I must enjoy
'my *Liberty* in *that*, as *you* do your selves. But for the *Manner, this*, and all
70 'that was blame-worthy in it, was wholly *my own*; and whatsoever I
'might alledge for my own Justification therein before *Men*, I waive it,
'as now setting my self before another *Judgment-Seat*. However, what I
'wrote was upon *great Provocation*, and to vindicate my self and others from
'great Aspersion; yet that was no sufficient Warrant for me to allow any
75 '*Distemper of Spirit* in my self; and I doubt I have been too prodigal of my
'*Brethren's Reputation*; I might have maintained my Cause without casting
'any Blemish upon others, when I made that my Conclusion, *And now*
'*let Religion and sound Reason give Judgment in the Case*; it look'd as if I
'arrogated too much unto *my self*, and too little to *others*. And when I
80 'made that Profession, *That I would maintain what I wrote before all the*
'*World*, though such Words might modestly be spoken, yet I perceive

71   waive/wave

'an unbeseeming *Pride* of my own Heart breathing in them. For these 'Failings I ask Pardon both of God and Man.

85
Sic ait, & dicto citius Tumida Æquora placat,
Collectasq; fugat Nubes, Solemq; reducit.[10]

This *acknowledging Disposition* in the Governour, made them all *acknowledge*, that he was truly *a Man of an excellent Spirit*. In fine, the *Victories* of an *Alexander*, an *Hannibal*, or a *Cæsar* over *other Men*, were not so Glorious, as the *Victories* of this great Man over *himself*, which also at
90 last prov'd *Victories* over *other Men*.

§. 9. But the stormiest of all the *Trials* that ever befel this Gentleman, was in the Year 1645. when he was in *Title* no more than *Deputy-Governour* of the Colony. If the famous *Cato* were Forty-four times call'd into Judgment, but as often acquitted; let it not be wondred, and if our Famous
95 *Winthrop* were one time so. There hapning certain Seditious and Mutinous Practices in the Town of *Hingham*, the *Deputy-Governour* as legally as prudently interposed his *Authority* for the checking of them: Whereupon there followed such an *Enchantment* upon the minds of the *Deputies* in the
99 General Court, that upon a scandalous Petition of the Delinquents unto *them*, wherein a pretended Invasion made upon the *Liberties* of the *People* was complained of the *Deputy-Governour*, was most Irregularly call'd forth unto an Ignominious *Hearing* before them in a vast Assembly whereto with a *Sagacious Humility* he *consented*, although he shew'd them how he might
5 have *Refused* it. The result of that *Hearing* was, That notwithstanding the touchy *Jealousie* of the *People* about their *Liberties* lay at the bottom of all this Prosecution, yet Mr. *Winthrop* was publickly Acquitted, and the Offenders were severally Fined and Censured. But Mr. *Winthrop* then resuming the Place of *Deputy-Governour* on the Bench, saw cause to speak
10 unto the *Root of the Matter* after this manner. 'I shall not now speak any 'thing about the past *Proceedings* of this Court, or the *Persons* therein 'concerned. Only I bless God that I see an Issue of this troublesome 'Affair. I am well satisfied that I was publickly *Accused*, and that I am 'now publickly *Acquitted*. But though I am justified before *Men*, yet it
15 'may be the *Lord* hath seen so much amiss in my Administrations, as 'calls me to be *humbled*; and indeed for me to have been thus charged by '*Men*, is it self a Matter of *Humiliation*, whereof I desire to make a right 'use before the *Lord*. If *Miriam*'s Father spit in her Face, she is to be '*Ashamed*. But give me leave before you go, to say something that may
20 'rectifie the *Opinions* of many *People*, from whence the *Distempers* have

3 Ignominious/Ignominous   4 *Humility/Humilitude* C.M.

[10] "Thus he speaks, and swifter than his word he calms the swollen seas, puts to flight the gathered clouds, and brings back the sun."*

'risen that have lately prevailed upon the *Body* of *this* People. The
'Questions that have troubled the Country have been about the *Au-*
'*thority of the Magistracy*, and the *Liberty of the People*. It is *You* who have
'called *us* unto this Office; but being thus *called*, we have our *Authority*
25 'from *God*; it is the *Ordinance* of *God*, and it hath the *Image* of *God* stamped
'upon it; and the contempt of it has been vindicated by *God* with terrible
'*Examples* of his *Vengeance*. I intreat you to consider, That when you
'chuse *Magistrates*, you take them from among your selves, *Men subject*
'*unto like Passions with your selves*. If you see *our* Infirmities, reflect on *your*
30 '*own*, and you will not be so severe Censurers of *Ours*. We count him a
'*good Servant* who *breaks not his Covenant*: The *Covenant* between *Us* and
'*You*, is the *Oath* you have taken of *us*, which is to this Purpose, *That*
'*we shall govern you, and judge your Causes, according to God's Laws, and our*
'*own, according to our best Skill*. As for our *Skill*, you must run the hazard
35 'of it; and if there be an Error, not in the *Will*, but only in the *Skill*, it
'becomes *you* to bear it. Nor would I have you to mistake in the Point of
'your own *Liberty*. There is a *Liberty* of corrupt Nature, which is affected
'both by *Men* and *Beasts*, to do what they list; and this *Liberty* is inconsis-
'tent with *Authority*, impatient of all Restraint; by this *Liberty*, *Sumus*
40 '*Omnes Deteriores*:[1] 'Tis the Grand Enemy of *Truth* and *Peace*, and all the
'*Ordinances* of God are bent against it. But there is a Civil, a Moral, a
'*Federal Liberty*, which is the proper End and Object of *Authority*; it is
'a *Liberty* for that only which is *just* and *good*; for this *Liberty* you are to
'stand with the hazard of your very *Lives*; and whatsoever Crosses it, is
45 'not *Authority*, but a *Distemper* thereof. This *Liberty* is maintained in a
'way of *Subjection* to *Authority*; and the *Authority* set over you, will in all
'Administrations for your good be quietly submitted unto, by all but
'such as have a Disposition to *shake off the Yoke*, and lose their true *Liberty*,
'by their murmuring at the Honour and Power of *Authority*.

50 The *Spell* that was upon the Eyes of the People being thus dissolved,
their *distorted* and *enraged* notions of things all vanished; and the People
would not afterwards entrust the Helm of the *Weather-beaten* Bark in
any other Hands, but Mr. *Winthrop's*, until he Died.

§. 10. Indeed such was the *Mixture of distant*[1] *Qualities* in him, as to
55 make a most admirable *Temper*; and his having a certain *Greatness of Soul*,
which rendered him Grave, Generous, Courageous, Resolved, Well-
applied, and every way a *Gentleman* in his Demeanour, did not hinder
him from taking sometimes the old *Romans* way to avoid Confusions,
namely, *Cedendo*;[2] or from discouraging some things which are agreeable

57 Demeanour/Deameanour

[1] "We are all the worse."*

---

[1] "*Distant*," in the obsolete sense of widely differing.
[2] "By yielding."*

60 enough to most that wear the Name of *Gentlemen.* Hereof I will give no
Instances, but only *oppose* two Passages of his Life.

In the Year 1632. the Governour, with his Pastor Mr. *Wilson,* and some
other Gentlemen, to settle a good understanding between the Two
Colonies, travelled as far as *Plymouth,* more than Forty Miles, through an
65 Howling Wilderness, no better accommodated in those early Days, than
the *Princes* that in *Solomon's* time saw *Servants on Horseback,* or than *Genus*
and *Species* 3 in the old Epigram, *going on Foot.* The difficulty of the *Walk,*
was abundantly compensated by the Honourable, *first* Reception, and
then Dismission, which they found from the Rulers of *Plymouth;* and by the
70 good Correspondence thus established between the New Colonies, who
were like the floating Bottels wearing this Motto, *Si Collidimur, Frangimur.* 4
But there were at this time in *Plymouth* two Ministers, 5 leavened so far
with the Humours of the *Rigid Separation,* that they insisted vehemently
upon the Unlawfulness of calling any *unregenerate* Man by the Name of
75 *Good-man such an One,* until by their indiscreet urging of this Whimsey, the
place began to be disquieted. The wiser People being troubled at these
Trifles, they took the opportunity of Governour *Winthrop's* being *there,*
to have the thing publickly propounded in the Congregation; who in
answer thereunto, distinguished between a *Theological* and a *Moral*
80 *Goodness;* adding, that when *Juries* were first used in *England,* it was usual
for the *Crier,* after the Names of Persons fit for that Service were called
over, to bid them all, *Attend, Good Men, and True;* whence it grew to be a
Civil Custom in the *English Nation,* for Neighbours living by one another,
to call one another *Good-man such an One:* And it was pity now to make a
85 stir about a *Civil Custom,* so innocently introduced. And that Speech of
Mr. *Winthrop's* put a lasting stop to the Little, Idle, Whimsical *Conceits,*
then beginning to grow Obstreperous. Nevertheless there was one *Civil
Custom* used *in* (and in few *but*) the *English Nation,* which this Gentleman
did endeavour to abolish in *this Country;* and that was, *The usage of Drink-*
90 *ing to one another.* For although by *Drinking to one another,* no more is meant
than an act of *Courtesie,* when one going to *Drink,* does Invite another to
do so too, for the same Ends with himself; nevertheless the Governour
(not altogether unlike to *Cleomenes,* of whom 'tis reported by *Plutarch,*
ἄκοντι οὐδεὶς ποτήριον προσέφερεν, *Nolenti poculum nunquam præbuit,*) 6
95 considered the *Impertinency* and *Insignificancy* of this Usage, as to any of
those Ends that are usually pretended for it; and that indeed it ordinarily
served for *no Ends* at all, but only to provoke Persons unto *unseasonable,*
and perhaps *unreasonable* Drinking, and at last produce that abominable

3 "*Genus* and *Species,*" used figuratively for "a Scholar."*
4 "If we collide, we break."*
5 Ralph Smith and Roger Williams.*
6 "Never offered a wine cup to one who was unwilling." Cleomenes reigned as king of
Sparta from *c.*235 to 219 B.C.*

99 *Health-Drinking*, which the *Fathers* of old so severely rebuked in the *Pagans*, and which the *Papists* themselves do Condemn, when their Casuists pronounce it, *Peccatum mortale, provocare ad Æquales Calices, & Nefas Respondere*.[7] Wherefore in his own most Hospitable House he left it off; not out of any silly or stingy *Fancy*, but meerly that by his *Example* a

5 greater *Temperance*, with *Liberty* of *Drinking*, might be Recommended, and sundry *Inconveniences* in Drinking avoided; and his *Example* accordingly began to be much followed by the sober People in *this Country*, as it now also begins to be among Persons of the *Highest* Rank in the *English Nation* it self; until an *Order of Court* came to be made against that

10 *Ceremony* in Drinking, and then the *old Wont* violently returned, with a *Nitimur in Vetitum*.[8]

§. 11. *Many were the Afflictions of this Righteous Man!* He lost much of his Estate in a Ship, and in an *House*, quickly after his coming to *New-England*, besides the Prodigious Expence of it in the Difficulties of his first coming

15 hither. Afterwards his assiduous Application unto the Publick *Affairs*, (wherein *Ipse se non habuit, postquam Respublica eum Gubernatorem habere coepit*)[1] made him so much to neglect his own *private Interests*, that an *unjust Steward*[2] ran him 2500 *l.* in Debt before he was aware; for the Payment whereof he was forced, many Years before his Decease, to sell

20 the most of what he had left unto him in the Country. Albeit, by the observable Blessing of God upon the *Posterity* of this *Liberal Man*, his Children all of them came to fair Estates, and lived in good Fashion and Credit. Moreover, he successively Buried Three *Wives*; the First of which was the Daughter and Heiress of Mr. *Forth*, of *Much Stambridge*[3] in *Essex*,

25 by whom he had *Wisdom with an Inheritance*; and an excellent Son.[4] The Second was the Daughter of Mr. *William Clopton*, of *London*, who Died with her Child, within a very little while. The Third was the Daughter of the truly Worshipful Sir *John Tyndal*, who made it her whole Care to please, First *God*, and then her *Husband*; and by whom he had Four

30 Sons,[5] which Survived and Honoured their Father. And unto all these, the Addition of the *Distempers*, ever now and then raised in the *Country*, procured unto him a very singular share of Trouble; yea, so hard was the Measure which he found even among Pious Men, in the Temptations of a *Wilderness*, that when the *Thunder* and *Lightning* had smitten a *Wind-*

35 *mill*, whereof he was Owner, some had *such things in their Heads*, as pub-

---

11 *Vetitum*/*Vetnum*   17 *coepit*/*cæpit*

[7] "It is a mortal sin to challenge anyone to a drinking match, and wrong to respond to it."*

[8] "We strive for what is forbidden."*

---

[1] "He did not possess himself after the state began to possess him as governor."*

[2] James Luxford.*

[3] Or Great Stambridge.

[4] John Winthrop, Jr.

[5] Stephen, Deane, Adam, Samuel.

lickly to Reproach this *Charitablest* of Men, as if the *Voice of the Almighty* had rebuked, I know not what *Oppression*, which they *judged* him Guilty of: Which things I would not have mentioned, but that the Instances may fortifie the Expectations of my *best Readers* for such Afflictions.

40 §. 12. He that had been for his Attainments, as they said of the blessed *Macarius*,[1] a Παιδαριογέρων, *An old Man, while a young One*, and that had in his *young Days* met with many of those *Ill Days*, whereof he could say, he had *little Pleasure in them*; now found *old Age* in its Infirmities advancing *Earlier* upon him, than it came upon his much longer lived *Progenitors*.

45 While he was yet Seven Years off of that which we call *the grand Climacterical*,[2] he felt the Approaches of his *Dissolution*; and finding he could say,

> *Non Habitus, non ipse Color non Gressus Euntis,*
> *Non Species Eadem, que fait ante, manet.*[3]

he then wrote this account of himself, *Age now comes upon me, and In-*
50 *firmities therewithal, which makes me apprehend, that the time of my departure out of this World is not far off. However our times are all in the Lord's Hand, so as we need not trouble our Thoughts how long or short they may be, but how we may be found Faithful when we are called for.* But at last when *that Year* came, he took a *Cold* which turned into a *Feaver*, whereof he lay *Sick* about a Month,
55 and in that *Sickness*, as it hath been observed, that there was allowed unto the *Serpent* the *bruising of the Heel*; and accordingly at the *Heel* or the *Close* of our Lives the *old Serpent* will be Nibbling more than ever in our Lives before; and when the Devil sees that we shall shortly be, *where the wicked cease from troubling*, that *wicked One* will *trouble* us more than ever;
60 so this eminent Saint now underwent sharp Conflicts with the *Tempter*, whose *Wrath* grew *Great*, as the *Time* to exert it grew *Short*; and he was Buffetted with the Disconsolate Thoughts of Black and Sore *Desertions*, wherein he could use that sad Representation of his own Condition.

> *Nuper Eram Judex; Jam Judicor; Ante Tribunal,*
65 > *Subsistens paveo, Judicor ipse modo.*[4]

But it was not long before those *Clouds* were Dispelled, and he enjoyed in his Holy Soul the *Great Consolations of God!* While he thus lay *Ripening* for Heaven, he did out of Obedience unto the *Ordinance* of our Lord, send for the *Elders of the Church* to *Pray* with him; yea, they and the whole
70 Church *Fasted* as well as *Prayed* for him; and in that *Fast* the venerable *Cotton* Preached on *Psal.* 35. 13, 14. *When they were Sick, I humbled my self*

64 *Tribunal/Tribunat*

[1] Macarius, a fourth-century Egyptian monk. Παιδαριογερων is a compound of παιδάριον, a youth, and γερων, an old man.*
[2] The sixty-third year. Winthrop died in his sixty-second.
[3] "There remains not the appearance, not even the color, nor the way of life, and not the same aspect, of that which was before."*
[4] "Once I was a judge; now I am judged. I stand trembling before the tribunal, now I myself am judged."*

with Fasting; I behaved my self as though he had been my Friend or Brother; I bowed down heavily, as one that Mourned for his Mother: From whence I find him raising that Observation, *The Sickness of one that is to us as a*
75 *Friend, a Brother, a Mother, is a just occasion of deep humbling our Souls with Fasting and Prayer;* and making this Application, 'Upon this Occasion we 'are now to attend this Duty for a *Governour,* who has been to us as a '*Friend* in his *Counsel* for all things, and *Help* for our *Bodies* by *Physick,* for 'our *Estates* by *Law,* and of whom there was no fear of his becoming an
80 '*Enemy,* like the *Friends* of *David:* A *Governour* who has been unto us as a '*Brother;* not usurping *Authority* over the Church; often speaking his '*Advice,* and often contradicted, even by Young Men, and some of low 'degree; yet not replying, but offering Satisfaction also when any 'supposed Offences have arisen; a *Governour* who has been unto us as a
85 '*Mother,* Parent-like distributing his *Goods* to Brethren and Neighbours 'at his first coming; and *gently* bearing our *Infirmities* without taking 'notice of them.

Such a *Governour* after he had been more than *Ten* several times by the People chosen their *Governour,*[5] was *New-England* now to lose; who having,
90 like *Jacob,* first left his *Council*[6] and *Blessing* with his Children gathered about his Bed-side; and, like *David, served his Generation by the Will of God,* he *gave up the Ghost,* and *fell asleep* on *March* 26. 1649. having, like the dying Emperour *Valentinian,* this above all his other *Victories* for his Triumphs, *His overcoming of himself.*
95 The Words of *Josephus* about *Nehemiah,* Governour of *Isreal,* we will now use upon this Governour of *New-England,* as his

EPITAPH.

Ἀνὴρ ἐγένετο χρηστὸς τὴν φύσιν, καὶ δίκαιος,
99 Καὶ περὶ τοὺς ὁμοεθνεῖς φιλοτιμότατος·
Μνημεῖον αἰώνιον αὐτῳ καταλιπὼν τὰ τῶν
Ἱεροσολύμων τείχη.

VIR FUIT INDOLE BONUS, AC JUSTUS:
ET POPULARIUM GLORIÆ AMANTISSIMUS:
5 QUIBUS ETERNUM RELIQUIT MONUMENTUM,
Novanglorum MOENIA.[7]

92 having/Having	99 τοὺς/τὺς
98 χρηστὸς/χρησὸς	

[5] Winthrop, governor of the Massachusetts Bay Company at the time of the migration, was elected governor of the colony in 1631, 1632, 1633, 1637, 1638, 1639, 1642, 1643, 1646, 1647, 1648.

[6] That is, "advice."

[7] "He was a man by nature of splendid mien and just, and most zealous for the honor of his countrymen, leaving for them an eternal memorial—the wall of Jerusalem." Mather's Latin translation adapts Josephus' lines by substituting the walls of "Novanglorum" for those of "Ἱεροσολύμων."*

CHAP. V.

SUCCESSORS.

§. 1. ONE as well acquainted with the Matter, as *Isocrates*, informs us,
10   That among the *Judges* of *Areopagus* none were admitted, πλὴν
οἱ καλῶς γεγονότες, καὶ πολλὴν ἀρετὴν καὶ σωφροσύνην ἐν τῷ βίῳ
ἐνδεδειγμένοις, *unless they were Nobly Born, and Eminently Exemplary for
a Virtuous and a Sober Life.* The Report may be truly made concerning the
Judges of *New-England*, tho' they were not *Nobly Born*, yet they were
15 generally *Well Born*; and by being *Eminently Exemplary for a Virtuous and a
Sober Life*, gave Demonstration that they were *New-born*.[1] Some Account
of them is now more particularly to be Endeavoured.

  We read concerning *Saul*, [1 Sam. 15. 12.] *He set up himself a place.* The
Hebrew Word, יָד there used, signifies *A Monumental Pillar.* It is accord-
20 ingly promised unto them who *please God*, [Isa. 56. 5.] *That they shall have
a Place and a Name in the House of God*; that is to say, a *Pillar* Erected for
Fame in the Church of God. And it shall be fulfilled in what shall now be
done for our *Governours* in this our *Church-History*. Even while the *Massa-
chusettensians* had a *Winthrop* for their *Governour*, they could not restrain
25 the Channel of their *Affections* from running towards another Gentleman
in their *Elections* for the Year 1634. particularly, when they chose unto the
Place of *Governour Thomas Dudley*, Esq; one whom after the Death of the
Gentleman abovementioned, they again and again Voted into the Chief
Place of Government. He was Born at the Town of *Northampton*, in the
30 Year 1574.[2] the only Son of Captain *Roger Dudley*, who being Slain in
the Wars, left this our *Thomas*, with his only Sister, for the *Father of the
Orphans*, to *take them up*. In the Family of the Earl of *Northampton*[3] he had
opportunity perfectly to learn the Points of *Good Behaviour*; and here
having fitted himself to do many other Benefits unto the World, he next
35 became a *Clerk* unto Judge *Nichols*,[4] who being his Kinsman by the
Mother's Side, therefore took the more special notice of him. From his
Relation to this *Judge*, he had and used an Advantage to attain such a
Skill in the *Law*, as was of great Advantage to him in the future changes
of his Life; and the *Judge* would have preferred him unto the higher
40 Imployments, whereto his prompt *Wit* not a little recommended him, if

----

[1] That is, reborn in Christ.*

[2] Dudley was born in 1576. Mather is correct concerning Dudley's age at his death on
July 31, 1653. (See p. 232, l. 25.)

[3] William Compton (*c.*1568–1630), second Baron Compton, created Earl of Northampton
in 1618.

[4] Augustine Nichols (1559–1616), appointed justice of the court of common pleas and
knighted in 1612; of Puritan tendencies, he was quoted as saying that Puritan sermons "come
nearest to my conscience, and doe mee the most good."*

he had not been by Death prevented. But before he could appear to do much at the *Pen*, for which he was very well Accomplished, he was called upon to do something at the *Sword*; for being a Young Gentleman well-known for his Ingenuity, Courage and Conduct, when there were
45 Soldiers to be raised by Order from Queen *Elizabeth* for the *French* Service, in the time of King *Henry* the Fourth, the Young Sparks about *Northampton* were none of them willing to enter into the Service, until a *Commission* was given unto our Young *Dudley* to be their *Captain*; and then presently there were *Fourscore* that Listed under him. At the Head of
50 these he went over into the Low Countries, which was then an *Academy* of *Arms*, as well as *Arts*; and thus he came to furnish himself with Endowments for the *Field*, as well as for the *Bench*. The Post assigned unto him with his Company, was after at the Siege of *Amiens*, before which the *King* himself was now Encamped; but the Providence of God so
55 Ordered it, that when both Parties were drawn forth in Order to Battel, a Treaty of *Peace* was vigorously set on Foot, which diverted the Battel that was expected. Captain *Dudley* hereupon returned into *England*, and settling himself about *Northampton*, he Married a Gentlewoman[5] whose Extract and Estate were Considerable; and the Scituation of his Habita-
60 tion after this helped him to enjoy the Ministry of Mr. *Dod*, Mr. *Cleaver*, Mr. *Winston*, and Mr. *Hildersham*,[6] all of them Excellent and Renowned Men; which *Puritan Ministry* so seasoned his Heart with a Sense of Religion, that he was a Devout and Serious Christian, and a Follower of the Ministers that most effectually Preached *Real Christianity* all the rest of his
65 Days. The Spirit of *Real Christianity* in him now also disposed him unto *Sober Non-Conformity*; and from this time, although none more hated the *Fanaticisms* and *Enthusiasms* of Wild *Opinionists*, he became a *Judicious Dissenter* from the *Unscriptural Ceremonies* retained in the Church of *England*. It was not long after this that the Lord *Say*,[7] the Lord *Compton*,[8]
70 and other Persons of Quality, made such Observations of him, as to commend him unto the Service of the Earl of *Lincoln*, who was then a

---

43 Gentleman/Gentlemen

---

[5] Dorothy Yorke (1583-1634).*

[6] John Dod (1549?-1645), staunch nonconformist minister at Hanwell, Oxfordshire, until suspended by Bishop Bridges in 1604; he then moved to Canons Ashby, Northamptonshire, where he was "silenced" by Archbishop Abbott in 1611. From 1624 until his death, rector of Fawsley in the same county. Mr. Winston was probably John Winston, B.A. Oxford 1603, who also served at Canons Ashby. Mr. Cleaver remains unidentified. On Arthur Hildersham see Bk. I, p. 152, l. 18 and notes.*

[7] William Fiennes (1582-1662), eighth Baron Saye and Sele until raised to the viscountcy in 1624. (See Bk. I, p. 167, l. 34.)

[8] Spencer Compton (1601-1643), second Earl of Northampton, succeeding his father in 1630; he was killed on the battlefield at Hopton Heath defending the king's cause.

Young Man,[9] and newly come unto the Possession of his *Earldom,* and of
what belonged thereunto. The Grand-father of this Noble Person had
left his Heirs under vast Entanglements, out of which his Father was
75 never able to Extricate himself; so that the Difficulties and Incumbrances
were now devolved upon this *Theophilus,* which caused him to apply
himself unto this our *Dudley* for his Assistances, who proved so Able, and
Careful, and Faithful a *Steward* unto him, that within a little while the
Debts of near Twenty Thousand Pounds, whereinto the *Young Earl* found
80 himself desperately Ingulphed, were happily waded through; and by his
Means also a *Match* was procured between the *Young Earl* and the Daughter
of the Lord *Say,*[10] who proved a most Virtuous Lady, and a great Blessing
to the whole Family. But the Earl finding Mr. *Dudley* to be a Person of
more than ordinary Discretion, he would rarely, if ever, do any Matter of
85 any Moment without his Advice; but some into whose Hands there fell
some of his Manuscripts after his leaving of the Earl's Family, found a
Passage to this purpose. *The Estate of the Earl of* Lincoln, *I found so, and so
much in Debt, which I have discharged, and have raised the Rents unto so many
Hundreds Per Annum; God will, I trust, bless me and mine in such a manner. I
90 can, as sometimes* Nehemiah *did, appeal unto God, who knows the Hearts of all
Men, that I have with Integrity discharged the Duty of my Place before him.*

I had prepared and intended a more *particular Account* of this Gentleman; but not having any opportunity to commit it unto the *Perusal* of any
Descended from him, (unto whom I am told it will be unacceptable for
95 me to Publish any thing of this kind, by *them* not *Perused*) I have laid it
aside, and summed all up in this more *General Account.*

It was about Nine or Ten Years, that Mr. *Dudley* continued a *Steward*
unto the Earl of *Lincoln;* but then growing desirous of a more private
99 Life, he retired unto *Boston,* where the Acquaintance and Ministry of
Mr. *Cotton*[11] became no little Satisfaction unto him. Nevertheless the Earl
of *Lincoln* found that he could be no more without Mr. *Dudley,* than
Pharaoh without his *Joseph,* and prevailed with him to resume his former
Employment, until the Storm of Persecution upon the *Non-Conformists*
5 caused many Men of great Worth to Transport themselves into *New-
England.* Mr. *Dudley* was not the least of the Worthy Men that bore a part
in this Transportation, in hopes that in an *American* Wilderness they might
peaceably attend and enjoy the pure Worship of the Lord Jesus Christ.
When the first Undertakers for that Plantation came to know him, they

87–88 *so much/so, much*

9 Theophilus Clinton (1600?–1667) succeeded to the earldom in 1619. His father, Thomas,
held the title only from 1616 to 1619; his grandfather Henry Clinton held the earldom from
1585 to 1616.
10 Bridget, whom the *"Young Earl"* married in or before 1622.
11 John Cotton was vicar of St. Botolph's in Boston, Lincolnshire, from 1612 to 1633.

10 soon saw *that* in him, that caused them to chuse him their *Deputy-
Governour*, in which Capacity he arrived unto these Coasts in the Year
1630. and had no small share in the Distresses of that Young Plantation,
whereof an account by him written to the Countess of *Lincoln* has been
since Published unto the World.[12] Here his *Wisdom* in managing the most
15 weighty and thorny Affairs was often signalized: His *Justice* was a perpetual Terror to Evil Doers: His *Courage* procured his being the first
Major-General[13] of the Colony, when they began to put themselves into a
Military Figure. His *Orthodox Piety* had no little Influence into the Deliverance of the Country, from the Contagion of the *Familistical Errors,*
20 which had like to have overturned all.[14] He dwelt first at *Cambridge*; but
upon Mr. *Hooker's* removal to *Hartford,* he removed to *Ipswich*; nevertheless, upon the Importunity and Necessity of the Government for his
coming to dwell nearer the Center of the whole, he fixed his Habitation
at *Roxbury,* Two Miles out of *Boston,* where he was always at Hand upon
25 the Publick Exigencies. Here he died, *July* 31. 1653. in the Seventy-
Seventh Year of his Age; and there were found after his Death, in his
Pocket, these Lines of his own Composing, which may serve to make up
what may be wanting in the Character already given him.

        Dim Eyes, Deaf Ears, Cold Stomach, shew
30   *My Dissolution is in View.*
        Eleven times Seven near liv'd have I,
        And now God calls, I willing Die.
        My Shuttle's shot, my Race is run,
        My Sun is set, my Day is done.
35   *My Span is measur'd, Tale is told,*
        My Flower is faded, and grown old.
        My Dream is vanish'd, Shadow's fled,
        My Soul with Christ, my Body Dead.
        Farewel Dear Wife, Children and Friends,
40   *Hate Heresie, make Blessed Ends.*
        Bear Poverty, live with good Men;
        So shall we live with Joy agen.
        Let Men of God in Courts and Churches watch
        O're such as do a Toleration *hatch,*
45   *Lest that Ill Egg bring forth a Cockatrice,*
        To poison all with Heresie and Vice.
        If Men be left, and otherwise Combine,
        My Epitaph's, 𝕴 𝔇𝔶'𝔡 𝔫𝔬 𝔏𝔦𝔟𝔢𝔯𝔱𝔦𝔫𝔢.

19 *Familistical/Famalistical*

[12] In 1696.*
[13] Dudley was made major general in 1644.
[14] The antinomian affair.

But when I mention the *Poetry* of this Gentleman as one of his Ac-
50 complishments, I must not leave unmentioned the Fame with which the
Poems of one descended from him have been Celebrated in both *Englands.*
If the rare Learning of a *Daughter*,[15] was not the least of those bright
things that adorn'd no less a Judge of *England* than Sir *Thomas More*; it
must now be said, that a Judge of *New-England*, namely, *Thomas Dudley,*
55 Esq; had a *Daughter*[16] (besides other Children) to be a *Crown* unto him.
Reader, *America* justly admires the Learned Women of the other *Hemi-*
sphere. She has heard of those that were *Tutoresses* to the Old Professors
of all Philosophy: She hath heard of *Hippatia*,[17] who formerly taught the
Liberal Arts; and of *Sarocchia*,[18] who more lately was very often the Mod-
60 eratrix in the Disputations of the Learned Men of *Rome:* She has been
told of the Three *Corinna*'s,[19] which equall'd, if not excell'd, the most
Celebrated *Poets* of their Time. She has been told of the Empress *Eudocia*,[20]
who Composed Poetical Paraphrases on Divers Parts of the *Bible*; and
of *Rosuida*,[21] who wrote the *Lives* of Holy Men; and of *Pamphilia*,[22] who
65 wrote other Histories unto the Life: The Writings of the most Renowned *Anna Maria Schurman*,[23] have come over unto her. But she now
prays, that into such Catalogues of *Authoresses*, as *Beverovicius, Hottinger,*
and *Voetius*,[24] have given unto the World, there may be a room now
given unto Madam 𝔄𝔫𝔫 𝔅𝔯𝔞𝔡𝔰𝔱𝔯𝔢𝔢𝔱, the Daughter of our Governour
70 *Dudley*, and the Consort of our Governour *Bradstreet*, whose *Poems,*
divers times Printed, have afforded a grateful Entertainment unto the
Ingenious, and a Monument for her Memory beyond the Stateliest
Marbles. It was upon these *Poems* that an Ingenious Person bestowed this
Epigram:

62 *Eudocia/Endocia* C.M.   66 *Schurman/Schurnian* C.M.

[15] Margaret More Roper.*

[16] Anne (1612–1672), married to Simon Bradstreet.

[17] Hypatia, Neoplatonic philosopher, mathematician, and teacher at Alexandria; murdered
in 415 by Cyril, Christian patriarch, and his monks.

[18] Margherita Sarocchia (Sarrochi, d. 1618), Neapolitan poetess.*

[19] Corinna of Tanagra (*c.*500 B.C.), celebrated Greek lyric poetess, a contemporary of
Pindar. Suidas mentions also a Corinna the younger and a Corinna of Thespiae.*

[20] The Empress Eudocia (*c.*401–*c.*460), wife of Theodosius II. She was the author of a verse
paraphrase of the Octateuch.*

[21] Roswitha, Hroswitha, or Hrotsuitha (*c.*935–*c.*1000), a celebrated German poetess of the
tenth century, reputed author of six Latin comedies in imitation of Terence, a poetic history
of her cloister, saints' lives, and other works in verse.*

[22] Pamphila, a learned Roman or Greek lady of the first century A.D., celebrated for voluminous histories.*

[23] Anna Maria van Schurman (1607–1678), a learned lady of Utrecht.*

[24] Jan van Beverwijck (1594–1647), a Dutch physician and voluminous writer, who wrote
a book on the excellence of the female kind; Johann Heinrich Hottinger (1620–1667), Swiss
theologian and orientalist; Gijsbert Voet (1588–1676), Dutch Calvinist theologian, vigorous
opponent of Arminianism.*

75   *Now I believe* Tradition, *which doth call*
        The Muses, Virtues, Graces, Females *all.*
        Only they are not Nine, Eleven, *or* Three;
        Our Auth'ress *proves them but an* Unity.
        Mankind, *take up some Blushes on the score*;[25]
80   *Monopolize* Perfection *hence no more.*
        In your own Arts confess your selves outdone;
        The Moon *hath totally Eclips'd the* Sun:
        Not with her Sable Mantle muffling him,
        But her bright Silver *makes his* Gold *look dim*:
85   *Just as his Beams force our pale Lamps to wink,*
        And Earthly Fires *within their Ashes shrink.*

What else might be said of Mr. *Dudley*, the Reader shall Construe from
the Ensuing

EPITAPH.

90   *Helluo Librorum, Lectorum Bibliotheca*
        Communis, Sacræ Syllabus Historiæ.
        Ad Mensam Comes, hinc facundus, Rostra disertus,
        (Non Cumulus verbis, pondus, Acumen erat,)
        Morum acris Censor, validus Defensor amansq;
95   *Et Sanæ & Canæ Catholicæ fidei.*
        Angli-novi Columen, Summum Decus atq; *Senatus*;
        Thomas Dudleius, *conditur hoc Tumulo.* E.R.[26]

§. 2. In the Year 1635. at the Anniversary Election, the Freemen of the
99 Colony testified their grateful Esteem of Mr. *John Haines*, a Worthy
Gentleman, who had been very Serviceable to the Interests of the Colony,
by chusing him their *Governour*.[1] Of him in an Ancient Manuscript I find

---

[25] That is, on the score between men and women, men must enter blushes to their debit.

[26] "Glutton of choice books, general library, register of sacred history; table companion,
hence ready of speech, eloquent on the platform, concise, weighty, and pointed in language;
a sharp censor of manners, a strong and loving defender of the sound and ancient orthodox
faith; chief pillar and ornament of the New England Senate, Thomas Dudley, is buried in
this tomb."

Jonathan Belcher (1681/82–1757), Governor of Massachusetts and New Hampshire from
1730 to 1741, recorded a rather different epitaph for Governor Dudley. To a friend, Joseph
Pitkin, he wrote in August 1732: "Strict justice is the rule ... It was wrote over Gov* Tho*
Dudley's Tomb,—

> Here lyes Tho* Dudley, that trusty old stud,
> A bargain's a bargain & must be made good."*

---

[1] John Haynes (1594–1654) arrived in Massachusetts Bay with John Cotton and Thomas
Hooker in 1633. He was elected an Assistant in 1634 and to the governorship in 1635.

this Testimony given; *To him is* New-England *many ways beholden; had he*
done no more but stilled a Storm of Dissention, which broke forth in the beginning
5 *of his Government; he had done enough to Endear our Hearts unto him, and to*
account that Day happy when he took the Reins of Government into his Hands.[2]
But this Pious, Humble, Well-bred Gentleman, removing afterwards into
Connecticut,[3] he took his turn with Mr. *Edward Hopkins,*[4] in being every
other Year the *Governour* of that Colony. And as he was a great Friend of
10 *Peace* while he lived, so at his Death he entred into that *Peace* which
attends the End of the *perfect* and *upright* Man, leaving behind him the
Character sometimes given of a *Greater,* tho' not a *Better,* Man, [*Vespasian*]
Bonis Legibus multa correxit, sed exemplo probæ vitæ plus effecit apud populum.[5]

§. 3. Near Twenty Ships from *Europe* visited *New-England* in the Year
15 1635. and in one of them was Mr. *Henry Vane,*[1] (afterward Sir *Henry*
Vane) an Accomplished Young Gentleman, whose Father was much
against his coming to *New-England*; but the King, upon Information of
his Disposition, commanded him to allow his Son's Voyage hither, with
a Consent for his continuing Three Years in this Part of the World.
20 Although his Business had some Relation to the Plantation of *Connecticut,*
yet in the Year 1636. the *Massachuset*-Colony chose him their *Governour.*
And now, Reader, I am as much a *Seeker* for his *Character,* as many have
taken him to be a *Seeker* in *Religion,* while no less Persons than Dr.
Manton[2] have not been to *seek* for the *Censure* of *A Wicked Book,* with which
25 they have noted the *Mystical Divinity,* in the Book of this Knight, Entituled, *The Retired Man's Meditations.* There has been a strange variety of
Translations bestowed upon the *Hebrew Names* of some *Animals* mentioned
in the *Bible: Kippod,* for Instance, which we translate a *Bittern*; R.
Salomon[3] will have to be an *Owl,* but *Luther* will have it be an *Eagle,* while
30 *Pagnin*[4] will have it be an *Hedg-hog,* but R. *Kimchi*[5] will have it a *Snail*;

30 *Pagnin/Paynin*

[2] As governor he pronounced the sentence of banishment on Roger Williams.*
[3] In 1637.*
[4] For Edward Hopkins (1600–1657), see chap. 7 below.
[5] "He corrected many things by good laws, but accomplished more among the people by
the example of a good life."*

[1] For Henry Vane, see above p. 220, l. 72.*
[2] Thomas Manton (1620–1677), probably the most popular of the Presbyterians, was in
1658 nominated by Parliament to draw up, together with Richard Baxter and others, "Fundamentals of Religion." He shared Baxter's dislike for Vane's *The Retired Man's Meditations*
(London, 1655), which seemed to deal in "Mystical Divinity." Baxter considered Manton
"an able, judicious, faithful Man."*
[3] Rabbi Solomon Bar Isaac (1040–1105), known as Rashi, celebrated commentator on
the Bible and Talmud.
[4] Sante Pagnino (1470–1541), of Lucca, Hebraist, author of a translation of the Bible and
of a *Thesaurus Linguae Sanctae.*
[5] Rabbi David Kimchi (1160–1235), French scholar famous for his exposition of Hebrew
grammar and his lexicon of the Bible, of which Pagnino's *Thesaurus* is essentially an elaboration.

such a Variety of Opinions and Resentments[6] has the *Name* of this Gentleman fallen under; while some have counted him an Eminent *Christian*, and others have counted him almost an *Heretick*; some have counted him a Renowned *Patriot*, and others an Infamous *Traitor*. If *Barak* signifie
35 both to *Bless* and to *Curse*; and Εὐλογεῖν[7] be of the same Significancy with Βλασφημεῖν,[8] in such Philology as that of *Suidas* and *Hesychius*;[9] the Usage which the *Memory* of this Gentleman has met withal, seems to have been Accommodated unto that *Indifferency* of Signification in the Terms for such an Usage.
40   On the one side, I find an Old *New-English* Manuscript thus reflecting, *His Election will remain as a Blemish to their Judgments who did Elect him, while* New-England *remains a Nation; for he coming from* Old-England, *a Young Unexperienced Gentleman, (and as young in Judgment as he was in Years) by the Industry of some that could do much, and thought by him to play their own Game,*
45 *was presently Elected Governour; and before he was scarce warm in his Seat, began to Broach New Tenets; and these were agitated with as much Violence, as if the Welfare of* New-England *must have been Sacrificed rather than these not take place.*[10] *But the Wisdom of the State put a Period to his Government; necessity caused them to undo the Works of their own Hands, and leave us a Caveat, that all*
50 *good Men are not fit for Government.* But on the other side, the Historian who has Printed *The Trial of Sir* Henry Vane, *Knt.*[11] *at the* King's Bench, Westminster, June 2. *and* 6. 1662. *with other occasional Speeches; also his Speech and Prayer on the Scaffold,*[12] has given us in him the Picture of nothing less than an *Heroe*. He seems indeed by that Story to have suffered
55 *Hardly* enough, but no Man can deny that he suffered *Bravely:* the *English* Nation has not often seen more of *Roman*, (and indeed more than *Roman*) Gallantry, out-facing *Death* in the most *pompous Terrors*[13] of it. A great Royalist, present, at his Decollation, swore, *He died like a Prince:* He could say, *I bless the Lord I am so far from being affrighted at Death, that I*
60 *find it rather shrink from me, than I from it!* He could say, *Ten Thousand Deaths rather than Defile my Conscience; the Chastity and Purity of which I value beyond all this World; I would not for Ten Thousand Worlds part with the Peace and Satisfaction I have in my own Heart.* When mention was made of the

---

[6] In the sense of feelings or emotions of any kind.

[7] To praise.

[8] To slander.

[9] Suidas, a Greek lexicographer of the eleventh century; Hesychius (fl. fifth century), a grammarian of Alexandria.

[10] A reference to Vane's role in the antinomian controversy.*

[11] Published anonymously in 1662.

[12] Vane was executed for high treason, having been arrested by Charles II's order soon after the Restoration.

[13] That is, bravery exemplifying heroic Roman virtues. "Pompous Terrors" are terrors heightened by the solemnity and pomp of a state trial.

Difficult Proceeding against him, all his reply was, *Alas, what a Do do*[14]
65 *they keep to make a poor Creature like his Saviour!* On the Scaffold they did,
by the Blast of Trumpets in his Face, with much Incivility, hinder him
from speaking what he intended; which Incivility he aforehand suspecting, committed a true Copy of it unto a Friend before his going
thither; the last Words whereof were these, *As my last Words I leave this*
70 *with you, That as the Present Storm we now lye under, and the dark Clouds that*
yet hang over the Reformed Churches of Christ, (which are coming thicker and
thicker for a Season) were not unforeseen by me for many Years past; (as some
Writings of mine declare) so the coming of Christ in these Clouds, in Order to a
speedy and sudden revival of his Cause, and spreading his Kingdom over the Face
75 *of the whole Earth, is most clear to the Eye of my Faith, even that Faith in which I*
Die. His Execution was *June* 14. 1662. about the Fiftieth Year of his Age.

§. 4. After the Death of Mr. *Dudley*, the Notice and Respect of the
Colony fell chiefly on Mr. *John Endicot*,[1] who after many Services done for
the Colony, even before it was yet a *Colony*, as well as when he saw it
80 grown into a *Populous Nation*, under his Prudent and Equal Government,
expired in a good Old Age, and was Honourably Interr'd at *Boston*,
March 23. 1665.

The Gentleman that succeeded Mr. *Endicot*, was Mr. *Richard Belling-*
ham,[2] one who was bred a *Lawyer*, and one who lived beyond Eighty, well
85 esteemed for his laudable Qualities; but as the *Thebans* made the Statues
of their Magistrates *without Hands*, importing that they must be no
Takers; in this fashion must be formed the *Statue* for this Gentleman; for
among all his Virtues, he was noted for none more, than for his notable
and perpetual hatred of a *Bribe*, which gave him, with his Country, the
90 Reputation of Old Claimed by *Pericles*, to be, φιλόπολίς τε καὶ
χρημάτων: κρείσσων: *Civitatis Amans, & ad pecunias Invictus*.[3] And as he
never *took* any from any one *living*; so he neither could nor would have
given any to *Death*; but in the latter end of the Year 1672. he had his
Soul gathered not with Sinners, whose Right Hand is full of Bribes, but with
95 such as *walk in their uprightness.*

---

[14] The *Tryal* (p. 81) reads, "what ado they keep." The *Magnalia* version may be a printer's
error. It is possible, however, that Mather, with his love of wordplay, enjoyed combining
"Do" in the seventeenth-century sense of "stir" or "fuss" with the intensive verb "do"
as a stylistic embellishment.

---

[1] John Endecott (born *c.*1589) was governor of the advance group who came to Salem in
1628 (see above Bk. I, p. 149, l. 83), and held office until Winthrop was elected governor. He
served as governor in 1644, 1649, 1651–1653, and 1655–1664.*
[2] Richard Bellingham (1592–1672) was a former member of Parliament and a patentee of
the charter. He came to New England in 1634 and was the following year elected deputy
governor. He defeated Winthrop for the governorship in 1641, served again in 1654, and from
1665 until his death.*
[3] "A good patriot and superior to the influence of money."*

The Gentleman that succeeded Mr. *Bellingham,* was Mr. *John Leveret,*[4] one to whom the Affections of the Freemen were signalized, in his quick advances through the lesser Stages of Office and Honour unto the highest 99 in the Country; and one whose *Courage* had been as much Recommended by Martial Actions abroad in his Younger Years, as his *Wisdom* and *Justice* were now at Home in his Elder. The *Anniversary Election* constantly kept him at the Helm from the time of his first Sitting there, until *March* 16. 1678. when *Mortality* having first put him on severe *Trials* of his 5 *Passive-Courage,* (much more difficult than the *Active*) in pains of the *Stone,* released him.

Pater Patriæ:[1] *Or, The LIFE of* SIMON BRADSTREET, *Esq;*

—Extinctus amabitur idem.[2]

THE Gentleman that succeeded Mr. *Leveret,* was Mr. *Simon Bradstreet,* 10 the Son of a Minister in *Lincolnshire,*[3] who was always a *Non-Conformist* at home, as well as when Preacher at *Middleburgh* abroad. Him the *New-Englanders* in their Addresses full of profound Respects unto him, have with good reason called, *The venerable* Mordecai[4] *of his Country.* He was born at *Horbling, March* 1603. His Father (who was the Son of a 15 *Suffolk* Gentleman of a fine Estate) was one of the First Fellows in *Immanuel*-Colledge, under Dr. *Chaderton,*[5] and one afterwards highly esteemed by Mr. *Cotton,*[6] and by Dr. *Preston.*[7] Our *Bradstreet* was brought up at the Grammar School, until he was about Fourteen Years Old; and then the Death of his Father put a stop for the present unto the Designs

[4] John Leverett (born 1616) was a prosperous merchant in foreign trade. Of a military bent, he was a member of the Ancient and Honorable Artillery Company, 1638–1668, and in 1644 went to England to take up a command in the Parliamentary army. He was major general of all Massachusetts forces from 1663 to 1673; governor from 1673 to 1678.

[1] "Father of his country."
[2] "He, too, will be beloved when his light is quenched."*
[3] Simon Bradstreet the elder studied at Christ's College, Cambridge, before becoming a Fellow of Emmanuel College. He was vicar of Horbling, Lincolnshire, 1596–1621; returned as "nonconformable" in 1611.*
[4] Mordecai, the cousin of Esther, was "great among the Jews, and accepted of the multitude of his brethren, seeking the wealth of his people, and speaking peace to all his seed" (Esth. 10.3). In this sentence, Mather shifts awkwardly from Simon the elder to "Him," the younger.
[5] Laurence Chaderton (1536?–1644), Puritan preacher and first master (1584–1622) of Emmanuel College, founded by Sir Thomas Mildmay, of Puritan sympathies, to train up godly ministers.
[6] For John Cotton, see *Magnalia,* Bk. III, pt. 1, chap. 1.
[7] John Preston (1587–1628) was Chaderton's successor at Emmanuel, and a principal architect of covenant doctrine.

20 of his further Education. But according to the *Faith* of his Dying Father,
that *he should be well provided for,* he was within Two or Three Years after
this taken into the Religious Family of the Earl of *Lincoln,* (the best
Family of any Nobleman then in *England,*) where he spent about Eight
Years under the Direction of Mr. *Thomas Dudley,* sustaining successively
25 divers Offices. Dr. *Preston* then (who had been my Lord's Tutor) moved
my Lord, that Mr. *Bradstreet* might have their permission to come unto
Immanuel Colledge,[8] in the Capacity of Governour to the Lord *Rich,*[9] the
Son of the Earl of *Warwick;* which they granting, he went with the Doctor
to *Cambridge,* who provided a Chamber for him, with Advice that he
30 should apply himself to Study until my Lord's Arrival. But he afterwards in a Writing of his, now in my Hands, made this humble Complaint; *I met with many Obstacles to my Study in* Cambridge; *the Earl of*
Lincoln *had a Brother there, who often called me forth upon Pastimes. Divers*
Masters of Arts, and other Scholars also, constantly met, where we spent most part
35 *of the Afternoons many times in Discourse to little purpose or profit; but that seemed*
an easie and pleasant Life then, which too late I repented. My Lord *Rich* not
coming to the University, Mr. *Bradstreet* returned after a Year to the Earl
of *Lincolns;* and Mr. *Dudley* then removing to *Boston,* his Place of *Steward*
unto the Earl was conferred on Mr. *Bradstreet.* Afterwards he with much
40 ado obtained the Earl's leave to Answer the Desires of the Aged and
Pious Countess of *Warwick,*[10] that he would accept the *Stewardship* of her
Noble Family, which as the former he discharged with an Exemplary
Discretion and Fidelity. Here he Married the Daughter of Mr. *Dudley,*[11]
by whose perswasion he came in Company with him to *New-England,*
45 where he spent all the rest of his Days, Honourably serving his Generation. It was counted a singular Favour of Heaven unto *Richard Chamond,*
Esq;[12] one of *England's Worthies,* that he was a *Justice of Peace* near
Threescore Years; but of *Simon Bradstreet,* Esq; one of *New-England's*
Worthies, there can more than this be said; for he was chosen a *Magistrate*
50 of *New-England* before *New-England* it self came into *New England;* even
in their first great Voyage thither *Anno* 1630. and so he continued annually
chosen; sometimes also their *Secretary,* and at last their *Governour,* until
the Colony had a share in the general Shipwrack of *Charters,* which the

34 *Arts/Art*

[8] Bradstreet was admitted sizar July 2, 1617; matriculated 1618; B.A. 1620; M.A. 1624.*
[9] Robert Rich (1611–1659), styled Lord Rich after the accession of his father to the earldom of Warwick in 1619. His father (1587–1658), the second earl, was early associated with colonial projects, and was a member of the Council for New England (cf. above Bk. I, p. 167, l. 36). He allied himself with the Puritan opposition to the court, and was a strong defender of the Puritan clergy.
[10] Frances (Wray) Rich, widow of the first Earl of Warwick. Bradstreet became her steward in 1628.
[11] In 1628. See above p. 233, l. 55.
[12] Of Cornwall.*

Reign of King *Charles* II. brought upon the whole *English* Nation. Mr.
55 *Joseph Dudley* was placed, *Anno* 1685. as *President*[13] over the Territory for
a few Months, when the *Judgment* that was entred against the *Charter*[14]
gave unto the late King *James* II. an opportunity to make what Alterations he pleased upon the Order of things, under which the Country had
so long been Flourishing. But when the short *Presidentship* of that *New-*
60 *English* and well Accomplished Gentleman, the Son of Mr. *Thomas*
Dudley abovementioned, was expired, I am not in a Disposition here to
relate what was the Condition of the Colony, until the *Revolution* whereto
their Condition compell'd them.[15] Only I have sometimes, not without
Amazement, thought of the Representation which a Celebrated *Magician*
65 made unto *Catherine de Medicis*, the *French* Queen, whose Impious Curiosity led her to desire of him a *Magical Exhibition* of all the Kings that had
hitherto Reigned in *France*, and yet were to Reign. The Shapes of all the
Kings, even unto the Husband of that Queen successively showed themselves, in the *Enchanted Circle*, in which that Conjurer had made his In-
70 vocations, and they took as many *Turns* as there had been Years in their
Government. The Kings that were to come, did then in like manner successively come upon the Stage, namely, *Francis* II. *Charles* IX. *Henry* III.
Henry IV. which being done, then Two Cardinals, *Richlieu* and *Mazarine*
in Red Hats, became visible in the Spectacle:[16] But after those Cardinals,
75 there entred 𝔚𝔬𝔩𝔲𝔢𝔰, 𝔅𝔢𝔞𝔯𝔰, 𝔗𝔶𝔤𝔢𝔯𝔰, and 𝔏𝔦𝔬𝔫𝔰, to consummate the
Entertainment. If the People of *New-England* had not Imagined, that a
Number of as *Rapacious Animals*[17] were at last come into their Government, I suppose they would not have made such a *Revolution* as they did,
on *April* 18. 1689.[18] in conformity to the Pattern which the *English*
80 *Nation* was then setting before them. Nevertheless, I have nothing in this

---

60 Accomplished/Acccomplished

[13] Joseph Dudley (1647–1720) was made "President of the Council and Governor of
Massachusetts, New Hampshire, and the Kings Province of Rhode Island." While his commission was made out on September 27, 1685, he did not arrive in Boston to take over the
provisional government until May of 1686.*
[14] The Massachusetts charter was declared vacated on October 23, 1684.
[15] The regime of Sir Edmund Andros lasted from December 20, 1686, until, in the April
1689 uprising in Boston, he was seized and imprisoned.*
[16] Catherine de Medici (1519–1583), Italian-born queen of Henry II, was the mother of
three French kings, Francis II, Charles IX, and Henry III, who reigned respectively 1547–
1559, 1560–1574, and 1574–1589. Catherine was abhorred by Protestants for her role in the
St. Bartholomew's Day massacre. Henry IV ruled 1589–1610; power under his son Louis XIII
was firmly in the hands of his chief ministers: Cardinal Richelieu (1585–1642), and the
Italian-born Cardinal Mazarin (1602–1661), whose power continued unabated until his
death in the early years of the reign of Louis XIV.*
[17] The New Englanders were particularly outraged by Andros' "Rapacious" taxation of
the colony.*
[18] Massachusetts lost no opportunity of calling attention to its own revolution as evidence
of its loyalty to William III.

Paragraph of our History to Report of it, but that Mr. *Bradstreet* was at this time alive; whose Paternal Compassions for a Country, thus remarkably *his own,* would not permit him to decline his Return unto his former *Seat* in the Government, upon the Unanimous Invitation of the
85 People thereunto. It was a Remark then generally made upon him, *That though he were then well towards Ninety Years of Age, his intellectual force was hardly abated, but he retained a Vigour and Wisdom that would have recommended a younger Man to the Government of a greater Colony.* And the wonderful Difficulties, through which the Colony under his discreet Conduct
90 waded, until the Arrival of his Excellency, Sir *William Phips,*[19] with a Commission for the Government, and a *New Charter* in the Year 1692. gave a Remarkable *Demonstration* of it. Yea, this Honourable *Nestor*[20] of *New-England,* in the Year 1696. was yet alive; and as *Georgius Leontinus,*[21] who lived until he was an Hundred and Eight Years of Age, being asked
95 by what means he attained unto such an Age, answered, *By my not Living Voluptuously;* thus this excellent Person attained his good old Age, in part, *By Living very Temperately.* And the *New-Englanders* would have counted it their Satisfaction, if like *Arganthonius,*[22] who had been Fourscore Years
99 the Governour of the *Tartessians,* he might have lived unto the Age of an Hundred and Twenty; or, even unto the Age of *Johannes de Temporibus,*[23] who was Knighted by the Emperour *Charlemaign,* and yet was Living till the Emperour *Conrade,*[24] and saw, they say, no fewer Years than *Three Hundred Threescore and One.* Though, *To be Dissolved and be with Christ,*
5 was the Satisfaction which this our *Macrobius*[25] himself was with a weary Soul now waiting and longing for; and Christ at length granted it unto him, on *March* 27, 1697. *Then* it was, that one of the oldest Servants that God and the King had upon Earth, drew his *Last,* in the very place where he drew his *First American* Breath. He Died at *Salem,* in a Troublesome
10 Time, and entred into everlasting Peace. And in Imitation of what the Roman Orator said upon the Death of *Crassus,* I will venture to say, *Fuit hoc, luctuosum suis, Acerbum Patriæ, Grave Bonis Omnibus: Sed ei tamen*

9 *First American/First, American*   12 *ei/ii*

[19] See Appendix, "Life of Sir William Phips."
[20] Nestor of Pylos, the oldest and most experienced of all the Greek chieftains who went to Troy.
[21] Gorgias Leontinus (c.483–375 B.C.), orator and teacher of rhetoric. Plato gave Gorgias' name to one of his dialogues.*
[22] Arganthonius, king of Tartessus in Asia Minor.*
[23] Johannes de Stampis, or de Temporibus, called "John of the Times" because of the several ages through which he lived, partly in Germany, where he was born, and partly in France, where he died.*
[24] That is, from the lifetime of Charlemagne (c.724–814) to that of Conrad III (1093–1152).
[25] The Macrobii were an Ethiopian race said by Pliny to live up to one hundred forty years.*

Reipublicae casus Secuti sunt, ut mihi non Erepta Bradstreeto *Vita, sed donata mors esse videatur.*[26]

15   The Epitaph on that famous Lawyer, *Simon Pistorius,*[27] we will now Employ for this Eminently Prudent and Upright Administrator of our *Laws.*

EPITAPH.

SIMON BRADSTREET.

20

*Quod Mortale fuit, Tellus tenet; Inclyta Fama
Nominis haud ullo stat violanda Die.*[28]

And Add,

*Extinctum luget quem tota Nov-Anglia Patrem,
O Quantum Claudit parvula Terra Virum!*[29]

25

CHAP. VI.

בעלינפש Id est, Viri Animati:[1] *Or, ASSISTANTS.*

THE Freemen of *New-England* had a great variety of Worthy Men, among whom they might pick and chuse a Number of MAGIS-STRATES to be the *Assistants* of their GOVERNOURS, both in
30 directing the General Affairs of the Land, and in dispensing of Justice unto the People. But they wisely made few Alterations in their Annual *Elections*; and they thereby shew'd their Satisfaction in the wise and good Conduct of those whom they had *Elected.* If they called some few of their *Magistrates* from the *Plough* to the *Bench,* so the Old *Romans* did some of their
35 *Dictators*; yea, the greatest Kings in the World once carried *Plough-shares* on the top of their *Scepters.* However, the Inhabitants of *New-England*

---

13   *Reipublicae/Rempublicam*

[26] "This brought lamentation to his friends, sorrow to his country, and regret to all good men; but the national misfortunes that followed have been such as to make me feel that the powers above did not rob Bradstreet of life, but vouchsafed to him the gift of death."*

[27] Saxon jurisconsult and chancellor (1489–1562).

[28] "Earth holds what of him was mortal; the glorious fame of his name stands inviolable by time."*

[29] "A little earth shuts in how great a man, whom, as a father dead, all New England mourns."*

---

[1] That is, "Conscientious Men."*

never were so unhappy as the Inhabitants of *Norcia*, a Town scarce Ten Leagues from *Rome*; where they do at this Day chuse their own *Magistrates*, but use an exact Care, *That no Man who is able to Write, or to Read, shall be*
40 *capable of any share in the Government.* The Magistrates of *New-England* have been of a better Education. Indeed, several deserving Persons, who were joined as *Associates* and *Commissioners* unto these, for the more effectual Execution of the Laws in some *Emergencies*, cannot be brought into our *Catalogue*; but the *Names* of all our *Magistrates*, with the *Times*
45 when I find their first Advancement unto that Character, are these.

MAGISTRATES of the *Massachuset*-Colony.[2]

John Winthrop, Gov.		*Roger Ludlow*,	1630
Thomas Dudley, Deputy Gov.		*Edward Rossiter*,	1630
Matthew Cradock,	1629	*John Endicot*,[4]	1630
50 *Thomas Goff*,	1629	*John Winthrop*, Jun.	1632
Sir *Richard Saltonstal*,	1629	*John Haines*,	1634
Isaac Johnson,	1629	*Richard Bellingham*,	1635
Samuel Aldersey,	1629	*Atterton Hough*,	1635
John Venn,	1629	*Richard Dummer*,	1635
55 *John Humfrey*,	1629	*Henry Vane*,	1636
Simon Whetcomb,	1629	*Roger Harlackenden*,	1636
Increase Nowel,	1629	*Israel Stoughton*,	1637
Richard Perry,	1629	*Richard Saltonstal*,	1637
Nathanael Wright,	1629	*Thomas Flint*,	1643
60 *Samuel Vassal*,	1629	*Samuel Symons*,	1643
Theophilus Eaton,	1629	*William Hibbons*,	1643
Thomas Adams,	1629	*William Tynge*,	1643
Thomas Hutchins,	1629	*Herbert Pelham*,	1645
George Foxcroft,	1629	*Robert Bridges*,	1647
65 *William Vassal*,	1629	*Francis Willoughby*,	1650
William Pinchon,	1629	*Thomas Wiggan*,	1650
John Pocock,	1629	*Edward Gibbons*,	1650
Christopher Cowlson,	1629	*John Glover*,	1652
William Coddington,	1629	*Daniel Gookin*,	1652
70 *Simon Bradstreet*,[3]	1629	*Daniel Denison*,	1654
Thomas Sharp,	1629	*Simon Willard*,	1654

52   *Bellingham/Billingham*   56   *Whetcomb/Whercomb*
53   *Aldersey/Aldersley*   56   *Harlackenden/Hartackenden*

[2] In Appendix S of his edition of Winthrop's *History* (2:380–483), James Savage lists the Massachusetts assistants "From the Magnalia, Book II, Chap. 6. with corrections and additions," and adds brief identifying biographical data. The present editors have made certain further corrections.

[3] Coddington and Bradstreet were chosen at Southampton March 18, 1629/30.*

[4] Rossiter and Endecott were elected in October 1629, not 1630.*

	Humphrey Atherton,	1654	*John Richards,*	1680
	Richard Russel,	1659	*John Hull,*	1680
	Thomas Danforth,	1659	*Bartholomew Gidney,*	1680
75	*William Hawthorn,*	1662	*Thomas Savage,*	1680
	Eleazer Lusher,	1662	*William Brown,*	1680
	John Leveret,	1665	*Samuel Appleton,*	1681
	John Pinchon,	1665	*Robert Pike,*	1682
	Edward Tyng,	1668	*Daniel Fisher,*	1683
80	*William Stoughton,*	1671	*John Woodbridge,*	1683
	Thomas Clark,	1673	*Elisha Cook,*	1684
	Joseph Dudley,	1676	*William Johnson,*	1684
	Peter Bulkley,	1677	*John Hawthorn,*	1684
	Nathanael Saltonstal,	1679	*Elisha Hutchinson,*	1684
85	*Humphrey Davy,*	1679	*Samuel Sewal,*	1684
	James Russel,	1680	*Isaac Addington,*	1686
	Samuel Nowel,	1680	*John Smith,*	1686
	Peter Tilton,	1680		

Major-Generals of the Military Forces in the Colony, successively chosen.[5]

90	*Thomas Dudley.*	[1644]	*Humphfry Atherton.*	[1652]
	John Endicot.	[1645]	*Daniel Denison.*	[1653]
	Edward Gibbons.	[1649]	*John Leveret.*	[1663]
	Robert Sedgwick.	[1652]	*Daniel Gookin.*	[1681]

Secretaries of the Colony, successively chosen.[6]

95	*William Burgis.*	[1629]	*Increase Nowel.*	[1636]
	Simon Bradstreet.	[1634]	*Edward Rawson.*	[1650]

That these *Names* are proper and worthy to be found in our *Church-History*, will be acknowledged, when it is considered, not only that they
99 were the *Members of Congregational Churches,* and by the *Members of the Churches* chosen to be the *Rulers* of the *Commonwealth*; and that their exemplary Behaviour in their *Magistracy* was generally such as to *adorn the Doctrine of God our Saviour,* and according to the Old *Jewish* Wishes, *prohibitum est Homini, instar principis Dominari super populum, & cum elatione*
5 *Spiritus, sed,* בעכוה זידאה *cum mansuetudine ac Timore:*[7] But also that their

89 successively/successfully C.M.   94 successively/successfully C.M.

[5] Dates in brackets supplied from the *Mass. Records.**

[6] Dates in brackets supplied from the *Mass. Records.* Nowel assumed the duties of the office in 1636, but he was not officially appointed until 1639.**

[7] "It is forbidden to man to rule like a prince over a people, and with a proud spirit, but he should exercise authority with meekness and fear."**

Love to, and Zeal for, and Care of these *Churches*, was not the least part of their Character.

The Instances of their Concern for the Welfare of the *Churches* were innumerable. I will single out but one from the rest, because of some
10 Singular Subserviency to the Designs of our *Church-History*, therein to be propos'd. I'll do it only by Transcribing an Instrument, published *Anno* 1668. in such Terms as these.

To the Elders and Ministers of every Town within the Jurisdiction of the Massachusets *in* New-England, *the Governour and Council sendeth Greeting.*

15 *Reverend and Beloved in the Lord,*

'WE find in the Examples of Holy Scripture, that *Magistrates* have not 'only excited and commanded all the People under their Govern-'ment, *to seek the Lord God of their Fathers, and do the Law and Commandment,* '(2. Chron. 14. 2, 3, 4. Ezra 7. 25, 26, 27.) but also stirred up and sent
20 'forth the *Levites*,[8] accompanied with other Principal Men, to *Teach the* '*good Knowledge of the Lord throughout all the Cities*, (2. Chron. 17. 6, 7, 8, 9.) 'which Endeavours have been Crowned with the Blessing of God.

'Also we find that our Brethren of the *Congregational* Perswasion in '*England*, have made a good Profession in their Book, Entituled, *A*
25 '*Declaration of their Faith and Order*, (Page 59. Sect. 14.) where they say, '*That altho' Pastors and Teachers stand especially related unto their particular* '*Churches, yet they ought not to neglect others Living within their Parochial* '*Bounds; but besides their constant publick Preaching to them, they ought to enquire* '*after their profiting by the Word, Instructing them in, and Pressing upon them,*
30 '*(whether Young or Old) the great Doctrines of the Gospel, even personally and* '*particularly, so far as their Strength and Time will permit.*

'We hope that sundry of you need not a *Spur* in these things, but are 'conscienciously careful to do your Duty. Yet, forasmuch as we have 'cause to fear that there is too much Neglect in many places, notwith-
35 'standing the *Laws* long since provided therein, we do therefore think it 'our Duty to emit this *Declaration* unto you, earnestly Desiring, and, in 'the Bowels of our Lord Jesus, requiring you to be very Diligent and 'Careful to *Catechise* and Instruct all People (especially the *Youth*) under 'your Charge, in the sound Principles of Christian Religion; and that not
40 'only in *Publick*, but privately *from House to House*, as Blessed *Paul* did; '(*Act*. 20. 20.) or at least, Three, Four, or more Families meeting to-'gether, as Time and Strength may permit; taking to your Assistance such 'godly and grave Persons as to you may seem most expedient: And also 'that you Labour to Inform your selves (as much as may be meet) how

---

[8] The descendants of Levi, that is, priests.

45 'your Hearers do profit by the Word of God, and how their Conversa-
'tions do agree therewith; and whether the Youth are Taught to Read
'the *English* Tongue: Taking all occasions to apply suitable *Exhortations*
'particularly unto them, for *the Rebuke of those that do evil, and the En-*
'*couragement of them that do well.*

50   'The effectual and constant Prosecution hereof, we hope will have a
'Tendency to promote the *Salvation of Souls*; to suppress the Growth of
'*Sin* and Profaneness; to beget more Love and *Unity* among the People,
'and more *Reverence* and Esteem of the *Ministry:* And it will assuredly be
'to the enlargement of your *Crown*, and Recompence in *Eternal Glory.*

55 *Given at* Boston, *the* 10th *of* March, 1668. *by the Governour and Council, and*
    by them Ordered to be Printed, and sent accordingly.

Edward Rawson, *Secret.*[9]

CHAP. VII.

Publicola Christianus.[1] *The LIFE of* EDWARD HOPKINS, *Esq*;
60   *Governour of* CONNECTICUT-*COLONY.*

Superiores sint, qui superiores esse sciunt.[2]

§. 1. WHEN the Great God of Heaven had carried his *Peculiar People*
    into a *Wilderness*, the *Theocracy*, wherein he became (as he was
for *that Reason* stiled) *The Lord of Hosts*, unto them and the *Four* Squadrons
65 of their *Army*, was most eminently display'd in *his* Enacting of their *Laws*,
his Directing of their *Wars*, and his Electing and Inspiring of their
Judges. In some resemblance hereunto, when *Four* Colonies of Christians
had marched like so many *Hosts* under the Conduct of the good Spirit
of our Lord Jesus Christ into an *American* Wilderness, there were several
70 Instances wherein that *Army* of *Confessors* was under a *Theocracy:* For
their *Laws* were still Enacted, and their *Wars* were still Directed by the
Voice of God, as far as they understood it, speaking from the *Oracle*
of the *Scriptures*; and though their *Judges* were still *Elected* by themselves,
and not *Inspired* with such extraordinary Influences as *carried* them of
75 Old, yet *these* also being singularly furnished and offered by the special
Providence of God unto the Government of his *New-English* People,

---

[9] Rawson was secretary of the colony until 1686, thirty-six years in all.

[1] "The Christian Patriot."
[2] "Let them be superior who know they are superior."*

were so eminently acted by *His Graces,* and *His Precepts,* in the Discharge
of their Government, that the Blessed People were still sensibly *Governed
by the Lord of All.* Now among the First *Judges* of *New-England,* was
80 𝕰𝖉𝖜𝖆𝖗𝖉 𝕳𝖔𝖕𝖐𝖎𝖓𝖘, Esq; in whose time the *Colony* of *Connecticut* was favoured
with *Judges as at the first;* and put under the Power of those with whom it
was a Maxim, *Gratius est pietatis Nomen, quam potestatis.*[3]

§. 2. The Descent and Breeding of Mr. 𝕰𝖉𝖜𝖆𝖗𝖉 𝕳𝖔𝖕𝖐𝖎𝖓𝖘, (who was
Born, I think, near *Shrowsbury,*[1] about the Year 1600.) first fitted him for
85 the Condition of a *Turky-Merchant,*[2] in *London;* where he lived several
Years in good Fashion and Esteem, until a powerful Party in the Church
of *England,* then resolving not only to *separate* from the Communion of
all the *Faithful* that were Averse to certain confessedly *unscriptural* and
uninstituted Rites in the Worship of God, but also to *Persecute* with de-
90 stroying Severities those that were *Non-Conformists* thereunto, compelled a
considerable Number of good Men to seek a shelter among the Salvages
of *America.* Among these, and with his Excellent Father-in-Law, Mr.
Theophilus Eaton,[3] he came to *New-England;* where then removing from
the *Massachuset*-Bay unto *Hartford* upon *Connecticut*-River, he became a
95 *Ruler* and *Pillar* of that Colony, during the time of his Abode in the
Country.

§. 3. In his Government he acquitted himself as the *Solomon* of his
Colony, to whom *God gave Wisdom and Knowledge, that he might go out and*
99 *come in before the People;* and as he was the *Head,* so he was the *Heart* of
the People, for the Resolution *to do Well,* which he maintained among
them. An *unjust Judge* is, as one says, *A cold Fire, a dark Sun, a dry Sea, an
ungood God, a* contradictio in Adjecto.[1] Far from such was our *Hopkins;*
no, he was, δίκαιον ἔμψυχον, a meer piece of *Living Justice.* And as he
5 had no *separate Interests* of his own, so he pursued their *Interests* with such
an unspotted and successful Fidelity, that they might call him as the
Tribe of *Benjamin* did their Leader in the Wilderness, *Abidan,* that is to
say, *Our Father is Judge. New-England* saw little *Dawnings,* and *Emblems,*
and *Earnests* of the Day, *That the greatness of the Kingdom under the whole
10 Heaven shall be given unto the People of the Saints of the most High,* when such
a *Saint* as our 𝕳𝖔𝖕𝖐𝖎𝖓𝖘 was one of its Governours. And the Felicity which
a Great Man has Prognosticated for *Europe, That God will stir up some
happy Governour in some Country in Christendom, indued with Wisdom and
Consideration, who shall discern the true Nature of Godliness and Christianity,*

---

[3] "More agreeable is the name of dutiful conduct than of power."*

---

[1] Shrewsbury. Mather's spelling reflects the pronunciation both of his time and the present.
[2] That is, a dealer in goods from Turkey and the Levant.
[3] Eaton was actually stepfather-in-law; he had married a widow, Anne Yale, whose daughter
by her first husband, also named Anne, married Hopkins.

---

[1] "A paradox."

15 *and the Necessity and Excellency of serious Religion, and shall place his Honour and Felicity in pleasing God, and doing Good, and attaining Everlasting Happiness, and shall subject all Worldly Respects unto these High and Glorious Ends:* This was now Exemplified in *America.*

§. 4. Most Exemplary was his *Piety* and his *Charity*; and while he
20 governed *others* by the *Laws* of God, he did *himself* yield a profound Subjection unto those *Laws.* He was exemplarily watchful over his own Behaviour, and made a continual *Contemplation* of, and *Preparation* for *Death,* to be the Character of his *Life.* It was his manner to *Rise early,* even before Day, to enjoy the Devotions of his *Closet*: after which he spent
25 a considerable time in Reading, and Opening, and Applying the *Word* of God unto his *Family,* and then *Praying* with them: And he had one particular way to cause Attention in the People of his Family, which was to ask any Person that seemed Careless in the midst of his Discourse, *What was it that I Read or Spoke last?* Whereby he Habituated them unto
30 such an Attention, that they were still usually able to give a ready Account. But as for his *Prayers,* they were not only *frequent,* but so *fervent* also, that he frequently fell a *Bleeding* at the Nose through the *Agony* of Spirit with which he labour'd in them. And, especially when imploring such *Spiritual Blessings,* as, *That God would grant in the End of our Lives, the*
35 *End of our Hopes, even the Salvation of our Souls,* he would be so Transported, that the Observing and Judicious Hearers would say sometimes upon it, *Surely this Man can't be long out of Heaven.* Moreover, in his Neighbourhood he not only set himself to Encourage and Countenance real *Godliness,* but also would himself kindly visit the *Meetings* that the Religious Neigh-
40 bours privately kept for the Exercises of it; and where the least Occasion for *Contention* was offered, he would, with a prudent and speedy Endeavour, Extinguish it. But the *Poor* he so considered, that besides the *Daily Reliefs* which with his own Hands he dispenced unto them, he would put considerable Sums of Money into the Hands of his Friends,
45 to be by them employed as they saw *Opportunity to do good unto all, especially the Houshold of Faith.* In this thing he was like that Noble and Worthy *English* General,[1] of whom 'tis noted, *He never thought he had any thing but what he gave away*; and yet after all, with much humility he would profess, as one of the most Liberal Men that ever was in the World often would,
50 *I have often turned over my Books of Accounts, but I could never find the Great God charged a Debtor there.*

§. 5. But *Suffering* as well as *Doing* belongs to the Compleat Character of a *Christian*; and there were several *Trials* wherein our Lord called this

20   yield/yeild

[1] Sir John Norris (1547?–1597), regarded as one of the most skillful and successful military officers of his day.*

Eminently Patient Servant of his to *Suffer the Will of God.* He Conflicted
55 with *Bodily Infirmities,* but especially with a Wasting and a Bloody *Cough,*
which held him for Thirty Years together. He had been by *Persecutions*
driven to cross an *Ocean,* to which he had in his Nature an *Antipathy;*
and then a *Wilderness* full of such Crosses as attend the *beginning of a
Plantation,* exercised him. Nevertheless there was one Affliction which
60 *continually dropt* upon him above all the rest, and that was this, He Married
a Daughter which the Second Wife of Mr. *Eaton* had by a former Husband; one that from a Child had been Observable for Desirable Qualities.
But some time after she was Married she fell into a Distempered *Melan-
cholly,* which at last Issued in an Incurable *Distraction,* with such Ill-
65 shaped *Ideas* in her Brain, as use to be formed when the *Animal Spirits*
are *fired* by Irregular Particles, fixed with Acid, Bilious, Venemous Fer-
ments in the Blood. Very Grievous was this Affliction unto this her worthy
Consort, who was by temper a very Affectionate Person: And who now
left no part of a tender Husband undone, to *Ease,* and, if it were possible,
70 to *Cure* the Lamentable Desolation thus come upon, *The Desire of his
Eyes;* but when the Physician gave him to understand, that no means
would be likely to *Restore* her *Sense,* but such as would be also likely to
Hazard her *Life,* he Replied with Tears, *I had rather bear my Cross unto the
End that the Lord shall give!* But upon this Occasion he said unto *her* Sister,[1]
75 who, with all the rest related unto *her,* were as dear unto him as *his own;
I have often thought, what should be the meaning of the Lord, in chastising of me
with so sharp a Rod, and with so long a Stroke!* Whereto, when she Reply'd,
*Sir, nothing singular has, in this Case, befallen you; God hath afflicted others in
the like way; and we must be content with our Portion:* He Answered, *Sister,*
80 *This is among the Lord's Rarities. For my part I cannot tell what Sore to lay my
Hand upon: However, in General, my Sovereign Lord is Just, and I will justifie
him for ever: But in Particular, I have thought the matter might lye here: I
promised my self too much Content in this Relation and Enjoyment; and the Lord
will make me to know that this World shall not afford it me.* So he wisely,
85 meekly, fruitfully bore this heavy *Affliction* unto his *Dying Day;* having
been taught by the Affliction to *Die Daily,* as long as he *Lived.*

§. 6. About Governour *Eaton,* his Father-in-Law, he saw cause to say
unto a *Sister-in-Law,*[1] whom he much valued; *I have often wondred at my
Father and your Father; I have heard him say, That he never had a Repenting, or a*
90 *Repining Thought,* about his coming to New-England: *Surely, in this Matter
he hath a Grace far out-shining Mine. But he is our Father! I cannot say, as he
can, I have had hard work with my own Heart about it.* But upon the Death of

---

[1] Mrs. Hopkins had no full sister. She had two halfsisters, Mary and Hannah, to either of
whom Mather may be referring.*

---

[1] The sister-in-law may have been the wife of either of her full brothers, David and Thomas,
or possibly of her halfbrother Samuel.*

his Elder Brother, who was *Warden of the Fleet*,[2] it was necessary for him to Return into *England*, that he might look after the Estate which then fell
95 unto him; and accordingly, after a Tempestuous and a Terrible Voyage, wherein they were eminently endangered by *Fire*, accidentally enkindled on the Ship, as well as by *Water*, which tore it so to Pieces, that it was Towed in by another Ship, he at length,

99   *Per Varios Casus; per tot Discrimina Rerum,*[3]

arrived there. *There* a great Notice was quickly taken of him: He was made *Warden of the Fleet*, Commissioner of the Admiralty, and the Navy-Office, a Parliament-Man; and he was placed in some other considerable Stations: In all which he more than answered the Expectations of those
5 who took him to be a Person *Eminently Qualified for Publick Service*. By these Employments, his design of Returning to *New-England*, with which he left it, was diverted so far, that he sent for his Family; and about the time that he looked for them, he being advantaged by his great Places to employ certain Frigots for their safety on the Coast, by that means had
10 them safely brought unto him. When they were with him in *London*, one of them told him how much his Friends in *New-England* Wish'd and Pray'd for his Return: And how that Passage had been used in our Pub-lick Supplications for that Mercy, *Lord, If we may win him in Heaven, we shall yet have him on Earth:* But he Reply'd, *I have had many Thoughts about*
15 *my Return, and my Affections have been bent very strongly that way; and tho' I have now, blessed be God, received my Family here, yet that shall be no hindrance to my Return. I will tell you, though I am little worth, yet I have that Love which will dispose me to serve the Lord, and that People of his. But as to that matter, I incline to think they will not win it in Heaven; and I know not whether the Terrors*
20 *of my dreadful Voyage hither might not be ordered by the Divine Providence, to Stake me in this Land, being in my Spirit sufficiently loth to run the hazard of such another. I must also say to you, I mourn exceedingly, and* I fear, I fear, *the Sins of* New-England *will e're long be read in its Punishments. The Lord has planted that Land with a* Noble Vine; *and* Blessed hast thou been, O Land, in thy
25 Rulers! *But, alas! for the generality they have not considered how they were to* Honour the Rules of God, *in Honouring of those whom God made* Rulers *over them; and I fear they will come to smart by having them set over them, that it will be an* hard Work to Honour, *and that will hardly be capable to manage their Affairs.*
30 §. 7. Accordingly he continued in *England* the rest of his Days, in several places of Great *Honour* and *Burden* faithfully serving the Nation;

---

[2] Henry Hopkins, warden of the Fleet Prison. Mather's chronology is incorrect; Hopkins returned to England in 1652, two years before his brother's death.*
[3] "Through divers mishaps; through so many perilous chances."*

but in the midst of his *Publick* Employments most exactly maintaining the *Zeal* and *Watch* of his own private *Walk with God.* His *Mind* kept continually Mellowing and Ripening for *Heaven*; and one Expression of
35 his *Heavenly Mind,* among many others, a little before his End, was, *How often have I pleased my self with thoughts of a joyful Meeting with my Father* Eaton! *I remember with what pleasure he would come down the Street, that he might meet me when I came from* Hartford *unto* New-Haven: *But with how much greater Pleasure shall we shortly meet one another in Heaven!* But as an
40 *Heavenly Mind* is oftentimes a *Presaging Mind,* so he would sometimes utter this *Presage* unto some that were Near and Dear unto him; *God will shortly take the* Protector[1] *away, and soon after that you will see great Changes overturning the present Constitution, and sore Troubles come upon those that now promise better things unto themselves.* However, he did not Live to see the
45 Fulfilment of this *Prediction.*

§. 8. For the *time now drew near that this Israelite was to Die!* He had been in his Life troubled with many *Fears of Death*; and after he fell Sick, even when he drew very near his Death, he said with Tears, *Oh! Pray for me, for I am in extream Darkness!* But at length, on a Lord's Day, about the very
50 time when Mr. *Caryl*[1] was publickly praying for him, his Darkness all vanished, and he broke forth into these Expressions, *Oh! Lord, thou hast kept the best Wine until the last! Oh! Friends, could you believe this? I shall be blessed for ever, I shall quickly be in Eternal Glory. Now let the whole World count me Vile, and call me an Hypocrite, or what they will, I matter it not;*[2]
55 *I shall be blessed; there is reserved for me a Crown of Glory. Oh! Blessed be God for Jesus Christ! I have heretofore thought it an hard thing to die, but now I find that it is not so. If I might have my choice, I would now chuse to die; Oh! my Lord, I pray thee send me not back again into this Evil World, I have enough of it; no, Lord, now take me to Glory, and the Kingdom that is prepared for me!* Yea,
60 the standers by thought it not possible for them to utter exactly after him, the *Heavenly Words* which now proceeded from him; and when one of them said, *Sir, The Lord hath enlarged your Faith*; he replied, *Friend, this is Sense; the Lord hath even satisfied my Sense; I am sensibly satisfied of Everlasting Glory!* Two or Three Days he now spent in *Prayers* and *Praises,* and in
65 Inexpressible *Joys*: In which time, when some Eminent Persons of a very *Publick* Station and Imployment came to Visit him, unto *them* he said, *Sirs, Take heed of your Hearts while you are in your Work for God, that there be no root of bitterness within you. It may be pretended your Desires are to serve God, but if there are in you secret Aims at advancing of your selves, and your own*
70 *Estates and Interests, the Lord will not accept your Services as pure before him.*

---

[1] Oliver Cromwell.

---

[1] Joseph Caryl (1602–1673), Puritan divine and Biblical expositor; minister at St. Magnus, near London Bridge, until ejected in 1662.
[2] That is, "I regard it not."

But at length in the Month of *March*, 1657. at *London* he expired; when being opened, it was found that his *Heart* had been unaccountably, as it were, Boiled and Wasted in Water, until it was become a little brittle Skin, which being touch'd, presently dropp'd in pieces. He had often 75 wished, upon some great Accounts, that he might live till the beginning of this Year; and now when he lay a dying, he said, *Lord! Thou hast fulfilled my Desires according to thy Word, that thou wilt fulfil the Desires of them that fear thee.*

Now from the Tombstone of another Eminent Person, we will fetch 80 what shall here be a proper

Part of EDWARD HOPKINS, Esq;

EPITAPH.

But Heaven, *not brooking that the* Earth *should share*
In the least Atom *of a Piece so rare,*
85 *Intends to Sue out, by a* New Revise,
His Habeas Corpus *at the* Grand Assize.

CHAP. VIII.

SUCCESSORS.

§. 1. $\mathbf{A}$Lternately, for the most part every other Year, Mr. *Hains*, 90 whom we have already mentioned elsewhere, took a turn with Mr. *Hopkins* in the Chief place of Government. And besides these, (Reader, the *Oracle* that once Predicted Government unto a Θ,[1] would now and here Predict it unto a W.) there were Mr. *Willis*, Mr. *Wells*, and Mr. *Webster*,[2] all of whom also had Opportunity to express their Liberal and 95 Generous Dispositions, and the *Governing Virtues* of Wisdom, Justice and Courage, by the Election of the Freemen in the Colony before its being United with *Newhaven*.[3] Had the Surviving Relations of these Worthy Men sent in unto me a Tenth Part of the *Considerable* and *Imitable* Things 99 which occurr'd in their *Lives*, they might have made more of a Figure in

81–82 Part of *EDWARD HOPKINS*, Esq; / EPITAPH
    EPITAPH / Part of *EDWARD HOPKINS*, Esq;

[1] Theta.*

[2] George Willis (Willys, d. 1645), governor of Connecticut 1642; Thomas Wells (Welles, d. 1660), governor or lieutenant governor from 1654 until his death; John Webster (d. 1661), governor in 1656.

[3] The union of the two colonies was established by royal charter in 1662, but because of the resistance of New Haven was not finally effected until 1665.*

this our *History*; whereas I must now Sum up all, with assuring my Reader, that it is the want of *Knowledge* in *Me*, and not of *Desert* in *Them*, that has confined us unto this Brevity.

§. 2. After the Union of *Connecticut* with *Newhaven*, there were in Chief Government Mr. *Leet*,[1] whom we have already paid our Dues unto; and Mr. *Treat*,[2] who is yet living, a Pious and a Valiant Man, and (if ever *Annosa Quercus*[3] be an Honourable thing!) worthy to be Honoured for *An Hoary Head found in the Way of Righteousness*: Besides, Mr. *Winthrop*,[4] of whom anon, Reader, expect a Compleater History.

CHAP. IX.

Humilitas Honorata.[1] *The LIFE of* THEOPHILUS EATON, *Esq*; *Governour of* NEW-HAVEN *COLONY*.

Justitiæ Cultor, Rigidi Servator Honesti, In Commune Bonum.[2]

§. 1. IT has been enquired, why the Evangelist *Luke* in the *First* Sacred History which he Addressed unto his Fellow-Citizen, gave him the Title of *The Most Excellent Theophilus*, but in the *next* he used no higher a Stile than plain *Theophilus?* And though several other Answers might be given to that Enquiry, 'tis enough to say, That neither the *Civility* of *Luke*, nor *Nobility* of *Theophilus*, were by Age abated; but *Luke* herein considered the Disposition of *Theophilus*, as well as his own, with whom a reduced[3] Age had render'd all *Titles of Honour* mere *Disagreeable Superfluities*. Indeed nothing would have been more unacceptable to the Governour of our *New-Haven Colony*, all the time of his being so, than to have been Advanced and Applauded above the rest of Mankind; yet it must be *now* Published unto the Knowledge of Mankind, that *New-England* could not of his Quality show a *More Excellent Person*, and this was *Theophilus Eaton*, Esq; the first Governour of that Colony. *Humility* is a Virtue whereof *Amyraldus*[4] observes, *There is not so much as a*

6 ever/even   21 mere/more
19 *Theophilus/Theoplilus*

[1] For William Leet (*c.*1613–1683), see chap. X, sec. 2, below.*
[2] Robert Treat (1622?–1710), commander of Connecticut troops in King Philip's War; governor 1683–1698. (See *Magnalia*, Bk. VII, chap. VI.)
[3] "An aged oak."*
[4] John Winthrop, Jr., on whom see chap. XI below.

[1] "Humility honored."
[2] "Cultivator of justice, guardian of uncompromising honesty for the general good."*
[3] "Reduced" in the sense of "brought to a state of gravity or composure."*
[4] Moyses Amyraldus (Moise Amyraut, 1596–1664), a French Protestant divine.*

Shadow of Commendation in all the Pagan Writers. But the Reader is now con-
30 cerned with Writings which will *Commend* a Person for *Humility*; and
therefore our *EATON*, in whom the shine of every Virtue was particularly set off with a more than ordinary Degree of *Humility*, must now be
propos'd as *Commendable.*

§. 2. 'Tis *Reported*, that the Earth taken from the Banks of *Nilus*, will
35 very strangely Sympathize with the place from whence it was taken, and
grow moist or dry according to the Increase and the Decrease of the
River. And in spite of that *Popish Lie* which pretends to observe the
contrary, this thing has been signally *Moraliz'd* in the daily Observation,
that the *Sons of Ministers*, though betaking themselves to other Imploy-
40 ments, do ordinarily carry about with them an Holy and Happy Savour
of their *Ministerial Education.* 'Twas remarkably Exemplified in our
Theophilus Eaton, who was Born at *Stony-Stratford* in *Oxfordshire*,[1] the
Eldest Son to the Faithful and Famous *Minister* of the place.[2] But the
Words of Old used by *Philostratus*[3] concerning the Son of a Great Man,
45 *As for his Son I have nothing else to say, but that he was his Son*; they could not
be used concerning our *Theophilus*, who having received a good Education
from his *Pious Parents*, did live many Years to Answer that Education in
his own *Piety* and *Usefulness.*

§. 3. His Father being removed unto *Coventry*, he there at School fell
50 into the Intimate Acquaintance of that Worthy *John Davenport*, with
whom the Providence of God many Years after united him in the great
Undertaking of settling a Colony of Christian and Reformed Churches
on the *American Strand.* Here his Ingenuity and Proficiency render'd him
notable; and so vast was his *Memory*, that although he wrote not at the
55 Church, yet when he came home, he would, at his Father's Call, *repeat*
unto those that met in his Father's House, the *Sermons* which had been
publickly Preached by others, as well as his own Father, with such exactness, as astonished all the Neighbourhood. But in their after Improvements,[1] the *Hands* of Divine Providence were laid *across* upon the Heads
60 of *Theophilus Eaton* and *John Davenport*; for *Davenport*, whose Father was
the *Mayor* of *Coventry*, became a *Minister*; and *Eaton*, whose Father was
Minister of *Coventry*, contrary to his Intentions, became a *Merchant.* His
Parents were very loth to have complied with his Inclinations; but their
Compliance therewithal did at last appear to have been directed by a
65 special Favour of Heaven unto the Family, when after the Death of his
Father, he, by this means, became the *Joseph*, by whom his *Mother* was

---

[1] Stony Stratford is in Buckinghamshire, not Oxfordshire.
[2] Richard Eaton, curate of Stony Stratford; subsequently (1591) vicar of Trinity Church,
Coventry, and later of Great Budworth, in Cheshire.
[3] Philostratus "the Athenian" (*c.*170–245), a Greek sophist of the Roman imperial period.*

---

[1] That is, employments.

maintained until she died, and his Orphan *Brethren* and *Sisters* had no small part of their Subsistence.

§. 4. During the time of his hard Apprenticeship he *behaved himself*
70 *wisely*; and his *Wisdom*, with God's *Favour*, particularly appeared in his chaste Escape from the *Snares* of a Young Woman in the House where he lived, who would fain have taken him in the *Pits* by the *Wise Man* cautioned against, and who was herself so taken *only* with his most Comely Person, that she dy'd for the *Love* of him, when she saw him gone
75 too far to be obtained: Whereas, by the like *Snares*, the Apprentice that next succeeded him was undone for ever. But being a Person herewithal most signally *Diligent in his Business*, it was not long before the *Maxim* of the *Wise Man* was most literally accomplished in his coming to *Stand before Princes*; for being made a *Freeman* of *London*, he applied himself unto
80 the *East-Country* Trade, and was publickly chosen the *Deputy-Governour* of the Company, wherein he so acquitted himself as to become considerable. And afterwards going himself into the *East-Country*, he not only became so well Acquainted with the Affairs of the *Baltick-Sea*, but also became so well Improved in the Accomplishments of a *Man of Business*, that the
85 King of *England*[1] imploy'd him as an *Agent* unto the King of *Denmark*. The Concerns of his *Agency* he so discreetly managed, that as he much obliged and engaged the *East-Land* Company, (who in Token thereof presented his Wife with a Bason and Ewer double gilt, and curiously wrought with Gold, and weighing above Sixty Pound,) so he found much
90 Acceptance with the King of *Denmark*, and was afterwards used by that Prince to do him no little Services. Nevertheless he kept his Integrity amongst the Temptations of that Court, whereat he was now a *Resident*; and not seldom had he most Eminent Cause to acknowledge the *Benignity* and *Interposal* of Heaven for his Preservations; once particularly, when
95 the King of *Denmark* was beginning the King of *England's* Health, while Mr. *Eaton*, who disliked such *Health-Drinking*, was in his Presence; the King fell down in a sort of a Fit, with the Cup in his Hand, whereat all the Nobles and Courtiers wholly applied themselves to convey the King
99 into his Chamber, and there was no notice taken who was to Pledge his Health; whereby Mr. *Eaton* was the more easily deliver'd from any share in the Debauch.

§. 5. Having arrived unto a fair Estate, (which he was *first* willing to do, he Married a most Virtuous Gentlewoman, to whom he had first
5 Espoused himself after he had spent Three Years in an Absence from her in the *East-Country*. But this dearest and greatest of his *Temporal* Enjoyments proved but a *Temporal* one; for living no longer with him than to render him the Father of Two Children, she almost *killed him* with her

---

[1] Charles I.

own *Death*;[1] and yet at her Death she expressed herself wondrous willing
10 *to be Dissolved, and to be with Christ, from whom* (she said) *I would not be
detained one Hour for all the Enjoyments upon Earth.* He afterwards Married
a Prudent and Pious Widow, the Daughter of the Bishop of *Chester*;[2]
unto the Three former *Children* of which Widow, he became a most
Exemplary, Loving and Faithful *Father*, as well as a most Worthy *Husband*
15 unto herself, by whom *he* afterwards had *Five* Children, *Two* Sons and
Three Daughters. But the Second of his Children by his latter Wife
dying some while before, it was not long before his Two Children by his
former Wife were smitten with the *Plague*, whereof the Elder died,[3] and
his House thereupon shut up with a, *Lord have Mercy!* However the *Lord*
20 had this *Mercy* on the Family, to let the Distemper spread no further;
and so Mr. *Eaton* spent many Years a Merchant of great Credit and
Fashion in the City of *London*.

§. 6. At length Conformity to *Ceremonies* Humanely Invented and
Imposed in the Worship of God, was urged in the Church of *England*
25 with so much Rigour, that Mr. *Davenport* was thereby driven to seek *a
Refuge from the Storm* in the Cold and Rude Corners of *America*. Mr. *Eaton*
had already assisted the New *Massachuset-Colony*, as being one of the
Patentees for it; but had no purpose of removing thither himself, until
Mr. *Davenport*, under whose Excellent Ministry he lived, was compelled
30 unto a share in this Removal. However, being fully satisfied in his own
Conscience, that *Unlawful things* were now violently demanded of him,
he was willing to accompany his *Persecuted Pastor* in the Retreat from
Violence now Endeavoured, and many Eminent *Londoners* chearfully
engaged with him in this Undertaking. Unto *New-England* this Company
35 of good Men came in the Year 1637. where chusing to be a distinct Colony
by themselves, more Accommodated unto the Designs of *Merchandize*
than of *Husbandry*, they sought and bought a large Territory in the *Southern* Parts of the Country for their Habitations. In the Prosecution hereof,
the chief Care was devolved upon Mr. *Eaton*, who with an Unexempled
40 Patience took many tedious and hazardous Journies through a Desolate
Wilderness full of Barbarous *Indians*, until upon Mature Deliberation he
pitched upon a place now called *New-Haven*, where they soon formed a
very regular Town; and a number of other Towns along the Sea side were
quickly added thereunto. But by the Difficulties attending these Journies,
45 Mr. *Eaton* brought himself into an extream Sickness; from which he
recovered not without a *Fistula* in his Breast, whereby he underwent

13 which/whic   14 Loving/Living C.M.

[1] Name unknown; she apparently died in 1617.
[2] His second wife, Anne Yale, was the widow of Thomas Yale (d. 1619), by whom she had
three children: David (1613–1690), Anne (1615–1698), and Thomas (1618–1683). Her father
was Bishop George Lloyd (1560–1615).*
[3] In 1625.

much Affliction. When the *Chirurgeon* came to Inspect the Sore, he told him, *Sir, I know not how to go about what is necessary for your Cure*; but Mr. *Eaton* answered him, *God calls you to do, and me to suffer!* And God accord-
50 ingly strengthened him to bear miserable Cuttings and Launcings of his Flesh with a most Invincible Patience. The *Chirurgeon* indeed *made* so many Wounds, that he was not able to *Cure* what he had made; another, and a better, Hand was necessarily imployed for it; but in the mean while great were the *Trials* with which the God of Heaven exercised the
55 Faith of this his Holy Servant.

§. 7. Mr. *Eaton* and Mr. *Davenport* were the *Moses* and *Aaron* of the Christian Colony now Erected in the South-West Parts of *New-England*; and Mr. *Eaton* being *yearly* and *ever* chosen their Governour, it was the Admiration of all Spectators to behold the *Discretion*, the *Gravity*, the
60 *Equity* with which he still managed all their Publick Affairs. He carried in his very Countenance a *Majesty* which cannot be described; and in his Dispensations of *Justice* he was a *Mirrour* for the most Imitable *Impartiality*, but Ungainsayable *Authority* of his Proceedings, being awfully sensible of the Obligations which the *Oath* of a *Judge* lays upon him.
65 *Ils sont plus tenus de raison de garder Leur Serment, que doubter mort, ou aucune forfeiture:*[1] And hence he, who would most patiently bear *hard things* offered unto his *Person* in *private* Cases, yet would never pass by any *Publick* Affronts, or Neglects offered when he appeared under the Character of a *Magistrate*. But he still was the Guide of the *Blind*, the Staff of the
70 *Lame*, the Helper of the *Widow* and the *Orphan*, and all the Distressed; none that had a *Good Cause* was afraid of coming before him: On the one side, *In his Days did the Righteous flourish*; on the other side, *He was the Terror of Evil Doers.* As in his Government of the *Commonwealth*, so in the Government of his *Family*,[2] he was Prudent, Serious, Happy to a
75 Wonder; and albeit he sometimes had a large *Family*, consisting of no less than *Thirty Persons*, yet he managed them with such an *Even Temper*, that Observers have affirmed, *They never saw an House ordered with more Wisdom!* He kept an Honourable and Hospitable *Table*; but one thing that still made the Entertainment thereof the better, was the continual
80 Presence of his Aged *Mother*, by feeding of whom with an Exemplary *Piety* till *she died*, he ensured his own *Prosperity* as long as *he lived*. His *Children* and *Servants* he would mightily Encourage unto the Study of the *Scriptures*, and Countenance their Addresses unto himself with any of their *Enquiries*; but when he discerned any of them sinfully negligent
85 about the Concerns either of their General or Particular *Callings*, he would admonish them with such a Penetrating Efficacy, that they could

65 *que doubter/doubter*   *aucune/aucutie*

[1] "They are more bound to keep their oath than to fear death or any forfeiture."
[2] In the sense of household.

scarce forbear falling down at his Feet with *Tears*. A *Word* of his was enough to steer them!

§. 8. So *Exemplary* was he for a *Christian*, that one who had been a 90 *Servant* unto him, could many Years after say, *Whatever Difficulty in my daily Walk I now meet withal, still something that I either saw or heard in my Blessed Master* Eaton's *Conversation, helps me through it all; I have Reason to bless God that ever I knew him!* It was his Custom when he first rose in a *Morning,* to repair unto his *Study*; a Study well Perfumed with the *Meditations* and 95 *Supplications* of an Holy Soul. After this, calling his *Family* together, he would then read a Portion of the *Scripture* among them, and after some Devout and Useful *Reflections* upon it, he would make a Prayer not long, but Extraordinary Pertinent and Reverent; and in the *Evening* some of 99 the same Exercises were again attended. On the *Saturday* Morning he would still[1] take notice of the Approaching *Sabbath* in his *Prayer*, and ask the Grace to be *Remembring* of it, and *Preparing* for it; and when the Evening arrived, he, besides this, not only *Repeated* a Sermon, but also *Instructed* his People, with putting of *Questions* referring to the Points of 5 Religion, which would oblige them to Study for an *Answer*; and if their Answer were at any time insufficient, he would wisely and gently Enlighten their Understandings; all which he concluded with *Singing of a Psalm*. When the *Lord's Day* came, he called his *Family* together at the time for the Ringing of the First Bell, and *repeated* a Sermon, whereunto 10 he added a Fervent *Prayer*, especially tending unto the Sanctification of the *Day*. At *Noon* he sang a *Psalm*, and at *Night* he retired an Hour into his *Closet*; advising those in his House to improve the same time for the good of their own Souls. He then called his *Family* together again, and in an obliging manner conferred with them about the things with which 15 they had been Entertained in the House of God, shutting up all with a *Prayer* for the Blessing of God upon them all. For Solemn Days of *Humiliation*, or of *Thanksgiving*, he took the same Course, and Endeavoured still to make those that belonged unto him, understand the meaning of the Services before them. He seldom used any *Recreations*, but being a great 20 *Reader*, all the time he could spare from Company and Business, he commonly spent in his Beloved *Study*; so that he merited the Name which was once given to a *Learned Ruler* of the *English Nation*, the Name of *Beauclerk*:[2] In Conversing with his Friends, he was Affable, Courteous, and generally *Pleasant*, but *Grave* perpetually; and so Cautelous[3] and 25 Circumspect in his Discourses, and so Modest in his Expressions, that it became a Proverb for Incontestable Truth, *Governour* Eaton *said it.*

But after all, his *Humility* appeared in his having always but *Low*

---

[1] Always, invariably.
[2] Henry I.*
[3] Cautious, heedful.

Expectations, looking for little Regard and Reward from any Men, after
he had merited as highly as was possible by his *Universal Serviceableness.*

30 §. 9. His Eldest Son he maintained at the *Colledge* until he proceeded
Master of Arts; and he was indeed the Son of his *Vows,* and a Son of great
Hopes.[1] But a severe *Catarrh* diverted this Young Gentleman from the Work
of the Ministry whereto his Father had once devoted him; and a Malignant Fever then raging in those Parts of the Country, carried off him

35 with his Wife within Two or Three Days of one another. This was counted
the sorest of all the Trials that ever befel his *Father* in the *Days of the Years
of his Pilgrimage;* but he bore it with a Patience and Composure of Spirit
which was truly admirable. His dying Son look'd earnestly on him, and
said, *Sir, What shall we do!* Whereto, with a well-ordered Countenance, he

40 replied, *Look up to God!* And when he passed by his Daughter drowned in
Tears on this Occasion, to her he said, *Remember the Sixth Commandment,
Hurt not your self with Immoderate Grief; Remember* Job, *who said,* The Lord
hath given, and the Lord hath taken away, Blessed be the Name of the
Lord! *You may mark what a Note the Spirit of God put upon it;* in all this *Job*

45 sinned not, nor charged God foolishly: *God accounts it a charging of him
foolishly when we don't submit unto his Will patiently.* Accordingly he now
governed himself as one that had attained unto the Rule of *Weeping as
if he wept not;* for it being the *Lord's Day,* he repaired unto the Church in
the *Afternoon,* as he had been there in the *Forenoon,* though he was never

50 like to see his Dearest Son alive any more in this World. And though
before the First Prayer began, a Messenger came to prevent Mr. *Davenport's* praying for the *Sick* Person, who was now *Dead,* yet his Affectionate
Father alter'd not his Course, but *Wrote* after the Preacher[2] as formerly;
and when he came Home he held on his former Methods of Divine

55 Worship in his Family, not for the Excuse of *Aaron,* omitting any thing in
the Service of God. In like sort, when the People had been at the Solemn
Interment of this his Worthy Son, he did with a very Unpassionate Aspect
and Carriage then say, *Friends, I thank you all for your Love and Help, and
for this Testimony of Respect unto me and mine: The Lord hath given, and the*

60 *Lord hath taken; blessed be the Name of the Lord!* Nevertheless, retiring
hereupon into the Chamber where his Daughter then lay Sick, some Tears
were observed falling from him while he uttered these Words, *There is
a difference between a sullen Silence or a stupid Senslesness under the Hand of
God, and a Child-like Submission thereunto.*

65 §. 10. Thus continually he, for about a Score of Years, was the *Glory*

48 *he/we*

[1] Samuel Eaton (1630–1655), A.B. Harvard 1649; one of the five original Fellows of the
Harvard Corporation under the college charter of 1650. He moved to New Haven in 1653,
where he died.*

[2] Took notes on the sermon, a common practice. Many early notebooks kept in this way
have been preserved.*

and *Pillar* of *New-Haven* Colony. He would often say, *Some count it a great matter to* Die *well, but I am sure 'tis a great matter to* Live *well. All our Care should be while we have our* Life *to use it well, and so when Death puts an end unto* that, *it will put an end unto all our Cares.* But having Excellently man-
70 aged his *Care to Live Well,* God would have him to *Die well,* without any room or time then given to take any *Care* at all; for he enjoyed a Death *sudden* to every one but himself! Having Worshipped God with his Family after his usual manner, and upon some Occasion with much Solemnity charged all the Family to carry it well unto their Mistress
75 who was now confined by Sickness, he Supp'd, and then took a turn or two abroad for his Meditations. After that he came in to bid his Wife *Good-night,* before he left her with her *Watchers;* which when he did, she said, *Methinks you look sad!* Whereto he reply'd, *The Differences risen in the Church of* Hartford *make me so;* she then added, *Let us e'en go back to our*
80 *Native Country again;* to which he answered, *You may,* [and so she did] *but I shall Die here.*[1] This was the last Word that ever she heard him speak; for now retiring unto his Lodging in another Chamber, he was overheard about midnight fetching a *Groan;* and unto one, sent in presently to en-quire how he did, he answered the Enquiry with only saying, *Very Ill!*
85 And without saying any more, he fell *asleep in Jesus:* In the Year 1657. *loosing Anchor* from *New-Haven* for the better

> ——*Sedes, ubi Fata, Quietas*
> *Ostendunt.*[2]

Now let his *Gravestone* wear at least the following

90   **EPITAPH.**

NEW-ENGLAND's Glory, *full of* Warmth *and* Light,
Stole away (*and* said nothing) *in the Night.*

CHAP. X.

SUCCESSORS.

95 §. 1. **W**HEN the Day arrived in the *Anniversary Course* for the Freemen of the Colony to Elect another Governour in the place of the Deceased *Eaton,* Mr. *Davenport* Preached on that Passage of the Divine

---

86   better/better.

   [1] After her husband's death, Mrs. Eaton did return to England, with her son Theophilus and her daughter Hannah. Theophilus went to live in Dublin; Hannah married William Jones in 1659 and returned to New Haven.
   [2] "Habitation, where the Fates promise peace."*

Oracle, in *Josh.* 1. 1, 2. *Now after the Death of* Moses, *the Servant of the Lord,*
99 *it came to pass that the Lord spake unto* Joshua, *the Son of* Nun, Moses *Minister,*
saying, Now arise thou and all this People. The Colony was abundantly
sensible that their **Eaton** had been a Man of a *Mosaic* Spirit; and that
while they chose him, as they did every Year of his Life among them to be
their Governour, they could not chuse a better. But they now considered
5 that Mr. *Francis Newman,*[1] who had been for many Years the Secretary
of the Colony, was there a *Minister* to their *Moses,* as he had been otherwise his intimate Friend, Neighbour, Companion and Counsellor. For
this Cause the Unanimous *Choice* of the Freemen fell upon this Gentleman
to succeed in the Government. And I shall have given a sufficient History
10 of his Government; which *through Death was not suffered to continue* above
Three or Four Years, by only saying, *That he walk'd exactly in the Steps*
of his Predecessor.

§. 2. Upon the setting of Mr. *Francis Newman,* there arose Mr. *William*
Leet,[1] of whom let not the Reader be displeased at this brief Account.
15 This Gentleman was by his *Education* a *Lawyer,* and by his Imployment a
Register[2] in the *Bishop's Court.* In that Station, at *Cambridge,* he observed
that there were Summoned before the Court certain Persons to answer
for the *Crime* of going to *hear Sermons abroad,* when there were *none* to be
heard in their own Parish Churches at home; and that when any were
20 brought before them for *Fornication* or *Adultery,* the Court only made
themselves merry with their *Peccadillo's;* and that these latter Transgressors were as favourably dealt withal, as ever the *Wolf* was when he
came with an *Auricular Confession* of his Murders to his Brother *Fox* for
Absolution; but the former found as hard measure as ever the poor *Ass,*
25 that had only taken a *Straw* by mistake out of a Pilgrim's Pad, and yet
upon *Confession,* was by Chancellour *Fox* pronounced *Unpardonable.* This
Observation extreamly scandalized Mr. *Leet,* who always thought, that
Hearing a good Sermon had been a lesser Fault than *Lying with one's Neighbour's*
Wife: And had the same Resentments[3] that *Austin* sometimes had of the
30 Iniquity which made *the Transgression of a Ceremony more severely repre-*
hended than a Transgression of the Law of God; but it made an Everlasting
Impression upon his Heart, when the Judge of the Court furiously de-
manded of one then to be censured, *How he durst be so bold as to break the*
Laws of the Church, in going from his own Parish to hear Sermons abroad? And
35 the Honest Man answered, *Sir, How should I get Faith else? For the Apostle*
saith, Faith comes by Hearing the Word Preached; which Faith is necessary to
Salvation; and Hearing the Word is the Means appointed by God for the obtaining

---

[1] Governor 1658–1661.

[1] Governor of New Haven Colony 1661–1664; governor of Connecticut 1676–1683.

[2] That is, registrar.

[3] Feelings, emotions.

and encreasing of it: And these Means I must use, whatever I suffer for it in this World. These Words of that Honest Man were Blessed by God with such
40 an Effect upon the Mind of Mr. *Leet,* that he presently left his *Office* in the Bishop's Court, and forsaking that *Untoward Generation* of Men, he associated himself with such as would go *Hear the Word, that they might get Faith;* and in *Hearing* he did happily get the *Like precious Faith.* On this, and *for* this, he was exposed unto the *Persecution,* which caused him to
45 retire into *New-England* with many Worthy Ministers and other Christians in the Year 1639. In that Country he settled himself under the Ministry of the Excellent Mr. *Whitfield*[4] at *Gilford,* where being also chosen a *Magistrate,* and then *Governour* of the *Colony;* and being so at the Juncture of time, when the *Royal Charter* did join *Connecticut* and *New-Haven,* he
50 became next unto Governour *Winthrop,* the *Deputy-Governour* of the whole; and after the Death of Mr. *Winthrop,* even until his own Death, the *Annual Election* for about a *Decad* of Years together still made him *Governour.* But in his whole Government he gave continual Demonstrations of an *Excellent Spirit,* especially in that part of it where the *Reconciliation*
55 and the *Coalition* of the Spirits of the People under it was to be accomplished. Mr. *Robert Treat*[5] is the Follower of his *Example,* as well as the Successor in his *Government.*

CHAP. XI.

Hermes Christianus.[1] *The LIFE of* JOHN WINTHROP, *Esq; Governour*
60 *of* CONNECTICUT *and* NEW-HAVEN *United.*

—*Et Nos aliquod Nomenq; Decusq; Gessimus.*—[2]

§. 1. IF the Historian could give that Character of the best *Roman Emperor,* that he was *Bonus a Bono, Pius a Pio,*[3] the *Son* of a *Father* like himself, our History may affirm concerning a very good
65 *New-English Governour* also, that he was the *Father* of a *Son* like himself. The Proverb of the *Jews* which doth observe, *That Vinegar is the Son of Wine;* and the Proverb of the *Greeks,* which doth observe, *That the Sons of Heroes are Trespassers,* has been more than once contradicted in the happy Experience of the *New-Englanders:* But none of the least remarkable

---

[4] Henry Whitfield (1597–*c.*1657).*
[5] Governor 1683–1687, 1689–1698.*

---

[1] "A Christian Hermes."*
[2] "We, too, bore some name and renown."*
[3] "A good son of a good father, and a pious son of a pious father."*

70 Contradictions given to it has been in the Honourable Family of our
𝔚𝔦𝔫𝔱𝔥𝔯𝔬𝔭𝔰.

§. 2. The Eldest Son of 𝔍𝔬𝔥𝔫 𝔚𝔦𝔫𝔱𝔥𝔯𝔬𝔭, Esq; the Governour of one
Colony, was 𝔍𝔬𝔥𝔫 𝔚𝔦𝔫𝔱𝔥𝔯𝔬𝔭, Esq; the Governour of another, in, therefore
happy, *New-England*, born *Feb.* 12. 1605. at *Groton* in *England*. His *Glad*
75 *Father* bestowed on him a liberal Education at the University, first of
Cambridge[1] in *England*, and then of *Dublin* in *Ireland*; and because *Travel*
has been esteemed no little Accomplisher of a *Young Gentleman*, he then
Accomplished himself by Travelling into *France, Holland, Flanders, Italy,*
Germany, and as far as *Turky* it self; in which places he so improved his
80 Opportunity of Conversing with all sorts of Learned Men, that he returned home equally a Subject of much *Experience*, and of great *Expectation*.

§. 3. The Son of *Scipio Africanus* proving a degenerate Person, the
People forced him to pluck off a Signet-Ring, which he wore with his
Father's Face engraven on it. But the Son of our Celebrated Governour
85 *Winthrop*, was on the other side so like unto his Excellent Father for early
Wisdom and Virtue, that arriving at *New-England* with his Father's
Family, *Nov.* 4. 1631. he was, though not above Twenty Three Years of
Age,[1] by the Unanimous Choice of the People, chosen a *Magistrate* of
the Colony, whereof his Father was the *Governour.* For this Colony he
90 afterwards did many Services, yea, and he did them *Abroad* as well as
at Home; very particularly in the Year 1634. when returning for *England,*
he was by bad Weather forced into *Ireland*, where being invited unto the
House of Sir *John Clotworthy*,[2] he met with many Considerable Persons,
by conferring with whom, the Affairs of *New-England* were not a little
95 promoted; but it was another *Colony* for which the Providence of Heaven
intended him to be such another *Father*, as his own Honourable *Father*
had been to *this.*

§. 4. In the Year 1635. Mr. *Winthrop* returned unto *New-England,*
99 with Powers from the Lord *Say* and the Lord *Brook*, to settle a Plantation
upon the *Long River* of *Connecticut*,[1] and a Commission to be himself the
Governour of that Plantation. But inasmuch as many good People of the
Massachuset-Colony had just before this taken Possession of Land for a
New-Colony thereabouts,[2] this Courteous and Peaceable Gentleman gave
5 them no Molestation; but having wisely Accommodated the Matter

[1] An error. Although his brother Forth studied at Cambridge, there is no evidence that
John, Jr., did; he entered Trinity College, Dublin, at the age of sixtreen.

[1] Winthrop, Jr., was elected in 1632. Having been born February 12, 1605/6, he was
therefore "not above" twenty-six years of age.
[2] Sir John Clotworthy, first Viscount Massereene (d. 1665), defender of Irish Presbyterians,
opponent of Strafford, active in proceedings against Laud.*

[1] The Connecticut River.
[2] The Connecticut Colony at Hartford, under the leadership of Hopkins, Haynes, and
Thomas Hooker.

with them, he sent a convenient number of *Men,* with all Necessaries, to Erect a Fortification at the Mouth of the River, where a *Town,* with a *Fort,* is now distinguished by the Name of *Say-Brook;* by which happy Action, the *Planters* further up the River had no small Kindness done
10 unto them; and the *Indians,* which might else have been more Troublesome, were kept in Awe.

§. 5. The Self-denying Gentleman, who had imployed his *Commission* of *Governour* so little to the Disadvantage of the Infant-Colony at *Connecticut,* was himself, e're long, by *Election* made *Governour* of that Colony.[1]
15 And upon the *Restoration* of King *Charles* II. he willingly undertook another Voyage to *England,* on the behalf of the People under his Government, whose Affairs he managed with such a Successful Prudence, that he obtained a *Royal Charter* for them, which Incorporated the Colony of *New-Haven* with them, and Invested both Colonies, now happily United,
20 with a firm Grant of *Priviledges,* beyond those of the Plantations which had been settled before them. I have been informed, that while he was engaged in this Negotiation, being admitted unto a private Conference with the King, he presented His Majesty with a Ring, which King *Charles* I. had upon some Occasion given to his Grandfather; and the
25 King not only accepted his Present, but also declared, that he accounted it one of his *Richest Jewels;* which indeed was the Opinion that *New-England* had of the Hand that carried it. But having thus laid his Colony under Everlasting Obligations of Gratitude, they did, after his return to *New-England,* express of their Gratitude, by saying to him as the *Israelites*
30 did unto *Gideon, Rule thou over us, for thou hast delivered us;* chusing *him* for their *Governour* twice Seven Years together.[2]

§. 6. When the Governour of *Athens* was a *Philosopher,* namely *Demetrius,*[1] the Commonwealth so flourished, that no less than Three Hundred Brazen Statues were afterward by the Thankful People Erected
35 unto his Memory. And a *Blessed Land* was *New-England,* when there was over part of it a Governour, who was not only a *Christian* and a *Gentleman,* but also an Eminent *Philosopher;* for indeed the Government of the *State* is then most successfully managed, when the measures of it are, by a *Wise Observer,* taken from the Government of the *World;* and very un-
40 reasonable is the *Jewish* Proverb,

Ne Habites in urbe ubi caput urbis est Medicus.[2] But highly reasonable the Sentence of *Aristotle, Ubi præses fuerit Philosophus, ibi Civitas erit Fœlix;*[3] and this the rather for what is truly noted by *Thucydides, Magistratus est*

---

[1] In 1657.
[2] From 1659 until his death.

---

[1] Demetrius of Phaleron, "guardian" of Athens from 318 to 307 B.C.*
[2] "Dwell not in a city where the head of the city is a physician."*
[3] "Where the leader is a philosopher, there the state will be happy."*

Civitatis Medicus.[4] Such an one was our 𝔚intℌrop, whose Genius and
45 Faculty for *Experimental Philosophy*, was advanced in his *Travels* abroad,
by his Acquaintance with many Learned *Virtuosi*. One Effect of this
Disposition in him, was his being furnished with *Noble Medicines*, which
he most Charitably and Generously gave away upon all Occasions;
insomuch that where-ever he came, still the Diseased flocked about him,
50 as if the Healing Angel of *Bethesda* had appeared in the place; and so
many were the *Cures* which he wrought, and the *Lives* that he saved, that
if *Scanderbeg*[5] might boast of his having slain in his Time Two Thousand
Men with his own Hands, this Worthy Person might have made a far
more desirable *Boast* of his having in his Time *Healed* more than so many
55 Thousands; in which Beneficence to Mankind, there are of his Worthy
Children, who to this Day do follow his Direction and Example. But it
was not unto *New-England* alone that the Respects of this Accomplished
Philosopher were confined. For, whereas in pursuance of the Methods
begun by that Immortally Famous *Advancer of Learning*, the most Illus-
60 trious Lord Chancellor *Bacon*, a Select Company of Eminent Persons,
using to meet in the Lodgings of Dr. *Wilkins*[6] of *Wadham* Colledge in
Oxford, had laid the Foundation of a Celebrated *Society*, which by the
Year 1663. being Incorporated with a *Royal Charter*,[7] hath since been
among the Glories of *England*, yea, and of *Mankind*; and their Design was
65 to make Faithful Records of all the Works of *Nature* or of *Art*, which
might come under their Observation, and Correct what had been *False*,
Restore what should be *True*, Preserve what should be *Rare*, and Render
the Knowledge of the World, as well more *Perfect* as more *Useful*; and by
multiplied Experiments both of *Light* and *Fruit*,[8] advance the *Empire* of
70 Man over the whole visible Creation; it was the Honour of Mr. *Winthrop*
to be a Member of this *Royal Society*. And accordingly among the *Philosophical Transactions* Published by Mr. *Oldenburgh*,[9] there are some notable
Communications from this Inquisitive and Intelligent Person, whose
Insight into many Parts of the *Creation*, but especially of the *Mineral*
75 *Kingdom*,[10] was beyond what had been attained by the most in many
Parts of *America*.

4 "The magistrate is the physician of the state."

5 The real name of Scanderbeg (1403?–1468) was George Castriota. He was reared as a
Moslem in Turkey, with the Turkish name of Iskander Bey. He returned to his ancestral
Albania, and became a Christian; as a leader of his people, he repelled the Turks in historic
battles and became renowned as both an Albanian and a Christian hero.*

6 John Wilkins (1614–1672), Warden of Wadham 1648–1659, first secretary of the Royal
Society, Bishop of Chester from 1668.

7 The Royal Society of London for Improving Natural Knowledge was chartered in 1662.*

8 That is, both basic knowledge and the useful application of knowledge.

9 Henry Oldenburg (1616?–1677), second secretary of the Society and the first editor of
the *Transactions*.*

10 A reference to Winthrop's promotion of the mining and working of iron.*

§. 7. If one would therefore desire an exact Picture of this Worthy Man, the Description which the most Sober and Solid Writers of the Great *Philosophick Work* do give of those Persons, who alone are qualified
80 for the Smiles of Heaven upon their Enterprizes, would have exactly fitted him. He was a *Studious, Humble, Patient, Reserved* and *Mortified*[1] Person, and one in whom the Love of *God* was Fervent, the Love of *Man* sincere: And he had herewithal a certain *Extension of Soul*, which disposed him to a *Generous Behaviour* towards those, who by Learning,
85 Breeding and Virtue, deserve Respects, though of a Perswasion and Profession in Religion very different from *his own*; which was *that* of a Reformed *Protestant*, and a *New-English Puritan*. In sum, he was not more an *Adeptist* in those Noble and Secret *Medicines*, which would reach the *Roots* of the Distempers that annoy Humane Bodies, and procure an
90 *Universal Rest* unto the *Archæus*[2] on all Occasions of Disturbance, than he was in those *Christian Qualities*, which appear upon the Cure of the Distempers in the Minds of Men, by the Effectual *Grace* of our Lord Jesus Christ.

§. 8. In the Year 1643. after divers *Essays* made in some former Years,
95 the several Colonies of *New-England* became in *Fact*, as well as *Name*, 𝔘𝔫𝔦𝔱𝔢𝔡 𝔆𝔬𝔩𝔬𝔫𝔦𝔢𝔰. And an Instrument was formed, wherein having declared, *That we all came into these parts of* America *with the same End and Aim, namely, to advance the Glory of our Lord Jesus Christ, and enjoy the Liberties*
99 *of the Gospel with Purity and Peace*, it was firmly agreed between the several Jurisdictions, that there should yearly be chosen *Two Commissioners* out of each, who should meet at fit Places appointed for that purpose, with full Powers from the *General Courts* in each, to Concert and Conclude Matters of General Concernment for *Peace* or *War* of the several Colonies
5 thus *Confederated*. In pursuance of this Laudable *Confederacy*, this most Meritorious *Governour* of *Connecticut* Colony accepted the Trouble of appearing as a *Commissioner* for that Colony, with the rest met at *Boston*, in the Year 1676. when the Calamities of the *Indian-War*[1] were distressing the whole Country: But *here* falling Sick of a Fever, he dy'd on *April* 5.
10 of that Year, and was Honourably Interred in the same Tomb with his Honourable Father.

§. 9. His Father, as long ago as the Year 1643. had seen Cause to Write unto him an Excellent Letter, wherein there were these among other Passages.

88 *Adeptist/Adoptist* C.M.

[1] That is, dead to sin or to the world; having the appetites and passions in subjection.
[2] In Greek, ἀρχᾶιος, an old medical term for the essential vital principle of the body.

[1] King Philip's War.

15 'You are the Chief of *Two* Families; I had by your Mother *Three*
'*Sons* and *Three Daughters*, and I had with her a *Large Portion* of outward
'Estate. These now are all *gone*; Mother *gone*; Brethren and Sisters *gone*;
'you only are left to see the Vanity of these *Temporal things*, and learn
'*Wisdom* thereby, which may be of more use to you, through the Lord's
20 'Blessing, than all that *Inheritance* which might have befallen you; And
'for which this may stay and quiet your Heart, *That God is able to give*
'*you more than this*; and that it being spent in the furtherance of *his Work*,
'which hath here prospered so well, through his Power hitherto, you and
'yours may *certainly expect a liberal Portion in the Prosperity and Blessing thereof*
25 '*hereafter*; and the rather, because it was not *forced* from you by a Father's
'Power, but freely *resigned* by your self, out of a Loving and Filial Respect
'unto me, and your own readiness unto the Work it self. From whence,
'as I do often take Occasion to Bless the Lord for you, so do I also Com-
'mend you and yours to his *Fatherly Blessing*, for a plentiful Reward to be
30 'rendred unto you. And doubt not, my Dear Son, but let your *Faith* be
'built upon his Promise and Faithfulness, that as he hath carried you
'hitherto through many Perils, and provided liberally for you, so he will
'do for the time to come, and will *never fail you, nor forsake you.*——*My Son,*
'the *Lord knows* how Dear thou art to me, and that my Care has been more
35 'for thee than for my self. But *I know* thy Prosperity depends not on my
'Care, nor on *thine own*, but upon the Blessing of our *Heavenly Father*;
'neither doth it on the things of this World, but on the *Light of God's*
'*Countenance*, through the Merit and Mediation of our Lord Jesus Christ.
'It is *that* only which can give us *Peace of Conscience* with *Contentation*;[1]
40 'which can as well make our Lives Happy and Comfortable in a *mean*
'Estate, as in a *great* Abundance. But if you weigh things aright, and sum
'up all the Turnings of Divine Providence together, you shall find great
'Advantage.—The Lord hath brought us to a *Good Land*; a Land, where
'we enjoy outward *Peace* and *Liberty*, and above all, the *Blessings of the*
45 '*Gospel*, without the Burden of *Impositions* in Matters of *Religion*. Many
'Thousands there are who would give *Great Estates* to enjoy our Condition.
'Labour therefore, my good Son, to increase our *Thankfulness* to God for
'all his Mercies to thee, especially for that he hath revealed his *Ever-*
'*lasting Good-will* to thee in Jesus Christ, and joined thee to the visible
50 'Body of his *Church*, in the Fellowship of his People, and hath saved thee
'in all thy *Travails* abroad, from being Infected with the *Vices* of these
'Countries where thou hast been, (a Mercy vouchsafed but unto few
'Young Gentlemen *Travellers*.) Let *him* have the Honour of it who kept

26 Loving/Living C.M.

[1] In the obsolete sense of "satisfied condition," "the fact of being satisfied."

'thee. *He* it was who gave thee Favour in the Eyes of all with whom thou
55 'hadst to do, both by Sea and Land; *He* it was who saved thee in all
'Perils; and *He* it is who hath given thee a Gift in Understanding and
'Art; and he it is who hath provided thee a Blessing in Marriage, a
'Comfortable Help, and many Sweet Children; and hath hitherto pro-
'vided liberally for you all: And therefore I would have you to *Love*
60 'him again, and *Serve* him, and *Trust* him for the time to come. Love and
'Prize that *Word of Truth*, which only makes known to you the Precious
'and Eternal Thoughts and Councils of the *Light Inaccessible*. Deny your
'*own Wisdom*, that you may find his; and esteem it the greatest Honour
'to lye under the Simplicity of the Gospel of *Christ Crucified*, without which
65 'you can never enter into the *Secrets of his Tabernacle*, nor enjoy those
'sweet things which *Eye hath not seen, nor Ear heard, nor can the Heart of*
'*Man conceive*; but God hath granted unto some few to know them even
'in this Life. Study well, my Son, the saying of the Apostle, *Knowledge*
'*puffeth up*. It is a *good Gift* of God, but when it lifts up the Mind above the
70 '*Cross of Christ*, it is the *Pride of Life*, and the High-way to *Apostacy*, where-
'in many Men of great Learning and Hopes have perished.—In all the
'Exercise of your *Gifts*, and Improvement of your *Talents*, have an Eye
'to your *Master's End*, more than your *own*; and to the *Day of your Account*,
'that you may then have your *Quietus est*,[2] even, *Well done, Good and Faith-*
75 '*ful Servant!* But my last and chief Request to you, is, that you be careful
'to have your *Children* brought up in the Knowledge and Fear of God, and
'in the Faith of our Lord Jesus Christ. *This* will give you the best *Comfort*
'of them, and keep them sure from any *Want* or *Miscarriage:* And when
'you part from them, it will be no small joy to your Soul, that you *shall*
80 '*meet them again in Heaven!*

Doubtless, the Reader considers the *Historical* Passages in this Extract
of the Letter thus Recited. Now, but by making this Reflection upon the
Rest, that as the *Prophetical Part* of it was notably fulfilled in the Estate,
whereto the good Providence of God Recovered this Worthy Gentleman
85 and his Family, so the *Monitory Part* of it was most Exemplarily attended
in his Holy and Useful Conversation. I shall therein briefly sum up the
Life of a Person whom we shall call a *Second* unto none of our *Worthies*,
but as we call him our *Second Winthrop*.

EPITAPHIUM.

90   Abi Viator;
Et Luge plures Magistratus in Uno periisse.
                    Redi Viator.

[2] "He is quit."

95
Non Periit, *sed ad Cælestem Societatem*
Regia Magis Regiam,
Vere Adeptus,
Abiit:
WINTHROPUS, *Non minor magnis Majoribus.*[3]

CHAP. XII.

99
ASSISTANTS.

MAGISTRATES[1] of *Connecticut*-Colony, before *New-Haven* Colony was
actually annexed unto it, were, (besides the two Alternately, for
the most Part, Elected Governours, *HOPKINS*, and *HAINS*.)[2]

Roger Ludlow,	1636	John Cullick,	1648
5 John Steel,	1636	Henry Clark,	1650
William Phelps,	1636	John Winthrop,	1651
William Westwood,	1636	Thomas Topping,	1651
Andrew Ward,	1636	John Talcot,	1654
Thomas Wells,	1637	John Ogden,	1656
10 William Swayn,	1637	Nathan Gold,	1657
Matthew Mitchel,	1637	Matthew Allyn,	1658
George Hull,	1637	Richard Treat,	1658
William Whiting,	1637	Thomas Baker,	1658
John Mason,	1637	[John] Mulford,	1658
15 George Willis,	1639	Alexander Knowles,	1658
John Webster,	1639	John Wells,	1658
William Ludlow,	1640	Robert Bond,	1659
William Hopkins,	1642	[Thurston] Rayner,	1661
Henry Woolcot,	1643	John Allyn,	1662
20 George Fenwick,	1644	Daniel Clark,	1662
[John] Cosmore,	1647	Samuel Sherman,	1662
John Howel,	1647	John Young,	1664

17 *Bond/Band*

---

[3] "Epitaph. Go, wayfarer, and bewail many magistrates who have died in this one. Return, traveler. He has not died, but, one who has truly Succeeded, has gone to a heavenly society more royal than the Royal Society: Winthrop, not inferior to the great elders of his name."*

---

[1] Before the union of Connecticut and New Haven, the term "Magistrates" was applied to the officers called "Assistants" in Massachusetts and Plymouth.

[2] The first six names are from the list of commissioners appointed by the General Court of Massachusetts on March 3, 1636, to administer justice in the settlement then forming on the Connecticut River. Forenames in brackets are supplied from Savage's *Genealogical Dictionary* and from the *Public Records of the Colony of Connecticut* (15 vols., Hartford, 1850–1858).*

MAGISTRATES of *New-Haven* Colony, before *Connecticut*-Colony could
accomplish its Coalition therewith, were, (besides the Governours else-
25 where mentioned) [3]

Stephen Goodyear,[4]	1637	*[John] Astwood,*	1653
Thomas Grigson,[5]	1637	*Samuel Eaton,*	1654
Richard Malbon,[6]	1637	*Benjamin Fen,*	1654
William Leet,	1637	*Matthew Gilbert,*	1658
30 *John Desborough,*[7]	1637	*Jasper Crane,*	1658
[Edmund] Tapp,[8]	1637	*Robert Treat,*	1659
William Fowler,[9]	1637	*William Jones,*[11]	1662
Francis Newman,[10]	1653		

MAGISTRATES after the Two Colonies were content, according to
35 their Charter, to become ONE, were,[12]

John Winthrop, Gov.	1665	*John Talcot,*	1665
John Mason,	1665	*Henry Woolcot,*	1665
Matthew Allyn,[13]	1665	*John Allyn,*	1665
Samuel Willys,	1665	*Samuel Sherman,*	1665
40 *Nathan Gold,*	1665	*James Richards,*	1665

23 MAGISTRATES/MAGISTATES

[3] Mather should probably be partially exonerated for the errors and incompleteness of
his New Haven data since the organization and administration of the colony developed in
ways that differed from the settlements with which he was familiar. Records were often frag-
mentary or scattered among town records, even in some cases lost. He should, however,
have been easily able to ascertain that 1638 and not 1637 was the year of the New Haven
settlement.

For the first year the plantation operated under a business agreement, probably made in
England, and a Plantation Covenant. Then in October 1639 a permanent government was
instituted, with the magistrate (Theophilus Eaton) and four deputies operating as a court.
Within the next few years, six settlements were established which in 1643 were consolidated
into the New Haven Colony. This jurisdiction was governed by a General Court to which
the towns sent deputies, and in which justice was administered by a court of magistrates,
one from each town. New Haven dominated the colony, of which Eaton was the first governor.

Under these circumstances, Mather's difficulty in establishing a list of magistrates equivalent
to those of other colonies is understandable. Forenames in brackets are supplied from Savage,
*Genealogical Dictionary.**

[4] One of the wealthiest merchants joined with Eaton in the settlement of New Haven in
1638. His wife was lost on the "phantom" ship in 1646.*

[5] Arrived New Haven 1638; lost on "phantom" ship.*

[6] Arrived New Haven 1638; one of the leading merchants.*

[7] Samuel (not John) Desborough arrived in New Haven in 1639.*

[8] Settled in Milford in 1639.*

[9] Settled in Milford in 1639.*

[10] For Newman, see above p. 261, ll. 5, 13.

[11] The husband of Hannah Eaton, arrived in Boston in July 1660, soon thereafter removed
to New Haven.*

[12] On January 5, 1665, New Haven formally submitted to the union with Connecticut.*

[13] Matthew Allyn's name does not appear in the list of those chosen at the annual election
held May 11, 1665, but his name is included in the list of magistrates present at a meeting of the
Connecticut Court October 12, 1665.*

William Leet,	1665	Thomas Topping,	1674
William Jones,	1665	Matthew Gilbert,	1677
Benjamin Fen,	1665	Andrew Leet,	1678
Jasper Crane,	1665	John Wadsworth,	1679
45 Daniel Clark,[14]	1666	Robert Chapman,[16]	1681
Alexander Bryant,[15]	1668	James Fitch,	1681
James Bishop,	1668	Samuel Mason,	1683
Anthony Howkins,	1668	Benjamin Newberry,[17]	1685
Thomas Wells,	1668	Samuel Talcot,	1685
50 John Nash,	1672	Giles Hamlin,[18]	1685
Robert Treat,	1673		

While the Colonies were Clusters of *Rich Grapes*, which had a *Blessing* in them, such *Leaves* as these (which is in the *Proverbs* of the Jewish Nation, a Name for *Magistrates*) happily defended them from the *Storms* 55 that molest the World.

Those of the least Character[19] among them, yet came up to what the *Roman* Commonwealth required in their *Magistrates*.

Populus Romanus delegit Magistratus, quasi Reipublicæ Villicos, in quibus, si qua præterea est Ars, facile patitur; sin minus, virtute eorum & Innocentia Contentus 60 *est.* Cic. Orat. Pro Plan.[20]

46   Bryant/Bryans   53   them, such/them. Such

[14] Daniel Clark was named secretary in 1665; he did not become a magistrate until 1667.*
[15] Bryant was first elected in 1667.*
[16] Chapman was earlier elected in 1669 as well as in 1681.*
[17] Newberry (or Newbury) had also been elected in 1666 and 1667.*
[18] Hamlin had also been elected in 1667.*
[19] That is, status, rank, position.
[20] "This is how the Roman people selects its magistrates. For they are, as it were, stewards of the Republic. If in addition to the necessary moral qualities, they are experts in any direction, the people is well pleased, if not, then uprightness and integrity are quite enough for it."*

THE Author of the following Narrative,[1] is a Person of such well known Integrity, Prudence and Veracity, that there is not any cause to Question the Truth of what he here Relates. And moreover, this Writing of his is adorned with a very grateful Variety of Learning, and doth contain
65 such surprizing workings of Providence, as do well deserve due Notice and Observation. On all which accounts, it is with just Confidence recommended to the Publick by

April 27.
1697.

Nath. Mather,
John Howe,
70   *Matth. Mead.*

[1] *Pietas in Patriam* was first published in 1697 in London. This "recommendation" was written by Cotton Mather's uncle Nathanael. He persuaded John Howe, a prominent non-conformist minister, and Matthew Mead, an Independent divine, to sign it with him. None of the three signers had ever seen Cotton, but all knew and respected his father Increase. Their readiness to praise Cotton was probably dictated by hope that his book might serve to refute the charges brought against Increase by Elisha Cooke and his followers and by other "Tories" who disapproved his acceptance of the new Charter and his choice of Phips as governor.*

[The heading on the opposite page was photographed from the 1702 edition of the *Magnalia*, courtesy of the Houghton Library, Harvard University. Line numbers and footnote references have been added. For footnotes see p. 274.]

Pietas in Patriam:[1]

THE

LIFE

OF HIS

EXCELLENCY

Sir 𝕎illiam 𝕡hips, Knt.

**Late Captain General, and Governour in Chief of the Province
of the *Maſſachuſet-Bay,***

NEW-ENGLAND.

**Containing the Memorable *Changes* Undergone, and *Actions* Per-
formed by Him.**

Written by one intimately acquainted with Him.

Diſcite Virtutem ex Hoc, verumque Laborem.[2]

To his Excellency the Earl of Bellomont,[3] *Baron of* Coloony *in* Ireland, *General Governour of the Province of* Maſſachuſets *in* New-
England, *and the Provinces annexed.*

May it please your Excellency,

THE Station in which the Hand of the God of Heaven hath disposed
His Majesties Heart to place your Honour, doth so manifestly
entitle your Lordship to this ensuing Narrative, that its being thus
Presented to your Excellencies Hand, is thereby both Apologized for
and Justified. I believe, had the Writer of it, when he Penned it, had
any Knowledge of your Excellency, he would himself have done it, and
withal, would have amply and publickly Congratulated the People of

95 *New-England,* on account of their having such a Governour, and your
Excellency, on account of your being made Governour over them. For
though as to some other things it may possibly be a place to some Persons
not so desirable, yet I believe this Character may be justly given of them,
99 that they are the best People under Heaven; there being among them,
not only less of open Profaneness, and less of Lewdness, but also more of
the serious Profession, Practice, and Power of Christianity, in proportion
to their number, than is among any other People upon the Face of the
whole Earth. Not but I doubt,⁴ there are many bad Persons among them,
5 and too many distemper'd Humours, perhaps even among those who are
truly good. It would be a wonder if it should be otherwise; for it hath of
late Years, on various accounts, and some very singular and unusual
ones, been a Day of sore Temptation with that whole People. Nevertheless, as I look upon it as a Favour from God to those Plantations, that
10 he hath set your Excellency over them, so I do account it a Favour from
God to your Excellency, that he hath committed and trusted in your
Hand so great a part of his peculiar Treasure and precious Jewels, as are
among that People. Besides, that on other accounts the Lord Jesus hath
more of a visible Interest in *New-England,* than in any of the Outgoings
15 of the *English* Nation in *America.* They have at their own Charge not only
set up Schools of lower Learning up and down the Country; but have
also erected an University, which hath been the happy Nursery of many
Useful, Learned, and excellently Accomplished Persons. And moreover,
from them hath the blessed Gospel been Preached to the Poor Barbarous,
20 Savage *Heathen* there; and it hath taken such Root among them, that
there were lately four and twenty Assemblies in which the Name of the
Lord Jesus was constantly called on, and celebrated in their own Language. In these things *New-England* outshineth all the Colonies of the
English in those goings down of the Sun. I know your Excellency will
25 Favour and Countenance their University, and also the Propagating of
the Gospel among the Natives; for the Interest of Christ in that Part of the
Earth is much concerned in them. That the God of the Spirits of all

97 things/thiugs

¹ "Love to one's Country." Cotton Mather finished the *Pietas* in 1696 and gave the manuscript
to Phips's widow, hoping that "in Time convenient" it might "be sent to *London* to bee there
published." He declared that the book was written to show the divine "wisdom and grace"
revealed in Phips's career and to serve his "Lord Jesus." The manuscript was duly sent abroad
to Nathanael Mather, who had it published. Mather first saw the finished volume in late
December of 1697 and promptly decided to reprint it in his *Magnalia* as an Appendix to
Book II. The *Magnalia* version was printed from the 1697 edition.*
² "Learn virtue and true labor from him."*
³ Richard Bellomont was appointed governor of New England in 1696 but did not come
to Boston until 1699.*
⁴ That is, "Fear."

Flesh would abundantly replenish your Excellency with a suitable
Spirit for the Service to which he hath called your Lordship, that he
30 would give your Honour a prosperous Voyage thither, and when there,
make your Excellency a rich Blessing to that People, and them a rejoicing to your Excellency, is the Prayer of,

My Lord,

April 27.
1697.

Your Excellencies most

35

Humble Servant,

Nath. Mather.

THE

LIFE

Of His EXCELLENCY

40 ## Sir *WILLIAM PHIPS*, Knt.

LATE

GOVERNOUR

OF

NEW-ENGLAND.

45 §. 1. I F such a Renowned Chymist, as *Quercetanus*,[1] with a whole Tribe
of *Labourers in the Fire*, since that Learned Man, find it no easie
thing to make the common part of Mankind believe, That they can take
a *Plant* in its more vigorous Consistence, and after a due *Maceration*,
Fermentation and *Separation*, extract the *Salt* of that *Plant*, which, as it were,
50 in a *Chaos*, invisibly reserves the *Form* of the whole, with its vital Principle;
and, that keeping the *Salt* in a *Glass* Hermetically sealed, they can, by
applying a *Soft Fire* to the *Glass*, make the *Vegetable* rise by little and little
out of its *Ashes*, to surprize the Spectators with a notable Illustration of
that *Resurrection*, in the Faith whereof the *Jews* returning from the Graves
55 of their Friends, pluck up the *Grass* from the Earth, using those Words of the
Scripture thereupon, *Your Bones shall flourish like an Herb:*[2] 'Tis likely, that
all the Observations of such Writers, as the Incomparable *Borellus*, will
find it hard enough to produce our Belief, that the *Essential Salts* of
Animals may be so Prepared and Preserved, that an Ingenious Man may
60 have the whole *Ark* of *Noah* in his own Study, and raise the fine *Shape*
of an *Animal* out of its Ashes at his Pleasure: And, that by the like Method
from the *Essential Salts of Humane Dust*, a Philosopher may, without any
Criminal *Necromancy*, call up the *Shape* of any *Dead* Ancestor from the
Dust whereinto his Body has been Incinerated. The *Resurrection of the*
65 *Dead*, will be as Just, as Great an Article of our *Creed*, although the
Relations of these Learned Men should pass for *Incredible Romances:* But

---

[1] Joseph du Chesne (1546?–1609), physician to Henry IV of France. A posthumous collection of his writings was published at Frankfort in 1648 as *Quercetanus* [du Chesne Latinized]
Redivivus, seu Ars Medico-Hermetica.*
[2] Isa. 66.14.*

yet there is an *Anticipation* of that Blessed *Resurrection*, carrying in it some Resemblance of these *Curiosities*, which is performed, when we do in a *Book*, as in a *Glass*, reserve the History of our Departed *Friends*; and by 70 bringing our *Warm Affections* unto such an History, we revive, as it were, out of their *Ashes*, the true *Shape* of those Friends, and bring to a fresh View, what was *Memorable* and *Imitable* in them. Now, in as much as *Mortality* has done its part upon a Considerable Person, with whom I had the Honour to be well acquainted, and a Person as *Memorable* for the 75 Wonderful *Changes* which befel him, as *Imitable* for his *Virtues* and *Actions* under those *Changes*; I shall endeavour, with the *Chymistry* of an Impartial *Historian*, to *raise* my Friend so far out of his *Ashes*, as to shew him again unto the World; and if the Character of *Heroick Virtue* be for a Man to *deserve well of Mankind, and be great in the Purpose and Success of Essays to do* 80 *so*, I may venture to promise my Reader such Example of *Heroick Virtue*, in the Story whereto I invite him, that he shall say, it would have been little short of a *Vice* in *me*, to have withheld it from him. Nor is it any *Partiality* for the Memory of my Deceased Friend, or any other Sinister Design whatsoever, that has Invited me to this Undertaking; but I have 85 undertaken this Matter from a sincere Desire, that the Ever-Glorious Lord *JESUS CHRIST* may have the Glory of his *Power* and *Goodness*, and of his *Providence*, in what he did for such a Person, and in what he disposed and assisted that Person to do for him. Now, *May he assist my Writing, even he that prepared the Subject, whereof I am to Write!*

90 §. 2. So *obscure* was the *Original* of that Memorable Person, whose *Actions* I am going to relate, that I must, in a way of Writing, like that of *Plutarch*, prepare my Reader for the intended Relation, by first searching the *Archives* of Antiquity for a *Parallel*. Now, because we will not *Parallel* him with *Eumenes*,[1] who, though he were the Son of a Poor Carrier, 95 became a Governour of Mighty Provinces; nor with *Marius*,[2] whose mean Parentage did not hinder his becoming a Glorious Defender of his Country, and Seven times the Chief Magistrate of the Chiefest City in the Universe: Nor with *Iphicrates*,[3] who became a Successful and Re- 99 nowned General of a Great People, though his Father were a *Cobler*: Nor with *Dioclesian*,[4] the Son of a poor *Scrivener*: Nor with *Benosus*,[5] the Son of a poor *School-Master*, who yet came to sway the Scepter of the *Roman* Empire: Nor, lastly, will I compare him to the more late Example of the Celebrated *Mazarini*,[6] who though no Gentleman by his Extraction,

---

[1] Eumenes, Thracian general. On the death of Alexander, whom he had served as principal secretary, he became governor of Cappadocia and Paphlagonia.*

[2] Caius Marius (155?–86 B.C.), Roman general, seven times named consul of Rome.*

[3] Iphicrates, Athenian general of the fourth century B.C.*

[4] Diocletian (245–313), Roman Emperor 284–305.

[5] Bonosus, Roman general of the third century A.D.*

[6] Mazarin.

5 and one so sorrily Educated, that he might have wrote *Man*, before he could write at all; yet ascended unto that Grandeur, in the Memory of many yet living, as to Umpire the most Important Affairs of *Christendom:* We will decline looking any further in that *Hemisphere* of the World, and make the *Hue and Cry* throughout the Regions of *America*, the *New World*,

10 which *He*, that is becoming the Subject of our History, by his *Nativity*, belong'd unto. And in *America*, the first that meets me, is *Francisco Pizarro*,[7] who, though a *Spurious Offspring*, exposed when a *Babe* in a Church-Porch, at a sorry Village of *Navarre*, and afterwards employ'd while he was a *Boy*, in keeping of Cattel, yet, at length, stealing into

15 *America*, he so thrived upon his Adventures there, that upon some Discoveries, which with an handful of Men he had in a desperate Expedition made of *Peru*, he obtain'd the King of *Spain's* Commission for the Conquest of it, and at last so incredibly enrich'd himself by the Conquest, that he was made the first Vice-Roy of *Peru*, and created Marquess of

20 *Anatilla.*

To the Latter and Highest Part of that Story, if any thing hindred His Excellency Sir *WILLIAM PHIPS*, from affording of a *Parallel*, it was not the want either of *Design*, or of *Courage*, or of *Conduct* in himself, but it was the Fate of a *Premature Mortality*. For my Reader now being satisfied, that

25 a Person's being *Obscure* in his *Original*, is not always a Just Prejudice to an Expectation of *Considerable Matters* from him; I shall now inform him, that this our *PHIPS* was Born *Feb*. 2. *A. Dom*. 1650. at a despicable Plantation[8] on the River of *Kennebeck*, and almost the furthest Village of the Eastern Settlement of *New-England*. And as the *Father* of that Man,[9]

30 which was as great a Blessing as *England* had in the Age of that Man, was a *Smith*, so a *Gun-Smith*, namely, *James Phips*, once of *Bristol*, had the Honour of being the *Father* to him, whom we shall presently see, made by the God of Heaven as great a Blessing to *New-England*, as that Country could have had, if they themselves had pleased. His fruitful *Mother*, yet

35 living, had no less than *Twenty-Six* Children, whereof *Twenty-One* were Sons; but Equivalent to them all was *WILLIAM*, one of the youngest, whom his *Father* dying, left young with his *Mother*, and with her he lived, *keeping of Sheep in the Wilderness*, until he was Eighteen Years Old; at which time he began to feel some further Dispositions of Mind from that

40 *Providence* of God which *took him from the Sheepfolds, from following the Ewes great with Young, and brought him to feed his People*. Reader, enquire no

---

[7] Francisco Pizarro (*c*.1471–1541), born at Trujillo in Estremadura (not Navarre), the illegitimate son of an infantry officer.

[8] 1650/51. The "Plantation" was probably the present Phipsburg, Maine, on the west side of the Kennebec river.

[9] Mather's reference is to Thomas Cromwell (*c*.1485–1540), Earl of Essex and lord high chamberlain under Henry VIII.

further who was his *Father?* Thou shalt anon see, that he was, as the *Italians* express it, *A Son to his own Labours!*

§. 3. His Friends earnestly solicited him to settle among them in a
45 Plantation of the *East*; but he had an Unaccountable *Impulse* upon his Mind, perswading him, as he would privately hint unto some of them, *That he was Born to greater Matters.* To come at those *greater Matters,* his first Contrivance was to bind himself an Apprentice unto a *Ship-Carpenter* for Four Years; in which time he became a Master of the *Trade,* that
50 once in a Vessel of more than *Forty Thousand Tuns,* repaired the Ruins of the Earth; *Noah's,* I mean; he then betook himself an Hundred and Fifty Miles further a Field, even to *Boston,* the Chief Town of *New-England*; which being a Place of the most Business and Resort in those Parts of the World, he expected there more Commodiously to pursue the *Spes*
55 *Majorum & Meliorum,*[1] Hopes which had inspir'd him. At *Boston,* where it was that he now learn'd, first of all, to *Read* and *Write,* he followed his Trade for about a Year; and by a laudable Deportment, so recommended himself that he Married a Young Gentlewoman of good Repute, who was the Widow of one Mr. *John Hull,* a well-bred Merchant, but the
60 Daughter of one Captain *Roger Spencer,* a Person of good Fashion, who having suffer'd much damage in his Estate, by some unkind and unjust Actions, which he bore with such Patience, that for fear of thereby injuring the Publick, he would not seek Satisfaction. *Posterity* might afterward see the Reward of his *Patience,* in what Providence hath now done
65 for one of his own *Posterity.* Within a little while after his Marriage, he indented with several Persons in *Boston,* to Build them a Ship at *Sheepscoat*[2] River, Two or Three Leagues Eastward of *Kennebeck*; where having Lanched[3] the Ship, he also provided a *Lading* of Lumber to bring with him, which would have been to the Advantage of all Concern'd. But
70 just as the Ship was hardly finished, the Barbarous *Indians* on that River, broke forth into an Open and Cruel War upon the *English*; and the miserable People, surprized by so sudden a storm of Blood, had no Refuge from the Infidels, but the *Ship* now finishing in the Harbour. Whereupon he left his intended *Lading* behind him, and instead thereof,
75 carried with him his old Neighbours and their Families, free of all Charges, to *Boston*; so the *first Action* that he did, after he was his own Man, was to *save his Father's House,* with the rest of the Neighbourhood, from Ruin; but the Disappointment which befel him from the Loss of his other *Lading,* plunged his Affairs into greater Embarasments with such as had em-
80 ploy'd him.

63 Satisfaction./Satisfaction,

[1] "Hopes of greater and better things."*
[2] Now Sheepscot.
[3] "Lanch" was the obsolete form of "launch."

§. 4. But he was hitherto no more than beginning to make *Scaffolds* for further and higher *Actions!* He would frequently tell the Gentlewoman his Wife, That he should yet be *Captain of a King's Ship*; That he should come to have the *Command of better Men* than he was now accounted himself; and,

85 That he should be Owner of a *Fair Brick-House* in the *Green-Lane*[1] of *North-Boston*; and, That, it may be, this would not be all that the Providence of God would bring him to. She entertained these Passages with a sufficient Incredulity; but he had so *serious* and *positive* an Expectation of them, that it is not easie to say, what was the *Original* thereof. He was of

90 an Enterprizing *Genius*, and naturally disdained *Littleness*: But his Disposition for *Business* was of the *Dutch* Mould, where, with a little shew of *Wit*, there is as much *Wisdom* demonstrated, as can be shewn by any Nation. His Talent lay not in the *Airs* that serve chiefly for the pleasant and sudden Turns of *Conversation*; but he might say, as *Themistocles*,

95 *Though he could not play upon a Fiddle, yet he knew how to make a little City become a Great One.* He would *prudently* contrive a weighty Undertaking, and then patiently pursue it unto the End. He was of an Inclination, cutting rather like a *Hatchet*, than like a *Razor*; he would propose very

99 Considerable Matters to himself, and then so *cut through* them, that no Difficulties could put by the *Edge* of his Resolutions. Being thus of the *True Temper*, for doing of *Great Things*, he betakes himself to the *Sea*, the Right *Scene* for such Things; and upon Advice of a *Spanish Wreck* about the *Bahama*'s, he took a Voyage thither; but with little more suc-

5 cess, than what just served him a little to furnish him for a Voyage to *England*; whither he went in a Vessel, not much unlike that which the *Dutchmen* stamped on their *First Coin*, with these Words about it, *Incertum quo Fata ferant.*[2] Having first informed himself that there was another *Spanish Wreck*, wherein was lost a mighty Treasure, hitherto

10 undiscovered, he had a strong Impression upon his Mind that *He* must be the Discoverer; and he made such Representations of his Design at *White-Hall*, that by the Year 1683. he became the Captain of *a King's Ship*, and arrived at *New-England* Commander of the *Algier-Rose*, a Frigot of Eighteen Guns, and Ninety-Five Men.

15 §. 5. To Relate all the *Dangers* through which he passed, both by Sea and Land, and all the Tiresome Trials of his *Patience*, as well as of his *Courage*, while Year after Year the most vexing Accidents imaginable delay'd the Success of his Design, it would even Tire the patience of the Reader: For very great was the Experiment that Captain *Phips* made of

20 the *Italian* Observation, *He that cann't suffer both Good and Evil, will never come to any great Preferment.* Wherefore I shall supersede all *Journal* of his

---

[1] A street in the then stylish North End of Boston, near the present Salem and Charter Streets.

[2] "Uncertain whither the fates lead."*

Voyages to and fro, with reciting one Instance of his Conduct, that show'd him to be a Person of no contemptible Capacity. While he was Captain of the *Algier-Rose,* his Men growing weary of their unsuccessful Enter-
25 prize, made a Mutiny, wherein they approach'd him on the Quarter-Deck, with Drawn Swords in their Hands, and required him to join with them in Running away with the Ship, to drive a Trade of Piracy on the *South Seas.* Captain *Phips,* though he had not so much of a Weapon as an *Ox-Goad,* or a *Jaw-bone* in his Hands, yet like another *Shamgar* or
30 *Samson,* with a most undaunted Fortitude, he rush'd in upon them, and with the Blows of his bare Hands, *Fell'd* many of them, and *Quell'd* all the Rest. But this is not the Instance which I intended: That which I intend is, That (as it has been related unto me) One Day while his Frigot lay *Careening,*[1] at a desolate *Spanish* Island, by the side of a Rock, from
35 whence they had laid a Bridge to the Shoar, the Men, whereof he had about an *Hundred,* went all, but about Eight or Ten, to divert themselves, as they pretended, in the *Woods:* Where they all entred into an *Agreement,* which they Sign'd in a Ring, That about seven a Clock that Evening they would seize the Captain, and those Eight or Ten, which they knew
40 to be True unto him, and leave them to perish on this Island, and so be gone away unto the *South Sea to seek their Fortune.* Will the Reader now imagine, that Captain *Phips* having Advice of this Plot but about an Hour and half before it was to be put in Execution, yet within *Two Hours* brought all these Rogues down upon their Knees to beg for their
45 Lives? But so it was! For these Knaves considering that they should want a *Carpenter* with them in their *Villanous Expedition,* sent a Messenger to fetch unto them the *Carpenter,* who was then at Work upon the Vessel; and unto him they shew'd their *Articles*; telling him what he must look for if he did not *subscribe*[2] among them. The *Carpenter* being an honest
50 Fellow, did with much importunity prevail for one half hours Time to consider of the Matter; and returning to Work upon the Vessel, with a *Spy* by them set upon him, he feigned himself taken with a Fit of the *Cholick,* for the Relief whereof he suddenly run unto the Captain in the Great Cabbin for a *Dram*; where, when he came, his business was only in
55 brief, to tell the Captain of the horrible Distress which he was fallen into; but the Captain bid him as briefly return to the Rogues in the *Woods,* and Sign their *Articles,* and leave *him* to provide for the Rest. The *Carpenter* was no sooner gone, but Captain *Phips* calling together the few Friends (it may be seven or eight) that were left him aboard, whereof the Gunner
60 was one, demanded of them, whether they would stand by him in the Extremity, which he informed them was now come upon him; whereto they reply'd, *They would stand by him, if he could save them*; and he Answer'd,

[1] Laid on its side so that its bottom might be cleaned and calked.
[2] Agree to join them.

By the help of God he did not fear it. All their Provisions had been carried
Ashoar to a Tent, made for that purpose there; about which they had
65 placed several Great Guns to defend it, in case of any *Assault* from
Spaniards, that might happen to come that way. Wherefore Captain
Phips immediately ordered those Guns to be silently Draw'd and Turn'd;
and so pulling up the Bridge, he charged his Great Guns aboard, and
brought them to Bear on every side of the Tent. By this Time the *Army*
70 *of Rebels* comes out of the Woods; but as they drew near to the Tent of
Provisions, they saw such a change of Circumstances, that they cried out,
We are Betray'd! And they were soon confirm'd in it, when they heard the
Captain with a stern Fury call to them, *Stand off, ye Wretches, at your Peril!*
He quickly saw them cast into a more than ordinary Confusion, when
75 they saw *Him* ready to Fire his Great Guns upon them, if they offered
one Step further than he permitted them: And when he had signified
unto them his *Resolve* to abandon them unto all the Desolation which
they had purposed for *him*, he caused the *Bridge* to be again laid, and his
Men begun to take the Provisions aboard. When the Wretches beheld
80 what was coming upon them, they fell to very humble Entreaties; and at
last fell down upon their Knees, protesting, *That they never had any thing*
against him, except only his unwillingness to go away with the King's Ship upon
the South-Sea *Design: But upon all other Accounts, they would chuse rather to*
Live and Die with him, than with any Man in the World; however, since they
85 *saw how much he was dissatisfied at it, they would insist upon it no more, and*
humbly begg'd his Pardon. And when he judg'd that he had kept them on
their *Knees* long enough, he having first secur'd their *Arms*, received them
aboard; but he immediately weighed Anchor, and arriving at *Jamaica*,
he Turn'd them off. Now with a small Company of other Men he sailed
90 from thence to *Hispaniola*,[3] where by the Policy of his Address, he fished
out of a very old *Spaniard*, (or *Portuguese*) a little Advice about the true
Spot where lay the *Wreck* which he had been hitherto seeking, as un-
prosperously, as the *Chymists* have their *Aurifick Stone*:[4] That it was upon
a *Reef of Shoals*, a few Leagues to the Northward of *Port de la Plata*, upon
95 *Hispaniola*, a Port so call'd, it seems, from the Landing of some of the
Shipwreck'd Company, with a Boat full of Plate, saved out of their
Sinking Frigot: Nevertheless, when he had searched very narrowly the
Spot, whereof the old *Spaniard* had advised him, he had not hitherto
99 exactly lit upon it. Such *Thorns* did vex his Affairs while he was in the
Rose-Frigot; but none of all these things could retund[5] the Edge of his

67 Draw'd/Drawn'd   79 aboard/abroad

[3] Haiti.
[4] A stone supposedly capable of producing gold.
[5] To dull or blunt.

Expectations to find the *Wreck*; with such Expectations he return'd then into *England*, that he might there better furnish himself to Prosecute a *New Discovery*; for though he judged he might, by proceeding a little
5 further, have come at the right *Spot*, yet he found his present Company too ill a Crew to be confided in.

§. 6. So *proper* was his Behaviour, that the best Noble Men in the Kingdom now admitted him into their Conversation; but yet he was opposed by powerful Enemies, that Clogg'd his Affairs with such De-
10 murrages, and such *Disappointments*, as would have wholly Discouraged his Designs, if his Patience had not been *Invincible*. *He who can wait, hath what he desireth.* This his Indefatigable *Patience*, with a proportionable *Diligence*, at length overcame the Difficulties that had been thrown in his way; and prevailing with the Duke of *Albemarle*,[1] and some other Persons
15 of Quality, to fit him out, he set Sail for the *Fishing-Ground*, which had been so well *baited*[2] half an Hundred Years before: And as he had already discovered his *Capacity for Business* in many considerable Actions, he now added unto those Discoveries, by not only *providing* all, but also by *inventing* many of the Instruments necessary to the prosecution of his
20 intended *Fishery*. Captain *Phips* arriving with a Ship and a *Tender* at *Port de la Plata*, made a stout *Canoo* of a stately *Cotton-Tree*,[3] so large as to carry Eight or Ten Oars, for the making of which *Periaga*[4] (as they call it) he did, with the same industry that he did every thing else, employ his own *Hand* and *Adse*, and endure no little hardship, lying abroad in
25 the Woods many Nights together. This *Periaga*, with the *Tender*, being Anchored at a place Convenient, the *Periaga* kept Busking[5] to and again, but could only discover a *Reef of Rising Shoals* thereabouts, called, *The Boilers*, which Rising to be within Two or Three Foot of the Surface of the Sea, were yet so steep, that a Ship striking on them, would immedi-
30 ately sink down, who could say, *how many Fathom* into the Ocean? Here they could get no other Pay for their long *peeping* among the *Boilers*, but only such as caused them to think upon returning to their Captain with the *bad News* of their total Disappointment. Nevertheless, as they were upon the Return, one of the Men looking over the side of the *Periaga*,
35 into the calm Water, he spied a *Sea Feather*,[6] growing, as he judged, out o₁ a Rock; whereupon they had one of their *Indians* to Dive and fetch this *Feather*, that they might however carry home *something* with them, and

---

[1] Christopher Monck, second Duke of Albemarle (1653–1688), was the principal promoter of Phips's second voyage in search of sunken treasure; he was made governor general of Jamaica in 1687.*

[2] That is, rendered alluring.

[3] A species of large poplar.

[4] A Periaga or Periagua was an open flat-bottomed schooner-rigged vessel; a sort of two-masted sailing barge.

[5] Cruising about.

[6] A kind of coral or polyp.

make, at least, as fair a Triumph as *Caligula's*.[7] The *Diver* bringing up the *Feather*, brought therewithal a surprizing Story, That he perceived a
40 Number of *Great Guns* in the *Watry World* where he had found his *Feather*; the *Report* of which *Great Guns* exceedingly astonished the whole Company; and at once turned their *Despondencies* for their ill success into *Assurances*, that they had now lit upon the *true Spot* of Ground which they had been looking for; and they were further confirmed in these *Assurances*, when
45 upon further Diving, the *Indian* fetcht up a *Sow*,[8] as they stil'd it, or a Lump of Silver, worth perhaps Two or Three Hundred Pounds. Upon this they prudently *Buoy'd* the place, that they might readily find it again; and they went back unto their Captain whom for some while they distressed with nothing but such *Bad News*, as they formerly thought they
50 must have carried him: Nevertheless, they so slipt in the Sow of Silver on one side under the Table, where they were now sitting with the Captain, and hearing him express his Resolutions to wait still patiently upon the Providence of God under these Disappointments, that when he should look on one side, he might see that *Odd Thing* before him. At last he *saw*
55 it; seeing it, he cried out with some Agony, *Why? What is this? Whence comes this?* And then, with changed Countenances, they told him *how*, and *where* they got it: *Then*, said he, *Thanks be to God! We are made*; and so away they went, all hands to Work; wherein they had this one further piece of Remarkable Prosperity, that whereas if they had first fallen upon
60 that part of the *Spanish Wreck*, where the Pieces of Eight had been stowed in Bags among the Ballast, they had seen a more laborious, and less enriching time of it: Now, most happily, they first fell upon that Room in the *Wreck* where the *Bullion* had been stored up; and they so prospered in this *New Fishery*, that in a little while they had, without the loss of any
65 Man's Life, brought up *Thirty Two Tuns* of Silver; for it was now come to measuring of Silver by *Tuns*. Besides which, one *Adderly* of *Providence*,[9] who had formerly been very helpful to Captain *Phips* in the Search of this *Wreck*, did upon former Agreement meet him now with a little Vessel here; and *he*, with his few hands, took up about *Six Tuns* of Silver;
70 whereof nevertheless he made so little use, that in a Year or Two he Died at *Bermudas*, and as I have heard, he ran *Distracted* some while before he Died. Thus did there once again come into the Light of the Sun, a Treasure which had been half an Hundred Years *groaning under the Waters:* And in this time there was grown upon the Plate a Crust like

---

[7] The Roman Caligula in an expedition against Germany found there no enemies to fight; he therefore had his troops gather shells, calling them spoils from the ocean, a worthy tribute for the Capitol and Palatine.*

[8] In the now obsolete or rare sense of a large bar or mass of metal as obtained from a smelting furnace.

[9] Little is known about Abraham (or Abram) Atherly except that he was a seafarer in the West Indies and perhaps the Bermudas.*

75 *Limestone*, to the thickness of several Inches; which Crust being broken
open by Irons contrived for that purpose, they knockt out whole Bushels
of rusty Pieces of Eight which were grown thereinto. Besides that incredible Treasure of Plate in various Forms, thus fetch'd up, from Seven or
Eight Fathom under Water, there were vast Riches of *Gold*, and *Pearls*,
80 and *Jewels*, which they also lit upon; and indeed, for a more Compre-
hensive *Invoice*, I must but summarily say, *All that a* Spanish *Frigot uses
to be enricht withal.* Thus did they continue *Fishing* till their Provisions
failing them, 'twas time to be gone; but before they went, Captain
Phips caused *Adderly* and his Folk to swear, That they would none of
85 them Discover the Place of the *Wreck*, or come to the Place any more till
the next Year, when he expected again to be there himself. And it was
also Remarkable, that though the Sows came up still so fast, that on the
very last Day of their being there, they took up *Twenty*, yet it was afterwards found, that they had in a manner wholly cleared that Room of
90 the Ship where those *Massy things* were Stowed.

But there was one extraordinary Distress which Captain *Phips* now
found himself plunged into: For his Men were come out with him upon
Seamens Wages, at so much *per* Month; and when they saw such vast
Litters of Silver *Sows* and *Pigs*, as they call them, come on Board them
95 at the Captain's Call, they knew not how to bear it, that they should not
share all among themselves, and be gone to lead *a short Life and a merry*, in
a Climate where the Arrest of those that had hired them should not reach
them. In this terrible Distress he made his Vows unto Almighty God, that
99 if the Lord would carry him safe home to *England* with what *he* had now
given him, *to suck of the Abundance of the Seas, and of the Treasures hid in the
Sands*, he would for ever Devote himself unto the Interests of the Lord
Jesus Christ, and of his People, especially in the *Country* which he did
himself Originally belong unto. And he then used all the obliging *Arts*
5 imaginable to make his Men true unto him, especially by assuring them,
that besides their *Wages*, they should have ample *Requitals* made unto
them; which if the rest of his Employers[10] would not agree unto, he
would himself distribute his *own share* among them. Relying upon the
Word of One whom they had ever found worthy of their *Love*, and of their
10 *Trust*, they declared themselves *Content:* But still keeping a most careful
Eye upon them, he hastned back for *England* with as much *Money* as he
thought he could then safely *Trust* his Vessel withal; not counting it safe
to supply himself with necessary Provisions at any nearer Port, and so
return unto the *Wreck*, by which delays he wisely feared lest all might be
15 lost, more ways than one. Though he also left so much behind him, that
many from divers Parts made very considerable Voyages of *Gleanings*
after his *Harvest:* Which came to pass by certain *Bermudians*, compelling

10 Albemarle and the others who financed Phips's voyage.

of *Adderly's* Boy, whom they *spirited* away with them, to tell them the
exact place where the *Wreck* was to be found. Captain *Phips* now coming
20 up to *London* in the Year 1687. with near *Three Hundred Thousand Pounds
Sterling* aboard him, did acquit himself with such an Exemplary Honesty,
that partly by his fulfilling his Assurances to the Seamen, and partly
by his exact and punctual Care to have his Employers defrauded of
nothing that might conscienciously belong unto them, he had less than
25 *Sixteen Thousand Pounds* left unto himself: As an acknowledgment of which
Honesty in him, the Duke of *Albemarle* made unto his Wife, whom he
never saw, a Present of a *Golden Cup*, near a Thousand Pound in value.
The Character of an *Honest Man* he had so merited in the whole Course of
his Life, and especially in this last act of it, that this, in Conjunction with
30 his other serviceable Qualities, procured him the Favours of the Greatest
Persons in the Nation; and *he that had been so diligent in his Business, must
now stand before Kings, and not stand before mean Men.* There were indeed
certain *mean Men*, if base, little, dirty Tricks, will entitle Men to Meanness, who urged the King to seize his *whole Cargo*, instead of the Tenth,
35 upon his first Arrival; on this pretence, that he had not been rightly
inform'd of the *True state of the Case*, when he Granted the *Patent*, under
the Protection whereof these *particular Men* had made themselves Masters
of all this Mighty Treasure; but the King replied, That he had been
rightly informed by Captain *Phips* of the whole Matter, as it now proved;
40 and that it was the Slanders of one then present, which had, unto his
Damnage,[11] hindred him from hearkning to the Information: Wherefore
he would give them, he said, no Disturbance; they might keep what
they had got; but Captain *Phips*, he saw, was a Person of that Honesty,
Fidelity and Ability, that he should not want his Countenance. Accord-
45 ingly the King, in Consideration of the Service done by him, in bringing
such a Treasure into the Nation, conferr'd upon him the Honour of
Knighthood;[12] and if we now reckon him, *A Knight of the Golden Fleece*,[13]
the Stile might pretend unto some Circumstances that would justifie it.
Or call him, if you please, *The Knight of Honesty*; for it was *Honesty* with
50 *Industry* that raised him; and he became a Mighty River, without the
running in of Muddy Water to make him so. Reader, now make a Pause,
and behold *One Raised by God!*

§. 7. I am willing to Employ the Testimonies of others, as much as
may be, to support the Credit of my History: And therefore, as I
55 have hitherto related no more than what there are *Others* enough to

20   1687/1887 C.M.   55   *Others*/others *Others*
34   Tenth/Tenths

[11] An obsolete form of "damage."
[12] On June 28, 1687.
[13] In his oration at the Harvard Commencement on July 4, 1688, the Reverend William
Hubbard compared Phips to "Jason fetching the Golden Fleece."*

avouch; thus I shall chuse the Words of an Ingenious Person Printed at *London* some Years ago, to express the Sum of what remains, whose Words are these; 'It has always been Sir *William Phip*'s Disposition to 'seek the *Wealth* of his People with as great Zeal and Unweariedness, as
60 'our *Publicans* use to seek their *Loss* and *Ruin*. At first it seems they were 'in hopes to gain this Gentleman to their Party, as thinking him *Good* '*Natur'd*, and easie to be flattered out of his Understanding; and the 'more, because they had the advantage of some, no very good, Treatment 'that Sir *William* had formerly met with from the People and Govern-
65 'ment of *New-England*. But Sir *William* soon shewed them, that what they 'expected would be his *Temptation* to lead him into their *little Tricks*, 'he embraced as a Glorious Opportunity to shew his *Generosity* and '*Greatness of Mind*; for, in Imitation of the Greatest Worthies that have 'ever been, he rather chose to join in the Defence of his Country, with
70 'some Persons who formerly were none of his Friends, than become the 'Head of a *Faction*, to its Ruin and Desolation. It seems this Noble 'Disposition of Sir *William*, joined with that Capacity and good Success 'wherewith he hath been attended, in Raising himself by such an Occa-'sion, as it may be, all things considered, has *never happened to any before*
75 '*him*, makes these Men apprehensive;—And it must needs heighten their 'trouble to see, that he neither hath, nor doth spare himself, nor any 'thing that is near and dear unto him, in promoting the Good of his 'Native Country.

When Sir *William Phips* was *per ardua & aspera*,[1] thus raised into an
80 *Higher Orb*, it might easily be thought that he could not be without Charming Temptations to take the *way on the left hand*. But as the Grace of God kept him in the midst of none of the strictest Company, unto which his Affairs daily led him, from abandoning himself to the lewd Vices of *Gaming, Drinking, Swearing* and *Whoring*, which the Men *that*
85 *made* England *to Sin*, debauch'd so many of the Gentry into, and he deserved the Salutations of the *Roman* Poet:

> *Cum Tu, inter scabiem tantam, & Contagia Lucri,*
> *Nil parvum sapias, & adhuc Sublimia cures:*[2]

Thus he was worthy to pass among the Instances of *Heroick Vertue* for
90 that *Humility* that still Adorned him: He was *Raised*, and though he prudently accommodated himself to the *Quality* whereto he was now *Raised*, yet none could perceive him to be *Lifted up*. Or, if this were not *Heroick*, yet I will Relate one Thing more of him that must certainly be accounted so. He had in his own Country of *New-England* met with

66 him/them

[1] "Through difficulties and hardships."*
[2] "You, amid so great a disease and contagion of avarice, are wise, and seek higher things."*

95 *Provocations* that were enough to have Alienated any Man Living, that had no more than *Flesh and Blood* in him, from the Service of it; and some that were Enemies to that Country, now lay hard at him to join with them in their Endeavours to Ravish away their *Ancient Liberties*. But this

99 *Gentleman* had studied another way to *Revenge* himself upon his Country, and that was to serve it in all *its* Interests, with all of *his*, even with his *Estate*, his *Time*, his *Care*, his *Friends*, and his very *Life!* The old *Heathen* Virtue of PIETAS IN PATRIAM, or, *LOVE TO ONES COUNTRY*, he turned into *Christian*; and so notably exemplified it, in all the Rest of

5 his *Life*, that it will be an Essential *Thread* which is to be now interwoven into all that remains of his *History*, and his *Character*. Accordingly though he had the Offers of a very Gainful Place among the *Commissioners of the Navy*, with many other Invitations to settle himself in *England*, nothing but a Return to *New-England* would content him. And whereas the

10 Charters of *New-England* being taken away, there was a Governour[3] Imposed upon the Territories with as *Arbitrary* and as *Treasonable* a *Commission*, perhaps, as ever was heard of; a *Commission*, by which the Governour, with Three or Four more, none of whom were chosen by the People, had Power to make what *Laws* they would, and Levy *Taxes*,

15 according to their own Humours, upon the People; and he himself had Power to send the best Men in the Land more than Ten Thousand Miles out of it, as he pleased: And in the Execution of his Power, the Country was every Day suffering Intollerable *Invasions* upon their *Proprieties*, yea, and the Lives of the best Men in the Territory began to be practised

20 upon: Sir *William Phips* applied himself to Consider what was the most significant Thing that could be done by him for that poor People in their present Circumstances. Indeed, when King *James* offered, as he did, unto Sir *William Phips* an Opportunity to Ask what he pleased of him, Sir *William* Generously prayed for nothing but *this*, *That* New-England *might*

25 *have its lost Priviledges Restored.* The King then Replied, *Any Thing but that!* Whereupon he set himself to Consider what was the *next Thing* that he might ask for the Service, not of himself, but of his *Country*. The Result of his Consideration was, That by Petition to the King, he Obtained, with expence of some Hundreds of *Guinea's*, a *Patent*, which con-

30 stituted him *The High Sheriff of that Country*; hoping, by his Deputies in that Office, to supply the Country still with Consciencious Juries, which was the only Method that the *New-Englanders* had left them to secure any thing that was Dear unto them. Furnished with this *Patent*, after he had, in Company with Sir *John Narborough*,[4] made a Second Visit unto the

---

3 Sir Edmund Andros.*

4 Sir John Narbrough (1640–1688), Commissioner of the Navy, was in 1687 appointed commander in chief of a small squadron sent to the West Indies. Phips was captain of one of its ships.*

35 *Wreck*, (not so advantageous as the former for a Reason already mentioned) in his way he Returned unto *New-England*, in the Summer of the
Year 1688. able, after Five Years Absence, to Entertain his Lady with
some Accomplishment of his Predictions; and then Built himself a *Fair
Brick House* in the very *place* which he foretold, the Reader can tell how
40 many *Sections* ago. But the *Infamous Government* then Rampant there, found
a way wholly to put by the Execution of this *Patent*; yea, he was like to
have had his *Person* Assassinated in the Face of the Sun, before his own
Door, which with some further Designs then in his Mind, caused him
within a few Weeks to take another Voyage for *England*.

45   §. 8. It would require a long Summers-Day to Relate the Miseries
which were come, and coming in upon poor *New-England*, by reason of
the *Arbitrary Government* then imposed on them; a *Government* wherein, as
old *Wendover*[1] says of the Time, when *Strangers* were domineering over
Subjects in *England, Judicia committebantur Injustis, Leges Exlegibus, Pax*
50 *Discordantibus, Justitia Injuriosis*;[2] and *Foxes* were made the Administrators
of Justice to the *Poultrey*; yet some *Abridgment* of them is necessary for the
better understanding of the Matters yet before us. Now to make this
Abridgment Impartial, I shall only have Recourse unto a little Book,
Printed at *London*, under the Title of *The Revolution of* New-England
55 *Justified*; wherein we have a *Narrative of the Grievances* under the Male
Administrations[3] of that Government, written and signed by the chief
Gentlemen of the *Governour's Council*; together with the *Sworn Testimonies*
of many good Men, to prove the several Articles of the *Declaration*, which
the *New-Englanders* published against their Oppressors. It is in that Book
60 demonstrated.

    That the Governour neglecting the greater Number of his *Council*, did
Adhere principally to the Advice of a *few Strangers*, who were Persons
without any *Interest* in the Country, but of declared *Prejudice* against it,
and had plainly laid their *Designs* to make an Unreasonable *Profit* of the
65 poor People: And *four* or *five* Persons had the absolute Rule *over a Territory, the most Considerable of any belonging to the Crown.*

    That when *Laws* were proposed in the *Council*, tho' the *Major* part at
any time Dissented from them, yet if the Governour were positive, there
was no fair *Counting* the Number of *Councellors* Consenting, or Dissenting,
70 but the Laws were immediately *Engrossed, Published* and *Executed.*

    That this *Junto* made a *Law*, which prohibited the Inhabitants of any

39 he/we

    [1] Roger de Wendover, a monk and chronicler at St. Albans, died in 1236. His *Flores Histori-
arum*, a history of the world from the creation until 1235, was for the years from 1202 until
his death a firsthand authority.*
    [2] "Judgments were entrusted to the unjust, laws to outlaws, peace to quarrelers, and justice
to wrongdoers."*
    [3] An uncommon spelling for "Mal" in "Maladministration."*

Town to meet about their *Town-Affairs* above *once* in a Year; for fear, you must Note, of their having any opportunity to Complain of *Grievances*.

That they made another *Law*, requiring all Masters of *Vessels*, even
75 *Shallops* and *Woodboats*, to give *Security*, that no Man should be Transported in them, except his Name had been so many Days posted up: Whereby the Pockets of a few *Leeches* had been filled with *Fees*, but the whole Trade of the Country destroyed; and all Attempts to obtain a *Redress* of these Things obstructed; and when this *Act* had been strenu-
80 ously opposed in Council at *Boston*, they carried it as far as *New-York*, where a Crew of them enacted it.

That without any *Assembly*, they Levied on the People a *Penny* in the Pound of all their *Estates*, and Twenty-pence *per* Head, as *Poll-money*, with a Penny in the Pound for *Goods* Imported, besides a Vast *Excise* on
85 Wine, Rum, and other *Liquors*.

That when among the Inhabitants of *Ipswich*, some of the Principal Persons modestly gave Reasons why they could not chuse a *Commissioner* to *Tax* the Town, until the King should first be Petitioned for the Liberty of an *Assembly*, they were committed unto *Gaol* for it,[4] as an *High Mis-*
90 *demeanour*, and were denied an *Habeas Corpus*, and were dragg'd many Miles out of their own County to answer it at a Court in *Boston*; where *Jurors* were pickt for the Turn, that were not *Freeholders*, nay, that were meer *Sojourners*; and when the Prisoners pleaded the Priviledges of *English-men, That they should not be Taxed without their own consent*; they were
95 told, *That those things would not follow them to the ends of the Earth:* As it had been before told them in *open Council*, no one in the Council contradicting it, *You have no more Priviledges left you, but this, that your are not bought and sold for Slaves:* And in fine, they were all *Fined* severely, and laid under great
99 *Bonds* for their good Behaviour; besides all which, the *hungry Officers* extorted *Fees* from them that amounted unto an Hundred and Three-score Pounds; whereas in *England*, upon the like Prosecution, the *Fees* would not have been Ten Pounds in all. After which fashion the *Towns-men* of many other Places were also served.

5 That these Men giving out, That the *Charters* being lost, all the Title that the People had unto their Lands was lost with them; they began to *compel* the People every where to take *Patents* for their Lands: And accordingly *Writs of Intrusion* were issued out against the chief Gentlemen in the Territory, by the Terror whereof, many were actually driven to
10 Petition for *Patents*, that they might quietly enjoy the Lands that had been Fifty or Sixty Years in their Possession; but for these *Patents* there were such exorbitant Prices demanded, that Fifty Pounds could not

89 *Gaol/Goal*

---

4 Those imprisoned were the minister John Wise and five leading citizens.*

purchase for its Owner an Estate not worth *Two Hundred,* nor could all
the Money and Moveables in the Territory have defrayed the Charges
15 of *Patenting* the Lands at the Hands of these *Crocodiles:* Besides the considerable *Quit-Rents* for the King. Yea, the Governour caused the Lands
of *particular Persons* to be measured out, and given to his Creatures: And
some of his Council Petitioned for the *Commons* belonging to several Towns;
and the *Agents* of the Towns going to get a *voluntary Subscription* of the
20 Inhabitants to maintain their Title at Law, they have been dragg'd
Forty or Fifty Miles to answer as Criminals at the next Assizes; the
Officers in the mean time extorting Three Pounds *per* Man for fetching
them.

    That if these *Harpies,* at any time, were a little *out of Money,* they found
25 ways to Imprison the *best Men* in the Country; and there appeared not the
least *Information* of any Crime exhibited against them, yet they were put
unto Intollerable Expences by these Greedy Oppressors, and the Benefit
of an *Habeas Corpus* not allowed unto them.

    That packt and pickt *Juries* were commonly made use of, when under
30 a pretended *Form of Law,* the Trouble of some Honest and Worthy Men
was aimed at; and these also were hurried out of their own Counties to
be tried, when *Juries* for the Turn were not like to be found there, the
Greatest Rigour being used still towards the *soberest sort* of People, whilst
in the mean time the most horrid Enormities in the World, committed
35 by Others, were overlook'd.

    That the publick Ministry of the Gospel, and all *Schools of Learning,*
were discountenanced unto the Utmost.

    And several more such abominable things, too notorious to be denied,
even by a *Randolphian*[5] Impudence it self, are in that Book proved against
40 that *unhappy Government.* Nor did that most Ancient Set of the *Phœnician
Shepherds,* who scrued the Government of *Egypt* into their Hands, as old
Manethon[6] tells us, by their *Villanies,* during the Reigns of those Tyrants,
make a *Shepherd* more of an *Abomination* to the *Egyptians* in all after Ages,
than these *Wolves* under the Name of *Shepherds* have made the Remem-
45 brance of their *French Government*[7] an *Abomination* to all Posterity among the

32 there, the/there. The

   [5] Edward Randolph (1632–1703) won the hatred of New Englanders by serving in 1676
as an agent of the crown, sent with instructions to obtain information on the resources of
Massachusetts, its government and the temper of the people; his subsequent reports were largely
denunciatory. In 1678 he was named collector and surveyor of customs for all New England,
and in 1685 secretary and registrar of the newly created Dominion of New England. When
Andros was overthrown, he too was imprisoned. Later returned to England, he was freed
and subsequently (1691) named surveyor general of customs for all North America.
   [6] Manethon (fl. *c.*250 B.C.), author of a Greek history of Egypt.*
   [7] Many New Englanders cherished the notion that Andros and his followers, creatures
of the Catholic king, were secretly in league with the French against the English colonists.

New-Englanders: A *Government,* for which, now, Reader, as fast as thou wilt, get ready this Epitaph:

Nulla quæsita Scelere Potentia diuturna.[8]

It was under the Resentments of these Things that Sir *William Phips*
50 returned into *England* in the Year 1688. In which *Twice Wonderful-Year* such a *Revolution* was wonderfully accomplished upon the whole Government of the *English* Nation, that *New-England,* which had been a *Specimen* of what the whole Nation was to look for, might justly hope for a share in the General Deliverance. Upon this Occasion Sir *William* offered his
55 best Assistances unto that Eminent Person,[9] who a little before this Revolution betook himself unto *White-Hall,* that he might there lay hold on all Opportunities to procure some Relief unto the Oppressions of that afflicted Country. But seeing the *New-English* Affairs in so able an Hand, he thought the best Stage of *Action* for him would now be *New-England*
60 it self; and so with certain Instructions from none of the least considerable Persons at *White-Hall,* what Service to do for his Country, in the Spring of the Year 1689. he hastened back unto it. Before he left *London,* a Messenger from the Abdicated King[10] tender'd him the Government of *New-England,* if he would accept it: But as that excellent Attorney Gen-
65 eral, Sir *William Jones,*[11] when it was proposed that the *Plantations* might be Governed without *Assemblies,* told the King, *That he could no more Grant a Commission to levy Money on his Subjects there, without their consent by an Assembly, than they could Discharge themselves from their Allegiance to the* English *Crown.* So Sir *William Phips* thought it his Duty to refuse a *Govern-*
70 *ment without an Assembly,* as a thing that was Treason in the very *Essence* of it; and instead of Petitioning the succeeding Princes,[12] that his *Patent* for *High Sheriff* might be rendred Effectual, he joined in Petitions, that *New-England* might have its own old *Patent* so Restored, as to render ineffectual *that,* and all other Grants that might cut short any of its
75 Ancient Priviledges. But when Sir *William* arrived at *New-England,* he found a new Face of things; for about an Hundred Indians in the *Eastern Parts* of the Country, had unaccountably begun a War upon the *English* in *July,* 1688. and though the Governour then in the *Western Parts* had immediate Advice of it, yet he not only delayed and neglected all that

---

[8] "No power achieved by wrong-doing is lasting."*

[9] Increase Mather. For an account of his mission see introductory essay "Cotton Mather."

[10] James II fled London December 21, 1688; the supporters of William of Orange claimed his flight constituted abdication. The Prince of Orange, a Protestant, who had arrived with his army in England November 15 of the same year, assumed the executive powers of the king, although he was not officially crowned until 1689.

[11] Sir William Jones, a distinguished lawyer and attorney general from 1675 until 1679, argued against Charles II's dissolution of Parliament.*

[12] William and Mary.

80 was necessary for the *Publick Defence*, but also when he at last returned, he
manifested a most Furious Displeasure against those of the Council, and
all others that had forwarded any one thing for the security of the Inhabitants; while at the same time he dispatched some of his Creatures
upon secret Errands unto *Canada*, and set at Liberty some of the most
85 Murderous *Indians* which the *English* had seized upon.

This Conduct of the Governour, which is in a *Printed* Remonstrance [13]
of some of the best Gentlemen in the Council complained of, did extreamly dissatisfie the *Suspicious* People: Who were doubtless more
extream in some of their *Suspicions*, than there was any *real Occasion* for:
90 But the Governour at length raised an Army of a *Thousand English* to
Conquer this *Hundred Indians*; and this Army, whereof some of the chief
Commanders were *Papists*, underwent the Fatigues of a long and a cold
Winter, in the most *Caucasæan* [14] Regions of the Territory, till, without the
killing of *One Indian*, there were more of the poor People killed, than they
95 had Enemies there alive! This added not a little to the Dissatisfaction of
the People, and it would much more have done so, if they had seen what
the World had not *yet* seen of the *Suggestions* made by the *Irish Catholicks*
unto the Late King, published in the Year 1691. in the *Account of the*
99 *State of the Protestants in* Ireland, Licensed by the Earl of *Nottingham*,[15]
whereof one Article runs in these Express Terms, *That if any of the* Irish
cannot have their Lands in Specie, but Money in Lieu,[16] *some of them may Transport*
themselves into America, *possibly near* New-England, *to check the growing*
Independants *of that Country:* Or if they had seen what was afterwards
5 seen in a Letter from K. *James* to His *Holiness*, (as they stile his *Foolishness*)
the Pope of *Rome*;[17] that it was his full Purpose to have set up *Roman-*
Catholick Religion in the *English* Plantations of *America:* Tho' after all,
there is Cause to think that there was more made of the *Suspicions* then
flying like Wild-Fire about the Country, than a strong *Charity* would have
10 Countenanced. When the People were under these *Frights*, they had got
by the Edges a little Intimation of the then Prince of *Orange*'s glorious
Undertaking to deliver *England* from the *Feared* Evils, which were already

---

[13] That is, *A Narrative of the Proceedings of Sir Edmund Andros*, etc., for which see endnote to p. 289, ll. 55–57.

[14] That is, regions as wild and forbidding as the Caucasian mountains.*

[15] *The State of the Protestants in Ireland under the late King James's Government*, by William King (London, 1691). Daniel Finch (1647–1730), second Earl of Nottingham, a leader of the Tories, had won favor with some dissenters by his introduction of the Toleration Act and by his support of the defeated Comprehension Bill which would have enabled them to conform to the Church of England.

[16] That is, in the real, actual form of land, without any kind of substitution, as of money.

[17] Undoubtedly Innocent XII, pope from 1691 to 1700. Innocent XI had in 1688 acquiesced in the accession of William of Orange because he distrusted James II's ties to the French court. His successor Alexander VIII continued the papal hostility to Louis XIV for the next two years. James's third and last serious attempt at restoration to his throne failed in 1696, the year of the alleged letter.*

felt by *New-England*; but when the Person[18] who brought over a Copy of the Prince's *Declaration* was Imprisoned for bringing into the Country a
15 *Treasonable Paper*, and the Governour, by his Proclamation, required all Persons to use their *utmost Endeavours to hinder the Landing* of any whom the Prince might send thither, *this* put them almost out of Patience. And one thing that plunged the more Considerate[19] Persons in the Territory into uneasie thoughts, was the *Faulty Action* of some Soldiers, who upon the
20 Common *Suspicions*, deserted their *Stations* in the Army, and caused their Friends to gather together here and there in little Bodies, to protect from the Demands of the Governour their poor Children and Brethren, whom they thought bound for a *Bloody Sacrifice:* And there were also belonging to the *Rose-Frigot* some that buzz'd surprizing Stories about *Boston*, of
25 many Mischiefs to be thence expected.[20] Wherefore, some of the Principal Gentlemen in *Boston* consulting what was to be done in this Extraordinary Juncture, They all agreed that they would, if it were possible, extinguish all Essays in the People towards an *Insurrection*, in daily Hopes of Orders from *England* for their Safety: But that if the Country People by any vio-
30 lent Motions push'd the Matter on so far, as to make a *Revolution* un- avoidable, then to prevent the shedding of *Blood* by an ungoverned *Mobile*,[21] some of the Gentlemen present should appear at the Head of the *Action* with a *Declaration*[22] accordingly prepared. By the *Eighteenth* of *April*, 1689. Things were pushed on so far by the People, that certain
35 Persons first Seized the Captain of the *Frigot*, and the Rumor thereof running like Lightning through *Boston*, the whole Town was immediately in Arms, with the most *Unanimous Resolution* perhaps that ever was known to have Inspir'd any People. They then seized those Wretched Men, who by their innumerable *Extortions* and *Abuses* had made themselves the
40 Objects of *Universal Hatred*; not giving over till the *Governour* himself was become their *Prisoner:* The whole *Action* being managed without the least *Bloodshed* or *Plunder*, and with as much *Order* as ever attended any *Tumult*, it may be, in the World. Thus did the *New-Englanders* assert their Title to the Common Rights of *Englishmen*; and except the Plantations are
45 willing to Degenerate from the Temper of True *Englishmen*, or except the *Revolution* of the whole *English* Nation be condemned, their *Action* must so far be justified. On their late *Oppressors*, now under just Confinement, they took no other Satisfaction, but sent them over unto *White-Hall* for the Justice of the King and Parliament. And when the Day for the

---

[18] On April 4, 1689, John Winslow arrived in Boston with copies of the Prince of Orange's Declaration written in Holland on October 10, 1688.*

[19] That is, "Thoughtful."

[20] The sailors on the English warship in the harbor no doubt spread yarns about dire punishments in store for those who protested against Andros' rule.

[21] That is, a movable or excitable crowd; a shortened form of *Mobile vulgus*.

[22] For the "*Declaration*," see endnote to p. 289, ll. 58–59.

50 *Anniversary Election*, by their vacated *Charter*, drew near, they had many
Debates into what Form they should cast the Government, which was
till then Administred by a *Committee for the Conservation of the Peace*; com-
posed of Gentlemen whose *Hap* it was to appear in the Head of the late
Action; but their Debates Issued in this Conclusion; That the *Governour*
55 and *Magistrates*, which were in power before the late *Usurpation*, should
Resume their Places, and apply themselves unto the *Conservation of the
Peace*, and put forth what *Acts of Government* the Emergencies might
make needful for them, and thus to wait for further Directions from the
Authority of *England*. So was there Accomplished a *Revolution* which
60 delivered *New-England* from grievous Oppressions, and which was most
graciously Accepted by the *King* and *Queen*, when it was Reported unto
their Majesties. But there were new Matters for Sir *William Phips*, in a
little while, now to think upon.

§. 9. Behold the great things which were done by the Sovereign God,
65 for a Person once as little in his *own Eyes*, as in *other Mens*. All the Returns
which he had hitherto made unto the *God of his Mercies*, were but Pre-
liminaries to what remain to be related. It has been the Custom in the
Churches of *New-England*, still to expect from such Persons as they admitted unto constant Communion with them, that they do not only
70 Publickly and Solemnly *Declare* their *Consent* unto the *Covenant of Grace*,
and particularly to those Duties of it, wherein a *Particular Church-State* is
more immediately concerned, but also first relate unto the *Pastors*, and
by them unto the *Brethren*, the special Impressions which the *Grace* of
God has made upon their Souls in bringing them to this *Consent*. By this
75 *Custom* and *Caution*, though they cannot keep *Hypocrites* from their Sacred
Fellowship, yet they go as far as they can, to render and preserve themselves *Churches of Saints*, and they do further very much *Edifie one another*.
When Sir *William Phips* was now returned unto his *own House*, he began
to bethink himself, like *David*, concerning the *House* of the *God* who had
80 surrounded him with so many Favours in *his own*; and accordingly he
applied himself unto the *North Church*[1] in *Boston*, that with his open Profession of his Hearty Subjection to the *Gospel* of the Lord Jesus Christ, he
might have the *Ordinances* and the *Priviledges* of the *Gospel* added unto his
other Enjoyments. One thing that quickned his Resolution to do what
85 might be in this Matter expected from him, was a Passage which he heard
from a Minister[2] Preaching on the Title of the *Fifty-First* Psalm: *To make
a publick and an open Profession of Repentance, is a thing not mis-becoming the
greatest Man alive. It is an Honour to be found among the Repenting People of
God, though they be in Circumstances never so full of Suffering. A Famous Knight*
90 *going with other Christians to be Crowned with Martyrdom, observed, That his*

---

[1] The church of which the two Mathers were ministers, then in sole charge of Cotton Mather.
[2] The minister was Cotton Mather.*

Fellow-Sufferers were in Chains, from which the Sacrificers had, because of his Quality, excus'd him; whereupon he demanded, that he might wear Chains as well as they. For, *said he,* I would be a Knight of that Order too; *There is among our selves a Repenting People of God, who by their Confessions at their Admissions*
95 *to his Table, do signalize their being so; and thanks be to God that we have so little of Suffering in our Circumstances. But if any Man count himself grown too big to be a* Knight of that Order, *the Lord Jesus Christ himself will one Day be ashamed of that Man!* Upon this Excitation, Sir *William Phips* made his
99 Address unto a *Congregational-Church,* and he had therein one thing to propound unto himself, which few Persons of his Age, so well satisfied in *Infant-Baptism* as he was, have then to ask for. Indeed, in the Primitive Times, although the *Lawfulness* of *Infant-Baptism,* or the Precept and Pattern of *Scripture* for it, was never so much as once made a Question, yet
5 we find *Baptism* was frequently delayed by Persons upon several superstitious and unreasonable Accounts, against which we have such Fathers as *Gregory Nazianzen, Gregory Nyssen, Basil, Chrysostom, Ambrose,* and others, employing a variety of Argument. But Sir *William Phips* had hitherto delayed his *Baptism,* because the Years of his Childhood were spent where
10 there was no settled Minister, and therefore he was now not only willing to attain a good Satisfaction of his own Internal and Practical *Christianity,* before his receiving that *Mark* thereof, but he was also willing to receive it among those *Christians* that seemed most sensible of the *Bonds* which it laid them under. Offering himself therefore, first unto the *Baptism,* and
15 then unto the *Supper* of the Lord, he presented unto the Pastor of the Church, with his own *Hand-Writing,* the following *Instrument*; which because of the Exemplary *Devotion* therein expressed, and the Remarkable *History* which it gives of several Occurrences in his Life, I will here faithfully Transcribe it, without adding so much as one Word unto it.[3]
20   'The first of God's making me sensible of my *Sins,* was in the Year
'1674. by hearing your Father Preach concerning, *The Day of Trouble*
'*near.* It pleased Almighty God to smite me with a deep Sence of my
'miserable Condition, who had lived until then in the World, and had
'*done nothing for God.* I did then begin to think *what I should do to be saved?*
25 'And did bewail my *Youthful Days,* which I had spent *in vain:* I did think
'that I would begin to mind the *things of God.* Being then some time under
'your Father's Ministry, much troubled with my *Burden,* but thinking on
'that Scripture, *Come unto me, you that are weary and heavy Laden, and I will*
'*give you Rest*; I had some thoughts of drawing as near to the Communion
30 'of the Lord *Jesus* as I could; but the Ruins which the *Indian Wars*
'brought on my Affairs, and the Entanglements which my following the

---

[3] Cotton Mather may not have added anything to Phips's "Instrument," but the number of Biblical references in the long paragraph which follows make it clear that he had tutored its author, not hitherto well versed in Holy Writ.

'*Sea* laid upon me, hindred my pursuing the Welfare of my own Soul as I
'ought to have done. At length God was pleased to smile upon my *Out-*
'*ward Concerns*. The various *Providences*, both Merciful and Afflictive,
35 'which attended me in my Travels, were sanctified unto me, to make me
'*Acknowledge God in all my Ways*. I have divers Times been in danger of my
'*Life*, and I have been brought to see that I owe my *Life* to him that has
'given a *Life* so often to me: I thank God, he hath brought me to see my
'self altogether unhappy, without an Interest in the Lord Jesus Christ,
40 'and to close heartily with him, desiring him to Execute *All his Offices*
'on my Behalf. I have now, for some time, been under serious *Resolutions*,
'that I would avoid whatever I should know to be Displeasing unto God,
'and that I would *Serve him all the Days of my Life*. I believe *no Man will*
'*Repent the Service of such a Master*. I find my self *unable* to keep such
45 '*Resolutions*, but my serious *Prayers* are to the Most High, that *he* would
'*enable* me. God hath done so much for me, that I am sensible I owe my
'self to him; *To him would I give my self, and all that he has given to me*. I
'can't express his Mercies to me. But as soon as ever God had smiled
'upon me with a Turn of my Affairs, I had laid my self under the VOWS
50 'of the Lord, *That I would set my self to serve his People, and Churches here,*
'*unto the utmost of my Capacity*. I have had great Offers made me in *England*;
'but the Churches of *New-England* were those which my Heart was most
'set upon. I knew, *That if God had a People any where, it was here:* And I
'*Resolved to rise and fall with them*; neglecting very great Advantages for
55 'my Worldly Interest, that I might come and enjoy the Ordinances of the
'Lord Jesus here. It has been my Trouble, that since I came Home I
'have made no more haste to get into the *House of God*, where *I desire to*
'*be:* Especially having heard so much about the *Evil* of that Omission. I
'can do little for God, but I desire to wait upon him in his Ordinances,
60 'and to live to his Honour and Glory. My being Born in a part of the
'Country, where I had not in my *Infancy* enjoyed the *First Sacrament* of
'the *New-Testament*, has been something of a *Stumbling-Block* unto me.
'But though I have had Profers of *Baptism* elsewhere made unto me, I
'resolved rather to defer it, until I might enjoy it in the Communion of
65 'these Churches; and I have had awful Impressions from those Words of
'the Lord Jesus in *Mark*. 8. 38. *Whosoever shall be ashamed of me, and of my*
'*Words, of him also shall the Son of Man be ashamed*. When God had blessed
'me with something of the World, I had no Trouble so great as this,
'*Lest it should not be in Mercy*; and I trembled at nothing more than being
70 '*put off with a Portion here*. That I may make sure of *better things*, I now offer
'my self unto the Communion of this Church of the Lord JESUS.
    Accordingly on *March* 23. 1690. after he had in the Congregation of

66   *Mark/Matth.*

North-Boston given himself up, *first unto the Lord, and then unto his People,* he was *Baptized,* and so received into the *Communion* of the Faithful there.

75 §. 10. Several times, about, before and after *this time,* did I hear him express himself unto this purpose: *I have no need at all to look after any further Advantages for my self in this World; I may sit still at Home, if I will, and enjoy my Ease for the rest of my Life; but I believe that I should offend God in my doing so: For I am now in the Prime of my Age and Strength, and, I thank God, I can*
80 *undergo Hardship: He only knows how long I have to live; but I think 'tis my Duty to venture my Life in doing of good, before an useless Old Age comes upon me: Wherefore I will now expose my self, while I am able, and as far as I am able, for the Service of my Country: I was Born for others, as well as my self.* I say, many a time have I heard him to express himself: And agreeable to this
85 Generous *Disposition* and *Resolution* was all the rest of his Life. About this time *New-England* was miserably *Briar'd* in the Perplexities of an *Indian War;* and the Salvages, in the *East* part of the Country, issuing out from their inaccessible *Swamps,* had for many Months made their Cruel Depredations upon the poor *English* Planters, and surprized many of the
90 Plantations on the Frontiers, into Ruin. The *New-Englanders* found, that while they continued only on the *Defensive* part, their *People* were thinned, and their *Treasures* wasted, without any hopes of seeing a Period put unto the *Indian Tragedies;* nor could an Army greater than *Xerxes's*[1] have easily come at the seemingly contemptible handful of *Tawnies* which
95 made all this Disturbance; or, *Tamerlain,*[2] the greatest Conqueror that ever the World saw, have made it a Business of no *Trouble* to have *Conquered* them: They found, that they were like to make no Weapons reach their Enswamped Adversaries, except Mr. *Milton* could have shown them
99 how

> *To have pluckt up the Hills with all their Load,*
> *Rocks, Waters, Woods, and by their shaggy tops,*
> *Up-lifting, borne them in their Hands, therewith*
> *The Rebel Host to've over-whelm'd—*

5 So it was thought that the *English* Subjects, in these Regions of *America,* might very properly take this occasion to make an attempt upon the *French,* and by reducing them under the *English* Government, put an Eternal Period at once unto all their Troubles from the *Frenchified Pagans.* This was a Motion urged by Sir *William Phips* unto the General Court of

3 *borne/bore*

[1] Xerxes the Great, the Persian conqueror of Egypt and of Thermopylae and Athens in the fifth century B.C.
[2] Tamerlane or Tamburlaine (1336?–1405), a Mongol conqueror, sometimes called the "Prince of Destruction," invaded Turkestan, Persia, Central Asia, and Russia as far as Moscow, destroyed Delhi, and died while planning to conquer China.

10 the *Massachuset-Colony*; and he then made unto the Court a brave *Offer*
of his own Person and Estate, for the Service of the Publick in their present
Extremity, as far as they should see Cause to make use thereof. Whereupon
they made a *First Essay* against the *French*, by sending a Naval Force, with
about Seven Hundred Men, under the Conduct of Sir *William Phips*,
15 against *L'Acady*³ and *Nova Scotia*; of which Action we shall give only this
General and Summary Account; that Sir *William Phips* set Sail from
Nantascot, April 28. 1690. Arriving at *Port-Royal, May* 11. and had the
Fort quickly Surrender'd into his Hands by the *French* Enemy, who
despaired of holding out against him. He then took Possession of that
20 Province for the *English* Crown, and having Demolished the Fort, and
sent away the Garrison, Administred unto the Planters an *Oath of Allegiance* to King *William* and Queen *Mary*, he left what Order he thought
convenient for the Government of the Place, until further Order should
be taken by the Governour and Council of the *Massachuset*-Colony, unto
25 whom he returned *May* 30. with an acceptable Account of his Expedition,⁴ and accepted a Place among the *Magistrates* of that Colony, to
which the *Free-Men* had chosen him at their *Anniversary Election* Two Days
before.

Thus the Country, once given by King *James* the First unto Sir
30 *William Alexander*,⁵ was now by another Sir *William* recovered out of
the Hands of the *French*, who had afterwards got the Possession of it;
and there was added unto the *English Empire*, a Territory, whereof no
Man can Read Monsieur *Denys's Description Geographique & Historique
des Costes de l'Amerique Septentrionale*,⁶ but he must reckon the Conquest
35 of a Region so Improvable, for *Lumber*, for *Fishing*, for *Mines*, and for
Furrs, a very considerable *Service*. But if a smaller *Service* has, e'er now,
ever merited a *Knighthood*, Sir *William* was willing to Repeat his Merits
by Actions of the greatest *Service* possible:

*Nil Actum credens, si quid superesset agendum.*⁷

40 §. 11. The Addition of this *French* Colony to the *English* Dominion,
was no more than a *little step* towards a *greater Action*, which was first in

---

³ Acadia, i.e., Nova Scotia and westward to the Kennebec.

⁴ However acceptable Phips's report may have been to the people of Boston, he had showed
a "scandalous rapacity" at Port Royal, taking there much plunder for himself. Mather may
have known this because Phips was ordered by Governor Bradstreet to give back some of his
loot—an order he did not fully obey. But Mather either did not hear of this or, more probably,
chose not to mention it lest it tarnish his glorification of his subject.*

⁵ Sir William Alexander, Earl of Stirling (1567?–1640), was granted jurisdiction over Nova
Scotia and Canada in 1621.

⁶ Nicolas Denys (1598–1688) was a pioneer and trader in New France. In 1653–1654 he
bought the Gulf of St. Lawrence coast of Nova Scotia and New Brunswick from Canso to
the Gaspé Peninsula, including Prince Edward Island and other islands, and held a royal
commission as governor.*

⁷ "Thinking nothing done, if anything remained to be done."*

the Design of Sir *William Phips*, and which was, indeed, the *greatest Action* that ever the *New-Englanders* Attempted. There was a time when the *Philistines* had made some Inroads and Assaults from the *Northward*, upon
45 the Skirts of *Goshen*, where the *Israelites* had a Residence, before their coming out of *Egypt*. The *Israelites*, and especially that Active Colony of the *Ephraimites*, were willing to Revenge these Injuries upon their wicked Neighbours; they presumed themselves Powerful and Numerous enough to Encounter the *Canaanites*, even in their own Country; and they formed
50 a brisk *Expedition*, but came off unhappy Losers in it: the *Jewish Rabbins* tell us, they lost no less than *Eight Thousand* Men. The *Time* was not yet come; there was more *Haste* than good *Speed* in the Attempt;[1] they were not enough concerned for the *Counsel* and *Presence* of God in the Undertaking; they mainly propounded the *Plunder* to be got among a People,
55 whose Trade was that wherewith *Beasts* enriched them; so the business miscarried. This History the Psalmist going to recite, says, *I will utter dark Sayings of old*. Now that what befel Sir *William Phips*, with his whole Country of *New-England*, may not be almost forgotten among *the dark Sayings of old*, I will here give the true Report of a very memorable
60 Matter.

It was *Canada* that was the chief Source of *New-England*'s Miseries. *There* was the main Strength of the *French*; *there* the *Indians* were mostly supplied with Ammunition; *thence* Issued Parties of Men, who uniting with the Salvages, barbarously murdered many Innocent *New-Englanders*,
65 without any Provocation on the *New-English* part, except this, that *New-England* had Proclaimed King *William* and Q. *Mary*, which they said were *Usurpers*; and as *Cato* could make no Speech in the Senate without that Conclusion, *Delenda est Carthago*;[2] so it was the general Conclusion of all that Argued sensibly about the safety of that Country, *Canada must*
70 *be Reduced*. It then became the concurring Resolution of all *New-England*, with *New-York*, to make a Vigorous Attack upon *Canada* at once, both by Sea and Land.

And a Fleet was accordingly fitted out from *Boston*, under the Command of Sir *William Phips*, to fall upon *Quebeque*, the chief City of *Canada*.
75 They waited until *August* for some Stores of War from *England*, whither they had sent for that purpose early in the Spring; but none at last arriving, and the Season of the Year being so far spent, Sir *William* could not, without many Discouragements upon his Mind, proceed in a Voyage, for which he found himself so poorly provided. However, the Ships being
80 taken up, and the Men on Board, his usual Courage would not permit him to Desist from the Enterprize; but he set Sail from *Hull* near *Boston*, *August* 9. 1690. with a Fleet of *Thirty Two* Ships and Tenders; whereof

---

[1] An English proverb.*
[2] "Carthage must be destroyed."*

one, called *the Six Friends*, carrying Forty Four great Guns, and Two
Hundred Men, was *Admiral*.[3] Sir *William* dividing the Fleet into several
85 Squadrons, whereof there was *the Six Friends*, Captain *Gregory Sugars*
Commander, with Eleven more of the Admiral's Squadron, of which one
was also a Capital Ship, namely, *The John and Thomas*, Captain *Thomas
Carter* Commander; of the *Vice-Admirals*, the *Swan*, Captain *Thomas
Gilbert* Commander, with Nine more; of the *Rear-Admirals*, the *America-
90 Merchant*, Captain *Joseph Eldridge* Commander, with Nine more, and
above Twenty Hundred Men on Board the whole Fleet: He so happily
managed his Charge, that they every one of them Arrived safe at Anchor
before *Quebeck*, although they had as dangerous, and almost untrodden a
Path, to take *Un-Piloted*, for the whole Voyage, as ever any Voyage was
95 undertaken with. Some small *French Prizes* he took by the way, and set up
English Colours upon the Coast, here and there, as he went along; and
before the Month of *August* was out, he had spent several Days as far
onward of his Voyage, as between the Island of *Antecosta*,[4] and the *Main*.
99 But when they entred the mighty River of *Canada*, such adverse Winds
encountred the Fleet, that they were *Three Weeks* dispatching the way,
which might otherwise have been gone in *Three Days*, and it was the Fifth
of *October*, when a fresh Breeze coming up at *East*, carried them along by
the *North* Shore, up to the Isle of *Orleans*;[5] and then haling *Southerly*, they
5 passed by the *East* end of that Island, with the whole Fleet approaching
the City of *Quebeck*. This loss of Time, which made it so late before the
Fleet could get into the Country, where a cold and fierce *Winter* was
already very far advanced, gave no very *good* Prospect of Success to the
Expedition; but that which gave a much *worse*, was a most horrid *Mis-
10 management*, which had, the mean while, happened in the *West*. For a
Thousand *English* from *New-York*, and *Albany*, and *Connecticut*, with
Fifteen Hundred *Indians*, were to have gone over-land in the *West*, and
fallen upon *Mount-Royal*,[6] while the Fleet was to Visit *Quebeck* in the *East*;
and no Expedition could have been better laid than *This*, which was
15 thus contrived. But those *English* Companies in the *West*, marching as far
as the great Lake that was to be passed, found their *Canoos* not provided,
according to Expectation; and the *Indians* also were [*How?* God knows,
and will one Day Judge!] Dissuaded from Joining with the *English*; and
the Army met with such Discouragements, that they returned.

18 Judge!]/Judge!

[3] "Admiral," here in the sense of the ship in which the admiral of a fleet makes his headquarters.
[4] Anticosti, a flat and narrow island at the head of the Saint Lawrence, northeast of the
Gaspé Peninsula.
[5] The Island of Orleans, in the river close to Quebec.
[6] Montreal.

20   Had this *Western Army*[7] done but so much as continued at the *Lake*, the Diversion thereby given to the *French* Quartered at *Mount-Royal*, would have rendered the Conquest of *Quebeck* easie and certain; but the Governour of *Canada* being Informed of the Retreat made by the *Western-Army*, had opportunity, by the cross Winds that kept back the Fleet,
25 unhappily to get the whole Strength of all the Country into the City, before the Fleet could come up unto it. However, none of these Difficulties hindred Sir *William Phips* from sending on Shoar the following Summons, on *Monday* the Sixth of *October*.

Sir *William Phips*, Knight, General and Commander in Chief, in and over
30   Their Majesties Forces of *New-England*, by Sea and Land;
        To Count *Frontenac*,[8] Lieutenant-General and Governour for the *French* King at *Canada*; or in his Absence, to his Deputy, or Him, or Them, in Chief Command at *Quebeck*.[9]

*T*HE *War between the Two Crowns of* England *and* France, *doth not only*
35   *sufficiently* Warrant, *but the Destruction made by the* French *and* Indians, *under your Command and Encouragement, upon the Persons and Estates of Their Majesties Subjects of* New-England, *without Provocation on their part, hath put them under the* Necessity *of this Expedition, for their own Security and Satisfaction. And although the Cruelties and Barbarities used against them, by the*
40 French *and* Indians, *might, upon the present Opportunity, prompt unto a severe* Revenge, *yet being desirous to avoid all Inhumane and Unchristian-like Actions, and to prevent shedding of Blood as much as may be;*
        I the aforesaid Sir William Phips, *Knight, do hereby, in the Name, and in the Behalf of Their Most Excellent Majesties,* William *and* Mary, *King and*
45 Queen *of* England, Scotland, France *and* Ireland, *Defenders of the Faith; and by Order of Their said Majesties Government of the* Massachuset-*Colony in* New-England, *Demand a present Surrender of your Forts and Castles, undemolished, and the King's, and other Stores, unimbezzelled, with a seasonable Delivery of all Captives; together with a Surrender of all your Persons and Estates*
50 *to my Dispose: Upon the doing whereof you may expect Mercy from me, as a* Christian, *according to what shall be found for Their Majesties Service, and the Subjects Security. Which if you Refuse forthwith to do, I am come Provided, and am Resolved, by the help of God, in whom I trust, by Force of Arms, to Revenge*

44   William/Wiiliam

    [7] The unsuccessful leader of this "Western army" was Fitz-John Winthrop, direct descendant of the two Winthrops whom Mather had eulogized in earlier pages of the *Magnalia*.*
    [8] Louis de Buade, Comte de Frontenac (1620–1698), was in 1672 appointed governor of New France; called back to France in 1682, he was in 1689 once again made governor of the French in Canada.*
    [9] Mather's version of Phips's summons agrees perfectly with the account of it by the French.*

all Wrongs and Injuries offered, and bring you under Subjection to the Crown of
55 England; *and when too late, make you wish you had accepted of the Favour ten-*
dered.

Your Answer Positive in an Hour, returned by your own Trumpet, with the
Return of mine, is Required, upon the Peril that will ensue.

The Summons being Delivered unto Count *Frontenac,* his Answer was;
60 *That Sir* William Phips, *and those with him, were* Hereticks *and* Traitors
to their King, and had taken up with that Usurper, *the Prince of* Orange, *and*
had made a Revolution, *which if it had not been made,* New-England *and*
the French *had been* all One; *and that no other Answer was to be expected from*
him, but what should be from the Mouth of his Cannon.[10]
65   General *Phips* now saw that it must cost him *Dry Blows,*[11] and that he
must Roar his Perswasions out of the Mouths of *Great Guns,* to make himself Master of a City which had certainly Surrender'd it self unto him,
if he had arrived but a little sooner, and Summon'd it before the coming
down of Count *Frontenac* with all his Forces, to Command the oppressed
70 People there, who would have been, many of them, gladder of coming
under the *English* Government. Wherefore on the Seventh of *October,* the
English, that were for the Land-Service, went on Board their lesser
Vessels, in order to Land; among which there was a Bark, wherein was
Captain *Ephraim Savage,*[12] with sixty Men, that ran a-ground upon the
75 *North*-Shoar, near two Miles from *Quebeck,* and could not get off, but lay
in the same Distress that *Scæva*[13] did, when the *Britains* poured in their
Numbers upon the *Bark,* wherein he, with a few more Soldiers of *Cæsar's*
Army, were, by the disadvantage of the *Tide,* left Ashoar: The *French,*
with *Indians,* that saw them lye there, came near, and Fired thick upon
80 them, and were bravely Answered; and when two or Three Hundred of
the Enemy, at last planted a Field-Piece against the *Bark,* while the Wind
blew so hard, that no help could be sent unto his Men, the General advanced so far, as to Level Two or Three great Guns, conveniently enough
to make the Assailants Fly; and when the Flood came, the Bark happily
85 got off, without the hurt of one Man aboard. But so violent was the Storm
of Wind all this Day, that it was not possible for them to Land until the
Eighth of *October;* when the *English* counting every *Hour* to be a *Week*
until they were come to Battel, vigorously got Ashoar, designing to enter

70   gladder/glader

[10] Mather condenses Frontenac's answer, but gives its essential gist.*
[11] Ordinarily "dry blows" signified "blows without bloodshed," but in obsolete usage
meant simply "hard" or "severe." By employing it in this sense, Mather in effect indulged
in a pun.*
[12] Captain Savage, a trader in Boston, was in 1674 made a member of the artillery company
there, appointed its ensign four years later, and its captain in 1683.*
[13] A partisan of Julius Caesar.*

the *East*-end of the City. The *Small-Pox* had got into the Fleet, by which
90 Distemper prevailing, the number of Effective Men which now went
Ashoar, under the Command of Lieutenant General *Walley*,[14] did not
amount unto more than Fourteen Hundred; but Four Companies of
these were drawn out as *Forlorns*,[15] whom, on every side, the Enemy
fired at; nevertheless, the *English* Rushing with a shout, at once upon
95 them caused them to Run as fast as Legs could carry them: So that the
whole *English* Army, expressing as much Resolution as was in *Cæsar*'s
Army, when they first landed on *Britain*, in spight of all opposition from
the Inhabitants, marched on until it was dark, having first killed many
99 of the *French*, with the loss of but *Four* Men of their own; and frighted about
Seven or Eight Hundred more of the *French* from an Ambuscado, where
they lay ready to fall upon them. But some thought, that by *staying in the
Valley*, they took the way *never to get over the Hill:*[16] And yet for them to
stay where they were, till the smaller Vessels came up the River before
5 them, so far as by their Guns to secure the Passage of the Army in their
getting over, was what the Council of War had ordered. But the Violence
of the *Weather*, with the General's being sooner plunged into the heat of
Action than was intended, hindred the smaller Vessels from attending
that Order. And this Evening a *French* Deserter coming to them, assured
10 them, that Nine Hundred Men were on their March from *Quebeck* to
meet them, already passed a little Rivulet that lay at the end of the City,
but seeing them Land so suddenly, and so valiantly run down those that
first Encountered them, they had Retreated: Nevertheless, That Count
Frontenac was come down to *Quebeck* with no fewer than *Thirty Hundred*
15 Men to defend the City, having left but *Fifty* Souldiers to defend *Mount
Real*, because they had understood, that the *English* Army on that side,
were gone back to *Albany*. Notwithstanding this dis-spiriting Information,
the common Souldiers did with much vehemency Beg and Pray, that
they might be led on; professing, that they had rather lose their Lives
20 on the Spot, than fail of taking the City; but the more wary Commanders
considered how rash a thing it would be, for about Fourteen Hundred
Raw Men, tired with a long Voyage, to assault more than Twice as
many Expert Souldiers, who were *Galli in suo sterquilinio*, or *Cocks Crowing
on their own Dunghil.*[17] They were, in truth, now gotten into the grievous

---

13 Encountered/Encounted

[14] John Walley, second in command to Phips, was English-born but came to New England
with his father and settled in Barnstable, then part of Plymouth. He was a member of the
provincial council called in 1689 and was continued in office by Increase Mather through
his choice of councillors in 1691.*
[15] Troops sent to the front; vanguards.
[16] An adaptation of a proverb.*
[17] Compare the proverb, "Every cock is proud [bold] on his own dunghill." Cotton Mather
here puns on "gallus," cock, and "gallus," a Gaul or Frenchman.*

25 Case which *Livy* describes, when he says, *Ibi grave est Bellum gerere, ubi non consistendi aut procedendi locus*; *quocunque aspexeris Hostilia sunt omnia*;[18] look on one side or t'other, all was full of *Hostile Difficulties*. And indeed, whatever Popular Clamour has been made against any of the Commanders, it is apparent that they acted considerately, in making a *Pause*
30 upon what was before them; and they did a greater kindness to their Souldiers than they have since been thanked for. But in this time, General *Phips* and his Men of War, with their *Canvas Wings*, flew close up unto the West-end of the City, and there he behaved himself with the greatest Bravery imaginable; nor did the other Men of War forbear to follow his
35 brave Example: Who never discovered himself more in his Element, than when (as the Poet expresseth it,)

> *The Slaughter Breathing Brass grew hot, and spoke*
> *In Flames of Lightning, and in Clouds of Smoke:*

He lay within *Pistol-shot* of the Enemies Cannon, and beat them from
40 thence, and very much batter'd the Town, having his own Ship shot through in almost an Hundred Places with *Four and Twenty Pounders*, and yet but one Man was killed, and only Two Mortally Wounded Aboard him, in this hot Engagement, which continued the greatest part of that Night, and several Hours of the Day ensuing. But wondring
45 that he saw no *Signal* of any Effective Action Ashoar at the East-end of the City, he sent that he might know the Condition of the Army there; and received Answer, That several of the Men were so frozen in their Hands and Feet, as to be disabled from Service, and others were apace falling sick of the *Small-Pox*. Whereupon he order'd them on Board
50 immediately to refresh themselves, and he intended then to have renew'd his Attack upon the City, in the Method of Landing his Men in the Face of it, under the shelter of his great Guns; having to that purpose provided also a considerable number of well-shaped *Wheel-Barrows*, each of them carrying Two *Petarraro's*[19] apiece, to March before the Men, and
55 make the Enemy Fly, with as much Contempt as overwhelmed the *Philistines*, when undone by *Foxes* with *Torches* in their Tails; (remembred in an Anniversary Diversion[20] every *April* among the Ancient *Romans*, taught by the *Phenicians*.)
   While the Measures to be further taken were debating, there was made
60 an Exchange of Prisoners, the *English* having taken several of the *French* in divers Actions, and the *French* having in their Hands divers of the *English*,

---

[18] "It is difficult to wage war when there is no chance to halt or to proceed, and wherever one looks everything is hostile."*
[19] This probably means "peterero" or "pedrero," an old name for a very short piece of chambered ordnance—a small gun or cannon.*
[20] The "Diversion" was the annual Cerealia from April 12 to 20 in honor of Ceres.*

whom the *Indians* had brought Captives unto them. The Army now on Board continued still Resolute and Courageous, and on fire for the Conquest of *Quebeck*; or if they had missed of doing it by Storm, they
65 knew that they might, by possessing themselves of the Isle of *Orleans*, in a little while have starved them out. Incredible Damage they might indeed have done to the Enemy before they Embarked, but they were willing to preserve the more undefensible Parts of the Country in such a Condition, as might more sensibly Encourage the Submission of the
70 Inhabitants unto the Crown of *England*, whose Protection was desired by so many of them. And still they were loth to play for any lesser Game than the immediate Surrender of *Quebeck* it self. But e're a full *Council of War* could conclude the next Steps to be taken, a violent *Storm* arose that separated the Fleet, and the Snow and the Cold became so extream,
75 that they could not continue in those Quarters any longer.

Thus, by an evident *Hand of Heaven*, sending one unavoidable Disaster after another, as well-formed an Enterprize, as perhaps was ever made by the *New-Englanders*, most unhappily miscarried; and General *Phips* under went a very mortifying Disappointment of a Design, which his
80 Mind was, as much as ever any, set upon. He arrived *Nov.* 19. at *Boston*, where, although he found himself, as well as the Publick, thrown into very *uneasie* Circumstances, yet he had this to Comfort him, that neither his Courage nor his Conduct could reasonably have been Taxed; nor could it be said that any Man could have done more than he did, under
85 so many *Embarassments of his Business*, as he was to Fight withal. He also relieved the uneasiness of his Mind, by considering, that his Voyage to *Canada*, diverted from his Country an *Horrible Tempest* from an Army of *Boss-Lopers*,[21] which had prepar'd themselves, as 'tis affirmed, that Winter, to fall upon the *New-English* Colonies, and by falling on them,
90 would probably have laid no little part of the Country desolate. And he further considered, that in this Matter, like *Israel* engaging against *Benjamin*, it may be, we saw yet but the *beginning* of the matter: And that the way to *Canada* now being learnt, the Foundation of a Victory over it might be laid in what had been already done. Unto this purpose likewise,
95 he was heard sometimes applying the Remarkable Story reported by *Bradwardine*.[22]

'There was an *Hermit*, who being vexed with Blasphemous Injections 'about the Justice and Wisdom of Divine *Providence*, an Angel in Hu-
99 'mane Shape invited him to Travel with him, *That he might see the hidden 'Judgments of God.* Lodging all Night at the House of a Man who kindly

---

[21] A Dutch name for "woods runners," in general equivalent to the French "coureurs de bois." Like them the "Boss-Lopers" were not only expert traders with the Indians and at home in the woods, but also indomitable fighters in forest warfare.*

[22] Thomas Bradwardine (1290?–1349), educated at Oxford, later Archbishop of Canterbury. His lectures and his religious treatises won him the name of "Doctor Profundus."*

'entertain'd them, the Angel took away a valuable Cup from their
'Host, at their going away in the Morning, and bestowed this Cup upon
'a very *wicked Man*, with whom they lodged the Night ensuing. The Third
5 'Night they were most lovingly Treated at the House of a very Godly
'Man, from whom, when they went in the Morning, the Angel meeting a
'Servant of his, threw him over the Bridge into the Water, where he was
'drowned. And the Fourth, being in like manner most courteously
'Treated at the House of a very Godly Man, the Angel before Morning
10 'did unaccountably kill his only *Child*. The Companion of the Journey
'being wonderfully offended at these things, would have left his *Guardian:*
'But the Angel then thus Addressed him, *Understand now the secret Judg-*
'*ments of God! The first Man that entertained us, did inordinately affect that* Cup
'*which I took from him;* '*twas for the Advantage of his Interiour that I took it away,*
15 '*and I gave it unto the impious Man, as the present Reward of his good Works,*
'*which is all the Reward that he is like to have. As for our* Third *Host, the*
'*Servant which I slew had formed a bloody Design to have slain his Master, but*
'*now, you see, I have saved the Life of the Master, and prevented something of*
'*growth unto the Eternal Punishment of the Murderer. As for our* Fourth *Host,*
20 '*before his* Child *was Born unto him, he was a very liberal and bountiful Person,*
'*and he did abundance of good with his Estate; but when he saw he was like to*
'*leave such an Heir, he grew Covetous; wherefore the Soul of the Infant is Trans-*
'*lated into Paradise, but the occasion of Sin is, you see, mercifully taken away from*
'*the Parent.*

25 Thus General *Phips*, though he had been used unto *Diving* in his time,
would say, *That the things which had befallen him in this Expedition, were too
deep to be* Dived *into!*

§. 12. From the time that General *Pen*[1] made his Attempt upon
Hispaniola, with an Army that, like the *New-English* Forces against
30 *Canada*, miscarried after an Expectation of having little to do but to
Possess and Plunder; even to this Day, the general Disaster which hath
attended almost every Attempt of the *European* Colonies in *America*, to
make any considerable Encroachments upon their Neighbours, is a
Matter of some close Reflection. But of the Disaster which now befel
35 poor *New-England* in particular, every one will easily conclude none of
the least Consequences to have been the *Extream Debts* which that
Country was now plunged into; there being *Forty Thousand* Pounds, more
or less, now to be paid, and not a Penny in the Treasury to pay it withal.
In this *Extremity* they presently found out an *Expedient*, which may serve
40 as an *Example* for any People in other Parts of the World, whose Distresses

13   *did/dtd*   14   *'twas/twas*

[1] Sir William Penn (1621–1670) was appointed general and commander in chief of a fleet
sent against the Spanish West Indies. He was routed at Hispaniola, but captured Jamaica.*

may call for a sudden supply of *Money* to carry them through any Important *Expedition*.[2] The *General Assembly* first pass'd *an Act* for the Levying of such a Sum of *Money* as was wanted, within such a Term of time as was judged convenient; and this *Act* was a *Fund*, on which the *Credit* of such a
45 Sum should be rendered *passable* among the People. Hereupon there was appointed an able and faithful *Committee* of Gentlemen, who Printed, from *Copper-Plates*, a just Number of *Bills*, and Florished, Indented, and Contrived them in such a manner, as to make it impossible to Counterfeit any of them, without a speedy Discovery of the *Counterfeit*:
50 Besides which, they were all Signed by the Hands of *Three* belonging to that *Committee*. These *Bills* being of several Sums, from *Two Shillings*, to *Ten Pounds*, did confess the *Massachuset-Colony* to be *Endebted* unto the Persons, in whose Hands they were, the Sums therein expressed; and Provision was made, that if any *Particular Bills* were Irrecoverably Lost,
55 or Torn, or Worn by the Owners, they might be Recruited without any Damage to the *whole in general*. The *Publick Debts* to the *Sailors* and *Soldiers*, now upon the point of *Mutiny*, (for, *Arma Tenenti, Omnia dat, qui Justa negat!*[3]) were in these *Bills* paid immediately: But that further *Credit* might be given thereunto, it was Ordered that they should be accepted
60 by the Treasurer, and all Officers that were Subordinate unto him, in all *Publick Payments*, at Five *per Cent.* more than the Value expressed in them. The People knowing that the *Tax-Act* would, in the space of Two Years at least, fetch into the Treasury as much as all the *Bills of Credit*, thence emitted, would amount unto, were willing to be furnished with
65 *Bills*, wherein 'twas their Advantage to pay their *Taxes*, rather than in any other *Specie*; and so the *Sailors* and *Soldiers* put off their *Bills*, instead of *Money*, to those with whom they had any Dealings, and they *Circulated* through all the Hands in the Colony pretty Comfortably. Had the *Government* been so settled,[4] that there had not been any doubt of any

53   Persons/Person   54   Irrecoverably/Irrecoverable

[2] Mather, although not skilled in finance, had even before the Quebec debacle recognized the shaky financial state of New England. In 1690, before Phips sailed, he delivered the annual election sermon, published as *The Serviceable Man*, pointing out that French and Indian wars had been costly, trade was poor, money scarce, and some loans made at 12 percent. In the long paragraph which follows here, Mather argues the usefulness of issuing paper currency in such circumstances, and inveighs against those who disagreed and in some cases hampered its success. One of these was Thomas Savage, who, in his *Account*, estimated that the Quebec enterprise had put Massachusetts more than £50,000 in debt, and declared that soldiers and seamen who served in the undertaking could get only half the value of the paper bills with which they were paid. Here "*Expedition*," coupled with "*Extream*," "*Extremity*," "*Expedient*," is a striking example of Mather's delight in wordplay, emphasized by his use of italics.*

[3] "He who denies his due to the strong man armed grants him everything."*

[4] Although Andros was no longer governor, no one had been appointed in his place, and the new charter did not arrive until 1692. Meanwhile, the former government and its members remained in office, but many people felt that they were not secure enough to carry and meet such a credit as that of £40,000.*

70 Obstruction, or Diversion to be given to the Prosecution of the *Tax-Act*, by a *Total Change* of their Affairs then depending at *Whitehall*, 'tis very certain, that the *Bills of Credit* had been better than so much ready *Silver*; yea, the *Invention* had been of more use to the *New-Englanders*, than if all their *Copper Mines* had been opened, or the Mountains of
75 *Peru*⁵ had been removed into these Parts of *America*. The *Massachuset Bills of Credit* had been like the *Bank Bills* of *Venice*,⁶ where though there were not, perhaps, a *Ducat* of Money in the *Bank*, yet the *Bills* were esteemed more than Twenty *per Cent.* better than Money, among the Body of the People, in all their Dealings. But many People being afraid,
80 that the Government would in half a Year be so overturned, as to Convert their *Bills of Credit* altogether into *Wast Paper*, the *Credit* of them was thereby very much impaired; and they, who first received them, could make them yield little more than *Fourteen* or *Sixteen* Shillings in the Pound;⁷ from whence there arose those Idle *Suspicions* in the Heads of many
85 more Ignorant and Unthinking Folks concerning the use thereof, which, to the Incredible Detriment of the Province, are not wholly laid aside unto this Day. However, this Method of paying the *Publick Debts*, did no less than save the Publick from a perfect Ruin: And e're many Months were expired, the Governour and Council had the Pleasure of
90 seeing the *Treasurer* burn before their Eyes many a Thousand Pounds Worth of the *Bills*, which had passed about until they were again returned unto the Treasury; but before their being returned, had happily and honestly, without a Farthing of *Silver Coin*, discharged the *Debts*, for which they were intended. But that which helped these *Bills* unto much
95 of their *Credit*, was the Generous Offer of many Worthy Men in *Boston*, to run the Risque of selling their *Goods* reasonably for them: And of these, I think I may say, that General *Phips* was in some sort the *Leader*; who at the very beginning, meerly to Recommend the *Credit* of the *Bills*
99 unto other Persons, chearfully laid down a considerable quantity of *ready Money* for an equivalent parcel of them. And thus in a little time the Country waded through the Terrible *Debts* which it was fallen into: In this, though unhappy enough, yet not so unhappy as in the *Loss of Men*,⁸ by which the Country was at the same time consumed. 'Tis true,

---

⁵ Some copper-mining activity developed early in the seventeenth century in Massachusetts and elsewhere on the eastern seaboard of North America. John Winthrop, Jr., was active in the search for the metal. Peru was famous for the mineral wealth of its high mountains, which included copper as well as silver and gold.*

⁶ Mather follows here a book published in London in 1688, *A Model for . . . a Bank of Credit: With a Discourse in Explanation . . . Adapted to the Use of Any Trading Countrey, Where there is a Scarcity of Moneys: More Especially for his Majesties Plantations in America.*

⁷ Some shrewd Bostonians refused to accept the Bills at their face value. Soldiers and seamen were easy prey for them, and they and other citizens were thus "horribly injured" and in their eyes the government was made "Contemptible and not worthy to be trusted."*

⁸ About twenty or thirty men were killed, but one hundred fifty of the soldiers, "some of them persons of great worth," died of "Small Pox & a malignant feaver."*

5 there was very *little Blood* spilt in the Attack made upon *Quebeck*; and
there was a *Great Hand* of Heaven seen in it. The Churches, upon the
Call of the Government, not only observed a General *Fast* through the
Colony, for the Welfare of the Army sent unto *Quebeck*, but also kept the
Wheel of Prayer in a *Continual Motion*, by Repeated and Successive Agree-
10 ments, for Days of *Prayer* with *Fasting*, in their several Vicinities. On these
Days the Ferventest Prayers were sent up to the *God of Armies*, for the
Safety and Success of the *New-English* Army gone to *Canada*; and though
I never understood that any of the Faithful did in their *Prayers* arise to
any assurance that the Expedition should *prosper in all respects,* yet they
15 sometimes in their Devotions on these Occasions, uttered their Perswasion, that Almighty God had heard them in *this* thing, *that the* English
Army should not fall by the Hands of the French *Enemy.* Now they were marvellously delivered from doing *so;* though the Enemy had such unexpected Advantages over them, yea, and though the horrid *Winter* was
20 come on so far, that it is a Wonder the *English* Fleet, then Riding in the
River of *Canada*, fared any better than the Army which a while since
besieged *Poland*, wherein, of *Seventy Thousand* Invaders, no less than *Forty
Thousand* suddenly perished by the severity of the *Cold*, albeit it were but
the Month of *November* with them.[9] Nevertheless, a kind of *Camp-Fever*,
25 as well as the *Small-Pox*, got into the Fleet, whereby some Hundreds came
short of Home. And besides this Calamity, it was also to be lamented, that
although the most of the Fleet arrived safe at *New-England*, whereof
some Vessels indeed were driven off by Cross-Winds as far as the *West-
Indies*, before such Arrival; yet there were Three or Four Vessels which
30 totally miscarried: *One* was never heard of, a *Second* was Wreck'd, but
most of the Men were saved by another in Company; a *third* was Wreck'd
so that all the Men were either starv'd, or drown'd, or slain by the *Indians*,
except *one*, which a long while after was by means of the *French* restored:
And a *fourth* met with Accidents, which, it may be, my Reader will by
35 and by pronounce not unworthy to have been Related.

A *Brigantine*, whereof Captain *John Rainsford*[10] was Commander, having
about Threescore Men aboard, was in a very stormy Night, *Octob.* 28.
1690. stranded upon the desolate and hideous Island of *Antecosta*, an
Island in the mouth of the Mighty River of *Canada*; but through the
40 singular Mercy of God unto them, the Vessel did not, immediately, stave

32 so that/so, that

[9] In 1655 Charles X of Sweden launched a campaign to establish his mastery over the
Baltic. In the autumn he marched into Poland and quickly occupied Warsaw, Cracow, and
half of Poland. By the end of the winter, however, a combination of vigorous Polish resistance
and the rigors of fighting over the snowy plains and frozen marshes brought defeat to his
armies. News of this debacle would undoubtedly have reached New England.

[10] Captain John Rainsford, commander of the *Mary*, one of the admiral's squadron during
the attack on Quebec.*

to pieces, which if it had happened, they must have, one way or another, quickly perished. There they lay for divers Days, under abundance of bitter Weather, trying and hoping to get off their Vessel; and they solemnly set apart one Day for *Prayer* with *Fasting*, to obtain the Smiles of
45 Heaven upon them in the midst of their Distresses; and this especially, That if they must go Ashoar, they might not, by any stress of Storm, lose the *Provisions* which they were to carry with them. They were at last convinced, that they must continue no longer on Board, and therefore, by the Seventh of *November*, they applied themselves, all Hands, to get
50 their *Provisions* Ashoar upon the dismal *Island* where they had nothing but a sad and cold Winter before them; which being accomplished their Vessel *overset* [11] so as to take away from them all expectation of getting off the Island in it. Here they now built themselves Nine small *Chimney-less things* that they called *Houses*; to this purpose employing such *Boards* and
55 *Planks* as they could get from their shattered Vessel, with the help of *Trees*, whereof that squalid Wilderness had enough to serve them; and they built a particular *Store-House*, wherein they carefully Lodg'd and Lock'd the poor quantity of *Provisions*, which though scarce enough to serve a very abstemious Company for *one Month*, must now be so stinted,
60 as to hold out *Six* or *Seven*; and the Allowance agreed among them could be no better than for One Man, *Two Biskets, half a pound of Pork, half a pound of Flower, one Pint and a quarter of Pease, and two Salt Fishes per Week.* This little Handful of Men were now a sort of *Commonwealth*, extraordinarily and miserably separated from all the rest of Mankind; (but I
65 believe, they thought little enough of an *Utopia:* Wherefore they consulted and concluded such *Laws* among themselves, as they judged necessary to their subsistence, in the doleful Condition whereinto the *Providence* of God had cast them; now

—*Penitus toto divisos Orbe.* [12]

70 They set up *Good Orders*, as well as they could, among themselves; and besides their daily Devotions, they Observed the *Lord's Days*, with more solemn Exercises of Religion.

But it was not long before they began to feel the more mortal effects of the Straits whereinto they had been Reduced: Their *short* Commons, their
75 Drink of *Snow-Water*, their Hard, and Wet, and Smoaky *Lodgings*, and their Grievous *Despair of Mind*, overwhelmed some of them at such a rate, and so *ham-string'd* them, that sooner than be at the pains to go abroad, and cut their one Fuel, they would lye after a Sottish manner in

52 so as/so, as

[11] "Overset," here in the now rare sense of "capsize," "turn upside down."
[12] "Wholly sundered from all the world." *

the Cold; these things quickly brought *Sicknesses* among them. The
80 first of their Number who Died was their *Doctor*, on the 20*th* of *December*;
and then they dropt away, one after another, till between *Thirty* and
Forty of the *Sixty* were buried by their disconsolate Friends, whereof every
one look'd still to be the next that should lay his Bones in that Forsaken
Region. These poor Men did therefore, on *Monday* the Twenty Seventh of
85 *January*, keep a *Sacred Fast* (as they did, in some sort, a *Civil* one, every
Day, all this while) to beseech of Almighty God, that his *Anger* might be
turned from them, that he would not go on to cut them off in his *Anger*,
that the Extremity of the Season might be mitigated, and that they might
be prospered in some Essay to get Relief as the *Spring* should Advance
90 upon them; and they took *Notice* that God gave them a Gracious Answer
to every one of these Petitions.

But while the *Hand of God* was killing *so many* of this little *Nation*
(and yet uncapable to become a *Nation*, for it was, *Res unius Ætatis,*
populus virorum![13]) they apprehended, that they must have been under a
95 most uncomfortable Necessity to *kill* One of their Company.

Whatever *Penalties* they Enacted for other Crimes, there was One, for
which, like that of *Parricide* among the Antients.[14] they would have promised themselves, that there should not have been Occasion for any *Punish-*
99 *ments*; and that was, the Crime of *Stealing* from the Common-Stock of
their Provisions. Nevertheless they found their *Store-House* divers times
broken open, and their *Provisions* therefrom *Stolen* by divers unnatural
Children of the *Leviathan,* while it was not possible for them to preserve
their feeble Store-House from the *Stone-Wall-breaking* Madness of these
5 unreasonable Creatures. This Trade of *Stealing*, if it had not been stopp'd
by some *exemplary Severity*, they must in a little while, by *Lot* or *Force*,
have come to have *Canibally* devoured one another; for there was nothing
to be done, either at *Fishing*, or *Fowling*, or *Hunting*, upon that Rueful
Island, in the depth of a Frozen Winter; and though they sent as far as
10 they could upon Discovery, they could not find on the Island any *Living*
thing in the World, besides themselves. Wherefore, though by an *Act*
they made *Stealing* to be so *Criminal*, that several did Run the *Gantlet*
for it, yet they were not far from being driven, after all, to make one
Degree and Instance of it *Capital*. There was a wicked *Irishman* among
15 them, who had such a *Voracious Devil* in him, that after divers *Burglaries*
upon the *Store-House*, committed by him, at last he *Stole*, and *Eat* with such
a *Pamphagous*[15] *Fury*, as to Cram himself with no less than *Eighteen Biskets*

---

[13] "A thing of a single generation, a people of males."*
[14] The first Roman law against parricide (*c.*81 B.C.) provided that the murderer of a parent
should be bound in a sack and thrown into the sea; later laws extended punishments for
killing virtually any relative.
[15] "All-devouring, omniverous."*

at one *Stolen Meal*, and he was fain to have his Belly strok'd and bath'd before the Fire, lest he should otherwise have burst. This Amazing, and
20 indeed Murderous Villany of the *Irishman*, brought them all to their Wits Ends, how to defend themselves from the Ruin therein threatned unto them; and whatever *Methods* were proposed, it was feared that there could be no stop given to his *Furacious*[16] Exorbitancies any way but *One*; he could not be past *Stealing*, unless he were past *Eating* too. Some think therefore
25 they might have Sentenced the Wretch to Die, and after they had been at pains, upon Christian and Spiritual Accounts, to prepare him for it, have Executed the Sentence, by Shooting him to Death: Concluding Matters come to that pass, that if *they* had not Shot him, he must have *Starved* them unavoidably. Such an Action, if it were done, will doubtless
30 meet with no harder a Censure, than that of the Seven *Englishmen*, who being in a Boat carried off to Sea from St. *Christopher's*,[17] with but *one* Days Provision aboard for *Seventeen*, Singled out some of their Number by Lot, and Slew them, and Eat them; for which, when they were afterwards accused of *Murder*, the Court, in consideration of the *inevitable*
35 *Necessity*, acquitted them. Truly the *inevitable Necessity* of *Starving*, without such an Action, sufficiently grievous to them all, will very much plead for what was done (whatever it were!) by these poor *Antecostians*. And *Starved* indeed they must have been, for all this, if they had not Contrived and Performed a very desperate Adventure, which now remains to be
40 Related. There was a very diminutive kind of Boat belonging to their *Brigantine*, which they recovered out of the Wreck, and cutting this Boat in Two, they made a shift, with certain odd Materials preserved among them, to lengthen it so far, that they could therein form a *little Cuddy*, where Two or Three Men might be stowed, and they set up a *little Mast*,
45 whereto they fastened a little Sail, and accommodated it with some other *little Circumstances*,[18] according to their present poor Capacity.

On the Twenty Fifth of *March*, Five of the Company Shipped themselves upon this Doughty *Fly-Boat*, intending, if it were possible, to carry unto *Boston* the Tidings of their woful Plight upon *Antecosta*, and by help
50 from their Friends there, to return with seasonable Succours for the rest. They had not Sail'd long before they were Hemm'd in by prodigious Cakes of Ice, whereby their Boat sometimes was horribly wounded, and it was a Miracle that it was not Crush'd into a *Thousand Pieces*, if indeed a *Thousand Pieces* could have been Splintred out of so minute a *Cock-Boat*.
55 They kept labouring, and fearfully Weather-beaten, among enormous

[16] "Thievish," from the Latin "furax."
[17] Saint Christopher or Saint Kitts, an island in the British West Indies. Mather clearly found the story of the seven Englishmen in Wanley's *Wonders*, which he follows closely.*
[18] The repetition of "little" seems in the context painfully out of place; an example of Mather's insatiable delight in wordplay.

Rands[19] of Ice, which would ever now and then rub formidably upon them, and were enough to have broken the Ribs of the strongest Frigot that ever cut the Seas; and yet the signal Hand of Heaven so preserved this petty Boat, that by the Eleventh of *April* they had got a quarter of their
60 way, and came to an Anchor under Cape St. *Lawrence*,[20] having seen Land but *once* before, and that about seven Leagues off, ever since their first setting out; and yet having seen the *open* and *Ocean Sea not so much as once* in all this while, for the Ice that still encompassed them. For their support in this Time, the little Provisions they brought with them would not have
65 kept them alive; only they killed *Seale* upon the Ice, and they melted the upper part of the Ice for Drink; but fierce, wild, ugly *Sea-Horses*,[21] would often so approach them upon the Ice, that the fear of being devoured by them was not the least of their Exercises. The Day following they weighed Anchor betimes in the Morning but the *Norwest Winds* per-
70 secuted them, with the raised and raging Waves of the Sea, which almost continually poured into them; and Monstrous Islands of Ice, that seemed almost as big as *Antecosta* it self, would ever now and then come athwart them. In such a Sea they lived by the special assistance of God, until, by the Thirteenth of *April*, they got into an Island of *Land*, where they
75 made a Fire, and killed some Fowl, and some *Seale*, and found some *Goose-Eggs*, and supplied themselves with what Billets of Wood were necessary and carriageable for them; and there they stayed until the Seventeenth. Here their Boat lying near a Rock, a great Sea hove it upon the Rock, so that it was upon the very point of *oversetting*, which if it had,
80 she had been utterly disabled for any further Service, and they must have called that Harbour by the Name, which, I think, one a little more *Northward* bears, *The* Cape *without Hope*.[22] There they must have ended their weary Days! But here the good Hand of God again interposed for them; they got her off; and though they lost their *Compass* in this Hurry,
85 they sufficiently Repaired another defective one that they had aboard. Sailing from thence, by the Twenty-fourth of *April*, they made Cape *Brittoon*;[23] when a thick Fog threw them into a new Perplexity, until they were safely gotten into the Bay of *Islands*,[24] where they again wooded, and watred, and killed a few Fowl, and catched some Fish, and began to

69 weighed/weig hed

[19] Here in the obsolete sense of "pieces" or "masses."
[20] At the northern extremity of Cape Breton Island.
[21] Walruses.
[22] Cape Despair on the Gaspé Peninsula, about opposite the southern tip of Anticosti, at the entrance of Chaleur Bay.*
[23] Cape Breton.*
[24] White Island Bay on modern maps; about a third of the way down the coast of Acadia, somewhat northeast of Halifax.*

90 reckon themselves as good as *half way home*. They reached *Cape Sables*²⁵
by the Third of *May*, but by the Fifth all their Provision was again spent,
and they were out of sight of Land; nor had they any prospect of catching
any thing that lives in the *Atlantick*: which while they were lamenting
one unto another, a stout *Halibut* comes up to the top of the Water, by
95 their side; whereupon they threw out the Fishing-Line, and the Fish
took the Hook; but he proved so heavy, that it required the help of
several Hands to hale him in, and a *thankful Supper* they made on't. By
the Seventh of *May* seeing no Land, but having once more spent all
99 their Provision, they were grown almost wholly hopeless of Deliverance,
but then a Fishing Shallop of Cape *Ann*²⁶ came up with them, Fifteen
Leagues to the Eastward of that Cape. And yet before they got in, they
had so Tempestuous a Night, that they much feared perishing upon the
Rocks after all: But God carried them into *Boston* Harbour the Ninth of
5 *May*, unto the great surprize of their Friends that were in Mourning for
them: And there furnishing themselves with a Vessel fit for their Undertaking, they took a Course in a few Weeks more to fetch home their
Brethren that they left behind them at *Antecosta*.

But it is now time for us to return unto Sir *William!*
10 §. 13. All this while *CANADA* was as much written upon Sir *William*'s
Heart, as *CALLICE*, they said once, was upon Queen *Mary*'s.¹ He needed
not one to have been his daily Monitor about *Canada*: It lay down with
him, it rose up with him, it engrossed almost all his thoughts; he thought
the subduing of *Canada* to be the greatest Service that could be done for
15 *New-England*, or for the Crown of *England*, in *America*. In pursuance
whereof, after he had been but a few Weeks at Home, he took another
Voyage for *England*,² in the very depth of Winter, *when Sailing was now
dangerous*; conflicting with all the Difficulties of a tedious and a terrible
Passage, in a very little Vessel, which indeed was like enough to have
20 perished, if it had not been for the help of his generous Hand aboard, and
*his Fortunes in the bottom.*³

Arriving—*per tot Discrimina*,⁴ at *Bristol*, he hastned up to *London*; and
made his Applications to their Majesties, and the Principal Ministers of

---

²⁵ Cape Sable, the southernmost tip of Nova Scotia.
²⁶ Gloucester, on Cape Ann, the northernmost promontory of Massachusetts, was in Mather's
day, as now, a major fishing port.

---

¹ Mary of England was supposed to have died mourning the loss of Calais (Callice) from her
domain.*
² Phips was no doubt happy to go to London in the hope that success abroad might atone
for his failure in Canada and the hardships it had imposed on the Bostonians. He was also
glad to help Increase Mather, whose disciple he was, and then the most powerful of the
agents.*
³ That is, money brought with him in the hold.
⁴ "Through so many hazards."*

State, for assistance to renew an Expedition against *Canada*, concluding
25   his Representation[5] to the King with such Words as these:

'If Your Majesty shall graciously please to Commission and Assist me,
'I am ready to venture my Life again in your Service. And I doubt not,
'but by the Blessing of God, *Canada* may be added unto the rest of your
'Dominions, which will (all Circumstances considered) be of more
30   'Advantage to the Crown of *England*, than all the Territories in the
'*West-Indies* are.

The Reasons *here subjoined, are humbly Offered unto Your Majesties*
Consideration.

'*First*, The Success of this Design will greatly add to the Glory and
35   'Interest of the *English* Crown and Nation; by the Addition of the *Bever-*
'*Trade*, and Securing the *Hudson*'s *Bay* Company, some of whose *Factories*
'have lately fallen into the Hands of the *French*; and increase of *English*
'Shipping and Seamen, by gaining the Fishery of *Newfoundland*; and by
'consequence diminish the number of *French* Seamen, and cut off a great
40   'Revenue from the *French* Crown.

'*Secondly*, The Cause of the *English* in *New-England*, their failing in the
'late Attempt upon *Canada*, was their waiting for a Supply of *Ammunition*
'from *England* until *August*; their long Passage up that River; the *Cold*
'*Season* coming on, and the *Small-Pox* and *Fevers* being in the Army and
45   'Fleet, so that they could not stay Fourteen Days longer; in which time
'probably they might have taken *Quebeck*; yet, if a few Frigots be speedily
'sent, they doubt not of an happy Success; the Strength of the *French*
'being small, and the *Planters* desirous to be under the *English* Govern-
'ment.

50   '*Thirdly*, The *Jesuites* endeavour to seduce the *Maqua's*, and other *In-*
'*dians* (as is by them affirmed) suggesting the Greatness of King *Lewis*,
'and the Inability of King *William*, to do any thing against the *French*
'in those Parts, thereby to engage them in their Interests: In which, if
'they should succeed, not only *New-England*, but all our *American* Planta-
55   'tions, would be endangered by the great increase of Shipping, for the
'*French* (built in *New-England* at easie rates) to the Infinite Dishonour
'and Prejudice of the *English* Nation.

But now, for the Success of these Applications, I must entreat the
Patience of my Reader to wait until we have gone through a little more
60   of our History.

§. 14. The Reverend *INCREASE MATHER* beholding his Country
of *New-England* in a very Deplorable Condition, under a *Governour* that

---

[5] Phips was not a practiced writer, and it is probable that Cotton Mather, his pastor, or
Increase Mather, then in London, supplied the "words" used in his "Representation" to
the king.

acted by an Illegal, Arbitrary, Treasonable Commission, and Invaded *Liberty* and *Property* after such a manner, as that no Man could say any
65 thing was *his own*, he did, with the Encouragement of the Principal Gentlemen in the Country, but not without much Trouble and Hazard unto his own Person, go over to *Whitehall* in the Summer of the Year 1688. and wait upon King *James*, with a full *Representation* of their Miseries.[1] That King did give him Liberty of *Access* unto him, whenever he
70 desired it, and with many *Good Words* promised him to relieve the Oppressed People in many *Instances* that were proposed: But when the *Revolution* had brought the Prince and Princess of *Orange* to the Throne, Mr. *Mather* having the Honour divers times to wait upon the King, he still prayed for no less a Favour to *New-England*, than the full Restoration
75 of their *Charter-Priviledges*: And Sir *William Phips* happening to be then in *England*, very generously joined with Mr. *Mather* in some of those Addresses: Whereto His Majesty's Answers were always very expressive of his Gracious Inclinations. Mr. *Mather*, herein assisted also by the Right Worshipful Sir *Henry Ashurst*,[2] a most Hearty Friend of all such good
80 Men as those that once filled *New-England*, solicited the Leading Men of both Houses in the Convention Parliament, until a Bill for the Restoring of the Charters belonging to *New-England*, was fully passed by the Commons of *England*; but that Parliament being Prorogu'd, and then Dissolved, all that *Sisyphæan* Labour came to nothing. The Disappointments
85 which afterwards most wonderfully blasted all the hopes of the Petitioned Restoration, obliged Mr. *Mather*, not without the Concurrence of other Agents, now also come from *New-England*,[3] unto that Method of Petitioning the King for a *New* Charter, that should contain more than all the Priviledges of the *Old*; and Sir *William Phips*, now being again returned
90 into *England*, lent his utmost assistance hereunto.

The King taking a Voyage for *Holland* before this Petition was answered; Mr. *Mather*, in the mean while, not only waited upon the greatest part of the Lords of His Majesties most Honourable Privy Council, offering them a Paper of *Reasons for the Confirmation of the* Charter-Priviledges
95 *granted unto the* Massachuset-Colony; but also having the Honour to be

---

[1] Cotton Mather summarizes his father's achievements in England from 1688 until 1692, arguing the colonists' case against Andros, trying to achieve a restoration of the original charter, and finally defending his acceptance of the new one with Phips as governor of Massachusetts. Both Murdock, *Increase Mather*, chaps. 13, 14, and 15, and Palfrey, *History*, vol. 4, chap. 3, have useful accounts of Increase's successes and failures, and supply notes with references to important sources.*

[2] Sir Henry Ashurst (born *c.*1614) was the oldest son of a wealthy London merchant of the same name. He was made a baronet by James II in 1688 and until 1702 was an agent for New England.

[3] In early 1690 Elisha Cooke and Thomas Oakes were deputed by the General Court to be associate agents with Mather and Ashurst, and Ichabod Wiswall joined them in London as agent of Plymouth Colony.*

introduc'd unto the Queen, he assured Her Majesty, That there were none
in the World better affected unto their Majesties Government than the
People of *New-England*, who had indeed been exposed unto great Hardships
99 for their being so; and entreated, that since the King had referred the *New-
English* Affair unto the Two Lord Chief Justices, with the Attorney and
Solicitor General, there might be granted unto us what they thought was
reasonable. Whereto the Queen replied, That the Request was reasonable;
and that she had spoken divers times to the King on the behalf of *New-
5   England*; and that for her own part, she desired that the People there
might not meerly have Justice, but *Favour* done to them. When the King
was returned, Mr. *Mather*, being by the Duke of *Devonshire*⁴ brought
into the King's Presence on *April* 28. 1691. humbly pray'd His Majesties
Favour to *New-England*; urging, That if their Old Charter-Priviledges
10 might be restored unto them, his *Name* would be great in those Parts of
the World as long as the World should stand; adding,

Sir,

Y*OUR Subjects there have been willing to venture their Lives, that they may
enlarge your Dominions; the* Expedition *to* Canada *was a Great and Noble
15 Undertaking.*

*May it please your Majesty, in your great Wisdom also to consider the Cir-
cumstances of that People, as in your Wisdom you have considered the Circumstances
of* England, *and of* Scotland. *In* New-England *they differ from other Plantations; they are called* Congregational *and* Presbyterian. *So that such a Gover-
20 nour will not suit with the People of* New-England, *as may be very proper for
other* English *Plantations.*

Two Days after this, the King, upon what was proposed by certain
Lords, was very inquisitive, whether he might, without breach of Law,
set a Governour over *New-England*; whereto the Lord Chief Justice, and
25 some others of the Council, answered, That whatever might be the
Merit of the Cause, inasmuch as the *Charter* of *New-England* stood vacated
by a Judgment against them, it was in the King's Power to put them
under what *Form of Government* he should think best for them.

The King then said, 'That he believed it would be for the Advantage
30 'of the People in that Colony, to be under a Governour appointed by
'himself: Nevertheless' (because of what Mr. *Mather* had spoken to him)
'He would have the Agents of *New-England* nominate a Person that should
'be agreeable unto the Inclinations of the People there; and notwith-
'standing this, he would have Charter-Priviledges restored and confirmed
35 'unto them.

31 Nevertheless'/Nevertheless

⁴ William Cavendish, first Duke of Devonshire (1640–1707), advocated toleration for
nonconformists.

The Day following the King began another Voyage to *Holland*; and when the Attorney General's Draught of a Charter, according to what he took to be His Majesties Mind, as expressed in Council, was presented at the *Council-Board*, on the Eighth of *June*, some Objections then made,
40 procured an Order to prepare *Minutes* for another Draught, which deprived the *New-Englanders* of several *Essential Priviledges* in their other Charter. Mr. *Mather* put in his Objections, and vehemently protested, That he would sooner part with his *Life*, than consent unto those *Minutes*, or any thing else that should infringe any Liberty or Priviledge of Right
45 belonging unto his Country; but he was answered, That the Agents of *New-England* were not *Plenipotentiaries* from another Soveraign State; and that if they would not submit unto the King's Pleasure in the Settlement of the Country, they must *take what would follow*.

The dissatisfactory *Minutes* were, by Mr. *Mather*'s Industry, sent over
50 unto the King in *Flanders*; and the Ministers of State then with the King were earnestly applied unto, that every mistake about the good Settlement of *New-England* might be prevented; and the Queen her self, with her own Royal Hand, wrote unto the King, that the Charter of *New-England* might either pass as it was drawn by the Attorney General, or be
55 deferred until his own Return.

But after all, His Majesties Principal Secretary of State received a Signification of the King's Pleasure, that the Charter of *New-England* should run in the Main Points of it as it was now granted: Only there were several Important Articles which Mr. *Mather* by his unwearied
60 Solicitations obtained afterwards to be inserted.

There were some now of the Opinion, that instead of submitting to this New Settlement, they should, in hopes of getting a Reversion of the Judgment against the Old Charter, declare to the Ministers of State, That they had rather have no Charter at all, than such an one as was
65 now proposed unto Acceptance. But Mr. *Mather* advising with many unprejudiced Persons, and Men of the greatest Abilities in the Kingdom, *Noblemen, Gentlemen, Divines* and *Lawyers*, they all agreed, that it was not only a lawful, but all Circumstances then considered, a Needful thing, and a part of Duty and Wisdom to accept what was now offered, and
70 that a peremptory refusal would not only bring an Inconveniency, but a Fatal, and perhaps, a Final Ruin upon the Country; whereof Mankind would lay the blame upon the Agents.

It was argued, That such a Submission was no Surrender of any thing; that the Judgment, not in the Court of King's *Bench*, but in *Chancery*
75 against the Old Charter, standing on Record, the Patten was thereby Annihilated; that all attempts to have the Judgment against the Old Charter taken off, would be altogether in vain, as Men and Things were then disposed.

It was further argued, That the Ancient Charter of *New-England* was
80 in the Opinion of the Lawyers very Defective, as to several *Powers*,
which yet were absolutely necessary to the subsistence of the Plantation:
It gave the Government there no more Power than the Corporations
have in *England*; Power in Capital Cases was not therein particularly
expressed.

85 It mentioned not an *House of Deputies*, or an *Assembly of Representatives*;
the Governour and Company had thereby (they said) no Power to
impose Taxes on the Inhabitants that were not Freemen, or to erect
Courts of Admiralty. Without such Powers the Colony could not subsist;
and yet the best Friends that *New-England* had of Persons most Learned
90 in the Law, professed, that suppose the Judgment against the *Massachuset-*
Charter might be Reversed, yet, if they should again Exert such Powers
as they did before the *Quo Warranto* against their Charter, a new Writ
of *Scire Facias*[5] would undoubtedly be issued out against them.

It was yet further argued, That if an Act of Parliament should have
95 Reversed the Judgment against the *Massachuset-Charter*, without a Grant
of some other Advantages, the whole Territory had been, on many
Accounts, very miserably Incommoded: The Province of *Main*, with
Hampshire, would have been taken from them; and *Plymouth* would have
99 been annexed unto *New-York*; so that this Colony would have been
squeezed into an *Atom*, and not only have been render'd *Insignificant* in
its Trade, but by having its Militia also, which was vested in the King,
taken away, its *Insignificancies* would have become out of measure humbling; whereas now, instead of seeing any Relief by Act of Parliament,
5 they would have been put under a Governour, with a Commission,
whereby ill Men, and the King's and Country's Enemies might probably
have crept into Opportunities to have done Ten Thousand ill things,
and have treated the best Men in the Land after a very uncomfortable
manner.

10 It was lastly argued, That by the New Charter very great Priviledges
were granted unto *New-England*; and in some respects greater than what
they formerly enjoyed. The *Colony* is now made a *Province*, and their
General Court, has, with the King's Approbation, as much Power in
New-England, as the King and Parliament have in *England*. They have all
15 *English* Liberties, and can be touched by no Law, by no Tax, but of
their own making. All the Liberties of their Holy Religion are for ever
secured, and their Titles to their Lands, once for want of some Forms of

17 secured/se ured

[5] In other words, even if the "*Massachuset*-Charter might be Reversed," they could, by a
writ of "*Scire Facias*," be called upon to show cause why the charter should not be revoked,
just as by a writ of "*Quo Warranto*" the Colony had been called upon to show "by what
warrant" they held their old charter.

Legal Conveyance, contested, are now confirmed unto them. If an ill
Governour should happen to be imposed on them, what hurt could he
20 do to them? None, except they themselves pleased; for he cannot make
one Counsellor, or one Judge, or one Justice, or one Sheriff to serve his
Turn: Disadvantages enough, one would think, to Discourage any ill
Governour from desiring to be Stationed in those uneasie Regions. The
People have a Negative upon all the Executive Part of the Civil Govern-
25 ment, as well as the Legislative, which is a vast Priviledge, enjoyed by no
other Plantation in *America*, nor by *Ireland*, no, nor hitherto by *England*
it self. Why should all of this good be refused or despised, because of
somewhat not so good attending it? The Despisers of so much good, will
certainly deserve a Censure, not unlike that of *Casaubon*, upon some who
30 did not value what that Learned Man counted highly valuable, *Vix illis
optari quidquam pejus potest, quam ut fatuitate sua fruantur:* Much good may
it do them with their Madness! All of this being well considered, Sir
William Phips, who had made so many Addresses for the Restoration of
the Old Charter, under which he had seen his Country many Years
35 flourishing, will be excused by all the World from any thing of a Fault,
in a most unexpected passage⁶ of his Life, which is now to be related.

Sir *Henry Ashurst*, and Mr. *Mather*,⁷ well knowing the agreeable Disposition to do Good, and the King and his Country Service, which was in
Sir *William Phips*, whom they now had with them, all this while Prosecut-
40 ing his Design for *Canada*, they did unto the Council-Board nominate *him*
for the GOVERNOUR of *New-England*. And Mr. *Mather* being by the
Earl of *Nottingham*⁸ introduced unto His Majesty, said,

Sir,

I *Do, in the behalf of* New-England, *most humbly thank your Majesty, in that*
45 *you have been pleased, by a* Charter, *to restore* English *Liberties unto them,
to confirm them in their Properties, and to grant them some peculiar Priviledges. I
doubt not, but that your Subjects there will demean themselves with that dutiful
Affection and Loyalty to your Majesty, as that you will see cause to enlarge your
Royal Favours towards them. And I do most humbly thank your Majesty, in that*
50 *you have been pleased to give leave unto those that are concerned for* New-England
to nominate their Governour.

Sir William Phips *has been accordingly nominated by us at the Council-Board.
He hath done a good Service for the Crown, by enlarging your Dominions, and*

---

18 them./them   31–32 may it/may
29 *Casaubon/Causabon*

⁶ The "unexpected passage" was presumably Phips's years as governor.
⁷ It appears that the nomination of Phips was made by Ashurst and Mather without consultation with the other agents of the colonies.*
⁸ Daniel Finch (1647–1730), second Earl of Nottingham, was secretary of state under William
and Mary until 1693.*

reducing of Nova Scotia *to your Obedience. I know that he will faithfully serve*
55 *your Majesty to the utmost of his Capacity; and if your Majesty shall think fit to*
confirm him in that place, it will be a further Obligation on your Subjects there.

The Effect of all this was, that Sir *William Phips* was now invested with
a Commission under the King's Broad-Seal to be *Captain General*, and
Governour in Chief over the Province of the *Massachuset-Bay* in *New-England*:
60 Nor do I know a Person in the World that could have been proposed
more acceptable to the Body of the People throughout *New-England*, and
on that score more likely and able to serve the King's Interests among the
People there, under the Changes in some things unacceptable, now
brought upon them. He had been a *Gideon*, who had more than once
65 ventured his Life to save his Country from their Enemies; and they now,
with universal Satisfaction said, *Thou shalt rule over us.*[9] Accordingly,
having with Mr. *Mather* kissed the King's Hand on *January* 3d, 1691.
he hastned away to his Government; and arriving at *New-England* the
Fourteenth of *May* following, attended with the *Non-such-Frigat*, both of
70 them were welcomed with the loud Acclamations of the long *shaken*
and *shatter'd* Country, whereto they were now returned with a Settlement
so full of happy Priviledges.

§. 15. When *Titus Flamininus*[1] had freed the poor *Grecians* from the
Bondage which had long oppressed them, and the Herald Proclaimed
75 among them the Articles of their Freedom, they cried out, *A Saviour! A*
Saviour! with such loud Acclamations, that the very *Birds* fell down from
Heaven astonish'd at the Cry. Truly, when Mr. *Mather* brought with
him unto the poor *New-Englanders*, not only a *Charter*, which though in
divers Points wanting what both *he* and *they* had wished for, yet for ever
80 delivers them from Oppressions on their *Christian* and *English* Liberties,
or on their Ancient Possessions, wherein ruining *Writs of Intrusion* had
begun to Invade them all, but also a *GOVERNOUR* who might call
New-England his own *Country*, and who was above most Men in it, full of
Affection to the Interests of *his Country*; the sensible part of the People
85 then caused the Sence of the *Salvations* thus brought them to reach as far
as *Heaven* it self. The various little Humours then working among the
People, did not hinder the *Great and General Court* of the Province to
appoint a Day of Solemn *THANKSGIVING* to Almighty God, for

---

57 Effect/Effects   73 *Flamininus/Flaminius*

---

[9] See Judg. 8.22. Cotton Mather earlier used this same Biblical reference to designate John
Winthrop, Jr., as a Gideon.

---

[1] Titus Quinctius Flamininus (*c*.230–174 B.C.), a Roman general and statesman, defeated
Philip V of Macedon in 197 B.C., and in 195 B.C. proclaimed the freedom of Greece from
Macedonian rule.*

Granting (as the Printed Order expressed it)² *a safe Arrival to his Excellency*
90 *our Governour, and the Reverend Mr.* Increase Mather, *who have industriously
endeavoured the Service of this People, and have brought over with them a Settlement
of Government, in which their Majesties have graciously given us distinguishing
Marks of their Royal Favour and Goodness.*

And as the obliged People thus gave *Thanks* unto the God of Heaven,
95 so they sent an Address of *Thanks* unto Their Majesties, with other Letters
of *Thanks* unto some Chief Ministers of State, for the *Favourable Aspect*
herein cast upon the Province.

Nor were the People mistaken, when they promised themselves all the
99 kindness imaginable from this *Governour,* and expected, *Under his shadow
we shall live easie among the Heathen:* Why might they not look for *Halcyon*-
days, when they had such a *King's-Fisher*³ for their Governour?

Governour *Phips* had, as every raised and useful Person must have, his
Envious Enemies; but the palest Envy of them, who turned their worst
5 Enmity upon him, could not hinder them from confessing, *That according
to the best of his Apprehension, he ever sought the good of his Country:* His Country
quickly felt this on innumerable Occasions; and they had it eminently
demonstrated, as well in his promoting and approving the Council's
choice of good *Judges, Justices* and *Sheriffs,* which being once established,
10 no *Successor* could remove them, as in his urging the *General Assembly* to
make themselves happy by preparing a Body of good Laws as fast as they
could, which being passed by him in his time, could not be nulled by any
other after him.

He would often speak to the Members of the general Assembly in such
15 Terms as these, *Gentlemen, You may make your selves as easie as you will for
ever; consider what may have any tendency to your welfare; and you may be sure,
that whatever Bills you offer to me, consistent with the Honour and Interest of the
Crown, I'll pass them readily; I do but seek Opportunities to serve you; had it not
been for the sake of this thing, I had never accepted the Government of this Province;*
20 *and whenever you have settled such a Body of good Laws, that no Person coming
after me may make you uneasie, I shall desire not one Day longer to continue in the
Government.* Accordingly he ever passed every Act for the welfare of the
Province proposed unto him; and instead of ever putting them upon
Buying his Assent unto any good Act, he was much forwarder to give it,
25 than they were to ask it: Nor indeed, had the *Hunger of a Salary* any such
Impression upon him, as to make him decline doing all possible Service

---

² On June 8, 1692, the Court appointed July 14 as a day of "Thanksgiving" and printed
a proclamation ordering that the day be observed.*
³ Mather plays with the words "Halcyon" and "Kingfisher," the names of a species of
birds. They were in fable supposed to calm the sea in the winter solstice, to bring "*Halcyon*-days"
of quiet, undisturbed peace. Phips was the seafarer who brought the king wealth from the
sea and who also as governor brought halcyon days to New England.

for the Publick, while he was not sure of having any Proportionable or Honourable Acknowledgments.

But yet he minded the Preservation of the King's Rights with as careful
30 and faithful a Zeal as became a good Steward for the Crown: And, indeed, he studied nothing more than to observe such a Temper in all things, as to extinguish what others have gone to distinguish; even the Pernicious Notion of a separate Interest. There was a time when the *Roman* Empire was infested with a vast number of Governours, who were
35 Infamous for Infinite Avarice and Villany; and referring to this time, the Apostle *John* had a Vision of *People killed with the Beasts of the Earth.*

But Sir *William Phips* was none of those Governours; wonderfully contrary to this wretchedness was the Happiness of *New-England*, when they had Governour *Phips*, using the tenderness of a Father towards the
40 People; and being of the Opinion, *Ditare magis esse Regium quam Ditescere,*[4] that it was a braver thing to enrich the People, than to grow rich himself. A *Father*, I said; and what if I had said an *Angel* too? If I should from *Clemens Alexandrinus*, from *Theodoret*, and from *Jerom*, and others among the Ancients, as well as from *Calvin*, and *Bucan,*[5] and *Peter Martyr,*[6] and
45 *Chemnitius,*[7] and *Bullinger,*[8] and a Thousand more among the *Moderns*, bring Authorities for the Assertion, *That each Country and Province is under the special Care of some Angel, by a singular Deputation of Heaven assigned thereunto*, I could back them with a far greater Authority than any of them all. The Scripture it self does plainly assert it: And hence the most
50 Learned *Grotius*, writing of *Commonwealths*, has a Passage to this purpose, *His singulis, suos Attributos, esse Angelos, ex Daniele, magno consensu, & Judæi & Christiani veteres colligebant.*[9]

But *New-England* had now, besides the *Guardian-Angel*, who more invisibly intended its welfare, a *Governour* that became wonderfully
55 agreeable thereunto, by his whole Imitation of such a Guardian-Angel. He employed his whole Strength to guard his People from all Disasters, which threatned them either by Sea or Land; and it was remark'd, that nothing remarkably Disastrous did befal that People from the time of his Arrival to the Government, until there arrived an Order for his leaving it:

43   and others/and and others

[4] "It was more fit for a king to enrich others than to be rich himself."*

[5] Guillaume Bucan, author of theological works; his *A Body of Divinity* had a London edition in 1659.

[6] Pietro Martire Vernigli (1500–1562), known as Peter Martyr, was a Florentine by birth. Converted to the reformed religion, he was a professor at Oxford, Strasbourg, and Zurich, and was the author of theological treatises and commentaries.

[7] Martin Chemnitz.

[8] Heinrich Bullinger (1504–1575) was a Swiss reformer and historian; he exerted considerable influence on the later stages of the English Reformation.*

[9] "Old writers, both Jewish and Christian, agree, on the evidence of Daniel, that individuals have angels assigned to them."*

60 (Except one thing which was begun before he entred upon the Government:) [10] But instead thereof, the *Indians* were notably defeated in the Assaults which they now made upon the *English*, and several *French* Ships did also very advantageously fall into his Hands; yea, there was by his means a Peace restored unto the Province, that had been divers
65 Years languishing under the Hectic Feaver of a lingring War.

And there was this one thing more that rendred his Government the more desirable; that whereas 'tis impossible for a meer Man to govern without some *Error*; whenever this Governour was advised of any Error in any of his Administrations, he would immediately retract it, and revoke
70 it with all possible Ingenuity; [11] so that if any occasion of just Complaint arose, it was usually his endeavour that it should not long be complain'd of.

—*O, Fælices nimium, sua si Bona, noscant,*
Nov-Angli.— [12]

75 But having in a *Parenthesis* newly intimated, that his Excellency, when he entred on his Government, found one thing that was *remarkably Disastrous* begun upon it: Of that one thing we will now give some account.

Reader, prepare to be entertained with as prodigious Matters as can
80 be put into any History! And let him that writes the next *Thaumatographia Pneumatica*,[13] allow to these Prodigies the chief place among the Wonders.

§. 16. About the time of our Blessed Lord's coming to reside on Earth, we read of so many *possessed with Devils*, that it is commonly thought the *Number* of such miserable *Energumens* was then encreased above what has
85 been usual in other Ages; and the *Reason* of that Increase has been made a Matter of some Enquiry. Now though the *Devils* might herein design by *Preternatural Operations* to blast the *Miracles* of our Lord Jesus Christ, which point they gained among the Blasphemous *Pharisees*; and the *Devils* might herein also design a Villanous *Imitation* of what was coming
90 to pass in the *Incarnation* of our Lord Jesus Christ, wherein *God* came to *dwell in Flesh*; yet I am not without suspicion, that there may be something further in the Conjecture of the Learned *Bartholinus* hereupon, who says, It was *Quod judæi præter modum, Artibus Magicis dediti Dæmonem Advocaverint,*[1]

73   *noscant/norant*

[10] That is, the witchcraft tragedy.
[11] Ingenuousness.
[12] "O most happy New Englanders, if they recognize their blessings."*
[13] A writing dealing with the "wonders of the air." Cotton Mather's own *Wonders of the Invisible World* was thus a "Thaumatographia Pneumatica," and he uses this title for chapter 7 of Book VI of the *Magnalia*.

[1] "Because the Jews, given over beyond measure to magical tricks, called in the Devil as an adviser." Thomas Bartholin (1616–1680) was a Danish physician and scholar.*

the *Jews,* by the frequent use of *Magical Tricks,* called in the *Devils* among
95 them.[2]

It is very certain, there were hardly any People in the World grown
more fond of *Sorceries,* than that unhappy People: The *Talmuds* tell us of
the little *Parchments* with Words upon them, which were their common
99 *Amulets,* and of the *Charms* which they mutter'd over *Wounds,* and of the
various *Enchantments* which they used against all sorts of Disasters whatsoever. It is affirmed in the *Talmuds,* that no less than Twenty-four Scholars
in one School were killed by *Witchcraft*; and that no less than *Fourscore*
Persons were Hanged for *Witchcraft* by one Judge in one Day. The
5 *Gloss* adds upon it, *That the Women of* Israel *had generally fallen to the Practice
of Witchcrafts*; and therefore it was required, that there should be still
chosen into the Council one skilful in the *Arts of Sorcerers,* and able thereby
to discover who might be guilty of those *Black Arts* among such as were
accused before them.

10 Now the Arrival of Sir *William Phips* to the Government of *New-England,*
was at a time when a Governour would have had Occasion for all the
Skill in *Sorcery,* that was ever necessary to a *Jewish Councellor*; a time when
Scores of poor People had newly fallen under a prodigious *Possession of
Devils,* which it was then generally thought had been by *Witchcrafts*
15 introduced. It is to be confessed and bewailed, that many Inhabitants of
New-England, and Young People especially, had been led away with
little *Sorceries,* wherein they *did secretly those things that were not right against
the Lord their God*; they would often cure Hurts with *Spells,* and practise
detestable Conjurations with *Sieves,* and *Keys,* and *Pease,* and *Nails,* and
20 *Horse-shoes,* and other Implements, to learn the things for which they had
a forbidden and impious Curiosity. Wretched Books had stoln into the
Land, wherein Fools were instructed how to become able Fortune-
Tellers: Among which, I wonder that a blacker Brand is not set upon
that Fortune-Telling Wheel, which that Sham-Scribler, that goes under
25 the Letters of *R. B.*[3] has promised in his *Delights for the Ingenious,* as an
honest and pleasant Recreation: And by these Books, the Minds of many had
been so poisoned, that they studied this *Finer Witchcraft*; until, 'tis well,
if some of them were not betray'd into what is Grosser, and more Sensible and Capital. Although these *Diabolical Divinations* are more ordinarily
30 committed perhaps all over the *whole World,* than they are in the Country
of *New-England,* yet, that being a Country Devoted unto the Worship and
Service of the Lord *JESUS CHRIST* above the *rest of the World,* He

---

[2] Cotton Mather, who studied Hebrew at Harvard and felt that a knowledge of it was to
be valued, may have drawn on his own knowledge for the following paragraph, but it is
probable he relied principally on other sources.*

[3] "R.B." was Nathaniel Crouch (1632?–1752?), a miscellaneous writer, apprenticed to a
London stationer and later made free of the Stationers' Company; he issued several journals.*

signalized his Vengeance against these Wickednesses, with such extraordinary Dispensations as have not been often seen in other places.

35   The *Devils* which had been so play'd withal, and, it may be, by some
few Criminals more Explicitely engaged and imployed, now broke in
upon the Country, after as astonishing a manner as was ever heard of.
Some Scores of People, first about *Salem*,[4] the Centre and First-Born of
all the Towns in the Colony, and afterwards in several other places, were
40   Arrested with many *Preternatural Vexations* upon their Bodies, and a variety
of cruel Torments, which were evidently inflicted from the *Dæmons*,
of the *Invisible World.* The People that were *Infected* and *Infested* with such
Dæmons, in a few Days time arrived unto such a *Refining Alteration* upon
their Eyes, that they could see their Tormentors; they saw a *Devil* of a
45   Little *Stature*, and of a Tawny *Colour*, attended still with *Spectres* that
appeared in more Humane Circumstances.

These *Tormentors* tendred unto the afflicted a *Book*, requiring them to
Sign it, or to *Touch* it at least, in token of their consenting to be Listed
in the Service of the *Devil*; which they refusing to do, the *Spectres* under
50   the Command of that *Blackman*, as they called him, would apply themselves to Torture them with prodigious Molestations.

The afflicted Wretches were horribly *Distorted* and *Convulsed*; they were
Pinched Black and Blue: *Pins* would be run every where in their Flesh;
they would be *Scalded* until they had *Blisters* raised on them; and a
55   Thousand other things before Hundreds of Witnesses were done unto
them, evidently *Preternatural*: For if it were *Preternatural* to keep a rigid
Fast for *Nine*, yea, for *Fifteen* Days together; or if it were *Preternatural* to
have one's Hands *ty'd* close together with a *Rope* to be plainly seen, and
then by *unseen Hands* presently pull'd up a great way from the Earth
60   before a Croud of People; such *Preternatural* things were endured by them.

But of all the *Preternatural* things which befel these People, there were
none more *unaccountable* than those, wherein the prestigious *Dæmons*
would ever now and then cover the most *Corporeal* things in the World
with a *Fascinating Mist* of *Invisibility.* As now; a Person was cruelly assaulted
65   by a *Spectre*, that, she said, run at her with a *Spindle*, though no Body
else in the room could see either the *Spectre* or the *Spindle*: At last, in her
Agonies, giving a snatch at the *Spectre*, she pulled the *Spindle* away; and
it was no sooner got into her Hand, but the other Folks then present

---

4 That is, Salem Village (now Danvers), some four miles from the center of Salem. Early
in 1692 some young girls in the "Village" appeared to be tormented by witches, and at the
beginning of April warrants were issued and various persons accused of witchcraft haled into
court, examined, and questioned by John Hathorne and Jonathan Corwin (Curwin), both
Salem magistrates, who acted rather as prosecutors than as investigators. By April 11 when
Samuel Sewall went to Salem with William Stoughton, the deputy governor, and four other
magistrates, the meeting house was crowded and nearly a hundred of those interrogated by
Hathorne and Corwin were in jail awaiting trial.*

beheld that it was indeed a Real, Proper, Iron *Spindle*; which when they
70 locked up very safe, it was nevertheless by the *Dæmons* taken away to do
farther Mischief.

Again, a Person was haunted by a most abusive *Spectre*, which came to
her, she said, with a *Sheet* about her, though seen to none but her self.
After she had undergone a deal of Teaze from the Annoyance of the
75 *Spectre*, she gave a violent *Snatch* at the *Sheet* that was upon it; where-from
she tore a Corner, which in her Hand immediately was beheld by all
that were present, a palpable Corner of a *Sheet:* And her Father, which
was now holding of her, *catch'd*, that he might *keep* what his Daughter had
so strangely seized; but the *Spectre* had like to have wrung his Hand off,
80 by endeavouring to wrest it from him: However he still held it; and
several times this odd Accident was renewed in the Family. There
wanted not the *Oaths* of good credible People to these particulars.

Also, it is well known, that these wicked *Spectres* did proceed so far
as to steal several Quantities of Money from divers People, part of which
85 Individual Money was dropt sometimes out of the Air, before sufficient
Spectators, into the Hands of the Afflicted, while the *Spectres* were urging
them to subscribe their *Covenant with Death*. Moreover, *Poisons* to the
Standers-by, wholly *Invisible*, were sometimes forced upon the Afflicted;
which when they have with much Reluctancy swallowed, they have
90 *swoln* presently, so that the common Medicines for *Poisons* have been
found necessary to relieve them: Yea, sometimes the *Spectres* in the
struggles have so dropt the *Poisons*, that the Standers-by have smelt them,
and view'd them, and beheld the *Pillows* of the miserable stained with
them.

95 Yet more, the miserable have complained bitterly of *burning Rags* run
into their forceably distended *Mouths*; and though no Body could see
any such *Clothes*, or indeed any *Fires* in the Chambers, yet presently the
scalds were seen plainly by every Body on the Mouths of the Complainers.
and not only the *Smell*, but the *Smoke* of the Burning sensibly fill'd the
Chambers.

99 Once more, the miserable exclaimed extreamly of *Branding Irons*
heating at the Fire on the Hearth to mark them; now though the Standers-by could see no *Irons*, yet they could see distinctly the Print of them in
5 the Ashes, and *smell* them too as they were carried by the *not-seen Furies*,
unto the Poor Creatures for whom they were intended; and those Poor
Creatures were thereupon so *Stigmatized* with them, that they will bear
the *Marks* of them to their Dying Day. Nor are these the *Tenth Part* of
the *Prodigies* that fell out among the Inhabitants of *New-England*.

10 Flashy People may *Burlesque* these Things, but when Hundreds of the
most sober People in a Country, where they have as much *Mother-Wit*

88 *Invisible/Invisibly* C.M.   3–4 Standers-by/Sanders-by

certainly as the rest of Mankind, know them to be *True*, nothing but the absurd and froward Spirit of *Sadducism*[5] can Question them. I have not yet mentioned so much as one Thing that will not be justified, if it be required by the *Oaths* of more considerate Persons than any that can ridicule these odd *Phænomena*.

But the worst part of this astonishing *Tragedy* is yet behind; wherein Sir *William Phips*, at last being dropt, as it were from the *Machine of Heaven*,[6] was an Instrument of easing the Distresses of the Land, now *so darkned by the Wrath of the Lord of Hosts*. There were very worthy Men upon the Spot[7] where the *assault from Hell* was first made, who apprehended themselves call'd from the *God of Heaven*, to sift the business unto the bottom of it; and indeed, the continual *Impressions*, which the outcries and the havocks of the *afflicted People* that lived nigh unto them caused on their Minds, gave no little Edge to this Apprehension.

The Persons were Men eminent for *Wisdom* and *Virtue*, and they went about their enquiry into the matter, as *driven* unto it by a *Conscience* of Duty to God and the World. They did in the first Place take it for granted, that there are *Witches*, or wicked Children of Men, who upon *Covenanting* with, and *Commissioning* of *Evil Spirits*, are attended by their Ministry to accomplish the things desired of them: To satisfie them in which Perswasion, they had not only the *Assertions* of the *Holy Scripture*; Assertions, which the *Witch-Advocates* cannot evade without Shifts, too foolish for any *Prudent*, or too profane for any *Honest* Man to use; and they had not only the well-attested *Relations* of the gravest Authors from *Bodin* to *Bovet*, and from *Binsfeld* to *Bromhal* and *Baxter*;[8] to deny all which, would be as reasonable as to turn the Chronicles of all Nations into Romances of *Don Quixot* and the *Seven Champions*;[9] but they had also an *Ocular Demonstration* in one, who a little before had been executed for *Witchcraft*,

18   *Machine/Machin*

[5] An epithet applied to disbelief in spirits of any kind.*

[6] "Deus ex Machina," a proverb: "A God from the skies," used especially to indicate unexpected aid in an emergency.*

[7] Presumably the "Spot" was not only Salem and Salem Village but Massachusetts in general. Phips on May 29 appointed a Special Court of Oyer and Terminer, with Stoughton as chief justice, and John Richards, Nathaniel Saltonstall, Wait Winthrop, Bartholomew Gedney, Sewall, John Hathorne, and Peter Sergeant. Saltonstall disliked the methods of the judges and resigned. His place was filled by Corwin, who, like Hathorne, gave no mercy to any suspected witch.*

[8] Jean Bodin (1530–1596), though a liberal political philosopher, was a staunch believer in witchcraft; his *Démonomanie des sorciers* was published in 1580. Richard Bovet's *Pandæmonium* was published in 1684. Pierre Binsfeld (d. 1598), Flemish theologian, was the author of *De Confessionibus Maleficorum et Sagarum* (1591). The Reverend Thomas Bromhall's *Treatise of Specters* was published in 1658. Richard Baxter's *The Certainty of the World of Spirits* was published in 1691.*

[9] The *Most Famous History of the Seven Champions of Christendom* (London, 1596), a romance by Richard Johnson (1573–1659?); the seven were St. George of England, St. Denis of France, St. James of Spain, St. Anthony of Italy, St. David of Wales, St. Andrew of Scotland, St. Patrick of Ireland.

40 when *Joseph Dudley*, Esq; was the Chief Judge.[10] There was one whose
Magical Images were found, and who *confessing her Deeds*, (when a Jury
of Doctors returned her *Compos Mentis*[11]) actually shewed the whole
Court, by what *Ceremonies* used unto them, she directed her *Familiar Spirits*
how and where to Cruciate[12] the Objects of her Malice; and the Experi-
45 ments being made over and over again before the whole Court, the *Effect*
followed exactly in the Hurts done to People at a distance from her. The
Existence of such *Witches* was now taken for granted by those good Men,
wherein so far the generality of reasonable Men have thought *they ran
well*;[13] and they soon received the *Confessions* of some *accused* Persons to
50 confirm them in it; but then they took one thing more for granted,
wherein 'tis now as generally thought they *went out of the Way*.[14] The
Afflicted People vehemently accused several Persons in several Places,
that the *Spectres* which afflicted them, did exactly resemble *them*; until
the Importunity of the Accusations did provoke the Magistrates to
55 examine them. When many of the *accused* came upon their Examination,
it was found, that the *Dæmons* then a thousand ways abusing of the poor
afflicted People, had with a marvellous exactness *represented* them; yea, it
was found, that many of the *accused*, but casting their Eye on the *afflicted*,
the *afflicted*, though their Faces were never so much another way, would
60 fall down and lye in a sort of a Swoon, wherein they would continue,
whatever Hands were laid upon them, until the Hands of the *accused*
came to touch them, and *then* they would revive immediately: And it
was found, that various kinds of *natural Actions*, done by many of the
accused in or to their own Bodies, as *Leaning, Bending, Turning* Awry, or
65 *Squeezing* their Hands, or the like, were presently attended with the like
things *preternaturally* done upon the Bodies of the *afflicted*, though they
were so far asunder, that the *afflicted* could not at all observe the *accused*.
　　It was also found, that the Flesh of the Afflicted was often *Bitten* at such
a rate, that not only the *Print of Teeth* would be left on their *Flesh*, but
70 the very *Slaver* of Spittle too: And there would appear just such a *set of
Teeth* as was in the *accused*, even such as might be clearly distinguished
from other Peoples. And usually the *afflicted* went through a terrible deal
of seeming Difficulties from the tormenting *Spectres*, and must be long
waited on, before they could get a Breathing Space from their *Torments*
75 to give in their Testimonies.

---

[10] This execution, in the summer of 1688 when Dudley was judge of the superior court,
was the last for witchcraft ever carried out in Boston. The victim was one "Goody Glover,"
found guilty of afflicting the children of John Goodwin, a mason in Boston.*

[11] Of sound mind.*

[12] Obsolete for torment.

[13] They were right.*

[14] That is, followed the erroneous principle that when the specter of any man or woman of
the community appeared to those afflicted, the individuals so represented were in all likelihood
"in a *Confederacy*" with demons and thus deserving of death. The two Mathers opposed
judging any one guilty on the sole basis of "spectral evidence."*

Now many good Men took up an Opinion, That the *Providence* of God would not permit an *Innocent Person* to come under such a *Spectral Representation*; and that a concurrence of so many Circumstances would prove an *accused* Person to be in a *Confederacy* with the *Dæmons* thus afflicting of
80 the Neighbours; they judged, that except these things might amount unto a *Conviction*, it would scarce be possible ever to *Convict* a *Witch*; and they had some *Philosophical Schemes* of *Witchcraft*, and of the Method and Manner wherein *Magical Poisons* operate, which further supported them in their Opinion.

85 Sundry of the *accused* Persons were brought unto their *Trial*, while this Opinion was yet prevailing in the Minds of the *Judges* and the *Juries*, and perhaps the most of the People in the Country, then mostly Suffering; and though against some of them that were Tried there came in so much *other Evidence* of their Diabolical Compacts, that some of the most
90 *Judicious*, and yet *Vehement* Opposers of the Notions then in Vogue, publickly declared, *Had they themselves been on the Bench, they could not have Acquitted them*; nevertheless, divers were Condemned, against whom the *chief Evidence* was founded in the *Spectral Exhibitions*.

And it happening, that some of the *Accused* coming to confess themselves
95 *Guilty*, their *Shapes* were no more seen by any of the *afflicted*, though the Confession had been kept never so Secret, but instead thereof the *Accused* themselves became in all Vexations just like the *Afflicted*; this yet more confirmed many in the Opinion that had been taken up.

99 And another thing that quickned them yet more to Act upon it, was, that the Afflicted were frequently entertained with *Apparitions* of *Ghosts* at the same time that the *Spectres* of the supposed *Witches* troubled them: Which *Ghosts* always cast the Beholders into far more Consternation than any of the *Spectres*; and when they exhibited themselves, they cried out
5 of being *Murdered* by the *Witchcrafts*, or other Violences of the Persons represented in the *Spectres*. Once or Twice these Apparitions were seen by others at the very same time that they shew'd themselves to the *afflicted*; and seldom were they seen at all, but when something unusual and suspicious had attended the Death of the Party thus appearing.
10 The *afflicted* People many times had never heard any thing before of the Persons appearing in *Ghosts*, or of the Persons *accused* by the *Apparitions*; and yet the accused upon Examination have confessed the Murders of those very Persons, though these *accused* also knew nothing of the *Apparitions* that had come in against them; and the *afflicted* Persons likewise,
15 without any private Agreement or Collusion, when successively brought into a Room, have all asserted the same *Apparitions* to be there before them: These *Murders* did seem to call for an Enquiry.

On the other Part, there were many Persons of great Judgment, Piety

and Experience, who from the beginning were very much dissatisfied at
20 these Proceedings; they feared lest the *Devil* would get so far into the
Faith of the People, that for the sake of many *Truths*, which they might
find him telling of them, they would come at length to believe all his
Lies, whereupon what a Desolation of *Names*, yea, and of *Lives* also, would
ensue, a Man might without much *Witchcraft* be able to Prognosticate;
25 and they feared, lest in such an extraordinary Descent of *Wicked Spirits*
from their *High Places* upon us, there might such *Principles* be taken up, as,
when put into *Practice*, would unavoidably cause the *Righteous to perish
with the Wicked*, and procure the Blood-shed of Persons like the *Gibeonites*,
whom some learned Men suppose to be under a false Pretence of *Witch-*
30 *craft*, by *Saul* exterminated.

However uncommon it might be for *guiltless Persons* to come under such
unaccountable Circumstances, as were on so many of the Accused, they
held *some things there are, which if suffered to be Common, would subvert Government, and Disband and Ruin Humane Society, yet God sometimes may suffer such*
35 *Things to evene, that we may know thereby how much we are beholden to him for
that restraint which he lays upon the Infernal Spirits, who would else reduce a
World into a* Chaos.[15] They had already known of one at the Town of
Groton hideously agitated by *Devils*,[16] who in her Fits cried out much
against a very Godly Woman in the Town, and when that Woman
40 approached unto her, though the Eyes of the Creature were never so
shut, she yet manifested a violent Sense of her approach: But when the
Gracious Woman thus Impeached, had prayed earnestly with and for
this Creature, then instead of crying out against her any more, she
owned, that she had in all been deluded by the *Devil*. They now saw,
45 that the more the *Afflicted* were Hearkned unto, the more the number of
of the *Accused* encreased; until at last many scores were *cried out* upon,
and among them, some, who by the *Unblameableness*, yea, and *Serviceableness* of their whole Conversation, had obtained the Just Reputation of
Good People among all that were acquainted with them. The Character
50 of the *afflicted* likewise added unto the common Distaste; for though some
of *them* too were *Good People*, yet others of them, and such of them as were
most Flippent at *Accusing*, had a far other Character.

In fine, the Country was in a dreadful *Ferment*, and wise Men foresaw a
long Train of Dismal and Bloody Consequences. Hereupon they first
55 advised, that the *afflicted* might be kept asunder in the closest Privacy;

[15] Mather quotes, with minor alterations, part of the preface to Increase Mather's *Cases of
Conscience* (pp. A3–A4). This preface was written by Samuel Willard.*
[16] The unhappy woman was Elizabeth Knap. Samuel Willard, minister there from 1664
until 1676 and later at the Old South Church in Boston, studied her case for months. His
conclusion was: "thus much is cleare, shee is an object of pitye, & I desire that all that heare
of her would compassionate her forlorne state. Shee is . . . a subject of hope & therfore, all
meanes ought to bee used for her recoverye."*

and one particular Person [17] (whom I have cause to know) in pursuance of this Advice, offered himself singly to provide Accommodations for any *six* of them, that so the Success of more than ordinary *Prayer* with *Fasting*, might, with *Patience*, be *experienced*, before any other Courses were taken.

60　　And Sir *William Phips* arriving to his Government, after this *ensnaring horrible Storm* was begun, did consult the neighbouring Ministers of the Province, who made unto his Excellency and the Council a return, (drawn up at their desire by Mr. *Mather* the Younger, as I have been inform'd [18]) wherein they declared.

65　　*We judge, that in the Prosecution of these and all such* Witchcrafts, *there is need of a very Critical and Exquisite Caution: Lest by too much Credulity for things received only upon the* Devil's Authority, *there be a Door opened for a long Train of miserable Consequences, and Satan get an Advantage over us*; *for* we should not be Ignorant of his Devices.

70　　*As in complaints upon* Witchcrafts, *there may be Matters of* Enquiry, *which do not amount unto Matters of* Presumption; *and there may be Matters of* Presumption, *which yet may not be reckoned Matters of* Conviction; *so 'tis necessary that all Proceedings thereabout be managed with an* exceeding Tenderness *towards those that may be complained of; especially if they have been Persons*
75 *formerly of an* unblemished Reputation.

　　When the first Enquiry *is made into the Circumstances of such as may lye under any just Suspicion of* Witchcrafts, *we could wish that there may be admitted as little as is possible of such* Noise, Company, *and* Openness, *as may too hastily expose them that are Examined; and that there may nothing be used as a*
80 Test *for the Trial of the Suspected, the lawfulness whereof may be doubted among the People of God: But that the Directions given by such judicious Writers as* Perkins *and* Bernard,[19] *be consulted in such a Case.*

---

[17] Mather's hiding of his identity here may have impressed some readers with his modesty, but by the time the *Magnalia* was printed no one can have been deceived by it. Moreover he made no pretense of modesty when in May 1692 he wrote in his *Diary* (1:151–152): "In this *Evil-Time*, I offered, at the beginning, that if the *possessed* People, might bee scattered Far asunder, I would singly provide for six of them: and we would see whether without more bitter methods, *Prayer* with *Fasting* would not putt an End unto these heavy Trials: But my offer (which none of my Revilers would have been so charitable, as to have made) was not accepted."*

[18] A further instance of Mather's pretense that he was not the author of the *Pietas*. Phips had consulted the "neighboring Ministers" for their opinion of the methods used by the court of Oyer and Terminer which he had established with the advice of the Council. Cotton Mather was one of the twelve ministers, and drew up *The Return of Several Ministers Consulted by His Excellency And The . . . Council, Upon the Present Witchcrafts in Salem-Village*, dated at Boston, June 15, 1692, which was sent to the governor. There were eight sections in the *Return*, of which Mather below omits the first two and the eighth. Had the judges heeded the good advice given them by the ministers, particularly in sections six and seven, many lives would have been saved.*

[19] William Perkins (1558–1602), influential English Puritan theologian, wrote *A Discourse of the Damned Art of Witchcraft* (Cambridge, Eng., 1608), and Richard Bernard (1568–1641), English nonconformist divine, wrote *A Guide to Grand Jurymen . . . in Cases of Witchcraft* (London, 1627).*

Presumptions, *whereupon Persons may be committed, and much more* Convictions, *whereupon Persons may be condemned as guilty of* Witchcrafts, *ought*
85 *certainly to be more considerable, than barely the* accused *Persons being* represented *by a* Spectre *to the afflicted: Inasmuch as it is an undoubted and a notorious Thing, that a* Dæmon *may, by God's Permission, appear even to ill Purposes in the shape of an* Innocent, *yea, and a* Virtuous *Man: Nor can we esteem* Alterations *made in the* Sufferers, *by a* look *or* touch *of the* accused,
90 *to be an infallible Evidence of Guilt; but frequently liable to be abused by the* Devil's Legerdemains.

We know not whether some remarkable Affronts *given to the* Devils, *by our dis-believing of those Testimonies whose whole Force and Strength is from* them *alone, may not put a Period unto the Progress of a direful Calamity begun upon us,*
95 *in the* accusation *of so many Persons, whereof, we hope, some are yet* clear *from* the great Transgression *laid unto their Charge.*

The Ministers of the Province also being Jealous lest this *Counsel* should not be duly followed, requested the President of *Harvard*-Colledge to
99 Compose and Publish (which he did) some *Cases of Conscience* referring to these Difficulties:[20] In which Treatise he did, with Demonstrations of incomparable *Reason* and *Reading*, evince it, that *Satan* may appear in the Shape of an *Innocent* and a *Virtuous* Person, to afflict those that suffer by the *Diabolical Molestations:* And that the *Ordeal* of the *Sight*, and the
5 *Touch*, is not a Conviction of a *Covenant* with the Devil, but liable to great Exceptions against the *Lawfulness*, as well as the *Evidence* of it: And that either a Free and Fair *Confession* of the Criminals, or the Oath of two Credible Persons proving such Things against the Person accused, as none but such as have a Familiarity with the Devil can know, or do,
10 is necessary to the Proof of the Crime. Thus,

Cum misit Natura Feras, & Monstra per Orbem,
Misit & Alciden qui Fera Monstra domet.[21]

The *Dutch* and *French* Ministers in the Province of *New York*, having likewise about the same time their Judgment asked by the *Chief Judge*

---

[20] The reference is to Increase Mather's *Cases of Conscience*, which he completed on October 3, 1692, and read in manuscript to fourteen ministers of the "Cambridge Association," who endorsed it. The document was sent to Phips, who, aware of the rising popular dislike of the judges' methods, and also disturbed by queries from England, was impressed by Mather's reasoning and promptly replaced the witch court with a supreme court which, when it convened in January, acquitted all but three of the fifty accused; the three were pardoned by Phips himself. Cotton Mather meanwhile, had been writing his *Wonders of the Invisible World*, which was published shortly before the *Cases*. Increase must have found it difficult to admire or even to accept his son's clumsy and confused pages, but paternal affection conquered whatever distaste he felt, and in the "Postscript" to his *Cases* he stoutly declared that he had read and approved the *Wonders* before it was printed.*

[21] "When Nature sent wild beasts and monsters throughout the world, she also sent Hercules to subjugate them.*

15 of that Province,[22] who was then a Gentleman of *New-England*, they gave
it in under their Hands, that if we believe no *Venefick*[23] *Witchcraft*, we must
Renounce the *Scripture* of God, and the *Consent* of almost all the World;
but that yet the *Apparition* of a Person afflicting another, is a very Insufficient Proof of a *Witch*; nor is it Inconsistent with the Holy and
20 Righteous Government of God over Men, to permit the Affliction of the
Neighbours, by Devils in the *Shape* of *Good Men*; and that a *Good Name*,
obtained by a *Good Life*, should not be Lost by Meer *Spectral Accusations*.

Now upon a Deliberate Review of these things, his Excellency first
Reprieved, and then *Pardoned* many of them that had been Condemned;
25 and there fell out several strange things that caused the Spirit of the
Country to run as vehemently upon the *Acquitting* of all the *accused*, as it by
mistake ran at first upon the *Condemning* of them. Some that had been
zealously of the Mind, that the *Devils* could not in the *Shapes* of good Men
afflict other Men, were terribly Confuted, by having their own *Shapes*, and
30 the *Shapes* of their most intimate and valued Friends, thus abused. And
though more than twice Twenty had made such voluntary, and har-
monious, and uncontroulable Confessions, that if they were all *Sham*,
there was therein the greatest Violation made by the Efficacy of the
Invisible World, upon the *Rules of Understanding Humane Affairs*, that was
35 ever seen since *God made Man upon the Earth*, yet they did so recede from
their *Confessions*, that it was very clear, some of them had been hitherto,
in a sort of a *Præternatural Dream*, wherein they had said *of them selves*, they
knew not what themselves.

In fine, The last Courts that sate upon this *Thorny Business*, finding
40 that it was impossible to Penetrate into the whole Meaning of the things
that had happened, and that so many *unsearchable Cheats* were interwoven
into the *Conclusion* of a Mysterious Business, which perhaps had not crept
thereinto at the *Beginning* of it, they *cleared* the *accused* as fast as they *Tried*
them; and within a little while the *afflicted* were most of them delivered
45 out of their *Troubles* also: And the Land had Peace restored unto it, by
the *God of Peace, treading Satan under Foot. Erasmus*, among other Historians,
does tell us, that at a Town in *Germany*, a *Dæmon* appearing on the Top of
a Chimney, threatned that he would set the Town on *Fire*, and at length
scattering some Ashes abroad, the whole Town was presently and horribly
50 Burnt unto the Ground.

Sir *William Phips* now beheld such *Dæmons* hideously scattering *Fire*
about the Country, in the Exasperations which the Minds of Men were
on these things rising unto; and therefore when he had well Canvased a
Cause, which perhaps might have puzzled the Wisdom of the wisest Men

---

[22] The "*Dutch* and *French* ministers" who responded to the "*Chief Judge*" of New York were
Henricus Selijns and Godfrey Daillé. The judge was Joseph Dudley.*
[23] Poisonous, applied especially to practices associated with sorcery (obsolete).*

55 on Earth to have managed, without any *Error* in their Administrations, he thought, if it would be any *Error* at all, it would certainly be the *safest* for him to put a stop unto all future Prosecutions, as far as it lay in him to do it.[24]

He did so, and for it he had not only the Printed Acknowledgments of
60 the *New-Englanders*,[25] who publickly thanked him, *As one of the Tribe of* Zebulun, *raised up from among themselves, and* Spirited *as well as* Commissioned *to be the* Steers-man *of a Vessel befogg'd in the* Mare Mortuum[26] *of* Witchcraft, *who now so happily* steered *her Course, that she escaped Shipwrack, and was safely again Moored under the Cape of* Good Hope; *and cut asunder the*
65 Circæan[27] *Knot of Enchantment, more difficult to be Dissolved than the famous* Gordian *one of Old.*

But the *QUEEN* also did him the Honour to write unto him those Gracious Letters, wherein her Majesty commended his Conduct in these *Inexplicable* Matters. And I did right in calling these Matters *Inexplicable.*
70 For if, after the Kingdom of *Sweden* (in the Years 1669, and 1670.) had some Hundreds of their Children by Night often carried away by *Spectres* to an *Hellish Rendezvous*,[28] where the Monsters that so *Spirited* them, did every way *Tempt* them to Associate with them; and the Judges of the Kingdom, after *extraordinary Supplications* to Heaven, upon a strict En-
75 quiry, were so satisfied with the *Confessions* of more than Twenty of the *accused*, agreeing exactly unto the *Depositions* of the *afflicted*, that they put several Scores of *Witches* to Death, whereupon the Confusions came unto a Period; yet after all, the chiefest Persons in the Kingdom would Question whether there were any *Witchcrafts* at all in the whole Affair;
80 it must not be wondred at, if the People of *New-England* are to this Hour full of *Doubts*, about the *Steps* which were taken, while a *War* from the *Invisible World* was Terrifying of them; and whether they did not kill some of their *own side* in the *Smoke* and *Noise* of this Dreadful *War*. And it will be yet less wondred at, if we consider, that we have seen the whole

70 Years/Year   82 *Invisible/Invinsible* C.M.

[24] Samuel Sewall was the only one of the "witch judges" to confess guilt for his part in the Salem trials. On January 14, 1697, a "day of prayer with fasting" which had been commanded by the General Court of Massachusetts, his request for pardon was read before the congregation in which he worshipped. On the same occasion, twelve jurymen at the trials in 1692 publicly declared, with disarming naïveté: "We confess that we ourselves were not capable to understand nor able to withstand the mysterious delusions of the Powers of Darkness . . . but were for want of knowledge in ourselves and better information from others, prevailed to take up with such evidence . . . as . . . we justly fear was insufficient for the touching the lives of any (Deuteronomy 17.6)."*

[25] Cotton Mather may have had in mind the Harvard College *Theses Amplissimo, Honoratissimo, Pariter ac Perillustri viro D. Guilielmo Phipps,* a folio broadside published in Boston, July 1693.*

[26] "Dead Sea."

[27] That is, like a spell cast by the witch Circe.*

[28] This outbreak occurred at Mohra in Sweden.*

85 *English Nation* alarumed with a *Plot*,[29] and both *Houses of Parliament*,
upon good Grounds, Voting their Sense of it, and many Persons most
justly *Hang'd, Drawn and Quarter'd*, for their share in it: When yet there
are enough, who to this Day will pretend, that they cannot comprehend
how much of it is to be accounted *Credible*. However, having related
90 these wonderful Passages, whereof, if the *Veracity* of the Relator in any
one Point be contested, there are whole *Clouds of Witnesses* to vindicate it,
I will take my leave of the Matter with an wholesome Caution of
Lactantius, which, it may be, some other Parts of the World besides *New-
England* may have occasion to think upon: *Efficiunt Dæmones, ut quæ non
95 sunt, sic tamen, quasi sint, conspicienda Hominibus exhibeant.*[30]

But the *Devil* being thus vanquished, we shall *next* hear, that some of
his most devoted and resembling *Children* are so too.

§. 17. As one of the first Actions *done* by Sir *William*, after he came to
99 the Age of *Doing*, was to save the Lives of many poor People from the
Rage of the *Diabolical Indians* in the *Eastern* Parts of the Country, so now
he was come to the Government, his Mind was very vehemently set upon
recovering of those Parts from the Miseries, which a New and a Long
War of the *Indians* had brought upon them. His *Birth* and *Youth* in the
5 *East*, had rendred him well known unto the *Indians* there: he had Hunted
and Fished many a weary Day in his Childhood with them; and when
those rude Savages had got the Story by the End, that *he had found a Ship
full of Money, and was now become all one-a-King!*[1] They were mightily
astonished at it: But when they farther understood that he was become
10 the Governour of *New-England*, it added a further Degree of Consternation to their Astonishment. He likewise was better acquainted with the
Scituation of those Regions than most other Men; and he consider'd
what vast Advantages might arise to no less than the whole *English*
Nation, from the *Lumber*, and *Fishery*, and *Naval-stores*, which those Regions
15 might soon supply the whole Nation withal, if once they were well
settled with good Inhabitants.

Wherefore Governour *Phips* took the first Opportunity to raise an
Army, with which he Travelled in Person, unto the *East Country*, to find
out and cut off the Barbarous Enemy, which had continued for near four
20 Years together, making horrible Havock on the Plantations that lay all
along the Northern *Frontiers* of *New-England:* And having pursued those
worse than *Scythian Wolves*, till they could be no longer followed, he did

94 *Efficiunt/Ffficiunt*   18 unto/under C.M.
96 *Devil/Devils*

[29] The Gunpowder Plot of November 5, 1605.
[30] "Devils so work that things which are not appear to men as if they were real."*

[1] That is, "just like a king"; apparently direct quotation of the Indian manner of speech.

with a very laudable *Skill*, and unusual *Speed*, and with less *Cost* unto
the Crown, than perhaps ever such a thing was done in the World, erect
25   a strong *Fort* at *Pemmaquid*.

This *Fort* he contrived so much in the very Heart of the Country now
possessed by the Enemy, as very much to hinder the several Nations of
the Tawnies from *Clanning* together for the Common Disturbance; and
his Design was, that a sufficient Garrison being here posted, they might
30   from thence, upon Advice, issue forth to surprize that Ferocient[2]
Enemy. At the same time he would fain have gone in Person up the Bay
of *Funda*,[3] with a convenient *Force*, to have spoiled the Nest of Rebellious
Frenchmen, who being Rendezvoused at St. *John*'s, had a yearly Supply
of Ammunition from *France*, with which they still supplied the *Indians*,
35   unto the extream Detriment of the *English*; but his Friends for a long
time would not permit him to expose himself unto the Inconveniencies
of that Expedition.

However, he took such Methods, that the *Indian Kings of the* East,
within a little while had their Stomachs brought down, to sue and beg for
40   a *Peace:* And making their appearance at the New-Fort in *Pemmaquid*,
Aug. 11. 1693. they did there Sign an Instrument, wherein, lamenting
the Miseries which their Adherence to the *French Counsels* had brought
them into, they did for themselves, and with the Consent of all the *Indians*
from the River of *Merrimack*, to the most Easterly Bounds of all the Prov-
45   ince, acknowledge their Hearty Subjection and Obedience unto the
Crown of *England*, and Solemnly Covenant, Promise and Agree, to and
with Sir *William Phips*, Captain General and Governour in Chief over
the Province, and his Successors in that place, *That* they would for ever
cease all Acts of Hostility towards the Subjects of the Crown of *England*,
50   and hold a constant Friendship with all the *English*. *That* they would
utterly abandon the *French* Interests, and not Succour or Conceal any
Enemy *Indians*, from *Canada* or elsewhere, that should come to any of
their Plantations within the *English* Territories: *That* all *English* Captives,
which they had among them, should be returned with all possible speed,
55   and no Ransom or Payment be given for any of them: *That* Their Majesties Subjects the *English*, now should quietly enter upon, and for ever
improve and enjoy all and singular their Rights of Lands, and former
Possessions, within the Eastern Parts of the Province, without any
Claims from any *Indians* or being ever disturbed therein: *That* all Trade
60   and Commerce, which hereafter might be allowed between the *English*
and the *Indians*, should be under a Regulation stated by an Act of the

33   Rendezvoused/Rendezvouzed

[2] Ferocious.
[3] Bay of Fundy.

General Assembly, or as limited by the Governour of the Province, with the Consent and Advice of his Council. And *that* if any Controversie hereafter happen between any of the *English* and the *Indians,* no private Revenge
65 was to be taken by the *Indians,* but proper Applications to be made unto His Majesties Government, for the due remedy thereof: *Submitting themselves herewithal to be Governed by His Majesties Laws.*

And for the Manifestation of their *Sincerity* in the *Submission* thus made, the *Hypocritical Wretches* delivered *Hostages* for their Fidelity; and then set
70 their *Marks* and *Seals,* no less than Thirteen *Sagamores* of them, (with *Names* of more than a *Persian* length[4]) unto this Instrument.

The first Rise of this *Indian War* had hitherto been almost as dark as that of the River *Nilus:* 'Tis true, if any *Wild English* did rashly begin to provoke and affront the *Indians,* yet the *Indians* had a fairer way to obtain
75 Justice than by Bloodshed: However, upon the *New-English Revolution,* the State of the *War* became wholly *New:* The Government then employed all possible ways to procure a good Understanding with the *Indians;* but all the *English* Offers, Kindnesses, Courtesies were barbarously requited by them, with New Acts of the most perfidious Hos-
80 tility. Notwithstanding all this, there were still some *Nice People*[5] that had their Scruples about the *Justice of the War;* but upon this New Submission of the *Indians,* if ever those *Rattle-snakes* (the only *Rattle-Snakes,* which, they say, were ever seen to the Northward of *Merimack-River*) should stir again, the most scrupulous Persons in the World must own, *That it must*
85 *be the most unexceptionable piece of Justice in the World for to extinguish them.*

Thus did the God of Heaven bless the unwearied Applications of Sir *William Phips,* for the restoring of *Peace* unto *New-England,* when the Country was quite *out of Breath,* in its Endeavours for its own Preservation from the continual Outrages of an inaccessible Enemy, and by the *Poverty*
90 *coming in so like an armed Man,* from the unsuccessfulness of their former *Armies,* that it could not imagine how to take one step further in its Wars. The most happy Respite of *Peace* beyond *Merimack-River* being thus procured, the Governour immediately set himself to use all possible Methods, that it might be *Peace, like a River,* nothing short of *Everlasting.*

95 He therefore prevailed with Two or Three Gentlemen to join with him, in sending a Supply of *Necessaries for Life* unto the *Indians,* until the General Assembly could come together to settle the *Indian-Trade* for the Advantage of the Publick, that the *Indians* might not by Necessity be
99 driven again to become a *French* Propriety; altho' by this Action, as the Gentlemen themselves were great *Losers* in their Estates, thus *he* himself declared unto the Members of the General Assembly, that he would upon Oath give an Account unto them of all his own Gains, and count himself

[4] Mather is probably thinking of such lengthy names as Artaxerxes, Cambyses, Hystaspes.
[5] That is, fastidious, overly scrupulous.

a Gainer, if in lieu of all they would give him *one Beaver-Hat*. The same
Generosity also caused him to take many a tedious Voyage, accompanied sometimes with his *Fidus Achates*,[6] and very dear Friend, Kinsman and Neighbour, Colonel *John Philips*,[7] between *Boston* and *Pemmaquid*; and this in the bitter Weeks of the *New-English*, which is almost a *Russian* Winter.

He was a sort of *Confessor* under such Torments of *Cold*, as once made the *Martyrdom* of *Muria*, and others, Commemorated in Orations of the Ancients; and the *Snow* and *Ice* which *Pliny* calls, *The Punishment of Mountains*, he chearfully endured, without any other *Profit* unto himself, but only the *Pleasure* of thereby establishing and continuing unto the People the Liberty to *Sleep* quietly in their *warm Nests* at home, while he was thus concerned for them abroad. *Non mihi sed Populo*, the Motto of the Emperor *Hadrian*, was Engraved on the Heart of Sir *William*: NOT FOR MY SELF, BUT FOR MY PEOPLE: Or that of *Maximin*,[8] *Quo major, hoc Laboriosior*, the more Honourable, the more Laborious.

Indeed the *Restlesness* of his Travels to the *Southern* as well as the *Eastern* Parts of the *Country*, when the Publick Safety call'd for his Presence, would have made one to think on the Translation which the King of *Portugal*, on a very Extraordinary Occasion, gave the Fourth Verse in the Hundred and Twenty-first *Psalm*. *He will not Slumber, nor will he suffer to Sleep the Keeper of* Israel. Nor did he only try to *Cicurate*[9] the *Indians* of the *East*, by other Prudent and Proper Treatments; but he also furnished himself with an *Indian* Preacher of the Gospel, whom he carried unto the *Eastward*, with an Intention to Teach them the Principles of the *Protestant Religion*, and Unteach them the mixt *Paganry* and *Popery* which hitherto *Diaboliz'd* them. To *Unteach* them, I say; for they had been *Taught* by the *French* Priests *this* among other things, that the Mother of our Blessed Saviour was a *French Lady*, and that they were *Englishmen* by whom our Saviour was Murdered; and that it was therefore a *Meritorious* thing to destroy the *English* Nation. The Name of the Preacher whom the Governour carried with him, was *Nahauton*, one of the Natives; and because the passing of such Expressions from the Mouth of a poor *Indian*, may upon some Accounts be worthy of *Remembrance*; let it be *Remembred*, that when the Governour propounded unto him such a *Mission* to the *Eastern Indians*, he replied, *I know that I shall probably Endanger my Life, by going to Preach the Gospel among the Frenchified* Indians; *but I know that it will be a Service unto the Lord Jesus Christ, and therefore I will venture to go.*

---

6 "Faithful Achates," the friend of Aeneas.*
7 John Philips (d. 1726) was a prosperous citizen of Charlestown. Under the new charter, he was made colonel of militia. His daughter Abigail was Cotton Mather's first wife.*
8 Gaius Julius Verus Maximinus (173–239), Roman general, became emperor in 235.*
9 To tame (obsolete).

God grant that his *Behaviour* may be in all things, at all times, according to these his *Expressions!* While these things were doing, having Intelligence of a *French* Man of War expected at St. *John's*, he dispatched away the
45 *Non-such-Frigat* thither to intercept him; nevertheless by the gross *Negligence*, and perhaps *Cowardice* of the Captain, who had lately come from *England* with Orders to take the Command of her, instead of one who had been by Sir *William* a while before put in, and one who had signalized himself by doing of notable Service for the King and Country
50 in it, the *Frenchman* arrived unladed, and went away untouch'd. The Governour was extreamly offended at this notorious *Deficiency*; it cast him into a great Impatience to see the *Nation* so wretchedly served; and he would himself have gone to Saint *John's* with a Resolution to *Spoil* that Harbour of *Spoilers*, if he had not been taken off, by being sent for
55 home to *Whitehall*, in the very midst of his Undertakings.

But the Treacherous *Indians* being *poisoned* with the *French Enchantments*, and furnished with brave *New Coats*, and *New Arms*, and all new Incentives to *War*, by the *Man of War* newly come in; they presently and perfidiously fell upon two *English* Towns,[10] and Butchered and Captived
60 many of the Inhabitants, and made a *New War*, which the *New-Englanders* know not whether it will end until either *Canada* become an *English Province*, or that State arrive, wherein they *shall beat Swords into Plough-shares, and Spears into Pruning-hooks*. And no doubt, the taking off Sir *William Phips* was no small Encouragement unto the *Indians* in this
65 Relapse, into the Villanies and Massacres of a *New Invasion* upon the Country.

§. 18. Reader, 'tis time for us to view a little more to the *Life*, the *Picture* of the Person, the *Actions* of whose *Life* we have hitherto been looking upon. Know then, that for his *Exterior*, he was one *Tall*, beyond
70 the common Set of Men, and *Thick* as well as *Tall*, and *Strong* as well as *Thick:* He was, in all respects, exceedingly *Robust*, and able to Conquer such Difficulties of *Diet* and of *Travel*, as would have kill'd most Men alive: Nor did the *Fat*, whereinto he grew very much in his later Years, take away the Vigour of his Motions.

75 He was Well-set, and he was therewithal of a very *Comely*, though a very *Manly* Countenance: A Countenance where any true skill in *Physiognomy* would have read the Characters of a *Generous Mind*. Wherefore passing to his *Interior*, the very first thing which there offered it self unto Observation, was a most Incomparable *Generosity*.

80 And of this, besides the innumerable Instances which he gave in his usual Hatred of *Dirty* or *Little* Tricks, there was one Instance for which I must freely say, *I never saw Three Men in this World that Equall'd him*;

[10] On July 18, 1694, there was an attack in force "upon a village at Oyster river [now Durham], in New-Hampshire province," and attacks soon spread to other areas.*

this was his wonderfully *Forgiving Spirit*. In the vast Variety of *Business*, through which he *Raced* in his time, he met with many and mighty *In-*
85 *juries*; but although I have heard all that the most venemous *Malice* could ever *Hiss* at his Memory, I never did hear unto this Hour, that he did ever once deliberately *Revenge an Injury*.

Upon certain *Affronts* he has made sudden *Returns* that have shewed *Choler* enough, and he has by *Blow*,[1] as well as by *Word*, chastised *In-*
90 *civilities*: He was, indeed, sufficiently impatient of being *put upon*; and when *Base Men*, surprizing him at some *Disadvantages* (for else few Men durst have done it) have sometimes drawn upon him, he has, without the *Wicked Madness* of a *Formal Duel*, made them feel that he knew how to *Correct Fools*. Nevertheless, he ever declined a *Deliberate Revenge* of a *Wrong*
95 done unto him; though few Men upon *Earth* have, in their *Vicissitudes*, been furnished with such frequent *Opportunities* of *Revenge*, as *Heaven* brought into the Hands of this *Gentleman*.

Under great Provocations, he would commonly say, *'Tis no Matter, let*
99 *them alone; some time or other they'll see their Weakness and Rashness, and have occasion for me to do them a Kindness: And they shall then see I have quite forgotten all their Baseness.* Accordingly 'twas remarkable to see it, that few Men ever did *him* a *Mischief*, but those Men afterwards had occasion for him to do *them* a *Kindness*; and he did the *Kindness* with as forgetful a
5 *Bravery*, as if the *Mischief* had never been done at all. The Emperor *Theodosius* himself could not be readier to *Forgive*,[2] so worthily did he verifie that Observation.

Quo quisque est Major, magis est Placabilis Ira,
Et Faciles Motus, Mens Generosa capit.[3]

10   In those Places of *Power* whereto the Providence of God by several *Degrees* raised him, it still fell out so, that before his *Rise* thereunto he underwent such things as he counted very hard *Abuses*, from those very Persons over whom the Divine Providence afterwards gave him the *Ascendant*.
15   By such *Trials*, the Wisdom of Heaven still prepared him, as *David*

---

[1] Two instances of Phips's "*Returns*" by a "*Blow*" arose out of his insistence that as chief naval officer he had complete authority over all shipping entering the port. He early made an enemy of Jahleel Brenton, son of the governor of Rhode Island, who had been named collector of customs for the port of Boston. Phips prevailed over Brenton, beating him over the head with a cane in the process. He served Captain Short, master of the *Nonesuch* frigate, in like manner; in addition, he had Short seized and made off with his papers, money, and clothes.*

[2] Theodosius I won over the Goths by his readiness to pay honors to their fallen leader, Athanaric.*

[3] "The greater one is, the more placable one is in wrath, and a generous mind is easily moved."*

before him, for *successive Advancements*; and as he behaved himself with a marvellous *Long-suffering*, when he was *Tried*, by such Mortifications, thus when he came to be *advanced*, he convinced all Mankind, that he had perfectly Buried all the old Offences in an Eternal *Amnesty*. I was my Self
20 an *Ear-witness*, that one, who was an *Eye-witness* of his Behaviour under such *Probations* of his Patience, did, long before his Arrival to that Honour, say unto him, *Sir, Forgive those that give you these Vexations, and know that the God of Heaven intends, before he has done with you, to make you the Governour of* New-England! And when he did indeed become the *Governour of* New-
25 England, he shew'd that he still continued a *Governour of himself*, in his Treating all that had formerly been in ill Terms with him, with as much *Favour* and *Freedom*, as if there had never happened the least Exasperations: Though any Governour that Kens *Hobbianism*,[4] can easily contrive Ways enough to wreak a *Spite*, where he owes it.

30 It was with some *Christian Remark*, that he read the *Pagan-story* of the Renowned *Fabius Maximus*, who being preferred unto the highest Office in the Commonwealth, did, through a Zeal for his Country, overcome the greatest Contempts that any Person of Quality could have received. *Minutius* the Master of the Horse, and the next Person in Dignity to him-
35 self, did first privately Traduce him, as one that was *no Soldier*, and less *Politician*; and he afterwards did both by Speeches and Letters prejudice not only the *Army*, but also the *Senate* against him, so that *Minutius* was now by an unpresidented[5] Commission brought into an *Equality* with *Fabius*.

40 All this while the great *Fabius* did not throw up his Cares for the Commonwealth, but with a wondrous *Equality of Mind* endured equally the Malice of the *Judges*, and the Fury of the *Commons*; and when *Minutius* a while after was with all his Forces upon the Point of perishing by the victorious Arms of *Hannibal*, this very *Fabius*, not listening to the Dictates
45 of *Revenge*, came in and helped him, and saved him; and so by a rare Virtue, he made his worst *Adversaries* the Captives of his *Generosity*.

One of the Antients[6] upon such an History, cried out, *If Heathens can do thus much for the Glory of their Name, what shall not Christians do for the Glory of Heaven!* And Sir *William Phips* did so *much more* than *thus much*,
50 that besides his meriting the *Glory* of such a *Name*, as *PHIPPIUS MAXIMUS*,[7] he therein had upon him the Symptoms of a Title to the *Glory of Heaven*, in the *Seal* of his own *Pardon* from God. Nor was this *Generosity* in His EXCELLENCY the Governour of *New-England*,

---

[4] That is, one familiar with the political philosophy of Thomas Hobbes, which asserted the necessity of absolutist government in order to curb antagonisms between individual interests.

[5] Unprecedented.

[6] "One of the Antients" has not been identified.

[7] "The very great Phips."

55 unaccompanied with many other *Excellencies*; whereof the *Piety* of his
Carriage towards *God* is worthy to be first Mentioned.

It is true, He was very Zealous for all Men to enjoy such a *Liberty of
Conscience*, as he judged a *Native Right* of *Mankind:* And he was extreamly
Troubled at the *over-boiling Zeal* of some good Men, who formerly took
that wrong Way of reclaiming *Hereticks* by *Persecution.* For this *Generosity*,
60 it may be, some would have compared him unto *Gallio*, the Governour of
Achaia, whom our Preachers, perhaps with Mistake enough, think to be
condemned in the Scripture, for his not appearing to be a *Judge*, in
Matters which indeed fell not under his Cognizance.[8]

And I shall be content that he be compared unto that Gentleman; for
65 that *Gallio* was the Brother of *Seneca*, who gives this Character of him,
*That there was no Man who did not love him too little, if he could Love him any
more*; and, *That there was no Mortal so Dear to any, as he was to all*; and, *That
he hated all Vices, but none more than Flattery.*

But while the *Generosity* of Sir *William* caused him to desire a *Liberty
70 of Conscience*, his *Piety* would not allow a *Liberty of Prophaneness*, either to
himself or others. He did not affect any mighty *show* of Devotion; and
when he saw any that were *evidently careful* to make a *show*, and especially,
if at the same Time they were *notoriously* Defective in the Duties of
Common Justice or *Goodness*, or the Duties of the *Relations* wherein God had
75 *stationed* them, he had an extream Aversion for them.

Nevertheless he did show a Consciencious Desire to observe the Laws of
the Lord Jesus Christ in his *Conversation*; and he Conscienciously attended
upon the Exercises of *Devotion* in the Seasons thereof, on *Lectures*, as well
as on *Lord's Days*, and in the *Daily Sacrifice*, the Morning and Evening
80 Service of his own Family; yea, and at the *Private Meetings* of the Devout
People kept every *Fortnight* in the Neighbourhood.

Besides all this, when he had *great Works* before him, he would invite
good Men to come and *Fast* and *Pray* with him at his House for the Success
thereof; and when he had succeeded in what he had undertaken, he
85 would prevail with them to come and keep a Day of Solemn *Thanksgiving* with him. His *Love* to Almighty *God*, was indeed manifested by
nothing more than his *Love* to those that had the *Image* of God upon them;
he heartily, and with real *Honour* for them, *Loved all Godly Men*; and in so
doing, he did not confine *Godliness* to this or that Party, but where-ever
90 he saw the *Fear of God*, in one of a *Congregational*, or *Presbyterian*, or
Antipædobaptist,[9] or *Episcopalian* Perswasion, he did, without any Difference,
express towards them a Reverent Affection.

85–86   *Thanksgiving/Thansgiving*

[8] Gallio, Proconsul of Achaia, was the Roman official before whom the Jews accused the
apostle Paul (Acts 18.12–17).*
[9] One opposed to infant baptism.*

But he made no Men more welcome than those *good Men,* whose *Office* 'tis to promote and preserve *Goodness* in all other Men; even the
95 *Ministers* of the Gospel: Especially when they were such as faithfully discharged their Office: And from these at any time, the least Admonition or Intimation of any good thing to be done by him, he entertained with a most obliging Alacrity. His *Religion* in truth, was one Principle that added
99 *Virtue* unto that vast *Courage,* which was always in him to a Degree *Heroical.* Those terrible Nations[10] which made their Descents from the *Northern* on the *Southern* Parts of *Europe,* in those Elder Ages, when so to *swarm out* was more frequent with them, were inspired with a *Valiant Contempt of Life,* by the Opinion wherein their Famous *Odin*[11] instructed
5 them. *That their Death was but an Entrance into another Life, wherein they who died in Warlike Actions, were bravely Feasted with the God of War for ever:* 'Tis in-expressible how much the *Courage* of those fierce Mortals was fortified by that Opinion.

But when Sir *William Phips* was asked by some that observed his *Valiant*
10 *Contempt of Death,* what it was that made him so little afraid of *Dying,* he gave a better grounded Account of it than those *Pagans* could; his Answer was, *I do humbly believe, that the Lord Jesus Christ shed his Precious Blood for me, by his Death procuring my Peace with God: And what should I now be afraid of dying for?*

15 But this leads me to mention the *Humble* and *Modest* Carriage in him towards other *Men,* which accompanied this his *Piety.* There were certain *Pomps* belonging unto the several *Places of Honour,* through which he passed; *Pomps* that are very taking to Men of *little Souls:* But although he rose from so *little,* yet he discovered a Marvellous *Contempt* of those Airy
20 things, and as far as he handsomely could, he declined, being Ceremoniously, or any otherwise than with a *Dutch Modesty* waited upon. And it might more truly be said of him, than it was of *Aristides, He was never seen the Prouder for any Honour that was done him from his Countrymen.*

Hence, albeit I have read that Complaint, made by a Worthy Man,[12]
25 *I have often observed, and this not without some blushing, that even good People have had a kind of Shame upon them, to acknowledge their low beginning, and used all Arts to hide it.* I could never *observe* the least of that Fault in this Worthy Man; but he would speak of his own *low beginning* with as much Freedom and Frequency, as if he had been afraid of having it forgotten.

[10] The Scandinavian people who made raids and established settlements in the British Isles and many parts of Europe from about the eighth to the eleventh century.

[11] Odin (Othin, Wodan, Woden) was in Norse mythology "a God of the Ancient *Danes*" who, with the god Thor, was believed to preside over battles. "Some Learned Men" were "of Opinion, That this *Odin* . . . finding that he could not avoid Death . . . commanded his Body to be burnt as soon as he was dead, assuring them, that his Soul would return to *Asgardie* . . . there to live for ever . . . where the *Danes* placed there *Vall-holl,* or *Elysian Fields.*"*

[12] The "Worthy Man" has not been identified.

30   It was counted an Humility in King *Agathocles*,[13] the Son of a *Potter*, to
be served therefore in *Earthern Vessels*, as *Plutarch* hath informed us: It was
counted an Humility in Archbishop *Willigis*,[14] the Son of a *Wheelwright*,
therefore to have *Wheels* hung about his Bed-Chamber, with this Inscription, *Recole unde Veneris*, i. e. *Remember thy Original*. But such was the
35 *Humility* and *Lowliness* of this *Rising Man!* Not only did he after his return
to his Country in his Greatness, one Day, make a splendid Feast for the
Ship-Carpenters of *Boston*, among whom he was willing at his Table to
Commemorate the Mercy of God unto him, who had once been a *Ship-
Carpenter* himself, but he would on all Occasions *Permit*, yea, *Study* to
40 have his *Meannesses*[15] remembred.

Hence upon frequent Occasions of Uneasiness in his Government, he
would chuse thus to express himself, *Gentlemen, were it not that I am to do
Service for the Publick, I should be much easier in returning unto my broad Ax
again!* And hence, according to the *Affable* Courtesie which he ordinarily
45 used unto all sorts of Persons, (quite contrary to the *Asperity* which the
old Proverb expects in the *Raised*) he would particularly, when Sailing
in sight of *Kennebeck*, with Armies under his Command, call the Young
Soldiers and *Sailors* upon Deck, and speak to them after this Fashion;
*Young Men, It was upon that Hill that I kept Sheep a few Years ago; and since
50 you see that Almighty God has brought me to something, do you learn to Fear
God, and be Honest, and mind your Business, and follow no bad Courses, and you
don't know what you may come to!* A Temper not altogether unlike what the
advanced *Shepherd*[16] had, when he wrote the *Twenty-third* Psalm; or
when he Imprinted on the *Coin* of his Kingdom the Remembrance of his
55 Old Condition: For *Christianus Gerson*,[17] a Christianized *Jew*, has informed
us, That on the one side of *David's* Coin were to be seen his old *Pouch*
and *Crook*, the Instruments of *Shepherdy*; on the other side were enstamped
the Towers of *Zion*.

In fine, our Sir *William* was a Person of so sweet a Temper, that they
60 who were most intimately acquainted with him, would commonly
pronounce him, *The best Conditioned Gentleman in the World!* And by the
continual Discoveries and Expressions of such a *Temper*, he so gained the
Hearts of them who waited upon him in any of his Expeditions, that they
would commonly profess themselves willing still, *to have gone with him to
65 the end of the World.*

But if all other People found him so kind a *Neighbour*, we may easily
infer what an Husband he was unto his *Lady*. Leaving unmentioned that
Virtue of his *Chastity*, which the Prodigious Depravation brought by the

[13] Agathocles (361–289 B.C.), tyrant of Syracuse.*
[14] Archbishop of Mainz 975–1011.*
[15] That is, his humble beginnings.
[16] David.
[17] A German Hebraist (1569–1627), author of learned works on the Talmud.*

Late Reigns upon the Manners of the Nation,[18] has made worthy to be
70 mentioned as a *Virtue* somewhat *Extraordinary*; I shall rather pass on to say,
That the *Love*, even to *Fondness*,[19] with which he always treated her, was a
Matter not only of *Observation*, but even of such *Admiration*, that every one
said, *The Age afforded not a kinder Husband!*

But we must now return to our Story.

75 §. 19. When Persons do by Studies full of *Curiosity*,[1] seek to inform
themselves of things about which the God of Heaven hath forbidden our
Curious Enquiries, there is a marvellous *Impression*, which the *Dæmons* do
often make on the Minds of those their Votaries, about the *Future* or
Secret Matters unlawfully enquired after, and at last there is also an horri-
80 ble *Possession*, which those *Fatidic*[2] *Dæmons* do take of them. The *Snares* of
Hell, hereby laid for miserable Mortals, have been such, that when I
read the Laws, which *Agellius*[3] affirms to have been made, even in
Pagan Rome, against the *Vaticinatores*;[4] I wonder that no *English* Noble-
man or Gentleman signalizes his regard unto *Christianity*, by doing what
85 even a *Roman Tully* would have done, in promoting *An Act of Parliament*
against that *Paganish* Practice of *Judicial Astrology*, whereof, if such Men as
Austin were now living, they would assert, *The Devil first found it, and they
that profess it are Enemies of Truth and of God.*

In the mean time, I cannot but relate a wonderful Experience of Sir
90 *William Phips*, by the Relation whereof something of an *Antidote* may be
given against a *Poison*, which the Diabolical *Figure-Flingers*[5] and *Fortune-
Tellers* that swarm all the World over may insinuate into the Minds of
Men. Long before Mr. *Phips* came to be Sir *William*, while he sojourned
in *London*, there came into his Lodging an Old *Astrologer*, living in the
95 Neighbourhood, who making some *Observation* of him, though he had
small or no *Conversation* with him, did (howbeit by him wholly undesired)
one Day send him a Paper, wherein he had, with Pretences of a Rule in
Astrology for each Article, distinctly noted the most material Passages
99 that were to befal this our *Phips* in the remaining part of his Life; it was
particularly Asserted and Inserted, That he should be engaged in a
Design, wherein by Reason of Enemies at *Court*, he should meet with
much delay; that nevertheless in the *Thirty-Seventh* Year of his Life, he

82 *Agellius/Angellius* C.M. 93–94 sojourned in/sojourned in in

18 An allusion to the moral decline in England during the Restoration period.
19 That is, extravagant doting.

---

1 Anything strange, abstruse, or occult, often in a bad sense.
2 That is, having the power of prophecy.
3 Antonius Agellius (1532–1608), Italian cleric, distinguished for his erudition and knowledge
of ancient languages.*
4 Soothsayers.
5 Those who cast "figures," that is, astrological diagrams and horoscopes; usually used
contemptuously of pretenders to astrological lore (obsolete).

should find a *mighty Treasure*; that in the *Forty-First* Year of his Life, his
5 *King* should employ him in as great a *Trust beyond Sea*, as a Subject could
easily have: That soon after this he should undergo an hard *Storm* from
the Endeavours of his Adversaries to *reproach* him and *ruin* him; that his
Adversaries, though they should go very *near* gaining the Point, should
yet *miss* of doing so; that he should hit upon a vastly *Richer Matter* than
10 any that he had hitherto met withal; that he should continue *Thirteen
Years* in his *Publick Station*, full of Action, and full of Hurry; and the rest
of his Days he should spend in the Satisfaction of a *Peaceable Retirement*.

   Mr. *Phips* received this undesired Paper with Trouble and with Contempt, and threw it by among certain loose Papers in the bottom of a
15 Trunk, where his Lady some Years after accidentally lit upon it. His
Lady with Admiration saw, step after step, very much of it accomplished;
but when she heard from *England*, that Sir *William* was coming over with
a Commission to be Governour of *New-England*, in that very Year of his
Life, which the Paper specified; she was afraid of letting it lye any longer
20 in the House, but cast it into the *Fire*.

   Now the thing which I must invite my Reader to remark, is this, That
albeit Almighty God may permit the *Devils* to *Predict*, and perhaps to
Perform very many particular things to Men, that shall by such a *Pre-
sumptuous and Unwarrantable Juggle* as *Astrology* (so Dr. *Hall*[6] well calls it!)
25 or any other *Divination*, consult them, yet the *Devils* which *foretel* many
True things, do commonly *foretel* some that are *False*, and it may be,
propose by the things that are *True* to betray Men into some fatal Mis-
belief and Miscarriage about those that are False.

   Very singular therefore was the Wisdom of Sir *William Phips*, that as
30 he ever Treated these *Prophesies* about him with a most *Pious Neglect*, so
when he had seen all but the *Two last* of them very punctually fulfilled
yea, and seen the beginning of a Fulfilment unto the *last but one* also,
yet when I pleasantly mentioned them unto him, on purpose to *Try*
whether there were any occasion for me humbly to give him the serious
35 *Advice*, necessary in such a Case to Anticipate the *Devices of Satan*, he
prevented my Advice, by saying to me, Sir, *I do believe there might be a
cursed Snare of Satan in those Prophesies: I believe Satan might have leave to
foretel many things, all of which might come to pass in the beginning, to lay me
asleep about such things as are to follow, especially about the main Chance of all;*
40 *I do not know but I am to die this Year: For my part, by the help of the Grace of
God, I shall endeavour to live as if I were this Year to die.* And let the Reader
now attend the Event!

   §. 20. 'Tis a Similitude which I have Learned from no less a Person

25 *Devils/Devil*

[6] Joseph Hall (1574–1656), Bishop of Exeter and Norwich.*

than the great *Basil:*[1] That *as* the *Eye* sees not those Objects which are
45 applied close unto it, and even lye upon it; but when the Objects are to
some distance removed, it clearly discerns them: *So,* we have little sense
of the Good which we have in our Enjoyments, until God, by the removal
thereof, teach us better to prize what we once enjoyed. It is true, the
Generality of sober and thinking People among the *New-Englanders,*
50 did as highly value the *Government* of Sir *William Phips,* whilst he lived, as
they do his *Memory,* since his Death; nevertheless it must be confessed,
that the Blessing which the Country had in his indefatigable Zeal, to
serve the Publick in all it's Interests, was not so valued as it should have
been.

55 It was mention'd long since as a notorious Fault in *Old Egypt,* that it
was *Loquax & Ingeniosa in Contumeliam Præfectorum Provincia; si quis forte
vitaverit Culpam, Contumeliam non effugit:*[2] And *New-England* has been at
the best always too faulty, in that very Character, *A Province very Talkative,
and Ingenious for the vilifying of its Public Servants.*

60 But Sir *William Phips,* who might in a *Calm* of the Commonwealth have
administred all things with as General an Acceptance as any that have
gone before him, had the Disadvantage of being set at *Helm* in a time as
full of *Storm* as ever that *Province* had seen; and the People having their
Spirits put into a *Tumult* by the discomposing and distempering Variety
65 of Disasters, which had long been rendring the time Calamitous, it was
natural for them, as 'tis for all Men *then,* to be *complaining;*[3] and you may
be sure, the *Rulers* must in such Cases be always *complained* of, and the
chief Complaints must be heaped upon those that are *Commanders in
Chief.* Nor has a certain Proverb in *Asia* been improper in *America, He
70 deserves no Man's good Word, of whom every Man shall speak well.*

Sir *William* was very hardly *Handled* (or *Tongued* at least) in the Liberty
which People took to make most unbecoming and injurious Reflections
upon his Conduct, and Clamour against him, even for those very Actions
which were not only *Necessary* to be done, but highly *Beneficial* unto
75 themselves; and though he would ordinarily smile at their *Frowardness,*
calling it *his Country Pay,*[4] yet he sometimes resented it with some uneasiness; he seem'd unto himself sometimes almost as bad as Rolled
about in *Regulus's* Barrel;[5] and had occasion to think on the *Italian*
Proverb, *To wait for one who does not come; to lye a Bed not able to sleep; and to*

[1] St. Basil, Bishop of Caesarea 370–379.*
[2] "Free-spoken and ingenious in slandering the rulers in the province; if by chance anyone
avoided guilt, he did not escape slander."*
[3] Emerging from a political struggle that had threatened their existence, the New Englanders
were still beset by distrust of English intentions, and by fears of further Indian wars.
[4] Commodities raised or produced in the country and used as money.
[5] Marcus Atilius Regulus, Roman general in the first Punic War, was tortured by the
Carthaginians by being placed in a barrel or chest which was studded with nails pointed
inward.*

80 *find it impossible to please those whom we serve; are three Griefs enough to kill a Man.*

But as *Froward* as the People were, under the *Epidemical Vexations* of the Age, yet there were very few but would acknowledge unto the very Last, *It will be hardly possible for us to see another Governour that shall more intirely*
85 *Love and Serve the Country:* Yea, had the Country had the Choice of their own *Governour,* 'tis judged their *Votes,* more than Forty to One, would have still fallen upon him to have been the Man: And the *General Assembly* therefore on all occasions renewed their Petitions unto the King for his Continuance.

90   Nevertheless, there was a little Party of Men, who thought they must not *sleep till they had caused him to fall:* And they so vigorously prosecuted certain Articles before the Council-board at *Whitehall* against him, that they imagined they had gained an *Order* of His Majesty in Council, to suspend him immediately from his Government, and appoint a *Com-*
95 *mittee* of Persons nominated by his Enemies, to hear all *Depositions* against him; and so a Report of the whole to be made unto the King and Council.

But His Majesty was too well informed of Sir *William*'s Integrity to permit such a sort of Procedure; and therefore he signified unto His most
99 Honourable Council, that nothing should be done against Sir *William,* until he had Opportunity to clear himself; and thereupon he sent His Royal Commands unto Sir *William* to come over. To give any retorting Accounts of the Principal Persons who thus adversaried him, would be a Thing so contrary to the Spirit of Sir *William Phips* himself, who at his
5 leaving of *New-England* bravely declared that he *freely forgave them all*; and if he had returned thither again, would never have taken the least revenge upon them, that *This* alone would oblige me, if I had no other Obligations of Christianity upon me, to forbear it; and it may be, for some of them, it would be *to throw Water upon a drowned Mouse.*

10   Nor need I to produce any more about the *Articles* which these Men exhibited against him,[6] than *This*; that it was by most Men believed, that if he would have connived at some *Arbitrary Oppressions* too much used by some kind of Officers on the King's Subjects, *Few* perhaps, or *None* of those Articles had ever been formed; and that he apprehended
15 himself to be provided with a full *Defence* against them all.

Nor did His Excellency seem loth to have had his Case Tried under the Brazen Tree of *Gariac,* if there had been such an one, as that mentioned by the Fabulous *Murtadi,* in his Prodigies of *Egypt,*[7] a Tree which had

82   *Epidemical/Epedemical*   13   or/of   C.M.
83   but/that   C.M.

[6] A suit for damages brought by Joseph Dudley and Jahleel Brenton.*

[7] *The Egyptian History, Treating of the Pyramids, the Inundation of the Nile, and other Prodigies of Egypt . . . Written originally in the Arabian tongue by Murtadi the son of Gaphiphus . . . faithfully done into English by J. Davies of Kidwelly* (London, 1672).*

Iron Branches with sharp *Hooks* at the end of them, that when any false
20 Accuser approached, as the *Fabel* says, immediately flew at him, and
stuck in him, until he had ceased Injuring his Adversary.

Wherefore in Obedience unto the King's Commands, he took his leave
of *Boston* on the seventeenth of *November,* 1694. attended with all proper
Testimonies of Respect and Honour from the *Body* of the People, which
25 he had been the *Head* unto; and with *Addresses* unto their Majesties, and
the Chief Ministers of State from the General Assembly, humbly imploring, that they might not be deprived of the Happiness which they
had in such an *Head.*

Arriving at *Whitehall,* he found in a few Days, that notwithstanding all
30 the Impotent Rage of his Adversaries particularly vented and printed in
a *Villanous Libel,* as well as almost in as many other ways as there are
Mouths, at which *Fyal*[8] sometimes has vomited out its Infernal Fires, he
had all *Humane Assurance* of his returning in a very few Weeks again the
Governour of *New-England.*

35 Wherefore there were especially *two Designs,* full of Service to the whole
English Nation, as well as his own particular Country of *New-England,*
which he applied his *Thoughts* unto. *First,* He had a new *Scene* of Action
opened unto him, in an opportunity to supply the Crown with all *Naval
Stores* at most *easie Rates,* from those *Eastern* Parts of the *Massachuset*
40 Province, which through the Conquest that *he* had made thereof, came
to be Inserted in the *Massachuset*-Charter.[9] As no Man was more *capable*
than *he* to improve this Opportunity unto a vast Advantage, so his *Inclination* to it was according to his *Capacity.*

And he longed with some Impatience to see the King furnished from
45 his *own Dominions,* with such floating and stately Castles, those *Wooden-
Walls* of Great *Britain,* for much of which he has hitherto Traded with
Foreign Kingdoms. Next, if I may say *next* unto this, he had an Eye upon
Canada; all attempts for the reducing whereof had hitherto proved
Abortive.

50 It was but a few Months ago that a considerable Fleet, under Sir
Francis Wheeler,[10] which had been sent into the *West-Indies* to subdue
Martinico, was ordered then to call at *New-England,* that being recruited
there, they might make a further Descent upon *Canada;* but Heaven
frowned upon that Expedition, especially by a terrible Sickness, the most
55 like the *Plague* of any thing that has been ever seen in *America,* whereof
there Died, e'er they could reach to *Boston,* as I was told by Sir *Francis*

52 *Martinico/Martenico*

[8] Fayal, a volcanic island in the Azores.
[9] For Phips's "Conquest" of the "*Eastern Parts,*" see section 17 above.
[10] For Sir Francis Wheeler and the "terrible Sickness" in his fleet, see p. 183, ll. 68–70.

himself, no less than *Thirteen* Hundred Sailers out of *Twenty One*, and no less than *Eighteen* Hundred Soldiers out of *Twenty-four*.

60 It was now therefore his desire to have satisfied the King, that his whole Interest in *America* lay at Stake, while *Canada* was in *French* Hands: And therewithal to have laid before several Noblemen and Gentlemen, how beneficial an Undertaking it would have been for them to have pursued the *Canadian*-Business, for which the *New-Englanders* were now grown too Feeble; their Country being too far now, as *Bede* says *England*

65 once was, *Omni Milite & floridæ Juventutis Alacritate spoliata.*[11]

Besides these *two* Designs in the *Thoughts* of Sir *William*, there was a *Third*, which he had Hopes that the King would have given him leave to have pursued, after he had continued so long in his Government, as to have obtained the more *General Welfare* which he designed in the for-

70 mer Instances. I do not mean the making of *New-England* the Seat of a *Spanish Trade*, though so vastly profitable a thing was likely to have been brought about, by his being one of an Honourable Company engaged in such a Project.

But the *Spanish Wreck*, where Sir *William* had made his first *good*

75 *Voyage*, was not the *Only*, nor the *Richest* Wreck, that he knew to be lying under the Water. He knew particularly, that when the Ship which had Governour *Boadilla*[12] Aboard, was cast away, there was, as *Peter Martyr* says, an entire Table of *Gold* of *Three Thousand Three Hundred and Ten Pound Weight.*

80 The Duke of *Albemarle*'s Patent for all such *Wrecks* now expiring, Sir *William* thought on the *Motto* which is upon the Gold *Medal*, bestowed by the late King, with his *Knighthood* upon him, *Semper Tibi pendeat Hamus:*[13] And supposing himself to have gained sufficient Information of the right Way to such a *Wreck*, it was his purpose upon his Dismission

85 from his Government, once more to have gone unto his old *Fishing-Trade*, upon a mighty Shelf of Rocks and Bank of Sands that lye where he had informed himself.

But as the Prophets *Haggai* and *Zechariah*, in their *Psalm* upon the Grants made unto their People by the Emperors of *Persia* have that

90 Reflection, *Man's Breath goeth forth, he returns to his Earth; in that very Day his thoughts perish*, my Reader must now see what came of all these considerablȩ *Thoughts*. About the middle of *February*, 1694. Sir *William* found himself indisposed with a Cold, which obliged him to keep his Chamber; but under this Indisposition he received the Honour of a

88 Prophets/Prophet   91 *perish*, my/*perish*. My

---

[11] "Despoiled of young and active soldiery."*
[12] Francisco de Bobadilla (d. 1502), Spanish viceroy of the West Indies.*
[13] "May your hook always be hanging."*

95 Visit from a very Eminent Person at *Whitehall*, who upon sufficient
Assurance, bad him *Get well as fast as he could, for in one Months time he should
be again dispatched away to his Government of* New-England.

Nevertheless his Distemper proved a sort of *Malignant Feaver*, whereof
99 many about this time died in the City; and it suddenly put an End at
once unto his *Days* and *Thoughts*, on the Eighteenth of *February*; to the
extream surprize of his Friends, who Honourably Interr'd him in the
Church of St. *Mary Woolnoth*, and with him, how much of *New-England's*
Happiness!

5 §. 21. Although he has now *no more a Portion for ever in any Thing that is
done under the Sun*, yet Justice requires that *his Memory be not forgotten*. I
have not all this while said *He was Faultless*, nor am I unwilling to use for
him the Words which Mr. *Calamy*[1] had in his Funeral Sermon for the
Excellent Earl of *Warwick, It must be confessed, lest I should prove a Flatterer*,
10 *he had his Infirmities, which I trust Jesus Christ hath covered with the Robe of his
Righteousness: My Prayer to God is, that all his Infirmities may be Buried in the
Grave of Oblivion, and that all his Virtues and Graces may Supervive*; although
perhaps they were no *Infirmities* in that Noble Person, which Mr. *Calamy*
counted so.

15 Nevertheless I must also say, That if the Anguish of his Publick
Fatigues threw Sir *William* into any *Faults* of *Passion*; they were but *Faults*
of *Passion* soon Recall'd: And *Spots* being soonest seen in *Ermin*, there
was usually the *most* made of them that could be, by those that were
least *Free* themselves.

20 After all, I do not know that I have been, by any personal Obligations
or Circumstances, charmed into any *Partiality* for the *Memory* of this
Worthy Man; but I do here, from a real Satisfaction of Conscience
concerning him, declare to all the World, that I reckon him to have
been really a very *Worthy Man*; that few Men in the World rising from
25 so mean an *Original* as he, would have acquitted themselves with a
Thousand Part of his *Capacity* or *Integrity*; that he left unto the World a
notable Example of a Disposition to *do Good*, and encountred and overcame almost invincible *Temptations* in doing it.

And I do most solemnly Profess, that I have most conscienciously en-
30 deavoured the utmost Sincerity and Veracity of a *Christian*, as well as
an *Historian*, in the *History* which I have now given of him. I have not
written of Sir *William Phips*, as they say *Xenophon* did of *Cyrus, Non ad
Historiæ Fidem, sed ad Effigiem veri imperii*;[2] what *should* have been, rather
than what really *was*. If the *Envy* of his *few Enemies* be not now *Quiet*, I
35 must freely say it, That for many Weeks before he died, there was not one

---

[1] Edmund Calamy (1600–1666), English Presbyterian divine. For the Earl of Warwick,
who died April 19, 1658, see p. 239, l. 27.*
[2] "Aiming not at truth of history, but at a picture of true empire."*

Man among his *personal Enemies* whom *he* would not readily and chearfully have done all the kind Offices of a *Friend* unto: Wherefore though
the Gentleman in *England* that once published a Vindication of Sir
William Phips against some of his Enemies, chose to put the Name of
40 *Publicans*[3] upon them, they must in *this* be counted worse than the
Publicans of whom our Saviour says, *They Love those that Love them.*

And I will say this further, That when certain Persons had found the
Skull of a *Dead Man*, as a *Greek* Writer of Epigrams has told us, they all
fell a Weeping, but only one of the Company, who Laughed and Flouted,
45 and through an unheard-of Cruelty, threw *Stones* at it, which *Stones*
wonderfully rebounded back upon the Face of him that threw them, and
miserably wounded him: Thus if any shall be so *Unchristian*, yea, so
Inhumane, as libellously to throw Stones at so deserved a Reputation as
this Gentleman has died withal, they shall see a *Just Rebound* of all their
50 Calumnies.

But the Name of Sir *WILLIAM PHIPS* will be heard Honourably
mentioned in the *Trumpets* of *Immortal Fame*, when the Names of many that
Antipathied him will either be Buried in Eternal Oblivion, without any
Sacer Vates[4] to preserve them; or be remembred, but like that of *Judas*
55 in the Gospel, or *Pilate* in the Creed, with Eternal Infamy.

The old *Persians* indeed, according to the Report of *Agathias*,[5] exposed
their *Dead* Friends to be Torn in Pieces by *Wild Beasts*, believing that if
they lay long *unworried*, they had been *unworthy* Persons; but all attempts
of surviving Malice to demonstrate in that way the *worth* of this *Dead*
60 Gentleman, give me leave to *Rate off* with Indignation.

And I must with a like Freedom say, That great was the Fault of *New-
England* no more to value a Person, whose *Opportunities* to serve all their
Interests, though very Eminent, yet were not so Eminent as his *Inclinations*. If this whole Continent carry in its very Name of *AMERICA*, an
65 unaccountable *Ingratitude* unto that Brave Man who first led any numbers
of *Europeans* thither, it must not be wondred at, if now and then a particular Country in that Continent afford some Instances of *Ingratitude*:
But I must believe, that the Ingratitude of many, both to God and Man,
for such *Benefits* as that Country of *New-England* enjoy'd from a Governour
70 of their own, by whom they enjoyed *great quietness, with very worthy Deeds
done unto that Nation by his Providence*, was that which hastned the Removal
of such a *Benefactor* from them.

41 *them.*/*him.* C.M.

[3] This was *The Humble Address of the Publicans of New-England* quoted above by Mather in
section 7.
[4] "Sacred bard."*
[5] Agathias Myrinensis (A.D. *c.*536–582), Greek poet and historian, wrote of the struggles
of the Byzantine army against the Goths, Vandals, Franks, and Persians.*

However, as the *Cyprians* buried their Friends in *Honey*, to whom they gave *Gall* when they were Born; thus whatever *Gall* might be given to this 75 Gentleman while he lived, I hope none will be so base, as to put any thing but *Honey* into their Language of him now after his Decease. And indeed, since 'tis a frequent thing among Men to wish for the Presence of our *Friends*, when they are *dead* and *gone*, whom, while they were present with us, we undervalued; there is no way for us to fetch back our Sir 80 *William Phips*, and make him yet Living with us, but by setting up a *Statue* for him, as 'tis done in these Pages, that may out-last an ordinary *Monument*.

Such was the Original Design of erecting *Statues*, and if in *Venice* there were at once no less than an Hundred and Sixty-two Marble, and Twenty- 85 three Brazen *Statues*, erected by the Order, and at the Expence of the Publick, in Honour of so many Valiant Soldiers, who had merited well of that Commonwealth; I am sure *New-England* has had those, whose Merits call for as good an acknowledgment; and, whatever they did *before*, it will be well, if *after* Sir *William Phips*, they find many as meritori- 90 ous as he to be so acknowledged.

Now I cannot my self provide a better *Statue* for this Memorable Person, than the *Words* uttered on the occasion of his Death in a very great Assembly, by a Person of so Diffus'd and Embalm'd a Reputation in the Church of God, that such a Character from *him* were enough to 95 Immortalize the Reputation of the Person upon whom he should bestow it.

The *Grecians* employ'd still the most Honourable and Considerable Persons they had among them, to make a *Funeral Oration* in Commenda- 99 tion of Soldiers that had lost their Lives in the Service of the Publick: And when Sir *William Phips*, the Captain General of *New-England*, who had often ventured his Life to serve the Publick, did expire, that Reverend Person,[6] who was the President of the only University then in the *English America*, Preached a Sermon on that Passage of the Sacred Writ, Isa. 57. 1. 5 *Merciful Men are taken away, none considering that the Righteous are taken away from the Evil to come*; and in it gave Sir *William Phips* the following Testimony.

'This *Province* is Beheaded, and lyes a Bleeding. A GOVERNOUR is 'taken away, who was a *Merciful Man*; some think *too Merciful*: And if 10 'so, 'tis best Erring on *that* Hand; and a *Righteous Man*; who, when he 'had great Opportunities of gaining by *Injustice*, did refuse to do so.

'He was a known Friend unto the best Interests, and unto the *Churches* 'of God: Not *ashamed* of owning them: No, how often have I heard him 'expressing his Desires to be an Instrument of *Good* unto them! He was a

[6] Increase Mather.*

15 'Zealous *Lover* of his *Country*, if any Man in the World were so: He exposed
'*himself* to serve it; he ventured his *Life* to save it: In *that*, a true *Nehemiah*,
'a Governour that *sought the welfare of his People*.

'He was one who did not *seek* to have the Government cast upon him:
'No, but instead thereof to my Knowledge he did several times Petition
20 'the King, that this People might always enjoy the *great Priviledge of*
'*chusing their own Governour*; and I have heard him express his Desires,
'that it might be so, to several of the Chief Ministers of State in the Court
'of *England*.

'He is now Dead, and not capable of being *Flattered*: But this I must
25 'testifie concerning him, That though by the Providence of God I have
'been with him at Home and Abroad, near at Home, and afar off, by
'Land and by Sea, *I never saw him do any evil Action, or heard him speak any*
'*thing unbecoming a Christian*.

'The Circumstances of his Death seem to intimate the *Anger* of God,
30 'in that he was *in the Midst of his Days* removed; and I know (though *Few*
'did) that he had *great Purposes* in his Heart, which probably would have
'taken Effect, if he had lived a few Months longer, to the great Advantage
'of this Province; but now he is gone, there is not a Man Living in the
'World capacitated for those Undertakings; *New-England* knows not yet
35 'what they have lost!

The Recitation of a Testimony so *great*, whether for the *Author*, or the
Matter of it, has now made a *Statue* for the Governour of *New-England*,
which

Nec poterit Ferrum, nec edax abolere vetustas.[7]

40 And there now remains nothing more for *me* to do about it, but only
to recite herewithal a well-known Story related by *Suidas*, That an *Envious*
Man, once going to pull down a *Statue* which had been raised unto the
Memory of one whom he maligned, he only got this by it, that the *Statue*
falling down, knock'd out his Brains.

45 But *Poetry* as well as *History* must pay it's Dues unto him. If *Cicero*'s
Poem, intituled, *Quadrigæ*,[8] wherein he did with a *Poetical Chariot* extol
the Exploits of *Cæsar* in *Britain* to the very Skies, were now Extant in the
World, I would have Borrowed some *Flights* of *That* at least, for the
Subject now to be Adorned.

50 But instead thereof, let the Reader accept the ensuing *Elegy*.

---

[7] "Neither sword nor greedy time will be able to destroy."*
[8] A four-horse chariot.

UPON THE

DEATH

OF

Sir 𝔚illiam 𝔓hips, Knt.[1]

55 Late Captain General and Governour in Chief of the Province of the *Massachuset-Bay* in *New-England*, who Expired in *London, Feb.* 18 169⅘.

> *And to* Mortality *a Sacrifice*
> *Falls* He, *whose Deeds must* Him Immortalize!

60 R *Ejoice* Messieurs; Netops[2] *rejoice*; *'tis true,*
  Ye Philistines, *none will rejoice but* You:
  Loving of All *He Dy'd*; *who Love* him *not*
  Now, have the Grace of Publicans *forgot.*
  Our Almanacks *foretold a great* Eclipse,
65 *This they foresaw not, of our greater* PHIPS.
  PHIPS *our great* Friend, *our Wonder, and our Glory,*
  The Terror of our Foes, *the World's rare Story.*
  England *will Boast him too, whose Noble Mind*
  Impell'd by Angels, *did those* Treasures *find,*
70 *Long in the Bottom of the* Ocean *laid,*
  Which her Three Hundred Thousand *Richer made,*
  By Silver *yet ne'er Canker'd, nor defil'd*
  By Honour, *nor Betray'd when* Fortune *smil'd.*
  Since this bright Phœbus *visited our Shoar,*
75 *We saw no* Fogs *but what were rais'd before:*
  Those vanish'd too; harrass'd by Bloody Wars
  Our Land saw Peace, *by his most generous Cares.*
  The Wolvish pagans *at his dreaded Name,*
  Tam'd, shrunk before him, and his Dogs became!

---

[1] Mather, seeking a poem for Phips as worthy as Cicero's lost *Quadrigæ* was for Caesar, chose a broadside printed in Boston in 1695, "Lamentations Upon the Death of Sir William Phips," omitting the first lines and four others. The authorship was often attributed to Mather, but in 1944 Professor Harold S. Jantz showed it to be the work of one "Hincsman" or "Henchman."*

[2] The French and Indians. "Netop" was an Indian word meaning "friend," "companion," and was frequently used as a greeting. It was also sometimes used as a synonym for "Indian," as here.*

80 *Fell* Moxus *and fierce* Dockawando[3] *fall,*
Charm'd at the Feet of our Brave General.
   Fly-blow the Dead, *Pale* Envy, *let him not*
(What Hero *ever did?) escape a Blot.*
All is Distort *with an* Inchanted *Eye,*
85 *And* Heighth *will make what's* Right *still stand* awry.
He was, *Oh that* He *was! His* Faults *we'll tell,*
Such Faults *as these we* knew, *and* lik'd *them well.*

   Just to an Injury; denying none
Their Dues; but Self-denying *oft his own.*

90   *Good to a Miracle; resolv'd to do*
Good *unto All, whether they would or no.*
To make Us *Good, Great, Wise, and all Things else,*
He wanted but the Gift of Miracles.
On him, vain Mob, *thy Mischiefs cease to throw;*
95 Bad, *but alone in* This, *the* Times *were so.*

   Stout to a Prodigy; living in Pain
To send back Quebeck-Bullets *once again.*
Thunder, his Musick, sweeter than the Spheres,
99 *Chim'd Roaring* Canons *in his Martial Ears.*
Frigats *of armed Men could not withstand,*
'Twas try'd, the Force of his one Swordless Hand:
Hand, *which in one, all of* Briareus[4] *had,*
And Hercules's *twelve* Toils[5] *but* Pleasures *made.*

5   *Too* Humble; *in brave* Stature *not so* Tall,
As low in Carriage, *stooping unto all.*
Rais'd in Estate, in Figure and Renown,
Not Pride; *Higher, and yet not* Prouder *grown.*
Of Pardons *full; ne'er to* Revenge *at all,*
10 *Was that which* He *would* Satisfaction *call.*

   True to his Mate; from whom though often flown.
A Stranger yet to every Love but one.
Write Him *not* Childless, *whose whole People were*
Sons, Orphans *now, of His Paternal Care.*

13   Childless/Childness

   [3] Moxus and Dockawando (or Madockawando) were Indian chiefs.
   [4] In Greek mythology, one of three hundred-armed, fifty-headed giants, born of Earth and Heaven. Many myths were associated with them, especially that of their mighty deeds in support of Zeus in the war of the Titans against Olympus.*
   [5] Labors performed by Hercules during the twelve years he served Eurystheus of Tyrens to atone for murders committed during a fit of madness.

15   *Now lest* ungrateful Brands *we should incur,*
Your Salary we'll pay in Tears, *GREAT SIR!*

To England *often blown, and by his Prince*
Often sent laden with Preferments *thence.*
Preferr'd each Time He went, when all was done
20   *That* Earth *could do, Heaven fetch'd Him to a Crown.*

    'Tis He: *With* Him *Interr'd how great designs!*
Stand Fearless now, ye Eastern Firrs *and* Pines.
With Naval Stores *not to enrich the Nation,*
Stand, for the Universal Conflagration.
25   Mines, *opening unto none but Him, now stay*
Close under Lock and Key, till the Last Day:
In this, like to the Grand Aurifick Stone,[6]
By any but Great Souls *not to be known.*
And Thou Rich Table, with Bodilla[7] *lost,*
30   *In the Fair* Galeon, *on our* Spanish *Coast.*
In weight Three Thousand and Three Hundred Pound,
But of pure Massy Gold, lye Thou, *not found,*
Safe, since He's *laid under the* Earth *asleep,*
Who learnt where Thou dost under Water *keep.*

35   *But Thou Chief Loser, Poor* NEW-ENGLAND, *speak*
Thy Dues to such as did thy Welfare seek,
The Governour that vow'd to Rise and Fall
With Thee, Thy *Fate shows in* His *Funeral.*
Write now His *Epitaph, 'twill be* Thine own,
40   *Let it be this,* A PUBLICK SPIRIT's GONE.
Or, but Name PHIPS; *more needs not be exprest;*
Both Englands, *and next* Ages, *tell the Rest.*

The End of the Second BOOK.

[6] For "Aurifick Stone," see p. 282, l. 93.
[7] For "Bodilla," see p. 352, l. 77.

END NOTES

ABBREVIATIONS

AAS	American Antiquarian Society.
AAS *Proc.*	American Antiquarian Society *Proceedings*.
DAB	Dictionary of American Biography.
DAE	Dictionary of American English.
DNB	Dictionary of National Biography.
MHS	Massachusetts Historical Society.
MHS *Pub.*	Massachusetts Historical Society *Publications*.
MHS *Coll.*	Massachusetts Historical Society *Collections*.
MHS *Trans.*	Massachusetts Historical Society *Transactions*.
Mass. Records	Records of Governor and Company of the Massachusetts Bay.
Plym. Records	Records of the Colony of New Plymouth in New England.
Conn. Records	Public Records of the Colony of Connecticut.
Migne G	*Patrologiae Cursus Completus*: Series Graeca.
Migne L	*Patrologiae Cursus Completus*: Series Latine.
NED	*New English Dictionary*.
NEQ	*New England Quarterly*.
K.J.V.	King James Version.
A.V.	Authorized Version.

63:2   On Higginson see also *Magnalia*, Bk. III, pt. 2, chap. 1 (76a:13–76b:22); DAB; Sidney Perley, *The History of Salem, Massachusetts* (3 vols., Salem, S. Perley, 1924–1928), 2:287–289; and F. L. Weis, *The Colonial Clergy and the Colonial Churches of New England* (Lancaster, Mass., 1936).

63:8   For "Great and wonderful works," cf. Judg. 2.7, Pss. 40.5, 78.4, 92.5, 107.8, Matt. 7.22, Rev. 15.3.

The idea that the world was nearing its end and that nature was decaying was widespread in the seventeenth century. The "motivation" for this was "almost wholly Christian, and the ultimate dissolution of the world" was expected to result from its "corruption" and "Man's wickedness" (Victor Harris, *All Coherence Gone*, Chicago, University of Chicago Press, 1949, pp. 196, 229–231). Mather in the *Magnalia* emphasizes the idea that the sins and backslidings of New England presage doom. "In this Last Age" is not a biblical expression, but cf. "last days," II Tim. 3.1, Heb. 1.2, etc.; "the last time," I Pet. 1.5, I John 2.18; "these last times," I Pet. 1.20. For "Stirred up the Spirits," see II Chron. 36.22–23, Ezra 1.1, Hag. 1.14; for "*Pleasant Land*," Gen. 49.15, Ps. 106.24, and Dan. 8.9; for "Land of . . . *Nativity*," Gen. 11.28, Ruth 2.11, Jer. 46.16.

63:13–64:23   For "*Pure . . . Religion*," see James 1.27; for "*Daily Bread*," Matt. 6.11, Luke 11.3, and cf. Jer. 37.21; for "*seeking first . . . the Righteousness thereof*," Matt. 6.33; for "*Blessing*," Deut. 11.22–27; for "true and living God . . . served," cf. Jer. 10.10, I Thess. 1.9; for "*Ends of the Earth*," Deut. 33.17, Job 28.24, Pss. 65.5, 72.8, Isa. 40.28.

64:26–33   See Eccles. 1.4: "One generation passeth . . . another cometh." The familiar phrase, "declining years," used for "old age," may derive from the Biblical image of man as a shadow that declines; see Pss. 102.11, 109.23. For "*served the Will of God*," cf. also Judg. 2.7–10; for "*Foundation of many Generations*," Ps. 102.25–28; for "*Example*," John 13.15, I Tim. 4.12. For "*Faith* and *Order*," cf. I Cor. 16.10, 13; for "Light . . . *Words* of God," Josh. 3.9, Pss. 119, 105, 130, Rev. 17.17; for "*gathered unto their Fathers*," Judg. 2.10.

64:42–43   For "Increased and Blessed," see Isa. 51.2; for "*Day of small things*," Zech. 4.10. For "Ebenezer," see *Magnalia*, Bk. I, Appendix, p. 181, ll. 73–96.

64:46–48   The quotation alters slightly the Biblical text. Similar alterations occur often (see above, introductory essay "The Magnalia").

65:49–50   For the pillar of cloud and fire, see also Exod. 13.21–22, 16.10, Num. 14.14. For the typological interpretation of the pillar, see Samuel Mather, *The Figures or Types of the Old Testament* (London, 1705; first published in 1683, probably in Dublin), pp. 133–136. See also *Typology and Early American Literature* (Amherst, Mass., University of Massachusetts Press, 1972), particularly "Cotton Mather's Magnalia and the Metaphor of History" by Mason I. Lowance, Jr., pp. 139–160.

65:52–60   For "*Fatherly Chastisements*," see also Heb. 12.6–7, Rev. 3.19. For "*Formalities*" and "*Life* and *Power* of Godliness," cf. also II Tim. 3.5: "having a form of godliness, but denying the power thereof: from such turn away," and II Pet. 1.3. For "*Provoking Evils*," see Deut. 31.16–18, I Kings 16.7, 13; for "witness against us," Deut. 31.19, I Sam. 12.5, Mic. 1.2; for "*Judgments*," Ezek. 14.21, 25.11, Matt. 23.14.

65:60–61   "Warning-piece" was in the seventeenth century often used metaphorically in the titles of books. See, for example, "A Warning-piece for all wicked livers," 1683; "A Warning-piece for rash Swearers," 1674; "A Warning-peece to all backsliding Protestants," 1644 (Donald Wing, *Short-Title Catalogue of Books . . . 1641–1700*, 3 vols., New York, Index Society, 1945–1951, 3:453–454). "Murdering-pieces" were used especially on ships to clear the decks when they were boarded by enemies. See NED and *The New World of Words . . . Compiled by Edward Phillips* (7th edition, "By J.K.," London, 1720), under "Murderers."

65:62–64   In 1690 Sir William Phips led an attack on Port Royal in Nova Scotia and conquered the French fort there, but later in the year his expedition against Quebec was defeated. The French recaptured Port Royal in 1691 and in 1696 destroyed Fort William Henry in Pemaquid, in Maine, which the New Englanders had built. Such defeats stimulated fear of the Canadians and their Indian allies and involved Massachusetts in serious financial difficulties. See *Magnalia*, Bk. II, Appendix, "Pietas in Patriam," secs. 10–13, 17, pp. 298–316, 337.

65:63–64   For "*diminished . . . through Affliction, and Sorrow*," see Ps. 107.39.

65:65–67   For "*Light side*," see above, endnote to lines 49–50. For "*Glory of God*," cf. Exod. 40.34–35; for Glory "departed," cf. Ezek. 10.4, 18–19, 11.22–23; for "*Signs* . . ." cf. such Biblical texts as Num. 14.11, Deut. 6.22, 7.19.

66:79–81   For detailed exposition of covenant theory, see William Ames, *The Marrow of Sacred Divinity* (London, 1643); William Perkins, *Works*, Vol. I (London, 1626); John Preston, *The New Covenant, Or the Saints Portion* (London, 1629); Peter Bulkeley, *The Gospel-Covenant* (2nd ed., London, 1651); Thomas Hooker, *A Survey of the Summe of Church-Discipline* (London, 1648). See also Perry Miller, *The New England Mind: The Seventeenth Century* (Cambridge, Mass., Harvard University Press, 1954), chaps. 13 and 15 and Appendix B, "The Federal School of Theology"; and his "The Marrow of Puritan Divinity," in *Errand Into the Wilderness* (Cambridge, Mass., Harvard University Press, 1956), pp. 48–98.

66:84–85   For "*Faithfulness*," see Pss. 89.1, 119.20.

66:95   Higginson combines two verses; 44.1 should be 44.1–2.

66:6   The first English edition of Foxe's book was published in 1563, with the title: "Actes and Monuments of these latter and perillous dayes, touching matters of the Church . . . and . . . the persecutions & horrible troubles . . . wrought . . . by the Romishe Prelates, speciallye in . . . England and Scotlande, from the year a thousand." By 1684 eight other editions had been printed, with various emendations and additions. It is often called "Foxe's Book of Martyrs." For its influence on seventeenth-century English nonconformity, see William Haller, *The Elect Nation* (New York, Harper & Row, 1963), and J. F. Mozley, *John Foxe and his Book* (New York, Macmillan Co., 1940).

67:8   See Samuel Mather, *Figures*, p. 251: The "*Church of Rome* . . . once a true Church, and the Pastor thereof a true Minister, is now, so far declined . . . from the Primitive and Scripture Pattern, *That* [It] *is become the Whore* of Babylon, *and the Head of that Church, is Antichrist.* See *Rev.* 13." In that chapter "*the first Beast* . . . is the Church *of* Rome; the second . . . is the *Pope*" and "Antichrist." Compare also I John 2.18, 22, II John 7.

67:9   For "*successfully*," cf. Josh. 1.8.

67:16–19   For "*Good Hand of God*," see Ezra 7.9, 8.18, Neh. 2.1; for "*Good Success*," Josh. 1.8. For "*Desired*," "*Expected*," see Perry Miller and Thomas H. Johnson, *The Puritans* (New York, American Book Co., 1938), pp. 81–90, and K. B. Murdock, *Literature and Theology in Colonial New England* (Cambridge, Mass., Harvard University Press, 1949), chap. 3.

67:21   For "Raised up the Spirit," see Ezra 1.5, Jer. 51.11.

67:25   Compare John Milton, *The Reason of Church-Government* . . . (London, 1641), reprinted in Don M. Wolfe *et al.*, eds., *Complete Prose Works of John Milton* (New Haven, Yale University Press, 1953), 1:755: "Publick preaching indeed is the gift of the Spirit . . . but discipline is the practick work of preaching directed . . . as is most requisite to particular duty; without which it were all one to the benefit of souls as it would be to the cure of bodies, if all the Physitians should get into the severall Pulpits of the City, and assembling all the diseased . . . should begin" a lecture on a variety of diseases "to which perhaps none there present were inclin'd . . . without so much as feeling one puls." In calling Boston the "Metropolis" of English America, Higginson probably had in mind not only its population but its importance as a publishing center. "Measured by the number (not the quality) of imprints," it was by 1700 second in the British Empire only to London and surpassed even Cambridge and Oxford. See Samuel E. Morison, *The Puritan Pronaos* (New York, New York University Press, 1936), pp. 110–111. For data on the population of cities in the English colonies in America, see E. B. Greene and V. D. Harrington, *American Population before the Federal Census of 1790* (New York, Columbia University Press, 1932), *passim*.

67:26–27 According to *A Platform of Church Discipline . . . Agreed upon by the Elders: and Messengers of the Churches Assembled in the Synod at Cambridge in New England* (Cambridge, 1649), the "Teacher" of a church was "to attend to *Doctrine*, and therein to Administer a Word of *Knowledge*." The Pastor's special work was "*Exhortation*" and the administering "therein . . . a Word of *Wisdom*." In practice pastors and Teachers seem to have shared all ministerial duties. See *A Platform*, chap. 6, sec. 5; *Magnalia*, Bk. V, p. 27b, ll. 4–9, and Williston Walker, *The Creeds and Platforms of Congregationalism* (Douglas Horton, ed., Boston, Pilgrim Press, 1960), p. 211.

67:31 For "*Native Country*," cf. Jer. 22.10 and above, endnote to "Land of . . . *Nativity*," p. 63, l. 8.

67:34–68:38 For "Difficulties, Tears, Temptations," see Acts 20.19; for "*Memorials*," cf. Exod. 17.14, Ps. 135.13, Hos. 12.5, Matt. 26.13. "Form and Frame" have in rhetoric closely similar meanings—"plan, structure, order"—and Higginson probably used both simply for the stylistic effect of their alliteration.

68:40–42 In typology "The Temple was a very great and glorious *Type*; both the Temple and all the Concernments of it were mystical and significant of Gospel-Truths. The general Significations of the Temple were *Christ*, and the *Church*, and every individual *Saint* . . . The chief Builders were Types of Christ, whose Work and Office it is, to build the Temple of the Lord." Since "An Army of Workmen" were employed in building Solomon's temple, "all Hands should help to carry on Church-Work," with "both the Word and Spirit of God to direct them." See Samuel Mather, *Figures*, pp. 399, 342, and I Chron. 28.12, 19.

68:43–46 The epigram was written by Raimund Gaches, like Borel a native of Castres and was prefixed to Borel's *Historiarum, et Observationum Medicophysicarum, Centuriae IV* (Paris, 1656), [p. iii]. Higginson, who probably quoted from a secondary source, has "Cum" instead of the "Cui" of the original text and a comma after "opus" instead of a colon.

68:50 Compare Deut. 29.2, Josh. 23.3 for "Lord hath done for his People."

68:60 For Biblical references see below, line 68.

68:65 Thomas Fuller, *The Holy State and the Profane State* (London, 1642), has this maxim, probably derived from geometry and apparently once widely known, as "Rectum est index sui & obliqui." Fuller glosses it: "The lustre of the good . . . will sufficiently discover the enormity of those which are otherwise" (see M. G. Walten's edition, 2 vols., New York, Columbia University Press, 1938, 2:410). Compare also Owen Felltham, "On Censure," in *Resolves* (10th ed., London, 1677), p. 70: "The *crooked lines* help better to shew the *streight*."

69:77 Prov. 10.7.

69:78–89 Higginson here, and in the following paragraphs, "eighthly," "ninthly," and "lastly," summarizes "the theological meaning which the wilderness held for New Englanders when they looked back on their heroic period" (George H. Williams, *Wilderness and Paradise in Christian Thought*, New York, Harper & Row, 1962, p. 110, and his introductory essay, "The Idea of the Wilderness"). "Wilderness-condition," "A condition of straits, wants, deep distresses, and most deadly dangers." When God's people are in this condition, He "takes them by the hand . . . and leads them . . . to the land of Canaan. Ah! . . . God turns a wilderness into a paradise, a desert into a Canaan" (Thomas Brooks, *The Golden Key to Open Hidden Treasures*, London, 1675, in *Works*, ed. A. B. Grosart, Edinburgh, 1867, 5:473). See also Alan Heimert

"Puritanism, the Wilderness, and the Frontier," *NEQ*, 26:361–382 (September 1953). For "*Humbling . . . Providences*," see Exod. 20.18–20, Deut. 8.2–3, 15–16; for "*Massahs, Meribahs*," Num. 20.13, 24, 27.14, Deut. 6.16, 9.22, 33.8, Ps. 81.7. For "*prove us*," cf. Exod. 20.20, Deut. 33.8, Ps. 81.7; for "*hours of Temptation*," Ps. 95.8, Heb. 3.8; for "*keep his Commandments*," Deut. chap. 8.

69:90–91   For "*Generations . . . willing Mind*," see I Chron. 28.9.

69:97   For "*increased and multiplied*," see Jer. 3.16.

69:3–5   For "Cause them to *Return*," "*Return* again in Mercy," see Deut. 30.2, 3; for "*many Thousands*," Deut. 5.10.

69:6–70:19   A similar assertion of the New Englanders' filial respect for the English church is that of the Reverend William Hubbard: "It is hoped the church of Great Britain will not be unwilling to put in mind of her little sister, which as yet hath no breasts, and to take care what shall be done for her . . . To build upon her a palace of silver . . . is not now asked [Cant. 8.8–9] on her behalf . . . that she may have the continuance of all due means and encouragements for her building up in knowledge and faith, repentance and holiness, is all that is aimed at" (William Hubbard, *The History of New England*, Preface, p. xi). The preface was not printed until 1878, when a recently discovered manuscript of it was printed by the Massachusetts Historical Society for insertion in copies of the 1848 volume. The *History* was finished by 1682, but not published until 1815. Compare "*Church of God in* England" with "The Church of God at Corinth," I Cor. 1.2, II Cor. 1.1.

70:16–18   The Toleration Act of 1689, achieved by the efforts of the nonconformists and some members of the Church of England, recognized "the right of Dissenters to exist," but neither the Presbyterians nor the Congregationalists were strong enough to win complete acceptance of their politics. Since they shared the same basic creed, an attempt was made to unite them. The leaders were John Howe, Matthew Mead, and Increase Mather, who was in England from 1688 until 1692. A friend of both Mead and Howe, he was probably the "strongest influence" at the meeting of ministers from London or nearby, on April 6, 1691, which prepared *The Heads of Agreement*, published in that year in London. It was reprinted in Cotton Mather's *Blessed Unions* (Boston, 1692), and *Magnalia*, Bk. V, pt. 2, pp. 59–61. In England the plan for union failed and in New England its influence was short lived. See Holmes, *Cotton Mather*, 1:79–82; K. B. Murdock, *Increase Mather* (Cambridge, Mass., Harvard University Press, 1925), pp. 281–282; and Walker, *Creeds and Platforms*, chap. 14. For the "Fifth Commandment," see Exod. 20.12.

70:31–32   "Fathers did . . . acknowledge . . . *Imperfections* in our Way": John Robinson, the Pilgrims' English minister in Leiden from 1609 until 1620, "was very confident the Lord had more truth and light yet to breake forth out of his holy Word." See the "Brief Narrative" annexed to Edward Winslow, *Hypocrisie Unmasked* (London, 1646; reprinted, Providence, R.I., Club for Colonial Reprints, 1916), p. 97.

70:40–71:45   For "*thy great Name*," see Isa. 63.14; for "*Simplicity and Godly Sincerity*," II Cor. 1.12. For "People in their Generation," cf. Acts 13.36. For "Deliver their own Souls," see, for example, Job 33.28, Pss. 33.19, 120.2. For "*with him*," cf. also Rev. 22.12; for "Endeavours," II Cor. 13.4.

71:48–50   "Among the Holy Places, *Jerusalem* was very eminent, as . . . the Place of the Temple and Ark, and all the . . . Worship thereunto belonging, *Ps.* 76.2. *In* Salem [Jerusalem] *is his Tabernacle, and his Dwelling-place in* Sion. *Ps.* 87.2. *The Lord loveth the Gates of* Sion, *more than all the Dwellings of* Jacob. *Jerusalem* therefore is . . . a Type of the Church both Militant and Triumphant, Gal. 4.26" (Samuel Mather, *Figures*, p. 328). For Jerusalem as a type of the true Church of God, see also Joannes Cassianus, *Conlationes*, no. 14, sec. 8, in *Corpus Scriptorum Ecclesiasticorum* (ed. Michael Petschenig, Vienna, 1886), 13:408–409.

71:67   At the Synod of 1662 Richard and Increase Mather took opposite sides. Richard was strongly in favor of the Half-Way Covenant. Increase opposed it lest the churches weaken themselves by admitting to membership persons not genuinely possessed by devotion to God. The advocates of the Covenant argued that, unless it was agreed to, many young people would grow up without the instruction and inspiration the churches offered. Increase later changed his mind and in 1675 defended the Covenant in his *Discourse Concerning . . . Baptism* and his *First Principles of New-England*, both published in Cambridge in 1675. On the whole controversy and the result of the Half-Way Covenant, see *Magnalia*, Bk. V, pt. 3; Cotton Mather, *Parentator* (Boston, 1724), Article 12; Murdock, *Increase Mather*, pp. 80–85, 138; Walker, *Creeds and Platforms*, chap. 11; and Perry Miller, "The Half-Way Covenant," *NEQ*, 6:676–715 (1933).

72:75–98 For the Mather family in general, see H. E. Mather, *Lineage of Rev. Richard Mather* (Hartford, 1890); the "Pedigree" in the 1853–1855 edition of *Magnalia*, 1:xlii–xliii; John H. Sibley, *Biographical Sketches of Harvard University* (Vols. I–III, Cambridge, Mass., 1873–1875; Vol. 4, ed. Clifford K. Shipton, Cambridge, Mass., Harvard University Press, 1933); and Weis, *The Colonial Clergy*. For the writings of the Mathers, see T. J. Holmes, *Cotton Mather, Increase Mather* (2 vols., Cambridge, Mass., Harvard University Press, 1931), and *The Minor Mathers, A List of their Works* (Cambridge, Mass., Harvard University Press, 1940). For Richard Mather, see *Magnalia*, Bk. III, pt. 2, chap. 20; Increase Mather, *The Life and Death of Mr. Richard Mather* (Cambridge, Mass., 1670; reprinted in *Collections of the Dorchester Antiquarian and Historical Society*, No. 3 [Boston, 1850], pp. 37–94); DAB, DNB. For Samuel, see *Magnalia*, Bk. IV, pt. 2, chap. 2; DNB; DAB; and A.G. Matthews, *Calamy Revised* (Oxford, Clarendon Press, 1934), p. 343. For Nathanael, see DNB, Sibley, 1:157–161, and Holmes, *Minor Mathers*, pp. 37–50. For Increase Mather, see DNB, DAB; Cotton Mather, *Parentator*; Murdock, *Increase Mather*, and introductory essay, "Cotton Mather." For Eleazar, *Magnalia*, Bk. III, pt. 2, chap. 20, sec. 19–20. For Cotton Mather, see introductory essay "Cotton Mather," and bibliographical notes thereto, pp. 23–25. For Nathanael Mather, see Cotton Mather, *Early Religion Urged* (Boston, 1694); *Magnalia*, Bk. IV, pt. 2, chap. 10, and his "A Token for the Children of New-England" (Boston, 1700) in *Magnalia*, Bk. VI, Appendix, Example 3; Sibley, 3:321–323; and Holmes, *Minor Mathers*, pp. 33–35. The epitaph Higginson quotes was probably written by him. It was inscribed on Nathanael's gravestone. Some time after 1700 it was replaced by another stone with the epitaph: "An Aged person that had seen but Nineteen Winters in the World," possibly written by Cotton Mather himself. This still stands in the Charter Street burying ground in Salem (Perley, *History of Salem*, 3:232). For Samuel Mather, see T. J. Holmes, "Samuel Mather of Witney," in *Col. Soc. Mass. Pub.*, 26:312–322.

72:99–73:6 For Samuel Mather of Windsor, see Holmes, *Cotton Mather*, 2:834. For the "Great Divisions" in Windsor, see H. R. Stiles, *History of Windsor* (Hartford, Conn., 1891), pp. 190–219. For Warham Mather, see Sibley, *Biographical Sketches*, 3:319–320. For John Warham, see *Magnalia*, Bk. III, pt. 2, chap. 18.

73:9–16 "O Nimium Dilecte Deo." This phrase appears in Increase Mather's *A Historical Discourse Concerning the Prevalency of Prayer* (Boston, 1677; see reprint in S. G. Drake, *Early History of New England*, Boston, 1864, p. 250). It is from Claudian, "Panegyricus de Tertio Consolatu Honorii Augusti," line 96. The line beginning "Et Nati Natorum" is from Virgil, *Aeneid* III.98. "Patrum tu sequeris . . ." stems from Statius, *Thebaid* xii.857: "sed longe sequere et vestigia semper adora." Cotton Mather, in *Magnalia*, Bk. IV, pt. 2, chap. 4, p. 165, ll. 30–31, makes use of the same quotation, with "adorans" instead of "adora," and Higginson probably followed him.

73:25 In strict Calvinist circles of 1630, speculation about the end of the world, especially about whether Christ's second coming was to precede or follow the millennium, had been highly suspect, as tending to revolutionary action. By the end of the century, both Increase and Cotton Mather were subscribing to what Cotton called "Sober Chiliasm," namely, the opinion that Christ will physically appear, the earth will be refined by fire, and paradise will reign on earth for a thousand years (cf. II Pet. 3.7–10). To both of them, the declension for which they castigated the churches seemed evidence that the millennium was about to begin. In *A Midnight Cry* (Boston, 1692, p. 24), Cotton conjectured that "THE TIME OF THE END, seems just going to lay its Arrest upon us: and we are doubtless very near the Last Hours of that Wicked One, whom our Lord *Shall Destroy* with the Brightness of his Coming." The extraordinary explosion of witchcraft in Salem seemed to him evidence, as he declared in *The Wonders of the Invisible World* (Boston, 1693, p. 15), of "an unusual Range of the Devil among us, a little before the *Second Coming* of our Lord," and that "The Devils *Whole-time*, cannot but be very near its *End*" (p. 35). By 1710, both he and his father were ready to affirm their hope in the imminent triumph of good over evil. In that year were published Increase Mather's *A Discourse concerning Faith and Fervency in Prayer, and the Glorious Kingdom of the Lord Jesus Christ, on Earth, now Approaching*, and Cotton's *Bonifacius* (ed. David Levin, Cambridge, Mass.: Harvard University Press, 1966, p. 15), in which expectation centered on the year 1716: "M.DCC.XVI. is a-coming." In that same year, Cotton expressed the ultimate occasion for rejoicing: "There are many Arguments to perswade us that our Glorious LORD will have an Holy City in AMERICA" (*Theopolis Americana*, Boston, 1710, p. 43). The chiliasm of the Mathers receives extended treatment by Robert Middlekauff in *The Mathers: Three Generations of Puritan Intellectuals, 1596–1728* (New York, Oxford University Press, 1971); see especially pp. 179–187, 322–327.

73:17–26 For "*Covenant and Mercy to a thousand*, etc.," see Deut. 5.10, 7.9, I Kings 8.23, Neh. 9.32; for "Blessing of *Abraham*," Gen. 22. 17, 28.4. For "Mercy and Truth unto *Jacob*," cf. Pss. 25.10, 57.3, 61.7, 85.10, 86.15, 98.3, etc.; for "Mercies of *David*," see Isa. 55.3; for "*Grace* of our Lord," cf. Rom. 1.7, I Cor. 1.3, etc.; for "*Dominion, for Ever and Ever*," I Pet. 5.11, Rev. 1.6.

PREFATORY POEMS

74:1 Noyes was an "Excellent Friend" of Cotton Mather and contributed to the *Magnalia*, in addition to the verses which follow, a biographical sketch which Mather found "Elegant and Expressive"; see *Magnalia*, Bk. III, pt. 2, Appendix to chap. 25. See also H. S. Jantz, *The First Century of New England Verse* (Worcester, Mass., The Society, 1944), pp. 89–94, 240–242; Weis, *Colonial Clergy*; Sibley, 2:239–246; and Perley, *History*, 3:127.

74:12 See Sir John Davies, *Nosce Teipsum* (London, 1599, reprinted in Edward Arber, ed., *An English Garland*, London, 1895–1897, 5:170): "But as this world's sun . . . Makes the Moor black! and th'European, white! Th'American tawney! and th'East Indian red!" For the sons of Noah, see Gen. 5.32, 6.10, 7.13, 9.18–19, 10.1

74:21 Cotton Mather, in his *Bonifacius* (p. 4), defines a "Publick Spirit" as a "true man of honor," a "*benefactor* to mankind," who strips "himself of *emoluments* and *advantages*," and "never counts himself so well *advanced* as in *stooping* to do *good*." In his *Fair Weather* (Boston, 1692), p. 6, he wrote: "A *private Spirit* has prevailed, and the *Times* have been made *perillous*, by mens concernment for none but their own Cabin, while the whole Vessel has been in a Storm."

75:29 M. P. Tilley, in his *Dictionary of the Proverbs in England in the Sixteenth and Seventeenth Centuries* (Ann Arbor, Michigan University Press, 1950), p. 337, cites John Northbrook's *A Treatise against Dicing, Dancing, Plays and Interludes*, in which ignorance is "called the mother (not of devotion as the papistes tearme it) but of all mischiefe and vice"; and see Dr. Thomas Fuller's *Gnomologia: Adagies and Proverbs* (London, 1732): "Ignorance is the Mother of Romish Devotion." See also Robert

Burton, *The Anatomy of Melancholy*, pt. III, sec. 4, memb. 1, subsec. 2: "'Ignorance is the mother of devotion,' as all the world knows."

75:32   The Coverdale version was used in the Anglican *Book of Common Prayer* of 1662, a book not popular among New England Congregationalists. Noyes, however, probably found Coverdale's translation in the "Great Bible" of 1539 or in some one of the other Bibles prior to the King James Version. See F. L. Cross, *The Oxford Dictionary of the Christian Church* (London and New York, Oxford University Press, 1957), pp. 168–169, 317. Of course, the idea that man is or can be a beast or worm is common. Compare, for example, Job 25.6; Aristotle, *Politics* I.i.10–12; and Joseph Hall, *The Second Century of Meditations and Vows*, in *Works* (ed. Philip Wynter, Oxford, 1863), 7:485: "Mankind hath within itself its goats . . . wolves, dogs, swine . . . and whatever sorts of beasts: there are but a few men amongst men."

75:33   The pejorative use of "tradition" was common among Protestants opposed to Roman Catholic doctrines handed down through the centuries, and especially among the extreme reformers or Puritans who distrusted the honored traditions of both Rome and Canterbury. Harry Levin, in his brilliant "The Tradition of Tradition" (*Contexts of Criticism*, Cambridge, Mass., Harvard University Press, 1957, p. 58), says that for Milton "tradition is at best a 'broken reed': traditions are equated with 'superstitions' in *Paradise Lost* and with 'idolisms' in *Paradise Regained*."

75:36   According to Monsignor Knox, some "enthusiasts" held that "The Bible is not the Word of God, but a signification thereof . . . the Bible is but ink and paper, but the word of God is spirit and life," and believed there was no reason to read the Bible or to listen to sermons since the Scripture was a dead letter; they had "Father, Son and Spirit" within themselves (R. A. Knox, *Enthusiasm*, Oxford, Clarendon Press, 1950, pp. 172–173).

76:62   For "Heads of our Tribes," cf. also Deut. 5.23, I Sam. 15.17, I Kings 8.1, II Chron. 5.2.

76:69   Ross may, although his name is not given, have been the author of the *Apocalypsis*. Its "Epistle Dedicatory" to Edward Benlowes (1603?–1676) was signed "Jo. Davies," probably Sir John Davies (see above endnote on 74:12), and states that the book was written in Latin and translated by him, since its author feared it would be dangerous to have it printed in English over his own name.

76:71   "First Fruits alludes not only to the text from Exodus but also to *New Englands First Fruits* (London, 1643), which describes "the progresse of *Learning*, in the *Colledge* at CAMBRIDGE, in *Massacusets* Bay." Several times reprinted, it is reproduced in Samuel E. Morison, *The Founding of Harvard College* (Cambridge, Mass., Harvard University Press, 1935), Appendix D, pp. 419–447.

76:73   For "Lost its Savour," see Matt. 5.13 and Luke 14.34.

77:85   See also Pss. 36.9, 68.26, 114.7–8, Prov. 13.14, Jer. 2.13, 17.13, Rev. 7.17, 14.7; and Williams, *Wilderness and Paradise, passim*.

78:11   Noyes may have had in mind Wentworth Dillon, the Earl of Roscommon's *Essay on Translated Verse* (London, 1684): "Degrading prose explains his meaning ill, And shows the stuff, but not the workman's skill" (reprinted in Alexander Chalmers, *Works of the English Poets*, London, 1810, 8:26, ll. 43–44).

78:2   See K. B. Murdock, *The Portraits of Increase Mather* (Cleveland, W. G. Mather, 1924), p. 59; and *Congregational Quarterly*, 3:317, note 1.

78:6   The implications of the word *doctor* here and below extend beyond the simple definition of *teacher* or the designation of a formal academic degree. The "doctor" of a university could be considered·the successor of the prophets and apostles. The "Sons of the Prophets were the Scholars that dwelt and studied and worship'd in the Colleges of Israel"; the task of the prophet, apostle, or doctor was "the declaration of the divine will among men." See Williams, *Wilderness and Paradise*, pp. 191–195, and introductory essay, "The Idea of the Wilderness."

79:5   For Benjamin Tompson, see Howard J. Hall, ed., *Benjamin Tompson . . . His*

Poems (Boston, Houghton Mifflin, 1924); Jantz, *The First Century*, pp. 71–75, 157–167, 264–269; K. B. Murdock, *Handkerchiefs from Paul* (Cambridge, Mass., Harvard University Press, 1927), pp. xxx–xxxi, 3, 9–11, 20; Sibley, 2:103–111; Moses C. Tyler, *A History of American Literature, 1607–1765* (Ithaca, N.Y., Cornell University Press, 1949), pp. 274–276; DAB.

80:12–15 For "Familiar spirits," see Lev. 19.31, 20.6, 27, I Sam. 28.3, 7–9; for "Unseals . . . Tombs," cf. John 11.33–34.

80:21–22 For "Gems," see Exod. 25.7, 28.9–14; for "Heaven's open," cf. John 1.51.

80:23 "Acts were penned" suggests the Biblical book, "The Acts of the Apostles"— an appropriate allusion since the New England religious leaders of the past were in the eyes of their successors not only "saints" but in a sense "apostles," men who planted Christianity in a new region.

80:24 Although his name is here spelled *Thompson*, the accepted form is *Tompson*. According to Sibley (2:103), it was "so written by himself."

81:17 The "hand of God" was a common Biblical image. See, for example, Isa. 50.2, 59.1.

81:22–24 "Return" may allude to the adding of fifteen years to Hezekiah's life; see II Kings 20.1–11. For "Root . . . Fruit . . . Branches," cf. John 15.1ff.

81:33–34 Possibly suggested by I John 2.15–17.

81:36 Compare Rev. 9.20–21, 16.9, 11.

81:41 For Woodbridge see Weis, p. 236; Sibley, 2:465–470.

82:14 Compare Edward Taylor, "Prefatory Meditations," Series 2, in Donald E. Stanford, ed., *The Poems of Edward Taylor* (New Haven, Yale University Press, 1960), p. 283; "Hence make me, Lord, thy Golden Trumpet Choice And trumpet thou thyselfe upon the same"; and Cotton Mather, *Fair Weather*, p. 23: "Our honourable rulers will doubtless lend their Helping Hand, for the Redressing of every Evil, that hurts *Humane Society*, whereof . . . *They* are the Officers." "*We may Lift up our Voice like a Trumpet*, but the Strong holds of Sin are Stronger than those of Jericho: there must be *Swords* as well as *Trumpets*." For both "trumpets" and "swords," see Josh. chap. 6; see also I Cor. 15.51–52. For "Tombs Crack . . . Saints Rise," see Matt. 27.51–53. For "shine," cf. Dan. 12.3.

82:19 For Danforth, see Jantz, pp. 199–202, 106–110; Weis; Sibley, 2:507–514.

83:13 In his *Diary* (MHS *Coll.*, 1:259), Cotton Mather writes, "I distinguish the Friends of the *Reformation*, by the Name of *Eileutherians* (while I call its Foes, Idumeans)." He gives his reasons in *Eleutheria: Or, An Idea of the Reformation* (London, 1698), pp. 59, 63: the Eleutherians desire "That conscientious *Dissenters* from *established Rites*, may not be compelled, and harassed, and ruined with *Civil Penalties*." He continues: "If the Story of our King *Lucius*, the *first Christian King* they say in the World, were certain, we would respect the name the more, for that famous old *Eleutherius*, who thought that the *Faith of Christ, and the Old and New Testament* . . . was Law enough to govern the Church of *England*." The Idumeans are those "whose Grief it has been that ever the Reformation proceeded so far," and who "would monopolize unto themselves the name of *the Church of England*."

The story referred to by Mather was definitely not certain. The tradition that a British king named Lucius wrote concerning his desire to become a Christian to Eleutherius, pope from about 175 to 189, rested on the authority of Bede's *Historia Ecclesiastica Gentis Anglorum* (Bk. I, chap. IV). In his preface, Bede related that a "devout priest of the church of London" named Nothelm, "going after unto Rome was permitted by Gregory . . . to search the closets of the said holy Church of Rome, where he found out certain epistles . . . and at his return hath delivered unto us the said epistles to be put into our History" (see Loeb edition of Bede's *Historical Works*, 2 vols., ed. J. E. King, 1:5–7). Presumably Nothelm came upon a letter from Lucius, king of Edessa in Mesopotamia, whose headquarters were at Birtha (Britium), and, as J. E. King suggests (1:29n), confused *Britium* with *Brittania*. Mather would seem to have confused Lucius with the pope and thus provided his king with an etymology of freedom and love of liberty. In *Eleutheria* (p. 60), the first person praised by Mather for writing against "Persecution for Conscience sake" was "Doctor *Jewell*," and again in the General Introduction (108:90), a passage on the Eleutherians is shortly followed by a reference to the "great JUELS (109:10).

83:18   See *Magnalia*, Bk. VI, chap. 6, 61b:23–25; Weis, p. 171; and Sibley, 3:159–168.

84:9   For "*Garamantas et Indos*," see Virgil, *Aeneid* VI.794.

84:16   Grotius's *De Origine Gentium Americanarum*, a brief work of fifteen pages, was first published in Paris in 1642, and in Amsterdam probably in that same year. See Hendrik Cornelis Rogge, *Bibliotheca Grotiana* (The Hague, 1883), p. 29.

85:35   For "E Tenebris . . .," see Gen. 1.2–4.

85:36–37   For "*Ignotum Deum*," cf. Acts 17.22–23. "*Psalmos*" may be a reference to the famous *Bay Psalm Book* (Cambridge, Mass., 1640), a New England version of the Psalms, and the first book printed in North America.

85:38–39   Possibly there is here an analogy to Acts 2.5–11.

85:47   According to the NED, there was an edition of the *Gradus ad Parnassum* published in Cologne in 1687 and one in London in 1691.

86:67   For Arminianism, see Cross, *Dictionary*, pp. 87–88; for the attitude of New Englanders toward it, see Perry Miller, *The New England Mind: The Seventeenth Century*, pp. 367–369. Increase Mather, in a preface to Samuel Willard's *Covenant-Keeping* (Boston, 1682), listed among the errors of the times "Arminian Tenents about Universal Redemption, Free Will, Apostacy from Grace, &c." which were "inconsistent with the Covenant of Redemption." For the followers of Menno, see Cross, *ibid.*, p. 886, under "Mennonites." To orthodox New England Puritans, their rejection of infant baptism and of the participation of Christians in the magistracy were especially distasteful. Baruch Spinoza, a pantheist, ruled out all conceptions of a personal God, of the permanence of personality, and of immortality, and his religious ideas were purely rationalist. Compare Cross, *ibid.*, p. 1281.

86:80   For Selijns, see DAB; *Nieuw Nederlandsch Biografisch Wordenboek* (10 vols., Leiden, Sijthoff, 1911–1937), 3:1159–1166; and Henry C. Murphy, *Anthology of New Netherland* (New York, 1865), pp. 79–183, which contains a memoir and a collection of Selijns' verse.

GENERAL INTRODUCTION

89:4   Mather's Latin is an adaptation of Theodoret, *In Canticum Canticorum*, Bk. IV, sec. 1 (*Migne G*, 81:175–176). Mather considered Theodoret "the best Expositor of the Bible among all the *Fathers*" (*Manuductio ad Ministerium*, Boston, 1726, p. 89).

89:5   An echo of the opening words of the *Aeneid*, "arma virumque cano. . . ." For "*Wonders*," cf. Ps. 77.11: "I will remember the works of the Lord: surely I will remember thy wonders of old"; Deut. 4.34, in which God leads his people as "a nation from the midst of another nation, by temptations, by signs, and by wonders"; and Jer. 32.31, where God brings forth his people "out of the land of Egypt with signs, and with wonders . . ." For Mather, England is the Egypt of the Bible; New England, the new Israel.

89:6   In his "Quotidiana," vol. II, Mather noted, "Christianity may [as Mr. Herbert presaged, hoist sale for America," with a reference to Edwards' *Survey* (John Edwards, *A Compleat HISTORY or SURVEY Of all the Dispensations and Methods of RELIGION From the beginning of the World to the Consummation of all things*, 2 vols., London, 1699). The "Quotidiana," preserved at the American Antiquarian Society, are in four pocket-size books and cover the period 1696–1723. Only two bear volume numbers, and the other two are undated (cf. Holmes, *Cotton Mather*, 3:1308). A copy of Herbert's poems was in the Mather library, and he elsewhere quotes him. See below p. 113, ll. 59–60; p. 115, l. 59, and the title page of *The Christian Thank-Offering* (Boston, 1696), where he quotes the last stanza of Herbert's "Obedience," with the reference "*Herbert*. Pag. 98." This page reference agrees with all the seventeenth-century editions of Herbert's *Temple*; the spelling of the quoted lines follows that of the 1656 and later editions.

89:7   Mather's invocation of "the Holy Author of that Religion" parallels the invocation of the muses in *Aeneid* 1.8. Compare Milton's *Paradise Lost* I.6–26: "Sing, Heavenly Muse . . ." For "Conscience," i.e., inner knowledge of "*Truth*," cf. II Cor. 1.12-13. For the phrase "the *Truth* itself," see John 14.6.

89:9   For "*Wonderful Displays*," cf. Deut. 4.34, where "signs" is closely similar to "displays." Compare Ps. 60.4: "Thou hast given a banner to them that fear thee, that it may be displayed because of the truth." For "Power, Wisdom, Goodness, and Faithfulness," cf. Exod. 28.3; 31.3; Ps. 147.5.

89:10   "*Irradiate*" was a favorite word of Mather's. In his Diary for Sept. 9, 1696, for example, he wrote: "The Lord exceedingly irradiated my Soul, by His Good Spirit," and when he heard encouraging news about the possibilities of publishing the *Magnalia* (Jan. 7, 1698), he wrote, "Behold, the Faith which irradiated mee, the last *November*, answered!" The Diary from 1681 through 1701 uses forms of "irradiate" at least eleven times. See *Diary*, 1:204–247 and *passim*.

89:15   For "*Ends of the Earth*," cf. Matt. 12.42, Luke 11.31. For "Field," cf. Matt. 13.18: "The field is the world; the good seed are the children of the kingodm; but the tares are the children of the wicked one." Mather's "world," with its good seed and tares, was New England. Compare in this context Isa. 32.15–16: "Until the spirit be poured upon us from on high, and the wilderness be a fruitful field . . . Then judgment shall dwell in the wilderness and righteousness remain in the fruitful field." Verse 18 adds that "my people shall dwell" there. In the light of what follows, "field" may here have been intended to suggest also the "stage" on which the "actors" "acted."

89:18   The manner of introducing both the actors and the causes of action is again reminiscent of the epic tradition (e.g., *Aeneid* I.1, 8–12; Milton, *Paradise Lost* I.29, 34, 36, 38). "Actor," "stage" (and possibly "field"), and "action" in the sense of stage action were often used metaphorically by the New England colonists. The notion that "all the world's a stage" had a long secular history and was also used by religious writers. For example, Jonathan Mitchell, minister at Cambridge from 1650 to 1668, wrote: "This lower World was made but to be a Stage for men to act their parts on for a few ages, and then taken down: Hence it stands but on Crazy shows it may and will e'er long fall on heaps" (*A Discourse of the Glory*, London, 1677, pp. 69–70, quoted in Babette M. Levy, *Preaching in the First Half Century of New England History*, Hartford, American Society of Church History, 1945, p. 130). See Miss Levy's book, pp. 127–130, for further discussion of the religious use of the stage-world-actor figure.

89:20   "LIVES" is capitalized presumably in reference to Books II and III of the *Magnalia*, both devoted to biographies; "*lived*" may be italicized simply because of its relation to "LIVES." See the uses of "life" and "live" in Mather's *Manuductio* (e.g., pp. 3–5) for an indication of the meanings Mather—and his pious colleagues—gave the words. For Biblical usages, see Deut. 30.19–20, Rom. 1.17, 8.6, II Cor. 3.6, 13.4, Ps. 119.77.

89:21   For "*Examples*," cf. Jas. 5.10, I Pet. 2.21, and introductory essay "The Magnalia"; for "worthy of *Everlasting Remembrance*," cf. Ps. 112.6.

89:24   In the first use cited by the NED ([John Toland], *Paradoxes of State*, 1702, p. 13), the term "American Creolians" refers to persons of Spanish descent in the West Indies, and hence accords with usual modern usage. Bk. IV, pt. 2, of the *Magnalia* contains the lives of eleven ministers, not all born in America but all so far "Criolians" as to have been reared in New England and educated at Harvard. "Biography" was a relatively new word at the time of the *Magnalia*. See Donald A. Stauffer, *English Biography before 1700* (Cambridge, Mass., Harvard University Press, 1930), pp. 217–219. "Our *Biography*" seems to be used collectively—the "life" or "lives" of "our people" or "our colony" in the New World. For "*whole World*," see Rom. 1.8, I John 2.2.

90:30   "Tempestuated" occurs again (*Magnalia*, Bk. VII, chap. 6, sec. 14)—the only instance of its use given by the NED. The word was probably coined by Mather. Compare Ps. 11.6.

90:33   Compare Owen Feltham, *Resolves*, p. 236; "Observations that shall naturally arise from a *Rational Collection* are not to be denied, as the *Imbellishment* of a *well-prais'd work*."

90:37   See "The Life of Plutarch" in *John Dryden's Works* (ed. Scott and Saintsbury, London, 1882–1893), 17:56.

90:47   "Fidelity and Simplicity": II Cor. 1.12.

90:48–49   For "the Sum of the Matter," cf. Dan. 7.1, 28, Eccles. 12.13, Heb. 8.1. From here until the end of the paragraph Mather gives briefly the "Idea" and "History" of the "REFORMATION in the *English Nation*," one of the basic themes in the *Magnalia*. The passage is for the most part a summary version of his *Eleutheria*, pp. 35–37, sometimes agreeing word for word with that text. *Eleutheria* was written in 1696, sent to London to be printed in May 1698, and appeared there and in Boston later the same year. The *Magnalia* manuscript was not sent to London until thirteen months later, although the General Introduction was probably finished by August 1697. It seems clear that Mather was working on *Eleutheria* before he finished the *Magnalia*, and that then, or after the *Eleutheria* was printed but before the *Magnalia* manuscript was sent to England, he thriftily excerpted passages from it for the General Introduction of the latter.

90:50   Compare Pss. 4.3, 14.5, 24.6, 112.2, for the idea of the continuity of generations of "*Godly men*."

90:51–52   The italicized passage is from The Solemn League and Covenant (see Richard Baxter, *Reliquiae Baxterianae*, London 1696, p. 391), quoted in a fuller version in *Eleutheria*, p. 38. The full text appears in S. R. Gardiner, *Constitutional Documents*, 3rd ed. (Oxford, Clarendon Press, 1906), pp. 267–271.

90:53   *Antiquitates Judaicae*, VI.7.4. For "the words of *Samuel* to *Saul*," see I Sam. 15.22.

90:57–91:60   For a generation of evil men (in contrast to the generation of Godly men above), see Prov. 30.13–14; for such a generation with the power to persecute, see Mic. 2.1.

91:63–64   Foxe's 1702 text has "ease" for "else," following the 1685 edition, but earlier editions of the *Acts and Monuments* have "else," which is clearly the correct reading.

91:65–67   For "*Ignorance* and *Vanity*," see Eph. 4.17–18; for "*Administrations*," II Cor. 9.12; for "*Law of Christ*," John 1.17, Rom. 8.2, 10.4–6.

91:72   In *Eleutheria*, pp. 18–19, Mather wrote of "Our memorable *Wickliff*, who sounded the alarm of Reformation louder than any . . . before him," so that the whole world was "irradiated" by him.

91:73   Cranmer, during his imprisonment and trial for heresy, made several recantations of past "errors," but in the eyes of Protestants he redeemed himself on the scaffold where, in his last "confession," he reaffirmed his Protestant faith. The juxtaposition of Cranmer's "confessions" with Bucer's *Scripta Anglicana* suggests, however, that Mather, using the word somewhat loosely, may have intended the first and second Books of Common Prayer. Bucer's "Censura," or reflections on the first Book of Common Prayer, were subsequently published in his *Scripta Anglicana* (ed. Conrad Hubert, Basel, 1577), a collection containing all those of his works published in England.

91:76–77   Mather wrote that "bitter Heylin" was an "enemy to any *further progress* of the *Reformation*" (*Eleutheria*, pp. 45–46), and remarked that in his *Ecclesia Restaurata, or The History of the Reformation of the Church of England* (London, 1661, p. 34), Heylin declared that the Reformation began with "*preparatory Injunctions*" so that the people, "being prepared by little and little, might with more Ease and less Opposition, admit the *total Alteration, which was intended in due time to be introduced.*"

91:79–80   Compare also Rev. 6.11.

91:80–83   The quotation, which also appears in *Eleutheria*, p. 40, is from John Owen, *An Enquiry into the . . . Order and Communion of Evangelical Churches* (London, 1681), Preface, pp. 38–39; Mather changed "to seek" to "and seek." For Owen's views on progress in Reformation, see pp. 36–37. Owen, chaplain to Cromwell and vice-chancellor of Oxford, was admired in New England because he shifted from Presbyterianism to Independency, and because of his "profound learning." He was especially "great" in Mather's eyes because he wrote a laudatory preface for Increase Mather's *Some Important Truths* (London, 1674). Compare Bk. III, "Johannes in Eremo," Introduction, sec. 1.

91:84–89   Compare John Milton, "Of Reformation," in *Complete Prose Works* (1:585): "numbers of faithfull, and freeborn Englishmen, and good Christians have bin constrain'd to forsake their dearest home . . . whom nothing but the wide Ocean and the savage deserts of *America* could hide and shelter from the fury of the Bishops."

92:90–94   The New England settlers hoped to advance "Reformed Christianity so that . . . all Europe would imitate New England," to lead an exodus of saints to found "a Citty vpon a Hill" (*Winthrop Papers*, MHS *Coll.*, 2:295) as an example to the world.

92:96   Compare Rev. 3.2, 17.

92:99   For the idea but not the exact phrasing of this quotation, see Augustine, *Sermones ad Populum* (*Migne L*, 38:931): "ipsa est perfectio hominis, invenisse se non esse perfectum?" and *Contra Duas Epistolas Pelagianorum* (*Migne L*, 44:599).

92:1   I Tim. 4.6.

92:11–13   Mather took this story (see "Quotidiana," I, no. 21) from Samuel Ward, *The Life of Faith in Death* (London, 1627), p. 32. It is told of "Constantinus Northmannus" of Rouen (d. 1542) in Jean Crespin, *Actiones et Monumenta Martyrum* (Geneva, 1560), fol. 68a, which Foxe cited as his source in *Acts and Monuments* (London, 1641), 2:129b. Compare endnote to Bk. I, Introd., p. 115, ll. 52–54.

92:20–22   Compare Xenophon's *Cyropaedia* VIII.vii.24. Mather's translation echoes Eccles. 2.12.

92:24   *Sermones in Cantica, Migne L*, 183:976.

93:32–37   At the irenical Council of Poissy, 1561, the Cardinal's reply to Theodore Beza's defense of the Calvinist reformers was printed as *L'Oraison de Monseigneur le . . . Cardinal de Lorraine, faite en l'Assemblée de Poissy* (Rheims, 1561). Mather's quotation (see "Quotidiana," I, no. 295) is from a letter printed in *Petri Rami . . . Collectaneæ: Præfationes, Epistolæ, Orationes* (Paris, 1577), p. 257, which was in Increase Mather's library, and follows the text except for the change of "illas opes" to "opes illas."

93:39   The name "Puritan," proudly accepted by Mather and his fellow nonconformists, was probably first used derisively. The Anglican Thomas Fuller, whom Mather quotes approvingly in *Eleutheria*, pp. 45, 48–52, says that in 1563 those who refused the ceremonies and discipline of the English church were given "the odious name of purtans." Fuller wished "the word *puritan* were banished common discourse, because so various in the acceptions thereof" (*Church History of Britain*, ed. J. S. Brewer, Oxford, 1845, 4:327).

93:42   John Norton, *Three Choice . . . Sermons* (Cambridge, 1664), p. 7: "You may look at it [liberty] as a Power, as to any external restraint, or obstruction on mans part, to walk in the Faith, Worship, Doctrine and Discipline of the Gospel, according to the Order of the Gospel."

93:46–48   In Job 8.22, Bildad declares God will not cast away a perfect man, but "the dwelling place of the wicked shall come to naught." Increase Mather, in *A Discourse Concerning the Uncertainty of the Times of Men* (Boston, 1697), p. 35, wrote that "a blessed day to the visible Church" was near, but that "very Learned men" believed that in the promised "Glorious Times . . . *America* will be Hell." He expressed the fear that while some "Elect of God" will still be born in New England, "in process of Time, *New England* will be the wofullest place in all *America*, as some other parts of the World once famous for Religion are now . . . Emblems and Pictures of Hell." Cotton's father was arguing that New England must reform, and may have been thinking of the "learned man," Joseph Mede (Mead), of Cambridge University, who held that the devil, "being impatient of the sound of the Gospel and Cross of Christ in every part of this old world, so that he could in no place be quiet" and "foreseeing that he was like at length to lose all here," took to the New World as a place where he might establish a race "over which he might reign securely" (from a letter to Dr. William Twisse in *Works*, London, 1672, p. 800). Compare *Magnalia*, Bk. I, chap. 1, sec. 7; Bk. VI, chap. 7, secs. 1, 2.

93:52   For "Severities," cf. Rom. 11.22.

93:55   For the typological significance of the seven golden candlesticks, see Samuel Mather, *Figures*, pp. 390–394: "The end and use of the Church is to give Light, and to hold forth the Truth, as the Candlestick gave Light." The Church is golden because constituted of "visible Saints," who are "golden." The candlestick is also "a Type of the Ministry in the Church," because it supports "the light": "A Church without a Minister, is a Candlestick without a Light." Candlesticks also typified "the Light of the Word" and "the Sprit of God." There were seven in Revelation, and "seven is a number of perfection"; hence Cotton Mather numbers the churches "more than *twice Seven times Seven*." For "light in darkness," see Ps. 112.4.

94:67   The use of "polyantheae" and commonplace books in the seventeenth century was widespread; they were part of every scholar's stock in trade, but their abuse was also often criticized. The authors of Smectymnuus's *A Vindication of the Answer* (London, 1641, "To the Reader" [p. 61]', complain that they are accused of being "destitute of all learning as if our reading had never gone beyond a *Polyanthea*," and Robert Burton, *Anatomy of Melancholy* (2nd ed., Oxford, 1624, p. 121), speaks of one who, by "some trivantly *Polyanthean* helpes, steales and gleanes a few notes from other mens Harvests."

   In Section 4 and most of Section 5, Mather relies heavily on such "polyantheas," commonplace books, and encyclopedias. The notes which follow give the original source of his quotations whenever possible, succeeded by references to the secondary sources he drew them from. Many of them appear in more than one reference work, but ordinarily only one secondary source is given in each case. He used especially, as the annotations show, Degory Wheare, *Relictiones Hyemalis de Ratione et Methodus Legendi . . . Historias* (Cambridge, England, 1684) and its translation, *The Method and Order of Reading Histories* (London, 1685). Indeed, it is difficult not to conclude that Mather wrote this section with the *Relictiones* open before him, since he plucks out authors to cite, and judgments on them to quote, in the very order in which they appear (among others) in Wheare. Quoted less often are Johann Alsted, *Encyclopædia* (Herborn, 1630); Thomas Blount, *Censura Celebriorum Authorum* (London, 1690); Johan Heidfeld, *Sphinx Theologico-Philosophica* (Herborn, 1621); Joseph Lange, *Florilegii Magni seu Polyantheæ* (Leyden, 1648); Edward Leigh, *A Treatise of Religion and Learning* (London, 1656); and Nathaniel Wanley, *The Wonders of the Little World* (London, 1678). Of these, all but the Blount and the Wheare are known to have been in Mather's library or in that of his father, and these are quoted from often enough to make it certain that he used them.

94:72   Mather changes the order of the phrases of this widely known quotation from Cicero *De Oratore* II.ix.36. He quotes the passage again in his *Manuductio*, p. 58, in a context that might well be cited against his earlier practice: "The Praises of that Method [history] . . . that *Historians* usually begin their Works withal, and the Flourishes about, *Lux Veritatis, Vita Memoriæ, Magistra Vitæ*, and I know not what, are as unnecessary on *this* Occasion, as they are *that* whereon we commonly have them."

94:73–88   Wheare climaxes his *Relictiones* with a section in praise of church history (pp. 208–210): "*Sacra Historia* sola, quæ ab ipso rerum omnium primordio, fidele temporum exhibet testimonium, nec usquam vacillat. Hæc sola veritatis æternæ lux splendidissima." The attributes "dignity," "suavity," "utility" were frequently applied to such history, as for example by Alsted (*Encylopædia*, p. 1982b), in the paragraph-heading, "Materia historiæ sit gravis, suavis, et utilis." "Suavity"— sweetness, agreeableness—was often associated with spirituality. Wheare's treatment of "The Method and Order of Reading Church Histories" is contained in sections 32 through 45 of the *Relictiones*, and cites many of the writers Mather refers to.

On the Bible as history, see Wheare, p. 29. The story of the creation is told in chapters 1 and 2 of Genesis; the description of the tabernacle in chapters 25–40 of Exodus. For "more Precious than the *World*," see Isa. 11.12, II Pet. 2.4. For "*Redeemed* and *Purified*," see Deut. 15.15, 24.18, I Pet. 1.18, 22, etc. For "*Peculiar People*," see Deut. 14.2, 26.18, Titus 2.14, I Pet. 2.9. For "*Strangers* in *this World*," see I Chron. 16.19, I Pet. 2.11, *etc.* For "*Truths* and *Rules*," see, for examples, II Cor. 6.7, 11.10, Gal. 2.5, 6.16, Phil. 3.16, Col. 1.5, 3.15.

94:89–90   For "Dispensations," see Col. 1.25, Eph. 3.2.

94:91–95:94   For "Calamities," see Ps. 57.1; for "Deliverances," Ps. 44.4–5; for "Dispositions," cf. Acts 7.53; for "*Admiration* and *Admonition*," I Cor. 10.11.

95:97–98   For the image of Herodotus' history as a smoothly flowing river, see Wheare, *Relictiones*, p. 33, with a reference to Cicero *Orator* xii. 39.

95:4   For the quotation from Isaac Casaubon's preface to his edition of *Polybius* (Paris, 1609, [p. 35]), see Wheare, p. 37.

95:5–9   The epithet, Ἀττικὴ μέλιττα, applied to Xenophon, appears in Suidas, *Lexicon Graecum* (ed. I. Bekker, Berlin, 1854, p. 752), and was well known. Mather's immediate source was probably Wheare, p. 40, but the phrase can be found in a number of works, e.g. Alsted, *Encyclopaedia*, p. 1948b, and in Gerardus Vossius, *De Historicis Graecis* (Leyden, 1651), p. 21.

For the quotation from Justus Lipsius, "Notae ad I Liber Politicorum" (*Opera*, Wesel, 1675, 4:215), see Wheare, p. 41. Mather condenses the original "suavis ille, et fidus, certe circumspectus scriptor."

95:9–13   See Wheare, pp. 43–44. Mather probably found the Greek in Vossius, *De Historicis Graecis*, p. 169, quoted from Photius, *Bibliotheca*, cod. 70 (ed. I. Bekker, 1824, p. 35a).

95:15   In Wheare, p. 46, the praise of Curtius is quoted from Christoph Coler, "De Ordinando Studio Politico Epistola," in Hugo Grotius *et al.*, *Dissertationes de Studiis Instituendis* (Amsterdam, 1645), p. 188.

96:18–19   A variation of Lipsius' judgment of Plutarch, "digni tamen, si quid alius, Principe scriptor" (*Opera*, 4:215), which Mather follows Wheare (p. 47) in applying to Polybius.

96:20   While Mather implies a personal knowledge of Florus, his reference merely echoes Wheare's words, p. 52.

96:22–23   Wheare, pp. 55–56, gives in full the passage from Jean Bodin's *Methodus ad Facilem Historiarum Cognitionem* (Strassburg, 1598, p. 74).

96:24   Compare Wheare, p. 57, where "the famous critic" is the "famous Casaubon," and the passage, from the preface to *Polybius* [p. 37], appears in full.

96:31–33   Gaza is said to have named Plutarch when he was asked what author he would choose to save if he were to be deprived of all but one. See Wheare, p. 59. The story also appears in Blount, *Censura*, p. 101, where it is credited to Rolandus Maresius, *Epistolorum Philologicarum Libri Duo* (Paris, 1655), Lib. I, Epist. 24. John Spencer (d. 1680, librarian of Sion College, London; not to be confused with John Spencer of Corpus Christi, Cambridge), *Things New and Old* (London, 1658), p. 535, in a paragraph headed " *The* book of Scripture *to be preserved above all other books*," says that Guillaume Bude made the same asnwer to a similar question asked by Francis I. Mather's pious addition, "next unto the inspired oracles of the Bible," may have been suggested by Spencer's heading.

96:34   Only fragments of Polyhistor's work remain, and it is probable that Mather knew none of them, but it remained a name to conjure with as a synonym for one greatly learned.

96:39–42   Compare Richard Baxter, Introduction to *The Life and Death of Joseph Alleine* (London, 1673), pp. 13–14; Heinrich Cornelius Agrippa von Nettesheim, *De Incertitudine et Vanitate Scientarum* (Leyden, 1609), cap. v, "De Historia," fol. D5 verso: "Nam qui Herculem, Achillem, Hectorem . . . denique Xerxem, Cyrum, Darium . . . Caesarem miris laudibus depingunt: quid nisi magnos et furiosos latrones famosuqe orbis prædones descripserunt?" Mather knew both *The Life of Alleine* and *De Incertitudine*.

96:42–97:43   *Annals* iv.32. Tacitus does not say that great wars were the noblest historical material, but this is perhaps implied in both iv. 32 and iv. 33.

97:46–47   For *"Corruptions,"* see Isa. 38.17, John 2.6, Rom. 8.21, Gal. 6.8, II Pet. 1.4. For *"Afflictions,"* cf. Ps. 34.19, Acts 7.10, II Cor. 6.4, II Tim. 1.8, 3.11, I Pet. 5.9, Heb. 10.32, 33.

97:57–52   For a summary of these "questions," see the NED on the letters Z and H.

97:54   Seneca, "Ad Lucilium," in *Epistulae Morales* lxxxviii. 37.

97:57–60   The principles to be observed by an "Impartial Historian" as given by Mather are the standard ones enumerated over and over in sixteenth- and seventeenth-century compendia. Compare, for example, Owen Felltham's *Resolves*, pp. 235–237, on "History and Historians" (no. 38 of the "Second Century"), which could serve as an outline for much of Mather's Section 5.

97:58   The quotation from the section entitled "Historica" in Alsted's *Encyclopaedia*, p. 1983a, appears also in Increase Mather, *A Relation of the Troubles . . . in New England* (Boston, 1677), Pref., [p. 3], where it is ascribed to "a learned man in his *Historica*." Increase Mather has "h.e." for Alsted's *hoc est*, which, presumably correctly transcribed by Cotton, was corrupted by the printer to "et."

97:60–63   Polybius *Historiæ* I.xiv. 3–5; cited in Alsted, p. 1983a.

97:65   *How to Write History* 8.

97:63–72   Aubery's *Mémoires pour servir à l'histoire de Hollande* (Paris, 1687), was translated by Thomas Brown as *The Lives of the Princes of Orange* (London, 1693), the Preface of which (p. 4) was apparently Mather's source.

98:75–76   Mather probably quotes from Lange, *Florilegii*, 1:1197, where Agrippa von Nettesheim, *De Incertitudine* (cap. v, first sentence), is cited as source. Lange alters the text slightly and Mather follows Lange. Compare Diodorus Siculus *Bibliotheca Historica* X.xii.1.

98:76–82   For Tertullian's censure of Tacitus, see his *Apologeticus Adversus Gentes pro Christianis*, cap. 16 (*Migne L*, 1:420) and his *Ad Nationes*, Bk. I, sec. 11 (*Migne L*, 1:648). Mather probably relied on Wheare (*Relictiones*, p. 68), who quotes Casaubon's preface to Polybius, ([p. 38]), to the effect that Tacitus was "pernicious" since he wrote of the vicious, whose "ill examples" may be harmful because they "have the effect of precepts." Lipsius' judgment of Tacitus as "Acer Scriptor (dii boni!) et prudens" appears in the dedication to the Emperor Maximilian II of his edition of Tacitus (*Opera*, Anvers, 1585, [p. 47]), and Wheare quotes this as his source (*ibid.*,

p. 67). Mather's position is that virtues and vices ought to be not simply subjects of narration but also of serious moral reflection.

98:89 See Zacharias to Boniface, *Migne L*, 89:946–948. Mather seems to have taken the story ("*Quotidiana*," no. 35) from John Templer, *A Treatise Relating to the Worship of God*, London, 1694.

98:94 There is a possibility that the "Noble Historian" was Richard Montagu (1577–1641), bishop of Chichester and chaplain to James I. The likelihood of his being the one referred to rests on the circumstance that Wheare, in a marginal note to his *Method . . . of Reading History* (p. 235), refers to "Montague *in Praef ad Apparatum*. 10," seemingly applied to the "Reverend Bishop of *Chichester*," whom Wheare has been praising as a writer of religious history. As has been noted, Mather was following Wheare closely at this point. Montagu disliked the extremes of both Calvinism and Romanism. While Mather's quotation has not been found, we find a similar opinion expressed in a letter by Montagu to John Cosin, for a time Master of Peterhouse and Vice-Chancellor of Cambridge, namely, that his aim was "to stand in the gapp against puritanisme and popery, the Scilla and Charybdis of Ancient Piety" (Cosin, *Correspondence*, 2 vols., 1868–1870, 1:21).

98:1–2 The Latin quotation from Polybius, *Histories* II.61 is to be found in Lange, *Florilegii*, 1:1203.

98:4–5 See John Spencer, *Things New and Old*, p. 207 (par. 820, headed "*Conscientious Preachers* not to be slighted"), where one Dr. Web is quoted about "a godly Man, preaching before the King," who observed "*that the Ambassadours that come from* Placentia, *are welcome . . . whereas those that come from* Verona *are sleightly set by.*"

99:6–10 Polybius *Histories* I.xiv.4–6, quoted by Lange, 1:1203.

99:16 For Naphtali see Gen. 49.21; I Kings 7.14. Compare Higginson's comparison in the Attestation of the writing of the *Magnalia* to the building of a Temple, p. 68, ll. 41–42.

99:17–19 Polybius, *Histories* II.61, quoted by Lange, 1:1203.

99:21–22 The phrase appears in Jerome's *Epistolæ*, no. 22, "Ad Eustochium" (*Migne L*, 22:421), and is to be found in Blount, *Censura*, p. 92. For the Golden Calf, see Exod. 32.4.

99:27–34 The story of the pasquil on Pope Urban is told by James Howell, *Epistolæ Ho-Elianæ: Familiar Letters*, Bk. I, sec. 4: Letter 21, dated May 3, 1626 (ed. Joseph Jacobs, London, 1890, p. 237). Mario dell'Arco, in *Pasquino e le Pasquinate* (Milano, Martello, 1957), p. 131, says the subject of the lampoon was Pope Sixtus V.

99:31–34 For Peter's denial, see Matt. 26.69–75, Mark 14.66–72, Luke 22.55–62, John 18.15–18, 25–27. For Paul's persecutions, see Acts 8.1–3, 9.1–2.

99:39–100:49 Pierre Jurieu, *Histoire du Calvinisme et du Papisme mises en parallèle* (2nd ed., Geneva, 1823), 2:86–150; Jurieu presents an account of Mary Queen of Scots "jusqu'à sa sortie du royaume." In his *History of My Own Time*, Bishop Gilbert Burnet recorded a conversation in 1686 with Queen Mary, during which she asked "what had sharpened the king so much against Mr. Jurieu." He replied that it was in part because Jurieu "had writ with great indecency of Mary queen of Scots, which cast reflections on them that were descended from her." To this the Queen answered: "Jurieu was to support the cause that he defended, and to expose those that persecuted it, in the best way he could. And, if what he said of Mary queen of Scots was true, he was not to be blamed. . . . if princes would do ill things, they must expect that the world will take revenges on their memory." The volume in which this exchange was printed was not published until after Mather had finished his Introduction. He most probably got the story from his father, Increase, who while in England saw a good deal of Burnet, was aided by him in his quest for a new charter, and may well have been told the Queen's saying by him. The *Magnalia* version somewhat alters Burnet's record, perhaps because his father's memory was not exact or because Cotton Mather chose to embellish it. It is also possible that he got his version from some one of the many writers who published eulogies of the Queen after her death in 1694 and may have known the tale from hearsay. See the second edition of Burnet's *History* (6 vols., Oxford, 1833), 3:134–135; Murdock, *Increase Mather*, p. 211 and note; pp. 236, 264.

100:52–53 See Plato *Minos* 319.A3. In the Latin translation of Marsilio Ficino (*Platonis Opera Omnia*, Leyden, 1590, p. 46): "Deus quippe nimium indignatur, quoties quispiam illius similem improbar, aut probat dissimilem."

100:53–60 Mather also refers to the "incomparable Thuanus" in his *Manuductio*, p. 62, again noting the charge that his work contains "multa falsissima."

100:60–61 Erasmus, Mather records in his "Quotidiana," no. 38, "makes *Gregory* and *Theodorus* two distinct scholars of Origen, where tis notoriously known they were but two names of one and the same person." (See William Cave, *Antiquitates Apostolicae*, London, 1677, p. 170). The passage in question is from Erasmus, *Via Origenes*, "Instituit et *Theodorum* . . . , praeterea Gregorium quem Θαυμα Τουργὸν appellant."

100:63–65 Mather here relies on a statement by Samuel Herne in *Domus Carthusiana* (London, 1677), Pref., [p.10]: "Sir Richard Baker, Dr. Heylin, and Mr. Fuller say little of him, and that little very full of mistakes, for they call him Richard Sutton, and affirm he lived a Batchelor, and so by his single life had an opportunity to lay up a heap of mony; whereas his *dear wife* is, with much honour and respect, mentioned in his Will." Richard Baker, in *A Chronicle of the Kings of England* (London, 1643), p. 151, refers to him as "*Thomas Sutton*, Esquire . . . having always lived a Batchelour." Thomas Fuller, in *The Church History of Britain* (5:425–429), calls him Richard and says he "died a bachelor." In his *History of the Worthies of England* (London, 1662), Fuller called Sutton's benefaction "the masterpiece of Protestant English charity" (ed. P. A. Nuttall, New York, AMS Press, 1965, 2:294).

100:70–101:71 The Greek quotation is from Eusebius *Ecclesiastical History* 4.8. [121]. Compare Jerome, *De Viris Illustribus*, cap. 22 (*Migne L*, 23:673–674).

101:72–75 Mather probably drew on Vossius, *De Historicis Græcis*, p. 229, for his comments on Hegesippus.

101:79–81 Lange, *Florilegii*, 1:1202, with reference to Erasmus' *Parabolæ, sive Similia* (Strassburg, 1514), p. G iii.

101:83 See *Aesop: Fables* (tr. V.S.V. Jones, London, 1933, p.1), "The Fox and the Grapes."

101:84 Ovid *Tristia* I.7.31.

101:84–86 "Puerile Spoils of *Polyantheas*" comes oddly from Mather, who, as these notes show, constantly made use of such books. What he was in effect saying, however, was that the quotations he used were not "puerile" or "foolish" but deliberately chosen to give useful information and pleasure, or to add meaning to or clarify his text. See prefatory essay, "The Magnalia."

101:87–89 Ambrose, *Epistolæ, Migne L*, 16:1201

101:95–96 Erasmus, *Adagiorum Chiliades* (Frankfurt-am-Main, 1599), col. 389: "Omnis herus servo monosyllabum. Heris et potentibus brevissimo tantum verbulo est opus, ut vel annuant, vel renuant." See also William Lambarde, *Perambulation of Kent* (ed. 1826), p. 233: "Our speech at this day (for the most part) consisteth of words of one sillable. Which thing King Erasmus observing, merrily in his Ecclesiast, compareth the English toong to a Dogs barking, that soundeth nothing else, but Baw, waw, waw, in Monosillable. This was written in 1570." Increase Mather had in his library the London, 1596, edition of Lambarde's book.

101:98–102:3 For the story of the two statues made by Polyclitus, see Aelian *Varia Historia* xiv. 8 (ed. Rudolf Hercher, Leipzig, 1864–66, 2:161–162).

102:6 In his Diary for August 20, 1697, Mather copied a long passage from his manuscript of the General Introduction as it then stood. This he changed somewhat and added to in the final version which he sent to London to be printed. The manuscript passage begins with the words, "A Varietie of other Employments hath kept mee" (102:6 and runs to 106:34). The additions he made to the manuscript in the finished text of the *Magnalia* are indicated in the endnotes which follow. Changes in spelling, punctuation, capitalization, and italicization are not annotated. In the notes the transcription of the manuscript, now owned by the Massachusetts Historical Society, is that made by Anna M. Galvin for the Society's edition of the Diary, 1:229–231.

102:9–17   See Fuller, *Church History*, 5:387–388: "Indeed the Romanists herein may rise up and condemn those of the protestant confession; for . . . the Romish church doth not burden their professors with preaching, or any parochial incumbrances, but reserved them only for polemical studies: whereas in England the same man reads, preacheth, catechiseth, disputes, delivers sacraments, &c. . . . Besides the study of divinity, at the least two able historians were to be maintained in this college, faithfully and learnedly to record and publish to posterity all memorable passages in church and commonwealth."

102:23   Cicero *De Natura Deorum* III.ii.5. Compare *In Catilinam* IV.x.20. "Reader . . . *de Me*" was added to the manuscript version.

102:25–26   For "*Pastoral Watchfulness*," cf. Paul's instructions to Titus and Timothy on the duties of a minister, especially Titus chaps. 2 and 3, I Tim. chaps. 4 and 5, and II Tim. 4.1–8. See also Eph. 4.11–12. For ministers described as shepherds, see Jer. 3.15, 23.4, Ezek. 34.2–10, Zech. 10.2, 3, John 21.15, 16.

102:26–29   "Wherein . . . employ'd them all" was added to the manuscript version.

102:31–32   For "*Omitted*," cf. Matt. 23.23; for "*fulfill my Ministry*," II Tim. 4.5; for "Give myself wholly," I Tim. 4.15.

103:35–37   "My Reader . . *Negotii*" was added to the manuscript version. The editors have not discovered a source for the quotation. "Litany" seems to be used in the sense of any "continued repetition or recounting." Possibly Mather devised the sentence himself, but this seems unlikely.

103:38–39   See Diodorus *Histories* I.4.1; Jean Bodin, *Methodus*, pp. 82–83; Carlo Sigonio, *Opera* (1732–1737), 6:1009. Mather's immediate source may have been Blount's *Censura*, p. 43: "Sanè multa adeo sunt σφαλματα Diodori in *Olympiadum* annis, & *Romanis Magistratibus*, ut planè verisimile sit corruptis ac mutilis fastis usum esse. Sanè hoc nomine non a *Bodino* modò vapulat: sed ab ipso etiam *Sigonio* . . . & aliis *Chronographis* sæpitus reprehenditur."

103:44–45   *Coryats Crudities hastily gobled up in Five Moneths Travells . . newly Digested in the hungry aire of Odcom*, London, 1611.

103:46–47   The story is told in Aelian *Varia Historia* xii.41, as well as in Pliny *Historia Naturales* xxx.36, 80, and in Plutarch *Demetrius* xxii.2–3. The passage from "*Protogenes*" to "*Time* to do it" was added to the manuscript version.

103:52   In the prefatory "Ad doctorum lectorum" included in the first English edition of *Acts and Monuments* (1563), p. 2, and in most of the subsequent editions other than that of 1570, Foxe says that he had "barely eighteen full months" for the compilation of the book. In the 1570 and subsequent editions he speaks of "my former edition of *Acts and Monuments* so hastily rashed up at that present, in such shortnesse of time, as in the said Book thou mayest see . . . declared and signified" (ed. 1641, p. 920a).

103:54   "Glad, in the little" is, in the manuscript version, "glad, if in the little."

104:66–68   "For (tho' I am" to "*totum potest*" was added to the manuscript version. The source of the Jerome quotation has not been found.

104:68   *Institutiones Oratoriae* X.iii.23: "Neque enim se bona fide in multa simul intendere animus totum potest."

104:72   "For the most part" was added to the manuscript version.

104:88   "Arabian" was added to the manuscript version.

104:92–94   "Or, To have many Hundreds . . . hitherto imagined" was added to the manuscript version. For Christ "discovered" (revealed), cf. John 5.39, 15.26.

104:95–96   Compare Matt. 24.34, 26.54; Luke 4.21, John 17.12.

105:99–1   I Cor. 2.9–10, cf. Job 12.22.

105:3   The manuscript version has "one" instead of "a Person."

105:3   The earliest example of "authorism" in the NED is 1761; possibly the word here was Mather's own coinage.

105:4–5   For Mede see endnote above to Gen. Introd. p. 93, ll. 46–48. John Lightfoot was the author of *Horæ Hebraicæ* and many other tracts and works. Mather's "carefully selected and corrected" suggests that he wanted to appear more learned than the authors he named or to disguise the frequency with which he relied on them without "correction." The passage in parentheses was added to the manuscript version.

105:6–18   "Travellers tell us . . *than he found*" was added to the manuscript version. Mather's "Quotidiana," no. 27, gives his source as Richard Lassels, *The Voyage of Italy* (Paris, 1670, pt. I, p. 173). Mather condenses Lassels' account, and either he or his printer changed "a hundred thousand" to "a thousand."

105:15–18   Poole's *Synopsis Criticorum aliorumque Scripturae Interpretum* was first published in London, 5 vols., 1669–1676. The quoted passage is from the preface to the *Annotations upon the Holy Bible . . . By the late . . . Divine Mr. Matthew Poole . . . Being a Continuation of Mr. Poole's Work by certain judicious and learned Divines* (London, 2 vols., 1683–1685), 1 : A6 verso.

105:19–20   Ovid, "Epitaph on Phaëthon," *Metamorphoses* II.v.328; cf. Seneca *De Vita Beata* xx.2.

105:26   Matt. 16–19. Solomon's temple had gates overlaid with gold. The temple was, in typology, a symbol of "*Christ*, and the *Church*, and every individual *Saint*." Its doors were overlaid with gold and typified Christ, who "is the Door of Entrance and Admittence into the Temple and Presence of God, John 10.7, 9." It also signified "The Ordinance of Admission into the Church, or keeping or *shutting out*." The keys to it were only for those who, like Peter, were accepted by God, or "individual Saints." Mather is saying in effect that he collected for the *Biblia* notes which would illustrate God's truth and metaphorically would give them "golden keys" to the understanding of divine laws, or "the *Pandects* of Heaven." See Samuel Mather, *Figures*, pp. 339, 347.

105:27   "And curious" was added to the manuscript version.

105:28–29   For "*run and be glorified*," see II Thess. 3.1; for "*God of my Life*," see Ps. 42.8.

106:32   The manuscript of Mather's "Biblia Americana" is in the Massachusetts Historical Society. See Holmes, *Cotton Mather*, 2:729–735, 3:1305. Compare L. M. Friedman, "Biblia Americana: the First American Attempt at Post-Bibilical Jewish History," *Journal of Jewish Bibliography*, 3:19–21 (1942); and E. K. Rand, "Plymouth Plantation and the Golden Age," in *Col. Soc. Mass. Trans.*, 24:185 (1920–1922). See also introductory essays "Cotton Mather" and "The Magnalia."

106:41–42   The source of this quotation has not been found.

106:44   Ovid, *Tristia* I.i.1: "Parve—nec invideo—sine me, liber, ibis in urbem." Mather substitutes "sed" for "nec," thereby altering the sense to "though I envy you" instead of "I grudge it not." Apparently he was proud of this emendation, since he repeats it in the Introduction to his *Corderius Americanus* (Boston, 1708), p. A2. Samuel Sewall, who was an accomplished classicist, took him to task: "I cannot well brook your charging Ovid with Stumbling . . . *Parve, nec invideo* is a most Noble and excellent Exordium, becoming the Ingenious Author; and that way of marring it, that you speak of [*Sed* for *Nec*] would be a Blunder indeed; proper for an Envious Carper. The Poet Lov'd his Book . . . and could not envy it's going to Rome: for then he would not have sent it thither. And yet it was lawfull for him to lament, that he himself might not be the bearer" (Sewall, *Letter Book*. 6 MHS *Coll.*, 1:372–373).

106:45–46 See Alsted, *Encyclopaedia*, 6:1982a. For Luther's text, see *Geist aus Luther's Schriften* (4 vols., Darmstadt, 1828–1831), 2:298. For "*Heart of a Lion*," see II Sam. 17.10; for "Roaring Lion," cf. I Pet. 5. 8–9.

106:51–52 It has not been possible to determine Mather's exact source for the silkworm's motto. It may be found in a Catholic compendium by Philippus Picinellus, *Mundus symbolicus* (Cologne, 1687), Lib. VIII, chap. iii, p. 515, par. 129: "Homo, omnem in operando vanam gloriam effugere, suasque virtutes occultare desiderans, bombycem imitatur, qui calathisco suo texendo occupatus, sensim filorum cassibus totus obtegitur. Unde lemma: OPERITUR, DUM OPERATUR. Has virtutes Salomon in Divina sponsa observans, eam hortum conclusum cognominavit."

107:57–58 In the *Magnalia*, Bk. III, pt. 1, chap. 3, sec. 20, Mather calls "*Anagram-matizing* the *Names* of Men" a "certain little *Sport* of *Wit* . . . used as long ago at least as the Days of Old Lycophron," etc. For the anagram as a form of "wit" in the first half of the seventeenth century, see Murdock, *Handkerchiefs from Paul*, pp. liv-lvi, and the references given there, especially that to William Camden, *Remains Concerning Britaine* (London, 1870, from the 7th [1674] impression), pp. 182–184.

107:59–61 The name "Mather" occurs in John Selden, *De Diis Syris* (London, 1617), Syntagmata II, p. 165: "*Mader* enim siue *Mather* (vnde facilè Mitra de-flectitur) Persicè Genetricem seu Matrem interpretari ex R. Stadiae Pentateucho notauit doctissimus Raphalengius, si vis autem à Mithri quod Dominam denotet nò reclamo."

107:62 Compare Virgil *Aeneid* IX.427.

107:64–68 For "*Day . . . into Judgment*," see Eccles. 12.14; for "*Day* of the *Kingdom*," cf. Luke 1.32–33; for promises to David, cf. Isa. 55.3–4, II Sam. 7.8–16, 23.5; for "*Vanities*," see Eccles. 1.2, 5.7, 12.8; for "*Work . . . of his Neighbour*," see Eccles. 4.4.

107:70–74 In many early editions of Virgil there was included a life of the poet, formerly ascribed to Aelius Donatus, a Roman grammarian of the fourth century, or to Tiberius Claudius Donatus of the same period, but now generally accepted as the work of Gaius Suetonius Tranquillus, the second century biographer and his-torian (see *Suetonius*, Loeb ed., 2:464–483). The account of the "Obtrectatores Virgilio" listed by Mather is to be found in paragraphs 43 and 44 of Suetonius' life, which, according to H. Nettleship, *Ancient Lives of Virgil*, Oxford, 1879, was "origi-nally prefixed to the commentary by Aelius Donatus, and usually attributed to him." See also H. Rushton Fairclough in his Loeb edition of Virgil, 2:523.

107:74 Pliny, the younger, *Epistles* V.iii, defended himself for writing lascivious verses by asserting that Virgil had done so, too. Mather may have read Pliny, or have read of him in Vossius, *De Historicis Latinis* (Leyden, 1651), Bk. I, chap. 29, p. 154.

107:74–78 For Seneca on Virgil, see *Episulae Morales*, Letters 59, sec. 3, and 86, secs. 15 and 16. Jerome, *Epistolae*, no. 22, "Ad Eustochium" (*Migne L.* 22:416) reads: "Qui facit cum Psalterio Horatius? cum Evangeliis Maro? . . . simul bibere non debemus calicem Christi, et calicem dæmoniorum." Mather's Latin quotation is from a long interpolation beginning "Refert etiam Pedianum" in the life of Virgil by "Donatus" [Suetonius], which follows the paragraphs on Virgil's detractors in various editions of Virgil, e.g., that of Leyden, 1680. See Arnst Diehl, *Die Viae Virgilianae und ihre antiken Quellen* (Bonn, A. Marcus & E. Weber, 1911), p. 34; for Mather's "Expers," Diehl has "expertem," and for "esset" "fuisset."

108:80–81 J. C. Scaliger, *Poetices Libri Septem* I.ii (4th ed., Heidelberg, 1607, p. 10): "Respiciat ipse sese, quot ineptas, quot spurcas fabellas inserat: quas Græcanicum, scelus olentes sententias identidem inculcent. Certe Symposium, & Phaedrum, atque alia monstra operæ pretium fuerit nunquam legisse." Lactantius accuses

Aristotle of self-contradiction: see *Divinum Institutionum* I.v.22 (Basel, 1521), which Increase Mather owned.

108:82–84   Thomas Fuller, in his *Church History* (3:425), tells the story of Apollonia, concluding: "Were her stomach proportionable to her teeth, a county would scarce afford her a meal's meat." Fuller cites Chemnitius, "In his *Examination of the Council of Trent*, cap. de. Imag. pag. 1," on the belief that the teeth were effectual against the toothache. The *Examen Concilii Tridentini* was the most important work by the German Lutheran theologian Martin Chemnitz (1522–1586), published in four parts, 1565–1573.

108:87–89   Ignatius, *Epistola ad Romanos* iv. 1 (*Migne G*, 5:808); see also Eusebius, *Ecclesiastical History* III.xxxvi.12. The anecdote appears in Fuller, *Holy and Profane State*, 3:206: "But what said Ignatius? *I am Christs wheat, and must be ground with the teeth of beasts, that I may be made Gods pure manchet.*" Fuller's editor Walten cites (1:190) *Divi Irenaei Adversus Haereses* and *Annotationes* (Geneva, 1570), p. 353, ll. 13–14, as Fuller's source. The story is also to be found in Samuel Clarke, *The Marrow of Ecclesiastical Historie* (London, 1650), p. 7. Mather again refers to it in the *Magnalia*, Bk. VII, 5a:22. Compare Ps. 147.14.

108:90   For "Rage of *Envy*," see Ps. 7.6.

108:96   Howell, *Familiar Letters*, p. 337.

108:96–1   Howell, *ibid.*, p. 351.

108:7–8   For scourging by scorpions, see Deut. 8.15, I Kings 12.11, 14, Luke 10.19, Rev. 9.3–5, 10.

108:8–109:10   See Agrippa's *De Incertitudine*, "De Lectorem," *passim*.

109:10–28   Jewel's *Apologia Ecclesiae Anglicanæ* (London, 1562) was an important statement of the case of the Church of England against Rome, and Mather therefore could call him "Great" in spite of his later opposition to certain of the nonconformists' demands. Laurence Humphrey's *Ioannis Iuelli . . . vita et mors* (London, 1573), pp. 77–79, identifies the scholar as Edward "Year," his persecutor as one Welsh, a "fellow" of Corpus Christi. Mather took the story from Fuller's *Church History* (4:156–158). Fuller cites Humphrey as his source, calls Welsh the "Censor, as I take it," and says that the number of lines in the poem "were about eighty in all." The lines quoted by Mather are the first four and last two of a twelve-line stanza given by Fuller as a sample of the offending verses, which were entitled "Precatio contra Missam, Anno Mariæ primo per Edwardum Annum." Mather's translation follows that by Fuller except that he changes "young youth" to "O Youth," and "But trust me" to "Believe me." "Respondet" for "Respondit" in line one of the Latin was probably a printer's error. Compare also Thomas Fowler, *The History of Corpus Christi College* (Oxford, 1893), pp. 96–97; the appended "Catalogus" of members of the college lists "Thos. Walsthe" as "Socius" or Fellow (p. 380), and the scholar as "Edw. Anne" (p. 386).

109:32–35   It has thus far remained impossible to identify the "*Capsian* mountains in *Spain*." The geographical marvel which most closely approximates the lake described by Mather occurs in Boccaccio, *De montibus, syluis, fontibus, lacubus, fluminibus* (Venice, 1473), under "Montibus": "Canatus citerioris Hispaniae mons excelsus est, cuius (ut aiunt) in vertice lacus . . ." This lake is like Mather's in that, when a stone is thrown into it, a great storm arises. Unlike Mather's lake, there is no mention of smoke and a cloud, nor of any duration of time, and in Boccaccio, the presence of demons is conjectured. It is doubtful that Cotton Mather read Boccaccio; he may have seen this lake mentioned by Simon Maiolo, in his *Dies Caniculares*, *Illustrissimi et Reverendissimi Praesulis* (Mainz, 1610), p. 232. Maiolo follows Boccaccio's account of the lake on Mt. Canatus except that there is no mention of demons. Maiolo also cites "Lucius Marinæus Hisp. lib.i. in fin.," the reference being to Marinæus' *Hispaniæ illustratæ seu Rerum Urbiumque Hispaniæ, Lusitaniæ, Aethiopiæ et*

Indiæ Scriptorum varii (Frankfurt, 1603), p. 838, where there is a description by Heironymus Paulus Barcinonensis of a miraculous lake on Mt. Canatus, which is precisely located on the "hither" side of the Pyrenees, toward Gallia Narbonensis, and looking toward the fields of Ruscino. In this account the agitation of the lake is caused by waters boiling up through conduits from the underworld; the lake is definitely an abode of demons, and its waters poison vegetation. As Maiolo notes in his account, however, "tamen alii eiusdem naturæ laci, dequibus postea pluribus," and there were many accounts of such marvels of nature. Boccaccio also describes (under "Lacubus") a miraculous lake in the Apennines, named Scaphagiolus, near Pistoia, where great storms are generated when even the smallest object falls in "by chance," the force of whose winds uproots surrounding oak and fig trees. Mather's father Increase, in his *Remarkable Providences* (Boston, 1684), p. 100, refers to "strange Fountains in *New Spain*, which Ebb and Flow with the Sea," and to a "Pit near *St. Bartholmew's*" where, if a stone is thrown, a great clap of thunder is heard. Cotton Mather may well have been combining remembered details from accounts of several such phenomena.

109:39   For "Catholic Spirit of Communion," cf. I Cor. 10.16–17, II Cor. 12.13, 25–27.

110:44–48   This passage follows very closely the account in Louis Aubery's *Mémoires* (pp. 29–30) as translated by Thomas Brown, *Princes of Orange* (pp. 20–21).

110:56–57   *Responsio ad Rationes Decem Edmundi Campiani* (London, 1581), p. 9.

110:60   Martial, *Epigrams* VI.lx.

110:62   For "Communications," cf. Luke 24.17, Philem. 6.

110:64–65   Compare also Ezek. 34.27, 36.30, Luke 3.9, 6.43. "The tree as a symbol of spiritual life remained a precious and inspiring figure throughout Hebrew-Christian litrature. The tree of Eden stood for knowledge and life. The author of Revelation saw Christianity as the 'tree of life'" (Rev. 22.2, 14). See G. A. Buttrick *et al.*, eds., *The Interpreter's Bible* (New York, Abingdon Cokesbury Press, 1952–57), 2:438–439.

110:68   See Acts 7.57–60 for the stoning of Stephen. The epitaph is given by Venantius Fortunatus in his *Miscellanea* I.3 (*Migne L*, 88:67). For his "rock was Christ," cf. Matt. 16.18. In typology "rock" was a word with many implications. It represented Christ (I Cor. 10.4); the water that issued from it (Exod. 17.6) was Christ's spirit. For other typological interpretations and Biblicial references, see Samuel Mather, *Figures*, pp. 142–144.

110:69–72   At the Council of Constance, May 4, 1415, Wycliffe's remains were ordered dug up and burned. At the command of Pope Martin V, the order was carried out in 1428. Thomas Walsingham recounts this "monkery" under the heading "Rumores monachorum de morte Wiclif," in his *Historia Anglica* (Frankfurt, 1603), p. 313, which John Speed cites as his source in *The History of Great Britain* (London, 1614), p. 610. Fuller, in his *Church History* (2:425), under a 1430 heading, "A Monk's Charity to Wickliffe," also cites Walsingham, but his translation of the epitaph follows that of Speed: "The devil's instrument, church's enemy, people's confusion, heretic's idol, hypocrite's mirror, schism's broacher, hatred's sower, lie's forger, flattery's sink; who at his death despaired like Cain, and stricken by the horrible judgments of God, breathed forth his wicked soul to the dark mansion of the black devil." The version given by William Turner in his *Remarkable Providences* (p. 157, 3rd Alph.) exactly follows Speed. Any one of the last three might have been Mather's source since all were known to him.

111:75   The King James Version reads "disobedience" instead of "*Unperswadeableness,*" as does the 1599 English Bible. Mather's reading is that of John Trapp's commentary on Colossians 3.6: "Unpersuadable, uncounsellable persons, that regard not good courses or discourses" (*Commentary or Exposition upon . . . the New Testament*, 1st ed. London, 1656; ed. W. Webster, London, 1877, p. 618). The Greek Testament has ἀπειθεια.

111:85–86 Mather's reference is to Solomon Stoddard and the ministers of the Connecticut valley under his leadership, who, at the time Mather wrote, were inaugurating changes in church polity whereby all in a town not openly scandalous were not only admitted to the church but were brought to the sacraments. (See Miller, *Puritans*, New York, 1938, p. 770.)

111:91–5 There was no one whose support of the *"Congregational Church-Discipline"* of New England Mather would more eagerly invoke than that of Richard Baxter, whose life-long efforts, despite persecution, were directed toward church-concord. He had long associations with the Mathers, and as recently as Aug. 3, 1691, had written to Increase: "I am as zealous a lover of the New England Churches as any man, according to Mr. Noyes', Mr. Norton's, and Mr. Mitchael's, and the Synod's model. I love your father upon the letters I received from him. I love *you* better for your learning, labours, and peaceable moderation . . . I love your *son* better than either of you, for the excellent temper that appeareth in his writings." Mather printed the letter in the *Magnalia*, Bk. III, pp. 210–211, following the life of John Eliot, noting it has been written "upon the Sight of Mr. *Eliot's* LIFE, in a Former edition."

Baxter often did indeed sound like a Congregationalist: "A particular Church of Christs Institution . . . is, *A competent number of Neighbour-Christians, who by Christs appointment . . . are associated with one or more Pastors*, for the right worshipping of God in publick: (*Whether Parish Congregations be True Christian Churches*, London, 1684, pp. 2–3). At the same time, he always professed not to oppose prelacy as such, only "the old diocesan frame" (*The Autobiography of Richard Baxter*, ed. J. M. Lloyd Thomas, London, J. M. Dent & Sons, 1925, p. 155), although his definition of acceptable "Congregational Bishops" as "but the *Governors of true particular churches*" (p. 13 of "A Theological Dialogue" in *Whether Parish Churches*) obviously could never satisfy the established church. And certainly his statement "That I had rather the Church had a Liturgy (to make all foreknow what Worship they meet for) with free prayer also in its place, than to have either alone" (*ibid.*, p. 32) hardly accorded with New England doctrine. Baxter himself felt that his *Five Disputations of Church-Government and Worship* (London, 1659) correctly represented his ecclesiastical tenets (*Autobiography*, pp. 152–153). For sections relevant to Congregational polity, see particularly Disputation II, "Those who Nullify our present Ministry and churches which have not the Prelatical Ordination . . . do incur the guilt of grievous sin," and the section on Synods in Disputation III (pp. 347–348): "*Synods* . . . are not directly for *Government*, but for *Concord* and *Communion* of Churches . . . If any think that this doth too much favour the Congregational way, I must tell him that it is true and clear, that the Episcopal men that are moderate acknowledge it."

New England's greatest expositor of ecclesiastical doctrine was Thomas Hooker, in his *A Survey of the Summe of Church-Discipline*. For a description of New England Congregational church discipline, see Miller, *Orthodoxy in Massachusetts* (Cambridge, Mass.: Harvard University Press, 1933). particularly Chapter IV, "Non-Separating Congregationalism"; *The New England Mind: The Seventeenth Century*, particularly chap. XV, "The Church Covenant"; *The New England Mind: From Colony to Province* (Cambridge, Mass.: Harvard University Press, 1953), particularly pp. 216–225 for the dissensions and factional quarrels within the churches to which Mather is obviously referring in ll. 48–64. For the efforts of Cotton Mather and his father Increase to counteract those who "have an unhappy Narrowness of Soul" and to effect greater unity among Protestant bodies, see endnote to Attestation p. 70, ll. 16–19.

112:7–9 Mather here follows Matthew Henry's *An Account of the Life and Death of Mr. Philip Henry* (London, 1698), p. 8, which speaks of the quotation as the saying of "some Wise men." Mather changed the tenses of Matthew Henry's text, put Ussher first instead of last, and substituted "Breaches" for "Wounds." In J. B. Williams's edition of Matthew Henry's *Account* (London, 1825), p. 6, he annotates the passage in question: "Mr. Baxter used to say so. Neal's History of the Puritans, v. 3, p. 349, ed. 1795." Daniel Neal's *History* was first published in London in 1732–1738, more than forty years after Richard Baxter's death. Neal gives no authority for his attribution of the saying.

112:19–27 This passage, taken almost word for word from Heidfeld's *Sphinx* (p. 894), illustrates both Mather's reliance on books of reference and his occasional pedantic heaping up of more learned references than are necessary to illustrate his point. Here he gives four instances of "generosity" when, it seems, one or two would have sufficed.

113:48–49 Compare John 3.16, Rom. 5.16–17, Gal. 2.20, Eph. 5.2.

113:50–57 For "*give ourselves*," see II Cor. 8.5. The King James version has "they did, not as we hoped, but first gave their own selves to the Lord." "Hoped" here means "expected," translated in the 1599 Bible as "looked for." See also I Tim. 4.15. For "All that we *have*," cf. Luke 12.22–31; for "*Angels in Heaven*," Pss. 103.20, 148.2; for "higher Felicity," cf. Pss. 147.1, 149.1, 2, 5.

113:52–53 For "*King of Heaven*," see Dan. 4.37, Acts 7.49; for "*Lord of all things*," Matt. 11.25, Acts 17.24; for "*Angels of Light*," II Cor. 4.4, 6; for "*Love to glorifie*," Pss. 147.1, 148.2, 149.1, 2, 5, etc.

113:54–56 For "*Own thee alone*," see II Kings 19.15, Neh. 9.6, Ps. 83.18, Isa. 37.16; for "*Head*," I Cor. 11.3, Eph. 1.22, 4.15, Col. 1.18, 2.10; for "*Prince*," Isa. 9.6, Acts 5.31; for "*Law-giver*," Isa. 33.22, Jas. 4.12; for "*With thy own Blood*," acts 20.28, Heb. 13.12, Rev. 1.5, 5.9.

113:56–60 For "*Dispensations*," see Eph. 1.10, 3.2, Col. 1.25; for "*Preserved*," I Sam. 30.23, Pss. 16.1, 145.20, Jude 1; for "*Form*," Gen. 2.7, Isa. 43.21; for "*Shew forth thy Praises*," Pss. 9.14, 51.15, 79.13, Isa. 43.21; for "*Bless thy great Name*," Pss. 96.2 100.4, 145.1, 21; for "*Sprinkle . . with thy Blood*," Heb. 9.19–20, 10.22, I Pet. 1.2. Mather probably also remembered "The Printers Preface to the Reader" in George Herbert's "The Temple" (*Works*, p. 4): "when a friend went about to comfort him on his death-bed, he made answer, *It is a good work, if it be sprinkled with the bloud of Christ*."

113:61.62 For "*Truths and Ways*," see Deut. 5.33, Dan. 4.37, Luke 1.76, John 14.6, Rev. 15.3; for "*Prepared*," Ps. 103.19, Luke 1.17, I Cor. 2.9.

113:63–64 The quotation is in Leigh, *Religion and Learning*, p. 322, where it is said to have been written about himself by Nicolaus Selneceerus (Selnecker), professor of divinity at the University of Leipzig.

BOOK I

114:24 For "A FIELD . . . *Acted*," cf. General Introduction, p. 90, ll. 26, 32, and endnote thereto.

114:27 The Hebrew letters *Aleph*, *Yod*, and *He*, standing for the words *if wills the Lord*, are equivalent to the Latin *D.V.* (*Deo volente*) and were often placed at the beginning of a work to acknowledge reliance on God's grace. Compare James 4.15, Acts 18.21, I Cor. 4.19.

114:34 For "Quiet Seats," cf. II Chron. 14.1, 5, Ps. 107.30, I Tim. 2.1–3, Rev. 11.16–17.

114:40 For "Plantations," cf. Isa. 60.21.

115:47–48 For "*Corners*," cf. Rev. 7.1; for "*God in our Lord Jesus*," cf. II Cor. 13–14; for "*called upon*," see Gen. 4.26, Ps. 50.15, Jer. 33.3, Rom. 10.13, etc.

115:50–52 Villegagnon came to be hated by Protestants because, while seeming at first to support their cause, he later rejected it, quarreled with the pastors sent to Brazil from Geneva in 1557, and after their return executed three of the colonists for heresy. Lery and other Protestants accused him of having feigned interest in their cause in order to win support from Coligny and Calvin for colonizing ambitions. Jean Crespin's version of the Brazilian expedition is based on an account of the

"Persécution des fidèles en la terre de l'Amerique" which Lery in 1560 prepared for Crespin for a new edition of his *Histoire des martyrs persécutez et mis à mort pour la vérité de l'Evangile*. (See introduction by Charly Clerc to edition of Lery's *Histoire*, Paris, 1927, pp. 14–15.) Crespin's *Histoire*, first published in 1554, was frequently reprinted. For the account of the Brazil martyrs, see the Geneva edition of 1619, pp. 437–438, 440, 454–455. Lery's own *Histoire*, written in 1563, because of vicissitudes undergone by the manuscript, was not published until 1578. Lery's work was principally an account of the manners, customs, beliefs of the Brazilian Indians, as well as of the flora and fauna of the country. He remarks only briefly on the three martyrs (ed. Geneva, 1594, p. 346).

115:52–53   See Horace *Satires* I.1.120–121. Mather substitutes *lecti* (the excellent) for Horace's *lippi* (the blear-eyed).

115:56–57   For contemporary accounts of the massacres, see de Thou, *The History of the Bloody Massacre of the Protestants in France in the Year of our Lord 1572* (London, 1674), and Sir John Temple, *The Irish Rebellion . . . Together with the Barbarous Cruelties and Bloody Massacre Which Ensued* (London, 1646).

115:62   With the phrase "besides others," Mather would seem to be trying to magnify the range of his erudition. His source for these lines is entirely Leigh's *Religion and Learning* (pp. 340–341), where de Thou is called "a most faithful Historian, and the chief of those of this last Age. President of the Parliament at *Paris*." Leigh quotes "Sir *Simonds D'Ewes* his Primitive practice for preserving Truth. *Sect.* 16" as calling de Thou's history "the most exact and excellent that ever was written by a humane pen." The extract from Casaubon describing de Thou as "exemplum pietatis, integritatis, probitatis" (*Epistolae*, The Hague, 1638, p. 774) is also from Leigh. De Thou's account appears in his *Historiarum sui Temporis Libri CXXXVIII* (5 vols., Geneva, 1625–1630), Vol. I, Bk. 16.

116:72–74   Compare Jer. 22.10.

116:77–83   This last sentence contains phrases and echoes from Ps. 119.29, John 8.50, Neh. 5.19, 13.14, 22, 31, I Cor. 10.31.

116:85   *Aeneid* VI.687.

116:87–117:15   This section is abridged from Increase Mather's *A Dissertation Concerning the Future Conversion of the Jewish Nation*, probably first published in Boston in 1695 or 1696 (cf. Holmes, *Increase Mather*, 1:197). Cotton Mather made use of his father's book in several passages; here he is using chapter 8, pars. 3 and 4 (see 2nd ed., Boston, 1709), where Increase writes that "it is solidly refuted by *Basnagius* in *Exercitat. Historic. Critic.*" that the Apostles preached in America (see Basnage, *De Rebus Sacris et Ecclesiasticis, Exercitationes Historico-Criticae*, Utrecht, 1692, pp. 524–526). In a section on the topic whether "Apostoli ad omnia mundi climata perrexerint," Basnage undertook the following: "Profectionem Apostolicam in Americam ex Scriptura probari non posse, demonstratur." In addition, he argued that had such missions occurred, some record would surely have been found in the "annales evangelium." The opinions of Lactantius, Augustine, and Pope Zachary on the antipodes were often linked by Renaissance commentators. For the much debated question of the meaning of Christ's injunction to his Disciples to preach the gospel to all the world, see *Purchas His Pilgrimes* (London, 1625; cited from ed. Glasgow, 1905–1907, 1:136–139).

116:92   As translated by George Hakewill, *Apologie . . . of the Power and Providence of God* (London, 1630), p. 249. See Lactantius, "De Falsa Sapientia Philosophorum," caput 24, *Divinarum Institutionem* III (*Migne L*, 6:425–426).

117:2   Fuller, *Miscellanea Sacra*, Bk. 2, chap. 4 (Leyden, 1622, p. 1896), cited from *Critici Sacri* (Amsterdam, 1698), 8:903. Compare Acts 11.28.

117:15   *De Civitas Dei* 16.9 (*Migne L*, 41:487).

117:16   Although the King James Version, I John 5.19, reads "wickedness" instead of "wicked one," the Greek ἐν τῷ πονηρῷ may yield either meaning.

117:17   Compare Ezek. 29.3, Rev. 12.7–10, 20.1–2.

117:22 Flavio did not discover the loadstone; he developed an arrangement of the elements of the compass that greatly increased its usefulness for navigators. Compare Peter Heylin, *Cosmographie* (London, 1666), p. 1003: "In the year 1300. one *Flavio* of *Malphi* in the Realm of *Naples* found out the *Compass*," possibly Mather's source.

117:25 Compare Gal. 4.4 and Eph. 1.10 for "the fulness of Time." In 1684 Samuel Sewall asked Cotton Mather "why the Heart of America may not be the seat of the New-Jerusalem" (4 M.H.S. *Coll.* 8:516–517), referring to Dr. Twisse's letter to Joseph Mede (see Mede, *Works*, p. 798).

117:28 *Bibliotheca Historica* V.20.3.

117:31–33 *Timaeus* 24.E.

118:40 For "*Silver Trumpets*," cf. Num. 10.2.

118:47 Strabo *Geography* II.5.6. Compare Sir Thomas Browne, *Religio Medici* (in *Works*, ed. G. Keynes, 6 vols., London, Faber & Gwyer, Ltd., 1928), 1:68: "Judgments that wrap the church of God in Strabo's *cloak*."

118:54–55 Augustine, *In Joannis Evangelium Tractatus* 118.4 (*Migne L*, 35:1949). Mather's quotation is exact except for "Jesu" in place of Augustine's "Jesu Christi."

118:58 Cotton Mather refers to the story of Madoc, a Welsh prince said to have colonized America in 1170. All subsequent accounts of Madoc rely on David Powel, *The History of Cambria, now called Wales, written in the Brytish language . . . translated into English* (London, 1584), pp. 228–229. As evidences, Powel cites Montezuma's acknowledgment that the Mexican rulers were "descended from a strange nation, that came thither from a farre countrie"; "the people honored the crosse" [Mather's "popish reliques"]; they used "Brytish or Welsh" words. As an example, Powel cited "a certeine bird with a white head, which they call Pengwin, that is, white head." Mather may have found the account in John Ogilby's *America: Being an Accurate Description of the New World, etc.*, *Collected and translated* [out of Arnoldus Montanus] (London, 1670), pp. 36–37, who follows Powel closely, or in John Smith, "How Ancient Authors Report the New World was Discovered," in *Travels and Works of Captain John Smith* (ed. A. G. Bradley, 2. vols., New York, Franklin, 1966), 1:303–304.

119:67 From this point forward in his history of the New England settlements, Cotton Mather relied heavily on William Hubbard's *History of New England from the Year 1620 to the Year 1680*, to the complete manuscript of which Mather had access. (For the history of the publication of Hubbard's work, see endnote to Attestation, p. 69, l. 6–p. 70, l. 19. All citations in these notes are to the revised 1848 edition published by the Massachusetts Historical Society; the recovered pages will be referred to as Hubbard, *Rpp.*) Not only did Mather largely follow Hubbard's ordering of details, but he constantly paraphrased him, appropriated words and phrases, even repeated Hubbard's errors. Mather begins his close dependence on Hubbard on page 5 (*Rpp.*), where Hubbard has "Christopher Columbus, a Genoesian, had the happiness and honor first to discover"; Mather foregoes "happiness," retains "honor."

119:70 Vespucci's claims to have made four voyages to America and to have discovered the continent are not generally accepted today, but Mather's authorities do not question them. See Ogilby, *America* (pp. 60–65), who dates the first voyage 1497–1498; this is the voyage subject to the greatest doubt.

119:73 *Rerum Memorabilium sive Deperditarum, et contra recens Inventarum, Libri Duo*, Frankfort, 1660. Panciroli, however, classes America not as a *res deperdita*, but as a *res inventa*, and ascribed its discovery to Columbus (*Liber* II, p. 20).

119:75–78 Mather was misled concerning Drake's ship—and voyage—by his source, Heidfeld's *Sphinx* (pp. 344–345), the relevant passage being: "Accidit nostro seculo, vidit cum admiratione nostra aetas, ut navis e classe Castellae regum ductore Draco, nobilissimo Anglo, universum orbis terrarum ambitum circumlegerit & incolumis unde solverat, reversa sit. Unde merito Victoria appellata est, juxta hoc ejusdem apophthegmata.

> Prima ego velivolis ambivi cursibus orbem,
> Magellane, novo te duce ducta freto.

Sic et Ecclesia Christi totum circumgitavit orbem, ut nunc finem mundi haud procul abesse, credere fas sit." Heidfeld was, of course, completely in error in saying that "a ship from the fleet of the Kings of Castille, under Drake as leader, a most noble Englishman, circumnavigated the whole circuit of the globe and returned safe whence it set out. Whence deservedly it is called 'Victory,' along with this apothegm of the same.

> I first went about the world in my sail-driven coursings,
> Magellan, under you as leader, led by a new strait."

On the map of the Pacific Ocean by Ortelius, 1589 (reproduced in A. S. Hildebrand, *Magellan*, New York, Harcourt Brace & Co., 1924, p. 253), the apothegm encircles a drawing of the *Victory*, the "I" being "I, the ship," that went about, etc. It is extraordinary that Mather should have been so ignorant of the exploits of the great Sir Francis Drake as to accept Heidfeld's assigning him to a Spanish fleet. Perhaps he did sense something wrong, and for that reason dropped the second line of the apothegm, with its reference to Magellan.

Mather reverses Heidfeld's order, and the two lines following the apothegm appear as Mather's introduction to his reference to Drake, with its image of a ship as a metaphor of the church. Mather's uncle, Samuel, in his *Figures or Types*, wrote that "Noah was a Type of Christ *in regard of his saving those that did believe his teaching* . . . from the Common Deluge and Destruction." He "built the *Ark according to the Mind of God . . . All that God commanded so did he*. So Christ buildeth the Church in perfect Faithfulness to his Fathers Will, Heb. 3.2.3." That there were "*any great Ships* before the Flood is not probable: So that here it seems was the beginning of the Art of Navigation and Shipping" (p. 27), and "the Ark was a type of the Church." "The Church is resembled by a Ship: so Isa. 54.11. Here the Church is compared to a Ship, resembling somewhat in the Church" (p. 73).

119:80 An English translation by Sir Paul Rycaut of Garcilaso's *Commentarios Reales de los Incas* (Lisbon, 1609) was published in London in 1688 as *The Royal Commentaries of Peru*. It is difficult to believe Mather had not looked into it since his account of the pilot Sanchez closely parallels the wording and sequence of details on the first page of that work.

119:91–120:5 Mather paraphrases Hubbard (*Rpp.*, pp. 5–6) throughout this passage on the Cabots. For example, Hubbard's "notable discoveries" become Mather's "notable Enterprizes"; compare also Hubbard's "foundation and groundwork of those noble adventures made afterwards by some of the English nation" with Mather, lines 4–5. Sebastian's pension, according to Hubbard, was £166. 13s. 4d. For "in a good Old Age," see Gen. 25.8, Judg. 8.32, I Chron. 29.28.

120:8–9 These explorers and adventurers are all listed in Hubbard (*Rpp.*, pp. 6–7).

120:14–18 Mather is here abridging the account in Hubbard (*Rpp.*, pp. 8, 9). Hubbard is explicit in speaking of "that part of the country of Florida called Roanoke." After recounting the obliteration of the colony, he continues: "The planting of any place about Florida being thus nipped in the bud, if not blasted." He conjectures at some length concerning the significance of the name of Virginia Dare. Mather selected one of his conjectures, and followed his error in dating the child's birth. It was Raleigh who originally, in complement to the Queen, bestowed the name of Virginia on the territory, following the expedition of exploration he sent out in 1584 under Philip Amadas and Arthur Barlow.

120:18–19 An account of this voyage led by Captain Gosnold was written by John

Brereton, "one of the voyage," as *A Brief and True Relation of the Discovery of the North Part of Virginia . . . Made This Present Year 1602 . . .* see John Smith, *General Historie of Virginia*, London, 1624, in *Works*, 1:332–335). Brereton's narrative is the earliest of English eyewitness accounts of New England. A portion of it is included in Louis B. Wright, *The Elizabethans' America* pp. 137–144. In the following year was written "A relation of the Voyage made to Virginia . . . by Captaine Bartholomew Gilbert, in the yeere 1603. Written by Master Thomas Canner . . . his companion in the same Voyage" (see *Purchas His Pilgrimes*, 18:329–335).

120:21–25   Correctly given by Brereton (*Elizabethans' America*, p. 137). Mather's error was copied from Hubbard (Rpp., p. 9). Hubbard continues with Gosnold's "finding himself embayed with a mighty headland"; in Mather "he found himself Embayed within a mighty Head of Land".

121:30–32   Compare also Isa. 16.9, Jer. 40.10, 12, 48.32, Amos 8.1, 2, Mic. 7.1. The "*Summer-Fruits*" encountered on Cape Cod by Gosnold's companions were "strawberries, red and white, as sweet and much bigger than ours in England, raspberries, gooseberries, hurtleberries"; the "*Wild Creatures*," "great store of deer . . . and other beasts, as appeared by their tracks, as also divers fowls, as cranes, heronshaws, bitterns, geese, mallards, teals"; the "*wilder People* now surprized into Courtesie," "tall, big-boned men, all naked," who "gave us of their fish, ready boiled . . . They gave us also of their tobacco" (*Elizabethans' America*, p. 139).

121:33–34   Compare Hubbard (*History*, p. 11): "yet . . . the report they carried back was not like that of the unbelieving spies, for it gave encouragement."

121:38–39   The play on "Purchas" and "purchase" first appears in the Epistle to the Reader (p. [2]) of the 1614 edition of *Purchas His Pilgrimage; or, Relations of the World and the Relations observed in all Ages*, and is repeated in the 1617 and 1626 editions of that work; a copy of the 1617 edition was in the Mather library.

121:44   Compare George L. Kittredge, "Cotton Mather's Election into the Royal Society," *Col. Soc. Mass. Pub.*, 14:81–114, 281–292; and "Cotton Mather's Scientific Communications to the Royal Society," *AAS Proc.*, N.S., 26:18–57.

121:47–122:61   This account, with minor changes (e.g., "an animal" for "Behemoth, an amphibious animal"), is taken from Avril, *Voyages en Divers Etats D'Europe et D'Asie* (Paris, 1693), pp. 175–176.

122:66–68   What Mather presents as the "words" of Captain Waymouth is a composite of two sentences in Hubbard. The first (*Rpp.*, p. 12) states that it was "one main end of all the forementioned adventurers [among them Waymouth] . . . to plant the Gospel there." In the second (p. 14), Hubbard says that "Mr. Rosier, that came along with Capt. Weymouth," expressed their purpose "to propagate God's holy church, by planting Christianity in these dark corners of the earth." In calling Waymouth an "Historian," Mather perhaps confused him with James Rosier, "a gentleman employed in the voyage," who immediately upon their return wrote *A True Relation of the Most Prosperous Voyage Made This Present Year 1605 by Captaine George Waymouth* (London, 1605): "For we supposing not a little present private profit, but a public good, and true zeal of promulgating God's holy church, by planting Christianity, to be the sole intent of the honorable setters forth of this discovery" (as reprinted in 3 M.H.S. *Coll.* 8:153).

122:72   At least one copy of the *Magnalia* reads "*sola! End,*" corrected in other copies examined to "*sole end.*"

122:78   For Smith's map of New England, see *Works*, 2:694. A facsimile is published in William Bradford's *History of Plymouth Plantation*, ed. Worthington C. Ford (2 vols., Boston, Houghton Mifflin Company for M.H.S., 1912), 1:189.

122:81   Mather here paraphrases Hubbard (p. 14): "one of the principal daughters of the Chief Lady of the European world from whence she is descended."

122:82   The patent to the New England Council, which superseded the Plymouth Company, was sealed on November 3, 1620, and embraced all lands between 40 and 48 degrees north latitude. For the text, see Ebenezer Hazard, *Historical Collections* (2 vols., Philadelphia, 1792–1794), 1:103–118.

122:90–123:97 These lines again echo Increase Mather's *Dissertation Concerning . . . the Jewish Nation*, chap. 8, par. 3.

122:91 For "*Spied out,*" see Num. 13.16–17. Mather repeatedly played with the figure of the "spies," the men from Eshkol; it was one of his devices for sustaining the image of New England as the New Israel.

122:32–33 For "*Resting-place.*" see Num. 10.33; for "*Hiding-place,*" see Pss. 32.7, 119.114, Isa. 32.2.

123:98–20 Throughout section 7, Cotton Mather is very largely echoing or excerpting words and phrases from the *Jewish Nation* (chap. 8, pars. 3 and 4), particularly the passages on Gog and Magog and the New Jerusalem. For what was to be expected "at the descent of our Lord," cf. Rev. 20.4, 7, 8, 15, 21.4 ff.

123:10 *L'Oeconomie Divine* (7 vols., Amsterdam, 1687), 5:468–471.

123:16 For "Vanity," cf. Ps. 39.5, 11, Eccles. 1.2, 14, Isa. 40.17, 23.

123:19 The Grand Apostate and his Legions represented both the devil and his angels, and, by extension, the Roman Catholic Church. For their doom, cf. Matt. 25.41. For "deceive the Nations," cf. II Thess. 2.3–8.

123:25 *et seq.* For his two chapters on the Plymouth Colony, Mather continued his reliance on Hubbard, at the same time making liberal use of a manuscript copy of Bradfords' *History of Plymouth Plantation* (all citations are to the edition by W. C. Ford), of Nathaniel Morton's *New Englands Memoriall* (Cambridge, Mass., 1669; ed. Arthur Lord, Boston, Club of Odd Volumes, 1903), of Edward Winslow's *Hypocrisie Unmasked*, and occasionally of *Mourt's Relation* (London, 1622; ed. H. M. Dexter, Boston, 1865).

124:29–31 Compare Hubbard, p. 42.

124:31 Compare Eccles. 7.29.

124:46–53– Mather's passage on Robinson follows Hubbard (pp. 42–43) closely; for example, he takes over Hubbard's figure of Robinson as "*sowred* in his *younger* time." Hubbard has: "like some fruit, that before it is ripe is harsh, sour, and unpleasant . . . till it attain . . . the sweetness of riper age." Quite naturally Bradford had felt no need to excuse Robinson's Separatism and hence he makes no reference to his ecclesiastical controversy with "Dr. *Amiss*"; but for Mather, following Hubbard, it was advantageous to picture Robinson as finally weaned away from the Separatist position, the better to enshrine him among New England's progenitors. It should perhaps be noted that in Holland Dr. Ames was known by the Latin form *Amesius*, which adds point to the word play of "Amiss."

For Robinson's earlier opinion on Separation, see *An Answer to a Censorious Epistle* (1608), in *Works*, (ed. Robert Ashton, Boston, 1851), 3:405–420; *A Justification of Separation from the Church of England* 1610), in *Works*, Vol. 2; "Letters that passed betwixt Mr. Ames and Mr. Robinson touching the bitterness of the separation," *Works*, 3:85–89; Christopher Lawne *et al.*, *The Prophane Schism* (London, 1612), pp. 47–51. For his later position see *A Manumission to a Manuduction* (1615) in 4 M.H.S. *Coll.* 1:165–194. The *Treatise on the Lawfullness* is in *Works*, 3:337–393.

124:58 Note that Mather associates "embalmed" with the "ointment" of Eccles. 7.1; "A good name is better than a precious ointment."

125:60–70 These lines paraphrase Winslow, *Hypocrisie Unmasked* (p. 95). Indeed, lines 66–70 are, with the omission of a few words, direct quotation.

During the Pilgrims' Dutch sojourn, Leyden was a stronghold of Calvinist orthodoxy, and a refuge for others besides the English. The Walloons in Leyden were, according to Bradford (1:46), "of the french church in that citie"—that is, they followed the rigorously Calvinist French Confession. Large numbers of Walloons, refugees from the Inquisition, had fled to the Dutch provinces from their homes in southern Belgium still held by Spain. Their name derives from the Old French *Wallon* (Gualon). Their pastor Hommius was one of the most vigorous combatants against the Arminian Remonstrants, who favored revision of the Confession and Catechism of the Dutch Reformed Church. The conflict with Episcopius had all the ardour of political battle, since the Remonstrants were followers of John of Barneveldt, who wanted an Erastian national church and favored the unpopular truce with Spain, and the Calvinist Contra-Remonstrants, who were followers of Prince Maurice, in favour of a free church in a free state, and bent on continuing war with Spain. For a detailed account of the strife between the Calvinist and Arminian theologians, and churches, in Leyden, see H. M. Dexter, *The England and Holland of the Pilgrims* (Boston, Houghton Mifflin Company, 1905), pp. 525–592, *passim*, and *The Encyclopaedia of Religion and Ethics* (ed. J. Hastings, New York, Charles Scribner's Sons, 1928), 10:30–31.

125:65   In the Preface (p. [3]) to *The Principles of the Protestant Religion Maintained . . . Against . . . one George Keith, a Quaker* (Boston, 1690), by the "Ministers of Boston," namely, James Allen, Joshua Moody, Samuel Willard, and Cotton Mather, the "*great* Choak-weed *of the Christian* & Protestant *Religion*" has become Quakerism.

125:71–86   Mather follows his sources studiously in these lines. Hubbard (p. 42) speaks of the unwholesomeness of the "watery situation," and says it was "uncomfortable for their purses and estates." On p. 44 (where he writes, "see Morton, page 4") he lists further reasons for the desire of the English band in Leyden to leave, including not "losing their interest in the English nation," and "to enlarge his Majesty's dominion." Morton (*Memoriall*, pp. 3–4) follows his uncle Bradford's list of reasons (1:53–55)—the "great licentiousness of Youth in that Country," the fear that "their Posterity would in a few generations become *Dutch*," etc. But whereas all three, as in Morton's words, speak of "a great hope and inward Zeal they had of laying some good Foundation . . . for the propagating and advancement of the Gospel of the Kingdome of Christ in those remote parts of the World," Mather specifies that the zeal was for "the establishment of Congregational Churches."

125:92–126:8   For this entire passage, Mather follows Morton (p. 4), who in turn has followed Bradford (cf. Bradford, 1:98, for lines 97–1, and 1:44–46, for lines 1–8. During these years, almost all the Leyden magistrates sympathized with the Remonstrants, a circumstance which may account for their finding the Calvinist Walloons, led by Hommius, contumacious and quarrelsome (cf. Dexter, *England and Holland of the Pilgrims*, p. 570). The comparison of the removal from Leyden to the departure of the Israelites from Egypt is in Morton. For "Ten Years" (line 7), Bradford has twelve.

126:98   John 14.2.

126:9–11   The likening of the removal to Abraham's departure from the "*Caldean* Territories" is in Hubbard (p. 52); cf. Gen. 12.1, 2.

126:12 *et seq.*   From this point to the end of section 3, Mather's chief source was Hubbard (pp. 44–50). Hubbard begins thus: having "resolved upon their 'terminus a quo,' viz. to leave Holland, the next and no less difficult question was the 'terminus ad quem,'" and proceeds to the considerations on Guiana.

126:22   On page 47, Hubbard goes into greater detail concerning the "Persons about the Court" whose help was solicited, particularly Sir John Worstenholme, a letter to whom by William Brewster and John Robinson appears in Bradford (1:77–78). The negotiations with the Virginia Company are detailed in Bradford (1:65–96), including a letter from Sir Edwin Sandys to Robinson and Brewster (1:70–73).

126:23   Affirmation of agreement with the French—and Dutch Reformed—churches had become a point of policy with English protestants. Marian exiles in Frankfort in 1554 had subscribed to the doctrines and practices of the French church (cf. Bradford, 1:78 n. 3), and Robinson expressed the attitude of the Leyden church toward the French and Dutch churches: "we acknowledge [them] for true churches" (*Works*, 3:128). For Robinson and his congregation, this affirmation of solidarity was a politic assurance that they, like the French, would be submissive to lawful rulers:

"The oath of Supremacie we shall willingly take if it be required of us," Robinson and Brewster wrote to the negotiators in London (Bradford, 1:78–82). They then listed their "small differences . . . in some accidental circumstances" (such as praying with heads covered or uncovered, the length of service of elders and deacons, etc.) from the French.

Mather's reason for retaining this sentence from Hubbard (p. 47) was probably a desire both to exhibit the Leyden company as adhering to the "enlarged catholic spirit" which he and his father were so eagerly promoting at the time, and, by implication, to reinforce their own professions of allegiance to the throne.

126:27–30 It is not clear that the Archbishop did, in fact, give them any satisfaction. Winslow (*Hypocrisie Unmasked*, p. 90) says that when the King asked their agents to confer with "the Bishops of *Canterbury* and *London* . . . wee were advised to persist upon his [the King's] first approbation, and not to entangle ourselves with them." And Bradford (1:66–68) says "diverse of good worth laboured with the king to obtaine it . . . and some other wrought with the archbishop to give way thereunto, but it proved all in vaine. Yet thus farr they prevailed, in sounding his majesties mind, that he would connive at them, and not molest them." Winslow (p. 89) says that it was Sir Edwin Sandys "who procured Sir *Robert Nawnton* . . . to move his Majesty by a private motion to give way to such a people." A note (dated May 16, 1623) of a conversation held by Sir Nathaniel Rich and Captain John Bargrave concerning Sir Edwin Sandys states that Sandys had moved the Archbishop of Canterbury unseccessfully to "give leave to the Brownists and Separatists to go to Virginia." (*Hist. Mss. Com.*, Eighth Report, 2:45).

127:34–39 "This his Majesty said was a good and honest motion, and asking what profits might arise in the part wee intended (for our eye was upon the most Northern parts of *Virginia*) 'twas answered, Fishing" (Winslow, p. 90).

127:35–52 Here Mather drastically abridges his authorities. Both Bradford and, following him, Hubbard say that when the patent from the Virginia Company was sent to them in Leyden to sign, they heard "that sundrie Honourable Lords had obtained a large grante from the king, for the more northerly parts of that countrie, derived out of the Virginia patente, and wholy secluded from their Governmente, and to be called by another name, viz. New-England. Unto which Mr. Weston [an "adventurer"], and the cheefe of them, began to incline it was best for them to goe" (Bradford, 1:100–103). But, says Hubbard (p. 48), "the generality was swayed to the better opinion. Howbeit the Patent for the northern part of the Country not being fully settled at that time, they resolved to adventure with that Patent they had, intending for some place more southward than that they fell upon in their voyage, at Cape Cod."

The "*Articles*" stipulated by the adventurers (lines 12–13) are given in Hubbard (pp. 48–49), after Bradford (1:104–106). The "Division" is described by Bradford (1:103): "some of those that should have gone in England, fell of and would not goe; other merchants and friends that had offered to adventure their moneys withdrew, and pretended many excuses. Some disliking they wente not to Guiana; others againe would adventure nothing excepte they wente to Virginia. Some againe (and those that were most relied on) fell in utter dislike with Virginia, and would doe nothing if they wente thither. In the midds of these distractions, they of Leyden, who had put of their estates, and laid out their moneys, were brought into a greate streight, fearing what issue these things would come too; but at length the generalitie was swaid to this latter opinion."

127:53 *et seq.* The sources for section 4 are chiefly Morton (pp. 5–10) and Bradford (1:121–135). The first paragraph is very close to Bradford's account (1:121), although Bradford does not name the ships. The *Speedwell* is first named in Morton (p. 5). Details of the departure from Delft are also given by Winslow (p. 91).

127:60–61 Compare Heb. 11.10, 13–16.

127:63–67   Compare Mather's account of the mournful parting with Paul's farewell to Ephesus, Acts 20.37, 38.

128:70   For "*Companions of the Voyage,*" cf. Acts 19.29.

128:71   As given in a note by Bradford (1:126n.): "This was about .22. of July." Mather follows Morton (p. 10).

128:72–85   For the "Holy Counsels," cf. Acts 20.17–32. Robinson's pastoral letter is given in Bradford (1:130–135); Bradford calls it "so frutfull in it selfe . . . I thought meete to inserte in this place." See also Morton (pp. 6–9).

128:73   For "settle their *Peace*, etc.," cf. II Cor. 1.12, 4.2, 5.11, I Tim. 1.2, II Tim. 1.2.

128:90   For "*their* greater affliction," cf. Ps. 44.1–2.

128:93–95   Bradford names Reinolds (1:137) and attributes the dropping out of the *Speedwell* to the "cunning and deceite of the master" (1:149–150); Morton elaborates (pp. 10–11).

128:91–95   In these lines Mather adopts many phrases either from Morton (p. 11) or from Bradford at first hand: for example, "after longe beating at sea they fell with that land which is called Cape Cod" (1:151), and "Being thus arrived in a good harbor and brought safe to land, they fell upon their knees and blessed the God of heaven, who had brought them over the vast and furious ocean" (1:155).

128:3–5   Compare Ps. 65.5; the King James Version has "confidence" for "assurance." The 1559 English Bible has "hope" for "confidence." For "*Ends of the Earth,*" cf. General Introduction, 89:15 and endnote.

128:67   Compare *Aeneid* I.16–17.

129:12–30   For this passage, Mather's immediate source was Hubbard (pp. 50–51). The charge of duplicity against the shipmaster was first made by Morton (p. 12), on the basis, he said, of "late and certain Intelligence," namely, that the master had by "fraudulency and contrivance," and because he had been "fraudulently hired" by the Dutch, put on a "pretence of danger of the Sholes."

129:37–130:50   Mather follows Hubbard's account of the Frenchman's prophecy (pp. 54–55), again at second hand from Morton's *Memoriall* (p. 27). Thomas Morton united with Nathaniel Morton on this story of the Frenchman's curse (*New English Canaan*, Amsterdam, 1637, p. 23).

130:51 *et seq.*   Section 7 is largely a paraphrase of Hubbard (pp. 52–53). Compare the account in the "plaine stile" of Bradford (1:153–154): "It is recorded in scripture as a mercie to the apostle and his shipwraked company, that the barbarians shewed them no smale kindnes in refreshing them, but these savage barbarians . . . were readier to fill their sides full of arrows then other wise. And for the season it was winter, and they that know the winters of that cuntrie know them to be sharp and violent, and subjecte to cruell and feirce stormes . . . Besides, what could they see but a hidious and desolate wilderness, full of wild beasts and willd men? . . . For summer being done, all things stand upon them with a wetherbeaten face; and the whole countrie, full of woods and thickets, represented a wild and savage heiw."

130:51–53   For "*chosen Generation,*" cf. I Pet. 2.9; for "*a flight in the Winter,*" see Matt. 24.20, Mark 13.18.

130:61–62   Acts 28.1–2.

130:65   Acts 28.3.

130:70–73   For "*Abraham,* called out of *Ur,*" see Gen. 15.7, Neh. 9.7; for "*Land flowing with Milk and Honey,*" see Exod. 3.8; for "*Trial of the Faith,*" I Pet. 1.7.

130:81–82   An adaption of the *Aeneid* VII.229–230.

131:83–92   Mather, in a brief paragraph, hurries over an episode to which his predecessors devoted considerably greater detail. The want of a valid patent was deeply troubling to Bradford. The immediate necessity of formulating an "*Instrument*" was, he wrote (1:189–191), "occasioned partly by the discontented and mutinous speeches that some of the strangers amongst them had let fall from them in the ship; That when they came a shore they would use their owne libertie; for none had power to command them, the patente they had being for Virginia, with which the Virginia Company had nothing to doe. And partly that shuch an acte by them done . . . might be as firme as any patent, and in some respects more sure." In its first sentence the Compact protested loyalty to "our dread soveraigne Lord, King James." In place of Bradford's reasons, Morton repeats his charge of Dutch fraudulence, and briefly notes the need for "orderly carrying on of their affairs" (p. 14). Hubbard, in his account (p. 62), emphasizes not the settlers' loyalty as subjects but their possession of rights enjoyed under the laws of England. To Mather, at the end of the century, only the profession of loyalty to the crown called for reaffirmation.

131:93–1   From here to the end of section 8, Mather is closest to Morton's account (pp. 16–17), which is a condensation of Bradford (1:162–167). Bradford first likened the finding of Indian corn to the return of "the men from Escholl" (1:165). Both Morton and Hubbard retained the figure.

131:12 *et seq.*   Throughout section 9 Mather abridges, often quoting directly, Morton's *Memoriall* (pp. 18–22).

131:12–13   For "Supplications," cf. Dan. 6.11, 9.20, Job 8.5; for "Consultations." cf. Dan. 6.7.

131:12–19   Compare Bradford (1:167–168): "The month of November being spente in these affairs, and much foule weather falling in, the .6. of *Desember* they sente out their shallop againe with .10. of their principall men, and some sea men, upon further discovery, intending to circulate that deepe bay of Cap-Codd. The weather was very could, and it frose so hard as the sprea of the sea lighting on their coats, they were as if they had been glased." Note Mather's baroque elaboration of this last phrase into "glazed them with an immediate Congelation."

131:19   For "tarried that Night," cf. Gen. 19.2, 24.54, 28.11, 31.54, Num. 22.19, Ruth 3.13, II Sam. 19.7, Jer. 14.8.

132:20–21   See Bradford (1:168): "they made them selves a barricado with loggs and bowes." Morton follows Bradford's language closely here (p. 19).

132:30   For "God their Saviour," cf. Luke 1.47, I Tim. 1.1, 2.3, Tit. 1.3, 2.10, 3.4, Jude 25.

132:31–49   This material is covered in Bradford (1:170–177) and in Hubbard (pp. 56–57), but Mather still seems to be paraphrasing Morton (p. 21).

132:38–39   For other invocations of "the stone of help," cf. Attestation, 64:44–45, and Mather's *Bostonian Ebenezer* (1698), reprinted as the conclusion to Book I of the *Magnalia*. For the "*Lord's Day*," cf. Exod. 16.23.

132:43   An "encouraging Report," unlike that of the spies who "brought up an evil report of the land" (Num. 13.32).

132:44–45   For "pitch their Tents," cf. Gen. 12.8, 26.17, 31.25, Num. 1.52, 9.17, Deut. 1.33, etc.

132:47   Compare *Mourt's Relation* (p. 84): "he [Samoset] told vs the place where we now liue, is called, *Patuxet*." Later (p. 99) Mourt has "*Patuxet, alias New Plimmouth*."

132:50–53   In *Mourt's Relation* (p. 77): "the most losse was Maister *Carvers* and *William Bradfords*, who then lay sicke in bed, and if they had not risen with good speede, had been blowne up with the powder." The date was January 14.

132:53–133:62   Bradford says only (1:192) that, having "begune some small cottages for their habitation . . .they mette and consulted of lawes and orders, both for their civill and military Governmente, as the necessitie of their condition did require, still adding thereunto as urgent occasion in severall times, and as cases did require." Morton is even briefer (p. 22).

133:62 *et seq.*   While Mather continues to keep an eye on Morton's *Memoriall*, Hubbard was probably the principal source for section 10. Bradford gives the bare facts of the sickness (1:193–196).

133:67   Compare Hubbard (p. 58): their trials served "to remind them that they were pilgrims and strangers upon the earth." See also Morton (p. 5), and Heb. 11.15, I Peter 2.11.

133:67–78   In his account of the sickness, Mather's language is close to Morton (p. 22).

133:74   For "Submission to the Will of God," cf. James 4.7.

133:76   Compare II Cor. 5.4.

133:77   For "*Murmur,*" cf. I Cor. 10.10, John 6.43.

133:79–89   This special providence is celebrated by Hubbard (p. 58): "It had been a very easy matter for the savages at that time to have cut them all off, as they had done others before, had not God, by his special providence, laid a restraint upon them, as was promised of old to Israel . . . and if a great part of those had not been removed by death, it was feared they might all have perished for want of food, before any more supplies came from England." Compare also Morton (p. 23) on the mortality of the Indians.

133:84   For "*little Remnant,*" see also II Kings 19.4, 30, 31, II Chron. 30.6.

133:85   See also Dan. 9.23 and 10.11, both of which, in the 1611 King James Version, have "greatly beloved," but with marginal glosses giving the literal Hebrew meaning: "a man of desires."

133:86–87   For "People of God," see Heb. 4.9, 11.25; for "into a *Wilderness* to *Worship Him,*" cf. Exod. 3.18, 5.3, 8.27. For the theme of the wilderness church, see Introductory essay, "The Idea of the Wilderness of the New World."

133:89–90   Compare Bradford (1:198): "All this while the Indians came skulking about them, and would sometimes show them selves aloofe of, but when any approached near them, they would rune away." And Morton (p. 23): "The *Indians* . . . would shew themselves afarre off, but when they endeavoured to come near them, they would run away."

133:92   Compare Hubbard (p. 58): "the heathen, who were come, instead of hating, to fear this poor handful of people."

133:93–94   Where Mather writes of wolves and kids, Morton's metaphor is of lions and lambs (p. 23). Compare I Kings 20.27, Matt. 10.16, Luke 10.3, 12.32.

134:98–10   This paragraph is very close to Hubbard (p. 60), who begins his account by alluding to "Balaam's counsel," and concludes, "surely there is no enchantment against Jacob, nor divination against Israel." Cf. Num. 22.5–6, 23.23.

134:11   Hubbard does not mention the onset of spring, but Mourt speaks of "faire warme" days in early March (p. 82), Bradford of the "spring now approaching" (1:212), and Morton of "the Spring being now come" (p. 29). They had reason to remember.

134:13–19   Mather's principal source here is Hubbard (pp. 58–59). According to Mourt (p. 83), Samoset was from "Monchiggon," or Monhegan Island, and Squanto was one of twenty carried off from Patuxet by Captain Hunt (p. 91).

134:19–23   Mather's language suggests he took his account from *A briefe Relation of the Discovery and Plantation of New England* (London, 1622; cited from 2 M.H.S. *Coll.* 9:6): Hunt, when "ready to set sail, seized upon the poor innocent creatures that in confidence of his honesty had put themselves into his hands. And stowing them under hatches to the number of twenty-four, carried them into the Straits, where he sought to sell them for slaves, and sold as many as he could get money for." *Mourt's Relation* (p. 87) says Hunt took twenty Indians from Patuxet and seven from the Nausites. Captain John Smith provided authority for each of these calculations. In his *Description of New England* (1616), writing of his 1614 expedition, he denounces Hunt as follows: "I haue had many discouragements by the ingratitude of some, the malicious slanders of others . . . but chiefly by one *Hunt,* who was Master of the ship . . . yet he practiced to haue robbed mee of my plots [maps], and obseruations, and so to leaue me alone in a desolate Ile . . . hee abused the Saluages where hee came, and betrayed twenty seauen of these poore innocent soules, which he sould in *Spaine* for slaues; to mooue their hate against our Nation" (*Works*, 1:219). When later he came to write his *Generall Historie* (1624), he accused Hunt of treacherously seeking to prevent a plantation, "thereby to keepe this abounding Countrey still in obscuritie, that onely he and some few Merchants more might enioy wholly the benefit of the Trade," and that he "betraied foure and twenty of those poore Saluages aboord his ship: and most dishonestly, and inhumanely . . . for a little priuate gaine sold those silly Saluages for Rials of eight" (*Works*, 2:698–699). Mather, possibly because he had these conflicting numbers before him, seeks safety in "more than twenty."

134:23–31 Compare Mourt (p. 114): "We told them we were sorry that any English man should give them that offence, that *Hunt* was a bad man, and that all the English that heard of it condemned him for the same." Hubbard also recounts the Indian hostility caused by Hunt's perfidy (p. 39).

134:31–135:35 Squanto had been fortunate enough to get "away for *England*, and was entertained by a Merchant in *London*, and imployed to *Newfound-land* and other parts." (Morton, *Memoriall*, p. 25). The authority for his dwelling "in *Cornehill* with master *Iohn Slanie*, a Marchant," is Mourt (p. 91). For a letter from Thomas Dermer concerning his second New England voyage, of 1619–1620, to "his Worshipfull Friend M. Samuel Purchas," see *A Relation of Plymouth*, in *Purchas His Pilgrims* (19:333).

135:38–43 An account of Squanto's assistance to the settlers is given in Hubbard (pp. 59–60), but Bradford's simple testimonial is the most moving: "He directed them how to set their corne, wher to take fish, and to procure other comodities, and was also their pilott to bring them to vnknowne places for their profitt, and never left them till he dyed" (1:202–203). Compare also Morton (p. 25). For "instruct in the way," cf. Pss. 25.8, 32.8, Acts 18.25.

135:43–49 The terms of the agreement with Massasoit are given in Bradford (1:201–202), in Mourt (pp. 93–94), and in Morton (p. 24). The terms of the second agreement appear in Morton (p. 29) and in Hubbard (p. 61).

135:54–57 According to Bradford, the story was that the plague was "buried in the ground" (1:254). Edward Winslow, *Good Newes from New-England* (London, 1624, cited from Alexander Young, *Chronicles of the Pilgrim Fathers*, 2nd ed., Boston, 1844, pp. 291–292), elaborated, locating it "in our storehouse."

135:61 According to Bradford (1:221), the Narragansets "were a strong people, and many in number, living compacte togeather, and had not been at all touched with this wasting plague." Hubbard (p. 67) adds the information that they were "more potent than their neighbors . . . and grown very insolent also, as having escaped the late mortality, which made them aspire to be lords over their neighbors."

135:64 Compare Prov. 16.33, Job 34.13.

135:66 Horace *Odes* I.vi.9.

136:70 John Carver, on the signing of the Mayflower Compact, was confirmed as governor and was reelected the following March, but died a few weeks later. Hubbard (p. 67) calls him "a gentleman of singular piety, rare humility, and great condescendency; one also of a public spirit, as well as of a public purse, having disbursed the greatest part of that considerable estate God had given him, for the carrying on the interest of the company, as their urgent necessity required."

136:71 See *Magnalia*, Bk. II, chap. 1, sec. 2.

136:74–76 Compare Bradford (1:283) and Hubbard (p. 76); Mather has "them" instead of Bradford as the recipient of Squanto's prayer.

136:77 For the lines on Hobbamok, cf. Hubbard (p. 68).

136:80–84 Only Bradford mentions the "twelfe month" anniversary (1:231), which suggests that Mather was here making use of Bradford's history. The "Friends" were Robert Cushman, in the ship *The Fortune*, Thomas Barton master, with thirty-five persons. There is no statement in Bradford, Morton, or Smith that the passengers were all old friends from Holland. However, the list in the *Plymouth Colony Records*

(XII:5) contains the names of many who had been with the Pilgrims in Leyden (see also Bradford, 1:231; *Mourt's Relation*, pp. 62–63). Bradford (1:233) sadly remarked that "the plantation was glad of this addition of strenght, but could have wished that many of them had been of beter condition, and all of them beter furnished with provissions." Compare also Morton (p. 33), who notes that their want of provisions "was one cause of a great famine," and Hubbard (p. 69), who says they "overstored the Plantation with number of people in proportion to the provision."

136:85–87　The quotations, slightly abridged, from Peter Martyr, and the meditation thereon, are in Bradford (1:303–304), whom Morton follows almost word for word (pp. 44–45). Mather further abridges the second quotation, and changes "five dayes" to "three days." Morton had changed Bradford's "saturity" to "satiety," and Mather follows him. For Peter Martyr's text, correctly referred to by Bradford, see *De Nouo Orbe, or The Historie of the West Indies* (London, 1612), pp. 208, 94.

136:93–94　For "other Men . . . with ease," cf. John 4.38.

136:95–99　Bradford recounts the "pretie shift" they made to obtain and apportion food (1:274–275); cf. also Morton (p. 45).

136:1　Compare Ps. 116.12.

136:4–6　The letter that informed Bradford of the Virginia massacre was from the master of a fishing vessel, John Hudleston (cf. Bradford, 1:273). Bradford immediately continues (1:275–276) with the building of the fort, adding that "the hearing of that great massacre in Virginia, made all hands willing to despatch the same." Compare also Smith, *Generall Historie* (2:760), giving an abstract of "diuers Relations" received from New England: "Since the massacre in Virginia, though the *Indians* continue their wonted friendship, yet wee are more wary of them then before."

For "Nightly *Watch*," cf. Pss. 63.6, 119.148, 90.4, Matt. 14.25, Mark 6.48, Isa 21.11.

136:7–137:25　Mather follows Morton (*Memoriall*, pp. 37–38) and, less closely, Hubbard (p. 74) in his account of the drought, placing it in the year 1622. Bradford originally inserted an account of the drought at this date, but finding he had mistaken the year, he rewrote it in proper sequence, that is, in 1623 (1:324–325; cf. p. 276n).

137:19　Morton (p. 38) identifies the Indian as "Hobamak," and Mather quotes the Indian's words from him.

137:19–20　Compare Exod. 18.1, Ps. 20.6.

137:25　Compare Ps. 65.2, Prov. 15.29.

137:26–139:98　Mather' saccount is largely based on Winslow, *Good Newes from New England. Good Newes* was written to tell the story of Weston's "disorderly colony," who "were a stain to Old England that bred them . . . and . . . will be no less to New England in their vile and clamorous reports" (p. 276). In addition there are a number of verbal echoes of Morton's *Memoriall*.

137:27–30　These lines follow Morton (pp. 35–36), who says the two ships were the *Sparrow* and the *Charity*, with "sixty lusty men." According to Winslow (*Good Newes*, pp. 293, 296, and so in Bradford, 1:257, 262), the *Sparrow* arrived in May, and the two ships arriving together were the *Charity* and the *Swan* in July, "having in them some fifty or sixty men," who joined six or seven from the *Sparrow* who had stayed at Plymouth.

137:33–35　Although Mather's sources do not record the fact that Weston's men were Church-of-England men, Daniel Neal, *History of New England* (2nd ed., 2 vols., London, 1747, 1:112) says that Weston "obtained a Patent for Part of the Massachusetts Bay under pretence of Propagating the Discipline of the Church of England in America." The condemnation of the "Westonians" was unanimous. Morton (p. 36) calls them "an unruly company, and had no good government over them." Winslow (*Good Newes*, p. 297) accuses them of stealing the corn before it was ripe, and records that "though they received much kindness, set light both by it and by us, not sparing to requite the love we showed them, with secret backbitings, revilings, &c." Bradford had been warned. Weston had himself admitted that "ther are many of our people rude fellows," but added, "I hope . . . to reclaime them from . . . profanenes" (Bradford, 1:265–266). Robert Cushman had written Bradford, "The people which they cary are no men for us," and cautioned, "I pray you therefore signifie to Squanto, that they are a distinct body from us" (1:269–270). John Peirce wrote: "But as for Mr. Weston's company, I thinke them so base in condition . . . as in all appearance not fitt for an honest mans company" (1:271).

137:36   Compare Prov. 6.10–11, 24.33–34; see also Tilley, *Dictionary of the Proverbs in England*, I, 12: "Idleness is the key of beggary."

137:38   Winslow summarized the letter (*Good Newes*, pp. 328–330); cf. Bradford (1:286).

137:42

> Our Bretheren of *New England* use
> Choice *Malefactors* to excuse,
> And hang the *Guiltless* in their stead,
> Of whom the *Churches* have less need.

(*Hudibras*, Part II, Canto ii, vv. 409–412, in ed. by A. R. Waller, Cambridge, Eng., Cambridge University Press, 1905, p. 139). Butler had happily appropriated the story from Thomas Morton, who, in the book in which he paid his respects to New England, *The New English Canaan* (pp. 108–110), reported that a motion to hang a useless member of the community in the place of the one guilty of theft was rejected. Hubbard, in an obvious reference to Thomas Morton's report, notes that this "was the ground of the story with which the merry gentleman that wrote the poem called Hudibras did, in his poetical fancy, make so much sport" (p. 77).

137:46   Hubbard (p. 111), on a later occasion, gave an astringent assessment of the character of the man: "Captain Standish had been bred a soldier in the Low Countries, and never entered the school of our Savior Christ . . . or, if he was there, had forgot his first lessons, to offer violence to no man . . . A little chimney is soon fired; so was the Plymouth Captain, a man of very little stature, yet of a very hot and angry temper. The fire of his temper soon kindled and blown up into a flame by hot words, might easily have consumed all, had it not been seasonably quenched."

138:47   For "Lodging," cf. Gen. 32.13, 21, Num. 22.8, Josh. 4.3.

138:71–72   In *Good Newes* (pp. 338–339), Winslow reports graphically how the Indians, being lured into a closed room and the door shut, were fallen upon, three killed and a youth slain, "But it is incredible how many wounds these two pineses [braves] received before they died, not making any fearful noise, but catching at their weapons and striving to the last."

138:80   Winslow (*Good Newes*, p. 310) says the beheaded man, Wituwamat, was "a notable insulting villain, one who had formerly imbrued his hands in the blood of English and French . . . and derided their weakness, especially because, as he said, they died crying, making sour faces, more like children then men."

138:81   Compare Gen. 4.5–6.

138:83   Obtakiest, who was said to have joined the conspiracy somewhat reluctantly (*Good Newes*, p. 343).

139:91–92   "One Phineas Prat . . . saved his life by losing his way" (Hubbard, p. 78). The story is told in "A Decliration of the Affaires of the English People that first inhabited New-England," which Pratt submitted to the General Court in 1662 (see Holmes, *Increase Mather*, 2:465, and 4 M.H.S. *Coll.* 4:474–491). Increase Mather made use of the manuscript and printed excerpts from it in *A Relation of the Troubles which Have Happened in New-England*. Compare Matt. 10.39, 16.25, Mark 8.35, Luke 9.24.

139:95–96   Compare Acts 5.36, 38.

139:97–98   John Robinson, writing from Leyden after receiving a report of the expedition, gave Bradford a word of caution about Standish: "Upon this occasion let

me be bould to exhorte you seriou[s]ly to consider of the dissposition of your Captaine, whom I love, and am perswaded the Lord in great mercie and for much good
hath sent you him, if you use him aright. He is a man humble and meek amongst you,
and towards all in ordinarie course. But now if this be meerly from an humane spirite,
ther is cause to fear that by occasion, espetially of provocation, ther may be wanting
that tendernes of the life of man (made after Gods image) which is meete" (Bradford,
1:368–369).

139:99–140:29   Section 4 is an abridgement of Hubbard (pp. 81–83), with much of
his vocabulary and imagery retained.

139:99   It was in the name of John Peirce that the original patent was issued by the
Virginia Company under which the Pilgrims sailed for America. He was very early
associated with Weston in his dealings with the congregation in Leyden. Strong
resentment of what was felt to be his perfidious dealings with the Plymouth colony
was widespread. "But," as Bradford noted (1:306), "the Lord marvelously crost
him."

139:21   Hubbard said (p. 82) the 1629 patent was obtained "by the Earl of Warwick
and Sir Ferdinando Gorges's act."

140:30–141:81   Section 5 is for the most part a paraphrase of Morton's *Memoriall*
(pp. 53–61), although less slavish than was Mather's use of Hubbard in section 4.

140:30   Robinson died on March 1, 1625, after only a week's illness, thus putting to
an end the colonists' hope that he would join them (cf. Hubbard, p. 97).

140:32   A fusing of two biblical references: Amos 5.15 speaks of "the remnant of
Joseph," and Deut. 33.16 of Joseph as "He that was separated from his Brethren."

140:34   I Tim. 3.2 speaks of a bishop "apt to teach"; Mather substitutes "an elder
so apt to teach." "Elder Brewster," says Hubbard (p. 97), "was qualified both to
rule well, and also to labor in the word and doctrine, although he could never be
persuaded to take upon him the pastoral office, for the administration of the sacraments, &c."

140:36   Of Smith, Hubbard wrote (p. 97): "being much overmatched by him that he
was joined with in the presbytery [Elder Brewster], both in point of discretion to rule,
and aptness to teach, so as through many infirmities, being found unable to discharge
the trust committed to him with any competent satisfaction, he was forced soon after
to lay it down."

140:39–141:77   This account of John Lyford is substantially repeated in Bk. VII,
chap. 5, sec. 1, of the *Magnalia*. In a letter, Robert Cushman had described him (see
Bradford, 1:357–358) as "(we hope) an honest plaine man, though none of the most
eminente and rare. About chusing him into office use your owne liberty and discretion; he knows he is no officer amongst you, though perhaps custome and uni-
versalitie may make him forget him selfe. Mr. Winslow and my selfe gave way to his
going, to give contente to some hear, and we see no hurt in it, but only his great
charge of children."

140:48   In the King James Version of 1611, "divisions" in I Cor. 3.3 was glossed on
the margin as "factions."

140:49   To say that the letters "fell" into the governor's hands is an understatement.
"The Gov[erno]r and some other of his freinds . . . tooke a shalop and wente out
with the ship a league or .2. to sea, and caled for all Lifords . . . letters. . . . He found
above .20. . . . Most of the letters they let pas, only tooke copys of them, but some of
the most materiall they sent true copyes of them, and kept the originalls, least he
should deney them" (Bradford, 1:383; cf. Morton, pp. 54–55).

140:54–141:64   For Lyford's "*Repentance*," see Bradford (1:397), whom Morton
follows (p. 58). Bradford, and after him Morton, says he has "put it downe as I find
it recorded by some who tooke it from his owne words, as him selfe utered them."
Mather takes several liberties in his quotation. Lyford's repentance echoes words
and phrases from Deut. 21.8, Prov. 16.30, Isa. 6.10, 44.18, Gen. 4.14, Ps. 51.4.

141:65–67 "Samuell Fuller (a deacon amongst them), and some other tender harted men" (Bradford, 1:397).

141:67–68 Compare Jer. 14.14, 17.9, 23.26, Mark 7.22, Prov. 12.20.

141:69–74 ". . . his wife who was a prudent sober woman, taking notice of his false and deceitful carriage . . . related that he had a *Bastard* by another woman, before marriage with her, which he denied to her with an oath, but it afterwards appeared to be so: and another miscarriage of the like nature, more odiously circumstanced, was also discovered" (Morton, p. 60). The "odious" circumstances are detailed in Bradford (1:414–418).

141:77 Morton, following Bradford, writes that Lyford "shortly after died" (p. 61). Hubbard (p. 93) has "where he ended his days." Mather may have interpreted this to mean "ended his own *Life.*"

141:82–92 The opening passage of section 6 is somewhat distantly dependent on Morton's summary of the condition of the colony in 1642 (pp. 115–116). For that year Morton lists thirteen ministers, which in Mather becomes "above a dozen."

141:92–98 For Biblical references to distribution of lands, cf. Num. 33.54, 34.17, 18, Josh. 13.7, Ezek. 45.1, 47.21–22, 48.29. Mather is here closest to Morton (p. 65), but see also Bradford (1:372–373), and Hubbard (p. 98). Morton abridges the Pliny passage as given by Bradford, and Mather follows Morton (see Pliny *Natural History* XVIII.II.6–7).

142:4–8 For "*Whales,*" cf. Gen. 1.21. It would seem that, to begin with, the colonists chiefly took advantage of whales cast up on shore. Compare Winthrop in 1635 (1:187–188): "Some of our people went to Cape Cod, and made some oil of a whale, which was cast on shore. There were three or four cast up, as it seems there is almost every year."

142:9 Mather was probably told of the "Cow" and "Calf" whales by his cousin, John Cotton (1661–1706), who was from 1693 until his death pastor of the First Church of Yarmouth, Massachusetts. He and Cotton Mather, both grandsons of the famous John Cotton (1584–1652), studied at Harvard at the same time. For John Cotton the elder, see *Magnalia*, Bk. III, pt. 1, chap. 1. For John Cotton the younger, see Weis, *Colonial Clergy*, p. 62.

142:13–14 For "*draw forth their Breasts,*" see Lam. 4.3; for "*suck the abundance,*" see Deut. 33.19.

142:15–25 Mather opens section 7 with a summary of the virtues of the "Holy Souls" in "this Colony" in the language of Biblical allusion: "that are above" from Col. 3.2; "at rest" from Heb. 4.11; the "*Book of Life*" from Phil. 4.3; blessings rather than punishments unto the "Third and Fourth Generation" from Exod. 20.5; "*as they followed Christ*" from I Cor. 11.1.

142:26 *et seq.* Mather returns to Winslow's *Hypocrisie Unmasked* (pp. 92–101), again to demonstrate that there had always been concord between New England churches and other reformed churches, and, by implication, once more to attest the theological respectability of New England. Compare above, p. 126, l. 23, and endnote thereto.

142:33–37 Quoted from Winslow, pp. 94–95.

142:37–43 Quoted from Winslow, pp. 98–99. This passage is a pastiche of Biblical allusions: i.e., "Separation *from the World,*" II Cor. 6.17; "Saints by Calling," Rom. 1.7, I Cor. 1.2; "*shining forth,*" II Cor. 4.6, Ps. 80.1; "*secret things,*" Deut. 29.29; "*wallow,*" II Pet. 2.22; "*Holy things,*" Num. 18.32, Ezek. 22.8, 26, 44.8, 13; "*Communion of Saints,*" cf. II Cor. 8.4, and see the last paragraph of the Anglican creed; "leavened," I Cor. 5.6–8, Gal. 5.9.

143:49–50 "*Required,*" Isa 1.12; "*Holiness,*" II Cor. 7.1; "*Submission to every Ordinance,*" I Pet. 2.13, which reads, "submit yourself to every ordinance of man for the Lord's sake; whether it be to the king, as supreme, or unto governors," a text often turned against the Puritans.

143:54–55　The often repeated description of the congregation at Leyden and, later, the Plymouth settlers as Brownist was particularly troubling to the colony, since it carried the implication of rebellion against the crown. In his *Treatise of Reformation without tarrying for Anie* (Middelburg, 1582), Robert Browne had called for immediate reformation of the Church of England to make it conform to primitive Biblical practice, and affirmed the duty of Christians to disobey the orders of a prince who sought to compel observance of corrupt practices, and to separate completely from corrupt national churches.

It was precisely against charges that both the Plymouth colony and the Massachusetts Bay had usurped the civil powers of the King, and were "Schismaticks, Brownists, rigid Separatists," that *Hypocrisie Unmasked* was directed (cf. p. 93). For Cotton Mather, striving at the same time to maintain the Massachusetts theocracy and to affirm the colony's loyalty under a new royal charter, there was still a compelling need to deny that the colonies had ever been tainted with Brownism.

143:56　For "*Hour of Temptation*," cf. Rev. 3.10.

143:57–60　For justification of prophesying by the bretheren and the gift of prophecy, the Plymouth band could cite I Cor. 12.8–10, 28, 13.2. Hubbard (pp. 65–66), speaking of Brewster's congregation, says: "several of his people were well gifted, and did spend part of the Lord's day in their wonted prophesying, to which they had been accustomed by Mr. Robinson. Those gifts, while they lasted, made the burden of the other defect [lack of a pastor] more easily borne, yet was not that custom of the prophesying of private brethren observed afterwards in any of the churches of New England besides themselves, the ministers of the respective churches there not being so well satisfied in the way thereof, as was Mr. Robinson."

An exception occurred in 1631, necessitated by the return to England of John Wilson, pastor of the Boston church, to fetch his wife. Governor Winthrop wrote in his journal under date of March 29, 1631 (*The History of New England from 1630 to 1649*, ed. James Savage, 2. vols., Boston, 1853, 1:60): "Mr. Wilson, and divers of the congregation, met at the governour's, and there Mr. Wilson, praying and exhorting the congregation to love, etc., commended to them the exercise of prophecy in his absence, and designed those whom he thought most fit for it, viz., the governour, Mr Dudley, and Mr. Nowell the elder." In 1648 the official policy was enunciated in the Cambridge Platform (pub. Cambridge, 1649), that "attending to teach and preach the word is peculiar to" pastors and teachers, and not to be undertaken by ruling elders (Williston Walker, *Creeds*, p. 212). The practice of prophesying did continue in England, however. Compare the Savoy Declaration of 1658: "Although it be incumbent on the Pastors and Teachers of the churches to be instant in Preaching of the Word, by way of Office; yet the work of Preaching the Word is not so peculiarly confined to them, but that others also gifted and fitted by the holy Ghost for it . . . may publiquely, ordinarily and constantly perform it" (*ibid.*, p. 405).

143:60–62　A "Letter from the Governour and Magistrates of the Massachusetts Bay to the Commissioners of the United Colonies," dated Sept. 2, 1656 (in *Plymouth Records*, 10:155, and in Thomas Hutchinson, *A Collection of Original Papers*, Boston, 1769, pp. 283–284), draws the attention of the commissioners to the lack of support for the ministry in the Plymouth Colony, "so as many pious ministers of the gospell have (how justly we know not) deserted their stations, callings and relations."

143:62　Compare Matt. 27.45, Mark 15.33, Luke 22.53, 23.44.

143:64–65　Heb. 13.20.

143:66–69　Mather is here following Winslow (pp. 99–100), who identifies the minister who "*Questioned* and *Omitted*" the rite of infant-baptism as "Mr. *Hubbard* the Minister at *Hengam*." This was Peter Hobart, who had, with a number of followers, emigrated from Hingham in England in 1635 (cf. Morison, *Builders of the Bay Colony*, Houghton, Mifflin Co., Boston, 1930, p. 342). A similar spelling of his name appears in Edward Johnson's *Wonder-Working Providence of Sions Saviour in New England*

(London, 1654; cited from ed. J. F. Jameson, New York, C. Scribner's Sons, 1910, p. 115): "At this time also came to shore the servant of Christ Master Peter Hubbord." His unorthodoxy also included a strong Presbyterian predilection, or as Hubbard, who spells him "Hubbert," put it (p. 192), he was "not so fully persuaded of the Congregational discipline." His contentious spirit was most clearly demonstrated by his part in the Hingham affray in 1644 over the militia election (see Winthrop, *History*, 2:271–286, 288, 312–313; see also *Magnalia*, Bk. II, p. 223, l. 91–p. 224, l. 53. Johnson, writing in 1653, recorded (pp. 116–117) that the "Brotherly communion" of Hingham was "lessened by a sad unbrotherly contention" between factions in the church, which had "continued already for seven yeares space," and he concluded his account in verse:

> "Oh Hubbard! why do'st leave thy native soile?
> Is't not to war 'mongst Christ's true worthies here? . . .
> With humble, holy, learned men converse,
> Thee and thy flock they would in one unite,
> And all the fogs of selfe conceit disperse;
> Thee and thy sons the Lord Christ guide aright."

143:72   "Sectaries," that is, adherents of what were considered schismatical or heretical sects; they are compared to demons bent on destroying the good order of the churches. The Quakers, by renouncing all formalisms of creed, liturgy, priesthood, sacraments, in favor of an inward spiritual experience, were deemed extremely dangerous, as were the "Seekers," whose profession of ever seeking the true church seemed to negate the possibility of establishing any church estate whatsoever.

143:77–78   For participation in Synods, see *Hypocrisie Unmasked*, pp. 100, 101.

143:80–81   A likely source for Mather's quotation is Heidfeld's *Sphinx* (p. 489), where it is introduced as "Sane dictum est D. Bernhardi," with a marginal reference to "S. Bernhard Serm. 32 in Cant." (cf. *Migne L*, 183:150). Heidfeld has "suffocavit" rather than "devoravit." Hugh Peter wittily reversed the saying in his sermon, *God's Doings and Man's Duty* (London, 1646), p. 34: he refers to the quarrel that "grew among the two Pastors of these Churches [Rome and Byzantium], who should be called *Papa*," concluding that "Religion begot wealth, and the mother [Rome] devoured the daughter [Byzantium]."

143:83–84   For "*Power to get Wealth*," see Deut. 8.18.

144:86–87   See Amos 8.11–12: "Behold the days come, saith the Lord God, that I will send a famine in the land, not a famine of bread, not a thirst for water, but of hearing the words of the Lord: and they shall wander from sea to sea" and "shall run to and fro to seek the word of the Lord, and shall not find it." A gloss on Amos 8.13 in the 1599 English Bible explains that "they" were "idolators" who "did use to sweare by their idoles . . . as the Papists yet do by theirs." Mather thus implies that Plymouth settlers who failed to support their ministers were in effect encouraging some "miserable *Apostacy*" as dangerous as the "Darkness of Popery."

144:89   See Samuel Danforth's sermon, *A Brief Recognition of New England's Errand into the Wilderness* (Boston, 1670), and the title essay of Miller's *Errand into the Wilderness*, pp. 1–15. For Mather's contribution to the Jeremiad, cf. introductory essay, "The Magnalia," p. 43.

144:90   "Means of Grace" was used in the English Book of Common Prayer in the prayer for "General Thanksgiving" in the Order for Evening Prayer.

144:92   For "so great a Death," see II Cor. 1.10, cf. Ps. 79.11.

144:94   For "*Younger Sisters*," see Cant. 8.8.

144:95–96   Plymouth colony was incorporated into the Massachusetts Bay Colony in 1692.

144:93–145:40   Robinson's famous speech to the departing Pilgrims was first published by Winslow (*Hypocrisie Unmasked*, pp. 97–98). The address would seem to embody the substance of the sermon preached on Ezra 8.21, to which Bradford referred (1:121; cf. also p. 127, l. 56 above). Mather turns the address into the first person, and changes "ere long" to "quickly"; on p. 145, l. 36 "Godly Party" has become "Godly People." Dexter conjectured (pp. 407–409) that the famous words concerning "*further Light*" (p. 144, l. 19) referred to polity and not doctrine, and defended this position by noting that Winslow published it in a pamphlet defending the Plymouth colony against charges of separatist exclusiveness. As to Robinson's injunction to "study *Union*" (p. 145, l. 36), sometime after Robinson's death, Festus Hommius, by then rector of the Theological College at Leyden (an evidence of the victory of the Contra-Remonstrants), wrote that Robinson had ever been concerned to bring about the union of the English churches in Holland (cf. Bradford, 1:444n).

144:3–4   For "*God . . . Angels*," see I Tim. 5.21. For "*follow . . . Christ*," see I Pet. 2.21, I Cor. 11.1.

144:5–6   An echo of the words, but a reversal of the sense of Gal. 1.8–9.

144:15   For "*saw not all things*," see Heb. 2.8.

144:16–18   For "*Burning and Shining Lights*," see John 5.35. For "*whole Counsel of God*," see Acts 20.27.

145:25   For "*Scriptures of Truth*," cf. Dan. 10.21.

145:27   For "*Perfection of Knowledge*," see Job 37.16.

145:40   For "*Shepherds*," cf. Jer. 23.4.

145:42   "Commending . . . unto the Grace of God," Paul's customary valediction in his letters: Rom. 16.20, 24, I Cor. 16.23, II Cor. 13.14, etc.; cf. also Acts 14.26, Rev. 22.21.

145:43   For "*Flock*," see Ezek. 36.38.

145:45   Virgil *Eclogia* IV.1.

145:49–50   The presumption that Bishop Williams is the minister referred to rests on the following: in Thomas Fuller's comment on Calvin's "*tolerabiles ineptias*" (see note on line 53 below), he associates the response with Bishop Williams, adding, "In requital where of, bishop Williams was wont to say, that master Calvin had his *tolerabiles morositates.*" Later in his *Church History*, summing up the bishop's career (6:326), he writes: "Not out of sympathy to nonconformists, but antipathy to bishop Laud, he was favourable to some select persons of that opinion. Most sure it is, that in his greatness he procured for Mr. Cotton, of Boston, a toleration under the broad seal for the free exercise of his ministry, notwithstanding his dissenting in ceremonies, so long as done without disturbance to the church." It is not surprising that Mather should find the defender of his grandfather "Learned and Pious."

145:53   Epistle 2091, dated February 1556: "Calvin to the English in Frankfort," in *Opera* (ed. Baum, Cunitz, and Reuss, Brunsweig, 1863–1900), 15:394. The phrase is quoted in Fuller's *Church History*, 4:20, and in Peter Heylin's *Aerius Redivivus: Or, The History of the Presbyterians* (London, 1670), p. 15. The source of Mather's quotation has not been identified. However, the general tenor of the passage is to be found in a number of places in *Scrinia Reserata: A MEMORIAL offer'd to the Great Deservings of John Williams D. D. . . . Ld Bishop of Lincoln, and Ld Archbishop of York*, by John Hacket, London, 1693, as, for example, the accusation that Laud would not "seek them [the Puritans] with fair Entreaties, but went out to suppress the Ringleaders, or to make them fly the Kingdom. Bishop *Williams* perceived that this made the Faction grow more violent, to triumph against Justice, as it were Persecution, that the cutting of some great Boughs made the Under-woods grow the faster. His way to mitigate them, was to turn them about with the fallacy of Meekness: If they came to him, they had courteous Hospitality; if they ask'd his Counsel in Suits of Law, he gave them all the assistance; if some Ceremonies would [not] go down with them, he waited till their queasie Stomachs would digest the rest" (Part II, p. 86). Williams was notably conciliatory in the matter of placement of the communion table, a fact which, among other things, resulted in charges later being brought against him (cf. *Scrinia*, Part II, p. 101).

145:53 For "great Day," cf. Mal. 3.2, 4.1, 5.

146:55 For "lift up your Faces," cf. Ezra 9.6.

146:56 For "demand of you," cf. Job. 38.3, 40.7, 42.4. For "*Lambs*," John 21.15; cf. also Luke 8.29.

146:66–91 See Blackmore's *Prince Arthur* (London, 1695), pp. 18–19. Mather has changed "crawls" to "crawl'd" (line 66), "that" to "which" (line 69), and "Thirst" to "Heat" (line 88). He has also omitted two lines (between lines 83 and 84), possibly because he considered them too graphic.

146:86 For "Envy, Hate, Malice," cf. Tit. 3.3.

146:92–147:96 Compare Matt. 5.11. Mather increasingly stresses the theme of "Persecution" in his chapters on the Massachusetts Bay Company, often combined, as here, with insistence that the Laudian "*Party*" had "unjustly Challenged the Name of *the* Church of England." He could therefore go on to claim that the Massachusetts settlers had never separated from the true Church of England, but sought only to continue the work of reformation. For further references to persecution, see, for example, 150:29–33, 158:28–36, 160:75–84, and endnotes thereto. On non-separation, cf. 157:90–158:14, 159:60–66, and endnotes.

147:96 Compare Matt. 7.26–27.

147:97 For the "few attempts," see Hubbard, pp. 36–37, 104–106, 213–233. For a summary of the early "Designs," see Morison, *Builders of the Bay*, chapter 1.

147:5 For "*to this Day*," cf. Acts 26.22.

147:6 For "become of them," cf. Exod. 32.1, 23, Acts 7.40.

147:6–12 Mather may have received this story from his cousin John Cotton, minister at Hampton. "*Main End*" is here used in the sense of "chief aim or purpose." A few lines below (l. 2) it has the now archaic meaning of "a mainland, or continental land." Mather here indulges in a word-play on "main," carried out by "Aims" in l. 23.

147:23–24 Job 5.3, quoted in the same context in Hubbard, p. 105.

147:24–28 For the story of M. Finch, Mather undoubtedly relied on his father's *Relation of the Troubles*, p. 17, where Increase again utilized the narrative of Phineas Pratt for his account of how a multitude boarded the vessel, with "knives hid in the flappets which the Indians wear about their loins," concluding, "all killed" (see, 4 M.H.S. *Coll.* 4:479–480).

147:33–149:91 Section 3 is an abridged version of Hubbard, pp. 106–109.

148:37 For a full account of John White's role, see Morison, *Builders of the Bay*, pp. 21–50.

148:39 Mather follows Hubbard (p. 106) in dating the formation of the Company in 1624. They were for the most part of the Puritan party. Their settlement on Cape Ann, chiefly for fishing, was a failure, and the Company was dissolved in 1626.

148:41 Conant had originally gone to Plymouth, in 1623, but disliked its rigid Separatism. His brother John was one of the Dorchester Adventurers.

148:44 Hubbard gives the names of the "three Honest Men" (p. 107): John Woodberry, John Balch, and Peter Palfreys.

148:54 The date is Old Style, i.e., March 1627/28. Mather is here very close to Hubbard, p. 108. Compare Morison, *Builders of the Bay*, pp. 31–32, on this group.

148:62–66 Mather extends the abbreviated list given in Hubbard (p. 109) and arranges the names in the order in which they appear on the patent (see *Mass. Records*, 1:6).

149:73–76 Hubbard, whom Mather is following, quotes (p. 114) from the Patent: "to hold [as] of the manor of East Greenwich, in free and common soccage, and not in capite, or knight's service." "In capite" and "knight's service" mean tenure immediately from the crown, or under condition of performing military service. The ordinary form of "common soccage," which might stipulate determinate services, was in effect freehold. The date given is Old Style; the Charter was granted March 4, 1629. On this form of land tenure, see also Charles M. Andrews, *The Colonial Period of American History* (4 vols., New Haven, 1934–1938), 1:86.

149:85–91   Mather's "I have somewhere met with" must be described as studied disingenuousness, since he could have found his Hebrew etymology in either of two sources. John White's *Planter's Plea* (London, 1630), pp. 13–14, reads: "Some conceive, their Predecessors [the Indians] might have had some commerce with the *Iewes* in times past. . . . the name of the place, which our late Colony hath chosen for their seat, prooves to bee perfect Hebrew, being called *Nahum Keike*, by interpretation, *The bosome of consolation*." See also Joshua Scottow, *Narrative of the Planting of Massachusetts Colony* (Boston, 1694), p. 51, reprinted in 4 M.H.S. *Coll.* 4:351, who calls it *Naumkek* and gives the same translation; "bosom" is the more exact rendering than Mather's "haven." White says it was called Salem "in remembrance of a peace setled upon a conference at a generall meeting betweene them and their neighbours, after expectance of some dangerous jarre."

149:90–91   Compare Judg. 1.26, 15.19, Ezek. 20.29, Matt. 27.8 (in a quite different context).

149:92–150:7   Here Mather is relying on Hubbard, pp. 111–112. On Higginson and Skelton, cf. Morison, *Builders of the Bay*, pp. 37–38.

149:1   For "driven out," cf. I Sam. 26.19; for "Native Country," cf. Jer. 22.10.

150:3   The quotation is from Valerius Maximus, *Factorum dictorumque memorabilium* V.3.2. Mather's source was probably Heidfeld's *Sphinx* (p. 580) since the alteration of the original "ne ossa quidem mea habes" to "ne ossa quidem habebis" occurs in Heidfeld.

150:7   For "*Errand*," cf. endnote to p. 144, l. 89.

150:8–15   Mather's source here is Edward Johnson's *Wonder-Working Providence* (pp. 45–46), but he would also seem to have had open before him Hubbard's paraphrase (p. 113) of the same passage. Mather's grounds for calling Bright and Blackstone "*Clergy-Men*," that is, Church of England men, were a reference in Hubbard to Bright's "Conformity," and Johnson's observation that there was nothing left of Blackstone's "profession" but his "Canonical coate," which would be understood as an evidence of conformity. Compare also Morton's *Memoriall* (p. 74) on Bright as a "Conformist." Johnson said the stones were for "building the Temple," Hubbard, "the building." In Johnson, two "began to hew stones" but only "one of them began to build." In Hubbard, only one, Bright, hewed and built. Mather couples them throughout. It was Bright who "*betook himself to the Seas again*": he returned to England in 1630. Blackstone removed to the Boston peninsula in 1625— "*to Till the Land*"—and subsequently to Rhode Island in 1634. On Blackstone, see also *Magnalia*, Bk. III, Remarks, sec. 11.

For "*hew stones in the Mountains, for the Building of the Temple*," see I Kings 5.15, II Chron. 2.2; for "*Till the Land*," see Gen. 2.5, 3.23, II Sam. 9.10.

150:14–15   For "burying . . . among the Rubbish," cf. I Sam. 10.22.

150:17–26   Mather here clearly had access to the manuscript of Francis Higginson's *A true Relation of the last Voyage to New-England*, "written from New-England, July 24, 1629," first printed in Hutchinson's *A Collection of Papers Relative to the History of the Colony*, Boston, 1769 (see p. 37 for the seamen's words). Mather's language is close to Higginson's. The Biblical echoes are all in Higginson.

For "constantly served God," cf. Dan. 6.10, 13, 16, 20. For "*Reading, Expounding* and *Applying*," cf. Prov. 2.2, 22.17, 23.12, Eccles. 8.16, Luke 24.27. "Singing his praise" occurs throughout the Bible, especially in the Psalms. For "*seeking of His Face*" by "*Fasting* and *Prayer*," see Pss. 27.8, 35.13, Acts 14.23.

150:26–27   *Aeneid* I.204.

150:27   For "Haven," see Ps. 107.30.

150:29–33   The persecution of nonconformists by the "*English* Hierarchy" was being pressed by William Laud, appointed to the see of London in 1628. Mather elaborated the figure of torture by fire and ice in his *Eleutheria* (p. 34). Compare Rev. 15.12: "I saw as it were a sea of glass mingled with fire."

150:36–37   Ovid, *Metamorphoses* XV.22.

151:48–60   Mather's source for the "Computation" was Johnson (pp. 54–55). The "Cattel" included "Swine, Goates, Sheepe, Neate and Horse." The "Materials" included "Nayles, Glasse and other Iron-worke." Johnson first gave the number of ships as 298 (p. 58) but later corrected himself to 198 (p. 61). The ship that miscarried was the *Angel Gabriel*, lost in the hurricane of August 15, 1635. Richard Mather, who crossed in the companion vessel the *James*, recounted in his Journal that "the Angel Gabriel, being then at anchor at Pemmaquid, was burst in pieces and cast away in this storm, and most of the cattle and other goods, with one seaman and three or four passengers, did also perish therein" (Alexander Young, *Chronicles of the First Planters of the Colony of Massachusetts Bay*, Boston, 1846, p. 478); cf. also Winthrop, *History* (1:165); Scottow, *Narrative of the Planting* (p. 291); and Hubbard (p. 199). The last two said that none lost their lives.

151:50   For "Transportation" of possessions, cf. Eccles. 2.7.

151:58–59   For "*Perils of the Seas*," see Cor. 11.26.

151:62   For "stirring up the Spirits," see I Chron. 5.26, II Chron. 36.22, Ezra 1.1, Hag. 1.14.

151:63   Compare I Kings 8.14; II Chron. 25.17.

151:64–65   Compare Jer. 22.10.

151:73–152:14   The "General Considerations," written by John Winthrop before the migration and circulated in manuscript, first appeared in print in the *Magnalia*. Mather seems to have used Francis Higginson's copy, which was later printed in the Hutchinson *Papers*, pp. 27–29, and in the *Winthrop Papers*, 2:117–118. Mather gives some variant readings, omits a few lines, and essays to "improve" the language. By making it his "*First*" consideration, Winthrop emphasizes the conviction that Rome was the enemy most to be feared. His "*Secondly*" reflects the Puritan feeling that the Counter-Reformation was everywhere advancing in Europe, with no resistance from the Stuarts. The Elector Palatine, James I's son-in-law, had received no support against the Emperor of Germany, and French Protestants were prostrated after the fall of La Rochelle. At home it was only too apparent that Charles I's wife Henrietta Maria favored Papists. (For an excellent presentation of the melancholy state of Protestantism, see C. V. Wedgwood, *The King's Peace 1637–1641*, New York, Macmillan Company, 1955, pp. 113–133.) As for his "*Thirdly*," the great depression of the 1620's, especially in the cloth trade, reinforced a belief that "The Land grows weary of her *Inhabitants*." In both the Hutchinson and Winthrop *Papers*, the "Considerations" are followed by objections raised at the time to certain points, and Winthrop's answers to them.

152:79   For "*Desolations*," cf. Jer. 25.9.

152:81   For "*Refuge*," cf. Num. 35.11, Josh. 20.2, Isa. 4.6. For "*Destruction*," cf. Ezek. 32.9.

152:82   For "*Land grows weary*," cf. Levit. 18.25, Job 30.8.

152:87–92   For "*Excess of Riot*," cf. I Pet. 4.4. For "Scorn and Contempt," cf. Pss. 119.22, 44.13. For "upright Man," cf. Job. 12.4.

152:98–3   For "*Earth* is the *Lord's*," see Ps. 24.1. For "*Garden*," see Gen. 2.8, 15, 16. For "to be Tilled," see Gen. 2.15; the King James Version has "to dress it," but the Hebrew word is identical with "to till"; cf. also Gen. 3.23. For "Places of Habitation," see Ps. 33.14. For "profitable for . . . Man," see Tit. 3.8. For "lye waste," see Isa. 33.8, 34.10, Hag. 1.4.

152:6   Compare the Post-Communion Collect in the *Book of Common Prayer*.

152:15–17   Paraphrased from Hubbard (p. 116), including the references to Abraham "*calling on the Name*," for which see Gen. 12.8.

152:18–153:22   An abridgement of a Hubbard passage (p. 118). Hubbard referred to Hildersham as "that *malleus Brownistarum.*" For the "written word of God," cf. I Cor. 15.3, 4. The phrase appears frequently in the Psalms.

153:22–27   The extent to which the polity of the Salem church was modeled on the Separatist Plymouth pattern—was, in fact, determined by counsel given to Endecott by Deacon Fuller of Plymouth—has continued to be a subject of some controversy. Hubbard, whom Mather is following, reports (p. 115) Endecott's appeal to Governor Bradford in an outbreak of scurvy, and his subsequent thanks for Fuller's visit (for letter, see Bradford, 2:90–92), which added, "I am satisfied touching your judgments of the outward forme of Gods worship." However, later (p. 117) Hubbard writes that the "successors" to the first members of the Salem church were not "willing to own that they received their platform of church order from those of New Plymouth," and Winslow, in defending the colonists from charges of Separatism (*Hypocrisie Unmasked*, p. 92), insisted that "they set not the church at *Plimouth* before them for example, but the Primitive Churches were and are their and our mutuall patterns and examples." Compare also Morton, *Memoriall*, p. 77. For modern discussions of the question, see Morison, *Builders of the Bay* (pp. 38–41) and Miller, *Orthodoxy in Massachusetts* (pp. 127–137).

153:27   For "*Church-Order,*" cf. I Cor. 16.1.

153:28–36   A vivid contemporary account of the formation of the Salem church is provided by a letter of July 30, 1629, from Charles Gott to Governor Bradford (see Bradford's "Letter Book," 4 M.H.S. *Coll.* 3:67–68): "The 20. of July, it pleased yᵉ Lord to move yᵉ hart of our Govʳ to set it aparte for a solemne day of humilliation, for yᵉ choyce of a pastor and teacher." After an examination of Skelton and Higginson "concerning their callings," one from "yᵉ Lord," the second an "outward calling, which was from . . . a company of beleevers joyned together in covenante." Gott implies that such a company had already been joined, for he writes that "every member . . . are to have a free voyce," and continues: "Their choice was after this manner: every fit member wrote, in a note, his name whom the Lord moved him to think was fit for pastor, and so likewise, whom they would have for teacher; so the most voice was for Mr. Skelton to be Pastor, and Mr. Higginson to be Teacher." (For the function of these two offices, see above, endnote to Attestation, p. 67, ll. 25–26.) At that time, according to Gott, "the .6. of August is appoynted for . . . the choyce of elders and deacons." (Morton, in his *Memoriall*, p. 75, gives the date as August 6; Hubbard, p. 117, has August 9.) Morton reported that Bradford and some others, "coming by sea, were hindered by cross winds, that they could not be there at the beginning of the day, but they came into the assembly afterward, and gave them the right hand of fellowship." Mather, however, probably followed Hubbard's paraphrase of Morton, since he echoes Hubbard's "messengers of Plymouth church."

153:31–33   For "*Fasting* and *Prayer*, cf. Acts 14.23, I Cor. 7.5, Ps. 35.13, Dan. 9.3; for "*Confession of their Faith*, Matt. 10.32, Luke 12.8, Rom. 10.9, 14.11, Philip. 2.11, I John 4.15; for "Holy Covenant," see Luke 1.72; cf. also Dan. 11.28, 30.

153:31–33   Both Morton (pp. 75–76) and Hubbard (p. 119) use the phrase "a confession of faith and covenant," and both name Higginson as the author. According to Morton, "no man was confined unto that form of words, but onely to the Substance, End and Scope of the matter contained therein." On the question of whether two documents are to be inferred, see W. Walker, *Creeds*, p. 96, n. 6.

153:36–39   See Hubbard (p. 120) and Morton (p. 75), whom Mather was apparently consulting at this point.

153:39–40   The Salem covenant of 1629 was a simple and brief promise "to walk together" in all God's ways. In the renewal, "Seven Years after," it was repeated as the first sentence of the covenant, "expressed and inforced" by the addition of nine specific articles of promise (cf. Walker, *Creeds*, pp. 106, 110–111). At the time

Hugh Peter was ordained in 1636, the church was in a distracted state as a result of divisions arising during Roger Williams' brief pastorate, from 1634 until he was ordered out of the jurisdiction of the Bay in 1635. Specific promises of "*Watchfulness and Tenderness*" toward brethren, of avoiding "*Back-Bitings*," of "*lawful Obedience*," etc., were intended to stimulate repentance and reform. (See Walker, chap. 6: "The Development of Covenant and Creed in the Salem Church," pp. 93–115. For the texts of the covenants of 1629 and 1636, see pp. 116–118.)

153:43–47 The Puritan claim that their Church polity was entirely derived from the scriptures is here exemplified by Higginson's Biblical language. The covenants "with our Lord" were understood as both those with Israel and the new covenant fulfilled in Christ (cf. Luke 1.67–79, Heb. 9. 14–15, 13.20). For "*walk together*," see Amos 3.3; for "*walk . . . in all his Ways*," see Deut. 10.12, 11.22, 26.17, Josh. 22.5, I Kings 8.58; for "*Word of Truth*," see Ps. 119.43, II Cor. 6.7, Eph. 1.13, Col. 1.5, II Tim. 2.15, James 1.18; for "*to walk*," see Neh. 5.9, Mic. 4.5; for "*Power of Christ*," cf. II Cor. 12.9. Note that throughout "walk" is used with the religious connotation of "to live," "to comport oneself."

153:48 For "*Avouch the Lord*," see Deut. 26.17–18.

153:50–53 For "*Give . . . to the Lord*," cf. I Tim. 4.15; for "*Word of his Grace*," see Acts 14.3, 20.32; for "to cleave unto him," Deut. 30.20, Josh. 22.5; for "*contrary Ways*," cf. Levit. 26.21, 23, 24, 27, 28, 40, 41; for contrary "*Worship*," Acts 18.13.

153:55–57 For the list of offenses, see II Cor. 12.20; for "*bear and forbear*," cf. Gal. 6.2, Eph. 4.2, Col. 3.13; for "*give and forgive*," cf. Matt. 5.42, 10.8, 18.21–22, 19.21, Mark 11.25, Luke 6.37–38, 17.3–4, Eph. 4.32; for "*taught us*," cf. Matt. 5.2, John 8.2, II Thess. 2.15.

154:66–70 For "*in all Truth*," see John 16.13; for "*Truth and Peace*," II Kings 20.19, Esther 9.30, Isa. 39.8, Jer. 33.6, Zech. 8.16, 19; for "*those . . . without*," I Cor. 5.12; for "*Stumbling-block*," Levit. 19.14, Rom. 14.13; for "*appearance of Evil*," cf. I Thess. 5.22.

154:71–74 For "*Obedience*," cf. Rom. 13.1, Col. 3.20; for "*grieving their Spirits*," Isa. 54.6, Dan. 7.15, Eph. 4.30.

154:75–77 For "*approve . . . to the Lord*," see II Tim. 2.15; for "*shunning Idleness*," cf. Rom. 12.11, Heb. 6.12; for "*Lord's Stewards*," cf. I Cor. 4.1, Tit. 1.7.

154:78–81 For "*Teach our Children*" see Deut. 4.10, 6.7, 11.19; for "*Knowledge of God*," Prov. 2.5, Hosea 4.1, 6.6, Rom. 11.33, II Cor. 10.5, Col. 1.10; for "*may serve him*," Luke 1.74, from among many examples; for "*Blood . . . Covenant*." Exod. 24.8.

154:82–87 For "*Grace*," as interpreted in the Covenant of Grace, see Rom. 11.6; cf. also Josh. 24.25. "Renewing" or "owning" the Covenant in time became an institutionalized mechanism for reminding congregations of their obligations under the covenants they had entered into. The usual practice was to gather the congregation together upon some stated day of humiliation and, after a Jeremiad sermon, have them "renew" their church covenant. The *Result* of the Synod of 1679 (published as *The Necessity of Reformation*, Boston, 1679; Increase Mather was the chief penman), in answer to the question "What is to be done that so these Evils may be Reformed," in its Sections VIII, IX, and X devoted more space to covenant renewal than to any other recommended means of reformation. (See Walker, *Creeds*, pp. 435–437). At the time the people were anguished by the Indian wars and other disasters, Mather noted that they "with much solemn Fasting and Prayer . . . renewed their Covenants with God and one another" (*Magnalia*, Bk. V, pt. 4, sec. 2). He urged the same remedy in the year of witchcraft, 1692, saying that the churches could assist in the cure of witchcraft by doing "something extraordinary, in renewing of their Covenants, and in remembering and reviving the Obligations of what they have renewed" (*A Midnight Cry*, p. 67). After the Half-Way Covenant, renewal of the baptismal covenant was employed as a means of arousing halfway members to greater exertions. For covenant "renewal." see Miller, *From Colony to Province*, pp. 112–117; for days of humiliation, see Miller, "Declension in a Bible Common-wealth," in *Nature's Nation* (Cambridge, Mass., Harvard University Press, 1967), particularly pp. 14–17, 20–25, 52–53.

154:90–1 Paraphrased from Morton (p. 76), except that Mather expands the clause beginning "*Orally*." For "Blameless" and "Holy *Conversation*," see II Pet. 3.11, 14. To "Holy *Conversation*," Morton adds "viz. that they were without Scandal."

154:2–155:12 A combination of direct quotation and close paraphrase of Morton (pp. 77–78): "letters did pass between Mr. *Higginson*, and Mr. *Brewster* the reverend Elder of the church of *Plimouth*, and they did agree in their judgements, viz., con-cerning the *Church-Membership* of the Children with their parents, and that Baptism was a seal of their *Membership*, only when they were adult."

155:9 For "received unto the Table," cf. I Cor. 10.21.

155:10 For John Higginson, see Attestation, p. 63n, and Bk. III, pt. 2, chap. 1, sec. 15.

155:13–156:46 Section 8 is a close paraphrase of the section in Morton from the middle of page 76 to the middle of page 77, that is, the passage following what Mather used for the first half of Section 7 and preceding the last half of that section. Much of the language, including the italicized accusations and the ministers' replies, is directly reproduced.

155:20–22 The parenthetical "*Frankford*-Fashion" and the Latin tag are Mather's interpolations. The disputes over church order by Marian exiles in Frankfort in 1555 concluded with the more conservative faction wresting control. See *A Brief Discourse of the Troubles at Frankfort 1554–1558 A.D.* (Frankfort, 1575). Mather's source for the Latin quotation is Heidfeld's *Sphinx* (p. 324), where it is condensed from St. Bernard, "In Epiphania Domini," Sermon 3 (*Migne L*, 183:150).

155:22–23 They were indeed men of "Figure in the Place," being freemen of the Corporation, and appointed by the Company to Governor Endecott's council (cf. Morison, *Builders of the Bay*, p. 41).

155:38–40 The less politic Morton, whom Mather at this point sees fit to edit, says that Endecott "told them *that* New England *was no place for such as they*: and therefore he sent them back for *England* at the return of the *Ships* the same year."

155:41 For "*Threatnings*," see Acts 4.29.

156:48 Lange, *Florilegii* (2:2137), where it is ascribed to Pythagoras.

156:56–61 John Winthrop and John Humphry, who had been treasurer of the Dorchester Company of Adventurers. According to Hubbard (p. 124), whom Mather is here following, "Mr. Humphry not being ready to attend the service so soon, Mr. Thomas Dudley was (the next spring) chosen in his room." Hubbard also names the assistants. See also *Mass. Records*, 1:60.

156:59 For "After-Generations," cf. Ps. 102.18, Joel 1.3; for "*Glory*," cf. Luke 2.32, Prov. 17.6.

156:69 The correct spelling of the ship's—and the lady's—name was Arbella, and so it appears in Winthrop, in Hubbard, in the *Massachusetts Records*. However, Johnson's *Wonder-Working Providence* has Arrabella and Mather's parenthesis is close to Johnson's (p. 56). The tonnage of the vessel is given by Hubbard (p. 128). Compare C. E. Banks, *The Winthrop Fleet of 1630* (Boston, 1930).

156:70 See section 4 below; Winthrop, *History*, 1:40, note 2; and Edward Johnson, *Wonder-Working Providence*, p. 56.

157:73 According to Winthrop, *History* (1:29–34). See Hubbard (p. 132): "they kept a public day of thanksgiving, July the 8th, through all the Plantations, to give thanks to Almighty God for all his goodness . . . in their voyage."

157:74 Both British Sea and British Ocean appear on seventeenth-century maps showing the English Channel. See John Speed, *The Theatre of the Empire of Great Britain* (London, 1676), pp. 6–7, 9–10, 13–14.

157:74 Clement, *Stromata* V. Cap. 12 (*Migne G*, 9:118): cited in William Cave,

Apostolici (London, 1677), p. ix.

157:77 For "Heart of Stone," cf. Job 41.24.

157:77–79 Apparently Mather's source for John Winthrop's tearful leave-taking was Hubbard (p. 125). Johnson's rhapsodical and highly emotional version in *Wonder-Working Providence* (p. 52) does, however, contain the same reference to Paul's leave-taking from his friends (Acts 21.13) as is given by Hubbard, a fact which suggests a common source for both.

157:81 For "*Tears*," cf. Rev. 7.17, 21.4.

157:84 While the source of Mather's Latin has not been identified, the sense of Stouppe's quotation appears in his *Short and Faithful Account of the Late Commotions in the Valleys of the Piedmont*, 1655 (pp. 4–5, 78), which is included in *A Collection of the Several Papers Sent to his Highness the Lord Protector . . . Concerning the Bloody Massacres . . . by the Duke of Savoy's Forces*, London, 1655.

157:84–85 According to the anonymous *Thesaurus geographicus. A new body of geography* (1695), containing maps of North and South America and descriptions of the Eastern colonies, "*America* is bounded . . . by the *Atlantick* Ocean, or North Sea, which divides it from the old Continent, from which it is distant about 1000, or 1200 leagues, more or less, in several places" (p. 474).

157:86 Possibly an allusion to Matt. 7.14.

157:89–158:14 Again Mather seizes the opportunity to emphasize the non-separatist character of the New England Way. He devotes the entire section to reproducing, by paraphrase and direct quotation, *The Humble Request* (London, 1630), which was written by John White of Dorchester. White's convictions were sturdily non-separatist, and we cannot therefore attribute his profession of loyalty to "their *Dear Mother*," the Church of England, to policy alone. For some of the departing company, however, the protestation was obviously hedged with reservations. The passages in italics from line 2 on are direct quotation, with the single exception that Mather has "*Christ*" (line 8) instead of "Christ Jesus." Hubbard printed the *Request* (pp. 126–128), and it has been reprinted in the *Winthrop Papers* (2:231–233), and in Young, *Chronicles of Massachusetts* (pp. 295–296).

157:98–99 For "*Part* as they had obtained *Salvation*," cf. Acts 1.17, I Thess. 5.9, II Tim. 2.10. For "*sucked from her Breasts*," see Cant. 8.1.

157:1–2 For "recommend them" to "Mercies of God," cf. Acts 15.40, Rom. 12.1; for "springing out," cf. Ps. 85.11, Deut. 8.7; for "out of their own Bowels," cf. II Sam. 7.12, Isa. 48.19.

157:2–6 For "*You are not Ignorant*," cf. Rom. 1.13, I Cor. 10.1. For "*Spirit of God . . . Paul*," see Acts 17.16. For "*mention of the Church* at Philippi," see Philip. 1.3, 4, Rom. 1.9, I Thess. 1.2. All these references to Paul's prayers serve to intensify the entreaty to "*Reverend Fathers and Brethren*," as do the following: "same *Spirit*," as in I Cor. 12.4; "*we beseech you*," I Thess. 4.1, 10, 5.12; "*Remembrancers, to pray for us*," cf. II Tim. 1.3, Acts 12.5, I Thess. 1.3, 5.17.

158:8–13 For "*Brethren in Christ*," cf. Col. 1.2; for "*to give him no rest*," cf. Isa. 62.7. The concluding lines of the *Humble Request* weave together a number of Biblical echoes. Jer. 9. 1–2, "Oh that my head were waters, and mine eyes a fountain of tears, that I might weep day and night for the slain of the daughter of my people." "Oh that I had in the wilderness a lodging-place," suggests Isa. 1.8, "the daughter of Zion . . . left as a cottage in a vineyard" amid a desolate land. Similarly, the "Spirit of Supplication" from Eph. 6.18 is a call for prayers against "principalities, against powers, against the rulers of the darkness of this world, against spiritual wickedness in high places" (Eph. 6.12), against, that is, Laudian impositions and persecutions.

158:15–16 "Enlarged Soul" more commonly appears in Puritan parlance as "enlarged heart." Compare Ps. 119.32, Isa. 60.5, II Cor. 6.11.

158:28–159:44 See *Constitutions and Canons Ecclesiasticall* (London, 1604; ed. H. A. Wilson, Oxford, Clarendon Press, 1923). Mather singles out for comment Canons

4, 5, 6, 11, 17, 18, 19, 20. The entire section furnishes a summary of principal points at issue in matters of church polity, not only at the time of the Great Migration, but as they developed throughout the century in New and Old England. As always, Mather's purpose is to demonstrate that New England had never entertained separatist principles, had always been a loyal daughter of the Church of England.

158:40   For "Bowing at the *Name*," see Phil. 2.10.

159:48   For the composition of the Assembly, 151 persons in all, see A. F. Mitchell, *The Westminster Assembly of Divines* (Edinburgh, 1883). Among the laymen were John Pym, John Selden, Sir Henry Vane. The Church of England clerics included the Bishops of Exeter, Worcester, Armagh, and Bristol. Prominent among the Presbyterians were Edmund Calamy and William Twisse. Independents constituted the smallest group, among them Thomas Goodwin and Philip Nye, but they exercised considerable influence. The Scottish delegation consisted of five clerical and three lay Commissioners. The work of the Assembly embraced a revision of the 39 Articles, the formulation of the Westminster Confession, a Directory of Public Worship, and two Westminster catechisms, all of which were only partially and temporarily accepted in England.

159:56   *The King's Majesty's Declaration to His Subjects Concerning Lawful Sports to Be Used* was originally proclaimed in Lancashire in response to a petition from a delegation of servants, laborers, and mechanics complaining that they were allowed no recreation on Sunday afternoons. Many Puritan ministers who refused to read the declaration in their churches were suspended from or deprived of their livings.

159:56–58   In 1635 an ardent Laudian, Matthew Wren, was named Bishop of Norwich. He immediately began issuing "orders and directions" almost inquisitorial in character. He ordered that the prayer before the sermon be strictly according to the 55th Canon, and that no prayer be offered after the sermon (see Edward Cardwell, *Documentary Annals of the Reformed Church of England*, 2 vols., Oxford, 1839, 2:201). In less than two years, his visitation articles had fiercely roused the Puritans of East Anglia, who complained alike of the licensing and of the silencing of preachers and lecturers.

   The Puritan appetite for sermons and lectures was well-nigh insatiable. Strict Sabbath-keepers, the ministers preached sermons both morning and afternoon, and their sermons were frequently published. Lectures were a further means of winning over and educating the population. Some were given on Sunday afternoons, some on weekdays in churches, and festivals, fairs, and market days were favorite occasions. Many lectureships were endowed, in some cases by the Puritan gentry; often boroughs voted money to support lectureships (cf. L. J. Trinterud, "The Origins of Puritanism," *Church History*, 20:46). Under Laud, lecturers' opportunities were strictly limited, as were the number of sermons permitted. For example, Bishop Wren ordered (Cardwell, 2:206) that sermons were "required by the church of England only upon Sundays and holy-days in the forenoon, and at marriages, and are permitted at funerals, [but let] none presume to take upon them to use any preaching or expounding, or to have any such lecturing at any other time without express allowance from the bishop."

159:59   According to Puritans, the Laudian party not only retained popish superstitions and enforced their observance more rigorously than had their predecessors, but they also introduced "*New* Extravagancies," such as the removal of the communion table from the center of the church to a position within the chancel under the east wall, as if it were a high altar. No. 7 of the *Constitutions and Canons* (p. 19) declared "That the standing of the Communion-Table side-way under the East window of every Chancel or Chappel, is in its own nature indifferent, neither commanded nor condemned by the Word of God," and therefore no legitimate ground for complaint. For a list of innovations repugnant to Puritans, see Slingsby Bethel, *The Interest of the Princes and States of Europe* (London, 1680), p. 26. In this section, there are several parallels with Bethel's work, which Mather clearly had by him since he quotes from it directly at the conclusion of chapter 7. On Laudian innovations, see also Wedgwood, *King's Peace*, pp. 101–102.

159:62–63 For "Mother . . . honoured Her," cf. Exod. 20.12, Deut. 5.16; cf. also Cant. 8.1.

159:68 For "*envious Brethren*," cf. Gen. 37.11, Acts 7.9.

159:70 Mather is here referring to the period, from 1675 on, of Charles II's increasingly strenuous enforcement of the laws against nonconformists. His source for "*Bastards of the Church*" may have been Bethel's *Interest of Princes* (pp. 38–39), from a passage somewhat condensed by Bethel out of Edward Chamberlayne, *Angliae Notitia* (6th ed., London, 1672), pp. 38–39. In neither work is a "Prelate" or "Person of Quality" identified. Bethel (1617–1697), a staunch republican and vigorous advocate of both free trade and freedom of conscience, argues that "the Prince" would be better advised to ally himself with the Dutch than the French, and to show as much tolerance of the Presbyterians in England as of papists. "But this Gentleman" [the King?], Bethel writes, "doth not always ponder what he writes . . . Nor do I know how to reconcile his boasting of the transcending *charity* of the Church of *England* towards other Churches" with his "looking upon the Non-Conformists of *England* as Bastards."

160:79 On predestination the text most frequently quoted was Rom. 8. 28–30. Eph. 1.3–14 adds the factor of "election" according to the pleasure of God's will. II Tim. 1.9 pronounces election to be "not according to our works, but . . . His purpose and grace." According to Calvin, Christ's atoning death was proffered for the elect alone; it was Calvin who added the equally gratuitous reprobation of the damned. In effect, it was Calvin's form of the doctrine which was imposed by the Synod of Dort (1618–1619) and the Westminster Confession (1674). Compare Cross, *Dictionary of the Christian Church*, pp. 1098–1099.

For extended treatment of the nature and operation of the will, see Miller, *New England Mind: the Seventeenth Century*, Chapters VIII and IX.

See also *The Principles of the Protestant Religion Maintained* (pp. 103–108) for a careful discrimination between justification and sanctification. The question of the extent to which "evident sanctification" was a sign of "justification" was a central point at issue in the Antinomian controversy (cf. Hubbard, pp. 291–292), but Mather chooses not to consider it here.

As to perseverance, Calvin maintained that God would never permit the elect to fall away from Him. No man, of course, could infallibly know he was saved according to God's secret will; however, a fairly reliable test was thought to be his "perseverance" in sanctified behavior. Compare *Principles . . . Maintained*, pp. 6, 112–118.

160:89 This is the second of *Four Sermons* printed in London, 1642, with running pagination; the quotation is from p. 52. The same quotation from Symons, with a preceding sentence, is found at the beginning of Cotton Mather's *Wonders of the Invisible World* (Boston, 1693; ed. London, 1862, p. 9). Symons' theme is not so much a wish for New England's prosperity as a prophecy of hard times: "there will come Times in after Ages, when the *Clouds will over-shadow and darken the Sky there.*"

160:96–98 For "*King* Joash . . . at Home," cf. II Kings 14.10, II Chron. 25.19; for "God speed," cf. II John 10, 11.

160:99–2 For "No Man . . . better," see Luke 5.39.

160:3–161:23 Returning to his narrative, Mather again follows Hubbard (pp. 132–133), almost word for word on the death of Lady Arbella.

161:12–16 Mather derived his account of the "Noble Woman of Bohemia" from Samuel Clarke, *A Mirrour or Looking Glass* (London, 1657), p. 81.

161:19–20 William Camden, *Remains Concerning Britain*, p. 438: "She first deceas'd, he for a little tryed To live without her, lik'd it not, then dyed." Camden introduced the epithet as "Upon two Lovers who, being espoused, dyed both before they were married." With the gender of the pronouns changed, Sir Henry Wotton printed it as "Upon the Death of Sir Albert Morton's wife" (*Reliquiae Wottonianae*, London, 1685, p. 389), and Thomas Fuller applied it to the wife of Thomas Barington (*Worthies*, 1:528).

161:23–24 For "the *End . . . Peace*," see Ps. 37.37; for "*Peace*" and "*Joy*" cf. Rom. 14.17.

161:25–27 Close paraphrase of Johnson, *Wonder-Working Providence* (p. 65).

161:27–33 See Morton's *Memoriall* (pp. 83–84).

161:36–37 On the 5th of February, 1631, "Mr. William Peirse, in the ship Lyon of Bristol . . . brought store of juice of lemons, with the use of which many speedily recovered from their scorbutic distempers" (Hubbard, p. 139). For "out of those Distresses," cf. Ps. 107.6, 13, 19, 28.

161:37–162:48 In this passage, Cotton Mather relies closely on Johnson, *Wonder-Working Providence* (pp. 86–88).

161:41 For "Fruits of the Earth," cf. Isa. 4.2, James 5.7.

161:43 For "*Fast* and *Pray*," cf. Matt. 6.6, 17, Mark 9.29, I Cor. 7.5.

162:44–46 For "*poured out . . .* before him," see Lam. 2.19; for "*shower down . . . Rain*," Zech. 10.1; for "*while they were yet speaking*," Isa. 65.24.

162:50–57 Mather took his allusion to "*the last Meal in the Barrel*" (1 Kings 17.12) from Hubbard (p. 140), although Hubbard is here referring to the arrival of the *Lyon*. Mather's "several Ships," including that from the Lord Deputy of Ireland (named in Hubbard, p. 240), arrived in 1633; his source here was Johnson (p. 92), who also extols the equal sharing of supplies.

162:58 For "*thought for the Morrow*," cf. Matt. 6.34.

162:60 For a "Dish of *Clams*" as a symbol of extreme hardship, cf. Prefatory Poems, p. 81, l. 35.

Benjamin Tompson, in his *New Englands Crisis* (Boston, 1676), calls the days when the settlers were content with a fare of pumpkins and corn and ate "clamp-shells out of wooden Trayes" "golden times," which were "sin'd away for love of gold." (See Hall, *Poems of Tompson*, p. 49).

162:60–61 For "thanks to Heaven," cf. Mark 8.6, Acts 27.35, Rom. 14.6; for "*to suck the abundance*," etc., see Deut. 33.19.

162:63–78 For this paragraph, Mather weaves his sources together. For the "*Intestine Wars*," cf. Hubbard (p. 144), Johnson (pp. 78–79), and, briefly, Winthrop (*History*, 1:71). On Sagamore John's "hopefully" being "*Christianiz'd*" before his death, Mather's sources are somewhat ambiguous. According to Hubbard (p. 195), both "John Sagamore at Winnesimet" and "James Sagamore at Lynn" died: "It is said that those two promised, if they ever recovered, to live with the English, and serve their God." (Hubbard later, pp. 650–651, gives a more "literary" account of Sagamore John's death.) According to Johnson (pp. 79–80), "one of the chiefe Saggamores . . . whom the English named Saggamore John, gave some good hopes . . . much honour'd among the English, visiting a little before his death . . . Quoth hee, 'by and by . . . may be my two Sons live, you take them to teach much to know God.'" According to Winthrop (1:142–143), John Sagamore "left one Son, which he disposed to Mr. Wilson, the pastor of Boston, to be brought up by him . . . Divers of them, in their sickness, confessed that the Englishmen's God was a good God; and that, if they recovered, they would serve him. It wrought much with them, that when their own people forsook them, yet the English came daily and ministered to them." Johnson also speaks of the Englishmen's compassionate treatment of the Indians (p. 80). The allusion to *Golgotha* (see Matt. 27.33, Mark 15.22, John 19.17) is in Hubbard (p. 195). Johnson (p. 79) writes of the settlers' fairness in purchasing the land from the natives.

162:67 For "*great Plague*," cf. Num. 11.33, II Chron. 21.14.

162:72 For "*One* in *Ten*," cf. Neh. 11.1; for "left alive," cf. Num. 21.35.

162:79–163:85 Taken almost word for word from the beginning of Hubbard's Chapter XXV (p. 134). For the "*Family* of *Noah*," see Gen. 8.15–19.

163:87–98 Close paraphrase of Hubbard (p. 185). According to Hubbard, the "solemn *Fast*" was "partly in reference to the sickness and mortality ... and partly also for direction and blessing in choosing officers for their church."

163:87–7 Mather lists the first seven New England churches in the order given by Johnson (pp. 63–75), and he follows Johnson's errors. Winthrop and his company arrived in Massachusetts before the middle of July 1630 (cf. p. 157, l. 73 above). They soon went to Charlestown, and on August 27 called John Wilson as their Teacher (p. 163, ll. 91–92). This church shortly after removed to Boston as its First Church. According to Weis, the Dorchester church had meanwhile been organized on June 6, 1630; the Watertown church on June 30; Roxbury's in early 1632; Lynn's in August of that year, and the church in Charlestown, set up after its first church had moved to Boston, was established on November 2, 1632. (See Winthrop, *History*, 1:114n, and Weis, *Colonial Clergy*.)

163:89 Compare Joel 1.14, 2.15.

163:93–94 For "*Imposition of such Hands*," see Num. 27.18, 23, Deut. 34.9, Acts 6.6, 8.17, 13.3.

163:2 For "Issued out of," cf. Job 38.8, Ezek. 47.12; for "Care of the Church," I Tim. 3.5.

163:8–9 For "*Spirit* ... said unto them," cf. Rev. 2.7, 11, 17, 29; 3.6, 13, 22. For the "*Seven Churches*" as "*Golden Candlesticks*," see General Introduction, p. 93, l. 55, and endnote thereto.

163:11 The number twelve had many Biblical associations: for example, it was Jesus' age when he went to the Temple (Luke 2.42); cf. also Rev. 12.1, 21.12, 14, 21, 22.2.

163:14–164:20 In December 1634, the Commission for Foreign Plantations instructed the officers of the Port of London "not to suffer any person being a subsedyman [a man of means or substance liable for payment of subsidies granted to the Crown] to imbarke himselfe for any of the said plantations, without license from us his Maiesties commissioners, nor any person vnder the degree of a subsidyman without an attestation from two justices of the peace ... That he hath taken the oath of Supremacie and Allegiance, and the like Testimony from the Minister of the parish of his conversation and Conformity to the orders and discipline of the Church of England" (*Winthrop Papers*, 3:180).

Nevertheless, ways were found to escape the vigilance of the King's officers. On March 25, 1635, Emmanuel Downing wrote John Winthrop, Jr.: "There is one at the Custome howse apoynted to receive Certificates and give discharges to all such as shall goe to the pl[an]t[ation]. some that are goeing to N.E. went to him to know what they should doe. he bad them bring him any Certificate from Minister Church wardens or Justice that they were honest men and he would give them theire pass. they asked him what subsedy men should doe. he answered that he could not tell who were subsedy men, and would dischardge them vpon theire Certificates" (*Winthrop Papers*, 3:195).

The difficulties attendant on migrating appear in Philip Nye's letter of September 21, 1635, to John Winthrop, Jr.: "We haue sent you som servants but not so many as we purposed the reason is this   some of the Gentlemen of the North who lay som 3 or 4 Monthes in London transacting these affaires did thinke that their would have been no notice of their purpose and therevpon assumed to send vs vp servants but when they came down found the Countrie full of the reports of their going now those two (being Dep. leuetenants of the shire) did not care to moue any further in sending vp men for feare of increasing the reports; my lord Brooke likewise that vndertooke for xxtye failed likewise and sent vs not one" (*Winthrop Papers*, 3:211).

164:19–20 For "*Vproar*," cf. Acts 17.5; for "*let go*," see Exod. 4.21, 7.14, 8.32, 9.7, 17, 10.20, 27, 11.10.

164:24   The name of "Sir Arthur Hesilrige Barronet" appears on the agreement the Saybrook Company made with John Winthrop, Jr., July 7, 1635 (*Winthrop Papers*, 3:198). According to Thomas Hutchinson (*The History of the Colony and Province of Massachusetts-Bay*, ed. L. S. Mayo, 2. vols., Cambridge, Mass., Harvard University Press, 1936, 1:38–39), "many other persons of figure and distinction were expected to come over, some of which are said to have been prevented by express order of the King, as Mr. Pym, Mr. Hampden, Sir Arthur Haslerigg, Oliver Cromwell, &c. I know this is questioned by some authors, but it appears plainly by a letter from Lord Say and Seal to Mr. Vane, and a letter from Mr. Cotton to the same nobleman, as I take it, though his name is not mentioned, and an answer to certain demands made by him, that his Lordship himself and Lord Brooke and others were not without thoughts of removing to New-England".

The letters cited by Hutchinson are not reprinted, but Hampden's name is among the assignees of the Earl of Warwick's grant on the Narragansett River (Hutchinson, *History*, 1:57n). A letter from Cotton Mather's son Samuel (1706–1785) to his Tory son Samuel, June 9, 1784, suggests that Hutchinson may have had additional evidence: "There were several Letters I had, original Letters, written by the renowned Oliver Cromwell, to my Great-grandfather, Mr. John Cotton, which I sent to your careless Uncle, Mr. Hutchinson, and, as I suppose, they are irrevocably lost and gone: I furnished him, as I suppose you know, with most of the Materials, of which his History was composed" (see Holmes, *Increase Mather*, 1:82).

164:26   For "*Spirit of Prophecy*," see Rev. 19.10.

164:29–33   Mather's source for this passage on "divers Gentlemen in *Scotland*" is Hubbard (pp. 154–155): "About this time, or in the year 1634, letters were brought into the country from one Mr. Leviston, a worthy minister in the north of Ireland, (himself being of the Scottish nation,) whereby he signified that there were many Christians in those parts resolved to go thither, if they might receive satisfaction concerning some questions and propositions which he sent over." Hubbard's wording, from "whereby" on, exactly follows a Winthrop entry for July 1634 (*History*, 1:160), but in Winthrop the writer's name is spelled Levinston. This was the Reverend John Livingston, who, like a fellow Presbyterian minister, Robert Blair, had been deprived of his living in Scotland. Settled in Ireland with members of their congregations, they laid plans for migrating to New England. Blair's autobiography (see *The Life of Mr. Robert Blair*, Wodrow Society: Edinburgh, 1848, p. 105) continues the story: "About this time there came to us an English gentleman, whose name was Mr. Winthrop, from New England. This understanding gentleman being the son of the governor of that plantation . . . did earnestly invite and greatly encourage us to prosecute our intended voyage." In October of 1635, Governor Winthrop noted that the ship carrying his son to England had been forced by a storm to put in at Galloway. "Mr. Winthrop went to Dublin, and from thence to Antrim . . . to the house of Sir John Clotworthy, the evening before the day when divers godly persons were appointed to meet at his house, to confer about their voyage to New England" (*History*, 1:205–206). Livingston was obviously present at that meeting, for we have a letter, dated Jan. 5, 1634/5, from him to "Mr. Wynthorp," in which he regrets that "Hast to bee at my charge wes the reason why I come away so abruptly th'other day. I could have been glad to have had more tyme, and so to have been more refreshed with yowr company, But I hope the tyme may come when we may see one another in that land where a great part of my heart is already" (*Winthrop Papers*, 3:187–188). There were many difficulties and setbacks, however (cf. Blair, *Life*, p. 135). When the company finally sailed, September 9, 1636, they encountered such savage storms, with irreparable damage to their ship, that they turned back, "*Half-Seas* thorough" (Blair, pp. 143–146). Samuel Clarke, in his *Lives of Sundry Eminent Persons* (London, 1683, p. 219), among "Providences, Strange and Extraordinary," cites the saving of these "Divers choice Ministers and Christians in Ireland (Mr. *Blair*, Mr. *Levinston*, and Mr. *Mackleland*)" from the perils of the sea as an evidence of their true piety.

164:40 The Solemn League and Covenant proclaimed its purposes as the extirpation of popery and prelacy, the preservation of the rights of Parliaments and the liberties of the kingdoms, the defense of the King's "just powers" and the suppression of the "malignants" who sought to divide him from his people. The English were chiefly interested in obtaining a civil league against the Royalists; the Scottish interest was in the religious side of the agreement. After the rise of Cromwell and the Independents, it became a dead letter in England. Compare endnote to General Introduction, p. 90, ll. 51–52.

164:42–44 The figure of 4,000 for the number of arrivals in New England by 1640 is a surprising and probably erroneous computation. As early as May 1634, in a letter to Nathaniel Rich, Governor Winthrop had written "for the number of our people, we never took any surveigh of them . . . but I esteeme them to be in all about 4000 soules and vpwarde" (*Winthrop Papers*, 3:166). Increase Mather, in his *A Brief Relation of the State of New England* (London, 1689, p. 5; cf. Holmes, *I, Mather.* 1:76–82), wrote: "Some have observed, that since the year 1640, more people have removed out of *New England*, than have gone thither. Nevertheless, the four thousand, who did between that and the year 1620, transplant themselves into *New England*, are so marveilously increased, as that, if the computation fail not, they are now become more than Two hundred thousand Souls." Cotton Mather, however, seems not to have followed his father's *Relation*, but instead an anonymous pamphlet, *A Vindication of New-England* (Boston, 1690, pp. 22–23), in which he read: "3, or 4,000 of them— transplanted themselves . . . into that Howling wilderness of *America*. And coming over with the Royal consent and Charter, they purchased their possessions of the native Proprietors . . . and altho' in the last 50 years, more have gone out of it than ever went into it, yet hath New-England increased . . . to a people of perhaps more than 100,000 Souls." (See Holmes, *I. Mather*, 2:615). On the reverse migration, see W. L. Sachse, "The migration of New Englanders to England, 1640–1660," *American Historical Review*, 53:251–278 (Jan. 1948), and *The Colonial American in Britain*, Madison, Wis., University of Wisconsin Press, 1956.

164:47–50 Eutropius, *Historiae Romanae Brevarium* (ed. Mme Anna Dacier, Paris, 1683, p. 3): "Romanum imperium, quo neque ab exordio ullum fere minus, neque incrementis toto orbe amplius humana potest memoria recordari." The "saying of Eutropius about Rome" appears in the same form ["Nec minor," etc.] in Mather's "Quotidiana."

165:51–54 The Biblical echoes in these lines all heighten Mather's celebration of God's benevolent providence toward New England: His care of Jacob "in a waste howling wilderness" as "the apple of His eye" (Deut. 32.10); His promise (in Jer. 3.19), "I will . . . give thee a pleasant land"; and His conferring of the blessing on Joseph (Deut. 33.16): all "the precious things of the earth and the fulness thereof" on "him that was separated from his brethren."

165:62 Horace *Epistles* I.xi.27.

165:65–166:90 . For his account of the settling of Connecticut, Mather relies on Hubbard, Chapter XLI. Section 1 is taken from p. 305, including the figure of "an *Hive*, overstocked with *Bees*." For a detailed treatment of the founding of Connecticut see Miller, "Thomas Hooker and the Democracy of Connecticut," *Errand into the Wilderness*, pp. 16–47.

165:83–166:86 Mather followed exactly the introductory "Ad studiosos lectores" (page 2, 4 lines from the bottom of the page) in the Leyden, 1622, edition of Fernandez' *Commentarii in Visiones Veteris Testamenti*. It seems probable that he owned or had access to a copy of the book; his interest in typology (see introductory essay, "The

Magnalia," p. 45) would have led him to study any treatise on the figurative meaning of the "visions" of the Old Testament, and books published in Holland were often imported by Boston booksellers.

166:92   While referring to the leadership of Thomas Hooker in the removal, Mather chooses not to mention the possibility that desire for more land may not have been the only motivation, or as Hubbard hinted (pp. 305–306): "It was also said, that . . . there was . . . an impulsive cause, that did more secretly and powerfully drive on the business. Some men do not well like, at least, cannot well bear, to be opposed in their judgments and notions, and thence were they not unwilling to remove from under the power, as well as out of the bounds, of the Massachusetts. Nature doth not allow two suns in one firmament." Hutchinson named names (*History*, 1:40): "Mr. Hooker and Mr. Cotton were deservedly in high esteem; some of the principal persons were strongly attached to the one of them, and some to the other. The great influence, which Mr. Cotton had in the colony, inclined Mr. Hooker and his friends to remove to some place more remote from Boston than Newtown. Besides, they alledged . . . that they were straitened for room." Mather clearly wished to elide any suggestion of dissention between his grandfather and Hooker. See Miller, *Errand*, pp. 23–28. On the relations between Hooker and Cotton before they left England, see *Magnalia*, Bk. III. chap. 16, sec. 3.

166:94–95   Compare Num. 14.7.

166:96–1   The disposition of the churches is from Hubbard (pp. 307, 308).

166:3–9   Mather's account of the hardships suffered the first winter abridges Hubbard (p. 308), which is in itself a condensed account. According to Winthrop (*History*, 1:207), under date of Nov. 26, 1635, "There came twelve men from Connecticut. They had been twelve days upon their journey, and had lost one of their company, drowned in the ice by the way; and had been all starved, but that, by God's providence, they lighted upon an Indian wigwam." In an entry for Dec. 10 (1:208–209), Winthrop related that the *Rebecka* "was frozen twenty miles up the river, but a small rain falling set her free; but coming out, she ran on ground at the mouth of the river, and was forced to unlade. They came to Massachusetts in five days, which was a great mercy of God, for otherwise they had all perished with famine, as some did." Hooker, with the majority of the Connecticut settlers, did not remove until the spring of 1636.

166:11–17   The reference to the Pequot troubles follows Hubbard (pp. 306–307). For "subduing of the Quarrelsome Nation," cf. Neh. 9.24.

166:18   The "Countenance and Assistance" of Massachusetts Bay were not given as readily as Mather implies. When the removal was first proposed at a session of the General Court on September 4, 1634, it was strongly opposed (see Hubbard, pp. 172–175, and Winthrop, 1:167–168). As Hubbard put it (p. 306), "it might have been as well for the whole if they could have been included in one jurisdiction; for by that means their union together . . . had been much firmer and stronger." Nevertheless, Hubbard continued, the move to Connecticut was made "in the year 1635 . . . with the approbation of the authority of the Massachusetts." Again, Mather has chosen to play down any hint of discord.

167:28–30   Mather's source, followed closely, is Hubbard (p. 309). For the text of this compact, see Benjamin Trumbull, *A Complete History of Connecticut* (2 vols., New Haven, 1818), 1:498–502. On the relation of the *Fundamental Orders* to the "form of the Colony from whence they Issued," see Miller, *Errand*, pp. 37–47.

167:31   See Hubbard, p. 309. On Fenwick, see also p. 279.

167:35–36   The patent granted by the Earl of Warwick, known as "the old patent of Connecticut," was dated March 19, 1632. Compare Hubbard (pp. 309–310), and Trumbull (1:495–496).

167:49   See Hubbard (pp. 310–311). For the text of the charter, see Hazard (2:597–605) and B. P. Poore, *The Federal and State Constitutions, Colonial Charters, and Other Organic Laws of the United States* (2 vols., Washington, D.C., 1877), 1:252–257.

168:54–66   Section 4 is a paraphrase of Hubbard, retaining much of the language. For the contentions at Wethersfield, see pp. 313–314, from which Mather has borrowed the references to Abraham and Lot (Gen. 13.5–12) and to a "*Cottage in a Wilderness*" (Isa. 1.8), and the phrases "*Fire* of Contention" (Amos 7.4) and "beautiful Edifice" (for Hubbard's "beautiful habitation"). Mather has telescoped disputes that arose over a period of twenty years. The original dispute led to the founding of Stamford and Branford. Later disputes in the Hartford church after the death of Hooker spread to surrounding communities (see *Magnalia*, Bk. III, chap. 16, sec. 8), and men from Hartford, Wethersfield, and Windsor moved up the river to Springfield, Hadley, and Hatfield (cf. Hubbard, pp. 315–316). See also S. W. Adams, *The History of Ancient Wethersfield* (2 vols., New York, Grafton Press, 1904), 1:142–165; S. Judd, *History of Hadley* (Springfield, R. Huntting & Co., Mass., 1905), pp. 3–17; George Leon Walker, *History of the First Church in Hartford* (Hartford, Brown & Gross, 1884), pp. 146–181.

168:62   For "*Enlargements*," cf. Deut. 19.8, I Chron. 4.10.

168:67–169:88   Throughout Section 5 Mather closely follows Hubbard, pp. 317–320. Eaton had been one of the original patentees of the Massachusetts Bay Company. His interest in New England was partly religious, partly commercial. The company he and Davenport led constituted the wealthiest and commercially the ablest group which had yet emigrated. The Bay, where they landed, made every effort to persuade them to remain, but after nine months they removed to New Haven. Mather wrote later (*Magnalia*, Bk. II, p. 257, l. 56) that "Mr. Eaton and Mr. Davenport were the Moses and Aaron" of the New Haven colony.

169:84   "Take root," cf. 2 Kings 19.30, Ps. 80.9, Isa. 27.6, 37.31; etc.

169:86   For the New Haven "Agreement," see Trumbull, *Connecticut*, 1:502–506.

169:89–7   Abridged from Hubbard (pp. 321–322), with many phrases retained, such as "tradable estates," the ship "foundered in the Sea," "*Hopes* of their future Trade." Hubbard names Mr. Thomas Grigson as among the "Excellent Persons" who were lost; the "Manuscripts" as "some writings of Mr. Hooker's and Mr. Davenport's . . . which was a loss to the world itself." The lost writings by Hooker and Davenport were written to defend Congregationalism against two books published in England by Presbyterian apologists. Hooker's was his *Survey of the Summe of Church-Discipline*, written in answer to Samuel Rutherford's *The Due Right of Presbyteries* (1644). With considerable reluctance, he rewrote it: it was not published until 1648, a year after his death in 1647. Davenport's work was *The Power of Congregational Churches Asserted and Vindicated: In Answer to a Treatise of Mr. J. Paget.* (Paget's book was *A Defence of Church-government. Exercised in Presbyteriall, Classical, & Synodal Assemblies*, London, 1641.) He likewise rewrote his work; it too was published (London, 1672) only after the author's death, in 1670. See Franklin B. Dexter, "The Life and Writings of the Reverend John Davenport," *New Haven Historical Society Papers*, 2:229.

169:1–2   The NED cites this passage to illustrate the use of the word "tradable," which Mather borrowed from Hubbard's manuscript.

169:12–170:52   Hubbard (p. 322) agrees with Pierpont's letter on the circumstances of the voyage, but makes no mention of the phantom ship. Under date of January 1645/6, Winthrop briefly mentions a ship "forced to be cut out of the ice" (*History*, 2:311). His notice of the loss is also brief (2:325–326). A reference to the vision of the phantom ship is under date of June 1648 (2:399–400) rather than Pierpont's "*June* next ensuing."

169:18   According to Hubbard (p. 322), the ship was "ill built, very walt-sided, and, to increase the inconveniency thereof, ill laden." Winthrop said it was a ship of 80 tons; Pierpont increases its size to 150 tons. Andrews (*Colonial Period*, 2:176n) denies the Rhode Island origin of the ship, and argues convincingly for its having been built in New Haven.

170:24–25   See Ps. 119.94.

170:26   For "Heart began to fail her," cf. Gen. 42.28, Pss. 40.12, 73.26.

170:54   Samuel Mather of Witney, in his copy of the *Magnalia*, wrote in the margin opposite Pierpont's signature, "I have seen the original of this letter. S.M." (See Holmes, *The Minor Mathers*, p. 204).

170:57   Mather's claim that Pierpont's account was "as *undoubted*, as 'tis *wonderful*" must be viewed with considerable skepticism. Pierpont, born only in 1660, did not settle in New Haven until 1684, by which time the legend had clearly had time to grow. By then it had taken on certain characteristic attributes of all spectral vessels, such as that they always appear "sailing against the wind" and just "before sunset" (cf. John Livingston Lowes, *The Road to Xanadu*, Boston, Houghton Mifflin Co., 1927, pp. 276, 559–560).

170:58–171:72   Close paraphrase of Hubbard, pp. 325–327.

171:68–70   Compare Num. 14.31.

171:79–92   Section 7 derives entirely from Hubbard, who briefly defines the boundaries of the enlarged Connecticut Colony, p. 311. Mather takes his account of the negotiations leading to the joining of New Haven to Connecticut from pp. 331–332, including the allusion to Jephthah's daughter (Judg. 11.30–40). Hubbard describes the "Malignant *Fevers* and *Agues*" on pp. 324–325.

171:81   For Trumbull's narrative of the negotiations between New Haven and Connecticut, see 1:252–276; for the documents, see 1:515–521, 526–530.

171:81–90   For "the *God of Love and Peace*," see II Cor. 13.11. The phrase "children of God" recurs frequently in the New Testament. Compare Luke 20.36, Rom. 8.16, Gal. 3.26, etc. Mather's "these Children of God have not been without their *Chastisements*" reminds the reader of the "children which have not seen the chastisement of the Lord" (Deut. 11.2).

171:97   For settlements designed for the "*Fishing*-Trade" and "*Bever*-Trade," cf. Hubbard, chapter XXXI (pp. 213–233).

171:97–172:8   The northeast region was for some years the arena for all manner of disputes, between various patentees, between an Anglican and a Puritan party, between pastors of the several churches (cf. Hubbard, chap. XLIV). Relations with the Massachusetts Bay were not always cordial, since it was often an area of resort for persons inimical to or expelled from the Bay, such as, for example, the reverend John Wheelwright, Anne Hutchinson's brother-in-law, who in 1638 settled at Exeter, New Hampshire.

171:98   This oblique reference is Mather's only mention in Book I of the prolonged Antinomian controversy which disrupted the colony in 1636–1637 and led to the excommunication and banishment of Anne Hutchinson and her followers (cf. Hubbard, pp. 280–304). His purpose is clearly to blur the memory of his grandfather Cotton's role in the affair. Unable in his biographical sketch of John Cotton (Bk. III, chap. 1) to avoid reference to it, he devotes sections 21 and 22 entirely to defense of Cotton against those "venomous" souls who accused him of being in any way responsible for the Hutchinsonian heresy, managing in the process to omit any account of the doctrines at issue. When in his lives of other actors in the drama some mention is inescapable, he hurriedly makes brief references to "antinomian and familistical factions" and goes on to other matters (see, for example, the lives of Winthrop, Bk. II, chap. 4, sec. 8, of John Wilson, Bk. III, chap. 3, sec. 13, and of Thomas Shepard, Bk. III, chap. 5, sec. 12. (For a valuable examination of theological issues in the controversy, see Jesper Rosenmeier, "New England's Perfection: The Image of Adam and the Image of Christ in the Antinomian Crisis, 1634 to 1638," *William and Mary Quarterly*, Series 3, 27:435–459). For "Day of Temptation," cf. Rev. 3.10, Ps. 95.8, Heb. 3.8.

172:7–13   Mather writes as if there had been one "Application" made by the settlements in "*East Hampshire*" and "*Main*" to be taken under the protection of Massachusetts. Actually the absorption was a piecemeal, lengthy, and sometimes acrimonious process. The first movement was initiated in 1639. For his account

Mather may have drawn on both Johnson and Hubbard. According to Johnson (*Wonder-Working Providence*, pp. 206–207), "About this time the people inhabiting the Town of Dover ... (hearing and seeing with what sweet harmony, both in churches and civil Goverment, the Mattachusets peopled patten was carried on prosperously) desired greatly to submit unto the same ... and for that end they petitioned their General Cort to admit of them, and administer Justice as occasion served ... which accordingly was granted." Compare Hubbard (pp. 371–372): "On the other side, toward Pascataqua, some gentlemen ... finding they were not able to manage or carry on what they had taken in hand ... therefore petitioned the Massachusetts ... to accept of them into their government; which they did, not so much out of ambition of the power, as compassion to the poor inhabitants, who had been almost wearied out with dissensions ... both in their civil as well as church affairs ... So that, on Sept. 24, 1641, the inhabitants of the south side of Pascataqua, both at Dover and Strawberry Bank [Portsmouth] ... were declared to belong to the Massachusetts jurisdiction." Winthrop noted the beginning of negotiations in September 1639 (*History*, 1:384–385), and in February 1639/40, Edward Starbuck wrote to Winthrop on the possibility of bringing Dover under the jurisdiction of the Bay (*Winthrop Papers*, 4:185–188). After describing the contentions and strife around Piscataqua, Winthrop concluded (*History*, 2:33–34): "a good part of the inhabitants" offered "themselves again to the government of the Massachusetts ... The governour and council considered of their petition, and gave commission to Mr. Bradstreet, one of our magistrates, Mr. Peter and Mr. Dalton ... to go thither," and if they could not reconcile the quarreling factions, "to certify us" as agreeing.

Mather could find in Hubbard (pp. 542–543) an account of the next step, as of all subsequent ones in the proceedings: in 1651, "those on the other side in the Province of Maine ... urged with the like necessity ... for having run themselves aground in their government, and not well able to recover the stream again, they were willing to cast themselves upon the General Court of the Massachusetts, who, upon several considerations, past an order and declaration about their right and title thereunto ... On which account all the towns eastward of Pascataqua were, within the compass of the next two years, taken into the government of the Massachusetts in like manner." In 1652, the inhabitants of Kittery were summoned "to come in and own their subjection to the Massachusetts ... And being assembled together November 16th, that year, they submitted thereunto ... The like was done at Agamenticus the 22d of the same month, the place being afterward called York. In like manner in the year following ... Wells ... Saco ... Cape Porpoise ... submitted thereunto."

Contentions continued. Compare Hubbard (p. 584): "as to the Province of Maine, there were two sorts, that pretended a right to the government thereof: one that derived their power from Sir Ferdinando Gorges's title, the other derived theirs from the General Court of the Massachusetts." In 1665 royal commissioners intervened, saying neither side should extend power further until "his Magesty's pleasure were further known."

The final resolution is detailed at some length by Hubbard (pp. 593–601), "the occasion and manner, how it was brought about" in 1668. For a long time inhabitants east of the Saco River, most of them Episcopalians, had resisted being joined to Massachusetts. However, because "the people there [were] like to be reduced to a confused anarchy, for want of a settled order of government," "some principal persons" made application to the General Court. After considerable negotiations concerning the administration of the territories in question, agreement was signed on 23 October, 1668 (for the documents, see Hubbard, pp. 594–600). Hubbard's version concludes: "In this order and manner did the Province of Maine return to the government of the Massachusetts, without any other force, threatening, or violence, whatever hath been to the contrary judged, reported, and published by any other person, to the prejudice and disadvantage of the truth, and the credit of them that were called to act therein."

172:15   Ogilby's account (*America*, pp. 164–165) could not fail to outrage Massachusetts inhabitants. According to his version, "In the Year of our Lord 1665. his Majesties Commissioners for the Affairs of *New England*, being in the Province of *Mayne*, the People being much unsetled in Point of Government, by reason the Mattachusets Colony . . . did usurp compulsively a Power over them contrary to their wills; and the right of Sir *Ferdinando Gorges* Heir," petitioned them "to settle the Government." In the King's name the commissioners set up justices of the peace and other officers to govern until the King "had more leisure to determine it." Three years later, according to Ogilby, the "Bostoners" did, in July 1668, send warrants to the Court at York, demanding submission to the Bay. When the "King's Justices" demurred, showing their commission, "Major General *Leveret* told them, That he believ'd it might be the King's Hand, but he had a Commission from the general Court at *Boston*, which he would follow and observe by the help of God." While Hubbard does not name the "person" he accuses of "prejudice" (p. 601), he may well have been referring to this same passage, or possibly to similar strictures leveled by John Josselyn, the voyager, who lived with his brother Henry at Black Point between 1663 and 1671, and charged that "the Massachusets" entered the province of Maine "in a hostile manner with a Troop of Horse and Foot" (see *An Account of Two Voyages to New-England*, London, 1674, pp. 197–198).

172:15–16   Quoted in Lange, *Florilegii* (1:1200), from Ausonius, *In Didus Imaginem*, Epistle 118, line 15, which has *de me* instead of *veris*.

172:17   For the churches "along that Coast," see below p. 176, l. 47 to p. 177, l. 56.

172:21   For "Outgoings," cf. Josh. 17.9, 18, 18.19, 19.14, 22, 29, 33, Ps. 65.8.

172:25   Compare Gen. 27.27.

172:29   Compare Job 4.9, Amos 4.9, Hag. 2.17. For the unhappy story of the 1690 expedition against Canada, see section 11 of Mather's life of Sir William Phips, p. 299, *et seq.* above.

173:41–178:98   Except as otherwise noted the data for the notes on the list of ministers are taken from Weis, *The Colonial Clergy*, and Sibley, *Biographical Sketches*.

173:46   For John Cotton of Plymouth (1640–1699) and his somewhat checkered life, see *Diary*, 1:236, 277.

174:58   Compare Prov. 29.17, 18, and *Magnalia*, Bk. I, pt. 1, chap. 3, p. 144, l. 87.

174:59   In 1683 "inhabitants of the freeman's land at Fall River" were established as a township to be "called Freetowne." Part of Freetown was annexed to Fall River in 1803 and part to Fairhaven in 1815. (See Massachusetts Commissioner of Public Records of Parishes, Towns, and Counties, *Report on the Custody and Condition of the Public Records*, ed. Carroll D. Wright, Boston, 1889, p. 170). The first Congregational church at Freetown was established in 1704.

174:77   Cotton Mather unjustly suggests that the Anglican Church relied on itinerant preachers; in fact it seems to have had one minister and sometimes two from 1686 on. The first minister, John Ratcliffe, B.D., apparently came to New England at the instigation of Edward Randolph (cf. introductory essay "Cotton Mather," p. 13), who hoped to replace the Congregational hierarchy with an Episcopal one. For a time Ratcliffe's flock met in the Town House of Boston, but Governor Andros soon "arbitrarily quartered the congregation upon the meeting house of the South Church." This, of course, outraged its Congregational proprietors. Increase Mather in 1686 wrote and had published anonymously a *Brief Discourse Concerning the Unlawfulness of the Common Prayer Worship*, and Cotton Mather added to it an epistle "To the Reader," signing it "T.P." He was wrongly accused of having written the book itself and was therefore bound over for trial for having disseminated "scandalous libels against the church and government." After Andros's downfall in 1689 the indictment was quashed. By then, however, the Anglican worshippers had built a church of their own. This, the first King's Chapel, was replaced by the present building in 1750. Later in his life Mather was more tolerant toward other sects than his own, but when he wrote the *Magnalia* he could not resist minimizing the importance of the Episcopalians in Boston. See *Diary*, 1:133n; Justin Winsor, *The Memorial History of Boston* (4 vols., Boston, 1880–1881), 1:200–216; H. W. Foote, *Annals of King's Chapel* (Boston, 1882–1896); and, especially, Holmes, *Increase Mather*, 1:48–63.

176:33   For Higginson, see Attestation, p. 63n; for Noyes, Prefatory Poems, p. 74n.

176:40   Enfield, now in Connecticut, had a minister, Nathaniel Welch, who left there in 1689. His successor was not appointed until 1697, presumably too late for Mather's list.

177:50   For John Cotton of Hampton, see note to *Magnalia*, Bk. I, p. 147, ll. 6–12.

177:56   Neither Wells nor York seems to have had a minister when Mather wrote, but it is probable that John Hancock (Harvard, 1689) preached at both from 1692 to 1693. See W. D. Williamson in *Collections and Proceedings* of the Maine Historical Society, Series 2, 4:197 and 3:429–439.

177:57–58   The boundary between Massachusetts and Connecticut was a subject of debate, and some of the towns Mather lists as in Connecticut are now included in Massachusetts. For the movement of Connecticut settlers up the Connecticut Valley, see above p. 168, ll. 54–66, and endnote thereto.

177:78   Pescamsik is undoubtedly Mather's spelling of the Indian name for "Pantoosuck," "Pigscomscutt," or "Pigsumsuck." These names were applied to the region of Plainfield and nearby Canterbury, in the Quinebaug area of east Connecticut, to the northwest of Providence. (See "Quanabaug" on the map in the *Magnalia*.) Mather's "Joseph Mors" took his first degree from Harvard in 1695, taught school at Dedham until November 1696, and then "wandered to Providence." In 1698 he was asked to teach there for a year. Although there was no established church in the Quinebaug region until after 1700, it is probable that Mors found his way there in 1697 and taught or preached to the Indians and settlers before he returned to Providence, married there, in 1698, and returned to Massachusetts, where he took his second degree at Harvard in that year.

178:86   At least one copy of the 1702 *Magnalia* has "Andreter" for "Andrews" (more commonly spelled "Andrew"), presumably a typesetter's error which was corrected before the printing of the sheets for this page was finished.

178:13–15   For "Pestilential *Sicknesses*" and the "*Angel of Death*," cf. II Sam. 24.15–16.

178:16   A reference to Indian raids and wars. Compare Ps. 8.2.

179:23   For "*Upper*" and "*Nether-Springs*," see Josh. 15.19, Judg. 1.15.

179:25   *The Interest of Princes*, p. 78.

179:36   The year after Eliot's death, Mather published *The Triumphs of the Reformed Religion in America: The Life of the Renowned John Eliot* (see Prefatory Poems, p. 85, l. 36n). The words here given as direct quotation appear in "The Conclusion: Or, Eliot Expiring," as indirect address.

179:43   For "through the *Earth*," cf. Ps. 73.9.

THE BOSTONIAN EBENEZER

180:1   In his Diary on April 1, 1698, Mather wrote (1:256–257): "But one special Request, which I this Day made unto Heaven was; For the gracious Presence of the Lord Jesus Christ with mee, in my Design, on my Lecture the next week, to relate and improve the *History* of the Divine Dispensations, towards this Town; whereof I am a Native." On April 7 he reports: "The Lord having *helped* mee, beyond my expectation in praeparing a Discourse for the Lecture, Hee yett more gloriously *helped* mee, in uttering of it, unto a vast Assembly of His People . . . and the Hearts of the Inhabitants, of the Town, were strangely moved, by what was delivered among them. A Copy of the Discourse, was much desired; I gave it unto the Bookseller; entitling it, THE BOSTONIAN EBENEZER." Mather reproduces the first fifteen lines of that title-page, which concludes, "*Boston*, Printed by *B Green* & *F. Allen*, for *Samuel*

Phillips, at the Brick Shop. 1698." (Cf. Holmes, *Cotton Mather,* 1:97.) On the Ebenezer, cf. Attestation, p. 64, ll. 44–45, and endnote thereto.

180:16–17   This epigram was added to the original title-page of the *Ebenezer.* Mather's probable source was Alsted, *Encyclopaedia* (p. 1493a), from a collection of "Florilegium Politicum Ex Philippo Cominaeo." Mather omits the words "in toto Regno" after "Maximae." Philippe de Comines (Commynes), 1447–1511, French courtier and chronicler, served successively Charles the Bold, Louis XI, and Charles VIII. His *Memoires* are regarded as one of the classics of medieval history.

181:65–72   For the battle against the Philistines at Mizpeh, see I Sam. 7–11.

181:78   For the stone of Jacob, see Gen. 28.18, 35.14; for Joshua's, Josh. 24.26–27.

181:86–88   Compare Ps. 107.6, 13, 28.

182:2–3   Compare Judg. 16.28, Ezek. 3.11.

182:5 *et seq.*   In Mather's lecture, the "things to be Inculcated," or "uses," are greatly expanded at the expense of the "doctrine" and "reasons" of earlier Puritan sermon form. In his first "use," he introduces a second Biblical text, or theme: "His mercy endureth for ever."

182:14   That is, three score and ten. Compare Ps. 90.10.

182:20   For the water in Charlestown, see Robert C. Winthrop, "Boston Founded," in Justin Winsor, *The Memorial History of Boston,* 1:116, and Johnson, *Wonder-Working Providence,* p. 116. William Wood, who was in New England from 1629 to 1633, in his *New Englands Prospect* (London, 1634; ed. H. W. Boynton, Boston, 1898), wrote that the "greatest wants" of the Boston settlers were "Wood . . . and Medow-ground," so that they were "constrayned to fetch their building-timber, and fire-wood from the Islands in Boates and their Hay in Loyters [lighters]." Governor Winthrop himself wrote to his son that in the winter of 1637 "we at Boston were almost ready to break up for want of wood" (*History,* 1:472). Dorchester, Wood wrote, was "the greatest Towne in New England well wooded" and with "arable grounds," and the inhabitants of adjoining Roxbury were "all very rich" (p. 39). Johnson declared that Boston in the 1630's had been "a poor country village," but by 1650 was fit to be a "Mayor Town" (p. 247). Even before this, however, Boston had surpassed the other towns in population and prosperity and become the unquestioned capital city, Massachusetts' "Metropolis." It owed its success largely to its "safe and pleasant Harbor," ideally fitted for a port. The harbor had "but one common and safe entrance . . . not very broad," but with "roome for the Anchorage of 500 ships" (Wood, p. 3). Moreover, the hills of the peninsula and the islands in the bay were excellent sites for forts which could defend the town from enemy marauders. Ship building and trading by sea therefore developed rapidly. There seems to be no available source for Mather's assertion that Boston was once "proverbially" called "Lost Town." Perhaps it was, or he may simply have drawn that inference from Johnson's "poor country village."

182:20–21   For "*obtained help from God,*" see Acts 26.22, I Cor. 7.25.

182:23   Ps. 136. For the computation of twenty-six generations to the Psalmist, David, see Johann Alsted, *Thesaurus Chronologiæ* (Herborn, 1628), p. 35.

182:26   By employing the phrase "*Ab Urbe Condita*" for "this Town," Mather was in effect claiming that the founding of Boston signalized a new epoch comparable to that inaugurated by the founding of Rome. Livy entitled his history *Ab Urbe Condita.* Compare also Alsted's *Thesaurus* (p. [2]), where it appears as one category in the "Laterculum," or register, of various epochs in history.

182:29   Compare Bk. I, p. 162, ll. 50–57 on the famine of the winter of 1630–1631. Hubbard noted scarcity of provisions in 1635–1636 (p. 239) and in 1639–1640 (p. 423). Winthrop (*History,* 2:113) noted that by the end of April 1642 "Corn was very scarce all over the country . . . many families in most towns had none to eat, but were forced to live of clams, muscles, cataos, dry fish, etc."

182:30   Mather used the phrase "last meal" and quoted I Kings 17.12 (p. 162, ll.

50–57) with reference to the scarcity of food before the arrival of ships in the spring of 1631. He again cited the text in his life of Governor Winthrop in connection with the arrival of the *Lyon* in February 1631 (Bk. II, p. 217, l. 72). In his Diary for November 9, 1697, Cotton Mather wrote, "*A great Salvation* has this Year been granted unto this *Land.* We have with a *plentiful Harvest*, been saved from the *terrible Famine*, when a few Dayes of Drought more, would have rendred it irresistible." Thanks were offered in a "public *Thanksgiving*" on November 11 (*Diary*, 1:241).

182:31   Compare Matt. 15.33–36, Mark 6.35–40, Luke 9.13–16, John 6.9–11.

182:34–35   For "*Three last Years*," cf. II Sam. 21.1, I Chron. 21.12; for "*Shepherd* and *Feeder*," cf. Ps. 23.1, 5, Isa. 40.11.

183:37   For "*Arrows*," etc., cf. Prov. 26.18.

183:37–41   Smallpox visited Boston in 1666, resulting in forty deaths. A few cases appeared in 1675, but nothing of epidemic proportions (see Ernest Caulfield, "The Pursuit of a Pestilence," AAS *Proc.*, 60:28–29). The most severe epidemic of the disease came in 1678, with an estimated eight hundred victims (see Carl Bridenbaugh, *Cities in the Wilderness*, New York, Capricorn Books, 1955, pp. 86–87); Mather here estimates "about one Thousand." There were further epidemics in 1686 and 1690 (Hutchinson, *History*, 1:340). On the 1690 visitation, see also Sewall's *Diary* (1:320–324). Smallpox was by no means the only "Arrow of Death." There are records of pneumonia, yellow fever, influenza, and other diseases (Bridenbaugh, p. 240n, and Caulfield, pp. 26–32). For "long Home," cf. Eccles. 12.5.

Mather was to show himself increasingly concerned for the medical welfare of the colony, most notably in the great smallpox epidemic of 1721–1722, when he championed the cause of innoculation and Dr. Zabdiel Boylston's administration of that method of treatment. Dr. Walter Frankel, in an article entitled "Industrial Medicine's Hall of Fame: Cotton Mather, 1663–1728" (*Industrial Medicine and Surgery*, December 1963, pp. 251–524), praises his "progressive medical ideas and intelligence." He particularly emphasizes Mather's analysis (in *Angel of Bethesda*, 1724) of the relation between the diseases of craftsmen and the "Disaffection to the Business" which workers may exhibit, and calls him both "the father of occupational medicine in America" and "perhaps this country's first psychologist." Indeed, one might say that Mather showed himself the psychologist in his treatment of the bewitched Glover children whom he took into his home in 1688 (see below Bk. II, p. 333, ll. 56–59 and notes).

183:42   There are reported to have been in 1700 6,700 inhabitants in Boston (see Greene and Harrington, *American Population*, p.22n). Bridenbaugh (p. 143n) estimates 7,000.

183:43–44   For "*have Mercy upon us*," see Ps. 123.2, Luke 17.13; for "abandon'd Habitations," cf. Eccles. 12.4, Isa. 27.10.

183:46   Fire was a constant hazard. All contemporary records are filled with accounts of houses, churches, barns, haycocks, etc., consumed by fire. Lightning was a frequent cause. In his diary for April 29, 1695, Samuel Sewall wrote: "Mr. Cotton Mather dined with us . . . He had just been mentioning that more Ministers Houses than others proportionately had been smitten with Lightening; enquiring what the meaning of God should be in it" (*Diary*, 1:402).

183:49   Compare Ps. 127.1.

183:51–52   Compare Ps. 121.4.

183:52   The first of the "great" fires of Boston occurred on March 14, 1653; the exact extent is unknown. In 1672 there was a fire "at Mrs. Oliver's," which would be the dock area (Bridenbaugh, *Cities*, pp. 58, 60). Among the fires that would be fresh in Mather's mind was that of November 27, 1676, "enkindled at the north end of the town of Boston . . . whereby many other houses were consumed, together with the meeting house at that end of the said town" (see Hubbard, pp. 648–649), Shortly before this fire broke out, Increase Mather had a foreboding that his house would burn, and on November 19 he preached a sermon warning his flock. The next Sunday he preached on Rev. 3.3, and that night his house was destroyed by the fire (see his "Autobiography," ed. M. G. Hall, AAS *Proc.*, 71:302–303). On August 8, 1679, occurred the most spectacular of all. According to Hutchinson (1:295n). it began "about midnight," "at one Gross's house, the sign of the Three Mariners, near the dock." "The Public Diary of John Hull" (AAS *Trans. and Coll.*, 3:245) reported that by sunrise it had "consumed the body of the trading part of the town: from the Mill Creek to Mr. Oliver's dock, not one house nor warehouse left." Hubbard (p. 649) gave the loss as "a considerable part of the warehouses . . . and several dwelling houses of good value, to the number of twenty or thirty." It is to this fire that Cotton Mather refers below, p. 196, ll. 64–66.

183:58   For "Year of Salvations," cf. Isa. 49.8.

183:59–60   Mather wrote in his diary (1:241) that when the squadron was a "little way" from Boston, "the *Angel of the Lord went forth* and smote 'em with such a wasting Sickness, that the Loss of their Men by it, enfeebled 'em, so as to make 'em desert the Enterprise." (See P. F. X. Charlevoix, *Histoire et Description Générale de la Nouvelle France*, Paris, 1744, 2:319–322.) Charlevoix attributes the abandonment of the attempt upon Boston to head winds and scarcity of provisions. For "*Munition of Rocks*," see Isa. 33.16.

183:60–61   For streets running with "Blood and Gore," cf. Ezek. 28.23; for "Flames" ravaging "Substance," cf. Joel 1.19, 2.3, 5, Isa. 1.7.

183:64   W. T. Morgan, "The Expedition of Baron de Pointis against Cartagena," *American Hist. Rev.*, 37:237–254 (Jan. 1932); de Pointis published his *Relation* of it in 1698. See also D. W. Prowse, *History of Newfoundland* (2nd ed. London, 1896), pp. 214–222.

183:66–67   For "thy Soul is escaped," see Ps. 124.7; for "as a *Bird*," etc., Ps. 91.3, Prov. 6.5.

183:68   For "*vain Men*," cf. James 2.20.

183:68–70   See Mather, *Diary*, 1:166–167, and for the Martinique venture, *Magnalia*, Bk. II, p. 351, ll. 51–52. The "Autobiography of John Barnard" (3 MHS *Coll.* 5:181) records: "In June, 1693 . . . Sir Francis Wheeler, with his fleet, which had in vain made an attempt upon Martinico, came to Boston, and brought with him a violent and malignant distemper, called the scarlet fever, by which he lost many hundreds of his men. The distemper soon spread to Boston, of which many persons died, and that within two or three days of their being taken ill." Bridenbaugh makes no mention of scarlet fever, but lists an epidemic of yellow fever as occurring in 1693, and speaks of the frequency with which ships coming from the West Indies, where yellow fever was prevalent, acted as carriers of the disease (pp. 239–240). In his diary Mather acknowledges that the "Distemper," whatever it was, brought by the squadron "carried off" some of his "Neighbors," especially those "that spent their Time among" the soldiers from the ships. Sewall's *Diary* (1:380) says that the fever they brought continued until the middle of September, 1693. See also Hutchinson, *History*, 2:53–54, 71. What "*Plantation*" Mather had in mind is not clear, but in 1694 it was reported that in Stonington, Connecticut, a disease, probably influenza, killed twelve out of seventy who had it. In April there were similar deaths in Providence, Rhode Island, and in May in Rehoboth, Massachusetts. This disease of 1693–1694, whatever it was, seems not to have reached Boston. See Caulfield, "The Pursuit," p. 30.

184:77–78   Compare Isa. 30.20.

184:79   For "*Golden Candlesticks*," cf. General Introduction p. 93, l. 55 and endnote.

184:80   Christ called John the Baptist a "shining and burning" light: John 5.35.

184:81   The seven divines were John Wilson, John Cotton, John Norton, John Davenport, John Oxenbridge, and John Bailey of the First Church, and Thomas Thacher of the Old South. Among those who gave "transient Influences" were Joshua

Moody, who in 1683 left the First Church and ministered to Portsmouth, N.H., until his death in 1697, and John Mayo, who left the Second Church in 1673 in favor of Barnstable. Mather probably had also in mind as "transients" the pastors of the First Baptist Church, the French Huguenot Church, and the Anglican church founded in 1686.

184:83–84 For "Love, and Peace," cf. II Cor. 13.11; for "*Comforts of the Holy Spirit*," Acts 9.31.

184:89 For "*lifted up to Heaven*," cf. Matt. 11.23, Luke 10.15.

184:92 *et seq.* In Part II, Mather returns to his central theme of help, expounding the supernatural help, first, of God in the person of Christ, second, of Christ's sacrifice, the atonement, and third, of the angels. His text for this section is appropriately Isa. 42.8; "My glory will I not give to another"; see also Isa. 48.11.

184:96 For "*outcast Zion*," cf. Jer. 30.17.

184:2–3 On the ministry of Christ, cf. II Cor. 5.18–19; on "*bestowing*," cf. Isa. 63.7.

184:5–7 For "voice of God," cf. Ps. 29.3, 4, 5, etc.; for voice "from Heaven," cf. Matt. 3.17, Mark 1.11, Luke 3.22; for help from God, cf. Pss. 27.9, 54.4, I Chron. 12.18.

184:7–10 Mather based this story either on the version of it in Spencer, *Things New and Old* (p. 277) or on that in Clarke, *Mirrour* (p. 388). Both books he knew well. They identify the "Great Man" as Pope Adrian (Hadrian) VI. Spencer gives as his source the commentary on I Cor. 3.6 by David Pareus, a German Protestant theologian, from his *Opera Theologica, Pars Tertia* (Frankfort, 1642). I Cor. 3.6 is "I have planted, Apollos watered; but God gave the increase"; see also II Cor. 3.5: "Not that we are sufficient of ourselves; but our sufficiency is of God." For his version Clarke cites "Simps. Ec. Hist., probably Edward Simpson, D.D., of Trinity College, Cambridge, who published in London in 1652 his *Chronicon Historiam Catholicam complectens.* Clarke has "One to meet with his [Adrian's] folly and forgetfulnesse." In Spencer's version: "It is said of *Hadrian* the sixth, that having built a Colledge at *Lovain*, he set this Inscription on the front, in golden letters, *Trajectum plantavit, Lovanium rigavit, sed Caesar dedit incrementum* . . . A merry Passenger reproving his folly under-wrote, *Hic Deus nihil fecit.*"

185:12–13 Compare John 1.3.

185:16–17 Compare Pss. 30.9, 10, 54.5, Heb. 13.6.

185:19–21 Compare Ps. 118.22. In these lines Mather relates the "stone . . . refused" of the Psalmist, with all its resonance of exalted praise and thanks to Jehovah, not only to the stones of Jacob and Joshua and Samuel, but to Christ's use of the words of the Psalm in the parable of the wicked husbandmen, with its warning against turning to false protectors (Matt. 21.42, Mark 12.10, Luke 20.17; cf. also Pss. 27.5, 107.41, 148.1).

185:23–29 For the Hebrew Mauzzim of Dan. 11.38, the King James Version has "forces" and, in Dan. 11.39, "strongholds." For Mauzzim as "protectors," it seems likely that Mather consulted both Matthew Poole, *Annotations upon the Holy Bible* (London, 1688, vol. 2, commentary on Dan. 11.38), and Joseph Mede's commentary on the same text (*Works*, pp. 667–674). Poole cites Mede and paraphrases his definition fairly accurately, noting Mede's interpretation of Mauzzim as "Tutelar Gods which the *Romans* should worship with Christ, supposing them to be Angels or Saints," language echoed by Mather in lines 23–25. Mede refers only glancingly to popish reverence for saints' images; therefore Mather's emphasis on "Idolatrous Roman Catholicks" probably owes more to Poole's "the vulgar translates *Mauzzim, Protector*, and we know too well how the *Romanists* adorn the Churches and Shrines of these their Patrons and Tutelar Saints." On the "*Patronage*" by saints of particular peoples or towns, Mede writes at some length: "Mahuzzims or Protectors have by the Christian God been allotted . . . St. George for England, St. Andrew, Scotland, St. Denis, France, St. James, Spain, St. Mark, Venice," etc., to which Mather can add "Old Boston . . . Saint Botolph's Town." In his summing up Mede notes: "S. *Hilary* also will tell us, That neither the GUARDS of Saints nor [*Angelorum munitiones*] the BULWARKS of Angels are wanting to those who are willing to stand. Here *Angels* are *Mahuzzim*, as *Saints* were in the former," a passage which may well have been in Mather's mind when he speaks of the help of angels to towns, p. 187, ll. 93–94 below.

185:31   For "Rejoice in him," cf. Phil. 3.3.

185:31–32   Compare II Sam. 22.2, Ps. 18.2.

185:35   "Whose Name hath *Salvation in it*": in Hebrew ישועה is salvation, ישוע is Jesus.

185:37   See Matt. 26.19, 28.16: "then the eleven disciples went away into Galilee, into a mountain where Jesus had appointed them."

185:39   Edmund Dickinson, *Delphi Phoenicizantes, sive, Tractatus, in quo Graecos, quicquid apud Delphos celebre erat,* etc., Oxford, 1655, p. 52: "ne ab hostibus evocatus alio commigraret." In margin, "vide: Pliny 28. cap 6."

185:42–43   Here Mather combines a reference to God's help from Ps. 86.8 with a reference to God's strength as "Rock"—the stone of help—from I Sam. 2.2; cf. also Isa. 33.16.

185:46–49   Lactantius, *Divinarum Institutionum Libri* (*Migne L*, 6:177). Mather has inverted the order of several words.

186:56   On Christ's sacrifice as "*Purchasing*" help, cf. I Tim. 2.5–6, Tit. 2.14, I Pet. 2.24.

186:60   For "*Lamb of God*," cf. John 1.29; for "*Lamb slain*," cf. Rev. 5.6, 12.

186:63   For "*Mystery*," cf. footnotes to Book I, p. 118, l. 51; for "*Sacrifice for the whole Congregation*," cf. Lev. 16.33–34.

186:65–66   For "*Cry . . . to Heaven*," cf. I Sam. 5.12.

186:66–69   These lines weave together words and phrases from several Biblical texts: from Gen. 19.24–25 ("rained upon Sodom . . . out of heaven . . . overthrew those cities"); Jer. 20.16 ("cities which Jehovah overthrew, and repented not"); Deut. 29.23 ("like the overthrow of Sodom and Gomorrah . . . in his anger").

186:77   For "shaken *her Head* at you," cf. II Kings 19.21, Isa. 37.22.

186:80   For "*Sufferings*," etc., cf. II Cor. 1.5, I Pet. 1.11, 5.1

186:83–84   For "*Price of all our help*," cf. Philip. 3.14.

186:85   For "all our *Praise*," cf. Jer. 33.9.

186:86   For "Let the Lord . . . Glorified," cf. Isa. 66.5, Ps. 91.11. In this paragraph Cotton Mather follows many words, phrases, and Biblical references in Increase Mather's *Angelographia* (Boston, 1696). Both Mathers were convinced of the power of angels, good and bad. Increase wrote that "*Angels are Real beings*," "immortal," and "do not only deliver from Evil" but convey "by their Hands" also "positive Blessings and Benefits." He adds that "although Angelical Apparitions are not to be expected in these days; nevertheless *the Ministry of Holy Angels, doth continue still*" and "*Evil Angels have a fearful power over them that fear not God*" (*Angelographia*, pp. 5, 12, 42, 63, 84; quoted in Holmes, *Increase Mather*, 1:14–16).

186:87   For "Jacob," etc., see Gen. 28.12–22, 31.11–13.

187:93–94   The nature and function of the angels mentioned in the Bible had been debated for years. Benjamin Camfield, Rector of Aylston, England, who published in London in 1678 *A Theological Discourse of Angels, and Their Ministries*, was one of those who vigorously defended the idea that every Christian town had an angel to watch over it, citing a variety of Biblical passages and learned authorities (cf. Chap. 4, sec. 3, and marginal notes).

187:95   For "Scriptures of Truth," cf. Dan. 10.21.

187:96–97   The source of the Latin quotation has not been identified. Increase Mather, in his *Essay for the Recording of Illustrious Providences* (Boston, 1678), wrote "That holy Angels were frequently seen in old times, we are from the Scriptures of truth assured; and that the angelical ministration doth still continue, is past doubt,

Heb. 1.14 . . . They do invisably perform many a good office for the heirs of salvation continually" (ed. London, 1890, pp. 144–145).

187:98   Cotton Mather corrects " 1 Kings" in *Angelographia* to " 2 Kings."

187:3   Compare endnote to p. 183, ll. 59–60 above.

187:5–6   For "*Destroyers . . . Destruction*," cf. Mic. 2.10.

187:6–7   For "*Wall of Fire*," cf. Zech. 2.5.

187:8–13   For angelic help to Daniel, see Dan. 6.22; to Lot, Gen. 19.15–16; to
Elias, I Kings 19.5–8. For the "whole People of God in the Wilderness," see Exod.
16.4, 14–16. See also Increase Mather, *Angelographia* (pp. 28–29): "Everyman in the
Church of Israel did receive benefit by the Ministry of the Angels of Heaven:
they *All* did eat of the Manna . . . Therefore it is said that *Man did eat Angels Food*,
Psal. 78.25."

187:16   For "*See thou do it not*," see Rev. 19.10, 22.9.

187:18   For "*Bless ye*," etc., see Ps. 103.20.

187:20–21   For "*hope* in him," cf. Lam. 3.24; for "*as the Matter may require*," cf. I
Kings 8.59.

187:23   For "*Monumental Pillars*," cf. Josh. 4.1–9.

187:24   Ps. 78 is an epitome of God's magnanimous care for Israel and of the "wondrous works" done for His people. Hence its application by Mather to Boston as the
new Israel.

187:25–30   For "Hope in God," cf. Pss. 42.5, 11, 78.7; for "present help," cf. Ps. 46.1.

188:35–36   For "*help . . . in the time of need*," cf. Heb. 4.16.

188:37   For "Straits that may come," cf. Job 20.22.

188:51–52   For "stand still," etc., cf. Exod. 14.13.

188:53   For "*Widows* . . . provided for," see Ps. 146.9; cf. also I Tim. 5.16; for
"Handmaids," cf. Luke 1.38.

188:56–57   For " *The Lord is my Helper*," see Heb. 13.6.

188:66–68   Augustine, *Confessions* I.vi.7 (*Migne L*, 32:664).

188:69–189:70   For "*Nursing-Fathers*," see Num. 11.12; for "be not *froward*,"
etc., cf. Prov. 4.24.

189:70–71   For "thanks to God," cf. for example, Acts 27.35, Rom. 14.6, II Thess.
1.3, Eph. 5.20.

189:73–76   Ludovicus Caelius Rhodiginus (Lodovico Ricchieri), *Lectiones Antiquae*
(Frankfort, 1599), col. 858F: "Nam vt in Politicis Aristoteles præcipit,
Eunomia duplex creditur: vna quidem, vti est iuris constitutio recta: al-
tera, quum iuri sapienter, ac vt ratio dictat, constituto obedientes se homines
praestant. Denique eunomiam iudiciorum præsidem alteram, opinatur Demosthenes." "For as Aristotle teaches in the Politics, good order is a twofold creation:
one part consists in the correct establishment of law, the other, when wisely fixed
by law, and as reason dictates, in men excelling in obedience thereto. Finally,
Demosthenes postulated a further protection in the good order of the law courts."

189:79–80   For guidance to ministers on how to "approve themselves," see II Cor.
6.4; for "*Helpers of your Joy*," cf. II Cor. 1.24.

189:81–82   For "watch . . . give an account," see Heb. 13.17.

189:82–83   In his diary for October 18, 1685 (1:106), Cotton Mather professed
his and his father's willingness to die for "the Salvation of any Soul." See Acts
21.13.

189:85   For "*Converted unto me*," cf. Ps. 51.13.

189:87   For "*Rejoycing . . . unspeakable*," see I Pet. 1.8.

189:88   Very probably Mather referred here to such "revilers" as Elisha Cooke and
his allies. See introductory essay, "Cotton Mather," pp. 12–15.

189:95   See Rom. 15.30.

189:3–4   For " *Travel in Birth*," cf. Gal. 4.19.

190:28   For "*Fear of God*," cf. II Sam. 23.3.

190:34   For the parable of the talents, see Matt. 25.14–30.

190:40   See II Tim. 2.7.

190:41 *et seq.*   At the time he was writing the *Magnalia,* Mather was increasingly exhorting the populace to the practice of piety as a means of insuring God's continued favor to New England.

190:49–192:28   Mather's catalogue of impieties echoes the familiar inventory of evils in the *Result* of the Synod (Walker, *Creeds,* pp. 429–431). However, he considerably enlarges on that document's exhortations against drinking.

190:50   For "*What shall we render,*" see Ps. 116.12.

191:57–59   For "wonderfully saved," cf. Gen. 14.15–16; for "went on to Sin," cf. Gen. 18.20, 19.4–5; for "sent a *Fire,*" cf. Gen. 19.24–28.

191:66–70   During the seventeenth century, occasional students from both England and the other English colonies, as well as from the New Netherlands, were enrolled as students at Harvard College. The evidence would seem to indicate that the colony had more reason to complain of their behavior than had their parents and guardians of any "malignant" Boston influences. (See Morison, *The Founding of Harvard College,* pp. 259–260, and *Harvard in the Seventeenth Century,* 2 vols., Cambridge, Mass., Harvard University Press, 1936, 1:74, 77–78.)

191:70–72   Mather heard of the earthquake Aug. 4, 1692, and the next day wrote John Cotton of Plymouth: "The horrible Tidings of the Late Earthquake at Jamaica, on the 7th of June Last. When, on a fair Day the sea suddenly swell'd, and the Earth shook, and broke in many places; and in a Minutes time, the Rich Town of Port-Royal, the *Tyrius* of the whole English America, but a very Sodom for wickedness, was immediately swallow'd up . . . Behold, an Accident speaking to all our English America" (*Diary,* 1:142–143).

191:76–78   In his manuscript records of the Second Church, Mather wrote that on April 8, 1695, "Two young Women, belonging to our Communion . . . having been guilty of consulting an ungodly Fortune-teller, in the Neighbourhood . . . made a poenitent Acknowledgment of that Miscarriage, and so the Church was reconciled to them" (*Diary,* 1:180–181). See also Increase Mather, *Angelographia* (1696), p. 25: "I hear there are some such in this place, that have gone to an ungodly *Fortune-teller,* to reveal such things, as cannot be known, but by the help of Evil Angels."

191:83–85   In January of 1671/2, the Widow Alice Thomas, a tavern keeper, was tried and convicted in Suffolk County Court for providing "frequent secret and vnseasonable Entertainment in her house to Lewd Lascivious & notorious persons of both Sexes . . . she is a common Baud" (3 MHS *Coll.* 3:332). Shortly thereafter, May 15, 1672, the General Court enacted the colony's first law against erecting "a stew, whore house, or brothell house" (*Mass., Records,* 42:513).

192:95   See Samuel Adams Drake, *Old Boston Taverns and Tavern Clubs* (ed. W. K. Watkins, Boston, W. A. Butterfield, 1917), pp. 68, 118, 110.

192:99–3   Compare Giles Firmin, *The Real Christian: or a Treatise of Effectual Calling* (London, 1670), p. 92: "While he was sick indeed, then he might cry out of it . . . calling Ale-houses, Hell-houses."

192:4   For "*Hearken to me,*" cf. Judg. 9.7.

192:13   The *Result* of the Synod recommended that "those that shall without License from Authority sell any sort of strong drink, be exemplarily punished" (Walker, *Creeds,* p. 435).

192:19   See Luke 2.7.

192:20–21   For "*Works of Darkness,*" see Eph. 5.11; for "*Sun of Righteousness,*" see Mal. 4.2.

192:23   For "*Snares of Death,*" cf. II Sam. 22.6, Prov. 13.14, 14.27.

192:25   For "*Trust in the Lord,*" etc., see Ps. 37.3.

192:26–27   For "with a Little, better," cf. Prov. 15.16, 16.8.

192:31–193:43   Sabbath-breaking was the fifth in the list of evils drawn up by the

Synod of 1679 as provoking the Lord "to bring his Judgements on New-England." The Biblical text quoted by Mather for lines 37–38 is Neh. 13.18. This was misprinted as 3.18 in the *Result* of the Synod. The text quoted by Mather in lines 41–43 is Jer. 17.27, cited in the *Result*, where it is linked with Neh. 3.17, 18, a misprint in the *Result* for 13.17, 18. (See Walker, *Creeds*, p. 429, and *Magnalia*, Bk. V, pt. 4, ques. I, sec. 5, p. 88).

The Puritan Sabbath began at sundown on Saturday and ended at sundown on Sunday. In *Pray for the Rising Generation* (Boston, 1675; 2nd ed. 1685), Increase Mather included, as its second section, a sermon he preached on May 23, 1677, entitled "A Discourse Concerning the Danger of Apostacy." He deplored that on the "night after the Sabbath . . . there is more wickedness committed usually . . . than in all the week besides" (*Pray*, 2nd ed., p. 123; cf. also Holmes, *I. Mather*, 1:88–95). On the economic advantages of Sabbath-keeping, see Joshua Moody, *A Practical Discourse Concerning the Choice Benefits of Communion with God in his House* (Boston, 1685; 2nd ed. 1746, p. 14).

193:45–46 For "*hitherto* been a *Shield* unto us," cf. Ps. 18.35, Prov. 30.5, Eph. 6.16. For "*Ark* be in the Town," I Sam. 4.3, II Sam. 15.25, I Chron. 13.3.

193:47 For the "*Mortal Scourges*," see endnotes above to p. 183, ll. 37–41, on the smallpox, and to p. 183, ll. 68–70, on various "distempers."

193:51 For "*Destroying Angel*," cf. II Sam. 24.16, I Chron. 21.15. On the sparing of those "in the Communion of his *Churches*," cf. Richard Baxter on the plague in London: "At the first so few of the Religiouser sort were taken away, that (according to the mode of too many such) they began to be puffed up, and boast of the great difference that God did make: But quickly after, they all fell alike. Yet not many pious Ministers were taken away" (*Reliquiae Baxterianae*, London, 1696, pt. 3, p. 1).

193:55 For "*Upon the Glory*," see Isa. 4.5.

193:55–57 See Josephus *Antiquitates* XI.329–339, where he recounts that Alexander, in addition to sparing Jerusalem, greeted reverently the high priest of the temple, who came out to meet him, saying, "It was not before him that I prostrated myself, but the God of whom he has the honour to be the high priest." Compare also Poole's "Argument" to Zechariah in his *Annotations*: "Between Zechariah's Prophesying . . . to the death of Alexander Magnus . . . the Jews enjoyed the common peace with the Subjects of the Persian Empire, and the particular favour of Alexander the Conquerour, during his life."

193:59–62 Gregory Nazianzen, "Carmen de Vita Sua," *Migne G*, 37:1100: "tecum enim inquit aliquis, ejicies Triadem." In the story as told by William Cave in his *Ecclesiastici: or, the History of the Lives, Acts, Death, & Writings of the most Eminent Fathers of the Church* (London, 1683, p. 301), "Persons of all Ages, Sexes and Qualities . . . besought him not to desert his Flock . . . one of the Company telling him openly . . . Sir *with your departure you banish the Catholick Faith out of this City.*"

193:65 *et seq.* As the town prospered and differences in wealth increased, admonitions to observe equity and charity in all dealings were multiplied. See, for example, Urian Oakes, in *New-England Pleaded With* (1673), who speaks of much "Griping, and Squeezing, and Grinding the Faces of the poor" (p. 32). Increase Mather, in *The Day of Trouble Is Near* (Cambridge, 1674, p. 22), denounces excessive prices charged to the "poor man [who] cometh amongst you."

194:83–84 See II Cor. 8.2.

194:85 For "*Bread of Life*," see John 6.35, 48. On "*Subscriptions*" and "*Collections*," see, for example, a note by Sewall on Nov. 8, 1691: "a Contribution for the Fronteer Towns was called for" (*Diary*, 1:352).

194:87–88 Compare Acts 10.4.

194:89 Compare Tit. 3.1.

194:99–3 Compare the *Result* of the Synod (Walker, *Creeds*, p. 430) on the "abundance of Idleness, which brought ruinating Judgement upon Sodom."

194:3   Compare Prov. 14.34.

194:12–17   *God's Doings and Man's Duty*, p. 44. Compare Nathaniel Ward, *The Simple Cobbler of Agawam* (London, 1647), p. 61: "I thank God I have lived in a Colony of many thousand English almost these twelve years, am held a very sociable man; yet I may considerably say, I never heard but one Oath sworne, nor never saw one man drunke, nor ever heard of three women Adulteresses, in all this time, that I can call to minde." The source of both Ward's and Peter's affirmations may have been *New England's First-Fruits* (Morison, *Founding*, p. 443): "One may live there from yeare to yeare, and not see a drunkard, heare an oath, or meet a beggar."

195:19 *et seq.*   The first question posed by the Synod of 1679, "What are the Evils that have provoked the Lord to bring his Judgements on New-England," is answered by a resume of God's "publick Judgements": "his glitterring Sword," "mortal Contagion," "devouring Fires," "fearfull Desolations in the Earth" [i.e., earthquakes, droughts, etc.]. (See Walker, *Creeds*, pp. 426–427.) Later in the *Magnalia*, Mather multiplies instances of particular judgments. (Bk. VI, chap. 5, "The Second Sermon," pp. 31–37.)

195:20   For "*God of our Salvations*," cf. Ps. 65.5.

195:22   For "Twice beaten them," etc., cf. I Sam. 4.2, 10, 11.

195:26–28   For "*the Blood of the Righteous ABEL*," see Matt. 23.35. For the differing readings of I Sam. 6.18 current in Mather's time, see *Critici Sacri*, 2:618–623. In the original, Abel, the person, is אבל; Abel, the stone, is תבל, meaning "mourning."

195:35–37   Mather's probable source was a sermon by Thomas Fuller, entitled "Faction Confuted," in *Joseph's Partie-Colored Coat* (London, 1640), p. 177.

195:37   For "Blessed be God," cf. Pss. 66.20, 68.35, II Cor. 1.3.

195:38–39   Mather here employs the standardized vocabulary for lamenting religious declension. Compare the first "Evil" named by the Synod: "There is a great and visible decay of the power of Godliness" (Walker, *Creeds*, p. 427). Compare also II Tim. 3.5.

195:45–46   An allusion to the lepers baring their heads to the priests in Lev. 13.42–44.

195:47–48   Compare Rev. 2.5.

195:49–51   The note of threnody for departed ancestors is constant throughout the *Magnalia*, especially in Books II and III.

195:55–60   Mather's lament combines echoes of Zech. 1.5, Ps. 90.12, Job 7.10, 20.7, Pss. 46.4, 48.8, 87.3.

196:63–64   Compare James 1.9–10. On changes in possessions, see Miller, "Declension in a Bible Commonwealth," in *Nature's Nation* (Cambridge, Mass., Harvard University Press, 1967), pp. 40–41, 45–47.

196:66   For "Ruinous Heap," see II Kings 19.25, Isa 17.1, 37.26.

196:67–68   See *Magnalia*, Bk. II, p. 310, l. 26–p. 315, l. 5. See also Hutchinson, *History*, 1:352.

196:70–71   Compare Heb. 10.34, here combined with Luke 10.42.

196:73–78   Mather here possibly had in mind the following passage from Pausanias *Description of Greece* XXIV.6: "the Achaeans of the place removed some suppliants from the sanctuary and killed them. But the wrath of Poseidon visited them without delay; an earthquake promptly struck their land and swallowed up, without leaving a trace for posterity to see, both the buildings and the very site on which the city stood."

196:75   For "*First Fruits* unto God," cf. Rev. 14.4.

196:81–84   For "*Tott'ring House*," cf. Ps. 62.3; for "*Foundations . . . shaking*," cf. Isa. 24.18; for "*Whirlwinds . . . and they are Dead*," see Job 1.19.

196:86–87   Compare II Sam. 18.33, 19.4.

196:89–90   See Eccles. 12.1.

196:98–99   I Chron. 28.9.

BOOK II

197:1   For God as a shield see, for example, Gen. 15.1, Deut. 33.29, Pss. 3.3, 18.35, etc., and especially Ps. 47.9: "The princes of the people are gathered together, even the people of the God of Abraham: for the shields of the earth belong unto God."

197:13–14   Lange, *Florilegii*, 1:1199, where no source is given.

197:15–16   Mather's quotation is from the *Apophthegmata* of Conrad Lycosthenes, which was used by students at Harvard. Mather had a copy of the Geneva 1668 edition which he inscribed "Cottonus Matherus Liber, 1673." (See J. H. Tuttle, "The Libraries of the Mathers," AAS *Proc.*, New Series, 20:336, and Morison, *Seventeenth Century*, 1:178.) Lycosthenes attributes the quotation to Beccadelli, who was an admirer of Alphonso V of Aragon, the "Magnanimous," by heredity King of Sicily and by conquest of Naples. The quotation comes from Beccadelli's *De Dictis et Factis regis Alfonsi*, Pisa, 1485. In the London 1635 edition of Lycosthenes the quotation appears on pages 392 and 547.

197:17–18   Livy *Ab Urbe Condita* III.xx.5. Mather changes "deum" to "Dei."

197:19   Lange, *Florilegii*, 2:1947, has this quotation, except that "est" follows "Quisque." Lange cites "Vell. Paterc. 1.2," i.e., Gaius Velleius Paterculus (*c.* 19 B.C.–A.D. 30), the author of an epitome of Roman history, *Historiae Romanae* (see II.128), in which Paterculus has "neque novus his mos senatus populique est, putandi . . . quod optimum sit esse nobilissimum": "Nor is this a new fashion of the senate and the people to consider best that which is most noble." With a reference to "Vell. I.II." Justus Lipsius has "Tunc enim libens fatear, *Optimum quemquem, esse nobilissimum*" (*Opera*, 4:56). Probably Mather abbreviated "Paterculus" to "Pat" or "Paterc," which the printer misread as "Plato."

199:25–27   The substance of this Latin passage, but not the wording, is in Machiavelli's *Il Principe*, chapter 18. A translation of that work *Out of the Italian in to English*, by E[dward] Dacres had already appeared when Mather wrote (London, 1640), His Latin version follows closely an edition of Machiavelli's *Princeps*, dated 1595, with no indication of place of publication. A copy of this edition was among the six or seven hundred books from "the Remains of the Old Library of the Mathers" which in 1814 the Boston printer and collector, Isaiah Thomas, bought and gave to the American Antiquarian Society. This copy is inscribed "Matheri." Mather's phrase may be taken from some Latin commentary on Machiavelli's *Princeps* or, in accordance with his statement that the "Wicked Position" should never appear in English, he may have concocted a Latin version of his own.

199:31   Compare Rom. 14.12, Heb. 13.17.

199:32–33   When Justinian became emperor in 527, Agapetus presented to him a *Scheda regia sive de officio Boni Principis ad Imperaturum*. (See *Migne G*, 86:1163–1164.) The Latin translation in *Migne* has "Honore quolibet sublimiorem cum habeas dignitatem, o imperator, honora supra omnes qui hoc te dignatus est Deum," and a similar Latin version appears in a Leipzig 1669 edition of the *Scheda* (p. 7). Mather's immediate source was probably Alsted, *Encyclopaedia*, p. 1502.

199:34   For *"Rule over them,"* cf. Judg. 8.22–23.

199:35–36   Cicero *Pro Ligario* XII.38. Mather alters the word order, omitting "enim" after "Homines," and changing "deos" to "deum," "salutem" to "salute," and "dando" to "danda."

199:37   See also Josh. 24.31, Judg. 2.7.

199:42–44   For Rehoboam's rejection of his father's counsel, see I Kings 12.6–11, 22–24.

199:46   For "betrayed," see I Chron. 12.17.

199:47–50   Plutarch *Lives* ii.6 has "triremes" (τριήρεις), not "oars."

199:53   For oars, pilots, etc., cf. Ezek. 27.8, 27–29.

200:55–56   Cicero *De Finibus* III.vii.24 (the word being *gubernatio*). The reference to Plutarch should be to Plato *Republic* I.xviii.A. Mather may have abbreviated Plato to "Plat." which the printer misread as "Plut."

200:56–57 Compare James 3.4.

200:59–60 Prudentius, after retirement from his active career, turned to devout exercises and Christian writings. Symmachus, as a pagan worshipper, protested the removal from the Roman senate-house of the statue and altar of Victory and was therefore banished by the emperor Gratian. After Gratian's death in 383 Symmachus addressed a letter to the emperor Valentinian II, pleading for the restoration of the pagan symbols. This letter has been rated as the most interesting of his literary remains and provoked Prudentius's verse refutation in his "Contra Symmachum."

200:62 Probably from Lange, *Florilegii* (2:1648); "Magistratus, lex est loquens. Cic.3 *de leg.*" Cicero *De Legibus* III.i.2 has "vereque dici potest magistratum legem esse loquentem." See also Themistius, "De Imperatoris Theodosii Humanitate," in *Orationes* (Paris, 1618), p. 138; and Aristotle *Nichomachean Ethics* V.iv.7.

200:63–64 The word used by Homer is "θέμις," that which is established by custom rather than by statute.

200:65–66 Xenophon's *Cyropaedia*, Curtius' *De Rebus gestis Alexandri Magni*, and Pliny the younger's *Panegyricus ad Trajanum.*

200:69–70 Mather took this quotation not from Chaucer but from Josiah Dare, *Counsellor Manners His Last Legacy to His Son* (London, 1673), an etiquette book compiled, according to Dare, out of the dying advice of "an ancient *Gentleman*, called *Counsellor Manners*," who called his son to him and "brake with him in these *Terms*" (p. 1). Francis Manners (1578–1632), sixth earl of Rutland, was made Privy Councillor in 1617. Mather in his "Quotidiana" noted down ten consecutive passages from Manners, of which this is the first (Quotidiana no. 92): "It was the saying of old *English Chaucer*, that *to do the gentle deeds*, that makes the *Gentleman*" (pp. 3–4). Chaucer, *The Canterbury Tales*, "The Wife of Bath's Tale," has, lines 1115–1116, "To do the gentil dedes that he kan; Taak him for the grettest gentil man," and 1170, "he is gentil that dooth gentil dedis." The passage in the *Magnalia* follows exactly that in the Quotidiana.

201:76 Galeazzo Caraccioli, Marquis of Vico, was converted by a sermon of Peter Martyr (1500–1562), the reformer, and forced to leave his native land, give up his rank as Marquis, and endure the disapproval of his family. His life was written in Italian by Nicolo Balbani of Lucca, translated into Latin by Theodore Beza, and in 1608 into English by the ardent puritan, William Crashaw. Richard Bancroft, the Archbishop of Canterbury, ordered Crashaw in 1609 to retract the book, but after the Archbishop's death in 1610 a new edition was published in 1612 and at least three others in the years from 1639 to 1667. The title-page at first read *Newes from Italy of a Second Moses*, but later *The Italian Convert*. The book became well known in America and a copy was in John Harvard's legacy to Harvard College. Galeazzo was appropriately called a "Second Moses" since Moses was the adopted son of King Pharaoh's daughter, but was persuaded by God's command to lead the children of Israel in the wilderness (Exod. 5.2–10 and following chapters). Mather's label of "Galeacius Secundus" for Bradford was also appropriate. Galeazzo went from Italy first to Germany and then to Geneva; Bradford, fleeing from the "persecution" of the Anglicans, went first to Holland and then to New England. Galeazzo in Geneva quickly achieved leadership and was praised not only by Calvin but also by the local political leaders. Bradford in Plymouth was thirty times chosen Governor in the annual elections. See also endnote to p. 206, ll. 95–98.

201:78–79 No source for this repetitious passage has been found. It seems probable that Mather patched together a variety of Latin tags. See, for example, Cicero's "vacatione omnium rerum" in *Orationes In Verrem* II.v.22, and Horace *Epode* xvii.24: "Nullum ab labore me reclinat otium." Harvard students in Mather's day made much use of phrase books and thesauruses, like the *Apophthegmata* of

Lycosthenes, and Mather, as the *Magnalia* and his "Quotidiana" show, kept up for years his habit of gleaning from them.

201:80 *et seq.* Mather bases his account of Bradford on his *History of Plymouth Plantation.*

201:83 John Foxe, *Acts and Monuments*, 3:306–307. The account of John Leaf's martyrdom is included in the lengthy Bradford narrative.

201:85 *Acts and Monuments*, 3:280–362.

201:85–202:3 Compare Bradford, 1:16–30 and notes.

202:2–3 Matt. 6.33.

202:8–37 In this passage Mather closely follows Bradford, 1:32–34, echoing, for example, the language of the Dutchman's oath and the voyagers' not seeing "*Sun, Moon, or Star.*"

202:28–34 Compare Matt. 8.23–27.

202:36–37 Pss. 107.23–30, 145.19.

203:40 Heb. 11.13.

203:43–45 Compare II Kings 22.3–23.3, II Chron. 34.8–32; cf. also Jer. 2.8, Hosea 4.9.

203:52–53 II Tim. 3.15.

203:57–58 The "Young Man" may possibly have been John Smyth, a Fellow of Christ's College, Cambridge, and an A.M. in 1579. In 1584 he was ordained by the Bishop of Lincoln and for a time held an Anglican pulpit, but in 1602 was dismissed for having "preached 'untimely against divers men of good place.'" Leaving the established church, he founded in 1605 a separatist congregation at Gainsborough, Lincolnshire, and in 1608 moved with his family to Amsterdam. In Holland he became known as the "Se-baptist" (self-baptizer), and by the time of his death in 1612 had become famous for his unorthodox religious views and writings. By the time he began preaching in Lincolnshire after his ordination, he must have been at least in his late forties; Mather may have called him "young" derisively in the sense of "inexperienced" or "ignorant," having in mind his later downfall, or may simply have been unaware of Smyth's age at the time when he brought Bradford into the "fellowship" of the "professors." See DNB; Christopher Hill, *Society and Puritanism in Pre-Revolutionary England* (London, Secker and Warburg, 1964), p. 89 and note 3; and Bradford, 1:22 and notes 3, 4.

203:73–204:84 Mather probably found the "Answer" in unpublished manuscripts in Morton's possession. See H. M. Dexter, *The Pilgrims in England and Holland*, p. 391.

204:75 See II Pet. 1.10, 3.14.

204:91–95 See Bradford, 1:30–31.

204:98–4 Mather likens the "Officer" to the "Viper" of Acts 28.3–6. Ford (Bradford, 1:37n) suggests that the incident described in the *Magnalia* was probably a tradition in Mather's day.

204:7 For "*Shadow* of our Lord," see Pss. 63.7, 57.1, 91.1.

204:11 Compare Prov. 3.11.

205:17–18 Dorothy (May) Bradford, drowned in Cape Cod Harbor (Bradford, 2:399).

205:24 Gen. 30.27, Eccles. 1.16, Rom. 5.3–4.

205:30–44 For the Christmas episode see Bradford, 1:244–246 and notes. Compare II Thess. 3.10–12.

205:47 Deut. 8.3, Matt. 4.4.

205:52–206:58 For the decision to "settle Propriety" in land, see Bradford, 1:299–303; cf. also pp. 372–373, and Winslow, *Good Newes*, pp. 346–347.

206:59 Like Elisha, who had a double portion of Elijah's spirit; cf. II Kings 2.9.

206:61 For John Lyford and the trials he brought on the Plymouth Colony, see above, Bk. I, p. 140, l. 39–p.141, l. 77, and endnotes.

206:66–93 Mather embarks again on a refutation of charges that the Plymouth settlers were Brownists and Separatists. (On agreement with other Reformed churches, see Bk. I, p. 126, l. 23; p. 142, l. 26 *et seq.*, and endnotes; on Robinson and Separation, Bk. I, p. 124, ll. 46–55 and endnote.) What purports to be quotation (p. 206, ll. 66–68) is a paraphrase of a passage in Bradford, 1:423. Lines 74–90 are direct quotation with only few and minor changes from Bradford, 1:423–424.

206:77 The reference is to *Harmonia Confessionum. The Harmony of Protestant Confessions*, translated from the Latin by Peter Hall, published in 1586 and reprinted in 1643. See Ford's note 3 in Bradford, 1:423–424.

206:79–80 See I Cor. 11.1.

206:95–98 Mather counts the years from 1621 to 1657 inclusive. Bradford was in 1621 chosen governor to replace John Carver, who had died in April, but he was then recovering from a dangerous sickness and Isaac Allerton was chosen as an "Assistant" to him. Bradford died in early May of 1657 and so did not serve a full term as governor in that year. Thus the number of full years (thirty-five), less the five in which Winslow and Prince were elected, leaves a total of thirty in which he was governor. He was, however, chosen an Assistant in each year in which he was not governor. (See S. E. Morison in DAB, and Bradford, *History*, 2:216.)

207:99 See endnote above to p. 201, l. 76.

207:4–5 Matt. 16.24, Mark 8.34, Luke 9.23; cf. also Matt. 26.11, Mark 14.9.

207:5–12 For the story of the Patent, see Bradford, 2:282–288.

207:15–16 Matt. 19.29, Mark 10.29–30. Compare above, Bk. II, chap. 1.

207:17–19 By his first wife Dorothy, John; by his second wife, Alice (Carpenter, widow of Edward Carpenter), two sons, William and Joseph, and a daughter, Mercy (Bradford, 2:404n).

207:24–26 The evidence of Bradford's pursuit of the study of Hebrew appears on one of the blank leaves at the beginning of his history: "Though I am growne aged, yet I have had a longing desire, to see with my owne eyes, something of that most ancient language, and holy tongue, in which the Law, and oracles of God were write; and in which God, and angels, spake to the holy patriarks, of old time; and what names were given to things, from the creation. And though I cannot attaine to much herein, yet I am refreshed, to have seen some glimpse hereof; (as Moyses saw the land of Canan afarr of) my aime and desire is, to see how the words and phrases lye in the holy texte; and to discerne somewhat of the same, for my owne contente." (Quoted from Morison, *Of Plymouth Plantation*, New York, Alfred A. Knopf, 1952, p. xxviii. Compare also Isidore S. Meyer, "The Hebrew Preface to Bradford's History," *American Jewish Historical Society Pub.*, No. xxxviii, Part 4, June 1949.) See further "'With My Owne Eyes': William Bradford's *Of Plymouth Plantation*," by Jesper Rosenmeier, in *Typology and Early American Literature*, pp. 69–105. For "Oracles of God," see Rom. 3.2, Heb. 5.12.

207:32 See Gen. 6.9.

207:36–38 Compare II Cor. 12.2–4.

207:39–40 Compare Ephes. 1.14, Rom. 8.23.

208:44 Mather's probable source was Heidfeld's *Sphinx*, p. 1181, which has "O mihi si Similis Contingat Clausula Vitae." Compare Num. 23.10: "Let me die the death of the righteous, and let my last end be like his [Jacob's]."

208:48 Plato *Politicus* 268.B-C. Plato has $νομέα$ and $τροφòν$; Mather rightly puts them in the nominative singular, $νομεὺς$ and $τροφός$.

208:49–50 Compare I. Pet. 5.2–3; cf. also Ezek. 34.2–3.

208:53–56 The source of this quotation has not been identified.

208:57–65 Mather is here quoting, with only minor verbal changes, from Nathaniel Morton's notice of Winslow's death (*Memoriall*, p. 142), except for Mather's inserted parenthesis, which only serves to confuse the chronology. The spelling of Droitwich is Morton's. Thomas Dudley used the word "Plymotheans" in his letter to the countess of Lincoln (see Young, *Chronicles of Massachusetts*, p. 328), published in 1696; Mather may have adopted the word for his "*Plymouthean* Colony."

The 1624 return was from a trip to England whither he "was sent . . . to informe of all things, and procure shuch things as were thought needful for their present condition" (Bradford, 1:323–324; on this trip he published in London *Good Newes from New England*). Winslow's second trip to England was in 1630–1631 (Bradford, 2:99, 102, 157n). There were differences between the London investors and the Plymouth Colony. Hence Winslow was "*to see how the squares* [disputes, wrangles] *went . . .* and *to see how the accounts stood.*"

209:69–75   In 1634 Winslow's talents as negotiator again sent him to England, this time on behalf of both Plymouth and Massachusetts Bay, his mission arising out of conflicts over the limits and bounds between "the plantation of Pascataway" and the two Massachusetts colonies (see Bradford, 2:175 *et seq.*). In the course of an encounter between fishing parties, "one Hocking" of Piscataqua was killed. As Bradford noted (2:179), "The bruite of this was quickly carried all aboute, (and that in the worst manner)." Lord Say "and other gentlemen that were interested in that plantation" were disturbed, and the appointment of a new Commission for Regulating Plantations forebode trouble (Bradford, 2:183–186. For the Hocking affair, cf. also Winthrop, *History*, 1:136–145, 156, 163). Bradford, Winthrop and Dudley jointly commissioned Winslow "to informe and satisfie the Lord Say and others, in the former matter, as also to make answer and their just defence for the same . . . at Counsell-table, or els wher." Winslow was further "to signifie unto the partners in England, that the terms of their trade with the company here was out, and therfore he was sent to finishe the accounts with them." Winslow also carried with him "a great returne" of "coat-beaver" and "otter skines, which alltogeather rise to a great sume of money" (Bradford, 2:189–190; cf. also Winthrop, 1:138).

While on this mission, Winslow also petitioned the Commissioners for aid in preventing "the wrongs and incrochments that the French and other strangers both had and were like further to do unto them" (Bradford, 2:196; Morton, *Memoriall*, p. 94). He met with resistance from Sir Ferdinando Gorges, who believed the Massachusetts people had deprived him of some of his possessions and profits in New England (Bradford 2:199), and who, with the assistance of the Archbishop of Canterbury, got Thomas Morton to make complaints about his treatment by Plymouth; however the Commission "checked Morton." In the end of all, Winslow's mission had some success—in thwarting Gorges' "designe," for example—but he failed to gain full satisfaction on "that great debte which Mr. Allerton [a sometime agent of the colony] needlessly and unadvisedly ran you and us into," as James Sherley, one of the London investors wrote to Bradford (2:205).

209:77–82   The principal "Adversaries" whose "Designs" Winslow went in 1646 to thwart were a trio of assailants of the New England theocracy, William Vassal, Dr. Robert Child, and Samuel Gorton, who, in Morton's words, "sought to trouble their peace, and disturb, if not innovate their Government, by laying many scandals upon them . . . by Petitioning and Complaining to the *Parliament*" (*Memoriall*, pp. 123–124). Of them all Samuel Gorton was perhaps the most troublesome, not only to Massachusetts Bay but to Plymouth and Rhode Island. A kind of mystical Antinomian, he was, according to Morton, "a proud and pestilent Seducer" with "blasphemous and *Familistical Opinions*," who resorted to "surreptitious wayes" in dealing with two sachems of Shawomet, near Providence, as a result of which some "were deprived of their just Rights in Lands" (*Memoriall*, pp. 108–109). To the New Englanders, the idea that these troublemakers should enjoy a right of appeal to Parliament from the judgments of the colonies was intolerable. When Winslow arrived in London, he found copies of a volume by Gorton, *Simplicities Defense against the Seven-Headed Policy*, already on the book stalls. He responded with *Hypocrisie Unmasked*, to present "A True Relation of the Proceedings of the Governour and Company of the Massachusetts in New-England."

As much because of rapidly moving events in England as because of his presentation of his cause, Winslow won his case. As Bradford wrote in the last entry in his *History* (2:392–393), "Winslow did well answer their ends, and cleared them from any blame or dishonour, to the shame of their adversaries." How well he answered appears from the decision rendered by the Commission in a letter to Massachusetts, Plymouth, and Connecticut: "We . . . declare our tenderness of your just privileges, and of preserving entire the authority and jurisdiction of the several governments in New England" (Winthrop, 2:387). On Gorton's trouble-making in New England, see Winthrop, 2:165–169, 171–179, 188–189, 200–203; on Winslow's 1646 mission, see 2:346, 359, 364–367, 387–391. For the significance of this entire episode, see also Miller, *Orthodoxy in Massachusetts*, pp. 295–309.

209:82–83   For Hercules' strangling of the serpents, see Pindar *Nemean Odes* I.41–47. Crushing the serpents is at the same time a reference to Gen. 3.15 and especially to Rom. 16.20.

209:87–88   For "*Resurrection of the Just*," see Luke 14.14.

209:88–90   This passage echoes Morton's *Memoriall*, p. 124.

209:91–96   Mather's account of Winslow's last days combines direct quotation and paraphrase of Morton, *Memoriall*, p. 142.

209:98   During the life of Bradford, Prince was governor in 1634 and 1638.

209:4   See Morison, *Puritan Pronaos*, p. 86, and *Plymouth Colony Records*, 5:108.

209:5–6   Mather here seems to be relying on Morton, who details at some length the "storms" and "uncomfortable jarrs" that in 1657 threatened "the disturbing and shaking of many Towns and Churches" (*Memoriall*, p. 152). For a selection of materials on the religious troubles of Plymouth, see also Joseph B. Felt, *The Ecclesiastical History of New England* (2 vols., Boston, 1862), 2:166–171, 233–247.

210:7–8   On the "Gifts of Private Brethren," or "prophesying," see above Bk. I, p. 143, ll. 57–60 and endnote thereto. In England in 1635, Edward Winslow had been examined on this practice, particularly associated with Plymouth, by the Archbishop of Canterbury. Winslow "confessed that he had both spoken by way of exhortation to the people and married," explaining that in America "at such a time . . . necessity constrained them . . . to many things far differing from a settled common weale." He concluded that "having no Minister in seven or eight years at least, some of us must doe both." As a result, Winslow was committed "to the Fleete, and lay there .17. weeks" (Bradford, 2:202–203; see also Winthrop, 1:205). Winthrop himself had "exercised by way of prophecy" in 1634 at Agawam when they "wanted a minister" (*History*, 1:154–155). The charge made in 1657 was, of course, against the "Discountenance" rather than the want of "*Gospel Ministry*," but doubtless long familiarity with the practice contributed to its continuance.

210:9–14   Mather here follows Morton: at "the usual time for the renewing of our Election . . . Mr. *Thomas Prince* was by unanimous vote chosen Governour . . . chosen of God for us" as "an Instrument of much peace and settlement in this place, and to this people, in these times of trouble and confusion" (*Memoriall*, p. 151). The "*Adverse Party*" consisted almost entirely of "that pernicious sect called Quakers," but he notes that by 1659 "they have of late withered away in a great measure" (*Memoriall*, pp. 157–158). This happy turn of affairs could be attributed to the Court's passage in 1658, with Prince's sponsorship, of an act prohibiting all meetings and "entertainment" of Quakers (cf. Felt, *History*, 2:235–236).

210:27   For "*Walk* with God," cf. Deut. 5.33, Josh. 22.5; I Kings 8.36, Prov. 2.7, Jer. 6.16, Ezek. 37.24.

210:32   For Josiah Winslow (*c.* 1629–1680), see DAB.

210:36   Winslow was a member of the first class at Harvard but did not take a degree (Sibley, 1:16).

210:37   In 1659 Winslow became commander-in-chief of the colony, succeeding Myles Standish, who had died in 1656.

210:40   *Iliad* III.5.179: "βασιλεύς τ'ἀγαθὸς κρατερός τ'αἰχμητής," "a noble king and valiant spearman."

210:42–43   See *The Book of Cornelius Nepos on the Great Generals of Foreign Nations* XV.x.1–2.

210:45   On December 19, 1675, as commander-in-chief of the forces of the united colonies, Winslow won a decisive battle against the Narragansets, but with great loss of life.

211:49–50   Ovid *Metamorphoses* XII.6.5–616.

211:53–54   The source of the prophecy was William Lilly, *A Collection of Ancient and Moderne Prophesies* (London, 1645), pp. 1–6, where it is presented as by an "*Italian Monk* . . . Delivered to the *English* Ambassadour in *Rome*," who had solicited it on the part of Henry VII. In full it runs "*Mars. Puer. Alecto. Virgo. Vulpes. Leo. Nullus,*" who are identified as Henry VIII, Edward VI, Mary, Elizabeth, James, Charles, No one. Samuel Mather of Witney, in the copy of the *Magnalia* he began to prepare for an abridged edition, cites a later edition of Lilly, *Monarchy, or, No Monarchy* (London, 1651, p. 56), where the prophecy is very briefly stated, with the comment that Charles "had the signe of *Leo* ascending in his Nativity, one maine cause which made him so obstinate."

Perhaps the most plausible explanation for this insult to the then venerable Hinckley is that Mather retained strong resentment of Plymouth's attempt to obtain a separate charter in 1690–1691. As Hutchinson summarized events (*History*, 2:365), "Mr. Hinkley, their governor, wrote to Mr. Mather, the Massachusetts agent, to desire him to sollicit in their behalf, but the people refused to advance any money," largely because of dissensions among various towns and factions in the colony. "Mr. Wiswall, one of their ministers . . . went to England, but having no commission and, which is more fatal to those who have affairs at court, no money, he never made a public appearance, and served only to give offence to the ministry by offering exceptions to the proposal of joining Plimouth to the Massachusetts." The chief result of the interventions of Ichabod Wiswall, a stubborn and contentious man, was to get the colony annexed to New York instead, from which disposition they were "taken out . . . by Mr. Mather's interest."

The tone of letters between Increase Mather and Hinckley was courteous; both men had their troubles. Hinckley wrote frankly to Increase on October 16, 1691: "Though it would have been well pleasing to myself and to sundry others of the most thinking men, which are also desirous to support the ministry, and schools of learning, to have been annexed to Boston, yet the greatest part of the people and of our deputies are most desirous to obtain a charter for themselves," but "so far as I can discern, they had much rather be annexed to the Massachusetts than to New York" (4 MHS *Coll.* 5:287–288). When Cotton Mather heard of the course of events, he fired off a curt letter to Hinckley, telling him that if his father "had petitioned for a charter to be bestowed upon Plymouth by itself, there had none been obtained for you, nor for us neither." He held Hinckley responsible for "Mr. Wise-wall": "he came and told my father, your Colony would all curse him for it." Mather concluded: "if you find yourselves thereby plunged into manifold miseries, you have none to thank for it but one of your own . . . I pray the Wonderful Counsellor to direct you" (*ibid.*, pp. 248–249).

When he came to propose a list of names for the first councillors to serve under the new charter, Increase nominated Hinckley as one of them, evidence not only that he bore no ill will, but that he recognized the Plymouth governor's honorable position in the colony (see Murdock, *Increase Mather*, p. 250). Cotton's rage, however, apparently continued to burn. (For a list of references concerning Plymouth's efforts to obtain a new charter, as well as their expression of thanks to Increase Mather, see Murdock, *ibid.*, pp. 403–404).

211:56   See, for example, Cicero *In Catalinam* I.ii.4.

211:58   For "*Girdle of their Loins*," cf. Isa 5.27.

211:62   For "*Judges of the Land*," cf. Ps. 94.2.

211:68   Jerome, *Liber de Viris Illustribus*, cap. XLII, *Migne L*, 23:691.

211:70–212:74   See Pausanias *Description of Greece* II.vii.2: "they give the dead man's name . . . and bid him farewell," apparently a general practice, and not confined to kings. Mather's source was clearly William Turner's *Remarkable Providences* (p. 157, 3rd Alph.): "I have read of the People called *Sicyonians*, that they would have no Epitaph written upon the Tombs of their Kings, but only their Names, that they might have no Honour but what did result from their Merits."

212:81   For "*Seat of Judgment*," cf. Rom. 14.10.

213:5   Many parallels could suggest to Mather his designation of Winthrop as the "American Nehemiah." Nehemiah led the "remnant" of Judah after the Babylonian captivity, restored purity of religion, rebuilt the walls of Jerusalem (as Winthrop built the new Jerusalem in the wilderness), and presided over the "sealing of a covenant" to which all those who gave themselves to the "law of God" subscribed. (Cf. Neh. 9.38, 10.29–39.)

213:7   Cicero *Epistulae ad Familiares* XII.xxva.5.

213:8–16   Traditionally the lives of Lycurgus and Numa are the second pair of parallel biographies in Plutarch's *Lives*. The "Criminal Disorders" with which Lycurgus was charged were his harsh and cruel treatment of the Helots. Numa's piety was toward heathen gods, and his implied exercise of necromancy would of course be decried as "Heathenish Madness."

213:27   Probably William Winthrop (1529–1582). He was, however, son of the second Adam and half-brother to the third. For a letter of his to John Foxe, see *Winthrop Papers*, 1:15. For the Winthrop pedigree, see *Papers*, I, facing p. 1.

213:29   Philpot's martyrdom is recorded in Foxe, *Acts and Monuments*, 3:528–610; the fortuitous preservation of his writings is noted on p. 584.

214:39   That is, would rather study Calvin's *Institutes of the Christian Religion* than Coke's *Institutes*.

214:49   See Deut. 1.17: "Ye shall not respect persons in judgment; but ye shall hear the small as well as the great." Compare also Prov. 24.23, 28.21, Rom. 2.11, Eph. 6.9, Col. 3.25, James 2.9, I Pet. 1.17.

214:52   Under writs of oyer and terminer, the King's judges were empowered to hear and judge indictments for criminal offences.

214:54   See II Chron. 9.18–19. Compare also Francis Bacon, "Of Judicature," *Works* (ed. J. Spedding, 15 vols., Boston, 1857), 12:270: "Let judges also remember, that Salomon's throne was supported by lions on both sides."

214:56   Winthrop is again likened to Nehemiah, whose hospitality is celebrated in Neh. 5.17–18. Even on the occasion of his having been passed over for the governorship for the first time, in favor of Thomas Dudley, "the new governour and the assistants *were together entertained* at the house of the old governour, as before" (*History*, 1:158). However, this may have been, as Morison suggests, merely because he had already ordered the meal prepared in expectation of his own reelection (*Builders*, p. 87).

215:7   For keeping "Heart" and "House," cf. Prov. 4.23, I Tim. 3.4–5.

215:89–93   Compare Deut. 11.18–19.

215:2   Cleaves was what would now be called a slick operator, and he early seems to have had some connection with Morton. Their names were associated in a letter from Matthew Cradock to Winthrop in 1637 (*Winthrop Papers*, 3:379). Later that year Gorges wrote to Winthrop of Cleaves' "misreports" and double dealings;

he added that Cleaves may have been misled by "Moorton" (*Papers*, 3:492–493). In 1644 Edward Winslow in a letter to Winthrop calls "Cleves and Morton two of the arrantest known knaues that ever trod on New English shore" (*Papers*, 4:428). In Maine Cleaves and a henchman Tucker were at the center of fierce territorial disputes. (Gorges had written of the "generall dislike" which Cleaves aroused there.) On January 25, 1640/41, one Richard Vines of Saco wrote to Winthrop saying he wanted to "free my selfe from blame and the malice of Cleiues, who is a Fire brand of dissention and hath sett the whole Province together by the yeares" (*Papers*, 4:309), and in a later letter protesting the "evell practices" of Cleaves and Tucker in claiming jurisdiction over land not theirs, he warned that the two planned to go to Winthrop with "false certificates, leastwise fraudulently gotten." Vines further charged that they ignored the authority of Rigby and Gorges, even speaking of them in "seditious and mutinous" language (*Papers*, 4:441). On the Vines-Cleaves squabble, see also Winthrop (*History*, 2:186–187).

The dispute over the jurisdiction of Ligonia dragged on. Finally in 1646 both sides asked the Massachusetts Court to adjudicate. As reported by Winthrop, "The plaintiff [Cleaves] could not prove the place in question to be within his patent . . . the defendant had no patent of the province, but only a copy thereof attested by witnesses." As a result, a perplexed jury "gave in a non licet" and "persuaded the parties to live in peace" (*History*, 2:314–315). Cleaves always addressed Winthrop most respectfully (cf., for example, *Papers*, 4:433–434) and he doubtless thought he had more to gain by speaking well of him than by supporting Morton's charges.

215:5–6 Compare Ezra 6.10, I Tim. 2.1–2.

216:10 An account of another little book of "Three Leaves" appears in Clarke, *Mirrour or Looking Glass* (p. 540): "Bishop Babington had a little book containing three leaves which he turned over night and morning. The first leafe was black to mind him of hell and God's judgements due to him for sinne; the second red to mind him of Christ, and his passion; the third white to set forth God's mercy to him through the merits of his Son in his Justification."

216:13–40 The quotation (lines 13–18) is from Winthrop, *History*, 1:212, under date of July 18, 1636; the last sentence, "Lento Gradu," etc., does not appear there. The "Leading" persons who considered Winthrop too lenient were Dudley and Vane; the "Learned" counselors who recommended a "*stricter Discipline*" were the ministers John Cotton, Thomas Hooker, and John Wilson. The "several other Articles" are given in Winthrop, 1:213–214. For "seek the Honour of each other" (line 35), cf. Rom. 12.10. See also Plutarch *Moralia* 816.A: "But the honor of an office resides in concord and friendship with one's colleagues much more than in crowns and a purple-bordered robe."

216:43 For "Sanballat the Horonite and Tobiah the servant of Ammonite," see Neh. 2.10, 19, 4.1, 3, 6.1–14. They "mocked at the Jews" and were "wroth" at the rebuilding of the wall.

216:44–45 Luther, *Loci Communes* (ed. Fabricius, London, 1651), Quartae Classis, cap. 36, p. 103.

216:46–47 On the "part of a *Neighbour*," cf. Luke 10.27, 36.

217:50–51 For "*soft Raiment* . . . disagreeable to a *Wilderness*," see Matt. 11.7–8, Luke 7.24–25.

217:55–56 See Job 29.12–13.

217:62–63 An allusion to Ps. 78.19; cf. also Neh. 5.14–18.

217:65–67 Gen. 41.56.

217:69 Eccles. 11.1.

217:72–74 Mather repeatedly referred to the last "*Meal in the Barrel*," as, for example, Bk. I, p. 162, l. 50. The ship was the *Lyon*. (See Winthrop, *History*, 1:49, and Bk. I, p. 161, ll. 36–37 and endnote.)

217:75–76 On August 7, 1632, Winthrop noted that "for want of a public stock, [he] had disbursed all common charges out of his own estate" (*History*, 1:102). Evidence of public recognition of his generosity appears in an entry for July 2, 1633: "Court . . . agreed, that the governour, John Winthrop, should have, toward his charges this year, £150 . . . the money, which he had disbursed in public business, as officers' wages, etc. being between two and three hundred pounds" (1:124–125). In the account that he rendered to the General Court on September 4, 1634, he noted that during his terms as governor, "I have spent above £500 per annum, of which £200 per annum would have maintained my family in a private condition. So as I may truly say, I have spent, by occasion of my late office, above £1200" (*History*, 1:474–477; this accounting is also given in *Winthrop Papers*, 3:172–174).

217:78–79 Luke 14.12–14; Acts 20.35.

217:80–86 Quoted from Winthrop (1:92), but with some abridgement and a number of verbal changes, such as "*Civilities*" for "gratuities," "*God's Word*" for "God's rule," the rule being, "thou shalt take no gift: for the gift blindeth the wise, and perverteth the words of the righteous" (Exod. 23.8).

218:5–9 Plato *Republic* II.iv.C.

218:10 On "Popularity," see *History*, 1:103, where Winthrop, at a meeting held to resolve conflicts between him and Thomas Dudley, Deputy Governor, remarks that Dudley had "conceived" a "jealousy" "that the governour intended to make himself popular, that he might gain absolute power."

218:12 Luke 6.26.

218:19–24 For "*Envy*," see Eccles. 4.4; for "*stand before it*," see Prov. 27.4. Note Mather's word play of "*stand before*," "*not standing*," "*withstood*." Winthrop records two occasions when fear of "too *frequent Choice* of One Man" was voiced: in 1639, when, although Winthrop was reelected, some expressed "fear lest it might make way for having a governour for life" (*History*, 1:360); and in 1640, when Winthrop was passed over for Dudley, "lest the long continuance of one man in the place should bring it to be for life, and, in time, hereditary" (2:3).

218:24–25 On May 3, 1643, Mr. Ezekiel Rogers, pastor of the church in Rowley, preached the election sermon; he "dissuaded them earnestly from choosing the same man twice together, and expressed his dislike of that with such vehemency as gave offence." Nonetheless, Winthrop was reelected (2:119).

219:30–38 This was the election of 1641; Richard Bellingham was elected governor (Winthrop, *History*, 2:41–42), on whom see below p. 237, ll. 83–95.

219:39 For "*Frowardness*," see Prov. 10.32, 16.26.

219:41 "The Pazzians Conspiracie" was recounted by Thomas Fuller in *The Holy State and the Profane State* (2:421–424). He gives as his sources "Machiavels Florent. Hist. lib. 8. pag. 407 & sequent," "Mach. Disput. de Repub. lib. 3. cap. 6. p. 397," and "Mach, Disput. de Repub. lib. 3. cap. 6. p. 399."

219:43 The "Famous *Judges* Motto" is usually attributed to Sir Edward Coke, as in Fuller's *Worthies* (2:452), but David Lloyd, in *State-Worthies* (London, 1670), pp. 475–476), says of Lord Burleigh, "[it] was his saying, before it was *Sir Edward Cookes* Motto."

219:43–48 For the words of the "Oracles of God," see Prov. 14.30. Mather's source here may well have been J. Burroughes, *Irenicum* (London, 1646), p. 126: "The Holy Ghost sayes that *envie is rottennesse to the bones*; the same learned man *Guliel. Paris* applyes this to such as are chiefe in Church and Common-wealth, who are as it were the bones, the strength, the support of the societies whereof they are; *Envie*, sayes he, *is often found amongst them and it is rottennesse to them*." See Gulielmus Alvernus, *De Moribus*, cap. viii, in *Opera Omnia* (2 vols., Paris, 1674), 1:228, col. 2g: "Hi enim qui in corpore Ecclesiae fortissimi esse creduntur et velut ossa in corpore Ecclesiae, plerumque tabe hujusmodi contabescunt."

219:50–51 Prov. 15.1.

219:55–57 A probable source for the quotation from Theodosius is Samuel Clarke, *The Second Part of the Marrow* (London, 1650), p. 48, where the language is close to that of Mather.

219:57 For "*Meekness of Wisdom*," see James 3.13.

219:58–220:67 These lines follow closely a passage in Winthrop (*History*, 1:140), except for the omission of the names. The "sharp Letter" was in reply to a request from Winthrop that men from Newtown [Cambridge] give "help to the finishing of the fort at Boston."

220:72–86 Vane, as governor, headed a Boston party, their petition "being about a pretence of liberty, etc., (though intended chiefly for revoking the sentence given against Mr. Wheelwright.)" This sentence had been incurred at an earlier court, on February 9, 1636/37, because of a sermon "adjudged guilty of sedition, and also of contempt," but sentencing was "deferred till the next court" (*History*, 1:257–258). Winthrop, as Deputy Governor, marshalled the opposition to Vane's petition, and he was again elected governor; Mr. Vane, together with his supporters, was "quite left out." (For this entire episode, see *History*, 1:261–263.) For "*Dirt and Mire*" (line 81), see Isa. 57.20.

220:89 For "*doubled Respects*," cf. I Tim. 5.17.

220:90–221:36 The "*Antinomian* and *Familistical* Faction" included the majority of the members of the First Church of Boston, notable among them Henry Vane and Mrs. Anne Hutchinson. With her maintenance of such "gross errors" as the "indwelling of the Holy Ghost" and her speaking against "both magistry and ministry" after the manner of the sect known as the "Family of Love," she clearly menaced good order in church and state. The faction considered John Cotton, Teacher of the First Church, the only true expounder of the Covenant of Grace. Ranged against them were John Wilson, Pastor of the Boston church, and almost all the other clergy of the colony. For Mather, the problem was to veil the details of the controversy at the same time that he admitted that it nearly caused the "Ruin of the Country." (Cf. Bk. I, p. 171, l. 98 and endnote thereto.) Indeed, he gives the conflict epic stature by quoting the *Aeneid* (I.58–59). To follow the development of the controversy, see Winthrop, *History*, 1:239–243, 246, 248–259, 263–265, 281–282, 284–287 on the Synod at Newtown August 30, to September 22, 1637, and 292–298 on the General Court which assembled on November 2, 1637, at which John Wheelwright and Anne Hutchinson were banished and several other leading Antinomians disfranchised. For the documentary history of the affair, see *The Antinomian Controversy, 1636–1638* (ed. David D. Hall, Middletown, Conn., Wesleyan University Press, 1968).

What Mather presents as Winthrop's speech to the congregation transposes Winthrop's third person summary (1:299–301), with some elaboration, into direct discourse. The Biblical allusions all appear in Winthrop: for Uzziah's trespass (p. 221, ll. 20–22), see II Chron. 26.16–18; for Asa and the prophet (ll. 22–23), II Chron. 16.7–10; for "the Glory of God" (l. 32), I Cor. 10.31; for "*Hagar* and *Ishmael*" (l. 35), Gen. 21.9–14. (Cf. Miller, *Colony to Province*, pp. 57–63, for an analysis of the controversy.)

221:37–38 *Aeneid* I.154.

221:39–222:41 For the town's present to Winthrop, see *History*, 2:3–4.

222:41–46 The first occasion noted by Winthrop of the Deputies' resistance to the exercise of the negative voice by the Assistants was on September 4, 1634, at a meeting of the General Court in Newtown (*History*, 1:168–169).

222:46–48 See Pliny *Natural History* VIII.xliii. 104: "M. Varro auctor est a cuniculis suffossum in Hispania oppidum, a talpis in Thessalia, ab ranis civitatem in Gallia pulsam." In Pliny there is no mention of the German plague; Mather may have been utilizing the legend associated with the town of Hameln made use of by Browning for the "Pied Piper of Hamelin."

222:50–223:83 For the long saga of the sow and the contest over its ownership between "one Sherman's wife" and Captain Robert Keayne, see Winthrop, *History*, 2:83–86. The sow went astray in 1636; finally, at a court on June 22, 1642, the court found for the defendant, Keayne, with the magistrates overruling the deputies. "And because there was much laboring in the country upon a false supposition, that the magistrate's negative voice stopped the plaintiff in the case of the sow, one of the magistrates [Winthrop, then governor] published a declaration of the necessity of upholding the same." The dissension over the case did not end, and in 1643 it was again brought before the magistrates and elders (2:139–141). Winthrop states that "his speech is set down verbatim to prevent misrepresentation" (2:141–142), but Mather freely abridged it and "improved" the style. Winthrop concludes his account of "the sow business" by returning to the question of the negative voice (2:142–144). For his "Replye to the Answ: made to the Discourse about the Neg: vote," see *Winthrop Papers*, 4:380–391. For lines 68–70, cf. I Cor. 10.29; for lines 70–72, cf. I Cor. 4.3–5.

223:84–85 *Aeneid* I.142–143.

223:87 For a "*Man of an excellent Spirit*," cf. Prov. 17.27; Dan. 5.12, 6.3.

223:91–224:49 The account of the Hingham affair appears in Winthrop, *History*, 2:271–286. The squabble arose over the election of a militia captain. In 1645, Thomas Dudley was governor; Winthrop as Deputy Governor was a justice of the peace. He intervened in the Hingham quarrel, committing one faction for contempt of court, and the lower house of the General Court impeached him for exceeding his authority. He was tried and acquitted.

223:93–94 Sextus Aurelius Victor "De Viris Illustribus" 47.76 in *Historia Romana* (2 vols., London, 1829), 1:164: "ipse quadragies quater accusatus gloriose absolutus." Plutarch, however, in his *Lives* says he was a defendant no less than fifty times ("Cato Major" xv.5) and that on one occasion he was fined two talents (*ibid.* XIX.2). Some of Mather's possible secondary sources follow Plutarch: Wanley, *Wonders*, p. 167b, who cites Lipsius, *Monita et Exempla Politica*, p. 170, in *Opera*, Vol. IV; and Heidfeld, *Sphinx*, p. 751. Trapp's *Commentary* on Acts 25.6 (p. 479a) has 32 times; Clarke, *Mirrour*, has 46 times (p. 190).

223:4 "*Humilitude*" appears in the 1702 edition, and this instance is cited in NED. However, Mather corrected it to "*Humility*" as a typographical error.

223:10 For "*Root of the Matter*," cf. Job 19.28.

223:10–224:49 Mather's severely cropped and paraphrased version of Winthrop's sppech on liberty, delivered on July 3, 1645, obscures the magisterial sonorities of Winthrop's words, for which see the *History*, 2:279–282. Nonetheless, in Mather's version it gained wide European circulation. Compare *Universal History* (Modern Part, London, 1763), 39:292. Alexis de Tocqueville quoted a passage from it in chapter 2 of his *De la Democratie en Amerique*.

223:18 For Miriam, see Num. 12.14.

224:22–27 Compare Rom. 13.1–7, Tit. 3.1.

224:28–29 Acts 14.15; cf. also James 5.17.

224:30–31 Compare Ps. 89.34.

224:39–40 Terence, *Heauton Timorumenos*, Act III.483. In Winthrop (2:281), "omnes sumus licentia deteriores." "It was," says Spencer, "a grave and smart answer of Secretary *Walsingham* . . . when he was consulted by the Queen, about the lawfulnesse of Monopoly-Licences" (*Things New and Old*, ex. 1451, p. 504). Compare also Trapp on Matt. 4.6.

224:59 The context indicates that Mather did indeed intend "*Cedendo*," a reference to Ovid, *Ars Amatoria* II.197: "cedendo victor abibis." Mather's source may have been Melchior Adam, *Vitae Germanorum Theologorum* (Frankfort, 1653), p. 801. The proverb "Romani sedendo vincunt" (the Romans conquer by sitting) from Varro, *Rerum Rusticarum* I.2 (ed. G. Goetz, Leipzig, Blankenburgi, Kircher, 1912, p. 10), was also widely quoted in the period. Compare, for example, Erasmus, *Epitome Adagiorum* (Amsterdam, 1549), p. 510, and Trapp's *Commentary* (p. 328a) on Luke 14.31.

225:62–87   Winthrop's record of this visit to Plymouth is very brief (*History*, 1:109–110), and he does not give the question "publickly propounded," merely noting that after Williams and Smith had spoken, it was "desired the governour of Massachusetts" should also speak to the issue.

225:65–66   For "through an Howling Wilderness," cf. Deut. 32.10; for "*Servants on Horseback*," see Eccles. 10.7.

225:66–67   "*Dat Galenus opes, dat Justinianus honores, Sed genus et species cogitur ire pedes*": "The Rich Physician, honour'd lawyers ride, Whilst the poor scholar foots it by their side" (Robert Burton, *Anatomy of Melancholy*, p. I, sec.2, mem.3, subsec. 15, ed. Boston, 1859, 1:410). Burton gives his reference as "*Buchanan eleg. lib.*," which would be George Buchanan, *Franciscanus et fratres; Elegiarum Liber 1*, Geneva, 1584.

225:71   Mather's source may have been Trapp's *Commentary* (p. 42a) on Matt. 4.21: "The Low-Countrymen, suspecting the English (A.D. 1587), stamped money with two earthen pots swimming in the sea (according to the old fable) and wittily inscribed, *Si collidimur, frangimur*." Spencer also quotes the phrase (*Things New and Old*, Ex. 1173, p. 317): "it was of old the Dutch device, of two earthen Pots swimming upon the water, with this Motto, '*Frangimur si collidimur.*'" In 1588 and 1591, Dutch medals were struck bearing the two floating jars and the legend "*Frangimur si Collidimur.*" (See Pierre Bizot, *Histoire Métallique de la République de Hollande*, 2 vols., Amsterdam, 1688, 1:63***** and 63(*6) and plate opposite p. 73*.) Camden referred to such a "Medalia" (*Remains*, p. 384). Earlier the legend had appeared on a medal struck as a memorial of the Union of Utrecht, 1579; the city of Utrecht is in the background, with two ships in the foreground (Bizot, 1:40–41).

225:72–73   On Ralph Smith, see Bk. I, p. 140, l. 36 and endnote thereto; cf. also Bradford, *History*, 2:87n. Roger Williams arrived in Boston on February 5, 1631. In a letter to John Cotton of Plymouth, March 25, 1671, he wrote: "being unanimously chosen teacher at Boston . . . I conscientiously refused and withdrew to Plymouth, because I durst not officiate to an unseparated people" (Miller, *Roger Williams*, New York, Bobbs-Merrill Company, 1953, p. 239). Winthrop said nothing of his choice as teacher, simply stating that "Mr. Williams had refused to join with the congregation at Boston" because they had not made a "public declaration" of their separation from the Church of England (*History*, 1:63). Williams spent two years at Plymouth, preaching occasionally, but not officially ordained. In 1633 he was called to the church in Salem. For Cottom Mather on Williams, see *Magnalia*, Bk. VII, chap. 2.

225:87–226:11   Soon after his arrival Winthrop wrote (*History*, 1:44, under date of October 25, 1630): "The governour, upon consideration of the inconveniences which had grown . . . by drinking one to another, restrained it at his own table." Finally, in September 1639, at the General Court "an order was made to abolish that vain custom." (See *Mass. Records*, 1:271–272; Winthrop's record of this order was not entered in his Journal until December 1639, 1:390.)

225:93–94   "Agis and Cleomenes" XIII.4, in Plutarch's *Lives*.

226:3–11   For the remainder of his paragraph against health-drinking, Mather relies on the first chapter of his father's *A Testimony Against . . . Prophane and Superstitious Customs* (London, 1687). Increase inveighs against "Health-Drinking" as a pagan custom and "Poyson of the Devil," originating in Hell and used as a "Drink-offering to Satan." As for the judgment of "the *Fathers*," Increase notes: "That filthy and unhappy Custom (saith *Austin*) of *Drinking Healths is Reliquе of Paganism*," with a gloss "*De Tempore*, Serm. 131." and he also cites Ambrose as rebuking the pagans (p. 3). He admits (p. 7) that some "Popish-Authors" had "so much of Morality" as to write against "Healthings," mentioning especially

Pope Innocent III, who ordered "that if any of the clergy should be proved guilty of "Healthing," he should be suspended "*ab Officio & Beneficio*, without giving due Satisfaction for his offence." Mather cites as his authority "Matenesio, p. 3." Matensio (latinized Matenesius, Mathenesius) was an eccentric German scholar, Johann Friedrich von Mathenez, who published a book *De Ritu Bibendi super sanitate magnatum, pontificum, regum*, etc. (Cologne, 1611), a work which Mather cites five times in this first chapter, and which he may well have owned.

226:11 Ovid *Amores* III.iv.17 (ed. E. J. Kenney, Oxford, Clarendon Press, 1961, p. 75). The Ovid quotation appears in Fuller, *Church History*, 2:421.

226:12 For "*Many were the Afflictions*," etc., see Ps. 34.19.

226:12–20 As to the house, "The governour, having erected a building of stone at Mistick, there came so violent a storm of rain, for twenty-four hours, from the N.E. and S.E. as (it being not finished, and laid with clay for want of lime) two sides of it were washed down to the ground" (*History*, 1:75–76, Oct. 30, 1631). Then on April 10, 1633, Winthrop received news that a ship that had gone trading to Virginia had been cast upon a shoal, in which catastrophe "The governour of Massachusetts lost, in beaver and fish, which he sent to Virginia, etc., near £100" (1:120–121). In 1639 Winthrop learned that a dishonest agent in London had embezzled property in England (R. C. Winthrop, *Life and Letters of John Winthrop*, 2 vols., Boston, 1869, 2:253). On losses in America, see *History*, 2:3–4. In his will he details their effect on his estate (*ibid.*, 2:440, and *Papers*, 4:146–147).

226:16–17 The source of this quotation has not been found.

226:18–20 For the defalcations of Luxford, steward of Winthrop's farm Ten Hills on the Mystic River, see *Papers*, 4:163n, 174–176, 179–182, 199–200, 206, 208–210, 250, 252–253.

226:25 For "*Wisdom with an Inheritance*," see Eccles. 7.11.

226:33–34 For "Temptations of a *Wilderness*," cf. Ps. 95.8–9; for thunder and lightning as signs of God's displeasure, see Isa. 29.6.

227:36 For "*Voice of the Almighty*," cf. Ezek. 1.24, 10.5.

227:41 Sozomen, *Historia Ecclesiastica*, Bk. III, cap. 14 (*Migne G*, 67:1069), cited in Palladius, *Historia Lausiaca* (ed. Cuthbert Butler, Cambridge, Cambridge University Press, 1904), 17:1043b.

227:43 For "*Little Pleasure in them*," cf. Eccles. 12.1.

227:47–48 The *Elegies of Maximianus* I.211–212 (ed. Richard Webster, Princeton, Princeton University Press, 1900, p. 32). Compare Heidfeld, *Sphinx*, p. 1136, where the lines are wrongly ascribed to Cornelius Gallus, a Roman politician, poet, and soldier, who died in 26 B.C.

227:49–53 Winthrop's meditation on death appears in R. C. Winthrop's *Life and Letters*, 2:392, with the *Magnalia* as its source. The passage combines phrases from II Tim. 4.6, Ps. 31.15, I Cor. 4.2, Matt. 25.21, 23.

227:56–57 For "*bruising of the Heel*," see Gen. 3.15; for the "*old Serpent*," Rev. 12.9, 20.2.

227:59–60 For "*wicked cease from trembling*," see Job 3.17; for "that *wicked One*" as a designation for Satan, cf. I John 2.13, 14, 3.12, 5.18, Matt. 13.19, 38; for "Conflicts with the *Tempter*," cf. Matt. 4.3, I Thess. 3.5; cf. also Rev. 12.9, 12.

227:64–65 The source of this quotation has not been found.

227:67 Compare Job 15.11.

227:69 Compare James 5.14–15.

227:71–228:73 According to R. C. Winthrop (*Life and Letters*, 2:393), John Cotton's sermon is "not known to be extant." In quoting the text, Mather makes some alterations, such as "humbled my self" for "humbled my soul."

228:79–80 For becoming "an *Enemy*, like the *Friends of David*," see Pss. 35.15–16, 38.11. 41.9.

228:86 For "bearing our *Infirmities*," see Matt. 8.17, Rom. 15.1.

228:90–92 For the "*Council and Blessing*" of Jacob, see Gen. 49; for the death of David, see I Kings 2.1–10; for "*gave up the Ghost*," see, for example, Gen. 25.8, 17, 35.29, 49.33; for "*fell asleep*," see Acts 7.60, I Cor. 15.6, 18, II Pet. 3.4.

228:92–94 Compare Trapp, *Commentary* (p. 202b) on Matt. 16.24: "Valentinian the emperour dying, affirmed, that he was proud of one of his victories only, viz., that he had overcome his own flesh, that worst of enemies." Trapp's account is a fanciful elaboration of Ammianus Marcellinus *Res Gestae* XXX.6.3.

228:98–6 Josephus *Antiquitates* XI.183.

229:9–16 Isocrates *Areopagiticus* 147.37. The passage is quoted in Cave, *Antiquitates Apostolicae*, p. 66, citing "*Areop. 147 vid. Maxim. Prolog. Opera. S.Dionys. Praef. pag. 34*," where the English translation is the same as Mather's. For the "*Judges of Areopagus*," see Acts 17.19; for "*not Nobly Born*," I Cor. 1.26–27. By implication, Mather suggests that New England judges were raised up by Jehovah (cf. Judg. 2.16–18), and hence "*New-born*" (see John 3.3–7; cf. also John 1.12–13, I Pet. 1.23).

229:18–22 The Hebrew "**7ד'**" ordinarily means hand, but Mather is correct; here it means monument. By way of Isa. 56.5 Mather can thus equate those who "*please God*" with both Saul's monument and the "*Pillar*" of Rev. 3.12.

229:31–32 For God as the "Father of the Orphans," cf. Deut. 10.18, 14.29, 16.11, 14, 24.19–21, 26.12–13; "take them up" is an allusion to Ps. 27.10.

229:35 For Judge Nichols, see Fuller's *Worthies*, 2:512.

230:53 The French recaptured Amiens in September of 1597, and peace between France and Spain was concluded May 2, 1598.

230:58 See Anne Bradstreet's poem, "An Epitaph on my dear and ever honoured mother, Mrs. Dorothy Dudley," in *Works* (ed. J. H. Ellis, Charlestown, 1867), p. 369.

230:60–61 On John Dod, see Fuller, *Church History*, 4:305. On John Winston, see Henry Isham Longden, *Northamptonshire and Rutland Clergy* (15 vols., Northampton, 1938–1943), 15:149.

230:63 On "*Unscriptural Ceremonies*," see Bk. I, p. 159, l. 59 and endnote.

231:78 For "Faithful *Steward*," see I Cor. 4.2.

231:90–91 For Nehemiah's "appeal," see Neh. 1.11, 5.19, 13.14, 22, 21; for "*who knows the Hearts of all men*," see Acts 1.24.

231:92–96 The manuscript of Mather's "more particular account," some three or four times longer and long preserved among manuscripts of the Dudley family, was edited by C. Deane in MHS *Proc.*, 11:207–222, and issued separately, Cambridge, Mass., 1870 (edition cited). It is small wonder that certain Dudleys should have distrusted what Mather might write of them. In 1684 at a Boston town meeting, Increase aroused the citizens by comparing the greatness of the "fathers," including Thomas Dudley, with their degenerate descendants. He forced through a resolution condemning Joseph Dudley (Thomas's son), Simon Bradstreet (married to Anne Dudley), William Stoughton, and Peter Bulkeley as "Enemies of the Country" on the grounds that Dudley, Stoughton, and Bulkeley, although sent as agents to London to defend the Charter, had in fact acquiesced in its abrogation, and that Bradstreet as an assistant had supported them (see Everett Kimball, *The Public Life of Joseph Dudley*, N.Y., Longmans, 1911, pp. 17–18; see also Miller, *Colony to Province*, p. 139). Joseph Dudley was in England while Mather was putting together the *Magnalia*. However, John Quick, the London minister acting as Mather's agent with the publishers, reported in a letter of March 19, 1702, that the *Magnalia* biography of Dudley was submitted to Joseph in London and approved, with the alteration of only "one or two words." (See Murdock, *Cotton Mather: Selections*, New York, Harcourt, Brace & Co., 1926, pp. xlii, xliv.)

In the manuscript version of the life of Dudley, only "Mr. Dod" was named (see p. 230, l. 60), with the addition that "by being a follower of Mr. Dod, he came into the knowledge of the Lord Say & Lord Compton, & other persons of quality,

by whose means he was afterwards commended to the service of the earl of Lincoln"
(Deane, pp. 9–10). The *Magnalia* passage lines 73–79 is very close to the manuscript
version (p. 10); lines 87–91 are practically identical (p. 12), and there are other
resemblances between the two versions in the remainder of the sketch of Dudley.

231:3   For Pharoah and Joseph, see Gen. 41.32–57.

232:14   Dudley's letter to the countess of Lincoln was dated March 28, 1631; reprinted in Young, *Chronicles of Massachusetts*, pp. 301–340. Compare A. Jones,
The Life and Work of Thomas Dudley (Boston, 1899), pp. 437n and 437–452.

232:16   For "Terror to Evil Doers," cf. Rom. 13.3.

232:29–48   In the manuscript life (p. 19), Dudley's poem has "deed" for "Day"
in line 6, "meet" for "live" in line 14, and "I did no hurt to thine" in the last line.
Several of the verses contain Biblical echoes: "*My Shuttle's shot*," Job 7.6; "*my
Race is run*," Heb. 12.1; "*My Flower is faded*," Job 14.2, Ps. 103.15, James 1.10,
I Pet. 1.24; "*My Dream is vanish'd*," Job 20.8; "*Shadow's fled*," Job 8.9, 14.2, Ps.
144.4, Eccles. 8.13; "*Ill Egg*," Isa. 59.5.

233:52   Margaret More was said to have "attained to that skill in all learning and
languages that she became the miracle of her age" (Fuller's *Worthies*, 2:363).

233:55   For "to be a *Crown*," cf. Prov. 12.4, 17.6.

233:56–66   There were many possible sources for tales of "Learned Women."
Included in Diogenes Laërtius' *Historia Mulierum Philosopharum* were lives of Pam-
phila, Eudocia, and Hypatia (edited by Gilles Ménage in the two-volume 1692
Amsterdam edition of Laërtius, 2:489, 490–492, 491–495). Pamphila, Eudocia,
Anna Maria van Schurman, Margherita Sarocchia, and the three Corinna's are
listed, in that order, in Clarke, *Mirrour*, pp. 700–701; Clarke's reference for the three
Corinna's is Leigh, *Religion and Learning*, p. 171, according to whom "the first was a
Theban which overcame Pindar . . . five times. She put forth five books of epigrams;
the second was a Thespian very much celebrated by the Ancients, the third flourished
in the time of Ovid, and was very dear to him." For Corinna of Tanagra, see Pausanias *Description of Greece* IX.xxii.3. For Corinna the younger and Corinna of Thespiae,
see Suidas, *Lexicon*, p. 618. For Rosuida, see J. A. Fabricius, *Bibliotheca Latina Mediae
et Infimae Aetatis* (6 vols., Hamburg, 1734–1746), 3:824–834.

233:67–68   According to Tuttle, "Libraries of the Mathers" (AAS *Proc.*, New Series,
vol. 20), Jan van Beverwijck was represented by one volume (p. 317), Hottinger by
two (p. 332), and Voet by three (p. 353).

233:70   *The Tenth Muse Lately sprung up in America. or Several Poems, compiled with great
variety of Wit and Learning, full of delight*, was first printed in London in 1650. A second
edition was published in Boston in 1678.

234:75–86   The lines upon Anne Bradstreet appear in the second edition of her
poems signed B.W., probably Benjamin Woodbridge, one of the first settlers of
Andover, Massachusetts. Mather makes a few verbal changes: "or" for "nor"
in line 3, "an" for "one" in line 4, "hence" inserted in line 6, possibly intended as a
metrical improvement. See her *Works*, p. 89.

234:90   The tag "helluo librorum" may be found in many places. Heidfeld's *Sphinx*
(p. 929) has "*helluo librorum* dictus est," of Cato, citing Valerius Maximus (*Factorum
et Dictorum Memorabilium* VIII.vii.2). Cicero also describes Cato "quasi helluari
libris . . . videbatur" (*De Finibus* III.ii.7). Spencer uses the phrase "librorum
helluones" in the gloss to a paragraph headed "Man losing himself in the pursuit
after knowledge Extraordinary," where "Epicures of knowledge" are criticized for
neglecting the "chronicles of God" (*Things New and Old*, ex. 926, p. 238); Clarke
employs the phrase approvingly of an English minister (*Lives of Sundry Eminent
Persons*, London, 1683, p. 34). For Belcher's epitaph, see 6 MHS *Coll.* 6:479.

234:97   J. H. Ellis, editor of the *Works* of Anne Bradstreet, identifies "E.R." as
Ezekiel Rogers (p. lv), as does Jantz, *First Century of New England Verse*, p. 247.

235:6   See Winthrop, *History*, 1:204.

235:8   For "John Haynes of Connecticut," see Charles E. Cunningham, *NEQ*, 12:654–680.

235:10–11   Compare Ps. 37.37.

235:12–13   The sense of Mather's quotation from Vespasian, though not the exact words, appears in Sextus Aurelius Victor "De Caesaribus" 9.5 (*Historia Romana*, 1:257).

235:15–21   These lines echo Winthrop, 1:203. For Vane, see J. K. Hosmer, *The Life of Young Sir Henry Vane* (Boston, 1888). Mather undoubtedly disapproved of Vane's views, but recognized that he died a martyr. The account he gives of Vane is adroit in its evasion of any definite expression of opinion. See also a recent life by J. H. Adamson & H. F. Folland, *Sir Henry Vane*, Boston, Gambit, 1973, especially chapter four.

235:22–27   For "*Seeker*," see Bk. I, p. 143, l. 72 and endnote. Note Mather's wordplay with various meanings of "seeker" and "seek." Of Vane as a Seeker, Bishop Burnet wrote: "He had a head as darkened in his notions of religion, as his mind was clouded with fear: for though he set up a form of religion in a way of his own, yet it consisted rather in a withdrawing from all other forms, than in any new or particular opinions or forms; from which he and his party were called *seekers*, and seemed to wait for some new and clearer manifestations" (*History*, 1:294). Richard Baxter, speaking of the sects that "reigned" during the Rump Parliament (see *The Autobiography of Richard Baxter*, ed. J. M. Lloyd Thomas, London, J. M. Dent, 1925, p. 73), distinguished between the Seekers and the "Vanists (for I know not by what other name to make them known), who were Sir Henry Vane's disciples, [who] first sprang up under him in New England when he was governor there. . . . His unhappiness lay in this, that his doctrines were so cloudily formed and expressed that few could understand them, and therefore he had but few true disciples."

235:28–30   For "*Kippod . . . Bittern*," see Isa. 14.23, 34.11, Zeph. 2.14. Mather's source for his etymological bestiary has not been identified. Poole's *Annotations* (vol. I on Isa. 14.23) has "bittern," with the notation: "Others render the Word *Hedg-hog*, or *Porcupine*: But this not being considerable in itself . . . I shall not trouble the *English* Reader with any Discourse about it: And the Learned may consult my *Latin Synopsis*" (see 3:145). The K.J.V. has "bittern," the A.V. "porcupine."

236:34–36   Mather's source here may have been Fuller, *Holy and Profane State* (2:180–181): "The Hebrew word *Barac* signifies to blesse, and to curse; and 'tis the speakers pleasure if he use it in the worst acception. Fools of themselves are equally capable to pray and to swear."

236:40–50   The letter which Mather identifies as from "an Old *New-English* Manuscript" is also quoted, at somewhat greater length, by Hutchinson, who writes: "A letter, wrote from New England, shews the sense they had of him after they had made trial" (*History*, 1:57–58). One may perhaps assume that this letter was among the materials with which Cotton Mather's son Samuel said he had furnished the "careless" Mr. Hutchinson (see endnote to Bk. I, p. 164, l. 24). A very similar judgment was directed at young Vane by Hugh Peter at the General Court of October 1636: "Mr. Peter also besought him humbly to consider his youth, and short experience in the things of God, and to beware of peremptory conclusions, which he perceived him to be very apt unto" (Winthrop, *History*, 1:249). See also Hosmer, *Sir Henry Vane*, chapters 3 and 4, on Vane in New England. For Vane and the antinomian affray, see above p. 220, l. 72–p. 221, l. 36 and endnotes.

236:58–76   Much of the phrasing of these lines and all the italicized passages are taken from *The Tryal*: p. 89 for p. 236, l. 9; p. 79 for lines 59–60; p. 80 for lines 60–63; p. 81 for p. 237, ll. 64–65; p. 92 for lines 69–76.

237:73   For "*in these Clouds*," cf. Matt. 24.30, 26.64, Mark 13.26, 14.62, Rev. 1.7.

237:78   For John Endecott, see L. S. Mayo, *John Endecott: A Biography*, Cambridge, Mass., Harvard University Press, 1936.

237:80   For a "*Populous Nation,*" see Deut. 26.5.

237:84 *et esq.*   For his brief description of Bellingham, Mather may have been indebted to Hubbard (*History,* p. 610), who, while praising him as "a great justiciary . . . firm and fixed in any resolution he entertayned," acknowledges that he was "of larger comprehension than expression, like a vessel whose vent holdeth no good proportion with its capacity to contain, a disadvantage to a public person." He was not beloved by Governor Winthrop since in various disputes between the deputies and Winthrop over the negative voice, Bellingham sided with the deputies. In the controversy over the "sow business," Winthrop writes that "This stiffness of his and singularity in opinion was very unpleasing to all the company" (*History,* 2:139; see also p. 228).

Hubbard particularly praises Bellingham as "a notable hater of bribes." To be sure, Mather could have learned of this attribute by reading Bellingham's epitaph in the Granary burying ground: "Virtue's fast friend within this tomb doth lie, A foe to bribes, but rich in charity." Mather's source for his reference to Theban statues has not been found.

237:89–90   Thucydides *History* II.LX.5.

237:94–95   Mather here combines Ps. 26.9–10 with Isa. 57.2.

238:8   Horace *Epistles* II.I.14.

238:18   For Simon Bradstreet the elder, see J. A. Venn. *Alumni Cantabrigienses* (10 vols., Cambridge, Cambridge University Press, 1922–1954), 1:203.

239:27   Venn, *ibid.,* 1:203.

239:32–36   It seems clear that the quoted passage was in Cotton Mather's possession when he wrote, either in a copy or the original. Both he and his father were closely in touch with Simon Bradstreet until his death in 1697.

239:46–47   Fuller's *Worthies,* 1:329.

239:49   Bradstreet was elected an assistant at a meeting held at Southampton March 19, 1630 (*Mass. Records,* 1:69).

240:55   On Dudley's presidency, see Kimball, *Joseph Dudley,* pp. 22–38. Dudley was in some doubt concerning what his reception would be. He wrote to Increase Mather for advice and assistance (Hutchinson, *History,* 1:299n), but failed to obtain him as an ally.

240:61–63   For Cotton Mather on the tyranny of Andros, see below p. 288, l. 10– p. 292, l. 48. Mather's reference here to Dudley as "well Accomplished" (line 60) may perhaps be interpreted as cautious policy on his part or it may reflect the fact that by the later 1690's Dudley and the Mathers were being brought together by their common enemies, chiefly Elisha Cooke. (Cf. Kimball, *Joseph Dudley,* p. 74.)

240:64–76   See Eugene Defrance, *Catharine de Médicis, ses astrologues et ses magiciens-envoûtures* (Paris, Mercure de France, 1911), especially chapter 4 (pp. 125–144), "Le miroir magique," with references, and "Catherine de Médicis et l'évocation par le miroir magique" (p. 159), a reprint of an eighteenth-century engraving. Some have identified the magician as Nostradamus (Michel de Notredame); others as Cosmo Ruggiere of Florence.

240:77   See below p. 290, ll. 77–4.

241:93–97   Plato *Phaedrus* 261.C associates the two men Nestor and Gorgias: "unless you are disguising Gorgias under the name of Nestor." Both were famous in antiquity for their longevity. Mather's source was probably Wanley (*Wonders,* p. 48): "*Georgias Leontinus* a famous Philosopher liv'd in health till he was an hundred and eight years of age: and when it was asked of him by what means he attained to such fulness of days, his answer was, by not addicting himself to any voluptuous living." Georgias' answer appears in Athenaeus *Deipnosophistae* XII.548.2, where his age is given as 110 years, and in Eustathius *Commentarii ad Homeri Odysseam* (ed. J. A. G. Weigle, 2 vols., Leipzig, 1825, 1:53).

241:98–99   Again Wanley was undoubtedly Mather's source (*Wonders,* p. 48), with a reference to Herodotus (*History* I.163).

241:1 See Wanley, *Wonders*, p. 49. The great age of Johannes de Temporibus was a favorite exemplum with encyclopaedists of the age. Compare Alsted, *Thesaurus Chronologiae*, p. 306; Clarke, *Mirrour*, p. 354; Trapp on Matt. 32.27 (p. 235b); and Johannes Nauclerus, *Chronica* (Cologne, 1544), p. 753, who gives his age as 361 at his death in 1139 (Wanley has "*anno* 1146").

241:4 Mather here combines phrases from II Cor. 5.1 and Philip. 1.23.

241:5 Pliny *Natural History* VI.xxxv.190; VII.ii.28.

241:9–10 The Mathers had several reasons for thinking this was a "Troublesoms Time." They felt themselves threatened by Solomon Stoddard's revisions in ecclesiastical doctrine, by dissensions within Harvard College, of which Increase was president, and by Governor Bellomont and his council over a charter for the College, by demands from Elisha Cooke's party that Increase resign, indeed, by signs on all sides that their hegemony was rapidly waning.

241:12–242:14 The quotation is from Cicero *De Oratore* II.ii.8, with "Bradstreeto" substituted for "L. Crasso."

242:20–21 No source has been found for the epitaph on Pistorius (Pistoris). C. G. Jöcher, in *Allgemeines Gelehrten-lexicon* (4 vols., Leipzig, 1750–1751), 3:1597, writes that "In seinem Epitaphio wird ihm das Lob einer besondern Gelehrsamkeit und polit. Klugheit bengeleget," but does not quote the epitaph directly.

242:23–24 No source for these lines has been found; they are perhaps of Mather's own composition.

242:26 The Hebrew phrase means "one who is a master over his desires," that is, a conscientious man; hence Mather's plural "conscientious men."

242:35–36 Camden in his *Remains* (p. 367) speaks of "reverses in Roman Coyns, which were only historical memorials of their acts, as that of Claudius with a plowman at the plow." Mather has linked this bit of numismatic lore with the gold coin first issued by James I in 1604, sometimes called a "unite" to signify the union of the Scottish and English thrones, but popularly known as a "sceptre" because that symbol appeared on the obverse.

243:37–40 Mather repeats verbatim an anecdote about Norcia which he had used in *Little Flocks, Guarded Against Grievous Wolves, or Quakerism Display'd* (London, 1691), pp. 13–14.

243:69–70 *Mass. Records*, 1:69.

244:73–74 *Mass. Records*, 1:60.

244:89 For the Major-Generals, see *Mass. Records*, 2:66, 97, 116; 3:258, 277, 296; 4^2:71; 5:308.

244:94 For the Secretaries, see *Mass. Records*, 1:40, 118, 176, 236; 3:182.

244:2–3 Tit. 2.10.

244:4–5 Johann Buxtorf, *Florilegium Hebraicum* (Basel, 1648), p. 182. Mather correctly quotes the Hebrew words from Buxtorf's text.

245:13–246:57 Rawson's exhortation to the "*Elders and Ministers*" is listed in W. C. Ford, *Broadside and Ballads* (Boston, M.H.S., 1922), p. 7 (no. 36). Mather reproduces Rawson's text faithfully except for minor variations in punctuation and capitalization, and a few verbal variants: the omission of an introductory "WHEREAS" (p. 245, l. 16); the omission of "*of Judah*" after "*Cities*" (l. 21); the substitution of "Blessing of God" for "Gods blessing" (l. 22); the omission of "and Orthodox" after "sound" (l. 39); the transposition of "strength and time" (l. 42); and the insertion of "it" in "and will" (p. 246, l. 53).

245:25–31 *A Declaration of the Faith and Order Owned and Practised in the Congregational Churches in England; Agreed upon and Consented unto by their Elders and Messengers in their Meeting at the Savoy, October 12, 1658* (London, 1658; reprinted in Walker, *Creeds and Platforms*, pp. 354–408, the passage quoted being on p. 405). The lines before "*yet they*" (line 27), paraphrase the original: "they who are ingaged in the work of Publique Preaching, and enjoy the Publique Maintenance upon that account, are not thereby obliged to dispense the Seals to any other then such as (being Saints by Calling and gathered according to the Order of the Gospel) they stand related to, as Pastors or Teachers."

246:45   Compare Heb. 4.2.

246:53–54   Compare II Tim. 4.8, James 1.12, I Pet. 5.4, Rev. 2.10, 3.11.

246:61   The source of this quotation has not been found.

246:62–69   In a sentence compacted of Biblical echoes, Mather again reverts to his analogy of New England as a new Israel. For "Great God of Heaven," cf. Neh. 1.5; for "*Peculiar People*," Deut. 14.2, 26.18, Tit. 2.14, I Pet. 2.9; for "*Lord of Hosts*," Exod. 12.41, I Sam. 15.2. For the "*Four* Squadrons," see Num. 2.1–31, where the Lord commands Moses and Aaron in the "wilderness of Sinai" to dispose the tribes on the four sides of the tabernacle, north, south, east, west. Thereafter He instructs them (Num. 10.1–28) on how to signal the order of march to the four hosts: "Thus were the journeyings of the children of Israel according to their armies, when they set forward." For the "*Laws*," see Exod. 20; for the "*Wars*," cf., for example, Exod. 15.26, 17.11–16; for "*Judges*," or elders, cf. Num. 11.16–30. The "*Four* Colonies" which had marched into the "*American* Wilderness" were Plymouth, Massachusetts Bay, Connecticut, and New Haven.

247:78–79   See Acts 10.36. for "*Governed by the Lord of All*."

247:81   For "*Judges as at the first*," see Isa. 1.26.

247:82   See Tertullian *Apologeticus* XXXIV.2, where the phrase is a simple generalization. Clarke, *Mirrour*, p. 332 (ex. 30), has "Its said of *Augustus* the Emperour."

247:88–89   Mather reverts to themes already sounded, "*unscriptural* and *uninstituted* Rites" and "*Persecution*." Cf. above Bk. I, p. 146, l. 92 *et seq.*; p. 159, ll. 59, 66–67.

247:93–94   On the removal to Connecticut, see Bk. I, chap. 6, secs., 2 and 3.

247:95   For "*Ruler* and *Pillar*," cf. Gal. 2.9, Rev. 3.12.

247:97–98   II Chron. 1.10; cf. also I Kings 4.29, 5.12.

247:2   For "*unjust Judge*," see Luke 18.6.

247:7   For "*Abidan*," see Num. 1.11, 2.22, 7.60–65, 10.24.

247:8–9   For "*Dawnings*," cf. II Pet. 1.19; for "*Earnests*," cf. II Cor. 5.5, Eph. 1.14. The rest of the sentence is from Dan. 7.27.

247:12   The "Great Man" has not been identified.

248:23–26   For "*Rise early*" and "Devotions of his *Closet*," see Mark 1.35, Matt. 6.6; for teaching "unto his *Family*," see Deut. 6.7.

248:27–31   Compare "The Life and Death of Richard Blackerly," in Clarke, *Lives of Sundry Eminent Persons* (p. 58): "They sat round about the Table at his Expositions; and if he saw any behaving themselves as not minding, he would call out to that Youth by name, ask him what he had said last; by which means he made them constantly attentive."

248:31–33   Compare Luke 22.44.

248:34–35   This sentence combines a reference to Eph. 1.3, for "*spiritual Blessings*," with I Pet. 1.9; Mather substitutes "*our Hopes*" for "your Faith."

248:45–46   A rather free adaptation of Gal. 6.10.

248:46–48   See Trapp's *Commentary* on Luke 6.30 (*New Testament*, p. 316b): "General Norrice never thought he had that that he gave not away." See also Fuller, *Worthies*, 3:17–18.

248:49–51   See Howell, *Familiar Letters*, Bk. IV, Letter 36 (2:621), where the statement is attributed to "Cosmo" de Medici.

248:52–249:54   For "*Suffering*" and "*Doing*" that the Christian may "*suffer the Will of God*," cf. Rom. 8.17, Philip. 1.29, I Thess. 3.4, II Thess. 1.5, I Pet. 4.12–19.

249:58   For "full of such Crosses," cf. Matt. 10.38, 16.24, Mark 8.34, 10.21, Luke 9.23, 14.27.

249:59–86   In the spring of 1645, Hopkins brought her to Boston seeking help for "her sad infirmity, the loss of her understanding and reason . . . by occasion of her giving herself wholly to reading and writing, and had written many books." Winthrop's diagnosis was that "if she had attended her household affairs, and such things as belong to women, and not gone out of her way and calling to meddle in such things as are proper for men, whose minds are stronger, etc., she had kept her wits." Hopkins left her with her brother, "one Mr. [David] Yale, a merchant . . . But no help could be had." In his will, Hopkins expressed the "wish . . . that £150 per annum be yearly paid per my executor to Mr. David Yale, brother to my dear estranged wife, for her comfortable maintenance" (*History*, 2:265–266, 1:273n).

249:70–71 For "*The Desire of his Eyes*," see Ezek. 24.16.

249:73–74 Compare above line 58 and references.

249:74 Of three daughters born to Theophilus and Anne Yale Eaton, one died before the family removed to New England. Mary was married to Valentine Hill of Boston; for Hannah, see footnote to p. 260, l. 81. On the family of Theophilus Eaton, see DAB and James Savage, *A Genealogical Dictionary of the First Settlers of New England* (4 vols., Boston, 1860–1862; reissued Baltimore, Genealogical Publishing Co., 1965), 2:97.

249:76–77 On the chastisings of the Lord, cf. Deut. 8.5, Ps. 118.18, I Cor. 11.32, Heb. 12.5–11.

249:78–79 On afflictions and the duty to "be content," cf. I. Cor. 10.13, Philip. 4.11.

249:81–82 There are innumerable references to God as just; cf. for example, Gen. 18.25, Job 37.23, Ps. 11.7, Isa. 26.7, Rom. 9.14. For "*justifie Him*," cf. Rom. 8.30.

249:86 For "*Die Daily*," see I Cor. 15.31.

249:88 David Yale lived in Boston until his permanent return to England with his family in 1652. For the wife of Samuel Eaton, see below p. 259, ll. 34–35 and endnote; since they were married for less than a year, it is unlikely that she is the sister-in-law referred to.

250:93 Mather may have been confused by the fact that Hopkins, although absent in England, was reelected governor in 1654 because the colony hoped for his return (see Savage, *Genealogical Dictionary*, 2:461). His brother's death may have contributed to Hopkins' decision to remain in England. Henry Hopkins' will, dated December 30, 1654, was proved January 24, 1654/55, by Edward Hopkins, brother and sole executor (*New England Historical and Genealogical Register*, 38:314–315).

250:99 Virgil, *Aeneid* I.204.

250:1–3 Hopkins was made Warden of the Fleet by his brother's will. He was appointed a navy commissioner by Cromwell in December 1652 (see DNB and *Calendar of State Papers, Domestic Series*, 1652–1653, 1878, No. 45, p. 44). He became M.P. for Dartmouth in 1656.

250:24 For the "*Noble Vine*," see Isa. 5.2; Hopkins' fears for New England refer by implication to Isaiah's prediction that Israel's "vineyard" will be laid waste (verses 5–6). For "*Blessed . . . in thy Rulers*," cf. Eccles. 10.17.

251:33 "*Walk with God*," a common figure in the Bible, first occurring in Gen. 5.22, 24, 6.9.

251:46 See Gen. 47.29.

251:52 For "*best Wine*," see John 2.10.

251:55 For "*Crown of Glory*," see I Pet. 5.4.

251:57 For "*chuse to die*," cf. Phil. 1.21–23.

251:59 For "*Kingdom . . . prepared*," see Matt. 25.34, Mark 10.40.

251:63 For "*root of bitterness*," see Heb. 12.15; cf. also Deut. 29.18.

252:71 Hopkins' will was dated March 7, 1657; proved April 30, 1657 (*New England Historical and Genealogical Register*, 38:315–316).

252:76–78 Ps. 145.19.

252:82–86 See William Turner, *Compleat History of the Most Remarkable Providences* (London, 1697), which Mather knew. Part I, chap. 145, no. 77 has: "I have inserted in my Paperbook an Epitaph upon the Tomb of the Earl of *Warwick*, in whose Death the Family was extinct." There follows a verse of twelve lines, the last four of which are exactly those in the *Magnalia* except for capitalizations and italics. Turner gives as his source Matthew Barker's *Flores Intellectuales*, of which the first part was published in London in 1691, the second in 1692. The Earl of Warwick referred to was Ambrose Dudley (1528–1590), on whose death the honors became extinct until the earldom was recreated in 1618 in favor of Robert, third Baron Rich.

252:92 See Ammianus Marcellinus, XXIX.1.28–32, and Sextus Aurelius Victor, "Epitome" 48.3.4 (*Historia Romana*, 1:449); cf. also Sozomen, *Historia Ecclesiastica*, Bk. VI, cap. 35 (*Migne G*, 67:1400). A version appears in Camden, *Remains* (p. 264): "In the time of Valens divers curious men ... by the falling of a ring magically prepared upon the letter ΘΕΟΔ, judged that one Theodorus should succeed in the empire." According to Samuel Clarke, it was the emperor Constantius who "consulted with Necromancers, to know who would succeed him in the Empire: the devil answered ambiguously, that his name should begin with *Th*. Whereupon he put to death as many as were called *Theodorus*, *Theodotus*, *Theodosius* or *Theodulus*" (*A General Martyrologie*, London, 1651, p. 89). A like explication appears in Wanley, *Wonders*, p. 560 (no. 19).

252:97 On the union of Connecticut and New Haven, see Bk. I, chap. 6, sec. 7, and below, p. 264, ll. 18–21 with endnote and p. 270, ll. 34–35.

253:5 The reference to having "already paid our Dues unto" Mr. Leet suggests that Mather may have originally intended to place the lives of the governors of the New Haven colony before those of the Connecticut colony. As it stands, the whole of Section 2 is chronologically misplaced, belonging more properly to the end of Chapter 10.

253:7 See Ovid *Metamorphoses* XIII.799: "durior annosa quercus."

253:8 Prov. 16.31; cf. also Prov. 20.29, 12.28.

253:11 On Eaton, see Bk. I, p. 168, l. 67–p. 169, l. 88 and endnote thereto. Like many writers, Mather apparently sought the opinion of his friends on work in progress. On August 22, 1682, John Higginson wrote to Increase Mather: "I have lately received a large & excellent Narrative of the Life & Death of Mr. Eaton, Governor of New Haven, to be added to the rest" (*Mather Papers*, 4 MHS *Coll.* 8:282).

253:13 Lucan (on Cato Uticensis) The Civil War II.389–390. Mather substitutes "bonum" for "bonus."

253:14–17 The "*First* Sacred History" of Luke was his Gospel, the Acts his "*next*," which he addressed to "plain *Theophilus*" (Acts 1.1). Mather's source here may have been Sir John Lightfoot on "The Harmony of the four Evangelists," who notes in a marginal gloss that κράτιστε, "most excellent" (Luke 1.3), was a common "epithet for men of rank." Lightfoot identifies Theophilus as "In most probability, a Noble-man of *Antioch*, and fellow citizen with *Luke*; converted by *Paul* at his Preaching there." Luke went with Paul, "but *Theophilus* staying at *Antioch* after *Pauls* departure, what he wanted in verbal instruction from the mouth of his Master, when he went away, *Luke* doth in this his Gospel supply by writing" (see *Works*, 2 vols., London, 1684, 1:392). As to Theophilus' nationality, Poole, in the "Argument" to his commentary on Luke, writes, "*Whether by Nation, he was a* Syrian, *or a* Roman ... *is but an unprofitable speculation*."

253:21 According to NED, this use of "reduced" is confined to Thomas Fuller. However, it appears more than once in the *Magnalia*, perhaps from Mather's reading of Fuller.

253:28–254:29 Amyraldus, *A Treatise Concerning Religion* (London, 1660), p. 269: "Humility, of whose recommendation there is no footstep nor shadow to be found in their [the pagans'] writing."

254:34–35 Mather's source for earth from the Nile has not been found.

254:37–41 Thomas Hodges in *A Treatise of Marriage* (London, 1673, pp. 12–13) lists a number of famous sons of churchmen to refute the popish argument against a married clergy. See also Clarke, *A Collection of the Lives of Ten Eminent Divines* (London, 1662), p. 308, where he writes of the sons of Dr. Robert Harris: "And truly so well did they improve . . . that they became Masters of their particular Callings, which ministered unto him no small comfort . . . He was one of them in whose children that *Popish* slander concerning the ungraciousness of the children of the married Clergy, received a real confutation."

254:44–45 Philostratus *Vitae Sophistarum* II.17, where it is said of Rufus of Perinthus: "He died and left sons about whom I have nothing important to relate, except, indeed, that they were his offspring."

254:50 On John Davenport see Bk. I, p. 168, l. 67–p. 169, l. 7, and endnotes thereto; see also Bk. III, pt. 1, chap. 4.

254:53 See General Introduction, p. 89 l. 6, and endnote.

254:66–255:68 Compare Gen. 50.21.

255:69–70 For "*behaved himself wisely*," see I Sam. 18.14, 15, 30, Ps. 101.2.

255:71 Eaton's "chaste Escape" suggests Joseph's resistance to the wiles of Potiphar's wife (Gen. 39.7–9). With this allusion Mather combines the warning of the "*Wise Man*," Solomon, that "The mouth of strange women is a deep pit" (Prov. 22.14), a caution frequently repeated throughout Proverbs.

255:78–79 Prov. 22.29; Mather substitutes "Princes" for the Biblical "Kings." The prophecy is borne out below, line 85.

255:80 The Eastland Merchants were an ancient body of traders whose principal activity was in the Baltic. Rechartered by Elizabeth in 1579, the company flourished under the early Stuarts. See *The Acts and Ordinances of the Eastland Company* (ed. Maud Sellers, London, Royal Historical Society, 1906); Eaton is mentioned on pp. xli and xlii.

255:96 On health-drinking, see above p. 225, l. 87–p. 226, l. 11 and endnote; see also Bk. V, pt. 4: "Necessity for Reformation," ques. I, VIII.

256:10–11 See Philip. 1.23. Mather prefers the Wycliffe version, "be dissolved," rather than "depart," as in the K.J.V. Compare also II Cor. 5.1–8.

256:12 For the genealogy of Eaton's wife, see Col. Soc. Mass. *Pub.*, 25:417–419.

256:19 Compare Matt. 15.22, 17.15.

256:26 Compare Isa. 4.6.

256:31 For "*Unlawful things*," cf. Acts 10.28.

256:32–35 For the arrival of Eaton and Davenport in New England, see Winthrop, *History*, 1:272–273, and Hubbard, *History*, p. 262.

256:45 On Eaton's "extream Sickness," cf. Hubbard, *History*, p. 329: "Soon after his being in these parts he was in great hazard of life, by a cancerous sore . . . in his breast, which was not without great difficulty cured."

257:56 For Moses and Aaron, see Exod. 5.1, 4, 20, 6.20, 26–27, 7.6, 20, etc.

257:72–73 Mather combines phrases from Ps. 72.7 and I Pet. 2.14.

258:99–2 Compare Exod. 20.8.

258:10–12 Compare the injunctions of Deut. 5.12 and Matt. 6.6.

258:23 See Camden, *Remains*, p. 396: "King Henry the first, for his learning surnamed Beauclerc."

259:30 Sibley, 1:171–172.

259:31 For "Son of his *Vows*," see Prov. 31.2.

259:33–35 On November 17, 1654, Samuel Eaton married Mabel Haynes, widow of Governor John Haynes of Hartford, who had died earlier that year. Thus they were married less than a year.

259:36–37 Gen. 47.9.

259:41–42 Exod. 20.13, Deut. 5.17.

259:42–46 Job 1.21–22.

259:47–48 I Cor. 7.30.

259:53 Compare Hubbard, *History*, p. 330, where Eaton's "taking notes of the sermons he heard" is extolled.

259:55–56 Lev. 10.1–19, especially v. 19.

259:59–60 Again, Job 1.21.

260:66 For the image of the "*Pillar*," cf. Gal. 2.9, Rev. 3.12.

260:78–79 Dissension in the Hartford church arose initially over a successor to Thomas Hooker after his death in 1647. By 1653 a struggle between the two chief officers of the church and their factions had been intensified by a controversy over the rights of children of baptized parents who were not themselves church members, and for the next six years the church was in a turmoil. (See Walker, *First Church in Hartford*, pp. 151–175, and Miller, *Colony to Province*, pp. 93–102, 105–106; cf. also above Bk. I, p. 168, ll. 54–66.)

260:82–85 Compare Hubbard, *History*, pp. 329–330: "He died suddenly in the night ... He supped well ... in the night was heard to groan ... but before any could step into the chamber was near speechless, and within a very little time died." See I Thess. 4.14; cf. also Acts 7.60.

260:87–88 *Aeneid* I.205–206.

260:90–92 Mather has adapted the epitaph on Richard Vines, eminent puritan divine, from Clarke's *Lives of Sundry Eminent Persons* (p. 53): "Our *English Luther*, *Vines* (whose Death I weep), Sloth [stole] away (and said nothing) in a sleep."

261:22–26 Fables dealing with the wiles of Reynard the Fox proliferated throughout Europe in the Middle Ages. Doubtless Mather was familiar with them as they persisted in folklore. The earliest English version of the fox tricking the wolf into an "*Auricular Confession*" is the Middle English *The Fox and the Wolf*, where the wolf is beguiled into taking the fox's place at the bottom of a well. (See John E. Wells, *A Manual of the Writings in Middle English*, New Haven, Yale University Press, 1916, p. 183.) The sad case of the poor ass Mather could have found in Foxe, *Acts and Monuments* (ed. 1641), 1:511: "There is among other old and ancient records of antiquitie belonging to this present time, a certaine monument in verses ... entituled *Pœnitentiarius Asini*, the Asses confessor; bearing the date and year of our Lord in this number, *Completus, Ann.* 1343. In this treatise are brought forth the wolfe, the foxe, and the asse, comming to shrift and doing penance. First, the wolfe confesseth him to the foxe, who easily doth absolve him from all his faults ... In like manner the wolfe, hearing the foxes shrift, shewed to him the like favor againe. After this cometh the Asse to confession, whose fault was this; that he being hungry tooke a straw out from the sheaf of one that went in peregrination unto Rome. The Asse both repenting of this fact, and because he thought it not so hainous as the faults of the others, he hoped the more for his absolution. But what followed? After the silly Asse had uttered his crime ... the discipline of the law was executed upon him ... he was apprehended ... slaine, and devoured ... By the Wolfe no doubt was meant the Pope: But the foxe was resembled to the prelates, curtesans, priests, and the rest of the spiritualitie. Of the spiritualitie the lord pope is soone absolved, as contrarily, the pope soone dothe absolve them in like manner. By the asse is meant the poore laitie, upon whose backe the straite censure of the law is sharpely executed."

261:28–29 Compare Exod. 20.17.

261:29–31 Augustine, Epistle 119.1 (*Migne L*, 33:449).

261:35 The "*Honest Man's*" answer echoes Rom. 10.8–10, 14–15, 17.

262:41–43 For "*Untoward Generation*," see Acts 2.40; for "*Hear the Word*," again Rom. 10.17; for "Like *Precious Faith*," II Pet. 1.1.

262:47 On Whitfield, see *Magnalia*, Bk. III, pt. 4, chap. 4. Leet had become associated with Whitfield in England, and with him and four others bought land from the Indians where they established the town of Guilford. He was deputy governor of New Haven 1658–1661, governor 1661–1664. He was active in promoting the union of New Haven and Connecticut and in 1669 was elected deputy governor of the combined colony. He served as governor from 1676 until his death in 1683. (See DAB.)

262:54 For "*Excellent Spirit*," see Dan. 5.12, 6.3.

262:56 Treat took part in the settling of Milford, and served not only as a deputy and later as magistrate from that town, but as the chief military officer. Opposing the union with Connecticut, he removed for a time to Newark, New Jersey, but returned to Milford and was chosen an assistant in 1673. After Leet's death in 1683, he was governor, except for the Andros administration, until 1698. (See DAB.)

262:59 It is difficult to say on what precise grounds Mather assigned the epithet, "Christian Hermes," to Winthrop, Jr., since in various ages Hermes played many roles. Possibly it was from Hermes, the messenger of the gods, that Mather devised the metaphor. That Hermes, by extension, became a conductor of souls as well as of travelers on the earth—even in a "Wilderness"; in this sense, Mather may possibly have been alluding to the Greek text of Acts 14.12, where Paul was called Hermes ("τον δὲ παῦλον 'Ερμῆν") rather than Mercurius, as in the English versions. In the "Homeric" epic hymn to Hermes, he is a precocious child, an ideal ephebe. In short, a versatile Greek of many gifts. Since Mather earlier calls Winthrop a "Virtuoso" (Bk. I, p. 167, l. 43), perhaps this is the sense in which the epithet is most appropriate.

262:61 *Aeneid*, II.89–90.

262:63 Said of Constantine by Eusebius, *Ecclesiastical History* IX.ix.1.

262:66–67 Mather's source may have been Charles Chauncy's *Anti-Synodalia Scripta Americana* (1662), Preface, p. 6, where "that Hebrew proverb" appears in the same words. See also Sir John Lightfoot, *Works*, 2:612, with the gloss "Bava Meziah, fol. 83.2": "R. Eliezer b. R. Simeon, had laid hold on some Thieves. R. Joshua b. Korchab sent to him, saying, O thou Vinegar, the Son of good Wine, [i.e., O thou wicked Son of a good Father]"

262:67–68. Compare Lange, *Florilegii* (1:1049), where he gives a list of degenerate sons ("Heroum filij noxae").

263:82–84 The name of the son was Lucius (or Cnaeus) Cornelius Scipio. The story appears in Fuller, *Holy and Profane States*, 2:417; in Spencer, *Things New and Old*, p. 9 (no. 9), with a reference to Ammianus Marcellinus, and with "censors" in place of "people"; in Clarke, *Mirrour*, p. 78 (no. 14), with a reference to Valerius Maximus III.5.1; and in Wanley, *Wonders*, p. 366, with the same reference to Valerius Maximus, and "family" for "people." Any one of these might have been Mather's source.

263:93 It was at Sir John Clotworthy's house that Winthrop, Jr., met the "Scottish gentlemen" who thought to emigrate to New England (see endnote to Bk. I, p. 164, ll. 30–35). Following this meeting, letters from Clotworthy to Winthrop, Jr., show him active in sending goods and cattle, chiefly sheep, to New England. (See *Winthrop Papers*, 3:187, 190, 195–196, 4:230.)

264:18–21 The charter obtained by Winthrop, Jr., created a corporation under the name of the Governor and Company of the English Colony of Connecticut. It sanctioned the system of government already in existence, declared all acts of the general court valid under the seal of the colony, and made no reservation of royal or parliamentary control over legislation or the administration of justice. Hence the colony could look to its "*Priviledges*" as the supreme source of authority.

264:30 Judg. 8.22.

264:32–35 Pliny (*Natural History* XXIV.xii.27) gives the number of statues as 360, and that number appears in Diogenes Laërtius (*De Vitis . . . Clarorum Philosophorum* V.75, annotated by Isaac Casaubon, Thomas Aldobrandini, and Meric Casaubon, in 1692 Amsterdam edition, 1:306). Both Clarke (*Mirrour*, p. 315) and Wanley

(*Wonders*, pp. 414–415) tell the story, citing Pliny, but since they both say there were 200 statues, it is likely that either Pliny himself or some such work as that of Laërtius was Mather's source.

264:41   See Buxtorf, *Florilegium Hebraicum*, p. 186.

264:42   Lange, *Florilegii*, 2:1648.

264:43–265:44   Thucydides *History* VI.xiv.14.

265:50   John 5.2–4.

265:52   So great was the fame of Scanderbeg in history and romance that it is profitless to conjecture where Mather may have heard of his exploits. The figure of two thousand slain "with his own Hands" was often magnified. The earliest known *Scanderbegi Historia* dates from Venice, 1480. There followed many *Vitae* in Latin, French, and German, closely accompanied by imaginative glorifications in French, Italian, German and Spanish. (See Georges T. Petrovich, *Scanderbeg, Essai de bibliographie raissonnée*, Paris, 1881.) Margherita Sarrocchi, whom Mather had earlier praised as a learned lady (p. 233, l. 59), in 1606 published in Rome an Italian "poema heroico" entitled *La Scanderbeide* in fourteen cantos, and in 1690 *The Great Scanderbeg. A Novel done out of French* was published in London.

265:63   The earliest scientific society in England, founded in or a little before 1660, incorporated July 15, 1662; the charter was amended in 1663 and council meetings began that year.

265:70–76   John Winthrop, Jr., was a member from 1665. The *Philosophical Transactions* published communications from him on such subjects as the culture of maize, the starfish, the humming bird, dwarf oaks, wampum, etc. On his mining activities, see Winthrop, *History*, 2:261 and note.

266:95–99   The "several Colonies" were Plymouth, Massachusetts Bay, Connecticut, and New Haven. Their representatives met at the General Court held in Boston May 10, 1643 (Winthrop, *History*, 2:119–121). In lines 97–99 Mather quotes from the preamble to the Articles of Confederation drawn up at that time. (For the complete text, see Winthrop, 2:121–127). He omits the initial "WHEREAS," changes "one and the same" to "the same," substitutes "*Glory*" for "kingdom," and has "with Purity and Peace" for "in purity with peace."

267:15–268:80   The original of this letter has not been located; the *Winthrop Papers* reproduce Mather's text (4:366–367). The "*Two* Families" were the Winthrops and the family of his mother, Mary Forth, on whom see above p. 226, ll. 24–25. The three sons were John, Jr., Henry, and Forth. Of the sisters only Mary lived; the other, named Ann, died in infancy. (See *History*, 1:77nn.)

267:18   For "*Temporal things*," cf. II Cor. 4.18.

267:21–22   See II Chron. 25.9.

267:33   See Josh. 1.5; cf. also Heb. 13.5.

267:37–38   For "*Light of God's Countenance*," cf. Num. 6.26, Ps. 4.6, 44.3, Prov. 16.15.

267:39–41   For "*Peace of Conscience*," cf. Acts 23.1, 24.16, I Tim. 1.5, 19, 3.9; for contrast between "*mean*" and "*great*" abundance, cf. Philip. 4.11–12.

267:43–45   For "*Good Land*," cf. Exod. 3.8, Num. 14.7, Deut. 1.25, 35, 3.25, 4.21, 6.18, etc. For "*Blessings of the Gospel*," see Rom. 15.29.

268:61–62   For "*Word of Truth*," cf. Ps. 119.43, Acts 26.25, II Cor. 6.7, Eph. 1.13, Col. 1.5, II Tim. 2.15, James 1.18. For "*Light Inaccessible*," cf. I Tim. 6.16.

268:63–67   For "own *Wisdom*," cf. I Cor. 1.17–21; for "*Christ* Crucified," I Cor. 1.23, 2.2, 2.8; cf. also Gal. 2.20; for "*Secrets* of his Tabernacle," Ps. 27.5; for "*Eye hath not seen*," etc., I Cor. 2.9–10; cf. also Isa. 64.4.

268:68–69   For "*Knowledge puffeth up*," see I Cor. 8.1.

268:69–70   For "*good Gift*," cf. James 1.17; for "*Cross of Christ*" and "*Pride of Life*," Gal. 6.14, I John 2.16.

268:72–73   For the parable of the talents, see Matt. 25.14–23; for "*Day of your Account*," cf. also Luke 16.2.

268:79–80   Compare I Thess. 4.13–18, Rev. 20.12–13, 21.1–7.

268:89–269:97   Jantz (*First Century*, p. 229) believes this epitaph to be by Mather.

269:3   For the Connecticut commissioners, see *Mass. Records*, 1:170–171. Mather has omitted the names of two commissioners, William Pincheon [Pynchon] and Henry Smith, who became identified with Springfield. On June 2, 1641, Pincheon formally petitioned the Massachusetts General Court to include Springfield in its jurisdiction. Later that year commissioners were appointed to "lay out the South line" of the colony; their survey put the boundary line eight miles south of Springfield. (See *Mass. Records*, 1:320, 323.)

270:25   For a useful summary of the early years of the New Haven Colony, see Rollin G. Osterweis, *Three Centuries of New Haven, 1638–1938* (New Haven, Yale University Press, 1953), pp. 3–53. For "The fundamental articles, or original constitution of the colony of New Haven, June 4th, 1639," see Trumbull, *History of Connecticut*, 1:502–506. See also Isabel M. Calder, *The New Haven Colony* (New Haven, Yale University Press, 1934), especially pp. 55–66, 116–129, 162–171; Andrews, *Colonial Period*, 2:144–194. *The Records of the New Haven Jurisdiction* for the years 1644–1653 were lost, a circumstance reflected in the gap in Mather's listing.

270:26–27   For Goodyear, see Savage, 2:278; for Grigson, Savage, 2:315; for both, see Osterweis, *Three Centuries*, pp. 25, 45–46. For the "phantom ship" in which they perished, see above Bk. I, p. 169, l. 98–p. 170, l. 54.

270:28   Winthrop provides a titillating entry on Malbon under date of March 30, 1643 (*History*, 2:114): "There was a piece of justice executed at New Haven, which, being the first in that kind, is not unworthy to be recorded. Mr. Malbon, one of the magistrates there, had a daughter about [blank] years of age, which was openly whipped, her father joining in the sentence. The cause was thus. [large blank]."

270:29   For Leet, see above p. 261, l. 14–p. 262, l. 56.

270:30   For Desborough, see Savage, 2:41.

270:31   For Tapp, see Savage, 3:253. For Treat, see above p. 262, ll. 56–57.

270:32   For Fowler, see Savage, 2:195.

270:35   Compare Osterweis, *Three Centuries*, p. 62.

270:38   For Allyn, see *Conn. Records*, 2:13–14, 23.

271:45   For Clark, see *Conn. Records*, 2:13–14, 57. For Chapman, see *Conn. Records*, 2:104–105, 3:75.

271:46   For Bryant, see *Conn. Records*, 2:57.

271:48   For Newberry, see *Conn. Records*, 2:30–31, 57, 3:168.

271:51   For Hamlin, see *Conn. Records*, 2:57, 3:168.

271:52–55   For "Clusters of *Rich Grapes*," cf. Num. 13.23, Rev. 14.18. The Jewish proverb appears in Buxtorf's *Florilegium Hebraicum* (p. 182). The "Magistratus" in this proverb are not only like "folia," but "sunt quasi clypei." One may conjecture that here in Buxtorf Mather found his subtitle for Book II, "*Ecclesiarum Clypei.*"

271:58–60   Cicero *Pro Cnaeo Plancio Oratio* xxv.62. Mather has "*delegit*" for "deligit" and "*Villicos*" for "vilicos."

PIETAS IN PATRIAM

p. 272:61–70   Nathanael, son of Richard Mather, was born in England in 1631 and came to Massachusetts with his father in 1635. He took his M.A. at Harvard in 1647, but returned to the land of his birth, probably in 1650 and certainly prior to 1655. In either case he left New England before Cotton Mather was born. See DNB and Sibley, 1:157–161. John Howe, curate of Great Torrington, Devonshire, spent much time in London as a chaplain to Oliver Cromwell and his son Richard, "the Lord Protector." In London in 1658 Increase Mather met Howe, who was so much impressed by the New Englander that he appointed Increase to serve for a time as a substitute in his Torrington pulpit. When Increase was again in England from 1688 to 1692, Howe joined him in 1691 in an attempt to unify the Congregationalists and Presbyterians, as did Matthew Mead, who also accompanied Increase Mather at an audience with William III and urged the King to be kind to New England. For Howe, see DNB; Increase Mather, "Autobiography," p. 283; Cotton Mather, *Parentator*, pp. 18–19; and Murdock, *Increase Mather*, pp. 63–67. For Mead, see DNB; "Autobiography," p. 333; Murdock, p. 219. For the part he played together with Howe and Increase Mather in drawing up "The Heads of Agreement of 1691," see Williston Walker, *Creeds*, pp. 442–452. The text of the "Heads" follows on pages 455–462 and is in the *Magnalia*, Bk. V, pp. 59–61.

272:61　In Cotton Mather's *Diary*, in a passage preceding an entry dated March 21, 1696 (1:186–187), he wrote, "I considered that the memorable *Changes* undergone, and *Actions* performed, in the *Life* of our late Governour, Sir William *Phips*, had . . . many Things in them, to display the glorious *Power* . . . of the Lord *Jesus Christ*. Wherefore I did, with much Elaboration, write the History thereof . . . I entituled it . . . PIETAS IN PATRIAM: and how many wayes I have propounded to myself, in this Composure, to serve my Lord Jesus . . . it is needless for mee to mention." Mather probably wished to have the book published in London because he believed it would be better received there, where Phips had won considerable fame and a knighthood, than in Boston, where he had made many enemies. Mather also thought, rightly, that his uncle Nathanael, his fellow nonconformists, and others who revered Increase Mather would give the book all the support they could.

273:75　The DNB has "Phipps," the name of one or more English families, but Sir William himself and his compatriots in Massachusetts consistently used "Phips."

273:81　Why Mather tried to hide his authorship on the titlepages of both the 1697 edition of the *Pietas* and the reprint of it in the *Magnalia* is hard to explain. Perhaps some English readers were deceived, but surely few in New England were. When the first copy of the book arrived in Boston from London, Mather delightedly saw in it "a further Answer of" his "poor Prayers," and declared, "Our base *Tories* are in much Anguish at this book" (*Diary*, 1:245). Anguished or not, his enemies were quick to see that the *Pietas* was vulnerable to attack. It was not, as Mather pretended, a life by an unbiased author, but, in large measure, a piece of special pleading in defense of his father's and his own support of the new charter, a eulogy marred by errors, and as such easy to ridicule.

273:82　Mather's adaptation of the *Aeneid* XII.435.

273:83–85　News that Richard Coote, Earl Bellomont, was to be appointed Governor of New England spread in London in 1695 and reached Massachusetts in August of that year. In 1696 he was commissioned to govern Massachusetts, New Hampshire, and New York, with command of their military forces and those of Rhode Island, Connecticut, and the Jerseys. He arrived in New York in 1698 and a delegation from Massachusetts went to greet him there. He did not, however, come to Boston until May of the next year. He returned to New York in July 1700, and died there on March 5, 1701. See DNB, DAB, Sewall, *Diary*, 1:411, 413, 476, 2:20, 33, and E. E. Hale, "Lord Bellomont and Captain Kidd," in Justin Winsor, ed., *Memorial History of Boston*, vol. II, chap. 5. The DNB has "Bellamont" but Hale gives evidence that Coote used "Bellomont" (pp. 175–176, 183).

274:88–89　Compare Prov. 21.1.

274:12　For "peculiar Treasure," cf. Exod. 19.5, Ps. 135.4; for "precious Jewels," cf. Lam. 4.2, Mal. 3.17.

276:45　Mather's account of the chemist's art closely follows Wanley, *Wonders*, p. 227. Similar accounts of the "Resurrection" of plants appear in Browne, *Religio Medici*, pt. 1, sec. 48 (in *Works*, 1:60), and in Sir Matthew Hale's *Primitive Origination of Mankind* (London, 1677, p. 288), who concludes, "this hath been pretended, but I could never hear any Man speak it that saw it done."

276:56 Cotton Mather had this verse carved on the tombstone of his daughter who died on the "28d. 12 mo." (February) in 1696 (*Diary*, 1:185). The ritual of picking up grass was presumably also related to Isa. 44.3-4: "I will pour my spirit upon thy seed, and my blessings upon thine offspring. And they shall spring up as among the grass, as willows by the watercourses." Thus grass symbolizes those whose bones are to flourish.

276:60 For the "*Ark of Noah*," see Gen. 6.14-22.

276:63 For "criminal *Necromancy*," cf. Deut. 18.10-12.

277:67 For the "*Resurrection of the Dead*," see Matt. 22.31, Luke 20.35, Acts 17.32, 23.6, 24.15, etc.

277:94-3 For his paragraph on "persons . . . of mean and low Birth," Mather relies on Wanley, *Wonders*, Bk. VI, chap. 7, secs. 1, 7, 12, 15-18 (pp. 566-569); he condenses Wanley, but preserves much of the phraseology. Compare also Plutarch *Lives*, "Eumenes" 1.1, "Caius Marius" III.1; for Iphicrates Plutarch *Moralia*, "Sayings of Kings" 187.1; for Bonosus, Flavius Vopiscus in *Scriptores Historiae Augustae* (Loeb ed.) III.410-411.

278:29-31 See Wanley, p. 567 (Sec. 3).

278:38-41 Mather glorifies Phips by likening him to David; see II Sam. 7-8, Ps. 78.70-71.

279:43 "Everyone is the Son of his own works (work)." See Tilley, *Dictionary of Proverbs*, S 624, under date of 1659.

279:50-51 Gen. 6.14-22. Mather may have considered a three-dimensional cubit as equivalent to a ton; if so, the space in the Ark (length 300 cubits, breadth 50 cubits, height 30 cubits) would be 45,000 tons or "more than Forty Thousand."

279:54-55 Compare Cicero *De Senectute* VI.17.

279:60 Roger Spencer of Saco, Maine, was from 1653 until at least 1689 a ship captain. In 1653 he sailed to Charlestown, Massachusetts, and probably continued to ply between Charlestown and Saco for some years. He may have been the ship-carpenter to whom Phips was apprenticed for four years. (See Savage, *Genealogical Dictionary*, 4:148.)

279:77 For "*save his Father's House*," cf. Heb. 11.7, which reverts to the comparison with Noah.

280:91 Compare Tilley, D 657: "Dutchmen [Hollanders] be wise [have their wits] in their hands."

280:94-96 See "Themistocles" II.3 in Plutarch's *Lives*.

280:7-8 The coin was dated 1565. See Gérard Van Loon, *Histoire Métallique des XVII Provinces des Pays-Bas* (5 vols., The Hague, 1732-1737), 1:71. For the Latin phrase, see *Aeneid* III.7.

280:15-19 The *Pietas in Patriam* has often been considered totally unreliable because of its unduly eulogistic portrait of Phips, its glossing over of many of his faults, and its author's patent desire to defend Increase Mather's choice of Sir William as Governor. In this passage Cotton Mather is obviously less concerned with sparing his readers undue boredom than with an attempt to show Phips in the best possible light. In justice to Mather, however, it is important to remember that for much of his information he had to rely on what Phips himself had told him, which of course omitted the seamier side of the Governor's career. Also, various documents which revealed the shortcomings of that career were not available to Mather when he wrote the *Pietas*. For such documents and for balanced judgments of Sir William, see, for example, Viola F. Barnes, "The Rise of William Phips" and "Phippius Maximus," in *NEQ*, 1:271-294 and 532-553; Robert H. George, "The Treasure Trove of William Phips," *NEQ*, 6:294-318; and C. H. Karraker, "The Treasure Expedition of . . . Phips to the Bahama Banks," *NEQ*, 5:731-752, and Karraker, *The Hispaniola Treasure* (Philadelphia, University of Pennsylvania Press, 1934). Notes in all these supply references of value and the *Calendar of State Papers: Colonial*,

America and West Indies (cited hereafter as *C.S.P.*, *Col.*, *Am. and W.I.*) has of course relevant Phipsian data.

280:20–21 This suggests the proverb, "He that endures [who suffers] is not overcome [overcomes]." See Tilley, E 136.

281:29–30 For Shamgar and the Ox-Goad, see Judg. 3.31; on Samson and the Jaw-bone, see Judg. 15.15–17.

282:99 For "Thorns," cf. II Cor. 12.7; cf. also Num. 33.55, Judg. 2.3, etc.

283:11–12 Compare Tilley, D 213: "Desires are nourished by delay."

283:14 The Duke of Albemarle and others persuaded James II to grant a warrant giving the Duke or his deputy the right to search and take "all such wrecks" as they might find "in the Seas to the Windward of the North side of Hispaniola" and to keep their findings for their own use, except for a tenth part to be reserved for the "royal benefit." This was the basis of a joint-stock company under whose auspices Phips was to voyage again on a treasure hunt. See George, "The Treasure Trove," pp. 297–298, and notes.

284:38 "Caligula" IV.xlvi.1 in Suetonius *Lives of the Caesars*.

284:65–66 The treasure was at first measured by single "Peeces of Eight," but later "the bullion and coin were measured by weight." See George, "The Treasure Trove," p. 306.

284:66 The Providence of Mather's account was probably "New" Providence in the Bahamas, not to be confused with "Old" Providence of the Mosquito Coast in the Caribbean or with Providence, Rhode Island. (Cf. 2 M.H.S. *Proc.*, 13:8–11.) Atherly brought a shallop and divers to help Phips in return for a share of the booty. (See George, "The Treasure Trove," p. 307, and letter of Sir Robert Robinson, Governor of Bermuda, dated July 11, 1687, in *C.S.P.*, *Col.*, *Am. and W.I.*, 12:392, no. 1340.)

285:1–2 Deut. 33.19.

286:31–32 Prov. 22.29.

286:47 See Samuel Sewall, *Diary*, 1:219.

286:52 Compare Exod. 9.16, 17, Josh. 5.7–9, Judg. 2.16, 18, 3.9, 15.

287:58–78 Quoted from *The Humble Address of the Publicans of New-England to which KING you please* (London, 1691; reprinted in *Andros Tracts*, ed. W. H. Whitmore, 3 vols., Boston, 1868–1874, 2:264–265).

287:79 Livy *Ab Urbe Condita* XLIV.iii.3.

287:81 The allusion is to Gen. 13.9–12. Compare the reference to "lewd Vices" a few lines below, which echoes Gen. 13.13.

287:87–88 Horace *Epistles* I.xii.14–15.

287:92 For "lifted up," see Deut. 8.14–17, II Chron. 17.6, 26.16, 32.25, Ps. 24.4, Isa. 2.12, etc. Mather here contrasts what God has done (p. 286, l. 52 above) with man's self-exaltation in being "lifted up."

287:94–288:95 Phips, unbaptized and not a member of any church, had, of course, not been approved by the Boston clergy. He had been snubbed by the Congregational magistrates who knew "what he was and from whence" and scorned him. See Barnes, "The Rise of William Phips," pp. 276–277, 283–284.

288:97–98 The reference is to Edward Randolph, who hated the Congregational clergy, and to those others who advocated a Dominion government and urged the cancellation of the original charter of Massachusetts. See introductory essay, "Cotton Mather," p. 6 above.

288:10 Andros was anathema to the New England clergy and many other good citizens, but was supported by those who favored a Dominion government over one largely controlled by Congregationalists. For Andros's commissions as Governor, see *Col. Soc. Mass. Pub.*, 2:44–68.

288:15–17 Mather follows here, except for his "Ten Thousand," *The Revolution in New-England Justified* (see note on p. 289, ll. 54–55 below), which declares that Andros "had power himself alone to send the best and most useful men a thousand miles (and further if he would), out of the country." This was based on the King's first Commission to Andros, June 3, 1686, which gave him full power "to levy arms" and muster, command, or employ all "persons whatsoever" dwelling in the Royal "Territory and Domain of New England." These persons Andros could transfer "from one place to another" whenever needed for "resisting and withstanding" enemies, pirates, and rebels "both at land and sea," or, if occasion required, to serve beyond the limits of Andros's "Territory and Plantations or any of them." The second Commission, April 7, 1688, gave Andros the same authority (see *Col. Soc. Mass., Coll.*, 2:50, 58, 63; Peter Force, *Tracts and Other Papers Relating . . . to the Origin, Settlement, and Progress of the Colonies in North America*, 4 vols., New York, 1947, Vol. 4, no. 8, pp. 8–9). As the New Englanders saw it, this meant that their Governor could force them to go to sea for any distance he chose. Cotton Mather's "Ten Thousand" was almost certainly a misprint for "Two Thousand," which is the figure named in Increase Mather's *A Brief Relation of the State of New England*, London, 1689. (See reprint in Force, Vol. 4, no. 11, p. 6.) It is barely possible, however, that Cotton Mather's "Ten Thousand" was a characteristic Cottonian bit of hyperbole, used to adorn his prose and drive home his denunciation of Andros.

288:34 Narbrough had been one of those interested in the Duke of Albemarle's joint-stock company. See DNB and Karraker, *Hispaniola Treasure*, chap. 5.

289:40–41 Andros's Council of the Dominion had already appointed a Provost Marshal-General and ignored Phips's Patent. Outraged, he blamed Randolph and resolved to go to England to denounce him. The Congregational leaders who had once looked down on Sir William now greeted him as a champion of their cause. "Andros and his Council had unwisely alienated an unwelcome support, and the old regime had won a valuable convert." (See Barnes, "The Rise," pp. 285–286.)

289:41–43 Mather probably exaggerated whatever danger threatened Phips. Possibly he had in mind Randolph's attempts to arrest his father Increase in order to prevent his going to England to plead for a restoration of the charter.

289:48–50 Roger de Wendover's *Flores* was not published until the nineteenth century (ed. H. O. Coxe, 2 vols., London, 1841–1842), but his history was revised and continued in the *Chronica Majora* of Matthew Paris, his successor as chronicler at St. Albans. The passage cited by Mather, headed "*De afflictione misera gentis Anglorum*," refers to the year 1085; the "domineering Strangers" were the Normans, "et quanto magis principes loquebantur de recto et justitia, tanto major fiebat injuria; qui justiciarii vocabantur, omnis injustitiae fuerunt auctores, etc." First printed in London by Archbishop Parker in 1571, editions of the *Chronica* by Dr. William Wats were also published in 1640, 1644, and 1648, and were much utilized by other historians and compilers of encyclopaedias, from some one of whom Mather probably derived his epigrammatized form. (For the Mather passage, cf. 1684 ed., p. 12; see also Coxe, 2:23.)

289:50–51 Compare the proverb, "When the Fox preaches beware the geese," Tilley, F 656.

289:54–55 *The Revolution in New-England Justified and the People . . . Vindicated from the Aspersions Cast upon them by Mr. John Palmer* was published in Boston in 1691. The foreword was signed "E.R. & S.S.," presumably Edward Rawson (1615–1693), who was Secretary of the Colony from 1650 to 1686, and Samuel Sewall. (See *Andros Tracts*, ed. W. H. Whitmore, 3 vols., Boston, 1868–1874, 1:63–132; Force, *Tracts*, Vol. 4, no. 9.) The "aspersions" of John Palmer, a lawyer trained in England, who had been Andros's councillor and chief judge of the supreme court in New York, had appeared in his *An Impartial Account of the State of New England*, London, 1690. (See *Andros Tracts*, 1:21–61, and Morison, *Pronaos*, p. 194.) Mather's recital of the sins of the Andros regime is largely taken from *The Revolution . . . Justified*, "that Book" of line 59 below.

289:55–56 The NED cites an example of "male-administration," dated 1647. Perhaps Mather's printer dropped out the hyphen or he himself may have done so to emphasize the words by using two capital letters.

289:55–57 *A Narrative of the Proceedings of Sir Edmund Androsse and his Complices . . . By Several Gentlemen who were of his Council,* published in Boston February 4, 1690/91, and signed by William Stoughton, Thomas Hinckley, Wait Winthrop, Bartholomew Gedney, and Samuel Shrimpton. (See *Andros Tracts,* 1:133–147; Force, *Tracts,* Vol. 4, no. 9, pp. 51–59; and C. M. Andrews, *Narratives of the Insurrections,* New York, C. Scribner's Sons, 1915, pp. 239–249.)

289:58–59 *The Declaration of the Gentlemen, Merchants, and Inhabitants of BOSTON and the Countrey Adjacent* was dated April 18, 1689, and was written in large part by Cotton Mather. (See Holmes, *C. Mather,* 1:223–234; *Andros Tracts,* 1:11–20; Force, *Tracts,* Vol. 4, no. 10, pp. 6–13; and Andrews, *Narratives,* pp. 175–182.) In this pamphlet Mather denounced those "Strangers to, and haters of the People" whom Andros preferred, and by whom the New Englanders "were chiefly *squeez'd*," a "Crew of abject Persons, fetched from *New York,* to be Tools of the Adversary, standing at our right hand." Palmer recognized himself as one of the targets of this assault, and his *Impartial Account* was his answer. For others of the "abject Persons," see endnote to lines 61–66 below.

289:61–66 There were in all twenty-six members of Andros's council, including representatives from Plymouth, Massachusetts Bay, Rhode Island, Connecticut, Maine, and New Hampshire, of whom ordinarily no more than six or eight attended. Joseph Dudley and William Stoughton were appointed judges of the Superior Court and as such were the instruments for enforcing hated laws (cf. Palfrey, *History,* 3:520). Hutchinson lists the "*Strangers*" (*History,* 1:300–301): John Palmer of New York, Anthony Brockholt, New York, Robert Mason, New Hampshire, John Usher, Maine, Edward Randolph of the council, together with John West, New York, Bullivant, a physician from London, Graham, a New York merchant, named Andros's Attorney General, "and others, who were not of the council, were his confidents and advisers."

290:86–3 For Wise and the Ipswich affair, see *The Revolution . . . Justified* (Force, *Tracts,* Vol. 4, no. 9, pp. 13–17); MHS *Proc.* 12:109; J. B. Felt, *History of Ipswich, Essex, and Hamilton* (Cambridge, Mass., 1834), pp. 123–126, for extracts from the town records of Ipswich. Compare also Palfrey, *History,* 3:525–528, and Miller, *Colony to Province,* pp. 155–157. The judgments quoted by Mather (line 95 and lines 97–98) were pronounced by Joseph Dudley.

291:42 Manetho *Egyptiaca* Fr. 43. Compare Gen. 46.34.

291:43–44 Compare Ezek. 22.27, Zeph. 3.3, Matt. 7.15, 10.16, Luke 10.3, Acts 20.29.

292:48 Quintus Curtius *History of Alexander* X.i.6.

292:65–69 Mather took this passage from *The Revolution . . . Justified,* Force, *Tracts,* Vol. 4, no. 9, pp. 45–46. For Jones's attack on King Charles II's declaration justifying his dissolution of Parliament, April 8, 1681, see *A Just and Modest Vindication of the Proceedings of the Last Two Parliaments,* published anonymously in London in 1681, and reissued after Jones's death as *The Design of Enslaving England Discovered,* London, 1689. It is possible that these books, or at least the *Design,* were compiled by one Robert Ferguson (d.1714), a protestant educated probably at Aberdeen and expelled from his pulpit by the Act of Uniformity, 1662, and a gadfly involved in various attacks on the Stuarts, and nicknamed "the Plotter." Mather's quotation is not found in the *Design,* but its substance is. It is probable that he condensed some pages of it or copied the full passage from some other source.

293:93 Compare "inhospitalem Caucasum" in Horace *Odes* I.xxii.7; *Epodes* I.12; Seneca *Medea* 43; and "horrens Caucasus" in *Aeneid* IV.366–367.

293:98–99 See King's *State of the Protestants in Ireland* (p. 300): "Persuasions and

Suggestions the Irish Catholics make to his Majesty . . . found in Col. Talbot's house, July 1, 1671."

293:5–6 A book alleged to be a *Letter to the Pope* from James II, with *Animadversions on the Same,* was published in Boston in 1696. It was a request from the king for assistance in putting down the "Revolution." (See Charles Evans, *American Bibliography,* 12 vols., Chicago, 1903–1934, Vol. I, no. 742.)

294:13–15 According to an affidavit signed later by Winslow, he paid four shillings and sixpence for each copy of the "Declarations" in order to inform the New Englanders of the deliverance from arbitrary power they might hope for. Andros had him arrested, but he refused to say where the "Declarations" were because, he said, the Governor would not let the people have any news. Andros called him a "saucy fellow" and sent him to trial, denying his request to have a judge of his own choosing. He was jailed for bringing traitorous and treasonable libels and papers of news, although he offered security of two thousand pounds. See Savage, *Genealogical Dictionary; Andros Tracts,* 1:9, 78, 156; Holmes, *C. Mather,* 1:229, 233n. 4; J. B. Palfrey, *History,* 3:574–577; W. H. Whitmore, "The Inter-Charter Period," in Justin Winsor, ed., *Memorial History of Boston* (Boston, 1881), 2:12.

294:38–39 Joseph Dudley was one of those seized, in his case imprisonment being to save him from the angry mob. While in prison, he wrote on June 5, 1689, to Cotton Mather in an effort to justify his actions. He acknowledges that he is "very particularly pointed at and reflected upon as a great mover and instrument in the late alteration of Governm.ᵗ and many supposed hardships and oppressions which they have suffered." As to the tax impost, he insists that he "did publickly in Council . . . object to it," and that he had urged the calling of a "generall council" to consult on revenues since "it was too much for us few persons to resolve so great an affair." He also denied that he was ever "tainted or shaken with popery," or had ever received "one penny." He concluded by asking Mather to use his letter to correct the "false aggravated imputations referring to myself." (See 6 MHS *Coll.* 3:501–507.)

295:66 For "*God of his Mercies,*" see Luke 1.78, II Cor. 1.3, Eph. 2.4; cf. also Ps. 103.8, Isa. 30.18, 54.7, Lam. 3.32.

295:77 For "*Edifie one another,*" see Rom. 14.19; cf. also 15.2.

295:79 For "like *David,*" see I Chron. 17.1.

295:86–88 Mather added to his diary for 1685–1686 a list of the "Subjects" he had "principally insisted on" in his "public Ministry." He had, he wrote, "in particular, insisted on *Conviction,* in two Sermons, from Psal. 51.3." That verse, which no doubt struck home to Phips, reads: "For I acknowledge my transgressions: and my sin is ever before me." (See *Diary,* 1:116 and 2:826, col. 1.)

295:89–296:93 See Clarke, *Mirrour* (p. 434, no. 11), for Mather's immediate source. Clarke attributes the story to Thuanus, who "reports of *Ludovicus Marsacus,* a Knight of *France,* that when he was led to execution with other Martyrs that were bound with cords, and he, for his dignity was not bound, that he cried out . . . Give me my chain too, and let me be a Knight of the same Order."

296:97–98 Mark 8.38; Luke 9.26.

296:1–14 Mather clearly had to deal with the question of Sir William's baptism with extreme care. New England orthodoxy had from the outset insisted on the "*Lawfulness of Infant-Baptism,*" and had denounced antipaedobaptists as heretics. Hence his eagerness to demonstrate that Phip's unbaptized state was not due to any such "superstitious and unreasonable Accounts." For Puritan theory of the sacrament of baptism. cf. Miller, *Orthodoxy,* pp. 200–206.

296:24–26 For "*do to be saved,*" see Acts 16.30; for "*Youthful Days,*" Eccles. 11.10; for "*things of God,*" Matt. 16.23.

296:28–29 Matt. 11.28.

297:33–34 For "*Outward Concerns,*" cf. Neh. 11.16.

297:36 For "*Acknowledge God,*" cf. Prov. 3.6.

297:43   Compare Deut. 6.2.

297:62   For "*a Stumbling Block*," see Lev. 19.14, Rom. 14.13, I Cor. 8.9.

297:70   For "*put off with a Portion*," cf. Ps. 17.14.

297:70   For "*better things*," cf. Heb. 6.9, 11.40, 12.24.

298:83   For "*Born for others*," etc., cf. Rom. 14.7.

298:1-4   Milton, *Paradise Lost*, VI, 644-647, somewhat altered by Mather.

299:10-11   *Massachusetts Colonial Records*, quoted by Palfrey, 4:49.

299:16-28   See Francis Parkman, *France and England in North America under Louis XIV* (18th ed., Boston, Mass., 1887), pp. 235-240; Palfrey, 4:49; G. M. Wrong, *The Rise and Fall of New France* (2 vols., New York, Macmillan Co., 1928), 2:521-523.

299:33-34   The full title of Denys' work, published in two volumes in Paris in 1672, was *Description géographique et historique des Costes de l'Amérique septentrionale, avec l'histoire naturelle du Pais*. Despite its title, Denys' account is confined to Acadia. An English edition, ed. W. F. Ganong, with the title *Description and Natural History of the Coasts of North America*, was published in Toronto by the Champlain Society in 1908.

299:39   Lucan *The Civil War* II.657.

300:43-57   Mather here draws on a Rabbinic interpretation of Ps. 78.8-11. According to an ancient tradition there was a foray out of Egypt against the Philistines before the exodus led by Moses. The Ephraimites, the largest of the Israelite tribes, dwelt in a district on the northern border of Egypt (see I Chron. 7.20-28), and were prosperous and strong, but, in the Psalmist's words, "They kept not the covenant of God, and refused to walk in his law." The Ephraimites could thus stand as the "type" of the New Englanders, who "were not enough concerned for the *Counsel* and *Presence* of God in the undertaking," but rather were too much moved by the desire for profit. The Canadians and Indians were like the Philistines in residing to the north. One may also conjecture that the linking of the New Englanders and Ephraimites had a further typological significance. Ephraim was the younger of Joseph's two sons, but Jacob, on his death-bed had insisted on conferring the blessing on him rather than on his brother Manasseh, saying, "his seed shall become a multitude of nations" (Gen. 48.19). Thus the younger, "New" England, which had received such special blessings, would inevitably invite the wrath of God: as the Psalmist warned the disbelieving and disobedient, "*I will utter dark Sayings of old*" (Ps. 78.2).

   This *Magnalia* passage corresponds closely with Mather's notes on the 78th Psalm in his unpublished Biblical commentary, *Biblia Sacra*. Under v.9 he queries, "What and when was the disaster of the Ephraimites turning back in the day of Battle, whereof the Psalmist maketh mention?" He concludes, "it seems to have been a thing that happened before ever Israel came out of Egypt." In the *Biblia*, after "*Time* not yet come," he adds, "for the Israelites to be delivered, or the Canaanites to be destroyed."

300:52   See B. J. and H. W. Whiting, *Proverbs, Sentences, and Proverbial Phrases* (Cambridge, Mass., Harvard University Press, 1968), H 167; Tilley, H 197.

300:68   Florus, *Epitome Rerum Romanorum* I.xxxi.15.4; cf. also "Marcus Cato" xxvii.1 in Plutarch's *Lives*.

301:17-18   Compare Ps. 7.8, Eccles. 3.17, 11.5-9, etc.

302:20   Grandson of John Winthrop, Governor of Massachusetts, and son of John Winthrop, Jr., Governor of Connecticut (*Magnalia*, Bk. II, chaps. 4 and 11). For the "Mismanagement" by Fitzjohn, see Parkman, *Count Frontenac and New France under Louis XIV* (18th ed.), pp. 256-257 and note.

302:31   In addition to Parkman's excellent life of Frontenac, see biography by W. D. LeSeur, *Count Frontenac*, London, T. C. and E. C. Jack, 1906.

302:34-303:58   See Parkman, *Frontenac*, p. 266, for the accuracy of Mather's text.

303:59   According to John Wise of Ipswich, who went as a chaplain on Phips's expedition against Quebec, the bearer of the summons was Lieutenant Thomas Savage. Savage himself, however, did not mention this mission in his *Account of the Late Action of the New-Englanders Under the Command of Sir William Phips* (London, 1691), nor did he include anything about the summons or Frontenac's answer. It is probable that Wise's statement was correct, since his "Narrative" of the attempt and failure of the enterprise seems throughout based on sound information (see 2 MHS *Proc.*, 15:286).

303:60–64   See Parkman, *Frontenac*, pp. 267–268 and note. Mather quotes in part an anonymous account of the Quebec expedition (see 2 MHS *Proc.*, 15:313). This account was apparently sent to Increase Mather in England, as Wise's probably was also. Certainly both were available to Cotton Mather when he wrote. (Cf. 2 MHS *Proc.*, 15:282, 313, 319.)

303:65   In NED, *s.v.* Dry, I.12.

303:74   For Ephraim Savage, see Sibley, 2:128–130, and references given there.

303:76   Mather's reference to Scaeva is puzzling. Caesar's valiant centurion, Cassius Scaeva, fought bravely at Dyrrachium, where, while besieging a fortress, his shield was pierced by more than a hundred arrows (Caesar *De Bello Civili* III.53; cf. also Lucan *The Civil War* X.543–546). Mather perhaps assumed that Scaeva also served Caesar when he came to Britain, where the Romans were in fact handicapped by tides and shallow water (cf. *Caesar De Bello Gallico* IV.23–24). It has also been suggested that Mather had in mind not the centurion, but a Publius Scaeva mentioned in Dio Cassius's *Roman History* (XXXVII.53.3), who with others landed and disembarked their troops, thinking they could cross over to the mainland on foot. But in this affair all save Publius died after bravely defending themselves against the Lusitanians. Publius lost his shield and received many wounds, but leaped into the water and escaped by swimming. This hardly agrees with Mather's comparison to Savage's adventure, since he, although grounded by the tide and shot at by enemies, escaped safely with all his men.

304:91   When the attack on Quebec failed, Walley was blamed by many in Massachusetts. John Wise in his "Narrative" called Phips "the truly Valliant Knight General"; he referred to Walley merely as "John Walley, Esquire, Lieutenant General." (2 MHS *Proc.*, 15:283.) Moreover, throughout his account, Wise charged Walley with being "destitute of all proper care for the Management of the Army," writing that his "gravity" and pretense of deep thinking were "only the Invincible Arrest of fear." Repeatedly his narrative harps on the cowardice of the Lieutenant General (MHS *Proc.*, as above, especially pp. 290, 294–295). The anonymous account (MHS *Proc.*, p. 315) follows the same pattern: Phips "did acquit himself with the greatest bravery," but Walley was "not a lion but a frightened Hart." In rebuttal of such charges Walley wrote for "the honorable council of this Massachusetts . . . 27th Nov. 1690" a "Narrative of the Proceedings to Canada, soe far as concerned the land army" (printed as Appendix No. 21 in Hutchinson, *History*, vol. I), in which he tried to absolve himself from blame for the Quebec defeat. He was supported in this by Thomas Savage (cf. p. 303, l. 59 above), who in his *Action* addressed to his brother, Perez Savage, in London, wrote (p. 5), "You will without doubt hear many reflections upon Lieutenant General Walley: but he is not guilty of what they charge him with; but there are some, who to make themselves Faultless lay the Fault upon him."

304:96–97   Caesar, *De Bello Gallico* IV.24–26.

304:2–3   Compare Tilley, V 11.

304:23–24   See Seneca, *Ludus de Morte Claudii Caesaris vel Apocolocyntosis* 7.3. This was included in Erasmus' *Adagia*, and soon became a popular proverb. See Tilley, C 486, and Whiting and Whiting, *Proverbs, Sentences*, C 350.

305:25–26   See Livy *History* XXVIII.xlii.7: "non consistendi usquam locus, non procedendi; quacumque circumspexerit, hostilia omnia atque infesta." Mather may have been quoting from memory, or from some secondary source whose inaccuracies he copies.

305:37–38　The source of this quotation has not been identified.

305:53–54　According to the anonymous narrative, "The General Employed Carpenters to make wheelbarrows Each to carry two Pateraro's to march before our Men" (2 MHS *Proc.*, 15:314).

305:55–58　For the Philistines, see Judg. 15.1–5; for the Cerealia, see Ovid *Fasti* IV.686–712. According to Ovid, on the last day of the "Diversion," foxes were let loose with torches tied to their backs. He explains the practice by telling a story he heard from a hospitable host who gave him lodging when he was travelling to the Pelignian country in which he had been born. The tale was that the young son of a husbandman and his wife caught a fox, wrapped it in straw and hay, and set it on fire. The fox, fleeing through the fields, burned the crops. This incident, Ovid wrote, was forgotten, but it lived on as a memorial, "for to this day . . . to punish the species a fox is burned at the festival of Ceres, thus perishing itself in the way it destroyed the crops." In the light of this tale, it seems probable that Mather's "*Phenicians*" was a misprint for "*Pelignians.*"

306:76　For "*Hand of Heaven*" (that is, "hand of God"), cf. Ps. 10.12, 31.15, Eccles. 9.1, I Pet. 5.6.

306:87　For "an *Horrible Tempest*," see Ps. 11.6.

306:88　See "Bossloper" and "Coureurs de Bois" in DAE and in M. M. Matthews, *A Dictionary of Americanisms*, Chicago, University of Chicago Press, 1951. Mather's passage closely parallels one in an anonymous 1691 pamphlet, "Some Additional Considerations Addressed unto the Worshipful Elisha Hutchinson, Esq." [a member of the Council]: "for had they not gone with the Fleet to *Canada*, a thousand *Boss-Lopers* had been upon our Country Towns and laid them waste" (*Tracts Relating to the Currency of the Massachusetts Bay 1682–1720*, ed. Andrew McFarland Davis, Boston, 1902, p. 26).

306:91–92　For "*Israel* engaging against *Benjamin*," see Judg. 19.22–20.48.

306:97–307:24　The moral tale of the Hermit and the Angel is in Thomas Bradwardine's *De Causa Dei Contra Pelagium* (London, 1618), p. 281. Bradwardine gives his source as the *Exempla* of Jacques de Vitry (Jacobus Vitriaco), 1290–1361, French prelate, historian, and preacher. (See the edition by T. F. Crane, London, 1890, pp. 50–51, 179–182.) Mather's text appears to be a literal translation of Bradwardine's Latin. Mather might also have found the story in Jan Makowski (Johannes Maccovius), *Loci Communes Theologici* (Amsterdam, 1658, p. 407), which exactly reproduces Bradwardine except that Maccovius has "spiritu progresso blasphemiæ" for Bradwardine's "spiritu aggresso blasphemiæ," in Mather, "with Blasphemous Injections." The tale is also referred to by Increase Mather in *The Doctrine of Divine Providence Opened and Applyed* (Boston, 1684), A2 recto–A3 recto.

307:28　Penn, the father of William Penn, the founder of Pennsylvania, seems to have negotiated secretly with the exiled king, who knighted him at the time of the Restoration. (See DNB.)

307:36–38　See Mather's *The Serviceable Man, A Discourse Made unto the General Court of the Massachusets Colony . . . At the Election 28d. 3m. 1690*, pp. 3–4; see also Holmes, *C. Mather*, 3:969–973; and Savage, *Account*, p. 12.

307:39–308:56　For general comment and data concerning this long passage, cf. A. M. Davis, *Colonial Reprints, 1882–1732* (Boston: Prince Society, 1910. 1:21–24, 197–208), especially Mather's *Some Considerations on the BILLS of CREDIT Now passing in New-England* (Boston, 1691), reprinted in Davis, 1:189–196. For this pamphlet see Holmes, *C. Mather*, 3:1000–1003. It was addressed to "*The Worshipful, John Philips*," Mather's father-in-law. (See Holmes, *ibid.*, p. 1003, n. 1, and Davis, *Reprints*, 1:196.)

A copy of a Ten Shilling Bill is given in Thomas Savage's *Account*, p. 13. It is signed by a committee of three: "Penn Townsend, Adam Winthrop, Tim. Thornton." Townsend, a wine merchant in Boston, was active in political affairs and in 1698 was chosen a Councillor; Thornton was also a merchant and representative of Boston; and Adam Winthrop was a member of the Mathers' church and a Councillor of Massachusetts in 1689 and 1692. See Palfrey, *History*, 4:598–600, and Savage, *Genealogical Dictionary*, 4:318–319, 607, 292–293.

308:57–58 Lucan *The Civil War* I.348–349.

309:74–75 Winthrop, Jr., was an early promoter of mining in the colony (see above p. 265, l. 75 and notes on his interest in iron mining and smelting). Some time in 1644 he presented a petition to the General Court of Massachusetts, saying that "these plantacions much abounding with rockie hills the nurceries of mynes and mineralls may probablie conteyne not only the most necessarie mynes of Iron . . . but alsoe with mynes of lead, tynne, copper, and other metalls noe lesse profitable." He therefore "humblie entreates" the liberty "to him and his assignes to search for these mynes in all places within the Jurisdiction" (*Winthrop Papers*, 4:422–423). In a letter dated "30 (7) 48," his father Governor Winthrop informed him that "mr. Endecott hath founde a Copper mine in his owne grounde, mr. Ledder [a metals assayer] hath tryed it" (*Winthrop Papers*, 5:262). Apparently in Mather's day there was still the sanguine expectation that considerable deposits of copper remained to be found.

309:76 See Wing, M2312; Evans, No. 1703. Reprinted in Davis, *Reprints*, 1:153–187; the Mather passage appears on p. 175.

309:82–87 Compare Thomas Savage, *Account of the Late Action*, p. 12, and Davis, *Reprints*, 1:29.

309:4 See 2 MHS *Proc.*, 15:316.

310:9 Compare Ezek., chap. 1.

310:10 Compare Matt. 17.21, Mark 9.29, Acts 14.23.

310:11 I Sam. 17.45.

310:34–311:42 Compare 2 MHS *Proc.*, 15:316, to which Mather makes certain additions. His remark that "Accidents" may be worth recounting to his "Reader" applies to the next paragraphs of his text. For Rainsford, see MHS *Proc.* as above, p. 306.

311:69 Virgil, *Eclogues* I.66.

311:71 Compare Rev. 1.10.

312:85–87 Compare Joel 1.14, 2.12–13, Dan. 9.3–16.

312:92 Compare Pss. 10.12, 31.15, Eccles. 9.1, I Pet. 5.6, etc.

312:93–94 Lucius Annaeus Florus *Epitome* I.1.10.

312:3 Leviathan is mentioned in Job 41.1, Pss. 74.14, 104.26, and in Isa. 27.1 is seen as a figure for Satan (cf. Rev. 12.9, 20.2). Thus "Children of the Leviathan" equals "Children of the Devil."

312:4 Compare Isa. 22.5.

312:17 *The Magnalia* is the only instance of the use of "pamphagous" listed by the NED, with derivation from the Greek παν φαγειν. It is probable, however, that "pamphagous" is a misprint for "panphagous," since the substitution of "m" for "n" before "ph" is linguistically highly unlikely.

313:31 Wanley, *Wonders*, pp. 638–639. Wanley gives as his source Nicholas Tulp (1594–1674), a doctor and magistrate of Amsterdam.

314:82 It is difficult to chart precisely the course followed by the five voyagers. They had for the most part no adequate charts, and the islands and bays had unfamiliar French names. Mather's "Cape without Hope" appears on modern maps as Cape d'Espoir. However, Henry Popple's *Map of the British Empire in America* (London, 1733), Sheet 3, has "Cap Désespoir." See also Wrong, *Rise and Fall*, 1:51–52, and Denys, *Description and Natural History*, p. 220n.

314:87   Mather's spelling "Brittoon" is that used in the anonymous account of Phips's expedition in 2 MHS *Proc.*, 15:307.

314:88   This bay appears as "Baye des Toutes Iles" on the map of Jean Baptiste Bouguinon d'Anville, *Canada, Louisiane, et Terres Angloises*, Paris, 1755.

315:11   Queen Mary was said by Holinshed to have declared: "When I am dead and opened, you shall find 'Calais' lying in my heart" (*Oxford Dictionary of Quotations* 2nd ed., London, 1953, p. 333).

315:11–12   Perhaps a reference to Herodotus *History* V.105: "When King Darius was told that Sardis had been taken and burned . . . he commanded one of his attendants, every time dinner was set before him, to say thrice, 'Master, remember the Athenians.'"

315:17   It was decided by the Massachusetts authorities that Phips should go on business for the colony. The ostensible purpose was to obtain aid for a second enterprise against Canada, but there was also a hope that he might be useful at court by joining Increase Mather and the other agents of the colonies then trying to win the restoration of their charters. (See Murdock, *Increase Mather*, chaps. XIII, XIV; Palfrey, *History*, 4:50–58, etc.).

315:22   *Aeneid* I.204.

316:26–40   Compare Increase Mather, *Reasons for the Confirmation of the Charter Belonging to the Massachusetts Colony in New-England* (London, January or February 1690/91), which has on p. 4, "Reason 7": "His Majesties Subjects in New-England . . . have lately reduced the *French* in *Acady* unto Obedience to the Crown of *England*. If the like should be done in *Canada*, that would be worth Millions to the English *Crown* and Nation: not only in respect of the Bever-trade, but in that the *Fishery* of those parts and of *New-found-land* also, would be entirely in the hands of the English, to the great Encouragement of Trade . . . if his Majesty shall . . . please to restore his Subjects in *New-England* to their Ancient Priviledges, that will encourage them a second time to attempt the reducing of *Canada*, in which . . . (assisted with Frigates from *England*) . . . they shall have good success, a profitable . . . Addition will be made to our Kings Dominions." (Reprinted in *Andros Tracts*, 2:225–229; see also Holmes, *I. Mather*, 2:450–458.)

316:50–51   See *New-England's Faction Discovered*, London, 1690 (*Andros Tracts*, 2:218): "With those *Mohawks* and other *Indians* several *French* Priests and Jesuits have dwelt and inhabited, and endeavoured to propagate their Religion amongst them." Phips's warning against the "Interests" of the Jesuits probably carried special weight to King William, a Protestant, and even more to the many New Englanders who had been told that Sir Edmund Andros "hired the Indians to kill the English" and was himself a disciple of Rome, who gave to an Indian a book which he said was better than the Bible and "had in it the Picture of the Virgin *Mary*." In 1689 two Indians reported that "the *Maquas* Indians sent a Messenger . . . to inform that Sir E. A. had been tampering to engage them to fight against the English." The image they called up of Andros, sitting in his Wigwam, saying "O brave Indians," while those Indians, for whom he had more love than for the English, fought against the citizens of the colonies he ruled, was no doubt distorted, but was none the less widely accepted by his foes. (See *Revolution Justified*, in *Andros Tracts*, 1:103.)

316:61–322:72   Section 14, as has been pointed out, was out of place in a biography of Phips. In its praise of Increase Mather, it was, rather, a political document defending its subject against critics. (See introductory essays, "Cotton Mather" and "The Magnalia," pp. 5–8, 12–13 and 44.) Cotton Mather here gives so thorough an account of his father's sojourn in England from 1688 until 1692 that there is no need to annotate it in detail. In writing this section, Cotton Mather had access to his father's "Autobiography" (pp. 322–344), certain of Increase Mather's diaries, and his writings while in London, some of which he later used in his *Parentator*, the life of his father published in 1724. Especially useful was Increase's *Brief Account concerning Several of the Agents of New-England, their Negotiation at the Court of England,* London, 1691. This is reprinted in *Andros Tracts*, 2:271–296, and in C. M. Andrews, *Narratives of the Insurrections*, pp. 276–297. Andrews says the accuracy of the *Brief Account* is "beyond impeachment . . . As a defence of" Mather's "own course the narrative is convincing, and as an argument in behalf of the new charter it is a state paper of high rank." See also in addition to the sources already cited the reprints in vol. 2 of the *Andros Tracts* and Holmes, *I. Mather*, for his listing, with annotations of the printed works Increase wrote or helped to write between 1689 and 1691.

317:87 See introductory essay "Cotton Mather," p. 12, and for Wiswall endnote to Bk. II, p. 211, ll. 52–54.

317:94–95 See endnote to p. 316, ll. 26–40.

318:13–21 See Increase's "Autobiography," pp. 335–336.

321:29–31 The source of the Casaubon reference has not been found.

321:37 See Palfrey, 4:85, and notes.

321:42 It was to Nottingham that Phips reported later that year (Feb. 21, 1692/3) on the steps he had taken to end the witchcraft delusion, concluding: "peoples minds before divided and distracted by differing opinions concerning this matter are now well composed." (See 2 MHS *Proc.*, 1:342.)

322:73–77 The joyous "Acclamations" occurred at the Isthmian Games. The crying out of "A Saviour!" ($\Sigma\omega\tau\acute{\eta}\rho$) is reported by Polybius (*Histories* XVIII.46.12), but he makes no mention of the birds. Plutarch's life of Flamininus (x.4–6) identifies the birds as ravens. The only ancient historian who, like Mather, reported the feelings of the birds ("astonished at the Cry") was Valerius Maximus (*Factorum et Dictorum* IV.vIII.5), who described them as "attonitas parentesque" (astonished and trembling).

323:89–93 The italicised passage follows the text of "the Printed Order," except for its last three lines. The document was issued "By the Governour, Council, and Representatives . . . in an Assembly of their Majesties Province of the Massachusetts Bay." (See *Acts and Resolves . . . of the Province of Massachusetts Bay*, Boston, 1869, 8:9.) A copy of "the Printed Order" is in *Broadsides and Ballads*, no. 190.

323:95–97 Phips wrote to Nottingham telling him of the "good disposition of the people," and Cotton Mather followed suit, assuring the Earl that "the Generallity" of their Majesties' "subjects . . . doe with all thankfulness receive the favours which by the new Charter are granted to them." (See Palfrey, 4:90n, and Murdock, *Increase Mather*, p. 287 and note.)

323:99–1 See Lam. 4.20.

324:36 Compare Rev. 6.8.

324:39–40 Compare I Thess. 2.11.

324:40–41 See Samuel Clarke, *Mirrour*, p. 341, no. 77: "Ptolomaeus Lagi" had as a "usual saying . . . it was fit for a King rather to make others rich, then to be rich himselfe." Clarke takes this from Plutarch *Moralia* 181.34. Mather's Latin sentence here may be his translation from Plutarch's Greek but it seems probable he relied on *Aphorismes Civill and Militarie: Amplified with Authorities, and exemplified with Historie*, drawn from Francesco Guicciardini. This book, published in London in 1613 and again in 1629, was probably compiled by Sir Robert Dallington (1561–1637), and has (1613 ed.), as Aphorism 38, "It is more princely to enrich, than to be rich," followed by "Regium est ditare, non ditescere."

324:45 Bullinger's three-volume *Sermonium Decades* (London, 1584) was in Increase Mather's library.

324:46–48 For angels caring for countries and provinces, see, in general, Cross, *Oxford Dictionary of the Christian Church*. See also endnotes to Bk. I, p. 186, ll. 86, 93–94.

324:49 Compare Dan. 10.5–12, 12.1–7.

342:49–52 The editors have not found a precise source for this passage, but it seems probable that it was based on Grotius's comment on Matt. 18.10 in his *Opera Omnia Theologica*, 3rd ed., Amsterdam, 1679. Part of this is translated in Benjamin Camfield's *Theological Discourse of Angels*, London, 1678, p. 76: "It is evident . . . that . . . Angels are Ministers of Divine Providence . . . and besides the universal Providence over all there is a common providence, whereby God upholds the civil Societies of Men, which we call Republics. And, that each of these have their Angels, is with great consent both of Jews and Christians collected out of *Daniel*."

325:73–74   Mather alters Virgil, *Georgics* II.458–459. Thomas Fuller in his *Worthies of England* (1:263) has "O fortunati nimium bona si sua norint, Angligenæ."

325:82–83   See, for example, Matt. 4.24, 8.16, Mark 1.32, 5.15, 16, 18, Luke 8.36.

325:86–88   Matt. 12.22–37, Luke 11.14–26, Mark 3.22–30.

325:89–91   John 1.14; cf. also 14.10.

325:93   Mather extracts one clause from a sentence in Bartholin's *De Morbis Biblicis Miscellanea Medica* (2nd ed., Frankfurt, 1672, p. 65), which reads in full: "Inter Judæos numerus Dæmoniacorum insolitus fuit, & saepe in sacro Evangelio occurrit, sive quod praeter modum artibus magicis dediti Dæmonem advocaverint, sive quod summæ impietatis hanc pœnam meruerint à vindice Jehovah."

326:94–95   For magic, dreams, charms, etc., among the Jews, see John Lightfoot (*Works*, 1:371), and the Talmuds, Ben Sanhedrin 65[b], 57[b].

326:97–2   See, for example, Mishnah Shabbath VIII.3; Ben Shabbath 115[b], etc., and II Chron. 33.6. The editors have found no source for the killing of the twenty-four scholars; for the fourscore hanged in one day, see Mishna Sanhedrin VI.4; Ben Sanhedrin 45[b].

326:5–9   See Ben Sanhedrin 17[a], and, for the prevalence of sorcery among Jewish women, see especially Ben Sanhedrin 100[b]: "When your daughter grows up, she will probably practice magic."

326:17   II Kings 17.9.

326:24–26   Crouch was indeed a "Sham-Scribler." On page 205 of the *Delights* were "Directions for finding the Chances," a kind of lottery. Each reader chose at random one of the emblems in the book, some limited to men and others to women, each promising either good luck or bad. Crouch called this an "honest and pleasant recreation"; it was anathema to Mather, who regarded any lottery as a "finer form" of witchcraft.

327:38   For the Salem Village "witches," cf. Murdock, *Increase Mather*, p. 288; Chadwick Hansen, *Witchcraft at Salem* (New York, 1969), chap. 3. For Sewall's visit see his *Papers*, 1:358 and 359n.

327:47–49   In Isa. 28.15 the "covenant with death" is also "with hell," and it was generally believed that witches had made a formal covenant or compact with Satan. The court at Salem acted on the proposition that no innocent person could be represented by a specter, and that to be so represented was proof of a covenant with the devil. On the devil's compacts, see George Lyman Kittredge, *Witchcraft in Old and New England* (Cambridge, Mass., Harvard University Press, 1929), pp. 239–243.

329:13   The Sadducees were an exclusive priestly caste (see Ezek. 40.46), who ridiculed the doctrine of the resurrection (Matt. 22.23, Mark 12.18–27, Luke 20.27–40), and denied the existence of angels and spirits (Acts 23.8). Thus disbelievers in devils, demons, witches and their powers were regularly so designated, as, for example, by Increase Mather in *Cases of Conscience Concerning Evil Spirits* (Boston, 1693): "a Sadduce, [one] not believing that there are any Devils or any (to us) invisible world" (p. 11); "No man but a Sadduce doubts of the ill will of Devils" (p. 14).

329:19   The phrase was taken into Latin from the Greek. See Lucian *Hermotimus* 86: "θεὸς ἐκ μηχανῆς," "A god from the machine."

329:19–20   For the "Land . . . *darkened by the Wrath of the Lord of Hosts*," see Isa. 9.19.

329:20–21   All those chosen for the Court except Corwin and Sergeant had been officeholders in the colony before Increase Mather selected them under the new charter of 1691. For the members of the Court, see Hansen, p. 122; Murdock, pp. 249–50, 293n; Sewall, *Diary*, 1:339n; and C. W. Upham, *Salem Witchcraft*, Boston, 1967 (reprint ed., New York, Frederick Unger Publishing Co., pp. 251–252), which points out that those in the Court were of the "highest order," not only of the magistracy, but "of society generally." For the "*assault from Hell*," cf. II Sam. 22.6, Ps. 18.5, Matt. 16.18.

329:32   For Biblical references to the sin of witchcraft, see, among others, Exod. 22.18, Deut. 18.10, I Sam. 15.23, II Kings 9.22, II Chron. 33.6.

329:35–36   All of these "gravest Authors" were cited by Cotton's father Increase in *Cases of Conscience*, who refers to "*Binsfeldius* in his *Treatise*" (p. 5), "*Mr. Bromhall* in his *Treatise of Spectres*," and "*Mr. Bovet* in his *Pandemonium*" (p. 12). Increase refers again to "*Mr. Bromhals History*" on p. 45, and to Bodin's "*In Daemonomanie*" on pp. 45, 48. Of spectral evidence, Increase writes (p. 23): "my dearly honoured and never to be forgotten Friend Mr. *Richard Baxter* has given an Account in his book about Witchcrafts lately Published".

330:40   This is the first case presented in Cotton Mather's *Memorable Providences, Relating to Witchcrafts and Possessions* (Boston, 1689), Section VII, described by him in great detail. Mather took Martha, the eldest of the afflicted children, into his own home in an effort to cure her of her possession. See also Holmes, *C. Mather*, 2:553, 3:1255.

330:42   See, for example, Cicero *In Pisonem Oratio* XX.48.

330:43   For "*Familiar Spirits*," see, for example, Lev. 19.31, 20.6, Deut. 18.11, I Sam. 28.3, II Kings 21.6, I Chron. 10.13, II Chron. 33.6, Isa. 8.19.

330:48–49   For "*they ran well*," cf. Gal. 5.7.

330:51   For "*went out of the Way*," cf. Mal. 2.8, Rom. 3.12. On "spectral evidence," see, for example, Murdock, *I. Mather*, pp. 293–294 and notes; and especially Kittredge, *Witchcraft*, pp. 363–365. See also Holmes, *C. Mather*, 2:553, 3:1255, 1261n, etc.

331:81   On the necessity to "*Convict a Witch*," see Exod. 22.18.

332:20–23   On the Devil as a teacher of lies, cf. John 8.44.

332:27–28   For the "*Righteous to perish with the Wicked*," cf. Eccles. 7.15–17. For the slaying of the Gibeonites, see II Sam. 21.1–2. Increase employs this analogy, with the same reference, on p. 58 of *Cases*.

332:33–37   Compare Sewall, *Diary*, 1:367; for the fourteen ministers who signed the preface to *Cases of Conscience*, see Holmes, *I. Mather*, 1:115.

332:38   For Samuel Willard's comment on "the Strange Case of Elizabeth Knapp," see 4 MHS *Coll.* 8:570. Cotton Mather follows closely the story of the Groton woman as recounted in his father's *Remarkable Providences* (pp. 140–142): "There was a Maid in that Town (one *Elizabeth Knap*) who in the Moneth of *October*, Anno. 1671. was taken after a very strange manner, sometimes weeping, sometimes laughing, sometimes roaring hideously . . . She cried out in some of her Fits, that a Woman . . . was the cause of her Affliction . . . but the gracious Party thus accused and abused by a malicious Devil, Prayed earnestly with and for the Possessed creature; after which she confessed that Satan had deluded her; making her believe evil of her good Neighbour without any cause." In his *Cases* (p. 33), Increase refers to this earlier account.

333:58–59   For "*Prayer* with *Fasting*," see Matt. 17.21, Mark 9.29, Acts 14.23, for "with *Patience*, be experienced," see Rom. 3–4.

333:62–334:96   Of the *Return*, Cotton Mather wrote in his *Diary* (1:151), "it was *I* who drew it up." The *Return* was first printed as the last two pages of the "Post-script" to Increase's *Cases*. (Cf. Holmes, *I. Mather*, 1:115, *C. Mather*, 3:913; Chadwick Hansen, *Witchcraft at Salem*, pp. 123–125.) Of the sections omitted in the *Magnalia*, the first was introductory: "The Afflicted State of our poor Neighbours, that are now Suffering by Molestations from the Invisible World, we apprehend so deplorable, that we think their condition calls for the utmost Help of all persons in their several Capacities." The second was in a complimentary vein: "We cannot but with all Thankfulness Acknowledge, the Success which the Merciful God has given unto the Sedulous and Assiduous Endeavours of Honourable Rulers, to detect the Abominable *Witchcrafts*, which have been Committed in the Country; Humbly praying that the Discovery of those Mysterious and Mischievous Wickednesses, may be perfected." The eighth was hortatory: "Nevertheless, We cannot but humbly Recommend unto the Government, the speedy and vigorous Prosecution of such as have rendred themselves obnoxious [in the obsolete sense of "guilty" or "reprehensible"], according to the Direction given in the Laws of God, and the wholsome Statutes of the English *Nation*, for the Detection of Witchcrafts." For of course no one denied the existence of witches and the necessity of punishing them. In the sections printed in the *Magnalia*, there are minor changes in capitalization and punctuation from the text in *Cases of Conscience*, and "*dreadful Calamity*" becomes "*direful Calamity*" (line 62).

333:68–69   II Cor. 2.11; cf. also Eph. 4.27, 6.11.

333:82   In his *Cases of Conscience*, Increase quotes Perkins (p. 67): "I would . . . wish and advise all Jurors . . . to take heed that as they be diligent in zeal of Gods Glory, and . . . his Church, in detecting of Witches, by all sufficient and lawful means, so . . . they would be careful . . . not to Condemn any party Suspected upon bare Presumptions, without sound . . . proofs, that they be not guilty . . . of Shedding Innocent Blood." The *Cases* also quotes Bernard (pp. 35–37): "The naming of the suspected in their Fits, and what they have done here or there . . . is but a presumption, because this is only Devils Testimony, who can lye and that more often than Speak Truth . . . Be it far from good men to confirm any word of the Devil by Oath, if it be not an evident Truth without Devils Testimony." Like all New England Puritans, Cotton Mather was, of course, familiar with Perkins, and, in the long preamble to his *Wonders of the Invisible World*, he included "An ABSTRACT of Mr. PERKINS's Way for the Discovery of WITCHES" (pp. 14–17).

334:95–96   Compare Acts 23.29, II Tim. 4.16.

334:99–1   Increase's *Cases of Conscience* was apparently quickly printed and some copies at least were sold before the end of November. The dates of the earlier editions were given as 1693, but this seems to have been intentional post-dating, perhaps to agree with the expected editions to be issued in England. See introductory essay "Cotton Mather," pp. 10–11; Holmes, *I. Mather*, 1:106–110, 119–120, 123; cf. also Miller, *Colony to Province*, pp. 191–208.

334:8   For two "Credible Persons," see Deut. 17.6, 19.15, Matt. 18.16; cf. also Matt. 26.60.

334:11–12   The source of this quotation has not been found.

334:12–335:15   The questions were addressed to the ministers on October 5, 1692; their response, rejecting spectral evidence, was made on October 11, signed by "Henricus Selijns" and "Godefridus Dellius" (see 2 MHS *Proc.*, 1:348–358). The Dutch Selijns was a friend of Cotton Mather, and furnished a prefatory poem for the *Magnalia* (see above pp. 84–88). Tolerant in ecclesiastical matters, Selijns allowed the Reverend M. Daillé to preach to his French congregation in the Dutch church. (See DAB on Selijns.)

Joseph Dudley, after the Massachusetts revolution of April 1688, was released and sent to London, where he was charged by seven colonists with 119 illegal acts (*Andros Tracts*, 1:149–173). He was acquitted and shortly thereafter sent back to America as Chief of the Council for New York (see Kimball, *Public Life of Joseph Dudley*, pp. 58–60).

335:16   On "*Venefick Witchcraft*," see Kittredge, *Witchcraft*, chap. VI.

335:39   For "*Thorny Business*," cf. II Cor. 12.7.

335:46   Rom. 16.20.

335:46–50   In his *Wonders*, Mather had already employed the Erasmus reference in practically identical language (p. 46). Mather's source may have been Increase's longer and more detailed account in *Cases* (p. 18): "Both *Erasmus* and *Cardanus* write that the town of *Schiltach* in *Germany*, was in the Month of April .1533. Set on Fire by a Devil and Burnt to the Ground, in an Hours space." He gives as his source the *De Subtilitate Rerum*, "Lib. 19" (see 1664 ed., pp. 690–691), of Girolamo Cardano (1501–1576), Italian mathematician, physician, and astrologer. Erasmus' account is given in Epistle MCCLIII, dated July 1533. (See Erasmus, *Opera Omnia*, Leyden, 1703; reprinted 10 vols., London, 1962, 3^b:1473.)

335:51–336:58   In his *Diary* (1:151) Mather wrote: "Most of the Judges" in Salem showed "a most charming Instance of *Prudence* and *Patience*," and underwent "*Agony* of Soul: seeking the "Direction of Heaven," so that although he "could not allow the *Principles*, that some of the Judges had espoused," he "could not but speak honourably of their *Persons*, on all Occasions." (It is impossible to date this observation of Mather's precisely, since between mid-May and December his diary entries, while reflecting the unfolding of events, are undated.) The twelve jurymen were Thomas Fisk, William Fisk, John Batcheler, Thomas Fisk, Jr., John Dane, Joseph Evelith, Thomas Perly, Sr., John Peabody, Thomas Perkins, Samuel Sayer, Andrew Eliot, Henry Herrick, Sr. (See Sewall, *Diary*, 1:445–446n; Hansen, *Witchcraft*, pp. 209–210; G. L. Burr, *Narratives of the Witchcraft Cases* (New York, C. Scribner's Sons, 1914, reprint 1959), pp. 387–388.

336:59–60   See Evans, *American Bibliography*, No. 638, and W. C. Ford, *Broadsides and Ballads*, No. 199.

336:60–61   For the steadfastness of the tribe of Zebulun, cf. Judg. 6.35, I Chron. 12.33–40, Rev. 7.8.

336:65   Compare Increase Mather, *Cases*, p. 25: "The old Witch Circe by an inchanted Cup causes *Ulysses* his Companions to imagine themselves to be turned into Swine."

336:70–73   Mather had already written a lengthy account of the "late Outrage committed by a knot of Witches in Swedeland" in his *Wonders of the Invisible World*, pp. 48–51. He acknowledged his indebtedness to "the Acute Pen of the Excellent and Renowned Dr. [Anthony] *Horneck*," a German divine who came to England *c.* 1661, where he enjoyed great success both as a casuist and as an ecclesiastic. His translation from the German of *An Account of what Happened in the Kingdom of Sweden, in the Years 1669, 1670 and Upwards* was included in the 1682 edition of Joseph Glanvil's *Saducismus Triumphatus, or Full and Plain Evidences concerning Witches and Apparitions*. (For the passage used by Mather, see the 1726 [4th] edition, pp. 474 ff.) Increase in *Cases* (p. 20) also refers to the witchcrafts "done in *Sweedland* about Twenty Years ago, by means of a cursed Knot of Witches there."

337:91   For "*Clouds of Witnesses*," see Heb. 12.1.

337:93–95   Mather probably took this quotation from the title-page of his father's *Cases of Conscience*, where the source is given as "Lactantius Lib. 2. Instit. Cap. 15." (See *Divinae Institiones* II.xv, *Migne L*, 6:332.) Cotton follows exactly Increase's wording, which is a paraphrase rather than a direct quotation from Lactantius.

338:25   In 1699, Cotton Mather published anonymously in Boston *Decennium Luctuosum: An History of Remarkable Occurrences in the Long War, which New-England hath had with the Indian Salvages, from the year 1688, to the year 1698*. His authorship is made clear in a Diary entry (1:271; cf. Holmes, *C. Mather*, 1:222–223). He reprinted it in the *Magnalia*, Bk. VII, Appendix (pp. 57–118), and it was reprinted by Charles H. Lincoln, *Narratives of the Indian Wars 1675–1699* (New York, 1913), pp. 179–300. According to the *Decennium*, Sir William built the fort at Pemaquid "in pursuance of his Instructions from Whitehall . . . the Expense of maintaining it, when we were so much impoverished otherwise, made it continually complained of, as one of the Countryes Grievances" (Lincoln, *Narratives*, p. 241).

338:41 *et seq.*   Article XIX of Mather's *Decennium* (Lincoln, *Narratives*, pp. 249–251) presents the Treaty, which he here condenses, closely following the language of the original. It conferred, he said, "A Years Breathing Time" on the colony.

339:72–73   Ancient writers repeatedly commented on the mystery of the source of the Nile, among them Herodotus *History* II.28; Pliny *Natural History* V.x; Statius *Silvae* V.21. Wanley, *Wonders*, p. 402, cites these and others but concludes, with considerable unction, that it is now well "known" that it rises "near the Mountain of the Moon, not far from the famous Promontory of *Good Hope*."

339:89–90   For "*Poverty . . . like an armed Man*," see Prov. 6.11, 24.34.

339:94   For "*Peace, like a River*," see Isa. 48.18, 66.12.

340:6   *Aeneid* I.120, 174.

340:7   Savage, *Genealogical Dictionary*, 3:412–413.

340:11–13   The editors are unable to identify with certainty the "*Martyrdom of Muria.*" The presumption is that, as an example of "Torments of *Cold*," a place rather than a person is referred to. The reference to Pliny and "*The Punishment of Mountains*" ("poenas montium") would seem to bear this out. (See *Natural History* XIX.xix.55.) For a possible identification of Muria, see Meric Casaubon, *A Treatise Proving Spirits, Witches and Supernatural Operations* (London, 1672), p. 56. With a reference to Seneca, *Quaestiones Naturales* (IV.vi.2–vii.2), on snow, hail, and rain, Casaubon writes that there are men who, "by observing of the clouds, were able and skillful to foresee and foretel, when a storm of Hail was approaching. *Cleonis* was the place . . . by what he saith of it . . . (now *Morea*, under the Turk) of no very great fame, or name." The place was "very subject to storms of Hail." Seneca goes into detail about the sufferings of the inhabitants and the damage to crops. Morea in fact was a mountainous region in what is now Albania.

340:16   See Aelius Spartianus "Life of Hadrian" VIII.4 in *Scriptores Historiae Augustae*: "in senatu saepe dixit ita se rem publicam gesturum ut scirent populi rem esse, non propriam," or "in the senate he used to say that he would so administer the commonwealth that men would know that it was not his own but the people's." Mather's source was probably Wanley, *Wonders*, p. 463.

340:18–19   See Julius Capitolinus "The Two Maximini" VI.4 in *Scriptores Historiae Augustae*: "Ego vero, quo maior fuero, tanto plus laborabo," or "As for me, the greater I become, the harder I will work." Mather's wording of the motto is that in Wanley's *Wonders*, p. 464.

340:22–25   Compare K. J. V.: "Behold, he that keepeth Israel shall neither slumber nor sleep." The king of Portugal remains unidentified.

341:59   In Article XX of the *Decennium*, entitled "Bloody Fishing at Oyster River; and Sad Work at Groton," Mather gives an account of this attack and of the subsequent extension of Indian raids as far south as Groton, Massachusetts (Lincoln, *Narratives*, pp. 252–254).

341:62–63   See Isa. 2.4, Joel 3.10, Mic. 4.3.

342:88–91   See Hutchinson, *History*, 2:56–58, and Barnes, "Phippius Maximus," pp. 535–536, 539–541. For "*Base Men*," cf. Job. 30.8.

342:94   For "*Correct Fools*," cf. Prov. 19.29, 26.5.

342:5–6   Theodosius' charity toward his enemy is recounted in Book IV of Zosimus' *Historiae Novae Libri VI* (ed. Basel, 1576, pp. 73–74), and by Augustine, *Civita Dei*, V.xxvi (*Migne L*, 41:172–173).

342:8–9   Ovid *Tristia* III.5.31–32. Ovid has "*Irae*" rather than "*Ira.*"

342:15–343:16   Among David's "*Trials*," see, for example, I Sam. 18.9–11, 19.18, 22.1; for his "*Advancements*," II Sam. 7.8–9, Ps. 78.70–71.

343:30–46   See "Fabius Maximus" iv.1; v.4–6; xi–xiii in Plutarch's *Lives* as well as his *MCondita oralia* 195. See also Livy *Ab Urbe* xxii, xxvii–xxx.

343:47–49   No source for "One of the Antients" and quotation.

343:52   For "*Pardon* from God," cf. II Chron. 30.18, Neh. 9.17, Isa. 55.7, Mic. 7.18.

344:60–68   For Seneca's praise of his brother Gallio, see the preface, par. 9, to Bk. IV of his *Quaestiones Naturales.*

344:79   For "*Daily Sacrifice,*" cf. Exod. 29.38–41, Num. 28.23–24.

344:83–86   On "*Thanksgiving*" for "Success," cf. Ps. 50.23.

344:88–92   On antipaedobaptists, cf. General Introduction, footnote to p. 108, l. 1; Bk. II, endnote to p. 296, ll. 1–14. Mather's emphasis on Phips's tolerating temper was clearly intended to reassure English readers as to the general attitude of Massachusetts citizens toward churches outside the orthodox "New England Way." In actual fact, the Mather party, with a governor and council of their own choosing, immediately went to work, under Phips, reenacting old laws which provided state support for orthodox Congregational churches (cf. Barnes, "Phippius Maximus," p. 533), and Mather was undoubtedly well aware that charges had been made in Whitehall of attempts to reestablish the old theocracy. For "*Love*" to all "*Godly Men,*" cf. I John 4.20–21.

345:3–6   See *The Great Historical Geographical and Poetical Dictionary,* based on the work of Lewis Morery and Monsieur Le Clerk, added to by Edmond Bohun, and published in London in 1694. The quoted passage is in this volume attributed to "*Barthol. Antiq. Danic.,*" that is, the *Antiquitatum Danicorum* by Thomas Bartholinus, published in three volumes in 1689. Whether Cotton Mather had access to this work is not clear, but there is little doubt that he knew and paraphrased *The Great . . . Dictionary,* which was well known to booksellers in Boston. See T. G. Wright, *Literary Culture in Early New England 1620–1730* (New Haven, Yale University Press, 1920), pp. 118, 119.

345:12–14   Compare Eph. 2.14–18, Col. 1.20–23; cf. also Rom. 3.24–26, 5.1.

345:22–23   See "Aristides" III.3 in Plutarch's *Lives.* Mather's source may have been Clarke, *Mirrour,* p. 281 (ex. 18).

346:30–34   For Agathocles, see Plutarch "On Inoffensive Self-Praise" in *Moralia* 544.B–C. Mather's source may have been Spencer, *Things New and Old,* p. 53, Clarke, *Mirrour,* pp. 280–281, or Wanley, *Wonders,* pp. 233–234, all of whom juxtapose Agathocles and Willigis and furnish the details found in Mather.

346:46–47   Claudian *In Eutropium* I.181: "Asperius nihil est humili cum surgit in altum."

346:55–58   Mather's source for his reference to Gerson has not been found. The description of David's coin is, of course, an anachronism since coins were not introduced until the Persian period.

346:64–65   See Matt. 28.20.

347:76–77   For Biblical injunctions against soothsayers, see Jer. 27.9–10, Mic. 5.12, Zech. 10.2.

347:82–83   The editors have found no source on Agellius and the Laws against Vaticinatores.

347:85–86   The whole of Part II of Cicero's *De Divinatione* is an argument against reliance on any method of reading the future by "*Curious Enquiries*"—dreams, haruspices, spells, etc. For his argument against astrology, see II.xlii.87–xlvii.99. Meric Casaubon, in *A Treatise Proving Spirits,* p. 141, describes "*Judicial Astrology*" as practised by the ancients: "though apparently, it be more mysterious, and deal in things more specious and sublime: yet, in very deed, [it] is founded upon meer imaginary suppositions, and Poetical fictions, words and names, which have no ground at all in nature."

347:87–88   Compare Letter No. 57, par. 2, in the Loeb edition of the *Select Letters* of Augustine.

348:24   Compare Hall's Satire VII, on Judicial Astrology, in *Works,* 9:604–606.

348:35–37   For the "*Devices of Satan*," cf. II. Cor. 2.11; for the "*Snare of Satan*," cf. I Tim. 3.7, II Tim. 2.26.

349:44–46   See Letter II, par. 2, in Loeb edition of *Collected Letters of St. Basil* (1:8–9).

349:56–57   See Seneca "Ad Helviam Matrem de Consolatione" in *Moralia* xix.6: "loquax et in contumelias praefectorum ingeniosa provincia, in qua etiam qui vitaverunt culpam non effugerunt infamiam."

349:69–70   Compare the "Epitaph" on Sir William that Mather gives in his *Decennium* (Lincoln, *Narratives*, p. 216): "Bonus non est, qui non ad Invidium usque Bonus est," or "He is not good who is not good enough to be hated."

349:77–78   Mather's immediate source has not been identified. See, however, Joannes Zonaras *Epitome of History* VIII.xv (*Migne G*, 134:678). Zonaras, chronicler and theologian at Constantinople in the early twelfth century, and private secretary to the emperor Alexius I Comnenus, based his Roman history on Dio Cassius, whose first twenty books are not otherwise known except in fragments. It may therefore be assumed that his passage on Regulus follows Dio: "They cutt off his eyelids and for a time shut him up in darkness, then they cast him into some kind of specially constructed receptacle bristling with spikes, and made him face the sun ... and ... he perished." Compare also Cicero *De Officiis* III.xxvii.100, where he speaks of Regulus's "Exquisita supplicia." Regulus's heroic endurance was also celebrated by Horace *Odes* III.v, and by Augustine *Civita Dei* I.xv.

350:90–91   See Prov. 4.16. The "Party of Men" opposed to Phips contained several elements. Naturally Jahleel Brenton and Captain Short pressed their charges against him (cf. above p. 342, ll. 88–90). According to Hutchinson (2:59), "The prejudices were great against him in England. Mr. Dudley [Joseph], who was upon the spot and desired to succeed him, heightened them. There was a strong party against him also within the province," made up of both the aristocratic "dominion party" and the adherents of Elisha Cooke (see introductory essay "Cotton Mather," pp. 13, 18). Furthermore "Stoughton, the lieutenant governor ... was very cold in Sir William's interest." According to Sewall (*Diary*, 1:378, 379), Phips made Stoughton an enemy by his vigorous interference with the witchcraft trials, a fact which Phips had recognized in the letter he sent to Nottingham on February 21, 1692/3, writing that "the Lieut. Gov. ... was inraged & filled with passionate anger" because "I sent a reprieve whereby y.ᵉ execuçon was stopped." He continued that Stoughton "hath from the beginning hurried on those matters with great precipitancy & by his warrant hath caused the estates, goods & chattels of y.ᵉ executed to be seized & disposed of without my knowledge or consent." (See 2 MHS *Proc.*, 1:342). When he arrived in London, Phips "was sued by Dudley and Brenton, in actions of twenty thousand pounds damage ... What were the grounds of Dudley's action does not appear" (Hutchinson, 2:63; cf. also Kimball, *Joseph Dudley*, p. 67).

350:9   Compare Tilley, W 102.

350:11   See endnote to lines 90–91 above.

350:17–351:21   Mather's account of the Brazen Tree is abridged, but he employs words and phrases from Davies' rendering of Murtadi (pp. 14–15) so faithfully as to make it almost certain that he had the volume before him.

351:25   Hutchinson's *History* (2:59) casts a somewhat different light on the attitude of the "*General Assembly*": "An address was proposed and carried in the house of representatives, humbly praying his majesty, that the governor might not be removed; but of 50 present, 24 voted against it."

351:31   While Mather's wording, "printed in a *Villanous Libel*," suggests the publication of some book or pamphlet, he apparently meant only the preferring of public charges against Phips. See Murdock, *Increase Mather*, pp. 337–338 and notes.

352:64–65   See Bede's *Historia Ecclesiastica Gentis Anglorum*, Bk. I, Cap. xii: "omni armato milite, militaribus copiis universis, tota floridae iuventutis alacritate spoliata."

352:70–73 Nothing further is known of this project for Spanish trade according to Miss Barnes, "Phippius Maximus," p. 550.

352:76–79 See Peter Martyr d'Anghiera, *De Nouo Orbe, or the History of the West Indies*, p. 56 verso. Mather follows Peter Martyr's spelling "*Boadilla*" of the viceroy's name.

352:80 For the Duke of Albemarle's patent, see above 40b:27–28 and endnote.

352:82–83 Ovid *Ars Amatoria* III.425.

352:88–89 The ascription of authorship of Ps. 146 to Haggai and Zechariah is in the Hebrew Bible (see Robert Pfeiffer, *Introduction to the Old Testament*, rev. ed., New York, Harper & Brothers, 1948, pp. 641–642). This Psalm, of which Mather quotes v.4, has nothing to do with the Persian grants, but is a Halleluiah hymn. These grants were the restitution by Cyrus I, at the time when Haggai and Zechariah were exhorting the Jews to rebuild the Temple, of the treasure taken from the Temple by Nebuchadnezzar. (See Ezra, chaps. 5 and 6.) In the "Argument" to his commentary on the book of Haggai, Poole refers also to the "the bounty of Darius, and the contributions of others."

353:95 Miss Barnes reports no evidence on the "Eminent Person" other than Mather's reference ("Phippius Maximus," p. 551).

353:1 For "*Days* and *Thoughts*, cf. Ps. 146.4.

353:5–6 For "*Portion for ever*," etc., see Num. 18.8, Ps. 73.26, Eccles. 9.6; for "*Memory be not forgotten*," Eccles. 9.5.

353:8–9 Calamy's sermon was entitled *A Patterne for all, especially for Noble and Honourable Persons, to teach them how to die Nobly and Honourably*, London, 1658. Mather's quotation, from pp. 38–39, abridges Calamy's "*his failings*, and his *many infirmities*." Compare Rev. 7.14.

353:27 For Biblical admonitions to "*do Good*," see, for example, Ps. 37.3, 27, Prov. 11.17, Gal. 6.9–10.

353:32–33 Mather's probable source was Alsted, *Encyclopaedia* (p. 1984b), with a reference to Cicero's epistle "Ad Quatrum Fratrem" (*Epistles* I.1.23): "Cyrus ille à Xenophonte non ad historiæ fidem scriptus, sed ad effigiem justi imperii."

354:40 For "Publicans," see Matt. 5.46.

354:42–47 *Greek Anthology* IX.159.

354:54 Compare Horace *Odes* IV.ix.28.

354:54–55 For the "Infamy" of Judas, see Matt. 26.14–16, 25, 47–48, 27.3–5, Mark 14.10–11, Luke 22.3–6, 47–48, John 18.2, 3, 5, Acts 1.18. For that of Pilate, see the Nicene and Apostles' Creeds: "Suffered under Pontius Pilate, Was crucified, dead, and buried."

354:56–58 See Agathias *Historia* II.22 (*Migne G*, 88:1378): the Persians, "according to native rites, expose the naked corpse to be devoured by dogs and the obscene birds which feed upon cadavers." Compare Sir Thomas Browne, *Urn Burial* (*Works*, 4:10): "The *Persian magi* . . . being only solicitous about their bones, exposed their flesh to the prey of Birds and Dogges."

354:70 For "*quietness*" under a good governor, cf. I Chron. 22.9, Acts 24.2.

355:73 The source for Cyprians buried in honey has not been found. Herodotus (*History* I.198) gives it as a practice of the Assyrians in Babylon under the Persians: "The dead are embalmed in honey for burial."

355:83–84 The reference to statues in Venice has not been found.

355:97–99 Compare Wanley, *Wonders*, p. 647: "*Pericles* was the first in Athens, who . . . publickly extolled those who were slain in the *Peloponnesian* War in defence of their Country." The *Greek Anthology* has many examples of verses extolling the heroic dead, those of the poet Simonides (*c.* 556–467 b.c.) being among the most famous. See, for example, his epigram on the monument to the Greeks who fell at Thermopylae (Bk. VII.248): "Four thousand from Peloponnesus once fought here with three million," and (Bk. VII.253) "If to die well be the chief part of virtue, Fortune granted this to us above all others; for striving to endue Hellas with freedom, we lie here possessed of praise that groweth not old."

355:3 See Murdock, *Increase Mather*, p. 338.

355:12–13 For "*Churches* of God," see I Cor. 11.16, I Thess. 2.14, II. Thess. 1.4.

356:16–17 Compare Cotton Mather's characterization of Governor John Winthrop as "Nehemias Americanus" (Bk. II, p. 213, l. 5). For "*sought the welfare*," see Neh. 2.10.

356:30 For "*in the Midst of his days*," see Ps. 102.14.

356:39 Ovid *Metamorphoses* XV.872.

356:41–44 Suidas' story of the envious man and the statue has not been found.

357:54–359:42 According to Jantz, *First Century of New England Verse*, pp. 216–217, no printed copy of the broadside has been preserved, but the New York Historical Society has a contemporaneous manuscript copy of it in a commonplace book of Samuel Sewall. Mather follows the poem as Sewall has it, except for the omission of some eleven lines and the name of the author of the elegy. Jantz suggests that Sewall's ascription of it to "D. Hincsman" is an error for "R. Hincsman," made by Bartholomew Green, the printer, or by Sewall himself. Mr. Richard M. Hinchman of Groton, Massachusetts, has kindly helped the editors of the present volume, writing: "If one assumes that the initial "D" was an error . . . then there are several Henchmans or Hincksmans who . . . could have written the Phips elegy. The most likely alternate is (as noted by Jantz) Daniel's older brother Richard Henchman" (1655 or 1656–1724/5). "Personally, I think Jantz was too conservative in considering Richard as a *possible* alternate author; to me it seems *highly probable*, although there is no proof. While we know nothing of Richard's education, his age, occupation, and later ventures into verse make him the logical candidate . . . I guess we'll never know unless further evidence turns up someday; however, my vote would be in favour of Richard. Isn't it more likely that a professional schoolmaster, aged 40, with known leanings toward verse, wrote the elegy than a callow youth of 18, even though a junior at Harvard?" Mr. Hinchman of Groton notes that the "professional schoolmaster" taught at Dedham, Mass., 1681–1685, went to Yarmouth in 1686, and was employed at the Free [North] Writing School in Boston from 1700 to 1714/15. It is clear also that he and Samuel Sewall often exchanged verses: see *Sewall Papers*, 1:290n, 293, 314n.

357:60 For "Netop," see DAE.

357:61 Compare Judg. 16.23, where the Philistines rejoice at the humiliation of Samson.

357:62–63 An allusion to Matt. 5.46; cf. Mather's reference to the same text on p. 354, l. 40.

358:90–91 For "*resolv'd to do* Good, etc.," cf. Gal. 6.10.

358:93 For the "Gift of Miracles," see I Cor. 12.10, 28, 29, Gal. 3.5.

358:98 Compare Job. 38.7.

358:3 For Briareus, see especially Hesiod *Theogony*:149–153 for the birth and early history of the hundred-armed; 617–628 for attacks on them by their jealous father Uranus; 644–735 for the war of the Titans.

359:20 For "*Heaven fetch'd Him to a Crown*," cf. II Tim. 4.8, I Pet. 5.4, Rev. 2.10.

359:24 For the "Universal Conflagration," cf. II Pet. 3.7–12.

INDEX

INDEX

Abbot, George, Archbishop of Canterbury, 126
Adam, Melchior, 444
Adams, Eliphalet, 174
Adams, Thomas, 148, 243
Adderly (Atherly), Abraham, 284–285, 286, 462
Adderly, Samuel, 148
Addington, Isaac, 244
Aelian, 379, 380
Aelius Donatus, 382
Aelius Spartianus, 476
Aesop, 379
Agamemnon, 75
Agapetus, 199, 433
Agathias Myrinensis, 354, 479
Agathocles, 346, 477
Agellius, Antonius, 347
Agrippa von Nettesheim, Heinrich Cornelius, 108, 377, 383
Albemarle, second Duke of (Christopher Monck), 283, 285n, 286, 352, 462, 463, 479
Alden, John, 212
Aldersey, Samuel, 243
Alexander the Great, 193, 223, 277n, 431
Alexander, Sir William, 299
Allen, James, 174, 392
Allerton, Isaac, 436, 437
Allyn, John, 269, 270, 459
Allyn, Matthew, 269, 270
Alsop, Vincent, 30
Alsted, Johann: *Thesaurus Chronologiae* (1628), 424, 451; *Encyclopaedia* (1630), 38, 375, 376, 377
Alvarez, Fernando, Duke of Alva, 110
Amadas, Philip, 389
Ambrose, Saint, 101, 296, 379
Ames, William, 124, 364, 391
Ammianus Marcellinus, 447, 454, 457
Amyraldus, Moyses, 253, 454
Anabaptists, 108, 143, 155, 207
Andrews, C. M., 419, 459, 464, 471

Andrews, Samuel, 178
Andros, Sir Edmund: as royal governor, 172n, 240n, 308n, 317n, 422, 457, 462, 463, 464, 465; iniquities of regime of, 288–291, 463–464, 465; failure to protect against Indians, 292–293; suspected of Roman Catholic machinations, 293, 470; revolt against, 294, 295, 450
Angier, Samuel, 175
Anglican Church in Boston, 13, 174, 422–423, 427
Anne, Queen, 40
Anne, Edward, 383
Antinomianism, 75n; controversy concerning, 220–221, 232, 236, 413, 420; synod at Newtown, 443
Antipaedobaptists, 174, 344, 477
Apelles, 103
Apollonia, 108, 383
Apollonius, 211
Appleton, Samuel, 244
Archimelus, 112
Arganthonius, 241
Aristides, 345, 477
Aristotle, 108, 264, 369, 434
Arminianism, 371; Robinson and Episcopius debate on, 125, 392; of Church of England, 159
Arminius, Jacobus, 86, 88, 125n
Arnold, Samuel, 174
Arrianus, Flavius, 95
Articles of Confederation (1643), 266, 458
Ashurst, Sir Henry, 12–13, 317, 321
Astwood, John, 270
Athenaeus, 450
Atherton, Humphrey, 244
Atwood, John, 212
Aubery, Louis, sieur de Maurier, 97, 377, 384
Augustine, Saint, 92, 117, 118, 188, 261, 347, 374, 387, 388, 429, 456, 476, 477, 478